POETRY IN THEORY

JON COOK

POETRY IN THEORY

AN ANTHOLOGY 1900–2000

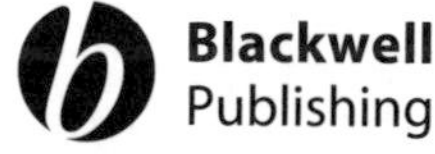

BLACKWELL PUBLISHING
350 Main Street, Malden, MA 02148-5020, USA
108 Cowley Road, Oxford OX4 1JF, UK
550 Swanston Street, Carlton, Victoria 3053, Australia

First published 2004 by Blackwell Publishing Ltd

Library of Congress Cataloging-in-Publication Data

Poetry in theory: an anthology, 1900–2000 / edited by Jon Cook.
p. cm.
Includes bibliographical references (p.) and index.
ISBN 0-631-22553-6 (hardcover : alk. paper) – ISBN 0-631-22554-4 (pbk. : alk. paper)
1. Poetry, Modern–20th century–History and criticism. 2. Poetry–History and criticism–Theory, etc. 3. Poetics. I. Cook, Jon

PN1271.P65 2004
809.1–dc22

2003022144

A catalogue record for this title is available from the British Library.

Set in 10/12.5 pt Minion
by Kolam Information Services Pvt. Ltd, Pondicherry, India
Printed and bound in the United Kingdom
by TJ International Ltd, Padstow, Cornwall

The publisher's policy is to use permanent paper from mills that operate a sustainable forestry policy, and which has been manufactured from pulp processed using acid-free and elementary chlorine-free practices. Furthermore, the publisher ensures that the text paper and cover board used have met acceptable environmental accreditation standards.

For further information on
Blackwell Publishing, visit our website:
http://www.blackwellpublishing.com

Contents

Part III 1940–1960 245

Part IV 1960–1980 359

Acknowledgments

I am especially grateful to the following for detailed criticism, advice, and encouragement: Denise Riley, Clive Scott, Richard Holmes, and my editor at Blackwells, Andrew McNeillie. Others have given helpful advice on particular texts or on the overall scope of this anthology. They include: Peter Bush, Jo Catling, Howard Caygill, Russell Celyn Jones, Sarah Churchwell, Jim Grant, Hannah Griffiths, Dennis Hirson, Matthew Hollis, Daniel Kane, Andrew Motion, Rupert Read, Vic Sage, Lyndsey Stonebridge, and George Szirtes. Thanks to Sally Shore for help in collecting some of the work included in this book, to Sarah Gooderson, Pam Lewis; and Mary Dortch for help in preparing the text, and to Karen Wilson at Blackwells.

I am grateful to the University of East Anglia for research grants that helped meet the costs of preparing the text. The Amsterdam School for Cultural Analysis at the University of Amsterdam gave me a research fellowship that enabled me to clarify my thinking about what should be included in this anthology and why. Many thanks to Thomas Elsaesser for his generous hospitality and stimulating conversation, and, similarly, to Murray Pearson and Atti Tordoir. Finally thanks to Alice Tomkins and to Diane De Bell. I hope, in Diane's case, that this is the book that she might once have found useful.

The editor and publisher wish to thank the following for permission to use copyright material.

Theodor Adorno for excerpt from *Notes to Literature*, vol. 1, edited by Rolf Tiedmann, translated by Shierry Weber Nicholsen (New York: Columbia University Press, 1991). Reprinted by permission of Columbia University Press.

Guillaume Apollinaire for excerpts from *Selected Writings*, translated by Roger Shattuck (New Directions, 1971). Copyright © 1971 by Roger Shattuck. Reprinted by permission of New Directions Publishing Corp.

John Ashbery for "The Invisible Avant-Garde" from *Reported Sightings: Art Chronicles 1957–1987* by John Ashbery, edited by David Bergman (Carcanet Press Ltd, 1989). Reprinted by permission of Georges Borchardt, Literary Agency, New York.

W. H. Auden for excerpts from *The Dyer's Hand and Other Essays*, by W. H. Auden (Random House, 1962). Copyright 1948, 1950, 1952, 1953, 1954, 1956, 1957, 1958, 1960, 1962 by W. H. Auden, used by permission of Random House, Inc.

Imamu Baraka for "Hunting Is Not Those Heads on the Wall" from *The Poetics of the New American Poetry*, edited by Donald Allen and Warren Tallman (Grove Press, 1974). Reprinted by permission of Sterling Lord Literistic, Inc. Copyright © 1973 by Amiri Baraka.

Roland Barthes for "Is there any poetic writing?" from *Writing Degree Zero* by Roland Barthes, translated by Annette Lavers. Translation copyright © 1968 by Jonathan Cape Ltd. Reprinted by permission of Hill & Wang, a division of Farrar, Straus and Giroux, Inc. and The Random House Group Limited.

Charles Bernstein for excerpt from *The L=A=N=G=U=A=G=E Book*, edited by Bruce Andrews and Charles Bernstein (Southern Illinois University Press, 1983). Used by permission of the author. Reprinted from *Content's Dream: Essays 1975–1984* (Sun & Moon Press, 1986; repr. Sun & Moon Classics, 1994; repr. Northwestern University Press, 2001).

Maurice Blanchot for excerpt from *The Space of Literature* by Maurice Blanchot, translated by Ann Smock (University of Nebraska Press, 1982). Reprinted by permission of the University of Nebraska Press. Translation © 1982 by the University of Nebraska Press. Originally published in France as *L'Espace litteraire*, © Editions Gallimard, 1955.

Eavan Boland for "The Woman Poet: Her Dilemma" from *Object Lessons: The Life of the Woman and the Poet in Our Time* by Eavan Boland (Carcanet Press, 1995). Reprinted by permission of Carcanet Press. Copyright © 1995 by Eavan Boland. Used by permission of W. W. Norton & Company, Inc.

André Breton for "The Automatic Message" from *What is Surrealism?*, edited and translated by F. Rosemount (Pluto Press, 1978). Reprinted by permission of Pluto Press.

Kenneth Burke for "The Poetic Process" from *Perspectives by Incongruity*, edited by Stanley Edgar Hyman (University of California Press, 1968). Reprinted by permission of the University of California Press. Copyright © 1968 The Regents of the University of California.

Hart Crane for "General Aims and Theories" from *The Complete Poems and Selected Letters and Prose of Hart Crane*, by Hart Crane, edited by Brom Weber (W. W. Norton, 1937). Copyright 1933, 1958, 1966 by Liveright Publishing Corporation. Copyright 1952 by Brom Weber. Used by permission of Liveright Publishing Corporation.

Robert Creeley for excerpt from *The Collected Essays of Robert Creeley* (University of California Press Ltd, 1989). Copyright © 1989 The Regents of the University of California.

Donald Davie for "What is Modern Poetry?" and "The Reek of the Human" from *Articulate Energy* (Routledge & Kegan Paul, 1955). Reprinted by permission of Taylor & Francis Books Ltd.

Paul de Man for "Intentional Structure of the Romantic Image" from *The Rhetoric of Romanticism* (Columbia University Press, 1984). Copyright © 1984 Columbia University Press. Reprinted with the permission of the publisher.

Jacques Derrida for excerpt from *A Derrida Reader: Between the Blinds*, edited with an introduction and notes by Peggy Kamuf (Columbia University Press, 1991, pp. 223–37, odd numbered pages only). Copyright © 1991 Columbia University Press.

Edward Dorn for "What I See in *The Maximus Poems*" from *The Poetics of the New American Poetry*, edited by Donald M. Allen and Warren Tallman (Grove Press, 1974). Copyright © 1961 by Edward Dorn. Used by permission of Grove/Atlantic, Inc.

Paul Éluard for excerpt from *Poetry's Evidence*, first published in *This Quarter*, September 1932, edited by André Breton. This copy from a text published by Arno Press and The New York Times, 1969. Copyright © Editions Gallimard, Paris, 1968.

William Empson for excerpt from *Seven Types of Ambiguity* (Chatto & Windus, 1930). Reproduced with permission of Curtis Brown Ltd., London on behalf of The Estate of William Empson. Copyright © William Empson 1930.

Hans Magnus Enzensberger for "A Modest Proposal for the Protection of Young People" from *Mediocrity and Delusion: Collected Diversions*, translated by Martin Chalmers (Verso, 1992). Reprinted by permission of Verso.

Shoshana Felman for "On Reading Poetry" from *The Literary Freud: Mechanisms of Defense and the Poetic Will*, editor Joseph H. Smith, assistant editor Gloria H. Parloff, editorial aides, Katherine S. Henry, Eve Nelson Shapiro (Yale University Press, 1980, pp. 119–48). This essay was later reprinted under the title "The Case of Poe: Implications/Applications of Psychoanalysis" as chapter two in *Jacques Lacan and the Adventure of Insight: Psychoanalysis in Contemporary Culture* by Shoshana Felman (Harvard University Press, 1987, pp. 27–52). Reprinted by permission of the author and Harvard University Press. Copyright © 1987 by the President and the Fellows of Harvard College.

Sigmund Freud for "Creative Writers and Day-dreaming" from the *Standard Edition of the Complete Psychological Works of Sigmund Freud*, vol. 7, translated and edited by James Strachey (London: Hogarth Press, 1959). © Copyrights, The Institute of Psychoanalysis and The Hogarth Press. Reprinted by permission of The Random House Group Ltd.

Gerard Genette for excerpt from *Figures of Literary Discourse* by Gerard Genette, translated by Alan Sheridan (Columbia University Press, 1982). English translation

Copyright © 1982 by Columbia University Press. Essays 1, 2, 3, 9, and 10 originally appeared in French in *Figures I*, copyright © 1966 Editions du Seuil. Essays 4, 5, 7, 8, and 11 originally appeared in *Figures II*, copyright © 1969 Editions du Seuil and essay 6 originally appeared in *Figures III*, copyright © 1972 Editions du Seuil. Reprinted by permission of Georges Borchardt, Inc. for Editions du Seuil.

Allen Ginsberg for excerpts from *Deliberate Prose: Selected Essays 1952–1995* by Allen Ginsberg, edited by Bill Morgan (HarperCollins, 2000). Copyright © 1999 by The Allen Ginsberg Trust. Reprinted by permission of HarperCollins Publishers Inc.

Robert Graves and Laura Riding for extracts from *A Survey of Modernist Poetry*, first published 1927. These extracts taken from 1969 edition published by Haskell House, New York. Excerpts from Chapter I and Chapter VII. Reprinted by permission of Carcanet Press on behalf of the Robert Graves Estate. Reprinted with permission of the Laura (Riding) Jackson Estate.

Seamus Heaney for excerpt from *The Redress of Poetry* by Seamus Heaney (Farrar, Straus and Giroux, 1995). Copyright © 1995 Seamus Heaney. Reprinted by permission of Farrar, Straus and Giroux Inc.

Martin Heidegger for excerpt from "The Ister Hymn" from *Hölderlin's Hymn "The Ister"/Martin Heidegger*, translated by William McNeill and Julia Davis (Indiana University Press, 1966). Reprinted by permission of the original German publisher Vittorio Klostermann GmbH, Frankfurt am Main, Germany.

Barbara Herrnstein Smith for "Closure and Anti-closure in Modern Poetry" from *Poetic Closure: A Study of How Poems End* (University of Chicago Press, 1968). Reprinted by permission of the University of Chicago Press and Barbara Herrnstein Smith.

Geoffrey Hill for "Poetry as Menace and Atonement" from *The Lords of Limit* (André Deutsch, 1984). Copyright © 1984 Geoffrey Hill.

Langston Hughes for "The Negro Artist and the Racial Mountain," first published in *The Nation*, June 1926. This copy from *Voices from the Harlem Renaissance*, edited by N. I. Higgins, Oxford University Press, New York, 1976. Reprinted by permission of *The Nation.*

T. E. Hulme for "Romanticism and Classicism" from T. E. Hulme, *Selected Writings*, edited by P. McGuinness (Manchester: Fyfield Books, Carcanet Press, 1998). Reprinted by permission of Carcanet Press Ltd.

Roman Jakobson for excerpts from *Style in Language*, edited by Thomas A. Seboek (MIT Press, 1960). Reprinted by permission of The MIT Press.

Randall Jarrell (1980) "The End of the Line" from *Kipling, Auden and Co.: Essays and Reviews, 1935–1964.* New York: Farrar, Straus and Giroux, 1980. First published in *The Nation*, February 21, 1942. Reprinted with permission of *The Nation.* http://www.thenation.com.

Velimir Khlebnikov for "On Poetry" and "On Contemporary Poetry" from *The Collected Works of Velimir Khlebnikov*, vol. 1, translated by Paul Schmidt, edited by Charlotte Douglas (Harvard University Press, 1987). Copyright © 1987 by the Dia Art Foundation. Reprinted by permission of the publisher.

Julia Kristeva for "The Ethics of Linguistics" from *Desire in Language: A Semiotic Approach to Literature and Art*, edited by Leon S. Roudiez, translated by Thomas Gora, Alice Jardine, and Leon S. Roudiez (Columbia University Press, 1980). Copyright © 1980 Columbia University Press. Reprinted with permission of the publisher.

Jacques Lacan for "The Agency of the Letter" from *Ecrits: A Selection*, translated from the French by Alan Sheridan (Tavistock Publications, 1977). Reprinted by permission of Routledge and W. W. Norton & Company, Inc.

Jacques Lacan, from *The Seminar of Jacques Lacan: Book II: The Ego in Freud's Theory and in the Technique of Psychoanalysis* by Jacques Lacan, translated by Sylvia Tomaselli. Copyright © 1978 by Editions du Seuil. English translation copyright © 1988 by Cambridge University Press. Used by permission of W. W. Norton & Company, Inc.

Jacques Lacan, from *The Seminar of Jacques Lacan: Book III: The Psychoses 1955–1956* by Jacques Lacan, translated by Russell Grigg. Copyright © 1981 by Editions de Seuil. English translation copyright © 1993 by W. W. Norton & Company, Inc. Used by permission of W. W. Norton & Company, Inc.

D. H. Lawrence for "Preface to the American Edition of *New Poems*" from *The Poetics of the New American Poetry*, edited by Donald Allen and Warren Tallman (Grove Press, 1974). Reprinted by permission of Pollinger Ltd.

F. R. Leavis for excerpts from Chapters I and III of *New Bearings in English Poetry* (Chatto & Windus, 1950). First published Chatto & Windus, 1932, excerpts taken from 1950 edition. Reprinted by kind permission of the Leavis Estate.

Federico García Lorca for "Play and Theory of the Duende" from *In Search of Duende*, translated by Christopher Maurer (New Directions, 1980). Copyright © 1955 by New Directions Publishing Corp., copyright © Herederos de Federico García Lorca, translation © Christopher Maurer and Herederos de Federico García Lorca. Reprinted by permission of New Directions Publishing Corp.

Mina Loy for "Modern Poetry" from *The Lost Lunar Baedeker: Poems of Mina Loy*, edited by Roger L. Conover (Farrar, Straus and Giroux and Carcanet, 1997). Reprinted by permission of Carcanet Press.

Filippo Marinetti for "Technical Manifesto of Futurist Literature" from *Marinetti: Selected Writings*, edited by R. W. Flint, translated by R. W. Flint and Arthur Coppotelli (London: Secker and Warburg, 1972). Translation copyright © 1972 by Farrar, Straus and Giroux, Inc. Reprinted by permission of Farrar, Straus and Giroux, Inc.

Czeslaw Milosz for excerpts from *The Witness of Poetry* by Czeslaw Milosz (Harvard University Press, 1983). Copyright © 1983 by the President and Fellows of Harvard College. Reprinted by permission of the publisher.

Frank O'Hara for "Personism: A Manifesto" from *The Poetics of the New American Poetry*, edited by Donald M. Allen and Warren Tallman (Grove Press, 1974). Copyright © 1961 by Frank O'Hara. Used by permission of Grove/Atlantic, Inc.

Marjorie Perloff for "Avant Garde or Endgame?" from *Radical Artifice* by Marjorie Perloff (University of Chicago Press, 1991). Reprinted by permission of the University of Chicago Press and the author, Marjorie Perloff.

Richard Poirier for excerpts from *The Renewal of Literature* by Richard Poirier (Random House, 1987). Copyright © 1987 by Richard Poirer. Used by permission of Random House, Inc.

Adrienne Rich for excerpt from "Blood, Bread, and Poetry: The Location of a Poet," from *Arts of the Possible: Essays and Conversations* by Adrienne Rich. Copyright © 2001 by Adrienne Rich. Used by permission of the author and W. W. Norton & Company, Inc.

I. A. Richards for excerpts from *Science and Poetry*, first published by Kegan, Paul, Trench & Trubner Ltd, London, and R. I. Severs, 1926. The complete, final, and revised text of *Science and Poetry*, from which the extract has been taken, can be read in Appendix 3, to John Constable, ed., *Principles of Literary Criticism*, vol. 3 in *Selected Works of I. A. Richards* (Routledge, 2001).

Rainer Maria Rilke for extracts from *Selected Letters*, translated by R. F. C. Hull (London, Macmillan, 1946). Reprinted by permission of Macmillan UK.

Gertrude Stein for excerpts from *Lectures in America* by Gertrude Stein (Random House, 1935). Copyright 1935 and renewed 1963 by Alice B. Toklas. Used by permission of Random House Inc.

Rabindranath Tagore for "Poet Yeats" from *Rabindranath Tagore: An Anthology*, ed. K. Dutta and A. Robinson (Picador, 1997). Reprinted by permission of Visva-Bharati University, Calcutta.

Edward Thomas for "North of Boston" from *A Language Not to be Betrayed: Selected Prose of Edward Thomas*, selected with an introduction by Edna Longley (Carcanet Press, 1981). Reprinted by permission of Carcanet Press Ltd.

Tristan Tzara for "Note on Poetry" from *Seven Dada Manifestos and Lampisteries*, translated by Barbara Wright (Calder, 1977). Reprinted by permission of Calder Publications Ltd., London.

Paul Valéry for excerpts from *The Collected Works of Paul Valery*, vol. 7, ed. Jackson Matthews (Routledge & Kegan Paul, 1958). Reprinted with permission of Editions Gallimard, Paris. Copyright © Editions Gallimard, Paris and with permission of Princeton University Press.

Helen Vendler for excerpt from *Soul Says: On Recent Poetry* by Helen Vendler (Belknap Press of Harvard University Press, 1995). Copyright © 1995 by the President and Fellows of Harvard College. Reprinted by permission of the publisher.

William Carlos Williams for "Prologue to *Kora in Hell*" from *Imaginations* (City Lights Books, 1973). Copyright © 1970 by Florence H. Williams. Reprinted by permission of New Directions Publishing Corp.

W. K. Wimsatt (1954) for "The Concrete Universal" from *The Verbal Icon: Studies in the Meaning of Poetry*, by W. K. Wimsatt, Jr., and two preliminary essays written in collaboration with Monroe C. Beardsley. Lexington, Ky.: University Press of Kentucky, pp. 69–83. Reprinted by permission of the University Press of Kentucky.

W. B. Yeats for "The Symbolism of Poetry" from *Essays and Introductions* by W. B. Yeats (London, Macmillan, 1961). Reprinted by permission of A. P. Watt Ltd., Literary Agents, London. Reprinted with the permission of Scribner, an imprint of Simon & Schuster Adult Publishing Group. Copyright © 1961 by Mrs W. B. Yeats.

Thomas Yingling for "The Homosexual Lyric" from *Hart Crane and the Homosexual Text* by Thomas Yingling (University of Chicago Press, 1990). Reprinted by permission of the University of Chicago Press.

Zukofsky, Louis (1981) "A Statement for Poetry" from *Prepositions: The Collected Critical Essays of Louis Zukofsky*. Reprinted by permission of Wesleyan University Press.

Every effort has been made to trace copyright holders and to obtain their permission for the use of copyright material. The editor and publisher will gladly receive any information enabling them to rectify any error or omission in subsequent editions.

Introduction

What difference does poetry make? How does poetry differ from other cultural forms and forces? These two questions recur in many of the pieces gathered in this anthology. The force and intensity, or the irony and the helplessness, of the answers given depend upon the description of another difference, that between modern poetry and the poetry that precedes it. What this difference amounts to is not a matter of settled agreement either about what modern poetry is or its value or its history. For T. S. Eliot, Adrienne Rich, or Derek Walcott these are momentous questions. Large issues about past traditions or political futures seem to depend on how poetry is written and how it is to be read. The right attunement of language to the world, the survival of modes of perception and feeling all become implicated in poetry's continuation.

From this perspective the difference between modern poetry and what precedes it is something more than the latest episode in the reforms or renewals of poetic style that regularly punctuate the history of poetry. In the seventeenth century, the poet John Donne wanted to roughen up the smooth textures of Petrarchan love poetry with vernacular idioms and rhythms. The eighteenth-century English critic, Samuel Johnson, praised his predecessor, John Dryden, for moving in another direction. Using an architectural analogy Johnson claimed that Dryden had found English poetry "brick" and "left it marble." He smoothed out the rough edges of English poetry, and, the implication is that in doing this he made it more civilized. These kinds of argument certainly enter into discussions about modern poetry. But the question of poetry's modernity has another implication. One way of understanding this is to change the metaphor used to describe change. Neither reform nor renewal is at issue, but revolution. A way of understanding this revolutionary perspective is to say that modern poetry begins by radically questioning what a poem is and by raising that question not just once but repeatedly. What is at issue then is not to do with altering something whose identity is generally agreed, but with creating poetry anew from the ground up. The idea of the modern does not just encompass poetry written in a particular time, so that all poetry written in the last twenty or forty or eighty years qualifies for the title. It comes to describe a particular kind of poetry, often described as "modernist" and distinguished from "traditional." And this produces a further turn in debate about whether it is only "modernist" poetry that can lay claim to being legitimately modern and what the formal features and cultural ambitions of this poetry should be.

Yet to others, such as Philip Larkin, this way of thinking about modern poetry could seem at best a distracting fuss and at worst a corruption of the art of poetry. From this perspective, despite all the talk of change, twentieth-century poetry was continuous with the poetry of the past, its essential forms and pleasures unaltered, or, at least, that was how things should be. The experiments associated with modernist poetry needed to be put in a specific and diminishing context. They were a noisy sideshow that had taken over what should have been the main event. The task was to restore a proper perspective.

Hence part of the history of debates about modern poetry was taken up with a resistance to the revolutions announced in the first decades of the twentieth century. To note this is to point to a continuing and unresolved issue that provokes a variety of responses. One is to see early twentieth-century poetic experiment as something that calls for remedial action. Another direction is indicated by Barbara Herrnstein Smith: the history of modern poetry, apart from being a "literary historian's nightmare," is best understood in terms of twentieth-century poetry's "stylistic multiplicity." Poetry has become a market with many niches. Those who like sonnets or villanelles can find them, but it's not hard to find free verse, drug poems, or sound poetry either, and, in every case, there will be arguments to justify any choice. A third response assumes that what is usually called "modernist poetry" is not a single phenomenon, nor does it leave a single recommendation for the poetry that succeeds it, other than the obligation to sustain the energies of experiment.

The temptation here is to say that in the twentieth century there is not poetry but "poetries"; that there is no longer a single state of the art, but many different states. While this may be true it is in danger of ignoring a risk and a possibility. The risk is that the conviction and seriousness of poets, critics, and theorists in arguing their case for poetry will be met with indifference. These arguments do not invite their readers to respond with a shrug of the shoulders as they gather another item in the checklist of "poetries," but with articulate agreement or disagreement. The possibility is that there is an alternative to the "literary historian's nightmare." There are patterns in the ways that modern poetry's past has been imagined, just as there are differences in judgment about the nature of poetic language or the characteristics of modern poetry that can speak to and against each other. Some of these patterns and differences are sketched in this introduction.

The Nineteenth Century

Writing in the early 1930s, the English critic F. R. Leavis, discerned a "new bearing" in English poetry by contrasting the work of T. S. Eliot, Ezra Pound, and Gerard Manley

Hopkins with a set of assumptions about poetry and its value that, in Leavis's view, had become dominant in the nineteenth century. The force of Leavis's argument derived from his belief that these assumptions were both pervasive and restrictive: "Poetry tends in every age to confine itself by ideas of the essentially poetical which, when the conditions that give rise to them have changed, bar the poet from his most valuable material" (p. 195).[1] The link between theory and practice is self-evident: inherited ideas about what poetry is will have a direct impact on the poetry that gets written. Critical intelligence would ideally work alongside poetic practice by subjecting these inherited ideas, often held as unconscious assumptions, to scrutiny and debate.

Leavis shared with Eliot and Pound a belief that the nineteenth century was a time when poetry went wrong. The same belief is echoed later in the twentieth century by the Irish poet, Eavan Boland, when she claims that nineteenth-century poetry tended towards a "debased romanticism... rooted in a powerful subliminal suggestion that poets are distinctive not so much because they write poetry as because in order to do so they have poetic feelings about poetic experiences" (p. 561). In Boland's case this "debased romanticism" stood between her and the poetry she wanted to write, not least because it appeared to reinforce the position of women as a "minority in the expressive poetic tradition." Leavis was not concerned with the gender of poets. In that sense the nineteenth century was put to different intellectual and ideological use in his argument. But he discerned in the nineteenth century the same idea that "certain things are poetical, e.g. flowers, dawn, dew, birds, love, archaisms and country place-names," and that the effect of the "poetical" is to put a barrier between poets and politically or morally important subject matter.

This critique of the nineteenth century is not unique to Leavis and Boland. It recurs in the work of writers otherwise as different from each other as Leavis is from Boland: Gertrude Stein and Ezra Pound for example. The repetitive character of the critique and its occurrence in different times and contexts suggest that the nineteenth century is the symptom of a wider malaise. For a number of twentieth-century poets and critics the nineteenth century is used to identify an anxiety about poetry becoming a standardized product, subject to a banal repetition of language and subject matter. This standardization makes one poem very much like another, and therefore compromises the claim of poetry to be an art if it is assumed that one of the things that makes something into a work of art is its uniqueness. Leavis asserted that this standardization is a "tendency in every age" and, therefore, not a burden unique to twentieth-century poetry.

But, in his very formulation of the problem, Leavis indicated something about its distinctive modernity. It resides in the traces of a philosophy of history that sets the realization of freedom as one of history's goals. The past is imagined as something that weighs upon the minds of the living and has to be cast off if freedom is to be realized. The scale of that emancipation – its difficulties, struggles, and triumphs – will depend upon what is defined as the inherited oppression. In the terms of this historical story, modern poetry has to overcome the stale habits and exhausted vocabularies of nineteenth-century poetry, a poetry that is failing to respond to its historical moment. And this, in turn, means challenging inherited assumptions about the identity of the poet and the poem.

The identity of the poet

The argument about the identity of the poet turned on an idea of impersonality regarded as a key element in the creation of a new twentieth-century poetry. Writing in 1919, T. S. Eliot insisted that poetry is "not the expression of a personality, but an escape from personality." Writing in 1950, Charles Olson wanted poets to become carpenters of language, ridding poetry of the "lyrical interference of the individual as ego, of the 'subject' and his soul." The very phrasing of the argument implied that poetry has been devalued or compromised by its association with expressions of personality. In Olson's case, this, in turn, was connected to one of poetry's major genres, the lyric.

What both writers rejected is a view epitomized by the nineteenth-century philosopher, John Stuart Mill, when he described poetry as "feeling confessing itself to itself in moments of solitude."[2] An awkward paradox hovered around Mill's remark, and it was one etched into the poetics of Romanticism from which it derived. If the poem was an auto-confession of feeling – feeling addressed to itself – it was also a means of presenting this curious privacy to the public. In the same essay Mill claimed that readers "overhear" poems, as though listening through a keyhole. The insistence on solitude, and the apparent absence of an audience, was bound up with a criterion of sincerity: if the expression of feeling was to be regarded as sincere it must not be obviously directed towards an audience, otherwise it was in danger of becoming an act of persuasion or an exhibitionistic display.

There is a multiplying anxiety at work here. On the side of the poet the expression of feeling opens up a risk that the feelings may not be understood, or not sympathetically received if understood; or that what is expressed may turn out to be deviant or disturbed in a way not anticipated by the poet; or that the language of the poem is made opaque by words overcharged with personal associations so that what seems important to the poet is trivial to the reader. In short, the danger is that the poet becomes the type of the egotist, demanding that private obsessions be treated as matters of general significance. On the side of the reader there is the possibility, again central to the poetics of Romanticism, of sympathetic communion with the feelings expressed in the poem, but this possibility exists alongside others: the reader as diagnostician of the poet's emotional and mental malaise, or as a voyeur caught in a guilty complicity with the poet's exhibitions of feeling, or as the subject of emotional manipulation.

The poetics of impersonality was an attempt to resist or evade this awkward inheritance. But it would be a mistake to believe that it corresponded to the emergence of a new kind of impersonal poem, or the separation of poetry from feeling or emotion. Eliot's account of impersonality, like Olson's, was not an accurate description of a new poetic practice, more an attempt to establish poetry's cultural authority and its claim upon the reader's attention. At issue was a relocation of both the place of feeling in poetry and the poet's autobiographical relation to the poem. The poet avoided identification as the expressive source of feelings embodied in language and passed over to the reader. At one level there was an attempt to locate the source of feeling in the condition of a whole society or historical epoch or mythical structure. Individual voices in poems such as Eliot's *Waste Land* or Olson's *Maximus Poems*, all rhetorically invented by the poet, display forms of feeling that are always more than just their own. The poet becomes the conductor of affective states whose origins are not readily identifiable. The poem becomes an artifact in which these affective states can be contemplated and perhaps shared by the reader. But these relocations do not simply make the poet impersonal. When Eliot wrote that "the progress of an artist is a continual self-sacrifice, a continual extinction of personality" he was actually establishing a context for the display of personality in the course of its repeated extinction and resurrection.[3]

The identity of the poem

Accounts of poetic impersonality were matched by redefinitions of the identity of the poem. Some of these were inspired by a wish to make the poem into something less fragile and more solid than words on a printed page. In his letter of 1903 written to Lou-Andreas Salomé, the Austrian poet, Rilke, set out his wish to make poems on the model of Rodin's paintings and sculptures. These could "implant the thing into the surrounding space... so that it does not move when you shake it. The *thing* is definite, the *art-thing* must be still more definite" (p. 36). Writing some forty years after Rilke, and in a different context and tradition, a similar aspiration is at work in the American poet Louis Zukofsky. For Zukofsky a good poem is "precise information on existence... [integrating] any human emotion, any discourse into an order of words that exists as another created thing in the world, to affect it and be judged by it" (p. 297). Poems were no longer the tremulous, dependent children of poets. They had to stand in the world with the solidity of something engineered or be before their readers in the way that paintings and sculptures stood before their viewers.

These imaginings of the poem as object are, of course, charged with metaphor – they are reminders that thinking about poetry is as much conducted by metaphors as by definitions and concepts. The poem's identity as an object is informed by the literal and symbolic space in which it is imagined. In Rilke's case this is obviously a space of art. His ideal of the "thing-poem" is born out of his observation of Rodin at work in his studio, and his envy of Rodin's artisan confidence in what he is doing.[4] But it is also an organic space – one in which the thing is implanted – and a context of practical activity in which something can take on the solidity of being. In this context the poem can become something more than a representation of something else. For Rilke this move beyond representation is bound up with the relation of the poem to the poet's subjectivity. In the same letter he writes that "in any successful poem of mine there is so much more reality than in any mood or tendency I may feel." For Zukofsky the space of the poem as "created thing" is different, at once more obviously technical in its emphasis on "precise information" and less fraught with existential anxiety than is the case with Rilke. Zukofsky's "created thing" is like a responsible citizen, democratically open to "any human discourse" but bounded, and hence capable of affecting the world and being judged by it. Zukofsky's poem is a recognizably American object, placed, by implication, in the ideal space of an energetic and democratic egalitarianism. By contrast, Rilke's "thing-poem" is surrounded by the tremulous anxieties of a European culture on the verge of war and revolution.

The recurrent idea of the poem as object constitutes a recognizable sequence in modernist poetics and, in Zukofsky's case, gave its name to a poetic movement, "Objectivism." But the poem as object or thing is only one amongst a number of metaphors for the poem's identity. The variety of metaphors – including the poem as machine, as confession, as image, as icon, as seductive dress, or as counter-weight – indicate that what is at stake in discussions of the identity of the poem is not just the apparent fact of its being printed as a shape on the page and read. Nothing, or little, can be taken for granted. What a poem is and how it might relate to its readers are issues that have to be returned to not just once but many times, and this has been interpreted either as a vexing sign of modern poetry's fragmentation or as a manifestation of its energetic experimentalism.

Rhythm

But something else drives this multiplication of metaphors and their corresponding ideas of the poem's identity. In the early years of the twentieth century – some would argue earlier – poets began to invent verse forms that broke from traditional meters. What had been one of the defining characteristics of poetry as a literary genre, and hence of the identity of the poem, was rejected. The rejection went under a number of names, notably, in the early years of the century, that of *vers libre* or "free verse," and it was often connected to the rejection of nineteenth-century precedent. In his instruction manuals for the writing of a new poetry, including *A Retrospect* published in 1918, Ezra Pound rejected a poetic rhythm composed in the "sequence of a metronome." As the context makes clear some of the worst offenders in this regard were nineteenth-century poets whose "words are shoveled in to fill a metric pattern or to complete the noise of a rhyme sound."

Equally didactic, the Russian poet Mayakovsky, writing in 1926, rejected "the learning up of other people's measurements: iambus, trochee, or even this much vaunted free verse" and demanded a "rhythm accommodating itself to some concrete situation, and of use only for that concrete situation" (p. 147). Mayakovsky's impatience with "other people's measurements" is indicative of at least two things: the rejection of traditional prosody was an international and cosmopolitan movement, with poets in one country aware of experiments in other places; and such was the controversy surrounding this break from inherited meters that "free verse" itself rapidly became identified as an experiment that had failed.

Statements like Pound's and Mayakovsky's can be readily found in a variety of contexts and traditions from the early twentieth century onwards. Some of them seem to be devoted to bringing controversy to an end, as in Amy Lowell's 1917 defense of *vers libre* as another "prosodic form"; others wanted to stir it up, as in Allen Ginsberg's rejection, published in 1961, of "fixed line count" as one amongst a number of formal conventions that distort "my own mind which has no beginning or end." But whatever the differences of accent and purpose they all share the same wish to reject or displace traditional meter as a central component of poetic form.

These rejections of conventional prosody seem to represent in an obvious way the break with an existing tradition of practice or belief that is one of the hallmarks of modernity; hence its place in the stories about modern poetry that stress its break from the nineteenth century. Yet this historical story is in need of immediate qualification. Amy Lowell, for example, did not regard *vers libre* as a break from past practice so much as a moment in the evolution of poetic forms, and one that called for a new way of communicating poetry through the spoken rather than the printed word. Her sense of poetry was capacious enough to allow old and new rhythms to coexist alongside each other.

Beyond any differences in historical accounting are further questions about what these new rhythms represent. Sometimes they appeared as something deeply intimate to the poet, a further reminder that modern poetry declared itself as much through its individualism as through its claim to impersonality. "A man's rhythm," wrote Pound, "must be interpretative, it will be, therefore, in the end his own, uncounterfeiting, uncounterfeitable" (p. 87). Pound's statement rehearses one of his familiar equivalencies between poetry and money. Here poetry is understood, paradoxically, as a currency that cannot be counterfeited, whereas it might be thought that it is a condition of a currency that it can be. But it also contains an echo of a classical maxim – "style is the man" – rewritten in a way that suggests a kind of character test: what is most a poet's own, what is least borrowed, what is more his than he perhaps knows, is rhythm. It interprets him. A similar sense of masculine intimacy and testing came from one of Pound's followers, Charles Olson, writing in 1950: "the line comes . . . from the breath, from the breathing of the man who writes, at the moment that he writes, and thus is, it is here that, the daily work, the WORK, gets in, for only he, the man who writes, can declare, at every moment the line its metric and its ending" (p. 291). But the gender here need not always be male. In 1925 Mina Loy described poetic rhythm as "the chart of a temperament."

The idea of rhythm as an intimate or individual signature of the poet is only one aspect of its significance. If rhythm is something that seems to come from deep within the poet as an individual and particular identity, it is not an exaggeration to suggest that it is also something like its opposite. Mayakovsky found it difficult to make up his mind about the location of rhythm, while providing numerous examples – "The sound of the sea, endlessly repeated . . . a servant who slams the door every morning" – of rhythm's origins in the external world (p. 147). Pound's formulations were not exactly contradictory, but they indicate a similar ambivalence. His assertion about rhythm as individual signature came in the same text as that where he commended the rhythm that comes from composing in the "sequence of the musical phrase." It is the ambivalence rather than its resolution that is significant. Rhythm's mobility, coming from within the self or outside it, indicates a hesitation before too strict a demarcation between "inner" self and "outer" world, and, hence, of placing the poem's origin too firmly in either.

What is common to this hesitation and double accounting is that rhythm marks the identity of the poem as a relation to something that is displayed within it and yet also exists beyond it. Such at least is one result of the frequent restatements of the significance of rhythm in modern poetry and poetics. The most strenuous of these formulations identify rhythm as the junction point between an absolute order and a particular moment in experience. Lawrence's account of free verse in his 1920 Preface to the American edition of his *New Poems* bears this kind of burden. Free verse fuses the personal and the impersonal, at once the "direct utterance from the instant whole man" and the "insurgent naked throb of the instant moment." This intensely metaphorical account of the poetic seeks to discover the absolute within experience rather than beyond it in the "seething poetry of the incarnate Now." But each "incarnate Now" is different from another, and so each must be differently realized: "The law must come new each time from within" (p. 109). Lawrence's invocation of the law invokes the idea that the poem's identity is not arbitrary or whimsically subjective but informed by what is necessary. It has to be as it is. But "within" is left grammatically and conceptually unresolved. It can be located in the poet or the instant, or both. Rhythm bears the poem beyond the representation or the commemoration of an experience. It is the moment when the distinction between the subject and the object of experience, the observer and the observed, dissolves.

Lawrence's Preface was an attempt to create an enabling myth about his poems or, from a more skeptical perspective, produce an effective advertisement for them. It did not correspond in any simple way to his poetry, which, in addition to experiments in rhythm, contains traditional forms and tender observations. His exalted claims might seem merely eccentric but they are not. Later in the century Julia Kristeva, drawing on the technical vocabularies of psychoanalysis and linguistics, bestowed upon rhythm an equally powerful function. In the work of the Russian poets Mayakovsky and Khlebnikov it marks the return of repressed libidinal drives in language, one side of a symbolic drama that pits the "paternal law" against desire. The high seriousness of this kind of claim about rhythm, and of the manifesto-like declaration of yet another new poetics, invited parody. In "Personism: a Manifesto," published in 1961, Frank O'Hara was clearly tired of such talk. Poking fun at the projective verse poetics of Olson and William Carlos Williams's preoccupation with measure, O'Hara translates a traditional idea about rhythm – that it ornaments the poem's subject – into the language of gay seduction: "if you're going to buy a pair of pants you want them to be tight enough so that everyone will go to bed with you" (p. 368). Rhythm makes language desirable and the more who are turned on by it the better.

For the early modernists in particular a polemic against the nineteenth century was useful in getting a new way of thinking about poetry started. Out of this thinking ideas emerged about the identity of the poet and the poem that in turn produced their legacies of elaboration and disagreement. But none of this amounted to an agreement amongst poets and critics about the definition of a new poetry. Lawrence's 1920 Preface is one example of the argument over the meaning of free verse and its value. Lawrence, like Mayakovsky, thought the Imagists had got it wrong. Their version of free verse wasn't really free at all. It was a weakly nihilistic gesture: breaking "the lovely form of metrical verse" and presenting it as "a new substance." Similarly ideas about poetic impersonality took on very different ideological meanings. In the work of T. S. Eliot and Charles Olson, it took on a religious connotation, in Eliot's case directed towards

Christianity, and, in Olson's, towards Buddhism. The Italian poet Marinetti was an advocate of impersonality too, and in a way that disposed him to sympathize with Mussolini's fascism in the 1920s. In his 1912 "Technical Manifesto of Futurist Literature," he issued a command to "Destroy the *I* in literature: that is psychology." But this concern to destroy in order to liberate a new creation was not the condition, as it was in Eliot, of a religious sacrifice of the self. What Marinetti hoped for was an impersonal "machine poem," a poem that worked like the cinema, "the dance of an object that divides and recomposes without human intervention" (p. 59).

The French poet, Apollinaire, writing within a few years of Marinetti, anticipated a similar migration of poetry into what were then the new technologies of sound and vision provided by film and the phonograph. A further variation on the idea of impersonality came with the work of the Surrealists. In the 1920s and 1930s Éluard and Breton developed the practice of automatic writing as the core technique of a new poetry. The practice was not simply confined to Surrealism. In the different context of his interests in the spirit world and mediums, W. B. Yeats had conducted experiments in automatic writing from as early as 1912. Like Éluard and Breton, Yeats believed that automatic writing gave access to images beyond the conscious mind and control of the poet.

The paradox of automatic writing was that it is a deliberate technique for doing away with all deliberation. Clearly the Surrealists' version of impersonality depended upon a different account from Eliot's of the self that had to be overcome. For Eliot it was the self of "personality and emotions." For Éluard and Breton it was the "ego," an identity based upon the repression of unconscious drives. What followed from these various versions of poetic impersonality could scarcely be more different. In Eliot's case it lead to poetry that, as F. R. Leavis acknowledged, may well be accessible only to a minority of readers. But automatic writing was conceived of as a technique open to all. It was part of the Surrealists' conviction that they had discovered a universal and authentic cultural form. Their version of the emancipation necessary to create a modern poetry consisted in the abolition of the poet and poetry as specialist categories. According to Breton "all men, all women, deserve to be convinced of the absolute possibility of their own appeal to that language which . . . is for each and every one the vehicle of a revelation" (p. 189). If one of the dreams of modern poetry was the creation of a poem so difficult that it challenged the very possibility of its interpretation, another was that everyone would become a poet.

Lyric

The question of poetic impersonality and the issue of modern poetry's relation to the nineteenth century find another focus in twentieth-century debates about lyric form. Charles Olson, as we have seen, wanted to be rid of the "lyrical interference of the individual ego." He associated the lyric with its Romantic and nineteenth-century versions, exactly that moment of "feeling confessing itself to itself in moments of solitude," that John Stuart Mill had identified as the essence of all poetry. For Olson this kind of expressiveness was fraught with self-importance. It prevented a democratic understanding that we are creatures of nature set alongside "those other creations of nature which we may, with no derogation, call objects." His irritation with the lyric had its precursor in Pound's desire for poetry without linguistic or emotional inflation. Marinetti's condemnation of the "I in literature" might seem to point in the same direction, but, in his case, what is envisaged is the abolition of one kind of lyricism and its replacement by another, a "lyricism of matter" that can celebrate a "strip of steel" or the "warmth of iron or wood."

In Apollinaire's essay, "The New Spirit and the Poets," the word "lyricism" was ambiguously placed. Apollinaire argued that free verse and typographic design might renew an exhausted lyricism but later in the same essay he argued that the new poetry will displace the lyric as the defining instance of poetry itself: "The new spirit... admits even hazardous literary experience, and those experiences are at times anything but lyric" (p. 78). The context suggests that "hazardous literary experience" included formal experiment for its own sake, a poetry of humor and ridicule, and a willingness to write in ways that will meet with condemnation or incredulity. Apollinaire's ambivalence about lyricism indicated a division in his thinking about the role of poetry in modernity: as a renewal of tradition or a belief that the authentically new called for a radical break from the past.

Olson, Apollinaire, and Marinetti were all preoccupied by a doubt about whether modern poetry could find a place for the expression of feeling and the presence of an individual voice associated with lyric. There was either no place for lyricism (Olson), some place for it (Apollinaire), or a new place (Marinetti). But for others the value of lyric form and its essential modernity was not open to doubt in this way. In his essay, "On Lyric Poetry and Society," written in the same decade as Olson's manifesto for projective verse, the German critic Theodor Adorno, argued that the lyric was the exemplary form of modern poetry. One reason for this dramatic difference in accounting for the lyric was Adorno's historical and conceptual understanding of modernity. Adorno identified the historical origins of modern poetry in the eighteenth century, not in a break from the nineteenth. His exemplary modern poet was Goethe, not, as it was for F. R. Leavis, T. S. Eliot. The basic dynamic of modern experience was not identified with the technological developments that excited Marinetti and Apollinaire, but rested in Adorno's interpretation of the typical social situation produced by capitalism, one that "every individual experiences as hostile, alien, cold, oppressive." The lyric poem arose as an essentially modern form of protest against this condition. But this protest was implicit. For Adorno the social significance of lyric poetry was not found in its explicit content but in what the very existence of the form presupposed: a subjective expression that, in order to exist at all, had to appear remote from society, and sought out a nature freed from economic exploitation. A central poetic trope of the nineteenth-century lyric, the projection of human feeling on to the natural world, was not a symptom of conceited anthropomorphism, but a utopian moment that restored to nature a dignity and life that "human domination has taken away from it."

Adorno argued that even the most ethereal and apparently private lyric could carry a utopian content, a longing for a world that is no longer "alien to the subject and to love for it as well." He did not conceive of subjectivity as something that gets in the way of objectivity, as did Anglo-American modernists such Olson, T. E. Hulme, or Pound. And the sources of his thinking in Marx did not lead him to celebrate the virtues of the "dry, hard, classical verse" that Hulme hoped would epitomize modern poetry. Celebrations of the objective carried another meaning for Adorno. They represented a further stage in the triumph of "reification," "the domination of human beings by commodities that has developed since the beginning of the modern era (p. 345)."

Great lyric poetry had the capacity momentarily to transcend this condition through its specific character as an art of language. It worked in a medium described by Adorno as "double": language informed subjective experience and was a condition of the most individual of experiences, but it was also made up of concepts that "established a relation to the universal and to society." Lyric poetry was an art of synthesis and reconciliation. It emerged from individual expression and the mark of individual voice was always present in it, not sacrificed or renounced to some larger power. But through individual expression something more than individual expression occurred. In Adorno's formulation "language acquired a voice." The relation of the individual to the collective was no longer one of antagonism or isolation. The movement and dynamism of lyric language represented the possibility of a fluid exchange between the individual and collective voices just as it intimated a sympathetic communion between the human and the natural worlds.

But lyric's modernity – beginning in the eighteenth century with the work of Goethe and continuing in the nineteenth in the work of Baudelaire, Morike, and Georg – was both troubled and threatened. Adorno's analysis of the direction of modern society was pessimistic. The imperatives of economic production, and the social forms associated with it, turned the individual into a set of administrative and economic functions that could be exchanged in the manner of commodities. As this happened the individuality vital to lyric was undermined, and the expression of individual voice became more mannered and artificial, increasingly isolated from the currents of collective experience that were vital to lyric's value as a modern form.[5]

Adorno's essay draws attention to what might appear to be an antithetical tradition in the interpretation of modern poetry, one that proposes the nineteenth century as the epoch of modern poetry, not its discredited precursor. And in Adorno's case the twentieth century threatened to become the time of poetry's terminal crisis, not of its rebirth and renewal. But the idea of an antithetical tradition implies too neat a distinction. The accounts of modern poetry's relation to the nineteenth century are created out of ambivalence. The Surrealist poets – Césaire, Breton, and Éluard – regarded their work as building on their nineteenth-century predecessors, Baudelaire, de Lautréamont, and Rimbaud. At the same time they condemned the nineteenth century as the era of bourgeois sterility. F. R. Leavis's scathing comments on nineteenth-century poetry did not stop him from including a nineteenth-century Anglo-Irish poet, Gerard Manley Hopkins, as one of the creators, along with T. S. Eliot and Ezra Pound, of a modern English poetry. D. H. Lawrence identified the nineteenth-century American poet, Walt Whitman, as the first poet of the "urgent, insurgent Now." Adorno's friend and colleague, Walter Benjamin, claimed that the publication of Charles Baudelaire's collection *Les Fleurs du Mal* in 1857 was the decisive event of modern poetry.

Equally, vocabularies of judgment derived from Romanticism were used to identify the modernity of work published in the twentieth century. Writing in 1914, Edward Thomas claimed Robert Frost's 1913 collection, *North of Boston*, as "one of the most revolutionary books of modern times" and identified its value in a language that echoed Wordsworth's justification of his and Coleridge's poetry in the 1800 *Preface to Lyrical Ballads*. Frost's poetry derived its language and meter from "common speech and common decasyllables." It was "free from the poetical words and forms that are the chief material of the secondary poets," and free too, Thomas implied, from the "discord and fuss" of free verse. It was possible for a book to be "revolutionary" and written in pentameters.

These various and divided responses to the nineteenth century raise a large question about what it is being made to stand for in twentieth-century reflections on modern poetry. Here only a sketch of an answer can be given. The attack on nineteenth-century poetry, especially evident amongst early twentieth-century writers, is part of a wider critique that, in a work such as Lytton Strachey's *Eminent Victorians*, questioned nineteenth-century morality or, in the case of Saussure's linguistics, its intellectual methods. Epochal change was called for in western culture generally and poetry was no exception to this demand. Writers who viewed nineteenth-century poetry as modern rather than pre-modern shared an assumption that one of poetry's central values lay in its power as a social critique. The terminology of this critique took various forms. It could be darkly glamorous, as in Éluard's association of the exemplary poets and thinkers of the nineteenth century with "The Evil principle... in opposition to bourgeois good." Or it could, more benignly, return us to a natural world that had been put in peril by the forces of industrial production.

But the idea that poetry is, in a sense basic to its value, opposed to the dominant or mainstream culture is only one side of the story of modern poetry's relation to the nineteenth century. The other, as I have already suggested, has to do with a recurrent belief about poetry's tendency to become precious, or stylized, or formulaic. Insofar as nineteenth-century poetry is identified with this tendency, it occupies a position in arguments about poetic language that will be occupied later by Eavan Boland's wariness about the "American workshop poem," or Adrienne Rich's impatience with poetry's incorporation in the academy. This kind of thinking indicates a typically modern preoccupation with originality or an equally typical modern anxiety about standardization. Poetry as practiced is in danger of becoming a claustrophobic inheritance. It needs to turn to something outside it that it is in danger of excluding. This can be a matter of how to get the impress of individual voice and experience into poetry, as it is for Eavan Boland, and then testing what it is that can make that voice more than just individual. But the belief that poetry has become standardized in a way that exlcudes individual experience is complicated by the recurrent anxiety about egotism that haunts discussions of modern poetry. For some critics the problem is that poetry becomes formulaic exactly because it is preoccupied with the self and its expressions. Edward Thomas thought Robert Frost's originality lay in his avoidance of the "egoistic rhetoric" that drew on the formulae of "poetical words." The danger of these words lay precisely in the fact that they might appear too much concerned with the poet's projection of his identity. For Thomas, poetry is renewed by its contact either with "non-poetic" idioms or with perceptions thought to be unclouded by habit or convention. It became better poetry by moving to the condition of prose.

Where and how these idioms and perceptions are to be identified is a recurrent preoccupation. Walter Benjamin noted Baudelaire's deliberate linguistic dissonance, his capacity to bring together in one poem contemporary urban idioms and the language of the French poetic tradition. Bringing street language into poetry has become one of the ways in which a poem can announce its modernity. But the renewal of poetic language can come from other sources. What Edward Thomas heard in Frost's poetry, the sound of "common words," had a rural not an urban context. Poetry escaped from "poetical words" by presenting language in its natural condition. But to invoke language in its natural condition is fraught with ambiguity and controversy. The ambiguity arises from different and often unstated assumptions about what is to count as natural; the controversy from the idea that language can have a natural condition at all. In Thomas's praise of Frost the idea of a natural language is derived from an assumption about the kind of language spoken by people who live close to nature. This language can return poetry to "common words," the words that we all supposedly share apart from linguistic differences created by ethnicity, class, gender, place, or profession. Or, as is the case with Pound's belief that "the proper and perfect symbol is the natural object," poetry gains an authority from nature by discovering a language that will give us an unadorned sense of natural things or states.

The list can be readily extended. Charles Olson's projective verse poetics discovered the connection between poetic language and nature in poetry's fidelity to the rhythms of embodied perception. Yet another direction of thinking and poetic practice, associated with the work of Heidegger and Blanchot, was concerned with a poetry that might reveal the inner nature or being of language itself. The poet, in Heidegger's formulation, "listens to the appeal of language" and it is in this listening that the nature of language will manifest itself. But, for Heidegger at least and those who followed him, this means removing poetic language from any contact with contemporary idioms because these show a language subjected to a relentless use far removed from listening; what he calls "an unbridled yet clever talking, writing and broadcasting of spoken words in which the being of language is abused" (p. 255). If language has a being, and if poetry has a special care for this being, from this perspective it is one endlessly threatened by the rapid cycling and recycling of language by technology.[6]

Tradition, Myth, Antiquity

Thinking about modern poetry in the twentieth century develops different accounts of the nineteenth century and these form a crucial element in historical narratives about how and when modern poetry emerges, and how the conditions of its emergence are a measure of its distinction. Understanding something quite specific to poetry – the value of poetic language, for example – depends upon understanding the place of poetry in a cultural and historical context. But reflection on modern poetry brings out another kind of relation between poetry and history. This is not so much to do with stories about modern poetry's emergence. Instead it identifies modern poetry's distinctive force as a special kind of archaeology, a capacity to bring a remote historic or mythical time into the present. Poetry shatters or overcomes historical time as a form of orderly sequence.

Eliot's essay, "Tradition and the Individual Talent," argued that poetic impersonality was dependent upon a concept of tradition. Eliot developed a dialectical account of the nature of tradition, a dialectic that brings what is temporally distant into the present moment at the same time as it invites a reflection on the present as part of a timeless order. The dedicated modern poet should write "not merely with his own generation in his bones, but with a feeling that the whole of the literature of Europe from Homer and within it the whole of the literature of his own country has a simultaneous existence and composes a simultaneous order." Poems in this exacting and ambitious project became the compositions of the tradition that also composed them. In the paradoxical time of tradition the dead come back to life and with a power that can seem greater than that of the living. According to Eliot the "best parts" of a modern poet's work will be those where "the dead poets, his ancestors, assert their immortality most vigorously" (p. 98). Like a figure in a Gothic fiction, the impersonal poet stands in the margin between the dead and the living, escaping from the emotional burdens of modernity by becoming a medium for the dead.[7]

Eliot's concept of tradition has its own pathos. It can only be acquired through "great labour." The order created out of the dialectical interaction between the poetry of the past and the present is felt to be a form of consolation in the face of the violence and disorder of modernity, whose most pressing example for Eliot was the First World War. The poetry of tradition, housed in its alternative order, holds out the possibility that this very disorder may itself be only a moment in a mythical and repetitive pattern of sacrifice and renewal. Walter Benjamin found in Baudelaire's poetry a similar encounter between a remote past and present time. In his interpretation of Baudelaire's poem, "The Swan," Benjamin detected the presence of figures from antiquity in the midst of modern urban experience. Again the poem is imagined as acting on time as well as within it. In this case the effect of bringing figures from the far past into the present is to bring time to a standstill. A mood and a perspective emerge out of this stasis. The energies of the modern city – its crowds, its commodities, its ceaseless transformations – momentarily fade away. Their place is taken by the figures of desolation and exile that haunt the modern city and the ancient world alike.

What Baudelaire and Eliot shared, despite their many differences, was a vision of modernity as "a destitute time," a phrase that Heidegger took over from the German poet, Hölderlin. The juxtaposition of a historically distant image or language with the present is a key element in the creation of this vision. Writing in the 1940s, Heidegger identified the cultural significance of modern poetry in these terms: modernity is understood as an epochal event, marking a major change in our experience of the world. The source of this change is the disappearance of the gods: "Night is falling. Ever since the 'united three' – Herakles, Dionysos, and Christ – have left the world, the evening of the world's age has been declining towards its night" (p. 251). Here, what is historically distant is also what is disappearing, something that leaves behind it only traces of its existence. His exemplary modern poet, Hölderlin, bears witness to this change and to the loss it brings with it: a loss described by Heidegger as the "complete absence of ground," or the "abyss." The task of poetry, in bearing witness, is twofold: to search out the traces of "divine radiance" that fitfully appear in the long night of modernity and, by doing this, anticipate and prepare for divinity's return.[8]

To think about poetry in this way is to give it a pivotal role in modern culture. One of poetry's oldest obligations, to commemorate, is redefined by Eliot, Benjamin, and Heidegger as a special form of witnessing, not just to a heroic individual, or to a specific event, but to a whole cultural epoch, the epoch of modernity. Poetry becomes a form of heroic action, something that defines or resists modernity as well as being defined by it. And if poetry is a kind of heroic action, then the poet is a kind of hero. The exact shapes of this heroism will vary from one writer to another. For Eliot the heroic poet is a figure of labor and sacrifice. For Benjamin, Baudelaire's heroic act is to absorb the shocks of modern experience and turn them into lyric poetry. For Heidegger the poet's courage is found in a special attunement to the vestiges of sacred experience in modernity's darkness. And each assumed what many other writers about modern poetry assume, that another side of this heroism is the act of writing poetry at all in a culture that appears either indifferent or hostile to it.

However, gloom is not all-pervasive, even amongst the gloomy. The belief that, as F. R. Leavis put it, "Poetry matters little to the modern world" has proved a fruitful myth, not least because the terms of the modern world's hostility or indifference can be endlessly reinvented in ways that make poetry distinctive. Similarly, the belief that poetry can splice the past into the present does not automatically lead to visions of modernity as desolation row. The notion of tradition has different inflections. In 1928 Robert Graves and Laura Riding argued that poetry is a form of autonomous energy, no different now from what it had been in Homeric times. Insofar as modern culture threatened this autonomy it did so by making poets believe that poetry must progress in the way that civilization is supposed to do.

In 1950 Louis Zukofsky affirmed a similar continuity between modern poetry and its archaic forms: "It is quite safe to say that the *means* and *objects* of poetry have been constant, that is, recognizably human since ca. 3000 B.C." (p. 298). There is an air of cool provocation about this kind of statement. Modern poetry distinguishes itself in a culture where change is the norm by not changing. Its capacity to defeat expectations about the effects of history becomes a source of its authority.

Writing in the mid-1970s, Derek Walcott transposed the authority of tradition into the context of debates about postcolonial culture. Acknowledging that the history of modern culture is a history of colonialism and its aftermath, Walcott contrasted two responses to this circumstance: one "whose muse of history has produced a literature of recrimination and despair, a literature of revenge written by the descendants of slaves or a literature of remorse written by the descendants of masters"; another that feels no obligation to make amends and reimagines the past as a "timeless, yet habitable moment." Walcott rejected "the literature of recrimination and despair" in favor of his own version of the heroic poet, "carrying entire cultures in his head, bitter, but unencumbered." The cultures of colonial power are open to imaginative appropriation. The imagination sustained by tradition discovers that the past repeats itself in the present and the Old World in the New, but this creates an "elation which sees everything as renewed," not "the jaded cynicism which sees nothing new under the sun" (pp. 421, 422).

Walcott imagined his hero poet as an extra-institutional figure, wandering through the wide spaces of the new world of the Americas. Tradition is something that can travel across continents and ideological debates. It is presented by Walcott as a method of poetic survival, and no longer carries the connotations of sacrifice and laborious submission that it did for Eliot. These different inflections of tradition point to the shifting nature of its presence in accounts of modern poetry: as authority and obligation in the case of Eliot; as a continuity of fundamental craft and technique in the case of Graves, Riding, and Zukofsky; as the basis for imaginative freedom in Walcott. Each of these inflections in turn indicates a judgment on modernity and the place of poetry within it.

Poetry's intimacy with tradition becomes a means of conferring value upon it. Its different inflections and restatements across the twentieth century suggest that this value cannot be taken for granted, that it must be constantly defended against implied or explicit threats. If one arc of argument is concerned with declaring modern poetry's distinction by its break from the past of yesterday, or last year, or the last century, another finds poetry's distinction in its relation to the past imagined as tradition. For a writer such as Walcott the concept of tradition can transform the past into a chosen rather than imposed inheritance. But for others what is imposed looms much larger and this adds a further complication to the question of tradition.

In 1926, the Harlem Renaissance writer Langston Hughes imagined American space dominated by the "racial mountain." The effects of this domination take two related forms. One is to inhibit the emergence of a poetic identity: the "negro poet" proud to live by that name. The other is to prevent the recognition of a black cultural tradition that draws on the energies of jazz, blues, and the speech idioms of black Americans. What Hughes proposed as an alternative to these constraints is in effect the creation of a tradition for the future, borne along by a messianic rhetoric that will overcome the subconscious message that "white is best" (p. 142).

The date of Hughes's essay is a reminder that modern poetry's implication in the politics of identity has a long history. Arguments about the value of poetry are embedded in narratives about identities affirmed in the face of repression and denial. Writing more than fifty years after Hughes, Adrienne Rich found an "aesthetic ideology" not a "racial mountain" standing between her and her ambition to become a woman poet. Overcoming this "aesthetic ideology" called for the invention of what is presented as a new poetry of personal testimony and inwardness, and a simultaneous rejection of "the dominant critical idea that the poem's text should be read as separate from the poet's everyday life in the world" (p. 510). This turn towards autobiographical form carried a double significance that is part of the persuasive intent of Rich's writing about poetry. On the one hand it stands opposed to the "aesthetic ideology" that denies any value or expression to the experiences of individual women's lives. On the other, it seeks to avert the dangers of narcissistic self-involvement by appeal to a kind of reading in which the reader will come to recognize her own experience in the experience of the poet.

Rich's essay might seem to represent another kind of transition, away from a poetry that finds its authority in literary tradition towards a poetry that draws its justifications from politics. What Eliot defined as a tradition in 1919 has by 1984 become what nineteenth-century poetry was for F. R. Leavis: the confining "ideas of the essentially poetical which . . . bar the poet from his most valuable material." A tradition that had to Eliot seemed beleaguered by modernity has taken on the insidious power of an "aesthetic ideology." It might be argued that this is one of the ways in which the conception of poetry as a critical art changes across the century. No longer concerned with defending the imaginary past of tradition, the new poetics is drawn into a more searching and self-conscious scrutiny that attempts to square the demands of social justice, individual conscience, and the art of poetry. Its starting point is to ask a question about what has been excluded, or silenced, or misheard by what Charles Bernstein has called "official verse culture."

But this kind of analysis seems at best partial. Langston Hughes's attack on the "racial mountain" is only one example from earlier in the twentieth century of the attempt to charge poetry with a political mission. In 1912, T. E. Hulme identified the new Imagist poetry of "accurate, precise and definite description" with a conservative political ideology, a view of human nature as "intrinsically limited, but disciplined by order and tradition to something fairly decent." Here the idea of tradition is implicated in a political rhetoric as it was to be later in T. S. Eliot's dream of an English culture ordered by the traditions of Anglican religion.

In 1926 Mayakovsky placed his new poetics squarely in the context of a revolutionary Marxist politics. His work provides a clear example of a poetics that uses politics as an alternative to tradition. Mayakovsky reimagined poetry as a proletarian art, with its own rules of production, and one whose value was defined by its contribution to class struggle, although the ironies that enter into the prose of *How Are Verses Made?* suggest that he was aware of the dangers of hyperbole that might enter into such a claim. Pound and Marinetti, although by very different routes, imagined that their ideas of poetic order and energy could find a political equivalent in fascism. In each case poetry is thought to take on new power and value, and often new readerships, by its association with politics, as if, by this association, it could be taken out of its place on the margins of culture.[9]

These imaginings of poetry's exaltation by politics are shadowed by a darker, more ironic counterpoint. The passage from poetic self-creation to the politics of identity is rarely straightforward, not least because the desired identity once achieved can in itself become constraining.[10] Writing within a decade of Adrienne Rich's essay, Eavan Boland, while respecting the force of Rich's analysis, found that "feminist ideology" was one of the cultural authorities that stood between her and what she wanted to write about. W. H. Auden, after a period in the 1930s when he wrote politically committed poetry, had second thoughts. By 1962 he argued that poetry and politics were best kept apart. Any political state modeled on ideals of poetic form was bound to be a tyranny. But Auden also discerned a change in the nature of modern politics itself: no longer concerned with the liberty of the citizen or the realization of the just state, politics had become the management of what was needed for human survival, concerned not with "human beings as persons and citizens but with human bodies" (p. 383). The modern collective was essentially a managed one, and poetry's antagonist was no longer the tyrant but the bureaucrat. The very possibility of a public realm of citizens or activists that poetry might help create or address had disappeared. So the "characteristic style of 'Modern' poetry is an intimate tone of voice, the speech of one person addressing one person, not a large audience." This intimate tone is part of poetry's capacity for self-creation, or, in Auden's case, self-preservation. The exemplary poem, or any work of art, reminds "the Management of something managers need to be reminded of, namely, that the managed are people with faces, not anonymous numbers" (p. 383). The political edge to this is ironic and forlorn. The face that poetry turns to its few readers, and the recognition it invites, are essentially private.

Imagined Readers

Auden typifies a certain style of thinking about the place of poetry in modern culture. It is imagined as existing outside major institutions and is valued for its quiet but determined resistance to what those institutions do and say. Its readers are valuable because they are in a minority. What the poem offers them is a kind of human recognition that is denied elsewhere. Poetry, in this view, is essentially an art of consolation, protecting human intimacy from the anonymizing power of modern experience. But Auden's belief that modern poetry is defined by its intimacy of address reminds us of a third identity in addition to that of the poet and the poem: that of the reader.

Writing about modern poetry has bestowed various identities on its readers, or sometimes appeared to ignore them altogether. In 1926 Robert Graves and Laura Riding wrote on behalf of the "plain reader" whose doubts about the credentials of modern poetry needed to be answered. In 1955 Donald Davie deplored the fact that modern poetry had lost touch with the "common reader." Other accounts have identified a reader likely to get things wrong. Thomas Yingling's 1990 study of Hart Crane cautioned against reading Crane's poetry as representing any external reality or inner state of mind. Instead Crane's lyrics should be read "as a constructed verbal artifact rather than as mimetic of any natural discourse" (p. 539). The mistaken reader, as with other varieties of the imagined reader, did not and does not correspond to any actual reader, although each may anticipate and even clarify an aspect of the experience of reading a poem. These various identities for the reader may be accepted by actual readers, or rejected, or briefly entertained. They contribute to the creation of contexts of reading, providing a vocabulary that may help readers understand how they do or should respond to a particular kind of poetry.

But two further identities for the reader need to be mentioned here, both arising from major institutional and intellectual changes in the way that modern poetry is, and has been, read. The first is a mode of reading poetry that requires the acquisition of techniques that are taught in schools and universities. Although this process did not begin in the twentieth century, it acquired a new institutional momentum, as well as an unprecedented conceptual and pedagogic complexity in the period after the First World War. The activity of studying poetry has sometimes been conducted under the banner of cultural or political redemption: teaching the art of reading poetry as a way of securing its readers from the desolating effects of science, or new media or modern power. This transformation of poetry into something that can be taught – requiring, as it does, the invention of the teachable poem – has produced its own sub-set of controversies in the history of thinking about poetry in the twentieth century, aspects of a long-standing debate about the place of poetry inside and outside the university.[11]

The second identity is the reader as critic or theorist. Here the reader becomes a writer with an ambition to put the results of reading into public circulation. Obviously this second identity is related to the first: writing about poetry has come out of universities and one of its motivations has been to teach how poetry should be read. But in an important sense this is not new. The tradition of writing about poetry in reviews, newspapers, and journals goes back to the eighteenth century, and pedagogic imperatives are never far from this kind of activity. What is new is the sheer scale and complexity of the enterprise.

More has been written about all kinds of poetry, including modern poetry, in the twentieth century than in any century preceding it. If the teaching of poetry has been an important stimulus, so has the identification of literature as a subject for university research. The repercussions of this particular episode in the history of poetry as an institution are complex, not least because they have affected the writing of poetry, as well as its reading. Eavan Boland's gloom, already mentioned, about the "American workshop poem" is one response to this. Through the development of creative writing courses, universities have become places where the writing as well as the reading of poems is taught. Apart from that development there has been a suspicion that poets have tended to write the kinds of poem that through their complex structures, their allusiveness, or their ideological tendency lend themselves to classroom treatment. In 1957 Philip Larkin deplored the "cunning merger between poet, literary critic and academic critic (three classes now notoriously indistinguishable)." Larkin saw more fuel in this for the poet's egotism – that modern ghost so difficult to lay to rest – and argued that the "cunning merger" undermined the reader's power to say "I don't like this, bring me something different" (p. 338).

But there is another and more productive history to be discerned here. Its starting points were in the late nineteenth and early twentieth centuries. They include the poetic experiments of the Russian poets, Khlebnikov and Mayakovsky, the work of the nineteenth-century French poets, Rimbaud and Mallarmé; the Anglo-American modernism of E. E. Cummings, T. S. Eliot, and Ezra Pound, and the critical responses provoked by this poetry. In 1965 the French critic Gerard Genette identified the question provoked by this kind of poetic experiment. The traditional distinction between poetry and prose, based upon the presence or absence of regular meters, had been effectively abolished by the work of Rimbaud and Mallarmé. In the absence of this traditional distinction, how was poetry now to be understood? For Genette, as for many others, this question has been approached by way of another about the nature of poetic language.

Language

Modernist experiment provoked a crisis in the theory as well as the practice of poetry. One result of this crisis was the creation of an informal, international research program

– one often not recognized as such – that has resulted in the reinvention of poetics as well as poetry. Its central question has been the one noted by Genette, that is to say, a question about the nature of poetic language. The concerns of an older poetics with how poems represent the world, or with how poetry is an expressive art, are certainly present in the twentieth-century reinvention of poetics, but they first have to be understood or framed as questions about poetic language and how it might differ from other written or spoken forms, such as prose, or the language or everyday speech.

It is out of this energetic contact between theory and practice that many of the central concepts of twentieth-century poetics have been created. They include the idea of ambiguity, given its special application to poetry in the work of William Empson in the 1930s. Empson began with a distinction between the role of ambiguity in everyday language and in poetry. Ambiguity in ordinary speech is something to be avoided because of its association with deceit, whereas in poetic language it is something to be celebrated because it charges language with a multiplicity of possible meanings that the poem can put into play.

Another example is Roman Jakobson's account from 1959 of the "poetic function." According to Jakobson, when language is working poetically all the elements that give form to a message – its sound texture, the ordering of its words, its rhythmic pulse – are brought to our attention, and they begin to dominate, but not exclude, other things that language does: expressing emotions, persuading someone of something, or saying something about the world and what is in it. The "poetic function" makes verbal signs "palpable," reminding us of their physical shape and presence. It provides an alternative principle of verbal structure, one in which the requirement to make a meaning clear is replaced by patterns of language or "verbal sequences" where rhythm, echoes of sound, the repetition of grammatical patterns, and other physical features of language come to predominate. But if the availability of meaning is delayed by the predominance of the poetic function, it is not obliterated by it. The "poetic function" in language promotes an experience of language that Jakobson, quoting the poet Gerard Manley Hopkins, calls "comparison for likeness' sake" and "comparison for unlikeness' sake" (pp. 357).

Poems are the force fields of such an experience of comparison. They build a language within a language, such that words connected by rhyme, rhythm, and other poetic devices create new possibilities of meaning. When the "poetic function" predominates a new grammar is built on top of the ordinary grammar of language, a mode of connecting words outside of the customary sequences of the written or spoken language. As with Empson's concept of ambiguity, the dividing line between poetic and other forms of language is not dogmatically drawn by Jakobson. The poetic function is at work in all language, but it comes to special prominence in poetry where the everyday requirements of clear and rapid communication do not predominate. If the experimental character of modern poetry provoked the questions that inform their work the answers they give apply to poetry as such: "the machinations of ambiguity are among the very roots of poetry" was Empson's claim (p. 171). He went on to apply the concept not just to poetry but to other literary genres. The boldness of Jakobson's account of poetic language was that he held it to be true universally of all poetry from whatever culture or historical period.

Other theorists, such as Roland Barthes, argued that modern poetry is a new event in the history of language. Barthes's historical starting point was the same as Genette's: the abolition of the traditional metrical distinction between prose and poetry. His description of modern poetry drew on the precedent of Tzara's avant-garde practice, as well as the work of modern French poets such as René Char. In Barthes's account modern poetry created an anti-grammar, a radical foregrounding of the poetic word shorn of its syntactical connections to other words. It returned language to enigma and a sense of sacred mystery, distanced from the usual civilities that attend literary writing. Meaning appeared at times as absent, and at others as excessively present; the poet initiated a discourse "filled with absences and overnourishing signs (p. 305)." Barthes shared with Genette a metaphor as well as a starting point, one that connected poetry to language under the conditions of a dream. In Genette's case the content of the dream derived from Mallarmé's poetics: the fantasy of creating a language that will overcome the arbitrary relation between words and what they stand for. Inventing a new theme in poetics, Genette called for a poetics of language, a taxonomy of dreams about language, in addition to dreams in language.

The disjunction between Empson and Jakobson on one side, and Genette and Barthes on the other, renews the question about how modern poetry is to be understood: a renewal of poetry as such or a radical break from the poetry of previous centuries. But the question remains productive and it echoes one raised much earlier in the twentieth century by a writer who was not a theorist of poetic language, but a poet and a reviewer of poetry. Earlier in this introduction I commented on Edward Thomas's response in 1914 to the publication of Robert Frost's *North of Boston*. One thing that made these poems revolutionary for Thomas was their power to raise what he called "the thrilling question: What is poetry?" Thomas's qualification of the question as "thrilling" is as important now as it was then. The danger is that the question can grow stale by repetition. One way of assessing the value of the texts gathered in this anthology is to decide whether they renew excitement and debate about the name and nature of modern poetry.

Poetry in Theory: A User's Guide

The texts collected in this anthology have been organized in a way that is intended to help its readers deepen their understanding of a range of related questions about poetic form and language; about the role of the poet and poetry in modern culture; about the relation of poetry to the other arts; and about what it is that makes modern poetry modern.

The texts have been put into a chronological order of their first date of publication. In a few cases the date has been determined by composition, not publication. Any decision to depart from the date of first publication has resulted from a concern with context. In the case of T. E. Hulme, for example, the date of the composition of "Romanticism and Classicism" has been used because it keeps Hulme's text close to those of Pound and Eliot, both of whom were influenced by Hulme's thinking about the requirements of modern poetry and its historical significance. In the case of the excerpt from Walter Benjamin's text on Baudelaire, the reasoning about context has been a little different. Benjamin was certainly influenced by Marxist debates in the 1930s about criticism and aesthetics – notably through his engagement with Brecht – but he gave an unprecedented philosophical depth and historical specificity to the Marxist analysis of poetry. His work then is of interest as much for its transformation of a context, one scarcely acknowledged at the time, as for its accord with it.

The basic chronological sequence is punctuated by a division into periods of twenty years. This division is not intended to correspond to series of distinct phases in thinking about poetry during the twentieth century. Nonetheless the texts gathered in each twenty-year period do share some thematic and conceptual affinities. The 1900–1920 section gathers a range of texts that illustrate the emergence of the different forms of poetic modernism from the avant-garde practice of Marinetti, the Russian Futurists, and Dada to the new poetics of Imagism and T. S. Eliot's account of poetic impersonality and tradition. Similarly the texts in the 1920–1940 section show, in the work of Graves and Riding and of F. R. Leavis, the early attempts to formulate the lasting significance and value of modernist poetry in English, at the same time as it shows in the texts of Breton, Éluard, and Mayakovsky the different directions taken by avant-garde experiment.

This pattern continues in the remaining sections of the anthology. In each twenty-year section there are texts that show the attempt to understand modernism as an uncompleted project, rather than something that came with explosive force in the early years of the twentieth century and then went into decline. At the same time it is possible to trace lines of writers who respond to each other across the different periods: from Pound and Williams at the beginning of the century to Olson and Zukofsky in the mid-century, for example, or, in the case of Dada and Surrealism, from Tzara to Éluard and Breton and then to Césaire. What is at issue in these responses is not simply a repetition of some single idea or belief about poetry, but a process of redefinition within what is a recognizably shared context of aspiration and assumption.

However, the grouping of texts into twenty-year periods offers important qualifications and alternatives to this pattern. In the period from 1900 to 1920, for example, Yeats's account of poetic symbolism has some technical similarities with Imagism, but a different view of what makes poetry valuable. Amy Lowell, a central figure in the Imagist movement, sees the new poetry as provoking a serious question about poetry as a spoken or written form, a question that does not concern T. E. Hulme or Ezra Pound. Edward Thomas's review of Robert Frost's *North of Boston* might seem a conservative reaction to the poetics of Imagism and free verse, but that is clearly not how he sees it. At any one moment there is always more than one game in town and the selections in this anthology are intended to give the reader the materials for understanding the diversity of thinking about modern poetry, for discovering its surprises as well as recognizing its familiar landmarks.

The decision to organize the anthology into twenty-year sections raised a question about the placing of work published in 1920, 1940, 1960, or 1980. Should it come at the end of one section or the beginning of another? In making decisions about this I have been guided by a sense of intellectual and artistic connection. For example, the pieces by Williams, Lawrence, and Fenollosa, with publication dates in 1920, are strongly connected to earlier discussions about free verse, Imagism, and the creation of a new poetry responsive to modern life. Similarly, the decision to place Roman Jakobson's paper at the end of the 1940–1960 section signals the fact that the formalist and structuralist ideas at work in the essay had a life before the 1960s as well as after them. Jakobson's thinking is rooted in the experiments of Mayakovsky, although "Closing Statement: On Linguistics and Poetics" had a considerable influence on the thinking about poetry in the years after its publication.

The value of an anthology depends on the intrinsic interest of the texts it contains, but also on the opportunities for comparison it creates. A sequential reading provides one basis for comparison, but the thematic index and the introductory notes to each text provide others. The thematic index provides a route through the anthology that is not chronologically sequential but arranged around certain key terms. Some of these are technical: ambiguity, image, the poetic, lyric, and free verse amongst them.

But technical terms are rarely just that. Free verse, for example, is a contested idea throughout the twentieth century because of the different connections that can be made between freedom in verse and other kinds of ethical and political freedom. Arguments about technique become arguments about ideology and the thematic index includes key terms that acknowledge this. So readers who want to trace arguments about poetry and politics, or poetry and gender will find guidance from the thematic index. The introductory notes provide basic information about the author of each text, and a brief summary of its content and significance. Again, where appropriate, the introductory notes make connections with other texts in the anthology.

The selection of texts has been guided by a number of criteria. One of these is to represent the diverse trends in thinking about poetry in the twentieth century. So the ideal of avant-garde experiment can be traced from Tzara's 1919 "Note on Poetry" through Olson's projective verse of 1950 to Marjorie Perloff's reflections on the continuing possibility of experimentalism at the century's end. The inclusion of material in translation – apart from reminding readers that significant thinking about modern poetry occurs in languages other than English – has provided some indication not only of modern poetry's cosmopolitan character, but its different national inflections. The question of where as well as when a self-consciously modern poetry arises is both problematic and fascinating. Apollinaire shares with Éluard and Césaire a belief that French poetry is the first to be authentically modern, whereas for Mayakovsky it is the Russian Revolution that creates the opportunity for the poetry of the future. F. R. Leavis wants to claim Ezra Pound and T. S. Eliot as English poets. Charles Olson's language implies that poetry's new frontier is in the United States. Adrienne Rich thinks that the same country is deeply antagonistic to poetry's flourishing. For Derek Walcott a different sense of the Americas, one that includes both North and South as well as the Caribbean, is the place where the "elemental privilege of naming the New World" arises.

Diversity is a criterion that has another application, one with a bearing on the anthology's title, *Poetry in Theory.* I have not adopted a canonical understanding of theory in selecting texts for inclusion. This anthology does not represent work drawn exclusively from the different theoretical schools – Marxism, feminism, deconstruction, psychoanalysis, new historicism, queer theory, postcolonialism – that have emerged since the early 1960s. Although texts are included that draw on and contribute to these different theoretical movements, I did not want to run the risk of dividing twentieth-century thinking about poetry into its pre-theoretical and theoretical phases, with the dividing line coming somewhere around 1960. To do so would narrow the range of what counts as theory. So this anthology contains texts from a variety of genres: lectures, manifestos, reviews, as well as essays and excerpts from books. I have not assumed that theory is defined by a particular tone, vocabulary, or set of concepts. The selection has been guided by a deliberate eclecticism of method and language. What all the texts have in common is their contribution to understanding the questions outlined at the beginning of this section.

But theory has another sense too, insofar as comparison between texts provokes theoretical questioning and debate. Theory, so to speak, occurs between the selected texts as well as within them. This eclecticism of approach, combined with the conviction that theory arises in acts of reading and comparison, also informs a decision not to make the difference between a modern and postmodern poetics into a major organizing principle of the anthology. A number of the texts included have been read as contributions towards a postmodern poetics, including those by Olson and Bernstein. But the division between the modern and the postmodern can obscure connections between, say, the work of Bernstein and Gertrude Stein. If Stein becomes a postmodernist before her time, the distinction between the modern and the postmodern begins to lose some of its cogency as the marker of a major historical transition. Whether postmodernism is, or is not, an aspect of modernism is a fascinating conceptual debate, and one that readers can follow up by using some of the books listed in this anthology's bibliography. But the anthology itself is not intended as a contribution to this debate. This is so not only for the reasons already stated, but also because there is a body of writing about poetry – including, in this anthology, the texts by Heaney, Milosz, and Vendler – that is only marginally involved in debating the distinction between the modern and the postmodern.

If diversity has been one criterion, another has been the inclusion of texts that are both prospective and retrospective. Both perspectives are involved in thinking about modern poetry. But there is a distinction to be made between those texts that attempt to create a new direction for poetry – by T. E. Hulme, Tristan Tzara, the Surrealists, Charles Bernstein, and the Language Poets – and those that look back on modern poetry as something that has already happened, and may either have ceased or be still in progress. This category of texts includes work by Benjamin, Heidegger, and Adorno; by Barthes, Genette, and Kristeva; by F. R. Leavis, Donald Davie, and Philip Larkin. These all provide in very different ways answers to the question about what makes modern poetry modern. They range from Benjamin's meditation on the heroism that lies at the heart of Baudelaire's modernity, to Genette's account of modern poetry's dream of language, to Philip Larkin's belief that modernist poetry is a piece of cunning intended to intimidate a readership.

In many cases these retrospective texts join another series of selections that formulate ideas about the nature of poetic language. This has provided another criterion for selection. As I have already indicated in this introduction, a number of writers in the twentieth century attempted to set out the distinguishing features of poetic language. These include, in this anthology, Barthes on poetic language, Empson on ambiguity, Genette on dreams of language, Jakobson on the poetic, and de Man's deconstruction of the tensions that lie at the heart of the Romantic image.

These three criteria – of diversity, of interaction between retrospect and prospect, of accounts of poetic language – work with an editorial intention that can be no more than a hope: that readers will find in the anthology materials for comparisons and contrasts of their own making. This hope is connected to what goes without being said, but has to be said. This anthology is a *selection.* For reasons of space I have had to exclude many texts that I would have liked to include. But it is exactly as a selection that an anthology of this kind can take on a critical value, insofar as it provokes debate about what should have been included and why.

Notes

1 Unless otherwise indicated in a note, all quotations are to texts included in the anthology. Page references are given in brackets after each quotation.

2 The quotation comes from Mill's essay "What is poetry?," first published in 1833. The text has been reprinted in J. B. Schneewind (ed.) *Mill's Essays on Literature and Society* (New York: Macmillan, 1965).

3 For a valuable study of impersonality in modern poetry see Maud Ellman, *The Poetics of Impersonality* (Cambridge, Mass: Harvard University Press, 1987).

4 Rilke also likes the fact the Rodin is a clear example of the artist as a worker. The implied problem is that writing poetry might not be work at all, and for a further response to this question see the subsequent quotation in this introduction from Charles Olson on rhythm.

5 The severity of Adorno's pessimism about the fate of poetry in modern culture was expressed in his essay "Cultural Criticism and Society": "To write poetry after Auschwitz is barbaric. And this corrodes even the knowledge of why it has become impossible to write poetry today." For the full text of the essay see T. W. Adorno, *Prisms,* translated by Samuel and Shierry Weber (Cambridge, Mass.: MIT Press, 1981).

6 For a critique of poetry's claim to be close to or identical with a natural source see Jacques Derrida, "Qual Quelle: Valery's Sources" in *The Margins of Philosophy,* translated by Alan Bass (Brighton: Harvester Press, 1982).

7 The value given to tradition in modernist poetics, as well as the stress on the poem's uniqueness, bears comparison with Walter Benjamin's analysis of the visual image in his essay, "The Work of Art in the Age of Mechanical Reproduction." There Benjamin argues that the aura attaching to visual images because of their uniqueness and their relation to tradition is shattered by mechanical reproduction. It could be argued that one strand of modernist poetics attempts to restore the poem's aura after its mechanical reproduction in the nineteenth century.

8 Frank Kermode has connected these aspects of Heidegger's thought to the later poetry of Wallace Stevens. See "Wallace Stevens: Dwelling Poetically in Connecticut" in *An Appetite for Poetry* (Glasgow: Fontana, 1990).

9 This is another indication of an affiliation between one form of modern poetry and Romanticism. For a major Romantic statement see Shelley's 1819 poem, "The Masque of Anarchy."

10 For a valuable discussion of the politics of identity and the languages of self-description see Denise Riley, *The Words of Selves* (Stanford: Stanford University Press, 2000).

11 For a fascinating discussion of the long history of poets and universities see Robert Crawford, *The Modern Poet* (Oxford and New York: Oxford University Press, 2001).

Part I
1900–1920

Chapter 1
W. B. Yeats

William Butler Yeats (1865–1939) was one of the leading Irish writers of the first half of the twentieth century. Whether as a poet, dramatist, essayist, or creator of cultural institutions Yeats was engaged in an intense and often troubled dialogue with Ireland's emergence as an independent nation. With the publication of his volume of poems, Responsibilities, *in 1914 his work gained increasing international recognition and in 1923 Yeats was awarded the Nobel Prize for Literature. In 1922 he became a senator of the Irish Free State.*

The following excerpt comes from "The Symbolism of Poetry", an essay first published in 1900 in The Dome *and included in Yeats's 1903 collection of essays,* Ideas of Good and Evil. *Influenced by French theories of poetic symbolism it develops its own distinctive account of the effects of juxtaposing images in poetry and establishes an important distinction between "emotional" and "intellectual" symbolism. As elsewhere in his work, "The Symbolism of Poetry" shows Yeats's abiding fascination with spiritualism and occult philosophy.*

The Symbolism of Poetry

I

...All writers, all artists of any kind, in so far as they have had any philosophical or critical power, perhaps just in so far as they have been deliberate artists at all, have had some philosophy, some criticism of their art; and it has often been this philosophy, or this criticism, that has evoked their most startling inspiration, calling into outer life some portion of the divine life, or of the buried reality, which could alone extinguish in the emotions what their philosophy or their criticism would extinguish in the intellect.

From *Essays and Introductions* (London: Macmillan, 1961), pp. 154–64.

They have sought for no new thing, it may be, but only to understand and to copy the pure inspiration of early times, but because the divine life wars upon our outer life, and must needs change its weapons and its movements as we change ours, inspiration has come to them in beautiful startling shapes. The scientific movement brought with it a literature which was always tending to lose itself in externalities of all kinds, in opinion, in declamation, in picturesque writing, in word-painting, or in what Mr. Symons has called an attempt "to build in brick and mortar inside the covers of a book"; and now writers have begun to dwell upon the element of evocation, of suggestion, upon what we call the symbolism in great writers.

II

In "Symbolism in Painting," I tried to describe the element of symbolism that is in pictures and sculpture, and described a little the symbolism in poetry, but did not describe at all the continuous indefinable symbolism which is the substance of all style.

There are no lines with more melancholy beauty than these by Burns:

> The white moon is setting behind the white wave,[1]
> And Time is setting with me, O!

and these lines are perfectly symbolical. Take from them the whiteness of the moon and of the wave, whose relation to the setting of Time is too subtle for the intellect, and you take from them their beauty. But, when all are together, moon and wave and whiteness and setting Time and the last melancholy cry, they evoke an emotion which cannot be evoked by any other arrangement of colours and sounds and forms. We may call this metaphorical writing, but it is better to call it symbolical writing, because metaphors are not profound enough to be moving, when they are not symbols, and when they are symbols they are the most perfect of all, because the most subtle, outside of pure sound, and through them one can best find out what symbols are....

All sounds, all colours, all forms, either because of their preordained energies or because of long association, evoke indefinable and yet precise emotions, or, as I prefer to think, call down among us certain disembodied powers, whose footsteps over our hearts we call emotions; and when sound, and colour, and form are in a musical relation, a beautiful relation to one another, they become, as it were, one sound, one colour, one form, and evoke an emotion that is made out of their distinct evocations and yet is one emotion. The same relation exists between all portions of every work of art, whether it be an epic or a song, and the more perfect it is, and the more various and numerous the elements that have flowed into its perfection, the more powerful will be the emotion, the power, the god it calls among us. Because an emotion does not exist, or does not become perceptible and active among us, till it has found its expression, in colour or in sound or in form, or in all of these, and because no two modulations or arrangements of these evoke the same emotion, poets and painters and musicians, and in a less degree because their effects are momentary, day and night and cloud and shadow, are continually making and unmaking mankind. It is indeed only those things which seem useless or very feeble that have any power, and all those things that seem useful or strong, armies, moving wheels, modes of architecture, modes of government, speculations of the reason, would have been a little different if some mind long ago had not given itself to some emotion, as a woman gives herself to her lover, and shaped sounds or colours or forms, or all of these, into a musical relation, that their emotion might live in other minds. A little lyric evokes an emotion, and this emotion gathers others about it and melts into their being in the making of some great epic, and at last, needing an always less delicate body, or symbol, as it grows more powerful, it flows out, with all it has gathered, among the blind instincts of daily life, where it moves a power within powers, as one sees ring within ring in the stem of an old tree. This is maybe what Arthur O'Shaughnessy meant when he made his poets say they had built Nineveh with their sighing; and I am certainly never sure, when I hear of some war, or of some religious excitement, or of some new manufacture, or of anything else that fills the ear of the world, that it has not all happened because of something that a boy piped in Thessaly. I remember once telling a seeress to ask one among the gods who, as she believed, were standing about her in their symbolic bodies, what would come of a charming but seeming trivial labour of a friend, and the form answering, "the devastation of peoples and the overwhelming of cities." I doubt indeed if the crude circumstance of the world, which seems to create all our emotions, does more than reflect, as in multiplying mirrors, the emotions that have come to solitary men in moments of poetical contemplation; or that love itself would be more than an animal hunger but for the poet and his shadow the priest, for unless we believe that outer things are the reality, we must believe that the gross is the shadow of the subtle, that things are wise before they become foolish, and secret before they cry out in the market-place. Solitary men in moments of contemplation receive, as I think, the creative impulse from the lowest of the Nine Hierarchies, and so make and unmake mankind, and even the world itself, for does not "the eye altering alter all"?

> Our towns are copied fragments from our breast;
> And all man's Babylons strive but to impart
> The grandeurs of his Babylonian heart.

III

The purpose of rhythm, it has always seemed to me, is to prolong the moment of contemplation, the moment when we are both asleep and awake, which is the one moment of creation, by hushing us with an alluring monotony, while it holds us waking by variety, to keep us in that state of perhaps real trance, in which the mind liberated from the pressure of the will is unfolded in symbols. If certain sensitive persons listen persistently to the ticking of a watch, or gaze persistently on the monotonous flashing of a light, they fall into the hypnotic trance; and rhythm is but the ticking of a watch made softer, that one must needs listen, and various, that one may not be swept beyond memory or grow weary of listening; while the patterns of the artist are but the monotonous flash woven to take the eyes in a subtler enchantment. I have heard in meditation voices that were forgotten the moment they had spoken; and I have been swept, when in more profound meditation, beyond all memory but of those things that came from beyond the threshold of waking life. I was writing once at a very symbolical and abstract poem, when my pen fell on the ground; and as I stooped to pick it up, I remembered some fantastic adventure that yet did not seem fantastic, and then another like adventure, and when I asked myself when these things had happened, I found that I was remembering my dreams for many nights. I tried to remember what I had done the day before, and then what I had done that morning; but all my waking life had perished from me, and it was only after a struggle that I came to remember it again, and as I did so that more powerful and startling life perished in its turn. Had my pen not fallen on the ground and so made me turn from the images that I was weaving into verse, I would never have known that meditation had become trance, for I would have been like one who does not know that he is passing through a wood because his eyes are on the pathway. So I think that in the making and in the understanding of a work of art, and the more easily if it is full of patterns and symbols and music, we are lured to the threshold of sleep, and it may be far beyond it, without knowing that we have ever set our feet upon the steps of horn or of ivory.

IV

Besides emotional symbols, symbols that evoke emotions alone, – and in this sense all alluring or hateful things are symbols, although their relations with one another are too subtle to delight us fully, away from rhythm and pattern, – there are intellectual symbols, symbols that evoke ideas alone, or ideas mingled with emotions; and outside the very definite traditions of mysticism and the less definite criticism of certain modern poets, these alone are called symbols. Most things belong to one or another kind, according to the way we speak of them and the companions we give them, for symbols, associated with ideas that are more than fragments of the shadows thrown upon the intellect by the emotions they evoke, are the playthings of the allegorist or the pedant, and soon pass away. If I say "white" or "purple" in an ordinary line of poetry, they evoke emotions so exclusively that I cannot say why they move me; but if I bring them into the same sentence with such obvious intellectual symbols as a cross or a crown of thorns, I think of purity and sovereignty. Furthermore, innumerable meanings, which are held to "white" or to "purple" by bonds of subtle suggestion, and alike in the emotions and in the intellect, move visibly through my mind, and move invisibly beyond the threshold of sleep, casting lights and shadows of an indefinable wisdom on what had seemed before, it may be, but sterility and noisy violence. It is the intellect that decides where the reader shall ponder over the procession of the symbols, and if the symbols are merely emotional, he gazes from amid the accidents and destinies of the world; but if the symbols are intellectual too, he becomes himself a part of pure intellect, and he is himself mingled with the procession. If I watch a rushy pool in the moonlight, my emotion at its beauty is mixed with memories of the man that I have seen ploughing by its margin, or of the lovers I saw there a night ago; but if

I look at the moon herself and remember any other ancient names and meanings, I move among divine people, and things that have shaken off our mortality, the tower of ivory, the queen of waters, the shining stag among enchanted woods, the white hare sitting upon the hilltop, the fool of Faery with his shining cup full of dreams, and it may be "make a friend of one of these images of wonder," and "meet the Lord in the air." So, too, if one is moved by Shakespeare, who is content with emotional symbols that he may come the nearer to our sympathy, one is mixed with the whole spectacle of the world; while if one is moved by Dante, or by the myth of Demeter, one is mixed into the shadow of God or of a goddess. So, too, one is furthest from symbols when one is busy doing this or that, but the soul moves among symbols and unfolds in symbols when trance, or madness, or deep meditation has withdrawn it from every impulse but its own. "I then saw," wrote Gérard de Nerval of his madness, "vaguely drifting into form, plastic images of antiquity, which outlined themselves, became definite, and seemed to represent symbols of which I only seized the idea with difficulty." In an earlier time he would have been of that multitude whose souls austerity withdrew, even more perfectly than madness could withdraw his soul, from hope and memory, from desire and regret, that they might reveal those processions of symbols that men bow to before altars, and woo with incense and offerings. But being of our time, he has been like Maeterlinck, like Villiers de l'Isle-Adam in *Axël*, like all who are preoccupied with intellectual symbols in our time, a foreshadower of the new sacred book, of which all the arts, as somebody has said, are beginning to dream. How can the arts overcome the slow dying of men's hearts that we call the progress of the world, and lay their hands upon men's heartstrings again, without becoming the garment of religion as in old times?

V

If people were to accept the theory that poetry moves us because of its symbolism, what change should one look for in the manner of our poetry? A return to the way of our fathers, a casting out of descriptions of nature for the sake of nature, of the moral law for the sake of the moral law, a casting out of all anecdotes and of that brooding over scientific opinion that so often extinguished the central flame in Tennyson, and of that vehemence that would make us do or not do certain things; or, in other words, we should come to understand that the beryl stone was enchanted by our fathers that it might unfold the pictures in its heart, and not to mirror our own excited faces, or the boughs waving outside the window. With this change of substance, this return to imagination, this understanding that the laws of art, which are the hidden laws of the world, can alone bind the imagination, would come a change of style, and we would cast out of serious poetry those energetic rhythms, as of a man running, which are the invention of the will with its eyes always on something to be done or undone; and we would seek out those wavering, meditative, organic rhythms, which are the embodiment of the imagination, that neither desires nor hates, because it has done with time, and only wishes to gaze upon some reality, some beauty; nor would it be any longer possible for anybody to deny the importance of form, in all its kinds, for although you can expound an opinion, or describe a thing, when your words are not quite well chosen, you cannot give a body to something that moves beyond the senses, unless your words are as subtle, as complex, as full of mysterious life, as the body of a flower or of a woman. The form of sincere poetry, unlike the form of the "popular poetry," may indeed be sometimes obscure, or ungrammatical as in some of the best of the *Songs of Innocence and Experience*, but it must have the perfections that escape analysis, the subtleties that have a new meaning every day, and it must have all this whether it be but a little song made out of a moment of dreamy indolence, or some great epic made out of the dreams of one poet and of a hundred generations whose hands were never weary of the sword.

Note

1 Burns actually wrote:
"The wan moon is setting ayont the white wave,"
but Yeats's version has been retained for the sake of his comments.

Chapter 2
Rainer Maria Rilke

Rainer Maria Rilke (1875–1926) was born in Prague as part of the city's German-speaking minority. Renouncing his early Catholicism, he developed a religious dedication to his role as a poet and to the possibility that poetry might provide a secular transcendence in the absence of traditional religious consolation. Under the influence of the French sculptor Rodin he developed his conception of the "thing-poem," a conception that indicates his preoccupation with the presence and authority of lyric poetry. He is best known for three works, the semi-autobiographical, Notebook of Malte Lauride Brigge, *published in 1914, and the two collections of poetry that he worked on intermittently from 1912,* The Duino Elegies *and* Sonnets to Orpheus, *both published in 1923. He is one of the most widely translated German poets of the twentieth century.*

Rilke did much of his thinking about poetry in the form of letters. Some of these were written to his wife, Clara, or to close friends, such as Lou Andreas-Salomé. Others were written to critics and translators of his work. The following excerpts are from three letters that he wrote between 1903 and 1925. The first shows Rilke using the example of Rodin to clarify his thinking about the artist as a creator of things, which have their own independent existence in the world. The second excerpt is about the emergence of an image out of the flux of perception. The third sets out Rilke's justification of his poetry and its distinctive modernity. The translation by R. F. C. Hull comes from an edition of Rilke's Selected Letters *published in 1946.*

To Lou Andreas-Salomé

Oberneuland bei Bremen
8 August 1903

When first I came to Rodin and took breakfast at his house out in Meudon with people with whom I did not become acquainted, with strangers at the table, I knew that his

From *Selected Letters*, trans. R. F. C. Hull (London: Macmillan, 1946), pp. 30–2, 34, 122–3, 392–6.

house meant nothing to him, a small and wretched requirement perhaps, a roof against rain and for sleep; and that it was no bother to him and no drag on his loneliness and concentration. Deep within him he bore the darkness, peace and shelter of a house, and he himself had become the sky above it and the wood around it and the distance and the great river that always flowed past. O what a solitary is this old man who, sunk in himself, stands fuller of sap than an old tree in autumn. He has grown deep; he has dug a deep hole for his heart, and its beating comes from a distance as from the middle of a mountain. His thoughts course round in him and fill him with heaviness and sweetness and do not expend themselves at the surface. He has grown blunt and hard against everything irrelevant, and as though surrounded by old bark he stands there among men. But to everything important he bares his breast, and he is all open when he is with *things*, or when animals and humans touch him quietly, like things. Here he is a learner and beginner and spectator and imitator of the Beautiful that has always been lost among those who sleep, among those who dream and take no part. Here he is the watcher whom nothing escapes, the lover who perpetually conceives, the patient heart that takes no count of time and has no thought of desiring the next thing. Always the thing he sees and surrounds with seeing is the only one for him, the world in which everything happens. When he forms a hand it is alone in space and there is nothing but a hand; and in six days God made only a hand and poured the waters round it and arched the skies above it; and he rested when all was finished, and it was a marvel and a hand.

And this way of looking and living is rooted so firmly in him because he acquired it as a craftsman: at the same time that he discovered this infinite, non-thematic, simple principle for his art, he won this great justice for himself, this equilibrium in face of the world which no name could disturb. Since it was given to him to see *things* in everything, he acquired the power to make them; for in this lies the greatness of his art. No longer does any movement mislead him, as he knows that there is movement even in the contour of a still plane, and only sees planes and systems of planes, which determine forms exactly and distinctly. There is nothing indefinite for him about an object that serves him as a model; thousands of little planes have here been fitted into space, and when he makes a work of art accordingly, his task is to implant the thing into the surrounding space more passionately, more firmly, and a thousand times better than before, so that it does not move when you shake it. The *thing* is definite, the *art-thing* must be still more definite; removed from all accident, reft away from all obscurity, withdrawn from time and given over to space, it has become enduring, capable of eternity. The model *seems*, the art-thing *is*. Thus the latter is an indescribable advance on the former, the calm and cumulative realisation of the desire-to-be which proceeds from everything in Nature. Hence the error that would see art as the vainest and most arbitrary of avocations, falls to the ground; art is the humblest service and is founded absolutely upon law. But all artists and all the arts are full of that error, and it was time for a very powerful personality to rise up against it; also, he had to be one who *did* things, who did not talk, who created without cease. From the very beginning his art had to be an actualisation (and as such diametrically opposed to music, which transforms the apparent realities of the daily world and still further de-actualises them into insubstantial, ephemeral appearances. Which is just the reason why this direct antithesis of art, this failure to condense, this temptation *towards diffuseness*, has so many friends and sympathisers and slaves, so many who are not free, chained to pleasure, who feel no inner intensity but only a stimulation from outside . . .) . . .

. . . O Lou, in any successful poem of mine there is so much more reality than in any mood or tendency I may feel. Where I create I am true, and I should like to find the strength to base my whole life on this truth, on this boundless simplicity and joy which are sometimes given me. When I first went to Rodin I was seeking this; for I had known bodingly for years about the measureless example and model of his work. Now that I have come from him I know that I too can demand and seek no other realisations than those of my work. . . . But how shall I begin to tread this path – where is the handcraft of my art, its least and deepest place where I could begin to be diligent? I will take every path back to that beginning, and all that I have done shall have been as nothing, less than the sweeping of a threshold to which the next visitor will bring the dust of the road again. I have patience for centuries in me and will live as though my time were very great. I will collect myself from everything that distracts me and out of my too facile proficiencies I will win back and husband the things that are mine. . . . Only *things* speak to me. Rodin's things, the things of the Gothic cathedrals, the things of Antiquity, all things that are perfect things. They point the way to the great archetypes: to the moving and living world, seen simply and without interpretation as a pure occasion for things. I begin to see anew: already flowers mean so infinitely much to me, and from animals have come strange intimations and promptings. And sometimes I perceive even people so, hands live somewhere, mouths speak, and I see everything more quietly and with greater justice.

To Clara Rilke

Capri, Villa Discopoli
8 March 1907

. . . Go on collecting impressions; don't think of letters which have to be informative and comprehensible; take in this and that with quick snatching-gestures: passing thoughts, ideas, fancies that suddenly flare up in you and last only a second under the influence of some occurrence; all those unimportant things that often become significant through a fleeting intensity of vision or because they take place on a spot where they are absolute in their irrelevance, unceasingly valid and profoundly meaningful for any personal insight which, rising up in us at the same moment, coincides pregnantly with that image. Looking is such a marvellous thing, of which we know but little; through it, we are turned absolutely towards the Outside, but when we are most of all so, things happen in us that have waited longingly to be observed, and while they reach completion in us, intact and curiously anonymous, *without our aid*, – their significance grows up in the object outside: a powerful, persuasive name, the only name these inner events could possibly have, a name in which we joyfully and reverently recognise the happenings within us, a name we ourselves do not touch, only apprehending it very gently, from a distance, under the similitude of a thing that, a moment ago, was strange to us, and the next moment will be estranged anew. It quite often happens now that some face affects me in this way; in the mornings, for instance, which generally start off with a lot of sun quite early, a mass of brightness – suddenly, in the shadow of a street, a face is held out to you and you see, under the influence of the contrast, its essence with such clarity (clarity of nuance) that the momentary impression involuntarily assumes the proportions of a symbol. More than ever I wish there were someone here who could paint; seriously paint. Only just recently, imagine: a green rectangular field running evenly towards the sloping, dark-blue sea, set beside it in such a way that you were unable to see the perpendicular drop of some old terrace which alone separated them. Sitting in this field a woman in rhubarb-red and orange, another passing to and fro in faded green beneath some white sheets and table-cloths hung up to dry on lines, animated in the most varied ways by the wind, now all hollow and drawn in, fall of luminous shadows, now dazzlingly blown out, and ever again interspersed with the distinct blue of the sea and over-arched by the perpetually descending sky....

To Witold von Hulewicz

Postmark: Sierre, 13.11.25

[This letter concerns the *Duino Elegies*, which Hulewicz was translating into Polish.]

...I am astonished that the *Sonnets to Orpheus*, which are at least as "hard", filled with the same essence, are not more helpful to your understanding of the Elegies. The latter were begun in 1912 (at Duino), continued fragmentarily in Spain and Paris till 1914; the Great War completely interrupted this, my greatest work, and when I ventured to take it up again here in 1922, the new Elegies found their termination forestalled by the tempestuous imposition, within a few days, of the Sonnets (which were *not* in my plan). These, and it cannot be otherwise, are of the same "birth" as the Elegies, and the fact that they arose suddenly in connection with the premature death of a young girl brings them still nearer to their original fountain-head; for this connection is another point of contact with the centre of that kingdom whose depth and influence we share, boundlessly, with the dead and the unborn. We, the men of the present and today, we are not for one moment content in the world of time, nor are we fixed in it; we overflow continually towards the men of the Past, towards our origin and towards those who apparently come after us. In that most vast, *open* world all beings are – one cannot say "contemporaneous", for it is precisely the passage of Time which determines that they all *are*. This transitoriness rushes everywhere into a profound Being. And thus all the manifestations of the Actual are not to be used as mere time-bound things, rather are they to be embodied, as far as lies within our power, in that nobler significance which we, too, share. Not, however, in the Christian sense (from which I always passionately dissociate myself); but, with a consciousness that is purely, deeply, serenely *earthly*, it behoves us to bring the things we here behold and touch within the greater, the very greatest circumference. Not into a Beyond whose shadow obscures the Earth, but into a Whole, into *the* Whole. Nature, and the objects of our environment and usage, are but frail, ephemeral things; yet, as long as we are here, they are *our* possession and our friendship, knowing our wretchedness and our joy, just as they were the familiars of our ancestors. Thus it is meet for us not only not to pollute and degrade the Actual, but, precisely because of the transitoriness which it shares with us, we should seize these things and appearances with the most fervent comprehension and transform them. Transform them? Yes, for such is our task: to impress this fragile and transient earth so sufferingly, so passionately upon our hearts that its essence shall rise up again, invisible, in us. *We are the bees of the Invisible. Nous butinons éperdument le miel du visible, pour l'accumuler dans la grande ruche d'or de l'Invisible.* The Elegies shew us engaged on this work, the work of the perpetual transformation of beloved and tangible things into the invisible vibration and excitability of our nature, which introduces new "frequencies" into the pulsing fields of the universe. (Since the various materials in the Universe are only varying coefficients of vibration, we build in this way not only intensities of a spiritual kind, but, who knows? new bodies, metals, nebulae and stars.) And this activity is sustained and accelerated by the increasingly rapid disappearance today of so much of the Visible which we cannot replace. Even for our grandfathers a house, a fountain, a familiar tower, their very clothes, their coat, was infinitely more, infinitely more intimate; almost every object a vessel in which they found something human or added their morsel of humanity. Now, from America, empty indifferent things crowd over to us, counterfeit things, the veriest dummies. A house, in the American sense, an American apple or one of the vines of that country has *nothing* in common with the house, the fruit, the grape into which have entered the hope and meditation of our forefathers. The lived and living things, the things that share our thoughts, these are on the decline and can no more be replaced. *We are perhaps the last to have known such things.* The responsibility rests with us not only to keep remembrance of them (that would be but a trifle and unreliable), but also their human or "laric" value ("laric" in the sense of household gods). The earth has no alternative but "laric" to become invisible – IN us, who with a portion of our being have a share in the Invisible, or at least the appearance of sharing; we who can multiply our possessions of the Invisible during our earthly existence, in us *alone* can there be accomplished this intimate and continual transmutation of the Visible into the Invisible... just as our own destiny becomes unceasingly MORE PRESENT, AND AT THE SAME TIME INVISIBLE, in us.

The Elegies set up this norm of existence: they affirm, they glorify this consciousness. They place it carefully among its own traditions, claiming in support of this assumption immemorial customs and rumours of customs and even evoking, in the Egyptian cult of the Dead, a foreknowledge of such affinities. (At the same time the "Land of the Threnodies" through which the Threnody Elder conducts the young man who has just died, is not to be identified with Egypt, it is only the reflection, so to speak, of the Nile country in the desert-like clarity of the dead man's mind.) If one makes the mistake of applying Catholic conceptions of death, the Hereafter and Eternity to the Elegies or Sonnets, one isolates oneself completely from their conclusions and becomes involved in a fundamental misunderstanding. The angel of the Elegies has nothing to do with the angel of the Christian heaven (rather with the angelic figures of Islam. . . .) The angel of the Elegies is that Being in whom the transmutation of the Visible into the Invisible, which we seek to achieve, is consummated. For the angel of the Elegies all the towers and palaces of the Past are existent *because* they have long been invisible, and the still existing towers and bridges of our world *already* invisible, although still materially enduring for us. The angel of the Elegies is that Being who stands for the recognition in the Invisible of a higher degree of reality. That is why he is "terrible" for us, because we, its lovers and transmuters, still cling to the Visible. – All the worlds in the Universe rush into the Invisible as into their next-deeper reality; a few stars undergo immediate sublimation and are lost in the infinite consciousness of the angels, – others are committed to beings who slowly and painfully transform them, beings in whose terror and rapture they attain their approaching consummation in the Invisible. We, let it be emphasised again, in the sense of the Elegies WE are the transmuters of the earth; our whole existence here, the flights and falls of our love, all strengthen us for this task (beside which there is really no other). (The Sonnets reveal single aspects of this activity, which is seen to take place under the name and guardianship of one dead, a young girl whose immaturity and innocence hold open the portals of the dead so that, departed from us, she now belongs to those powers which keep the one half of life fresh and open to that other half with its wide-open wound.) Elegies and Sonnets sustain one another at all points, – and I deem it an infinite grace that I have been able, with the same breath, to swell these two sails: the little rust-coloured sail of the Sonnets and the gigantic white canvas of the Elegies.

May you, dear friend, find here some counsel and instruction, and for the rest help yourself as best you may. For: I do not know whether I can ever say anything more.

Chapter 3
Sigmund Freud

Sigmund Freud (1856–1939) was the inventor of psychoanalysis, an account of the self and its troubles that has had an enormous influence on twentieth-century western culture. Freud's theory underwent a number of revisions during his lifetime, but his analysis of the self as divided between an unconscious and a conscious mind remained a constant. This division arose because of the nature of human biological drives and desires. According to Freud the shaping of a human animal into a cultural being depended upon the repression and reshaping of primary drives for gratification. This process of repression created the split between the unconscious mind, sometimes presented by Freud as the repository of repressed drives, and the conscious mind that regulated the human relation to reality. The result is that human beings always long for something they cannot have – the fulfillment of repressed desires – and this, according to Freud, was the source of their unhappiness even when they lived in conditions of material prosperity. In order to compensate for this loss we have invented substitute satisfactions, including art and religion. Freud's ideas have been attacked on both ideological and scientific grounds, but his work continues to be a source of debate and insight. Psychoanalysis has had effects on a wide range of activities, from the treatment of mental suffering to the development of advertising techniques and the interpretation of literature. The Surrealist movement was indebted to his work as was the early poetry of W. H. Auden. Freud spent most of his working life in Vienna, but was forced into exile by the Nazis in 1938 when he moved to London.

Freud was fascinated by the phenomenon of artistic creativity and wrote a number of studies of individual writers, including Dostoevsky and Goethe. "Creative Writers and Day-Dreaming" was first given as a lecture in December 1907 and published in the Neue Revue *the following year. Although Freud does not use examples from poetry, his argument applies as much to a lyric poem as to a popular narrative. In the excerpt that follows, he argues that creative writing is a form of day-dreaming in public. Like day-dreams, creative writing is motivated by unsatisfied wishes and the inventions of the writer seek to compensate for what Freud describes as an "unsatisfying reality." The art of poetry overcomes the audience's resistance to witnessing the fantasies of another both by disguising its content and by creating formal pleasures that enable the audience to participate in deeper psychic satisfactions. This is a modified version of the 1925 translation by I. F. Grant Duff, published in 1959.*

Creative Writers and Day-Dreaming

We laymen have always been intensely curious to know... from what sources that strange being, the creative writer, draws his material, and how he manages to make such an impression on us with it and to arouse in us emotions of which, perhaps, we had not even thought ourselves capable. Our interest is only heightened the more by the fact that, if we ask him, the writer himself gives us no explanation, or none that is satisfactory; and it is not at all weakened by our knowledge that not even the clearest insight into the determinants of his choice of material and into the nature of the art of creating imaginative form will ever help to make creative writers of *us*.

If we could at least discover in ourselves or in people like ourselves an activity which was in some way akin to creative writing! An examination of it would then give us a hope of obtaining the beginnings of an explanation of the creative work of writers. And, indeed, there is some prospect of this being possible. After all, creative writers themselves like to lessen the distance between their kind and the common run of humanity; they so often assure us that every man is a poet at heart and that the last poet will not perish till the last man does.

Should we not look for the first traces of imaginative activity as early as in childhood? The child's best-loved and most intense occupation is with his play or games. Might we not say that every child at play behaves like a creative writer, in that he creates a world of his own, or, rather, re-arranges the things of his world in a new way which pleases him? It would be wrong to think he does not take that world seriously; on the contrary, he takes his play very seriously and he expends large amounts of emotion on it. The opposite of play is not what is serious but what is real. In spite of all the emotion with which he cathects his world of play, the child distinguishes it quite well from reality; and he likes to link his imagined objects and situations to the tangible and visible things of the real world. This linking is all that differentiates the child's 'play' from 'phantasying'.

The creative writer does the same as the child at play. He creates a world of phantasy which he takes very seriously – that is, which he invests with large amounts of emotion – while separating it sharply from reality. Language has preserved this relationship between children's play and poetic creation. It gives [in German] the name of '*Spiel*' ['play'] to those forms of imaginative writing which require to be linked to tangible objects and which are capable of representation. It speaks of a '*Lustpiel*' or '*Trauerspiel*' ['comedy' or 'tragedy': literally, 'pleasure play' or 'mourning play'] and describes those who carry out the representation as '*Schauspieler*' ['players': literally

From the *Standard Edition of the Complete Psychological Works of Sigmund Freud*, vol. 7 (London: Hogarth Press, 1959), pp. 143–53.

'show-players']. The unreality of the writer's imaginative world, however, has very important consequences for the technique of his art; for many things which, if they were real, could give no enjoyment, can do so in the play of phantasy, and many excitements which, in themselves, are actually distressing, can become a source of pleasure for the hearers and spectators at the performance of a writer's work. . . .

As people grow up, then, they cease to play, and they seem to give up the yield of pleasure which they gained from playing. But whoever understands the human mind knows that hardly anything is harder for a man than to give up a pleasure which he has once experienced. Actually, we can never give anything up; we only exchange one thing for another. What appears to be a renunciation is really the formation of a substitute or surrogate. In the same way, the growing child, when he stops playing, gives up nothing but the link with real objects; instead of *playing*, he now *phantasies*. He builds castles in the air and creates what are called *day-dreams*. I believe that most people construct phantasies at times in their lives. This is a fact which has long been overlooked and whose importance has therefore not been sufficiently appreciated.

People's phantasies are less easy to observe than the play of children. The child, it is true, plays by himself or forms a closed psychical system with other children for the purpose of a game; but even though he may not play his game in front of the grown-ups, he does not, on the other hand, conceal it from them. The adult, on the contrary, is ashamed of his phantasies and hides them from other people. He cherishes his phantasies as his most intimate possessions, and as a rule he would rather confess his misdeeds than tell anyone his phantasies. It may come about that for that reason he believes he is the only person who invents such phantasies and has no idea that creations of this kind are widespread among other people. This difference in the behaviour of a person who plays and a person who phantasies is accounted for by the motives of these two activities, which are nevertheless adjuncts to each other. . . .

Let us now make ourselves acquainted with a few of the characteristics of phantasying. We may lay it down that a happy person never phantasies, only an unsatisfied one. The motive forces of phantasies are unsatisfied wishes, and every single phantasy is the fulfilment of a wish, a correction of unsatisfying reality. These motivating wishes vary according to the sex, character and circumstances of the person who is having the phantasy; but they fall naturally into two main groups. They are either ambitious wishes, which serve to elevate the subject's personality; or they are erotic ones. In young women the erotic wishes predominate almost exclusively, for their ambition is as a rule absorbed by erotic trends. In young men egoistic and ambitious wishes come to the fore clearly enough alongside of erotic ones. But we will not lay stress on the opposition between the two trends; we would rather emphasize the fact that they are often united. Just as, in many altar-pieces, the portrait of the donor is to be seen in a corner of the picture, so, in the majority of ambitious phantasies, we can discover in some corner or other the lady for whom the creator of the phantasy performs all his heroic deeds and at whose feet all his triumphs are laid. Here, as you see, there are strong enough motives for concealment; the well-brought-up young woman is only allowed a minimum of erotic desire, and the young man has to learn to suppress the excess of self-regard which he brings with him from the spoilt days of his childhood, so that he may find his place in a society which is full of other individuals making equally strong demands.

We must not suppose that the products of this imaginative activity – the various phantasies, castles in the air and day-dreams – are stereotyped or unalterable. On the contrary, they fit themselves in to the subject's shifting impressions of life, change with every change in his situation, and receive from every fresh active impression what might be called a 'date-mark'. The relation of a phantasy to time is in general very important. We may say that it hovers, as it were, between three times – the three moments of time which our ideation involves. Mental work is linked to some current impression, some provoking occasion in the present which has been able to arouse one of the subject's major wishes. From there it harks back to a memory of an earlier experience (usually an infantile one) in which this wish was fulfilled; and it now creates a situation relating to the future which represents a fulfilment of the wish. What it thus creates is a day-dream or phantasy, which carries about it traces of its origin from the occasion which provoked it and from the memory. Thus past, present and future are strung together, as it were, on the thread of the wish that runs through them.

A very ordinary example may serve to make what I have said clear. Let us take the case of a poor orphan boy to whom you have given the address of some employer where he may perhaps find a job. On his way there he may indulge in a day-dream appropriate to the situation from which it arises. The content of his phantasy will perhaps be something like this. He is given a job, finds favour with his new employer, makes himself indispensable in the business, is taken into his employer's family, marries the charming young daughter of the house, and then himself becomes a director of the business, first as his employer's partner and then as his successor. In this phantasy, the dreamer has regained what he possessed in his happy childhood – the protecting house, the loving parents and the first objects of his affectionate feelings. You will see from this example the way in which the wish makes use of an occasion in the present to construct, on the pattern of the past, a picture of the future.

...Our dreams at night are nothing else than phantasies like these, as we can demonstrate from the interpretation of dreams. Language, in its unrivalled wisdom, long ago decided the question of the essential nature of dreams by giving the name of 'day-dreams' to the airy creations of phantasy. If the meaning of our dreams usually remains obscure to us in spite of this pointer, it is because of the circumstance that at night there also arise in us wishes of which we are ashamed; these we must conceal from ourselves, and they have consequently been repressed, pushed into the unconscious. Repressed wishes of this sort and their derivatives are only allowed to come to expression in a very distorted form. When scientific work had succeeded in elucidating this factor of *dream-distortion*, it was no longer difficult to recognize that night-dreams are wish-fulfilments in just the same way as day-dreams – the phantasies which we all know so well.

So much for phantasies. And now for the creative writer. May we really attempt to compare the imaginative writer with the 'dreamer in broad daylight', and his creations with day-dreams? Here we must begin by making an initial distinction. We must separate writers who, like the ancient authors of epics and tragedies, take over their material ready-made, from writers who seem to originate their own material. We will keep to the latter kind, and, for the purposes of our comparison, we will choose not the writers most highly esteemed by the critics, but the less pretentious authors of novels, romances and short stories, who nevertheless have the widest and most eager circle of readers of both sexes. One feature above all cannot fail to strike us about the creations of these story-writers: each of them has a hero who is the centre of interest, for whom the writer tries to win our sympathy by every possible means and whom he seems to place under the protection of a special Providence. If, at the end of one chapter of my story, I leave the hero unconscious and bleeding from severe wounds, I am sure to find him at the beginning of the next being carefully nursed and on the way to recovery; and if the first volume closes with the ship he is in going down in a storm at sea, I am certain, at the opening of the second volume, to read of his miraculous rescue – a rescue without which the story could not proceed. The feeling of security with which I follow the hero through his perilous adventures is the same as the feeling with which a hero in real life throws himself into the water to save a drowning man or exposes himself to the enemy's fire in order to storm a battery. It is the true heroic feeling, which one of our best writers has expressed in an inimitable phrase: 'Nothing can happen to me!' It seems to me, however, that through this revealing characteristic of invulnerability we can immediately recognize His Majesty the Ego, the hero alike of every day-dream and of every story. . . .

If our comparison of the imaginative writer with the day-dreamer, and of poetical creation with the day-dream, is to be of any value, it must, above all, show itself in some way or other fruitful. Let us, for instance, try to apply to these authors' works the thesis we laid down earlier concerning the relation between phantasy and the three periods of time and the wish which runs through them; and, with its help, let us try to study the connections that exist between the life of the writer and his works. No one has known, as a rule, what expectations to frame in approaching this problem; and often the connection has been thought of in much too simple terms. In the light of the insight we have gained from phantasies, we ought to expect the following state of affairs. A strong experience in the present awakens in the creative writer a memory of an earlier experience (usually belonging to his childhood) from which there now proceeds a wish which finds its fulfilment in the creative work. The work itself exhibits elements of the recent provoking occasion as well as of the old memory.

Do not be alarmed at the complexity of this formula. I suspect that in fact it will prove to be too exiguous a pattern. Nevertheless, it may contain a first approach to the true state of affairs; and, from some experiments I have made, I am inclined to think that this way of looking at creative writings may turn out not unfruitful. You will not forget that the stress it lays on childhood memories in the writer's life – a stress which may perhaps seem puzzling – is ultimately derived from the assumption that a piece of creative writing, like a day-dream, is a continuation of, and a substitute for, what was once the play of childhood.

We must not neglect, however, to go back to the kind of imaginative works which we have to recognize, not as original creations, but as the re-fashioning of ready-made and familiar material. Even here, the writer keeps a certain amount of independence, which can express itself in the choice of material and in changes in it which are often quite extensive. In so far as the material is already at hand, however, it is derived from the popular treasure-house of myths, legends and fairy tales. The study of constructions of folk-psychology such as these is far from being complete, but it is extremely probable that myths, for instance, are distorted vestiges of the wishful phantasies of whole nations, the *secular dreams* of youthful humanity.

You will say that, although I have put the creative writer first in the title of my paper, I have told you far less about him than about phantasies. I am aware of that, and I must try to excuse it by pointing to the present state of our knowledge. All I have been able to do is to throw out some encouragements and suggestions which, starting from the study of phantasies, lead on to the problem of the writer's choice of his literary material. As for the other problem – by what means the creative writer achieves the emotional effects in us that are aroused by his creations – we have as yet not touched on it at all. But I should like at least to point out to you the path that leads from our discussion of phantasies to the problems of poetical effects.

... I have said that the day-dreamer carefully conceals his phantasies from other people because he feels he has reasons for being ashamed of them. I should now add that even if he were to communicate them to us he could give us no pleasure by his disclosures. Such phantasies, when we learn them, repel us or at least leave us cold. But when a creative writer presents his plays to us or tells us what we are inclined to take to be his personal day-dreams, we experience a great pleasure, and one which probably arises from the confluence of many sources. How the writer accomplishes this is his innermost secret; the essential *ars poetica* lies in the technique of overcoming the feeling of repulsion in us which is undoubtedly connected with the barriers that rise between each single ego and the others. We can guess two of the methods used by this technique. The writer softens the character of his egoistic day-dreams by altering and disguising it, and he bribes us by the purely formal – that is, aesthetic – yield of pleasure which he offers us in the presentation of his phantasies. We give the name of an *incentive bonus*, or a *fore-pleasure*, to a yield of pleasure such as this, which is offered to us so as to make possible the release of still greater pleasure arising from deeper psychical sources. In my opinion, all the aesthetic pleasure which a creative writer affords us has the character of a fore-pleasure of this kind, and our actual enjoyment of an imaginative work proceeds from a liberation of tensions in our minds. It may even be that not a little of this effect is due to the writer's enabling us thenceforward to enjoy our own day-dreams without self-reproach or shame. This brings us to the threshold of new, interesting and complicated enquiries; but also, at least for the moment, to the end of our discussion.

Chapter 4

T. E. Hulme

Thomas Ernest Hulme (1883–1917) was an English-born philosopher, literary theoretician, and poet who was identified by both Pound and Eliot as an intellectual and poetic precursor of their work. A restless figure, Hulme traveled in Canada and Europe, living in Brussels and Berlin as well as London. Pound published the ironically titled Complete Poetical Works of Hulme *in 1912 and regarded them as the precursors of Imagism. In his attempts to establish the philosophical and political implications of the modern movement in poetry and painting, Hulme drew on a wide range of European thinkers, including the French philosopher, Henri Bergson, and the German aesthetician, Worringer. He was fiercely conservative in his politics and identified himself closely with the right-wing group, Action Française. Hulme joined the British army at the outbreak of the First World War and was killed in a burst of artillery fire on September 28, 1917.*

"Romanticism and Classicism" was originally written as a lecture in 1911 or 1912. It was first published in Speculations, *a posthumous collection of his work, published in 1924. The following excerpt provides one of Hulme's fullest statements of the historical and cultural significance of poetic modernism, based in a contrast between a discredited romanticism and a new classicism, as well as setting out his credo for poetry based in a "visual, concrete" language.*

Romanticism and Classicism

I want to maintain that after a hundred years of romanticism, we are in for a classical revival, and that the particular weapon of this new classical spirit, when it works in verse, will be fancy. And in this I imply the superiority of fancy – not superior generally

From *Selected Writings*, ed. P. McGuiness (Manchester: Fyfield Books, Carcanet Press, 1998), pp. 68, 70–4, 75–6, 78–83.

or absolutely, for that would be obvious nonsense, but superior in the sense that we use the word good in empirical ethics – good for something, superior for something. I shall have to prove then two things, first that a classical revival is coming, and, secondly, for its particular purposes, fancy will be superior to imagination.

So banal have the terms Imagination and Fancy become that we imagine they must have always been in the language. Their history as two differing terms in the vocabulary of criticism is comparatively short. Originally, of course, they both mean the same thing; they first began to be differentiated by the German writers on aesthetics in the eighteenth century.

I know that in using the words 'classic' and 'romantic' I am doing a dangerous thing. They represent five or six different kinds of antitheses, and while I may be using them in one sense you may be interpreting them in another. In this present connection I am using them in a perfectly precise and limited sense. I ought really to have coined a couple of new words, but I prefer to use the ones I have used, as I then conform to the practice of the group of polemical writers who make most use of them at the present day, and have almost succeeded in making them political catchwords. I mean Maurras, Lasserre and all the group connected with L'Action Française.

At the present time this is the particular group with which the distinction is most vital. Because it has become a party symbol. If you asked a man of a certain set whether he preferred the classics or the romantics, you could deduce from that what his politics were....

Put shortly, these are the two views, then. One, that man is intrinsically good, spoilt by circumstance; and the other that he is intrinsically limited, but disciplined by order and tradition to something fairly decent. To the one party man's nature is like a well, to the other like a bucket. The view which regards man as a well, a reservoir full of possibilities, I call the romantic; the one which regards him as a very finite and fixed creature, I call the classical....

It would be a mistake to identify the classical view with that of materialism. On the contrary it is absolutely identical with the normal religious attitude. I should put it in this way: That part of the fixed nature of man is the belief in the Deity. This should be as fixed and true for every man as belief in the existence of matter and in the objective world. It is parallel to appetite, the instinct of sex, and all the other fixed qualities. Now at certain times, by the use of either force or rhetoric, these instincts have been suppressed – in Florence under Savonarola, in Geneva under Calvin, and here under the Roundheads. The inevitable result of such a process is that the repressed instinct bursts out in some abnormal direction. So with religion. By the perverted rhetoric of Rationalism, your natural instincts are suppressed and you are converted into an agnostic. Just as in the case of the other instincts. Nature has her revenge. The instincts that find their right and proper outlet in religion must come out in some other way. You don't believe in a God, so you begin to believe that man is a god. You don't believe in Heaven, so you begin to believe in a heaven on earth. In other words, you get romanticism. The concepts that are right and proper in their own sphere are spread over, and so mess up, falsify and blur the clear outlines of human experience. It is like pouring a pot of treacle over the dinner table. Romanticism then, and this is the best definition I can give of it, is spilt religion.

I must now shirk the difficulty of saying exactly what I mean by romantic and classical in verse. I can only say that it means the result of these two attitudes towards the cosmos, towards man, in so far as it gets reflected in verse. The romantic, because he thinks man infinite, must always be talking about the infinite; and as there is always the bitter contrast between what you think you ought to be able to do and what man actually can, it always tends, in its later stages at any rate, to be gloomy. I really can't go any further than to say it is the reflection of these two temperaments, and point out examples of the different spirits. On the one hand I would take such diverse people as Horace, most of the Elizabethans and the writers of the Augustan age, and on the other side Lamartine, Hugo, parts of Keats, Coleridge, Byron, Shelley and Swinburne.

I know quite well that when people think of classical and romantic in verse, the contrast at once comes into their mind between, say, Racine and Shakespeare. I don't mean this; the dividing line that I intend is here misplaced a little from the true middle. That Racine is on the extreme classical side I agree, but if you call Shakespeare romantic, you are using a different definition to the one I give. You are thinking of the difference between classic and romantic as being merely one between restraint and exuberance. I should say with Nietzsche that there are two kinds of classicism, the static and the dynamic. Shakespeare is the classic of motion.

What I mean by classical in verse, then, is this. That even in the most imaginative flights there is always a holding back, a reservation. The classical poet never forgets this finiteness, this limit of man. He remembers always that he is mixed up with earth. He may jump, but he always returns back; he never flies away into the circumambient gas.

You might say if you wished that the whole of the romantic attitude seems to crystallise in verse round metaphors of flight. Hugo is always flying, flying over abysses, flying up into the eternal gases. The word infinite in every other line.

In the classical attitude you never seem to swing right along to the infinite nothing. If you say an extravagant thing which does exceed the limits inside which you know man to be fastened, yet there is always conveyed in some way at the end an impression of yourself standing outside it, and not quite believing it, or consciously putting it forward as a flourish. You never go blindly into an atmosphere more than the truth, an atmosphere too rarefied for man to breathe for long. You are always faithful to the conception of a limit. It is a question of pitch; in romantic verse you move at a certain pitch of rhetoric which you know, man being what he is, to be a little high-falutin. The kind of thing you get in Hugo or Swinburne. In the coming classical reaction that will feel just wrong. For an example of the opposite thing, a verse written in the proper classical spirit, I can take the song from *Cymbeline* beginning with 'Fear no more the heat of the sun'. I am just using this as a parable. I don't quite mean what I say here. Take the last two lines:

> 'Golden lads and girls all must,
> Like chimney sweepers come to dust.'

Now, no romantic would have ever written that. Indeed, so ingrained is romanticism, so objectionable is this to it, that people have asserted that these were not part of the original song.

Apart from the pun, the thing that I think quite classical is the word lad. Your modern romantic could never write that. He would have to write golden youth, and take up the thing at least a couple of notes in pitch.

I want now to give the reasons which make me think that we are nearing the end of the romantic movement.

The first lies in the nature of any convention or tradition in art. A particular convention or attitude in art has a strict analogy to the phenomena of organic life. It grows old and decays. It has a definite period of life and must die. All the possible tunes get played on it and then it is exhausted; moreover its best period is its youngest. Take the case of the extraordinary efflorescence of verse in the Elizabethan period. All kinds of reasons have been given for this – the discovery of the new world and all the rest of it. There is a much simpler one. A new medium had been given them to play with – namely, blank verse. It was new and so it was easy to play new tunes on it.

The same law holds in other arts. All the masters of painting are born into the world at a time when the particular tradition from which they start is imperfect. The Florentine tradition was just short of full ripeness when Raphael came to Florence, the Bellinesque was still young when Titian was born in Venice. Landscape was still a toy or an appanage of figure-painting when Turner and Constable arose to reveal its independent power. When Turner and Constable had done with landscape they left little or nothing for their successors to do on the same lines. Each field of artistic activity is exhausted by the first great artist who gathers a full harvest from it.

This period of exhaustion seems to me to have been reached in romanticism. We shall not get any new efflorescence of verse until we get a new technique, a new convention, to turn ourselves loose in.

Objection might be taken to this. It might be said that a century as an organic unity doesn't exist, that I am being deluded by a wrong metaphor, that I am treating a collection of literary people as if they were an organism or state department. Whatever we may be in other things, an objector might urge, in literature in as far as we are anything at all – in as far as we are worth considering – we are individuals, we are persons, and as distinct persons we cannot be subordinated to any general treatment. At any period at any time, an individual poet may be a classic or a romantic just as he feels like it. You at any particular moment may think that you can stand outside a movement. You may think that as an individual you observe both the classic and the romantic spirit and decide from a purely detached point of view that one is superior to the other.

The answer to this is that no one, in a matter of judgment of beauty, can take a detached standpoint in this way. Just as physically you are not born that abstract entity, man, but the child of particular parents, so you are in matters of literary judgment. Your opinion is almost entirely of the literary history that came just before you, and you are governed by that whatever you may think. Take Spinoza's example of a stone falling to the ground. If it had a conscious mind it would, he said, think it was going to the ground because it wanted to. So you with your pretended free judgment about what is and what is not beautiful. The amount of freedom in man is much exaggerated. That we are free on certain rare occasions, both my religion and the views I get from metaphysics convince me. But many acts which we habitually label free are in reality automatic. It is quite possible for a man to write a book almost automatically. I have read several such products. Some observations were recorded more than twenty years ago by Robertson on reflex speech, and he found that in certain cases of dementia, where the people were quite unconscious so far as the exercise of reasoning went, that very intelligent answers were given to a succession of questions on politics and such matters. The meaning of these questions could not possibly have been understood. Language here acted after the manner of a reflex. So that certain extremely complex mechanisms, subtle enough to imitate beauty, can work by themselves – I certainly think that this is the case with judgments about beauty.

I can put the same thing in slightly different form. Here is a question of a conflict of two attitudes, as it might be of two techniques. The critic, while he has to admit that changes from one to the other occur, persists in regarding them as mere variations to a certain fixed normal, just as a pendulum might swing. I admit the analogy of the pendulum as far as movement, but I deny the further consequence of the analogy, the existence of the point of rest, the normal point. . . .

There is something now to be cleared away before I get on with my argument, which is that while romanticism is dead in reality, yet the critical attitude appropriate to it still continues to exist. To make this a little clearer: For every kind of verse, there is a corresponding receptive attitude. In a romantic period we demand from verse certain qualities. In a classical period we demand others. At the present time I should say that this receptive attitude has outlasted the thing from which it was formed. But while the romantic tradition has run dry, yet the critical attitude of mind, which demands romantic qualities from verse, still survives. So that if good classical verse were to be written tomorrow very few people would be able to stand it.

I object even to the best of the romantics. I object still more to the receptive attitude. I object to the sloppiness which doesn't consider that a poem is a poem unless it is moaning or whining about something or other. I always think in this connection of the last line of a poem of John Webster's which ends with a request I cordially endorse:

'End your moan and come away.'

The thing has got so bad now that a poem which is all dry and hard, a properly classical poem, would not be considered poetry at all. How many people now can lay their hands on their hearts and say they like either Horace or Pope? They feel a kind of chill when they read them.

The dry hardness which you get in the classics is absolutely repugnant to them. Poetry that isn't damp isn't poetry at all. They cannot see that accurate description is a legitimate object of verse. Verse to them always means a bringing in of some of the emotions that are grouped round the word infinite.

The essence of poetry to most people is that it must lead them to a beyond of some kind. Verse strictly confined to the earthly and the definite (Keats is full of it) might seem to them to be excellent writing, excellent craftsmanship, but not poetry. So much has romanticism debauched us, that, without some form of vagueness, we deny the highest.

In the classic it is always the light of ordinary day, never the light that never was on land or sea. It is always perfectly human and never exaggerated: man is always man and never a god.

But the awful result of romanticism is that, accustomed to this strange light, you can never live without it. Its effect on you is that of a drug....

...I must avoid two pitfalls in discussing the idea of beauty. On the one hand there is the old classical view which is supposed to define it as lying in conformity to certain standard fixed forms; and on the other hand there is the romantic view which drags in the infinite. I have got to find a metaphysic between these two which will enable me to hold consistently that a neo-classic verse of the type I have indicated involves no contradiction in terms. It is essential to prove that beauty may be in small, dry things.

The great aim is accurate, precise and definite description. The first thing is to recognise how extraordinarily difficult this is. It is no mere matter of carefulness; you have to use language, and language is by its very nature a communal thing; that is, it expresses never the exact thing but a compromise – that which is common to you, me and everybody. But each man sees a little differently, and to get out clearly and exactly what he does see, he must have a terrific struggle with language, whether it be with words or the technique of other arts. Language has its own special nature, its own conventions and communal ideas. It is only by a concentrated effort of the mind that you can hold it fixed to your own purpose. I always think that the fundamental process at the back of all the arts might be represented by the following metaphor. You know what I call architect's curves – flat pieces of wood with all different kinds of curvature. By a suitable selection from these you can draw approximately any curve you like. The artist I take to be the man who simply can't bear the idea of that 'approximately'. He will get the exact curve of what he sees whether it be an object or an idea in the mind. I shall here have to change my metaphor a little to get the process in his mind. Suppose that instead of your curved pieces of wood you have a springy piece of steel of the same types of curvature as the wood. Now the state of tension or concentration of mind, if he is doing anything really good in this struggle against the ingrained habit of the technique, may be represented by a man employing all his fingers to bend the steel out of its own curve and into the exact curve which you want. Something different to what it would assume naturally.

There are then two things to distinguish, first the particular faculty of mind to see things as they really are, and apart from the conventional ways in which you have been trained to see them. This is itself rare enough in all consciousness. Second, the concentrated state of mind, the grip over oneself which is necessary in the actual expression of what one sees. To prevent one falling into the conventional curves of ingrained technique, to hold on through infinite detail and trouble to the exact curve you want. Wherever you get this sincerity, you get the fundamental quality of good art without dragging in infinite or serious.

I can now get at that positive fundamental quality of verse which constitutes excellence, which has nothing to do with infinity, with mystery or with emotions.

This is the point I aim at, then, in my argument. I prophesy that a period of dry, hard, classical verse is coming. I have met the preliminary objection founded on the bad romantic aesthetic that in such verse, from which the infinite is excluded, you cannot have the essence of poetry at all.

After attempting to sketch out what this positive quality is, I can get on to the end of my paper in this way: That where you get this quality exhibited in the realm of the emotions you get imagination, and that where you get this quality exhibited in the contemplation of finite things you get fancy.

In prose as in algebra concrete things are embodied in signs or counters which are moved about according to rules, without being visualised at all in the process. There are in prose certain type situations and arrangements of words, which move as automatically into certain other arrangements as do functions in algebra. One only changes the X's and the Y's back into physical things at the end of the process. Poetry, in one aspect at any rate, may be considered as an effort to avoid this characteristic of prose. It is not a counter language, but a visual concrete one. It is a compromise for a language of intuition which would hand over sensations bodily. It always endeavours to arrest you, and to make you continuously see a physical thing, to prevent you gliding through an abstract process. It chooses fresh epithets and fresh metaphors, not so much because they are new, and we are tired of the old, but because the old cease to convey a physical thing and become abstract counters. A poet says a ship 'coursed the seas' to get a physical image, instead of the counter word 'sailed'. Visual meanings can only be transferred by the new bowl of metaphor; prose is an old pot that lets them leak out. Images in verse are not mere decoration, but the very essence of an intuitive language. Verse is a pedestrian taking you over the ground, prose – a train which delivers you at a destination.

I can now get on to a discussion of two words often used in this connection, 'fresh' and 'unexpected'. You praise a thing for being 'fresh'. I understand what you mean, but the word besides conveying the truth conveys a secondary something which is certainly false. When you say a poem or drawing is fresh, and so good, the impression is somehow conveyed that the essential element of goodness is freshness, that it is good because it is fresh. Now this is certainly wrong, there is nothing particularly desirable about freshness *per se*. Works of art aren't eggs. Rather the contrary. It is simply an unfortunate necessity due to the nature of the language and technique that the only way the element which does constitute goodness, the only way in which its presence can be detected externally, is by freshness. Freshness convinces you, you feel at once that the artist was in an actual physical state. You feel that for a minute. Real communication is so very rare, for plain speech is unconvincing. It is in this rare fact of communication that you get the root of aesthetic pleasure.

I shall maintain that wherever you get an extraordinary interest in a thing, a great zest in its contemplation which carries on the contemplator to accurate description in the sense of the word accurate I have just analysed, there you have sufficient justification for poetry. It must be an intense zest which heightens a thing out of the level of prose. I am using contemplation here just in the same way that Plato used it, only applied to a different subject; it is a detached interest. 'The object of aesthetic contemplation is something framed apart by itself and regarded without memory or expectation, simply as being itself, as end not means, as individual not universal.'

To take a concrete example. I am taking an extreme case. If you are walking behind a woman in the street, you notice the curious way in which the skirt rebounds from her heels. If that peculiar kind of motion becomes of such interest to you that you will search about until you can get the exact epithet which hits it off, there you have a properly aesthetic emotion. But it is the zest with which you look at the thing which decides you to make the effort. In this sense the feeling that was in Herrick's mind when he wrote 'the tempestuous petticoat' was exactly the same as that which in bigger and vaguer matters makes the best romantic verse. It doesn't matter an atom that the emotion produced is not of dignified vagueness, but on the contrary amusing; the point is that exactly the same activity is at work as in the highest verse. That is the avoidance of conventional language in order to get the exact curve of the thing.

I have still to show that in the verse which is to come, fancy will be the necessary weapon of the classical school. The positive quality I have talked about can be manifested in ballad verse by extreme directness and simplicity, such as you get in 'On Fair Kirkconnel Lea'. But the particular verse we are going to get will be cheerful, dry and sophisticated, and here the necessary weapon of the positive quality must be fancy.

Subject doesn't matter; the quality in it is the same as you get in the more romantic people.

It isn't the scale or kind of emotion produced that decides, but this one fact: Is there any real zest in it? Did the poet have an actually realised visual object before him in which he delighted? It doesn't matter if it were a lady's shoe or the starry heavens.

Fancy is not mere decoration added on to plain speech. Plain speech is essentially inaccurate. It is only by new metaphors, that is, by fancy, that it can be made precise.

When the analogy has not enough connection with the thing described to be quite parallel with it, where it overlays the thing it described and there is a certain excess, there you have the play of fancy – that I grant is inferior to imagination.

But where the analogy is every bit of it necessary for accurate description in the sense of the word accurate I have previously described, and your only objection to this kind of fancy is that it is not serious in the effect it produces, then I think the objection to be entirely invalid. If it is sincere in the accurate sense, when the whole of the analogy is necessary to get out the exact curve of the feeling or thing you want to express – there you seem to me to have the highest verse, even though the subject be trivial and the emotions of the infinite far away.

It is very difficult to use any terminology at all for this kind of thing. For whatever word you use is at once sentimentalised. Take Coleridge's word 'vital'. It is used loosely by all kinds of people who talk about art, to mean something vaguely and mysteriously significant. In fact, vital and mechanical is to them exactly the same antithesis as between good and bad.

Nothing of the kind; Coleridge uses it in a perfectly definite and what I call dry sense. It is just this: A mechanical complexity is the sum of its parts. Put them side by side and you get the whole. Now vital or organic is merely a convenient metaphor for a complexity of a different kind, that in which the parts cannot be said to be elements as each one is modified by the other's presence, and each one to a certain extent is the whole. The leg of a chair by itself is still a leg. My leg by itself wouldn't be.

Now the characteristic of the intellect is that it can only represent complexities of the mechanical kind. It can only make diagrams, and diagrams are essentially things whose parts are separate one from another. The intellect always analyses – when there is a synthesis it is baffled. That is why the artist's work seems mysterious. The intellect can't represent it. This is a necessary consequence of the particular nature of the intellect and the purposes for which it is formed. It doesn't mean that your synthesis is ineffable, simply that it can't be definitely stated.

Now this is all worked out in Bergson, the central feature of his whole philosophy. It is all based on the clear conception of these vital complexities which he calls 'intensive' as opposed to the other kind which he calls 'extensive', and the recognition of the fact that the intellect can only deal with the extensive multiplicity. To deal with the intensive you must use intuition. . . .

Chapter 5
Filippo Marinetti

Filippo Tommaso Marinetti (1876–1944) was an Italian writer who played a key role in the invention of Futurism, an avant-garde movement in art, literature, and music. Futurism celebrated the transformations in experience brought about by new technology and proposed that new art forms would have to be created to explore these transformations. Marinetti wrote experimental work in poetry, fiction, and drama. In later life he identified increasingly with Mussolini's fascist ideology.

Marinetti was an exuberant writer of manifestos. The "Technical Manifesto of Futurist Literature" was dated May 11, 1912 and was first published by Marinetti as a broadsheet newspaper. The following excerpt sets out the criteria for a new poetry alert to the possibilities of a world energized by technological innovation. Syntax as much as fixed meters stand in the way of a poetry that will embrace the expanding field of analogies opened up by new forms of movement. The images created by analogy will, in Marinetti's view, be free from the tendency in the poetry of the past to project human feelings on to the nonhuman world.

Technical Manifesto of Futurist Literature

Sitting on the gas tank of an airplane, my stomach warmed by the pilot's head, I sensed the ridiculous inanity of the old syntax inherited from Homer. A pressing need to liberate words, to drag them out of their prison in the Latin period! Like all imbeciles, this period naturally has a canny head, a stomach, two legs, and two flat feet, but it will never have two wings. Just enough to walk, to take a short run and then stop short, panting!

From *Marinetti: Selected Writings*, ed. R. W. Flint, trans. R. W. Flint and A. W. Coppotelli (London: Secker and Warburg, 1972), pp. 84–9.

This is what the whirling propeller told me, when I flew two hundred meters above the mighty chimney pots of Milan. And the propeller added:

1. One must destroy syntax and scatter one's nouns at random, just as they are born.
2. One should use infinitives, because they adapt themselves elastically to nouns and don't subordinate them to the writer's *I* that observes or imagines. Alone, the infinitive can provide a sense of the continuity of life and the elasticity of the intuition that perceives it.
3. One must abolish the adjective, to allow the naked noun to preserve its essential color. The adjective, tending of itself toward the shadows, is incompatible with our dynamic vision, because it supposes a pause, a meditation.
4. One must abolish the adverb, old belt buckle that holds two words together. The adverb preserves a tedious unity of tone within a phrase.
5. Every noun should have its double; that is, the noun should be followed, with no conjunction, by the noun to which it is related by analogy. Example: man-torpedo-boat, woman-gulf, crowd-surf, piazza-funnel, door-faucet.

Just as aerial speed has multiplied our knowledge of the world, the perception of analogy becomes ever more natural for man. One must suppress the *like*, the *as*, the *so*, the *similar to*. Still better, one should deliberately confound the object with the image that it evokes, foreshortening the image to a single essential word.

6. Abolish even the punctuation. After adjectives, adverbs, and conjunctions have been suppressed, punctuation is naturally annulled, in the varying continuity of a *living* style that creates itself without the foolish pauses made by commas and periods. To accentuate certain movements and indicate their directions, mathematical symbols will be used: + – ×: = and the musical symbols.
7. Up to now writers have been restricted to immediate analogies. For instance, they have compared an animal to a man or to another animal, which is almost the same as a kind of photography. (They have compared, for example, a fox terrier to a very small thoroughbred. Others, more advanced, might compare that same trembling fox terrier to a little Morse Code machine. I, on the other hand, compare it to gurgling water. In this there is an *ever-vaster gradation of analogies*, there are ever-deeper and more solid affinities, however remote.)

Analogy is nothing more than the deep love that assembles distant, seemingly diverse and hostile things. An orchestral style, at once polychromatic, polyphonic, and polymorphous, can embrace the life of matter only by means of the most extensive analogies.

When, in my *Battle of Tripoli*, I compared a trench bristling with bayonets to an orchestra, a machine gun to a fatal woman, I intuitively introduced a large part of the universe into a short episode of African battle.

Images are not flowers to be chosen and picked with parsimony, as Voltaire said. They are the very lifeblood of poetry. Poetry should be an uninterrupted sequence of new images, or it is mere anemia and green-sickness.

The broader their affinities, the longer will images keep their power to amaze. One must – people say – spare the reader's capacity for wonder. Nonsense! Let us rather worry about the fatal corrosion of time that not only destroys the expressive value of a masterpiece but also its power to amaze. Too often stimulated, have our old ears perhaps not already destroyed Beethoven and Wagner? We must therefore eliminate from our language everything it contains in the way of stereotyped images, faded metaphors; and that means almost everything.

8. There are no categories of images, noble or gross or vulgar, eccentric or natural. The intuition that grasps them has no preferences or *partis pris.* Therefore the analogical style is absolute master of all matter and its intense life.

9. To render the successive motions of an object, one must render the *chain of analogies* that it evokes, each condensed and concentrated into one essential word. . . .

10. To catch and gather whatever is most fugitive and ungraspable in matter, one must shape *strict nets of images or analogies,* to be cast into the mysterious sea of phenomena. Except for the traditional festoons of its form, the following passage from my *Mafarka the Futurist* is an example of such a strict net of images:

> All the bitter sweetness of past youth mounted in his throat, as the cheerful cries of boys rose from the schoolyard toward their teachers leaning on the parapets of the terraces from which ships could be seen taking flight. . . .

And here are two more nets of images:

> Around the well of Bumeliana, beneath the thick olive trees, three camels squatting comfortably on the sand were gargling with contentment, like old stone gutters, mixing the *chak-chak* of their spitting with the steady beat of the steam pump that supplies water to the city. Cries and Futurist dissonances, in the deep orchestra of the trenches with their winding depths and noisy cellars, as the bayonets pass and repass, violin bows that the sunset's ruddy baton inflames with enthusiasm. . . .
>
> It is the sunset-conductor whose wide sweep gathers the scattered flutes of tree-bound birds, the grieving harps of insects, the creak of branches, and the crunch of stones. It is he who suddenly stops the mess-tin kettledrums and the rifles' clash, to let the muted instruments sing out above the orchestra, all the golden stars, upright, open-armed, across the footlights of the sky. And here is the *grande dame* of the play. . . . Prodigiously bare, it is indeed the desert who displays her immense bosom in its liquefied curves, all glowing in rosy lacquer beneath the mighty night's cascading jewels. [*Battle of Tripoli*]

11. Destroy the *I* in literature: that is, all psychology. The man side-tracked by the library and the museum, subjected to a logic and wisdom of fear is of absolutely no interest. We must therefore drive him from literature and finally put matter in his place, matter whose essence must be grasped by strokes of intuition, the kind of thing that the physicists and chemists can never do.

To capture the breath, sensibility, and the instincts of metals, stones, wood, and so on, through the medium of free and whimsical motors. To substitute the human psychology, now exhausted, the lyric obsession with matter.

Be careful not to force human feelings onto matter. Instead, divine its different governing impulses, its forces of compression, dilation, cohesion and disaggregation, its crowds of massed molecules and whirling electrons. We are not interested in offering dramas of humanized matter. The solidity of a strip of steel interests us for itself; that is, the incomprehensible and nonhuman alliance of its molecules or its electrons that oppose, for instance, the penetration of a howitzer. The warmth of a piece of iron or wood is in our opinion more impassioned than the smile or tears of a woman.

We want to make literature out of the life of a motor, a new instinctive animal whose general instincts we will know when we have learned the instincts of the different forces that make it up.

For a Futurist poet, nothing is more interesting than the action of a mechanical piano's keyboard. The cinema offers us the dance of an object that divides and recomposes without human intervention. It also offers us the backward sweep of a diver whose feet leave the ocean and bounce violently back on the diving board. Finally, it shows us a man driving at two hundred miles an hour. These are likewise movements of matter, outside the laws of intelligence and therefore of a more significant essence.

Three elements hitherto overlooked in literature must be introduced:

1. Sound (manifestation of the dynamism of objects).
2. Weight (objects' faculty of flight).
3. Smell (objects' faculty of dispersing themselves).

To force oneself, for example, to render the landscape of smells that a dog perceives. To listen to motors and to reproduce their conversations.

Material has always been contemplated by a cold, distracted *I*, too preoccupied with itself, full of preconceived wisdom and human obsessions.

Man tends to foul matter with his youthful joy or elderly sorrows; matter has an admirable continuity of impulse toward greater warmth, greater movement, a greater subdivision of itself. Matter is neither sad nor gay. Its essence is courage, will power, and absolute force. It belongs entirely to the intuitive poet who can free himself from traditional, heavy, limited syntax that is stuck in the ground, armless and wingless, being merely intelligent. Only the unsyntactical poet who unlinks his words can penetrate the essence of matter and destroy the dumb hostility that separates it from us.

The Latin period that has served us up to now was a pretentious gesture with which the myopic and overweening imagination forced itself to master the multiform and mysterious life of matter. The Latin period, consequently, was born dead.

Deep intuitions of life joined to one another, word for word according to their illogical birth, will give us the general lines of an *intuitive psychology of matter.* This was revealed to me when I was flying in an airplane. As I looked at objects from a new point of view, no longer head on or from behind, but straight down, foreshortened, that is, I was able to break apart the old shackles of logic and the plumb lines of the ancient way of thinking.

All you Futurist poets who have loved and followed me up to now have, like me, been frenzied makers of images and courageous explorers of analogies. But your strict nets of metaphor are too disgracefully weighed down by the plumb line of logic.

I advise you to lighten them, in order that your immensified gesture may speed them farther, cast them over a vaster ocean.

Together we will invent what I call *the imagination without strings* [*l'immaginazione senza fili*]. Someday we will achieve a yet more essential art, when we dare to suppress all the first terms of our analogies and render no more than an uninterrupted sequence of second terms. To achieve this we must renounce being understood. It is not necessary to be understood. Moreover we did without it when we were expressing fragments of the Futurist sensibility by means of traditional and intellective syntax.

Syntax was a kind of abstract cipher that poets used to inform the crowd about the color, musicality, plasticity, and architecture of the universe. Syntax was a kind of interpreter or monotonous cicerone. This intermediary must be suppressed, in order that literature may enter directly into the universe and become one body with it.

They shout at us, "Your literature won't be beautiful! Where is your verbal symphony, your harmonious swaying back and forth, your tranquilizing cadences?" Their loss we take for granted! And how lucky! We make use, instead, of every ugly sound, every expressive cry from the violent life that surrounds us. We bravely create the "ugly" in literature, and everywhere we murder solemnity. Come! Don't put on those grand priestly airs when you listen to me! Each day we must spit on the *Altar of Art.* We are entering the unbounded domain of free intuition. After free verse, here finally are *words in freedom.*

In this there is nothing absolute or systematic. Genius has impetuous gusts and muddy torrents. Sometimes it imposes analytic and explanatory longueurs. No one can suddenly renovate his own sensibility. Dead cells are mixed with the living. Art is a need to destroy and scatter oneself, a great watering can of heroism that drowns the world. Microbes – don't forget – are essential to the health of the intestines and stomach. There is also a microbe essential to the vitality of *art, this extension of the forest of our veins,* that pours out, beyond the body, into the infinity of space and time.

Futurist poets! I have taught you to hate libraries and museums, to prepare you *to hate the intelligence,* reawakening in you divine intuition, the characteristic gift of the Latin races. Through intuition we will conquer the seemingly unconquerable hostility that separates out human flesh from the metal of motors.

Chapter 6
Rabindranath Tagore

Rabindranath Tagore (1861–1941) was a Bengali writer, educator, and political thinker who in 1912 published Gitanjali, *an influential collection of English translations of poetry he had written in Bengali. He was awarded the Nobel Prize for Literature in 1913. Tagore was a prolific writer in Bengali and English and published work in a number of different forms: poetry, short fiction, novels, and plays. Tagore's writing was at one with his political and cultural activism. He played an important role in the movement for Indian independence. The school and university he founded in 1922 at Santinikitan in northern Bengal set out a model for the kind of education he thought appropriate for an independent India.*

Tagore's essay on Yeats was first published in Bengali in 1912. In the following excerpt Tagore distinguishes two conditions of poetic inheritance: one dominated by imitation, the other identified by originality. But originality, in Tagore's understanding, combines the values of universality with a specific engagement with a national culture. Yeats's stature as a poet is, for Tagore, a measure of Ireland's emergence from a state of colonial dependency and he finds a ready parallel between Yeats's achievement in Ireland and the struggle for national independence in India.

Poet Yeats

. . . When I read today's English poets I am often struck by the thought that they are not poets of the world as a whole, but rather poets of the world of letters. Here in England poets have a long literary tradition, with a plentiful supply of similes, metaphors and other stylistic devices. The result is that they do not have to go to the springs of poetic inspiration to make poetry. Instead they emulate those *ustads* in music who no longer feel the call to sing from the heart and thereby reduce music to a series of phrases and

From *Rabindranath Tagore: An Anthology*, ed. Krishna Dutta and Andrew Robinson (London: Picador, 1997), pp. 215–20, 221.

tunes, however complex and adroit their technique may be. When passion does not come from deep sensitivity, it becomes just a series of well-crafted words. Then it has to make up for its lack of candour and inner assurance with exaggeration; since it cannot be natural, it resorts to artifice in order to prove its originality.

My meaning will become clearer if we compare Wordsworth with Swinburne. Swinburne is the principal poet of poetry as opposed to life. He is so extraordinarily adroit at verbal music that he is besotted by his skill. Out of suggestive sounds he fashions a gorgeously variegated tapestry of images. His is a striking achievement, no doubt; but it has not established him as a world poet.

The poetry of Wordsworth arose from the direct touch of the world upon his heart. Hence its simplicity – which is not the same thing as being easy of understanding by the reader. Whenever a poet writes out of a direct response to life, his poetry blooms like the flowers and fruits on a tree. It is not conscious of itself, nor does it feel obliged to present itself as being beautiful or deeply felt. Whatever it appears to be, it is: to appreciate and enjoy it is the onus upon the reader.

Certain individuals are born with a need for direct experience and they do not permit any barrier to come between that experience and its inner realization. With absolute self-confidence and sincerity, they express the essence of the natural and human worlds in their own idiom. They have the courage to break all the conventions of contemporary poetry.

Burns was born in an age of literary artifice. His feelings sprang straight from the heart and he could express them in words. And so he was able to pierce through the bonds of literary usage and give unrestrained expression to the soul of Scotland.

In our own time, the poetry of Yeats has been received very warmly for the same basic reason. His poetry does not echo contemporary poetry, it is an expression of his own soul. When I say 'his own soul', I ought to make the idea a bit clearer. Like a cut diamond that needs the light of the sky to show itself, the human soul on its own cannot express its essence, and remains dark. Only when it reflects the light from something greater than itself, does it come into its own. In Yeats's poetry, the soul of Ireland is manifest.

Again this statement requires some clarification. Consider how, when the sun shines upon clouds, different portions reflect back different colours, depending on their condition and position. But this variety of colours does not create a clash; there is harmony in it, which would be inconceivable with clouds made of painted cotton wool.

Thus, whether the country is Ireland, Scotland or anywhere else, the genius of its people gives its own hue to the light of universal humanity. Universal man is something many-splendoured.

But a universal poet, while reflecting universal ideas, also belongs to his country, and his ideas are coloured by the special passions of his native land. The one who can express these well is considered blessed. In our country Vaishnava poetry, by virtue of its being genuinely Bengali, must be considered world poetry. It gives the world its due, but in doing so, it adds a particular flavour, it renders the universal in a particular form.

Those who dedicate themselves to fighting life's battles must put on armour; they require protection against the world and the blows that fall upon them from all sides. But those whose only goal is self-expression, find lack of protection to be their proper garb. On meeting Yeats, I felt that here was such a man. Here was someone capable of comprehending the world through the untrammelled power of his soul. His gaze was different from that of other men: he saw not by learning, nor by habit, nor by imitation.

When a man has this kind of unmediated perception of the world and can convey it, we observe a similarity between his vision and the vision of previous men; and this is not accidental. For all those who look candidly, see similarly. The Vedic poets too saw the life spirit in nature. The rivers and clouds, dawn, fire and storm were not scientific facts to them but manifestations of the working of the divine law. Their own experiences of joy and sorrow seemed to be re-enacted in the earth and heavens in wonderful disguise. As it is in our minds, so it is throughout nature. The whole drama of the human heart, with its laughter and tears, its desires, fulfilments and failures, is played out on the grandest scale in the light and shade and colour of the firmament. So vast is it, we cannot grasp its totality, we see just its parts, the waters, the land: we miss the overall picture, the underlying structure of the play. Only when man casts off his blinkers of habit and learning, when he looks with his whole heart, does he perceive the great drama in all its epic yearning – and this he cannot express except through myths and metaphors. His mind is now awakened and he experiences a realization – that there is nothing in the world that is not within him also, and that whatever is within him is immanent in the world in a deeper form. He thus attains the vision of the poet, which is to say that he sees with his heart, not with his eyeball, nerves or brain. This is a truth not of objective fact, but of the inner eye. And the language of his expression is consonant; it is the language of melody and beauty, the most ancient of human languages. Even today, when a poet shares such a universal perception, he speaks in the same language used by the old poets – which is why, although such language is outdated in a scientific age, poets still use it. Every new human experience revivifies the old stories and leaves its mark upon them. It stimulates the poet's mind and naturally induces him to return to the ancient modes.

Yeats has made his poetry confluent with the ancient poetic tradition of Ireland. Because he has achieved this naturally, he has won extraordinary recognition. With all his vitality he has been in contact with this traditional world; his knowledge of it is not second-hand. And so he sees beyond the physical world: its mountains and open spaces are a mysterious field for him, traversable only by meditation. Had he tried to express this feeling through the channels of modern literature, his sentiment and vigour would have been spoilt; for such modernity is not really fresh, but rather something worn out, rendered stiff and unresponsive by constant use. It is like the ashes that hide the fire: the fire predates the ash and yet is always new; the ash is "modern" but decrepit. And so every time one finds that the real poetry cuts through the contemporary diction.

Everyone knows that for some time past Ireland has been undergoing a national awakening. As a result of the suppression of the Irish spirit by British rule, this movement has grown in strength. For a long time its chief expression was political, in the shape of a rebellion. But in due course it acquired a new form. Ireland now understood that she need depend on no one and stood ready to give of herself.

Her situation is reminiscent of our own country. Our educated community made a determined attempt to secure political rights. But in the course of this it became obvious that the leaders of the movement had no concern for the language, literature and traditions of the country. Their efforts were almost unrelated to the life of the vast majority of the people. Whatever they did in the way of national uplift was done in the English language and directed at the British Government. The idea that national work might involve the people as a whole, did not occur to them.

Fortunately, however, at least in Bengal, through our literature we started to find ourselves. The chief glory of Bankim Chandra [Chatterji] is that he ushered in an age in which Bengalis felt pleased and proud to speak and write in their own tongue. Before that we were just schoolboys, doing our English exercises using our dictionary and grammar book; and we treated our own language and literature with contempt. Suddenly, *Bangadarshan* appeared, and showed us our own power. We discovered that we too could create literature and that it could satisfy our mental hunger. Once begun, we could not stop. Before, we had shut our eyes and told ourselves that we had nothing; now, we went looking for our own wealth. Where previously in the pages of *Bangadarshan* Comte and Mill had reigned, our writers now assiduously enthroned indigenous gods.

This enterprise in due time spread itself through various fields of endeavour. Whether or not we would manage to increase the number of native seats in the legislative council had been something in the gift of the Government; but whether or not we would advance in the direction of national liberation, was dependent on our own will-power. We saw that any one of us willing to apply his powers in any sphere would help fit us to realize our national potential. The satisfaction inherent in this realization is the only true path of progress for us.

Arrogance accompanies the awakening of a sense of power and is an obstacle to the realization of truth. It inclines us to self-delusion rather than self-appraisal. It equates the bogus and the genuine, thus downgrading the genuine. It causes us to forget that only by clearly defining what we lack, may we truly understand what we have. Such clarity of self-knowledge is our sole means of access of strength. Arrogance obscures our grasp of the limits of our strength and leads us into weakness and futility. The foundation of our new pride must be truth: arrogance will get us nowhere. It is when arrogance repeatedly dashes itself against the fort of truth, to no avail, that we start to find our true selves.

In Ireland, as in our country, there has been an earnest effort to achieve self-expression. The first products of any such mental churning are bound to be frothy, and for a fair while it is not worth attaching much importance to what is often ludicrous – as witness, in Ireland, the work of the well-known writer George Moore, *Hail and Farewell.* But notwithstanding, a few Irish writers of real genius did find their voices and, by drawing upon the ancient stories and legends, gave new voice to the soul of Ireland. Yeats was one of them. He has won Ireland a place in world literature....

[The] notion of 'imaginative conviction' is profoundly true of Yeats. Imagination to him is not just the faculty of invention, it is the light whereby that which he sees is truly seized and becomes part of his life. In other words, imagination is not a mere device in his hands for making poetry, it is the stuff of life, which enables Yeats to extract sustenance from the world. Whenever I have chanced to meet him in private, I have sensed this. Though I have not yet had the opportunity to know him fully as a poet, by knowing him as a man I have come to feel that his is a soul in contact with life in all essentials.

Chapter 7
Edward Thomas

Edward Thomas (1878–1917) was born in London of Welsh parents. He first met the American poet, Robert Frost, in 1913, and it was through Frost's encouragement that Thomas became a serious poet in the last two and a half years of his life. For much of his career Thomas led a financially precarious and emotionally fragile life, writing reviews, biographies, and books based on his travels around Britain. In 1915 he joined the British Army. In 1917 he was killed at the battle of Arras. Most of his poetry was published posthumously. Its main subjects are the English rural landscape and those who lived and worked there. The violence of war and other more mysterious forms of psychological disturbance often haunt the peace offered by these rural settings.

Thomas wrote a number of reviews of Frost's 1914 collection, North of Boston. *In the two excerpts here – the first published in the* Daily News *in July 1914, the second in the* New Weekly *for August 1914 – Thomas sets out the arguments and the quotations that, for him, identify Robert Frost as the exemplary modern poet. They provide a muted alternative to the more assertive arguments about modern poetry put forward in the same period by T. S. Eliot, Amy Lowell, and Ezra Pound.*

Two Reviews of Robert Frost's *North of Boston*

This is one of the most revolutionary books of modern times, but one of the quietest and least aggressive. It speaks, and it is poetry. It consists of fifteen poems, from fifty to three hundred lines long, depicting scenes from life, chiefly in the country, in New Hampshire. Two neighbour farmers go along the opposite sides of their boundary wall, mending it and speaking of walls and of boundaries. A husband and wife discuss an old vagabond farm servant who has come home to them, as it falls out, to die. Two travellers sit outside a deserted cottage, talking of those who once lived in it, talking

From *A Language Not To Be Betrayed: Selected Prose of Edward Thomas*, selected by Edna Longley (Manchester: Carcanet Press, 1981), pp. 125–7, 128, 130.

until bees in the wall boards drive them away. A man who has lost his feet in a saw-mill talks with a friend, a child, and the lawyer comes from Boston about compensation. The poet himself describes the dreams of his eyes after a long day on a ladder picking apples, and the impression left on him by a neglected woodpile in the snow on an evening walk. All but these last two are dialogue mainly; nearly all are in blank verse.

These poems are revolutionary because they lack the exaggeration of rhetoric, and even at first sight appear to lack the poetic intensity of which rhetoric is an imitation. Their language is free from the poetical words and forms that are the chief material of secondary poets. The metre avoids not only the old-fashioned pomp and sweetness, but the later fashion also of discord and fuss. In fact, the medium is common speech and common decasyllables, and Mr Frost is at no pains to exclude blank verse lines resembling those employed, I think, by Andrew Lang in a leading article printed as prose. Yet almost all these poems are beautiful. They depend not at all on objects commonly admitted to be beautiful; neither have they merely a homely beauty, but are often grand, sometimes magical. Many, if not most, of the separate lines and separate sentences are plain and, in themselves, nothing. But they are bound together and made elements of beauty by a calm eagerness of emotion.

What the poet might have done, could he have permitted himself egoistic rhetoric, we have a glimpse of once or twice where one of his characters tastes a fanciful mood to the full: as where one of the men by the deserted cottage, who has been describing an old-style inhabitant, says:

'As I sit here, and often times, I wish
I could be monarch of a desert land
I could devote and dedicate for ever
To the truths we keep coming back and back to.
So desert it would have to be, so walled
By mountain ranges half in summer snow,
No one would covet it or think it worth
The pains of conquering to force change on.
Scattered oases where men dwelt, but mostly
Sand dunes held loosely in tamarisk
Blown over and over themselves in idleness.
Sand grains should sugar in the natal dew
The babe born to the desert, the sand storm
Retard mid-waste my cowering caravans –

There are bees in this wall.' He struck the clapboards,
Fierce heads looked out; small bodies pivoted.
We rose to go. Sunset blazed on the windows.

This passage stands alone. But it is a solitary emotion also that gives him another which I feel obliged to quote in order to hint at the poetry elsewhere spread evenly over whole poems. It is the end of 'The Wood Pile':

I thought that only
Someone who lived in turning to fresh tasks

Could so forget his handiwork on which
He spent himself, the labour of his axe,
And leave it there far from a useful fireplace
To warm the frozen swamp as best it could
With the slow smokeless burning of decay.

The more dramatic pieces have the same beauty in solution, the beauty of life seen by one in whom mystery and tenderness together just outstrip humour and curiosity. This beauty grows like grass over the whole, and blossoms with simple flowers which the reader gradually sets a greater and greater value on, in lines such as these about the dying labourer:

She put out her hand
Among the harp-like morning-glory strings
Taut with the dew from garden bed to eaves,
As if she played unheard the tenderness
That wrought on him beside her in the night.
'Warren,' she said, 'he has come home to die:
You needn't be afraid he'll leave you this time.'
'Home,' he mocked gently.
'Yes, what else but home?
It all depends on what you mean by home.
Of course, he's nothing to us, any more
Than was the hound that came a stranger to us
Out of the woods, worn out upon the trail.'
'Home is the place where, when you have to go there,
They have to take you in.'
'I should have called it
Something you somehow haven't to deserve.'

The book is not without failures. Mystery falls into obscurity. In some lines I cannot hit upon the required accents. But his successes, like 'The Death of the Hired Man', put Mr Frost above all other writers of verse in America. He will be accused of keeping monotonously at a low level, because his characters are quiet people, and he has chosen the unresisting medium of blank verse. I will only remark that he would lose far less than most modern writers by being printed as prose. If his work were so printed, it would have little in common with the kind of prose that runs to blank verse: in fact, it would turn out to be closer knit and more intimate than the finest prose is except in its finest passages. It is poetry because it is better than prose.

(*Daily News*)

This is an original book which will raise the thrilling question, What is poetry? and will be read and re-read for pleasure as well as curiosity, even by those who decide that, at any rate, it is not poetry. At first sight, some will pronounce simply that anyone can write this kind of blank verse, with all its tame common words, straightforward constructions, and innumerable perfectly normal lines. Few that read it through will have been as much astonished by any American since Whitman. Mr Frost owes nothing to Whitman, though had Whitman not helped to sanctify plain labour and ordinary men, Mr Frost might have been different. The colloquialisms, the predominance of conversation (though not one out of fifteen pieces has been printed in dramatic style), and the phrase 'by your leave' (which is an excrescence), may hint at Browning. But I have not met a living poet with a less obvious or more complicated ancestry. Nor is there any brag or challenge about this.

Mr Frost has, in fact, gone back, as Whitman and as Wordsworth went back, through the paraphernalia of poetry into poetry again. With a confidence like genius, he has trusted his conviction that a man will not easily write better than he speaks when some matter has touched him deeply, and he has turned it over until he has no doubt what it means to him, when he has no purpose to serve beyond expressing it, when he has no audience to be bullied or flattered, when he is free, and speech takes one form and no other. Whatever discipline further was necessary, he has got from the use of the good old English medium of blank verse....

Naturally, then, when his writing crystallizes, it is often in a terse, plain phrase, such as the proverb, 'Good fences make good neighbours', or 'Three foggy mornings and one rainy day / Will rot the best birch fence a man can build', or 'From the time when one is sick to death / One is alone, and he dies more alone', or 'Pressed into service means pressed out of shape.'

But even this kind of characteristic detail is very much less important than the main result, which is a richly homely thing beyond the grasp of any power except poetry. It is a beautiful achievement, and I think a unique one, as perfectly Mr Frost's own as his vocabulary, the ordinary English speech of a man accustomed to poetry and philosophy, more colloquial and idiomatic than the ordinary man dares to use even in a letter, almost entirely lacking the emphatic hackneyed forms of journalists and other rhetoricians, and possessing a kind of healthy, natural delicacy like Wordsworth's, or at least Shelley's, rather than that of Keats.

(*New Weekly*)

Chapter 8
Amy Lowell

Amy Lowell (1874–1925) began her career as a poet by writing in a style strongly influenced by the English Romantic poet, John Keats. In 1912 her reading of the Imagist poet, HD (Hilda Doolitle), opened up a new direction for her own work. In 1913, and again in 1914, she came to England from the United States to work with Ezra Pound, HD, and other poets associated with Imagism. Through her work as a poet, critic, editor, and public speaker Lowell became an energetic advocate for modernist poetry. Between 1914 and 1925 she published six further collections of her own poetry, edited three anthologies of Imagist poetry, wrote two pioneering critical studies of modern poetry, and a biography of Keats.

"Poetry as a Spoken Art" was published posthumously in 1930 in a collection of essays and lectures, Poetry and Poets: Essays by Amy Lowell. *Textual evidence suggests that "Poetry as a Spoken Art" was probably first given as a lecture at Brooklyn College in 1917 or 1918. In the following excerpt, Lowell argues that rhythm in poetry is subdued by the habit of silent reading from the printed page. The text contains one of her many justifications of* vers libre *and presents her credo for modern poetry: to restore "the audible quality to poetry."*

Poetry as a Spoken Art

To speak of poetry as a "spoken art," may seem, in this age of printing, a misnomer; and it is just because of such a point of view that the essential kinship of poetry and music is so often lost sight of. The "beat" of poetry, its musical quality, is exactly that which differentiates it from prose, and it is this musical quality which bears in it the stress of emotion without which no true poetry can exist. Prose itself when it is fused with emotion becomes rhythmic, and the rhythm in turn heightens the emotional

From *Poetry and Poets: Essays by Amy Lowell* (Boston and New York: Houghton Mifflin, 1930), pp. 10–15, 16–19, 20–3.

effect. The great orators of all time have been great because of their power to achieve this effect. Poetry and oratorical prose have this in common, that they are both intended primarily to be heard, not seen.

We moderns read so much more than we listen, that perhaps it is no wonder if we get into the habit of using our minds more than our ears, where literature is concerned, with the result that our imaginative, mental ear becomes absolutely atrophied. What I mean by our imaginative, mental ear is this: Most of us possess quite a handsome degree of visual imagination. In reading a book, we visualize its scenes. If we are reading about an orchard with an old stone seat set in an angle under blossoming boughs, we see the orchard, and the seat, with a good deal of distinctness, before us. Of course, the degree to which we see it depends upon how highly developed our imaginative power is. But I have never met any one so devoid of all such power as not to visualize to some extent the scenes of the story he was reading.

Now here is a curious thing: In the case of the average person, auditory imagination is not nearly so well developed as visual. Why this should be, I do not know. Possibly it is the writer's fault, or rather misfortune; it may be easier to convey the impression of a sight than of a sound. Whatever the cause may be that we do not hear things off paper as well as we see them, the fact, I believe, is indisputable.

No art has suffered so much from printing as has poetry. Our cheap processes of colour reproduction do not really reproduce the picture whose name they bear; they are merely so many shorthand notes upon it. If we have seen the picture, they serve to remind us of it; if we have not, they give us a kind of passport introduction to it when we meet it. They in no way attempt to replace the original picture; that exists apart from them, and no one would think of studying art by these reproductions alone. In the case of photographs, we have a still more restricted form of memoranda. For in photography, colours can only be given as light and shade. Photographs of paintings are more satisfactory than colour reproductions, because the imagination has more scope and does its work infinitely better than any mechanical colour process can do.

But take the case of poetry. Here we have no galleries of original pieces to which the art-hungry can turn. The reproduction, the printed book, is the only tangible substance which poetry has. If photography and colour-printing are the conventionalized symbols of pictures, how much slighter, less adequate, are the conventionalized symbols of poetry. Printed words, of no beauty in themselves, of no value except to rouse the imagination and cause it to function.

Again, take the case of music. Here we have a condition almost exactly similar to that of poetry, except for one thing. Printed notes are no more beautiful than printed words, but here comes in the one saving fact: nobody (except highly trained musicians) expects to *read* music, everybody insists upon *hearing* it.

Poetry is as much an art to be heard as is music, if we could only get people to understand the fact. To read it off the printed pages without pronouncing it is to get only a portion of its beauty, and yet it is just this that most people do.

Of course, the reason here is very simple. Wordsworth's "Ode to Immortality" is manufactured with the very same tools we employ when we order the dinner. The tools in both cases are words. Everybody uses words, and uses them all the time. The most uneducated peasant talks. Words are the birthright of humanity. To be dumb is to be deformed.

Using the common implements of all the world, poetry is treated with a cavalier ease which music escapes. A long and special training is required to learn and understand music. The layman does not carry a musical score home in his pocket to read in the evening. If he wants to hear Debussy's "L'Après-midi d'un Faune," for instance, he goes to a concert, where an orchestra of carefully trained musicians interprets it for him.

Poetry will come into its Paradise when carefully trained speakers make a business of interpreting it to the world. And poetry needs such interpretation, for I suppose it is only one reader out of a hundred (and I think that percentage is rather high than otherwise) who can possibly get all the beauty out of a poem.

Every one knows that poetry existed before printing, and I imagine there is no doubt that it existed before writing, although, of course, that cannot be proved. Even so recently as the Middle Ages, troubadours went from castle to castle chanting their poems to delighted listeners. For people listened then, partly because they could not read, and also because, even if they could, there were so few books. With the rise of printing, with the advent of a reading populace, poetry ceased to be chanted, ceased to be read aloud at all for the most part; and the poet has suffered as a composer would suffer whose works were doomed to be rendered by no finer instrument than an accordion.

Shakespeare is the greatest English poet who has ever existed, and doubtless he would have been considered so under all circumstances. But Shakespeare has certainly enjoyed one inestimable advantage over all purely lyric poets – he has been acted for three hundred years, and that means that he has been spoken. People have heard his poetry rendered by men and women of extraordinary genius, who have spent their lives in studying it. The world has been forced to receive his poetry, the whole of his poetry, all its beauty of sound and content. There has been no excuse for misunderstanding him, and he has not been misunderstood....

It is because we so seldom hear poetry adequately rendered that the art has for so long lapsed in popular favour. For years only those people trained to receive it as audible impression through the sense of sight have been able thoroughly to comprehend it. The few people who attempt to read it aloud are handicapped by the realization of the unusual quality of their task, and lose their sense of proportion and simplicity in the welter of artistic theories of expression which have gradually come into being. Let us examine a few of these theories, and see in what way they have hampered the enjoyment of poetry, and its simple, straightforward appeal....

Speaking lines in a modern play is a comparatively easy thing; reading poetry is quite different. In a play, one can rely to a certain extent upon acting, and upon one's fellow actors. In reading, one is all alone, and one must not act. I do not mean that one should not read with expression. I mean that it is more dangerous to overdo dramatic expression than to underdo it.

Reading is not acting, and the point cannot be too strongly insisted upon. The pitfall of all elocution-taught readers is that they fail to see this distinction. Great actresses like Sarah Bernhardt or Duse do not make this mistake; it is the little people who are not sure of their power of creating an effect by an inflection who fall into the error.

Again, the reader must not be confused with the impersonator. Impersonators act out their parts, although they are all alone upon the stage. They are approaching the brains of their audiences from the same standpoint as the actor. They are acting, in fact.

This point is the crux of the situation. In a play, the audience is intended to see the march of events with its physical eyes. It is, as it were, looking through a window at an actual scene. It must be made to feel the reality of what is before it. Even in mystical plays like Maeterlinck's "Pelléas and Melisande" the audience must have the sense of actuality. Dream world though it be, it is for the moment real.

In reading, the impression to be made upon an audience is achieved by quite other means. Here the audience must see nothing with its eyes which detracts from its mental vision. It must be made to imagine so vividly that it forgets the reader in the thing read. The dramatic quality of the piece must be given just in so far as it stimulates imagination, but never so far as to call attention to the reader as an actual personality.

... [T]here is a good tradition of speaking poetry, and ninety and nine bad traditions. Let us consider for a moment the bad traditions. (I shall take the word "reading" to imply the pronouncing of poetry aloud, whether it be done in character on the stage, or in *propria persona* from the platform.)

The first bad tradition is the mispronouncing of words. This starts from a misconception of the laws of English prosody, and a desire to heighten the poetical effect by some elegance other than those the author thought fit to insert.

The word most mispronounced in the whole vocabulary, by poetry readers and singers alike, is "wind." Unless the reader or singer is very well educated indeed, so well educated that he or she knows enough to be quite simple and natural, that unhappy word changes at once to "winde." Why? What is the reason for the change? The reason, in the case of nine readers out of ten, is merely that they have been taught to do it. But the reason which has actuated those teachers who have thought about the matter at all and not, themselves, repeated parrot-like from some earlier master, is based upon ignorance of the rules under which English poetry is written.

Why was "wind" ever pronounced "winde" in poetry, for it never is, and never was, in prose? Cannot we imagine the reason? Not a bad reason when one is in ignorance of any prosodic laws. It was because poets insisted upon rhyming it with "find," and "bind," and other words where the *i* was obviously long. To pronounce it with a long *i* saved the rhyming sound, thought these wiseacres, and that this pronunciation took all the windy connotations away from the word was to them of minor importance. Elocution teachers are seldom concerned with *le mot juste*; "winde" sounded like a perfect rhyme, "wind" did not, so "winde" it had to be.

But the good old English prosody which served Shakespeare, and Spenser, and Milton so excellently well, had one life-saving rule. It was that words spelt the same and pronounced differently, rhymed; as did also words pronounced the same and spelt differently. For instance, "plough" rhymed with "cow," an obvious chime, as we have recognized by spelling "bough" with an "ow" instead of the old "ough"; also "peak" rhymed with "break," and "push" with "rush," and "deaf" with "sheaf." All these non-chiming rhymes we have kept, probably because of the difficulty of changing them to fit. For we all balk at the "pake" of a mountain, or at a brook "rooshing" down a hill, and few of us can "pŭsh" ourselves to make such radical changes. It is true that in old times "deaf" was universally pronounced "deef," but good use has altered it to "deaf" without altering its co-rhymes, and he would be a bold man who should dare to speak of a "sheff" of wheat for any reason whatsoever. . . .

Now we understand how "wind" came to be tortured into "winde," and can see why the latter is never under any circumstances to be employed.

An important rule for the reading of poetry is never to mispronounce words. Give them the sound they have in everyday speech, and let the blunder of a false rhyme, if there be one, rest on the author.

Another of the bad traditions insists that poetry should be read as if it were prose. That is, that the reader should follow the punctuation marks and not the swing of the metre. This arose as a protest to the equally bad tradition which dropped the voice at the end of each line, regardless of the sense. Of course, monotony was the result of this latter practice. The sense of the poem was lost, while the rhythm was exaggerated out of all proportion.

People have often taken issue with the proposition that poetry should not be read as if it were prose. People who have not grasped the meaning, that is. "But," they say, "surely you don't like to have poetry read in a sing-song manner." Assuredly, I do not; and yet I say, unhesitatingly, that if one must choose between these two bad traditions, I prefer to have the rhythm over-accented than to have it lost sight of altogether. As a matter of fact, neither extreme is necessary. The good tradition, as is the way with good traditions, seeks the happy mean.

Blank verse is a long, stately metre composed of simple, dignified feet. It is rare to find a blank-verse poem in which the rhythms should be more than faintly indicated. But there are other metres in which the effect is entirely lost unless the rhythm is brought out so strongly as to become almost a lilt. We must suppose that the poet knew what he was about when he chose one metre rather than another. It is an impertinence to obscure his rhythm, and not give it its full value.

But, it may be asked, how is one to know when a rhythm is to be merely indicated, and when it is to be actively stressed? I can only reply that much experience is required to know this. But experience is a sure guide. Knowledge of an author's methods, sympathy with the aim of the poem, a realization that certain metres require certain renderings, all these things tell the reader what he should do. In the last analysis, it is common sense, and nowhere is common sense more needed than in the reading of poetry.

Take the case of "*vers libre*." For that to be misunderstood is both strange and unfortunate, since it owes its inception to no personal idiosyncrasy, but has been slowly evolved from existing laws. This is so little comprehended that hysterical people are constantly asking what it is, and whether it is prose or poetry, and is it destined entirely to supersede metrical verse.

To answer these questions categorically, let us begin with the last. Art has fashions; or if you prefer the term as more dignified, it is subject to the law of evolution. Differences are constantly being evolved; some are real changes, some only samenesses with a twist to them. Art, like life, has a queer way of revolving upon itself. Personally I feel that *vers libre* and metrical verse can exist side by side as cheerfully as do blank verse and quatrains. But this will not happen until people realize that *vers libre* is a prosodic form, and not an invitation to loose all the seven devils upon the reading public.

The second question, whether *vers libre* is poetry or prose, can be treated quite summarily. It is assuredly poetry. That it may dispense with rhyme, and must dispense with metre, does not affect its substance in the least. For no matter with what it dispenses, it retains that essential to all poetry: Rhythm.

Where stanzas are printed in an even pattern of metrical lines, some sense of rhythm can be gained by the eye. Where they are not, as in *vers libre*, the reading aloud becomes an absolute condition of comprehension. If the modern movement in poetry could be defined in a sentence, the truest thing which could be said of it, and which would include all its variations, would be that it is a movement to restore the audible quality to poetry, to insist upon it as a spoken art.

Chapter 9
Guillaume Apollinaire

Guillaume Apollinaire (1880–1918) was one of the leading poets and theoreticians of the French avant-garde in the early years of the twentieth century. The illegitimate child of an Italian father and Polish mother, he spent his early life living in different parts of Europe. In 1902 he settled in Paris, changed his name from Wilhelm de Kostrowitsky to Guillaume Apollinaire, and embarked on a literary career. His contact with Picasso, Braque, and others led him to write some of the earliest critical reflections on their work, The Cubist Painters, *published in 1913.* Alcools, *published in 1913 and* Calligrammes, *published in 1918, show the range and energy of his experiments with many aspects of poetic form. He invented new shapes for poems on the page, tested the limits of the unified lyric voice, and drew eclectically on different traditions and languages.*

The following excerpt is from "The New Spirit and the Poets," which was first given in 1917 as a talk at a meeting on "The New Spirit" held in Paris. Apollinaire confidently identifies France as world leader for modern poetry. His account of the possibilities of modernity is, like Marinetti's, exuberant and optimistic. Apollinaire sets out a program for the poetry of the future, one that will embrace new technologies of sound and image, moving poetry away from its identification with the printed word.

The New Spirit and the Poets

The new spirit which will dominate the poetry of the entire world has nowhere come to light as it has in France. The strong intellectual discipline which the French have always imposed on themselves permits them, as well as their spiritual kin, to have a conception of life, of the arts and of letters, which, without being simply the recollection of antiquity, is also not the counterpart of romantic prettiness.

From *Selected Writings of Guillaume Apollinaire*, trans. Roger Shattuck (New York: New Directions, 1971), pp. 227–32, 233–6, 237.

The new spirit which is making itself heard strives above all to inherit from the classics a sound good sense, a sure critical spirit, perspectives on the universe and on the soul of man, and the sense of duty which lays bare our feelings and limits or rather contains their manifestations.

It strives further to inherit from the romantics a curiosity which will incite it to explore all the domains suitable for furnishing literary subject matter which will permit life to be exalted in whatever form it occurs.

To explore truth, to search for it, as much in the ethnic domain, for example, as in that of the imagination – those are the principal characteristics of the new spirit.

This tendency, moreover, has always had its bold proponents, although they were unaware of it; for a long time it has been taking shape and making progress.

However, this is the first time that it has appeared fully conscious of itself. Up to now the literary field has been kept within narrow limits. One wrote in prose or one wrote in verse. In prose, rules of grammar established the form.

As for poetry, rimed versification was the only rule, which underwent periodical attacks, but which was never shaken.

Free verse gave wings to lyricism; but it was only one stage of the exploration that can be made in the domain of form.

The investigations of form have subsequently assumed a great importance. Is it not understandable?

How could the poet not be interested in these investigations which can lead to new discoveries in thought and lyricism?

Assonance, alliteration as well as rime are conventions, each of which has its merits.

Typographical artifices worked out with great audacity have the advantage of bringing to life a visual lyricism which was almost unknown before our age. These artifices can still go much further and achieve the synthesis of the arts, of music, painting, and literature.

That is only one search for attaining new and perfectly legitimate expressions.

Who would dare to say that rhetorical exercises, the variations on the theme of: *I die of thirst beside the fountain* did not have a determining influence on Villon? Who would dare to say the investigations of form of the rhetoricians and of the Marotic[1] school did not serve to purify the French style up to its flowering in the seventeenth century?

It would have been strange if in an epoch when the popular art *par excellence*, the cinema, is a book of pictures, the poets had not tried to compose pictures for meditative and refined minds which are not content with the crude imaginings of the makers of films. These last will become more perceptive, and one can predict the day when, the photograph and the cinema having become the only form of publication in use, the poet will have a freedom heretofore unknown.

One should not be astonished if, with only the means they have now at their disposal, they set themselves to preparing this new art (vaster than the plain art of words) in which, like conductors of an orchestra of unbelievable scope, they will have at their disposition the entire world, its noises and its appearances, the thought and language of man, song, dance, all the arts and all the artifices, still more mirages than Morgane could summon up on the hill of Gibel, with which to compose the visible and unfolded book of the future.

But generally you will not find in France the "words at liberty" which have been reached by the excesses of the Italian and Russian futurists, the extravagant offspring of the new spirit, for France abhors disorder. She readily questions fundamentals, but she has a horror of chaos.

We can hope, then, in regard to what constitutes the material and the manner of art, for a liberty of unimaginable opulence. Today the poets are serving their apprenticeship to this encyclopaedic liberty. In the realm of inspiration, their liberty can not be less than that of a daily newspaper which on a single sheet treats the most diverse matters and ranges over the most distant countries. One wonders why the poet should not have at least an equal freedom, and should be restricted, in an era of the telephone, the wireless, and aviation, to a greater cautiousness in confronting space.

The rapidity and simplicity with which minds have become accustomed to designating by a single word such complex beings as a crowd, a nation, the universe, do not have their modern counterpart in poetry. Poets are filling the gap, and their synthetic poems are creating new entities which have a plastic value as carefully composed as that of collective terms.

Man has familiarised himself with those formidable beings which we know as machines, he has explored the domain of the infinitely small, and new domains open up for the activity of his imagination: that of the infinitely large and that of prophecy.

Do not believe that this new spirit is complicated, slack, artificial, and frozen. In keeping with the very order of nature, the poet puts aside any high-flown purpose. There is no longer any Wagnerianism in us, and the young authors have cast far away all the enchanted clothing of the mighty romanticism of Germany and Wagner, just as they have rejected the rustic tinsel of our early evaluations of Jean-Jacques Rousseau.

I do not believe that social developments will ever go so far that one will not be able to speak of national literature. On the contrary, however far one advances on the path of new freedoms, they will only reinforce most of the ancient disciplines and bring out new ones which will not be less demanding than the old. This is why I think that, whatever happens, art increasingly has a country. Furthermore, poets must always express a milieu, a nation; and artists, just as poets, just as philosophers, form a social estate which belongs doubtless to all humanity, but as the expression of a race, of one given environment.

Art will only cease being national the day that the whole universe, living in the same climate, in houses built in the same style, speaks the same language with the same accent – that is to say never. From ethnic and national differences are born the variety of literary expressions, and it is that very variety which must be preserved.

A cosmopolitan lyric expression would only yield shapeless works without character or individual structure, which would have the value of the commonplaces of international parliamentary rhetoric. And notice that the cinema, which is the perfect cosmopolitan art, already shows ethnic differences immediately apparent to everyone, and film enthusiasts immediately distinguish between an American and an Italian film. Likewise the new spirit, which has the ambition of manifesting a universal spirit and which does not intend to limit its activity, is none the less, and claims to respect the fact, a particular and lyric expression of the French nation, just as the classic spirit is, *par excellence*, a sublime expression of the same nation.

It must not be forgotten that it is perhaps more dangerous for a nation to allow itself to be conquered intellectually than by arms. That is why the new spirit asserts above all an order and a duty which are the great classic qualities manifested by French genius; and to them it adds liberty. This liberty and this order, which combine in the new spirit, are its characteristic and its strength.

However, this synthesis of the arts which has been consummated in our time, must not degenerate into confusion. That is to say that it would be, if not dangerous, at least absurd, for example to reduce poetry to a sort of imitative harmony which would not have the excuse of exactness.

One is right to imagine that imitative harmony can play a role, but it will be the basis only of an art in which machinery plays a part; for example, a poem or a symphony composed on a phonograph might well consist of noises artistically chosen and lyrically blended or juxtaposed; whereas, for my part, I think it wrong that a poem should be composed simply of the imitation of a noise to which no lyric, tragic, or pathetic meaning can be attached. And if a few poets devote themselves to this game, it should be regarded only as an exercise, a sort of rough notation of what they will include in a finished work. The "brekeke koax" of Aristophanes' *Frogs* is nothing if one separates it from the work in which it takes on all its comic and satiric meaning. The prolonged "i i i i" sounds, lasting a whole line, of Francis Jammes' bird are a sorry harmony if they are detached from the poem to whose total fantasy they give precision.

When a modern poet notes in several lines the throbbing sound of an airplane, it must be regarded above all as the desire of the poet to accustom his sensibility to reality. His passion for truth impels him to take almost scientific notes which, if he wishes to present them as poems, have the faults of being *trompe-oreilles* so to speak, to which actuality will always be superior.

On the other hand, if he wants for example to amplify the art of the dance and attempt a choreography whose buffoons would not restrict themselves to *entrechats* but would utter cries setting off the harmony with an imitative novelty, that is a search which is not absurd, whose popular origins are found in all peoples among whom war dances, for example, are almost always embellished with savage cries.

To come back to the concern with truth and the verisimilitude which rules all investigation, all attempts, all efforts of the new spirit, it must be added that there is no ground for astonishment if a certain number or even a great many of them remain sterile for the moment and sink into ridicule. The new spirit is full of dangers and snares.

All that, however, belongs to the spirit of today, and to condemn categorically these trials and efforts would be to make an error of the kind which, rightly or wrongly, is attributed to M. Thiers in declaring that the railroads were only a scientific game and that the world could not produce enough iron to build rails from Paris to Marseilles.

The new spirit, therefore, admits even hazardous literary experience, and those experiences are at times anything but lyric. This is why lyricism is only one domain of the new spirit in today's poetry, which often contents itself with experiments and investigations without concerning itself over giving them lyric significance. They are materials which the poet amasses, which the new spirit amasses, and these materials will form a basis of truth whose simplicity and modesty must never give pause, for their consequences can be very great things.

At a later date, those who study the literary history of our time will be amazed that, like the alchemists, the dreamers and poets devoted themselves, without even the pretext of a philosopher's stone, to inquiries and to notations which exposed them to the ridicule of their contemporaries, of journalists and of snobs.

But their inquiries will be useful; they will be the foundation of a new realism which will perhaps not be inferior to that so poetic and learned realism of ancient Greece.

With Alfred Jarry, moreover, we have seen laughter rise from the lower region where it was writhing, to furnish the poet with a totally new lyricism. Where is the time when Desdemona's handkerchief seemed to be an inadmissible ridiculousness? Today even ridicule is sought after, it must be seized upon and it has its place in poetry because it is a part of life in the same way as heroism and all that formerly nourished a poet's enthusiasm.

The romantics have tried to give to things of rude appearance a horrible or tragic meaning. It would be better to say that they only worked for the benefit of what is horrible. They wanted to establish the horrible much more than the melancholy. The new spirit does not seek to transform ridicule; it conserves for it a role which is not without flavour. Likewise it does not seem to give a sense of nobility to the horrible. It leaves it horrible and does not debase the noble. *It is not a decorative art. Nor is it an impressionist art.* It is every study of exterior and interior nature, it is all eagerness for truth.

Even if it is true that there is nothing new under the sun, *the new spirit does not refrain from discovering new profundities in all this that is not new under the sun.* Good sense is its guide, and this guide leads it into corners, if not new, at least unknown....

There are a thousand natural combinations which have not yet been composed. Men will conceive them and use them to good purpose, composing thus with nature that supreme art which is life. These new combinations, these new works – they are the art of life, which is called progress. In this sense, progress exists. But if it is held to consist in an eternal becoming, a sort of messianism as appalling as the fable of Tantalus, Sisyphus, and the Danaidae, then Solomon was right over all the prophets of Israel.

What is new exists without being progress. Everything is in the effect of surprise. The new spirit depends equally on surprise, on what is most vital and new in it. *Surprise is the greatest source of what is new.* It is by surprise, by the important position that has been given to surprise, that the new spirit distinguishes itself from all the literary and artistic movements which have preceded it.

In this respect, it detaches itself from all of them and belongs only to our time....

Insofar as airplanes did not fill the sky, the fable of Icarus was only a supposed truth. Today, it is no longer a fable. And our inventors have accustomed us to greater prodigies than that which consists in delegating to men the function which women have of bearing children. I should say further that, these fables having been even more than realized, it is up to the poet to imagine new ones which inventors can in turn realize.

The new spirit requires that these prophetic ventures be accepted. It is why you will find traces of prophecy in most works conceived in the new spirit. The divine games of life and imagination give free rein to a totally new poetic activity.

It is that poetry and creation are one and the same; only that man can be called poet who invents, who creates insofar as a man can create. The poet is he who discovers new joys, even if they are hard to bear. One can be a poet in any field: it is enough that one be adventuresome and pursue any new discovery.

The richest domain being the imagination, the least known, whose extent is infinite, it is not astonishing that the name of poet has been particularly reserved for those who look for the new joys which mark out the enormous spaces of the imagination.

The least fact is for a poet the postulate, the point of departure for an unknown immensity where the fires of joy flame up in multiple meanings.

There is no need, in undertaking discovery, to choose with the reassuring support of any rules, even those decreed by taste, a quality classified as sublime. One can begin with an everyday event: a dropped handkerchief can be for the poet the lever with which to move an entire universe. It is well known how much an apple's fall meant to Newton when he saw it, and that scholar can thus be called a poet. That is why the poet today scorns no movement in nature, and his mind pursues discovery just as much in the most vast and evasive syntheses: crowds, nebulae, oceans, nations, as in apparently simple facts: a hand which searches a pocket, a match which lights by scratching, the cries of animals, the odor of gardens after rain, a flame which is born on the hearth. Poets are not simply men devoted to the beautiful. They are also and especially devoted to truth, insofar as the unknown can be penetrated, so much that the unexpected, the surprising, is one of the principal sources of poetry today. And who would dare say that, for those who are worthy of joy, what is new is not beautiful? Others will soon busy themselves about discrediting this sublime novelty, after which it can enter the domain of reason, but only within those limits in which the poets, the sole dispensers of the true and the beautiful, have advanced it.

The poet, by the very nature of his explorations, is isolated in the new world into which he enters the first, and the only consolation which is left to him is that, since men must live in the end by truths in spite of the falsehoods with which they pad them, the poet alone sustains the life whereby humanity finds these truths. This is why modern poets are above all singers of a constantly new truth. And their task is infinite; they have surprised you and will surprise you again. They are already imagining schemes more profound than those which created with Machiavellian astuteness the useful and frightful symbol of money.

Those who imagined the fable of Icarus, so marvellously realized today, will find others. They will carry you, living and awake, into a nocturnal world sealed with dreams. Into universes which tremble ineffably above our heads. Into those nearer and further universes which gravitate to the same point of infinity as what we carry within us. And more marvels than those which have been born since the birth of the most ancient among us, will make the contemporary inventions of which we are so proud seem pale and childish.

Poets will be charged finally with giving by means of lyric teleologies and arch-lyric alchemies a constantly purer meaning to the idea of divinity, which is so alive within us, which is perpetual renewal of ourselves, that eternal creation, that endless rebirth by which we live.

As far as we know, there are scarcely any poets today outside the French language.

All the other languages seem to keep silent so that the universe may hear the voices of the new French poets.

The entire world looks toward this light which alone illuminates the darkness which surrounds us.

Here, however, these voices which are being raised scarcely make themselves heard.

Modern poets, creators, inventors, prophets; they ask that what they say be examined in the light of the greatest good of the group to which they belong. They turn toward Plato and beg him, if he would banish them from the Republic, at least to hear them first.

France, the guardian of the whole secret of civilization, a secret only because of the imperfection of those who strive to divine it, has for this very reason become for the greater part of the world a seminary of poets and artists who daily increase the patrimony of civilization.

And through the truth and the joy they spread, they will make this civilization, if not adaptable to any nation whatever, at least supremely agreeable to all.

The French bring poetry to all people:

To Italy, where the example of French poetry has given inspiration to a superb young nationalist school of boldness and patriotism.

To England, where lyricism is insipid, and practically exhausted.

To Spain and especially in Catalonia, where the whole of an ardent young generation, which has already produced painters who are an honor to two nations, follows with attention the productions of our poets.

To Russia, where the imitation of French lyrics has at times given way to an even greater effort, as will astonish no one.

To Latin America, where the young poets write impassioned commentaries on their French predecessors.

To North America, to which in recognition of Edgar Poe and Walt Whitman, French missionaries are carrying during the war the fertile elements destined to nourish a new production of which we have as yet no idea, but which will doubtless not be inferior to those two great pioneers of poetry. . . .

The new spirit is above all the enemy of estheticism, of formulae, and of cultism. It attacks no school whatever, for it does not wish to be a school, but rather one of the great currents of literature encompassing all schools since symbolism and naturalism. It fights for the re-establishment of the spirit of initiative, for the clear understanding of its time, and for the opening of new vistas on the exterior and interior universes which are not inferior to those which scientists of all categories discover every day and from which they extract endless marvels.

Marvels impose on us the duty not to allow the poetic imagination and subtlety to lag behind that of workers who are improving the machine. Already, scientific language is out of tune with that of the poets. It is an intolerable state of affairs. Mathematicians have the right to say that their dreams, their preoccupations, often outdistance by a hundred cubits the crawling imaginations of poets. It is up to the poets to decide if they will not resolutely embrace the new spirit, outside of which only three doors remain open: that of pastiche, that of satire, and that of lamentation, however sublime it be.

Can poetry be forced to establish itself outside of what surrounds it, to ignore the magnificent exuberance of life which the activities of men are adding to nature and which allow the world to be mechanized in an incredible fashion?

The new spirit is of the very time in which we are living, a time rich in surprises. The poets wish to master prophecy, that spirited mare that has never been tamed.

And finally they want, one day, to mechanize poetry as the world has been mechanized. They want to be the first to provide a totally new lyricism for these new means of expression which are giving impetus to art – the phonograph and the cinema. They are still only at the stage of incunabula. But wait, the prodigies will speak for themselves and the new spirit which fills the universe with life will manifest itself formidably in literature, in the arts, and in everything that is known.

Note

1 From the French poet Clement Marot (1495–1544).

Chapter 10
Ezra Pound

Ezra Pound (1885–1972) moved from the United States to Europe in 1908, the year when he published his first book of poetry. Described by T. S. Eliot as "more responsible for the twentieth-century revolution in poetry than any other individual," he was one of the founders of the Imagist movement in poetry. His dedicated pursuit of new kinds of energy and immediacy in poetry was matched by his commitment to the work of other writers, including Yeats, Joyce, and Eliot. In 1920 he moved from London to Paris, and in 1925 to Rapallo in Italy. By this time Pound was engaged on his major project, a long, intricate, and finally unfinished sequence of poems, The Cantos. *In the Second World War he became a propagandist for Mussolini's fascist regime and was arrested as a war criminal in 1945. Judged unfit to plead he was held in a mental institution in Washington DC until 1958, when he returned to Italy.*

The following excerpts come from "A Retrospect," which includes some of Pound's writing about poetry from earlier in the decade, and was first published in 1918 in Pavannes and Divisions. *It is Pound's attempt to put the record straight about Imagism – the subject of conflicts between Pound and Amy Lowell – and it summarizes the significance of the "new fashion in poetry" he had done so much to instigate. Typically didactic and decisive in style, it sets out guidelines for the education of poets and the objectives of poetry. Both in its style and content, "A Retrospect" was to become an important reference point later in the century for a number of poets, including Zukofsky, Olson, and Creeley.*

A Retrospect

There has been so much scribbling about a new fashion in poetry, that I may perhaps be pardoned this brief recapitulation and retrospect.

From *Modern Poets on Modern Poetry,* ed. James Scully (London: Collins, 1966), pp. 30–5, 37–41, 43.

In the spring or early summer of 1912 'H. D.', Richard Aldington and myself decided that we were agreed upon the three principles following:

1. Direct treatment of the 'thing' whether subjective or objective.
2. To use absolutely no word that does not contribute to the presentation.
3. As regarding rhythm: to compose in the sequence of the musical phrase, not in sequence of a metronome.

Upon many points of taste and of predilection we differed, but agreeing upon these three positions we thought we had as much right to a group name, at least as much right, as a number of French 'schools' proclaimed by Mr. Flint in the August number of Harold Monro's magazine for 1911.

This school has since been 'joined' or 'followed' by numerous people who, whatever their merits, do not show any signs of agreeing with the second specification. Indeed *vers libre* has become as prolix and as verbose as any of the flaccid varieties that preceded it. It has brought faults of its own. The actual language and phrasing is often as bad as that of our elders without even the excuse that the words are shovelled in to fill a metric pattern or to complete the noise of a rhyme-sound. Whether or no the phrases followed by the followers are musical must be left to the reader's decision. At times I can find a marked metre in 'vers libres', as stale and hackneyed as any pseudo-Swinburnian, at times the writers seem to follow no musical structure whatever. But it is, on the whole, good that the field should be ploughed. Perhaps a few good poems have come from the new method, and if so it is justified.

Criticism is not a circumscription or a set of prohibitions. It provides fixed points of departure. It may startle a dull reader into alertness. That little of it which is good is mostly in stray phrases; or if it be an older artist helping a younger it is in great measure but rules of thumb, cautions gained by experience.

I set together a few phrases on practical working about the time the first remarks on imagisme were published. The first use of the word 'Imagiste' was in my note to T. E. Hulme's five poems, printed at the end of my 'Ripostes' in the autumn of 1912. I reprint my cautions from *Poetry* for March, 1913.

A few don'ts

An 'Image' is that which presents an intellectual and emotional complex in an instant of time. I use the term 'complex' rather in the technical sense employed by the newer psychologists, such as Hart, though we might not agree absolutely in our application.

It is the presentation of such a 'complex' instantaneously which gives that sense of sudden liberation; that sense of freedom from time limits and space limits; that sense of sudden growth, which we experience in the presence of the greatest works of art.

It is better to present one Image in a lifetime than to produce voluminous works.

All this, however, some may consider open to debate. The immediate necessity is to tabulate A LIST OF DON'TS for those beginning to write verses. I can not put all of them into Mosaic negative.

To begin with, consider the three propositions (demanding direct treatment, economy of words, and the sequence of the musical phrase), not as dogma – never consider anything as dogma—but as the result of long contemplation, which, even if it is some one else's contemplation, may be worth consideration.

Pay no attention to the criticism of men who have never themselves written a notable work. Consider the discrepancies between the actual writing of the Greek poets and dramatists, and the theories of the Graeco-Roman grammarians, concocted to explain their metres.

Language

Use no superfluous word, no adjective which does not reveal something.

Don't use such an expression as 'dim lands of *peace*'. It dulls the image. It mixes an abstraction with the concrete. It comes from the writer's not realizing that the natural object is always the *adequate* symbol.

Go in fear of abstractions. Do not retell in mediocre verse what has already been done in good prose. Don't think any intelligent person is going to be deceived when you try to shirk all the difficulties of the unspeakably difficult art of good prose by chopping your composition into line lengths.

What the expert is tired of to-day the public will be tired of to-morrow.

Don't imagine that the art of poetry is any simpler than the art of music, or that you can please the expert before you have spent at least as much effort on the art of verse as the average piano teacher spends on the art of music.

Be influenced by as many great artists as you can, but have the decency either to acknowledge the debt outright, or try to conceal it.

Don't allow 'influence' to mean merely that you mop up the particular decorative vocabulary of some one or two poets whom you happen to admire. A Turkish war correspondent was recently caught red-handed babbling in his despatches of 'dovegrey' hills, or else it was 'pearl-pale', and I can not remember.

Use either no ornament or good ornament.

Rhythm and rhyme

Let the candidate fill his mind with the finest cadences he can discover, preferably in a foreign language, so that the meaning of the words may be less likely to divert his attention from the movement; e.g. Saxon charms, Hebridean Folk Songs, the verse of Dante, and the lyrics of Shakespeare – if he can dissociate the vocabulary from the cadence. Let him dissect the lyrics of Goethe coldly into their component sound values, syllables long and short, stressed and unstressed, into vowels and consonants.

It is not necessary that a poem should rely on its music, but if it does rely on its music that music must be such as will delight the expert.

Let the neophyte know assonance and alliteration, rhyme immediate and delayed, simple and polyphonic, as a musician would expect to know harmony and counterpoint and all the minutiae of his craft. No time is too great to give to these matters or to any one of them, even if the artist seldom have need of them.

Don't imagine that a thing will 'go' in verse just because it's too dull to go in prose.

Don't be 'viewy' – leave that to the writers of pretty little philosophic essays. Don't be descriptive; remember that the painter can describe a landscape much better than you can, and that he has to know a deal more about it.

When Shakespeare talks of the 'Dawn in russet mantle clad' he presents something which the painter does not present. There is in this line of his nothing that one can call description; he presents.

Consider the way of the scientists rather than the way of an advertising agent for a new soap.

The scientist does not expect to be acclaimed as a great scientist until he has *discovered* something. He begins by learning what has been discovered already. He goes from that point onward. He does not bank on being a charming fellow personally. He does not expect his friends to applaud the results of his freshman class work. Freshmen in poetry are unfortunately not confined to a definite and recognizable class room. They are 'all over the shop'. Is it any wonder 'the public is indifferent to poetry'?

Don't chop your stuff into separate *iambs*. Don't make each line stop dead at the end, and then begin every next line with a heave. Let the beginning of the next line catch the rise of the rhythm wave, unless you want a definite longish pause.

In short, behave as a musician, a good musician, when dealing with that phase of your art which has exact parallels in music. The same laws govern, and you are bound by no others.

Naturally, your rhythmic structure should not destroy the shape of your words, or their natural sound, or their meaning. It is improbable that, at the start, you will be able to get a rhythm-structure strong enough to affect them very much, though you may fall a victim to all sorts of false stopping due to line ends and cæsurae.

The Musician can rely on pitch and the volume of the orchestra. You can not. The term harmony is misapplied in poetry; it refers to simultaneous sounds of different pitch. There is, however, in the best verse a sort of residue of sound which remains in the ear of the hearer and acts more or less as an organ-base.

A rhyme must have in it some slight element of surprise if it is to give pleasure; it need not be bizarre or curious, but it must be well used if used at all.

Vide further Vildrac and Duhamel's notes on rhyme in '*Technique Poétique*'.

That part of your poetry which strikes upon the imaginative *eye* of the reader will lose nothing by translation into a foreign tongue; that which appeals to the ear can reach only those who take it in the original.

Consider the definiteness of Dante's presentation, as compared with Milton's rhetoric. Read as much of Wordsworth as does not seem too unutterably dull.

If you want the gist of the matter go to Sappho, Catullus, Villon, Heine when he is in the vein, Gautier when he is not too frigid; or, if you have not the tongues, seek out the leisurely Chaucer. Good prose will do you no harm, and there is good discipline to be had by trying to write it.

Translation is likewise good training, if you find that your original matter 'wobbles' when you try to rewrite it. The meaning of the poem to be translated can not 'wobble'.

If you are using a symmetrical form, don't put in what you want to say and then fill up the remaining vacuums with slush.

Don't mess up the perception of one sense by trying to define it in terms of another. This is usually only the result of being too lazy to find the exact word. To this clause there are possibly exceptions.

The first three simple prescriptions will throw out nine-tenths of all the bad poetry now accepted as standard and classic; and will prevent you from many a crime of production. . . .

I do not like writing *about* art, my first, at least I think it was my first essay on the subject, was a protest against it. . . .

Credo

Rhythm. – I believe in an 'absolute rhythm', a rhythm, that is, in poetry which corresponds exactly to the emotion or shade of emotion to be expressed. A man's rhythm must be interpretative, it will be, therefore, in the end his own, uncounterfeiting, uncounterfeitable.

Symbols. – I believe that the proper and perfect symbol is the natural object, that if a man use 'symbols' he must so use them that their symbolic function does not obtrude; so that *a* sense, and the poetic quality of the passage, is not lost to those who do not understand the symbol as such, to whom, for instance, a hawk is a hawk.

Technique. – I believe in technique as the test of a man's sincerity; in law when it is ascertainable; in the trampling down of every convention that impedes or obscures the determination of the law, or the precise rendering of the impulse.

Form. – I think there is a 'fluid' as well as a 'solid' content, that some poems may have form as a tree has form, some as water poured into a vase. That most symmetrical forms have certain uses. That a vast number of subjects cannot be precisely, and therefore not properly rendered in symmetrical forms,

'Thinking that alone worthy wherein the whole art is employed'. I think the artist should master all known forms and systems of metric, and I have with some persistence set about doing this, searching particularly into those periods wherein the systems came to birth or attained their maturity. It has been complained, with some justice, that I dump my note-books on the public. I think that only after a long struggle will poetry attain such a degree of development, or, if you will, modernity, that it will vitally concern people who are accustomed, in prose, to Henry James and Anatole France, in music to Debussy. I am constantly contending that it took two centuries of Provence and one of Tuscany to develop the media of Dante's masterwork, that it took the latinists of the Renaissance, and the Pleiade, and his own age of painted speech to prepare Shakespeare his tools. It is tremendously important that great poetry be written, it makes no jot of difference who writes it. The experimental demonstrations of one man may save the time of many – hence my furore over Arnaut Daniel – if a man's experiments try out one new rime, or dispense conclusively with one iota of currently accepted nonsense, he is merely playing fair with his colleagues when he chalks up his result.

No man ever writes very much poetry that 'matters.' In bulk, that is, no one produces much that is final, and when a man is not doing this highest thing, this saying the thing once for all and perfectly; when he is not matching Ποιχιλόθρον', ἀθάνατ' Ἀφρόδιτα,[1] or 'Hist – said Kate the Queen', he had much better be making the sorts of experiments which may be of use to him in his later work, or to his successors.

'The lyf so short, the craft so long to lerne.' It is a foolish thing for a man to begin his work on a too narrow foundation, it is a disgraceful thing for a man's work not to show steady growth and increasing fineness from first to last.

As for 'adaptations'; one finds that all the old masters of painting recommend to their pupils, that they begin by copying masterwork, and proceed to their own composition.

As for 'Every man his own poet', the more every man knows about poetry the better. I believe in every one writing poetry who wants to; most do. I believe in every man knowing enough of music to play 'God bless our home' on the harmonium, but I do not believe in every man giving concerts and printing his sin.

The mastery of any art is the work of a lifetime. I should not discriminate between the 'amateur' and the 'professional'. Or rather I should discriminate quite often in favour of the amateur but I should discriminate between the amateur and the expert. It is certain that the present chaos will endure until the Art of poetry has been preached down the amateur gullet, until there is such a general understanding of the fact that poetry is an art and not a pastime; such a knowledge of technique; of technique of surface and technique of content, that the amateurs will cease to try to drown out the masters.

If a certain thing was said once for all in Atlantis or Arcadia, in 450 Before Christ or in 1290 after, it is not for us moderns to go saying it over, or to go obscuring the memory of the dead by saying the same thing with less skill and less conviction.

My pawing over the ancients and semi-ancients has been one struggle to find out what has been done, once for all, better than it can ever be done again, and to find out what remains for us to do, and plenty does remain, for if we still feel the same emotions as those which launched the thousand ships, it is quite certain that we come on these feelings differently, through different nuances, by different intellectual gradations. Each age has its own abounding gifts yet only some ages transmute them into matters of duration. No good poetry is ever written in a manner twenty years old, for to write in such a manner shows conclusively that the writer thinks from books, convention and *cliché*, and not from life, yet a man feeling the divorce of life and his art may naturally try to resurrect a forgotten mode if he finds in that mode some leaven, or if he think he sees in it some element lacking in contemporary art which might unite that art again to its sustenance, life.

In the art of Daniel and Cavalcanti, I have seen that precision which I miss in the Victorians, that explicit rendering, be it of external nature, or of emotion. Their testimony is of the eyewitness, their symptoms are first hand.

As for the nineteenth century, with all respect to its achievements, I think we shall look back upon it as a rather blurry, messy sort of a period, a rather sentimentalistic, mannerish sort of a period. I say this without any self-righteousness, with no self-satisfaction.

As for there being a 'movement' or my being of it, the conception of poetry as a 'pure art' in the sense in which I use the term, revived with Swinburne. From the puritanical revolt to Swinburne, poetry has been merely the vehicle – yes, definitely, Arthur Symon's scruples and feelings about the word not withholding – the ox-cart and post-chaise for transmitting thoughts poetic or otherwise. And perhaps the 'great Victorians', though it is doubtful, and assuredly the 'nineties' continued the development of the art, confining their improvements, however, chiefly to sound and to refinements of manner.

Mr. Yeats has once and for all stripped English poetry of its perdamnable rhetoric. He has boiled away all that is not poetic – and a good deal that is. He has become a classic in his own lifetime and *nel mezzo del cammin.* He has made our poetic idiom a thing pliable, a speech without inversions.

Robert Bridges, Maurice Hewlett and Frederic Manning are in their different ways seriously concerned with overhauling the metric, in testing the language and its adaptability to certain modes. Ford Hueffer is making some sort of experiments in modernity. The Provost of Oriel continues his translation of the *Divina Commedia.*

As to Twentieth century poetry, and the poetry which I expect to see written during the next decade or so, it will, I think, move against poppy-cock, it will be harder and saner, it will be what Mr. Hewlett calls 'nearer the bone'. It will be as much like granite as it can be, its force will lie in its truth, its interpretative power (of course, poetic force does always rest there); I mean it will not try to seem forcible by rhetorical din, and luxurious riot. We will have fewer painted adjectives impeding the shock and stroke of it. At least for myself, I want it so, austere, direct, free from emotional slither.

What is there now, in 1917, to be added?

Re vers libre

I think the desire for vers libre is due to the sense of quantity reasserting itself after years of starvation. But I doubt if we can take over, for English, the rules of quantity laid down for Greek and Latin, mostly by Latin grammarians.

I think one should write vers libre only when one 'must', that is to say, only when the 'thing' builds up a rhythm more beautiful than that of set metres, or more real, more a part of the emotion of the 'thing', more germane, intimate, interpretative than the measure of regular accentual verse; a rhythm which discontents one with set iambic or set anapæstic.

Eliot has said the thing very well when be said, 'No *vers* is *libre* for the man who wants to do a good job.'

As a matter of detail, there is vers libre with accent heavily marked as a drum-beat (as par example my 'Dance Figure'), and on the other hand I think I have gone as far as can profitably be gone in the other direction (and perhaps too far). I mean I do not think one can use to any advantage rhythms much more tenuous and imperceptible than some I have used. I think progress lies rather in an attempt to approximate classical quantitative metres (NOT to copy them) than in a carelessness regarding such things. . . .

Only emotion endures

'Only emotion endures.' Surely it is better for me to name over the few beautiful poems that still ring in my head than for me to search my flat for back numbers of periodicals and rearrange all that I have said about friendly and hostile writers.

The first twelve lines of Padraic Colum's 'Drover', his 'O Woman shapely as a swan, on your account I shall not die'; Joyce's 'I hear an army'; the lines of Yeats that ring in my head and in the heads of all young men of my time who care for poetry: Braseal and the Fisherman, 'The fire that stirs about her when she stirs'; the later lines of 'The Scholars', the faces of the Magi; William Carlos Williams's 'Postlude', Aldington's version of 'Atthis', and 'H. D.'s' waves like pine tops, and her verse in 'Des Imagistes' the first anthology; Hueffer's 'How red your lips are' in his translation from Von der Vogelweide, his 'Three Ten', the general effect of his 'On Heaven'; his sense of the prose values or prose qualities in poetry; his ability to write poems that half-chant and are spoiled by a musician's additions; beyond these a poem by Alice Corbin, 'One City Only', and another ending 'But sliding water over a stone'. These things have worn smooth in my head and I am not through with them, nor with Aldington's 'In Via Sestina' nor his other poems in 'Des Imagistes', though people have told me their flaws. It may be that their content is too much embedded in me for me to look back at the words.

I am almost a different person when I come to take up the argument for Eliot's poems.

Note

1 'Splendid-throned, deathless Aphrodite.'

Chapter 11
Tristan Tzara

Tristan Tzara (1896–1963) was a poet and theorist who helped initiate the Dada movement, one of the most influential of the early twentieth-century avant-gardes. Born in Romania as Sami Rosenstusck, by 1916 Tzara had moved to Zurich, the original city of Dada, before moving to Paris in 1920 where he began his collaboration with the founders of Surrealism. Dada was a polemical attack on European culture's basic assumptions about art and morality. Its experiments with random composition and with the idea of the art event as a happening formed a basis for later avant-garde movements.

Tzara's "Note on Poetry" was first published in Dada 4 et 5 *in Zurich in 1919. He asserts a separation of poetry from literature and the printed page. Instead poetry is imagined as a form of free energy with the power to transform human perception. The assertive and enigmatic style of Tzara's "Note" exemplifies Dada's rejection of the accepted procedures of rational argument and analysis. Both what it rejects and what it affirms are presented in a mix of polemical utterance and cryptic images.*

Note on Poetry

The poet of the last station has given up vain weeping; lamentation slows down progress. The humidity of past ages. People who feed on tears are contented and obtuse, they thread their tears behind the necklaces of their souls so as to cheat the snakes. The poet can go in for Swedish gymnastics. But for abundance and explosion he knows how to kindle hope TODAY. Whether tranquil, ardent, furious, intimate, pathetic, slow or impetuous, his burning desire is for enthusiasm, that fecund form of intensity.

To know how to recognise and pick up the signs of the power we are awaiting, which are everywhere; in the fundamental language of cryptograms, engraved on crystals, on

From *Seven Dada Manifestos and Lampisteries*, trans. Barbara Wright (London: Calder, 1977), pp. 75–8.

shells, on rails, in clouds, or in glass; inside snow, or light, or coal; on the hand, in the beams grouped round the magnetic poles, on wings.

Persistence quickens joy and shoots it like an arrow up to the celestial domes, to distil the quintessence from the waves of phlegmatic nourishment, creating new life. Flowing in all colours and bleeding amongst the leaves of all the trees. Vigour and thirst, emotion faced with a form that can neither be seen nor explained – that is poetry.

Let's not look for analogies in the various forms in which art is materialised; each must have its own liberty and its own frontiers. There are equivalents in art, each branch of the star develops independently, expands, and absorbs the world of its choice. But the parallelism that records the march of a new life will brand the era, without any theory.

To give each element its identity, its autonomy, the necessary condition for the creation of new constellations, since each has its own place in the group. The drive of the Word: upright, an image, a unique event, passionate, of dense colour, of intensity, in communion with life.

Art is a series of perpetual differences. For there is no measurable distance between "how are you?", the level on which people make their world grow, and human actions when seen from this angle of underwater purity. The strength to transmute this succession of ever-changing notions into *the instant* – that is the work of art. An Everlasting Sphere, a shape begotten by necessity, without a begetter.

The mind is alive with a new range of possibilities: to centralise them, to collect them under a lens that is neither material nor delimited – what is popularly called: the soul. The ways of expressing them, of transmuting them: the means. Bright as a flash of gold – the increasing beating of expanding wings.

Without pretensions to a romantic absolute, I present a few mundane negations.

A poem is no longer a formal act: subject, rhythm, rhyme, sonority. When projected on to everyday life, these can become means, whose use is neither regulated nor recorded, to which I attach the same weight as I do to the crocodile, to burning metals, or to grass. Eye, water, equilibrium, sun, kilometre, and everything that I can imagine as belonging together and which represents a potential human asset, is *sensitivity.* The elements love to be closely associated, truly hugging each other, like the cerebral hemispheres and the cabins of transatlantic liners.

Rhythm is the gait of the intonations we hear, but there is a rhythm that we neither see nor hear: the radius of an internal grouping that leads towards a constellation of order. Up to now, rhythm has been the beating of a dried-up heart, a little tinkle in putrid, padded wood. I don't want to put fences round what people call principles, when what is at stake is freedom. But the poet will have to be demanding towards his own work in order to discover its real necessity: order, essential and pure, will flower from this asceticism – (Goodness without a sentimental echo, its material side.)

To be demanding and cruel, pure and honest towards the work one is preparing and which one will be situating amongst men, new organisms, creations that live in the very bones of light and in the imaginative forms that action will take – (REALITY.)

The rest, called *literature*, is a dossier of human imbecility for the guidance of future professors.

The poem pushes up or hollows out the crater, remains silent, kills or shouts in an accelerating crescendo of speed. It will no longer depend on its visual image, on sense perception or on intelligence, but on its impact, or capability of transmuting the traces of emotions.

Comparison is a literary means which no longer satisfies us. There are different ways of formulating an image or of integrating it, but the elements will be taken from different and remote spheres.

Logic no longer guides us, and though it is convenient to have dealings with, it has become impotent, a deceptive glimmer, sowing the currency of sterile relativism, and we consider it from henceforth a light that has failed forever. Other creative powers, flamboyant, indefinable and gigantic, are shouting their liberty on the mountains of crystal and of prayer.

Liberty, liberty: not being a vegetarian, I'm not giving any recipes.

Obscurity must be creative if it is so pure a white light that it blinds our fellow-men. Where their light stops, ours starts. Their light is for us, in the fog, the microscopic and infinitely compact dance of the elements of darkness in imprecise fermentation. Is not matter in its pure state dense and unerring?

Under the bark of felled trees, I seek the image of things to come, of vigour, and in underground tunnels the obscurity of iron and coal may already be heavy with life.

Chapter 12
Velimir Khlebnikov

Velimir Khlebnikov (1885–1922) was a Russian poet and theorist who became a leading figure in the Russian Futurist movement of poets and painters. Khlebnikov was fascinated by words as entities with a structure that could be broken down and recomposed. Poetic experiment discovered the root meanings of words and developed new words and sound patterns out of them. It was on this basis that Khlebnikov developed the principle of "beyonsense" language. He believed that his poetic experiments would revive the magical powers of language and, in so doing, reveal truths about the structure of the world. Largely unpublished in his lifetime, Khlebnikov is now regarded as one of the pioneers of Russian modernism.

"On Poetry" and "On Contemporary Poetry" were both written in 1919 and the latter text was published in 1920. In "On Poetry" Khlebnikov draws attention to a poetic life in words that exceed the usual requirements of sense. He also distances himself from the demands of a socialist realism that would require writers to reflect the experience of their class. In the brief excerpt from "On Contemporary Poetry" included here, Khlebnikov identifies a double life in words, one of sound, the other of sense. In his view, the history of literary language oscillated between these two polarities.

On Poetry

People say a poem must be understandable. Like a sign on the street, which carries the clear and simple words "For Sale." But a street sign is not exactly a poem. Though it is understandable. On the other hand, what about spells and incantations, what we call magic words, the sacred language of paganism, words like "shagadam, magadam, vigadam, pitz, patz, patzu" – they are rows of mere syllables that the intellect can

From *Collected Works of Velimir Khlebnikov*, vol. 1, *Letters and Theoretical Writings*, ed. Charlotte Douglas, trans. Paul Schmidt (Cambridge, Mass.: Harvard University Press, 1987), pp. 370–3.

make no sense of, and they form a kind of beyonsense language in folk speech. Nevertheless an enormous power over mankind is attributed to these incomprehensible words and magic spells, and direct influence upon the fate of man. They contain powerful magic. They claim the power of controlling good and evil and swaying the hearts of lovers. The prayers of many nations are written in a language incomprehensible to those who pray. Does a Hindu understand the Vedas? Russians do not understand Old Church Slavonic. Neither do Poles and Czechs understand Latin. But a prayer written in Latin works just as powerfully as the sign on the street. In the same way, the language of magic spells and incantations does not wish to be judged in terms of everyday common sense.

Its strange wisdom may be broken down into the truths contained in separate sounds: *sh, m, v,* etc. We do not yet understand these sounds. We confess that honestly. But there is no doubt that these sound sequences constitute a series of universal truths passing before the predawn of our soul. If we think of the soul as split between the government of intellect and a stormy population of feelings, then incantations and beyonsense language are appeals over the head of the government straight to the population of feelings, a direct cry to the predawn of the soul or a supreme example of the rule of the masses in the life of language and intellect, a lawful device reserved for rare occasions. . . .

. . . [T]he magic in a word remains magic even if it is not understood, and loses none of its power. Poems may be understandable or they may not, but they must be good, they must be real.

. . . [I]t is clear that we cannot demand of all language: "be easy to understand, like the sign on the street." The speech of higher reason, even when it is not understandable, falls like seed into the fertile soil of the spirit and only much later, in mysterious ways, does it bring forth its shoots. Does the earth understand the writing of the seeds a farmer scatters on its surface? No. But the grain still ripens in autumn, in response to those seeds. In any case, I certainly do not maintain that every incomprehensible piece of writing is beautiful. I mean only that we must not reject a piece of writing simply because it is incomprehensible to a particular group of readers.

The claim has been made that poems about labor can be created only by people who work in factories. Is this true? Isn't the nature of a poem to be found in its withdrawal from itself, from its point of contact with everyday reality? Is a poem not a flight from the *I*? A poem is related to flight – in the shortest time possible its language must cover the greatest distance in images and thoughts!

Without flight from the self there can be no room for progression. Inspiration always belies the poet's background. Medieval knights wrote about rustic shepherds. Lord Byron about pirates, Buddha was a king's son who wrote in praise of poverty. Or the other way around: Shakespeare was convicted of theft but wrote in the language of kings, as did Goethe, the son of a modest burgher, and their writing is devoted to portrayals of court life. The tundras of the Pechersky region have never known warfare, yet there they preserve epic songs about Vladimir and his hero knights that have long since been forgotten on the Dnieper. If we consider artistic creativity as the greatest possible deviation of the string of thought from the axis of the creator's life, as a flight from the self, then we have good reason for believing that even poems about an assembly line will be written not by someone who works on an assembly line, but by someone from beyond the factory walls. And by the same token, once he withdraws from the assembly line, stretching the string of his soul to the fullest length, the assembly-line poet will either pass into the world of scientific imagery, of strange scientific visions, into the future of Planet Earth, like Gastev, or into the world of basic human values, like Alexandrovsky, into the subtle life of the heart.

On Contemporary Poetry

The word leads a double life. Sometimes it simply grows like a plant whose fruit is a geode of sonorous stones clustering around it; in this case the sound element lives a self-sufficient life, while the particle of sense named by the word stands in shadow. At other times the word is subservient to sense, and then sound ceases to be "all-powerful" and autocratic; sound becomes merely a "name" and humbly carries out the commands of sense; in this case the latter flowers in another round of this eternal game, producing a geode of stones of like variety. Sometimes sense says to sound "I hear and obey"; at other times pure sound says the same thing to pure sense.

This struggle between two worlds, between two powers, goes on eternally in every word and gives a double life to language: two possible orbits for two spinning stars. In one form of creativity, sense turns in a circular path about sound; in the other sound turns about sense. Sometimes sound is the Sun and meaning is the Earth; sometimes meaning is the Sun and sound is the Earth.

Either a land radiant with meaning or a land radiant with sound. And the tree of words clothes itself first in one resonance, then in the other; first it is festive, like a cherry tree decked with verbal blossoms, then it bears fruit, the succulent fruit of sense. It isn't hard to perceive that the time of verbal sound play is the marriage time of language, the courting season of words, while the time of words full of meaning, when the reader's bees hum busily, is the time of autumnal abundance, the time of families and offspring. . . .

Chapter 13
T. S. Eliot

Thomas Stearns Eliot (1888–1965) was the author of one of the defining works of poetic modernism, The Waste Land, *first published in 1922. Born in St. Louis, Missouri, and educated at Harvard where he studied philosophy, Eliot moved to Europe in 1914 when he met his fellow émigré poet, Ezra Pound. Pound encouraged Eliot's experimental poetry, including the work published in* Prufrock and Other Observations *in 1917 and played a decisive editorial role in the shaping of* The Waste Land. *From the 1920s onwards, Eliot's work as a poet, dramatist, and critic was increasingly shaped by his conservative vision of a Christian culture. His ideas about literature, culture, and religion had a considerable and, some would argue, oppressive influence on a generation of Anglo-American poets and critics. He was awarded the Nobel Prize for Literature in 1948.*

"Tradition and the Individual Talent" was first published as a two-part essay in The Egoist *in September and November 1919. "Reflections on Contemporary Poetry" was published in July 1919 in the same journal. In 1920 "Tradition and the Individual Talent" was one of the essays Eliot included in his collection,* The Sacred Wood, *but he did not reprint "Reflections on Contemporary Poetry" in his lifetime.*

"Tradition and the Individual Talent" sets out Eliot's requirements for the education of a modern poet by way of its two linked conceptions of tradition and poetic impersonality. Eliot argues that significant poetry is authored not just by an individual but by a culture. His account of tradition is concerned with defining the kind of cultural process that is a condition of this authorship. The First World War and its slaughter are not directly mentioned in Eliot's essay, but his version of tradition comes close to an act of mourning. It is a way of communing with the dead, as well as a way of overcoming the historical remoteness of dead writers by making their work live in the present. Works in the tradition have the funereal character of "monuments" and the living poet must find a place amongst them and, hence, move into a kind of deathliness.

"Reflections on Contemporary Poetry" shows Eliot using a review of three of his contemporaries to make a theoretical statement about the centrality of poetry of the past for contemporary poets. The review anticipates ideas about impersonality contained in "Tradition and the Individual Talent" but shows too how narrow the dividing line

between the impersonal and the personal could be. Clearly distinguishing between a conventional "admiration for the great" and his own idea of tradition, Eliot proposes that the relation between living and dead poets is a matter of passionate discoveries and attachments, something very different from an enforced veneration for the work of the past.

Tradition and the Individual Talent

I

In English writing we seldom speak of tradition, though we occasionally apply its name in deploring its absence. We cannot refer to "the tradition" or to "a tradition"; at most, we employ the adjective in saying that the poetry of So-and-so is "traditional" or even "too traditional." Seldom, perhaps, does the word appear except in a phrase of censure. If otherwise, it is vaguely approbative, with the implication, as to the work approved, of some pleasing archaeological reconstruction. You can hardly make the word agreeable to English ears without this comfortable reference to the reassuring science of archaeology.

Certainly the word is not likely to appear in our appreciations of living or dead writers. Every nation, every race, has not only its own creative, but its own critical turn of mind; and is even more oblivious of the shortcomings and limitations of its critical habits than of those of its creative genius. We know, or think we know, from the enormous mass of critical writing that has appeared in the French language the critical method or habit of the French; we only conclude (we are such unconscious people) that the French are "more critical" than we, and we sometimes even plume ourselves a little with the fact, as if the French were the less spontaneous. Perhaps they are; but we might remind ourselves that criticism is as inevitable as breathing, and that we should be none the worse for articulating what passes in our minds when we read a book and feel an emotion about it, for criticizing our own minds in their work of criticism. One of the facts that might come to light in this process is our tendency to insist, when we praise a poet, upon those aspects of his work in which he least resembles anyone else. In these aspects or parts of his work we pretend to find what is individual, what is the peculiar essence of the man. We dwell with satisfaction upon the poet's difference from his predecessors, especially his immediate predecessors; we endeavour to find something that can be isolated in order to be enjoyed. Whereas if we approach a poet without his prejudice we shall often find that not only the best, but the most individual parts of his work may be those in which the dead poets, his ancestors, assert their immortality most vigorously. And I do not mean the impressionable period of adolescence, but the period of full maturity.

Yet if the only form of tradition, of handing down, consisted in following the ways of the immediate generation before us in a blind or timid adherence to its successes, "tradition" should positively be discouraged. We have seen many such simple currents

From *Selected Essays*, 3rd edn. (London: Faber and Faber, 1951), pp. 13–18, 19–21.

soon lost in the sand; and novelty is better than repetition. Tradition is a matter of much wider significance. It cannot be inherited, and if you want it you must obtain it by great labour. It involves, in the first place, the historical sense, which we may call nearly indispensable to anyone who would continue to be a poet beyond his twenty-fifth year; and the historical sense involves a perception, not only of the pastness of the past, but of its presence; the historical sense compels a man to write not merely with his own generation in his bones, but with a feeling that the whole of the literature of Europe from Homer and within it the whole of the literature of his own country has a simultaneous existence and composes a simultaneous order. This historical sense, which is a sense of the timeless as well as of the temporal and of the timeless and of the temporal together, is what makes a writer traditional. And it is at the same time what makes a writer most acutely conscious of his place in time, of his contemporaneity.

No poet, no artist of any art, has his complete meaning alone. His significance, his appreciation is the appreciation of his relation to the dead poets and artists. You cannot value him alone; you must set him, for contrast and comparison, among the dead. I mean this as a principle of aesthetic, not merely historical, criticism. The necessity that he shall conform, that he shall cohere, is not one-sided; what happens when a new work of art is created is something that happens simultaneously to all the works of art which preceded it. The existing monuments form an ideal order among themselves, which is modified by the introduction of the new (the really new) work of art among them. The existing order is complete before the new work arrives, for order to persist after the supervention of novelty, the *whole* existing order must be, if ever so slightly, altered; and so the relations, proportions, values of each work of art toward the whole are readjusted; and this is conformity between the old and the new. Whoever has approved this idea of order, of the form of European, of English literature, will not find it preposterous that the past should be altered by the present as much as the present is directed by the past. And the poet who is aware of this will be aware of great difficulties and responsibilities.

In a peculiar sense he will be aware also that he must inevitably be judged by the standards of the past. I say judged, not amputated, by them; not judged to be as good as, or worse or better than, the dead; and certainly not judged by the canons of dead critics. It is a judgment, a comparison, in which two things are measured by each other. To conform merely would be for the new work not really to conform at all; it would not be new, and would therefore not be a work of art. And we do not quite say that the new is more valuable because it fits in; but its fitting in is a test of its value – a test, it is true, which can only be slowly and cautiously applied, for we are none of us infallible judges of conformity. We say: it appears to conform, and is perhaps individual, or it appears individual, and may conform; but we are hardly likely to find that it is one and not the other.

To proceed to a more intelligible exposition of the relation of the poet to the past: he can neither take the past as a lump, an indiscriminate bolus, nor can he form himself wholly on one or two private admirations, nor can he form himself wholly upon one preferred period. The first course is inadmissible, the second is an important experience of youth, and the third is a pleasant and highly desirable supplement. The poet must be very conscious of the main current, which does not at all flow invariably through the most distinguished reputations. He must be quite aware of the obvious fact that art never improves, but that the material of art is never quite the same. He must be aware that the mind of Europe – the mind of his own country – a mind which he learns in time to be much more important than his own private mind – is a mind which changes, and that this change is a development which abandons nothing *en route*, which does not superannuate either Shakespeare, or Homer, or the rock drawing of the Magdalenian draughtsmen. That this development, refinement perhaps, complication certainly, is not, from the point of view of the artist, any improvement. Perhaps not even an improvement from the point of view of the psychologist or not to the extent which we imagine; perhaps only in the end based upon a complication in economics and machinery. But the difference between the present and the past is that the conscious present is an awareness of the past in a way and to an extent which the past's awareness of itself cannot show.

Someone said: "The dead writers are remote from us because we *know* so much more than they did." Precisely, and they are that which we know.

I am alive to a usual objection to what is clearly part of my programme for the *métier* of poetry. The objection is that the doctrine requires a ridiculous amount of erudition (pedantry), a claim which can be rejected by appeal to the lives of poets in any pantheon. It will even be affirmed that much learning deadens or perverts poetic sensibility. While, however, we persist in believing that a poet ought to know as much as will not encroach upon his necessary receptivity and necessary laziness, it is not desirable to confine knowledge to whatever can be put into a useful shape for examinations, drawing-rooms, or the still more pretentious modes of publicity. Some can absorb knowledge, the more tardy must sweat for it. Shakespeare acquired more essential history from Plutarch than most men could from the whole British Museum. What is to be insisted upon is that the poet must develop or procure the consciousness of the past and that he should continue to develop this consciousness throughout his career.

What happens is a continual surrender of himself as he is at the moment to something which is more valuable. The progress of an artist is a continual self-sacrifice, a continual extinction of personality.

There remains to define this process of depersonalization and its relation to the sense of tradition. It is in this depersonalization that art may be said to approach the condition of science. I therefore invite you to consider, as a suggestive analogy, the action which takes place when a bit of finely filiated platinum is introduced into a chamber containing oxygen and sulphur dioxide.

II

. . . I have tried to point out the importance of the relation of the poem to other poems by other authors, and suggested the conception of poetry as a living whole of all the poetry that has ever been written. The other aspect of this Impersonal theory of poetry is the relation of the poem to its author. And I hinted, by an analogy, that the mind of the mature poet differs from that of the immature one not precisely in any valuation of "personality," not being necessarily more interesting, or having "more to say," but rather by being a more finely perfected medium in which special, or very varied, feelings are at liberty to enter into new combinations.

The analogy was that of the catalyst. When the two gases previously mentioned are mixed in the presence of a filament of platinum, they form sulphurous acid. This combination takes place only if the platinum is present; nevertheless the newly formed acid contains no trace of platinum, and the platinum itself is apparently unaffected: has remained inert, neutral, and unchanged. The mind of the poet is the shred of platinum. It may partly or exclusively operate upon the experience of the man himself; but, the more perfect the artist, the more completely separate in him will be the man who suffers and the mind which creates; the more perfectly will the mind digest and transmute the passions which are its material.

The experience, you will notice, the elements which enter the presence of the transforming catalyst, are of two kinds: emotions and feelings. The effect of a work of art upon the person who enjoys it is an experience different in kind from any experience not of art. It may be formed out of one emotion, or may be a combination of several; and various feelings, inhering for the writer in particular words or phrases or images, may be added to compose the final result. Or great poetry may be made without the direct use of any emotion whatever: composed out of feelings solely.... The poet's mind is in fact a receptacle for seizing and storing up numberless feelings, phrases, images, which remain there until the particles which can unite to form a new compound are present together.

If you compare several representative passages of the greatest poetry you see how great is the variety of types of combination, and also how completely any semi-ethical criterion of "sublimity" misses the mark. For it is not the "greatness," the intensity, of the emotions, the components, but the intensity of the artistic process, the pressure, so to speak, under which the fusion takes place, that counts....

The point of view which I am struggling to attack is perhaps related to the metaphysical theory of the substantial unity of the soul: for my meaning is, that the poet has, not a "personality" to express, but a particular medium, which is only a medium and not a personality, in which impressions and experiences combine in peculiar and unexpected ways. Impressions and experiences which are important for the man may take no place in the poetry, and those which become important in the poetry may play quite a negligible part in the man, the personality.

I will quote a passage, which is unfamiliar enough to be regarded with fresh attention in the light – or darkness – of these observations:

> And now methinks I could e'en chide myself
> For doating on her beauty, though her death
> Shall be revenged after no common action.
> Does the silkworm expend her yellow labours
> For thee? For thee does she undo herself?
> Are lordships sold to maintain ladyships
> For the poor benefit of a bewildering minute?
> Why does yon fellow falsify highways,

And put his life between the judge's lips,
To refine such a thing – keeps horse and men
To beat their valours for her?...

In this passage (as is evident if it is taken in its context) there is a combination of positive and negative emotions: an intensely strong attraction toward beauty and an equally intense fascination by the ugliness which is contrasted with it and which destroys it. This balance of contrasted emotion is in the dramatic situation to which the speech is pertinent, but that situation alone is inadequate to it. This is, so to speak, the structural emotion, provided by the drama. But the whole effect, the dominant tone, is due to the fact that a number of floating feelings, having an affinity to this emotion by no means superficially evident, have combined with it to give us a new art emotion.

It is not in his personal emotions, the emotions provoked by particular events in his life, that the poet is in any way remarkable or interesting. His particular emotions may be simple, or crude, or flat. The emotion in his poetry will be a very complex thing, but not with the complexity of the emotions of people who have very complex or unusual emotions in life. One error, in fact, of eccentricity in poetry is to seek for new human emotions to express; and in this search for novelty in the wrong place it discovers the perverse. The business of the poet is not to find new emotions, but to use the ordinary ones and, in working them up into poetry, to express feelings which are not in actual emotions at all. And emotions which he has never experienced will serve his turn as well as those familiar to him. Consequently, we must believe that "emotion recollected in tranquillity" is an inexact formula. For it is neither emotion, nor recollection, nor, without distortion of meaning, tranquillity. It is a concentration, and a new thing resulting from the concentration, of a very great number of experiences which to the practical and active person would not seem to be experiences at all; it is a concentration which does not happen consciously or of deliberation. These experiences are not "recollected," and they finally unite in an atmosphere which is "tranquil" only in that it is a passive attending upon the event. Of course this is not quite the whole story. There is a great deal, in the writing of poetry, which must be conscious and deliberate. In fact, the bad poet is usually unconscious where he ought to be conscious, and conscious where he ought to be unconscious. Both errors tend to make him "personal." Poetry is not a turning loose of emotion, but an escape from emotion; it is not the expression of personality, but an escape from personality. But, of course, only those who have personality and emotions know what it means to want to escape from these things....

Reflections on Contemporary Poetry

It is not true that the development of a writer is a function of his development as a man, but it is possible to say that there is a close analogy between the sort of experience

From *The Egoist*, July 1919, pp. 39–40.

which develops a man and the sort of experience which develops a writer. Experience in living may leave the literary embryo still dormant, and the progress of literary development may to a considerable extent take place in a soul left immature in living. But similar types of experience form the nourishment of both. There is a kind of stimulus for a writer which is more important than the stimulus of admiring another writer. Admiration leads most often to imitation, we can seldom remain long unconscious of imitating another, and the awareness of our debt naturally leads us to a hatred of the object imitated. If we stand toward a writer in this other relation of which I speak we do not imitate him, and though we are quite as likely to be accused of it, we are quite unperturbed by the charge. This relation is a feeling of profound kinship, or rather of a peculiar personal intimacy, with another, probably a dead author. It may overcome us suddenly, on first or after long acquaintance; it is certainly a crisis; and when a young writer is seized with his first passion of this sort he may be changed, metamorphosed almost, within a few weeks even, from a bundle of second-hand sentiments into a person. The imperative intimacy arouses for the first time a real and unshakeable confidence. That you possess this secret knowledge, this intimacy, with the dead man, that after a few or many years or centuries you should have appeared with this indubitable claim to distinction; who can penetrate at once the thick and dusty circumlocutions about his reputation, can call yourself alone his friend – it is something more than *encouragement* to you. It is a cause of development, like personal relations in life. Like personal intimacies in life, it may and probably will pass, but it will be ineffaceable.

The usefulness of such a passion is various. For one thing it secures us against forced admiration, from attending to writers simply because they are great. We are never at ease with people who, to us, are merely great. We are not ourselves great enough for that: probably not one man in each generation is great enough to be intimate with Shakespeare. Admiration for the great is only a sort of discipline to keep us in order, a necessary snobbism to make us mind our places. We may not be great lovers; but if we had a genuine affair with a real poet of any degree we have acquired a monitor to avert us when we are not in love. Indirectly there are other acquisitions: our friendship gives us an introduction to the society in which our friend moved; we learn its origins and its endings; we are broadened. We do not imitate, we are changed; and our work is the work of the changed man; we have not borrowed, we have been quickened, and we become bearers of a tradition.

I feel that the traces of this sort of experience are conspicuously lacking from contemporary poetry, and that contemporary poetry is deficient in tradition. We can raise no objection to "experiments" if the experimenters are qualified; but we can object that almost none of the experimenters hold fast to anything permanent under the varied phenomena of experiment. Shakespeare was one of the slowest, if one of the most persistent, of experimenters; even Rimbaud shows process. And one never has the tremendous satisfaction of meeting a writer who is more original, more independent, than he himself knows. No dead voices speak through the living voice; no reincarnation, no re-creation. Not even the *saturation* which sometimes combusts spontaneously into originality.

fly where men feel
The cunning axletree: and those that suffer
Beneath the chariot of the snowy Bear

is beautiful; and the beauty only appears more substantial if we conjecture that Chapman may have absorbed the recurring phrase in Seneca in

signum celsi glaciale poli
septem stellis Arcados ursæ
lucem verso termone vocat....
sub cardine
glacialis ursæ...

a union, at a point at least, of the Tudor and the Greek through the Senecan phrase.

In the books of verse I have undertaken to examine, this fertilisation is not very apparent. Mr Read's book is on a very high level of war poetry. It is the best war poetry that I can remember having seen. It is better than the rest because it is more honest; because it is neither Romance nor Reporting; because it is unpretentious; and it has emotion as well as a version of things seen. For a poet to observe that war is ugly and not on the whole glorious or improving to the soul is not a novelty any more: but Mr Read does it with a quiet and careful conviction which is not very common. His vision surpasses his ear; and he has, I guess, been impressed – how could he escape it? – by Wyndham Lewis, who is a visual and only occasionally an auditory writer. Mr Read is hampered by his imperfection of musical sense, in the production of *tone*: the effect that is to say, is a succession of effects of ideas and images, rather than the sharp and indefinable effect of the poem as a whole. Nevertheless, "The Happy Warrior" and parts of "Kneeshaw Goes to War," and particularly the prose sketch at the end, are decidedly successful.

M. Tristan Tzara, whose book bears the impression of the Collection Dada in Zurich, is very different. He goes in for tones, rather minor ones, and sometimes gets them, though at the vast sacrifice of everything else. He has assembled a kind of something which has the odd distinction of being neither verse nor prose nor prose-poem; his *tic-tac debile* is agreeably competent. This one opens rather pleasantly:

froid tourbillon zigzag de sang
je suis sans âme cascade sans
amis et sans talents seigneur
Je ne reçois pas regulièrement les
lettres de ma mère
qui doivent passer par la russie
par la norvège et par l'angleterre....

but at times he becomes difficult to follow:

bonjour sans cigarette tzantzana
ganga
bouzdouc zdouc nfounfa mbaah....

The only way to take this sort of thing is very seriously, and I have got the impression that M. Tzara is rather clever. At least it is a symptom of "experiment", and ought not to be put in the hands of the young. M. Tzara's work does not appear to have very deep roots in the literature of any nation.

A third violent contrast is Mr Conrad Aiken. He has written several books of verse, and is pretty well known in America. He has the distinction of believing in the long poem, and of having worked through and abandoned several forms of the long poem which he has probably perceived to be obsolete. He has discarded the Masefield poem; we infer from this that he has perceived that the older fashioned narrative poem cannot be taken seriously when it has Henry James or Tchekov to compete with in prose. "Senlin: a biography" can be read carefully and advantageously to see what Mr Aiken is attempting on his borderline of the subliminal. It cannot be said quite to succeed, and its Condor twilight is unsatisfying after the sharper outlines of Mr Read's vision. Mr Aiken has gone in for psycho-analysis with a Swinburnian equipment; and he does not escape the fatal American introspectiveness; he is oversensitive and worried. He is tangled in himself. The effect is of immaturity of feeling, not at all any lack of it. It is difficult for a writer to mature in America. This is a pity; if Mr Aiken were not so isolated, if he was in contact with European civilisation, he might go so very much farther; his attempt is more impressive than many English successes.

One ought properly at this point to revert to the question of tradition, and to the consideration of what, in the developing and maturing of verse, changes and what remains the same.

Chapter 14
D. H. Lawrence

David Herbert Lawrence (1885–1930) is best known today for his work as a novelist. Yet his poetry was a continuation of his novels by other means. Both were dedicated to finding a language that would present the intense, volatile relationship between conscious and unconscious life. Both were engaged in a polemic against the sacrifice of instinctive existence that Lawrence believed was the cost of modern civilization. Between 1913 and his death in 1930 he published seven collections of poetry, and two more were published immediately after his death.

Lawrence was a self-conscious, widely read, and often deliberately controversial writer. The preface to the American edition of New Poems, *published in 1920, had first appeared as an essay, "The Poetry of the Present", in issues 4 and 5 of* The Playboy *in 1919. In the preface, Lawrence identifies a new source and form for poetry in the "present moment." Lawrence found a precursor for his version of modern intensity in the work of the nineteenth-century American poet, Walt Whitman. This transmission of Whitman's work by way of Lawrence contributed later in the twentieth century to the work of Charles Olson and the Black Mountain poets. The influence of Whitman on Lawrence, as well as Lawrence's subsequent influence on American poetry, is one example amongst many of an Anglo-American poetic culture that emerged in the twentieth century.*

Preface to the American Edition of *New Poems*

It seems when we hear a skylark singing as if sound were running forward into the future, running so fast and utterly without consideration, straight on into futurity. And when we hear a nightingale, we hear the pause and the rich, piercing rhythm of recollection, the perfected past. The lark may sound sad, but with the lovely lapsing

From *The Poetics of the New American Poetry*, ed. Donald Allen and Warren Tallman (New York: Grove Press, 1974), pp. 69–74.

sadness that is almost a swoon of hope. The nightingale's triumph is a pæan, but a death-pæan.

So it is with poetry. Poetry is, as a rule, either the voice of the far future, exquisite and ethereal, or it is the voice of the past, rich, magnificent. When the Greeks heard the *Iliad* and the *Odyssey*, they heard their own past calling in their hearts, as men far inland sometimes hear the sea and fall weak with powerful, wonderful regret, nostalgia; or else their own future rippled its time-beats through their blood, as they followed the painful, glamorous progress of the Ithacan. This was Homer to the Greeks: their Past, splendid with battles won and death achieved, and their Future, the magic wandering of Ulysses through the unknown.

With us it is the same. Our birds sing on the horizons. They sing out of the blue, beyond us, or out of the quenched night. They sing at dawn and sunset. Only the poor, shrill, tame canaries whistle while we talk. The wild birds begin before we are awake, or as we drop into dimness, out of waking. Our poets sit by the gateways, some by the east, some by the west. As we arrive and as we go out our hearts surge with response. But whilst we are in the midst of life, we do not hear them.

The poetry of the beginning and the poetry of the end must have that exquisite finality, perfection which belongs to all that is far off. It is in the realm of all that is perfect. It is of the nature of all that is complete and consummate. This completeness, this consummateness, the finality and the perfection are conveyed in exquisite form: the perfect symmetry, the rhythm which returns upon itself like a dance where the hands link and loosen and link for the supreme moment of the end. Perfected bygone moments, perfected moments in the glimmering futurity, these are the treasured gemlike lyrics of Shelley and Keats.

But there is another kind of poetry: the poetry of that which is at hand: the immediate present. In the immediate present there is no perfection, no consummation, nothing finished. The strands are all flying, quivering, intermingling into the web, the waters are shaking the moon. There is no round, consummate moon on the face of running water, nor on the face of the unfinished tide. There are no gems of the living plasm. The living plasm vibrates unspeakably, it inhales the future, it exhales the past, it is the quick of both, and yet it is neither. There is no plasmic finality, nothing crystal, permanent. If we try to fix the living tissue, as the biologists fix it with formation, we have only a hardened bit of the past, the bygone life under our observation.

Life, the ever-present, knows no finality, no finished crystallisation. The perfect rose is only a running flame, emerging and flowing off, and never in any sense at rest, static, finished. Herein lies its transcendent loveliness. The whole tide of all life and all time suddenly heaves, and appears before us as an apparition, a revelation. We look at the very white quick of nascent creation. A water-lily heaves herself from the flood, looks around, gleams, and is gone. We have seen the incarnation, the quick of the ever swirling flood. We have seen the invisible. We have seen, we have touched, we have partaken of the very substance of creative change, creative mutation. If you tell me about the lotus, tell me of nothing changeless or eternal. Tell me of the mystery of the inexhaustible, forever-unfolding creative spark. Tell me of the incarnate disclosure of the flux, mutation in blossom, laughter and decay perfectly open in their transit, nude in their movement before us.

Let me feel the mud and the heavens in my lotus. Let me feel the heavy, silting, sucking mud, the spinning of sky winds. Let me feel them both in purest contact, the nakedness of sucking weight, nakedly passing radiance. Give me nothing fixed, set, static. Don't give me the infinite or the eternal: nothing of infinity, nothing of eternity. Give me the still, white seething, the incandescence and the coldness of the incarnate moment: the moment, the quick of all change and haste and opposition: the moment, the immediate present, the Now. The immediate moment is not a drop of water running downstream. It is the source and issue, the bubbling up of the stream. Here, in this very instant moment, up bubbles the stream of time, out of the wells of futurity, flowing on to the oceans of the past. The source, the issue, the creative quick.

There is poetry of this immediate present, instant poetry, as well as poetry of the infinite past and the infinite future. The seething poetry of the incarnate Now is supreme, beyond even the everlasting gems of the before and after. In its quivering momentaneity it surpasses the crystalline, pearl-hard jewels, the poems of the eternities. Do not ask for the qualities of the unfading timeless gems. Ask for the whiteness which is the seethe of mud, ask for that incipient putrescence which is the skies falling, ask for the never-pausing, never-ceasing life itself. There must be mutation, swifter than iridescence, haste, not rest, come-and-go, not fixity, inconclusiveness, immediacy, the quality of life itself, without denouement or close. There must be the rapid momentaneous association of things which meet and pass on the for ever incalculable journey of creation: everything left in its own rapid, fluid relationship with the rest of things.

This is the unrestful, ungraspable poetry of the sheer present, poetry whose very permanency lies in its wind-like transit. Whitman's is the best poetry of this kind. Without beginning and without end, without any base and pediment, it sweeps past for ever, like a wind that is forever in passage, and unchainable. Whitman truly looked before and after. But he did not sigh for what is not. The clue to all his utterance lies in the sheer appreciation of the instant moment, life surging itself into utterance at its very wellhead. Eternity is only an abstraction from the actual present. Infinity is only a great reservoir of recollection, or a reservoir of aspiration: man-made. The quivering nimble hour of the present, this is the quick of Time. This is the immanence. The quick of the universe is the *pulsating, carnal self*, mysterious and palpable. So it is always.

Because Whitman put this into his poetry, we fear him and respect him so profoundly. We should not fear him if he sang only of the "old unhappy far-off things," or of the "wings of the morning." It is because his heart beats with the urgent, insurgent Now, which is even upon us all, that we dread him. He is so near the quick.

From the foregoing it is obvious that the poetry of the instant present cannot have the same body or the same motion as the poetry of the before and after. It can never submit to the same conditions. It is never finished. There is no rhythm which returns upon itself, no serpent of eternity with its tail in its own mouth. There is no static perfection, none of that finality which we find so satisfying because we are so frightened.

Much has been written about free verse. But all that can be said, first and last, is that free verse is, or should be direct utterance from the instant, whole man. It is the soul and the mind and body surging at once, nothing left out. They speak all together. There is some confusion, some discord. But the confusion and the discord only belong to the reality, as noise belongs to the plunge of water. It is no use inventing fancy laws for free verse, no use drawing a melodic line which all the feet must toe. Free verse toes no melodic line, no matter what drill-sergeant. Whitman pruned away his clichés – perhaps his clichés of rhythm as well as of phrase. And this is about all we can do, deliberately, with free verse. We can get rid of the sterotyped movements and the old hackneyed associations of sound or sense. We can break down those artificial conduits and canals through which we do so love to force our utterance. We can break the stiff neck of habit. We can be in ourselves spontaneous and flexible as flame, we can see that utterance rushes out without artificial form or artificial smoothness. But we cannot positively prescribe any motion, any rhythm. All the laws we invent or discover – it amounts to pretty much the same – will fail to apply to free verse. They will only apply to some form of restricted, limited unfree verse.

All we can say is that free verse does *not* have the same nature as restricted verse. It is not of the nature of reminiscence. It is not the past which we treasure in its perfection between our hands. Neither is it the crystal of the perfect future, into which we gaze. Its tide is neither the full, yearning flow of aspiration, nor the sweet, poignant ebb of remembrance and regret. The past and the future are the two great bournes of human emotion, the two great homes of the human days, the two eternities. They are both conclusive, final. Their beauty is the beauty of the goal, finished, perfected. Finished beauty and measured symmetry belong to the stable, unchanging eternities.

But in free verse we look for the insurgent naked throb of the instant moment. To break the lovely form of metrical verse, and to dish up the fragments as a new substance, called *vers libre*, this is what most of the free-versifiers accomplish. They do not know that free verse has its own *nature*, that it is neither star nor pearl, but instantaneous like plasm. It has no goal in either eternity. It has no finish. It has no satisfying stability, satisfying to those who like the immutable. None of this. It is the instant; the quick; the very jetting source of all will-be and has-been. The utterance is like a spasm, naked contact with all influences at once. It does not want to get anywhere. It just takes place.

For such utterance any externally applied law would be mere shackles and death. The law must come new each time from within. The bird is on the wing in the winds, flexible to every breath, a living spark in the storm, its very flickering depending upon its supreme mutability and power of change. Whence such a bird came: whither it goes: from what solid earth it rose up, and upon what solid earth it will close its wings and settle, this is not the question. This is a question of before and after. Now, *now*, the bird is on the wing in the winds.

Such is the rare new poetry. One realm we have never conquered: the pure present. One great mystery of time is terra incognita to us: the instant. The most superb mystery we have hardly recognized: the immediate, instant self. The quick of all time is the instant. The quick of all the universe, of all creation, is the incarnate, carnal self. Poetry gave us the clue: free verse: Whitman. Now we know.

The ideal – what is the ideal? A figment. An abstraction. A static abstraction, abstracted from life. It is a fragment of the before or the after. It is a crystallised aspiration, or a crystallised remembrance: crystallised, set, finished. It is a thing set apart, in the great storehouse of eternity, the storehouse of finished things.

We do not speak of things crystallised and set apart. We speak of the instant, the immediate self, the very plasm of the self. We speak also of free verse.

All this should have come as a preface to *Look! We Have Come Through!* But is it not better to publish a preface long after the book it belongs to has appeared? For then the reader will have had his fair chance with the book, alone.

Chapter 15
William Carlos Williams

William Carlos Williams (1883–1963) worked for much of his life as a doctor in Rutherford, New Jersey. While he was a student at the University of Pennsylvania he began his friendship with Ezra Pound and Hilda Doolittle. Although Williams visited Europe he did not, as they did, stay there. Instead he dedicated himself to the invention of a specifically American poetics, one that would reflect the diversity of American speech and experience. He published novels, short stories, and essays as well as poetry. He dedicated the later part of his life to work on a contemporary epic, Paterson, *published in five volumes between 1946 and 1958. Like Pound, he became an important influence on the work of a number of American and English poets, including Charles Olson, Louis Zukofsky, and Charles Tomlinson.*

These excerpts come from the Prologue to Kora in Hell: Improvisations, *first published in 1920. The title,* Kora in Hell, *alludes to a Greek myth that tells the story of the descent of the goddess of spring into the underworld. Williams finds in the myth an allegory of his own condition as a poet, sustaining the hope of renewal through imagination in the midst of bleak surroundings. The prologue offers its readers a guide to the prose improvisations that make up the* Kora in Hell. *It combines a deliberately demotic style with a more intense, meditative idiom. Quoting letters from Hilda Doolittle and Wallace Stevens, Williams defines his stance in opposition to theirs, arguing for a poetry of multiple perspectives that renews our sensory attention to the world. His reservations about what HD and Stevens have to say about his work indicate his distrust of their adoption of European perspectives that fail to see the possibilities of a distinctively American poetics.*

Prologue to *Kora in Hell*

[to William Carlos Williams from Hilda Doolittle]

14 August 1916

Dear Bill –
I trust you will not hate me for wanting to delete from your poem all the flippancies. The reason I want to do this is that the beautiful lines are so very beautiful – so in the tone and spirit of your *Postlude* – (which to me stands, a Nike, supreme among your poems). I think there is *real* beauty – and real beauty is a rare and sacred thing in this generation – in all the pyramid, Ashur-ban-i-pal bits and in the Fiesole and in the wind at the very last.

I don't know what you think but I consider this business of writing a very sacred thing! – I think you have the "spark" – am sure of it, and when you speak *direct* are a poet. I feel in the hey-ding-ding touch running through your poem a derivative tendency which, to me, is not *you* – not your very self. It is as if you were *ashamed* of your Spirit, ashamed of your inspiration! – as if you mocked at your own song. It's very well to *mock* at yourself – it is a spiritual sin to mock at your inspiration –

Hilda

Oh well, all this might be very disquieting were it not that "sacred" has lately been discovered to apply to a point of arrest where stabilization has gone on past the time. There is nothing sacred about literature, it is damned from one end to the other. There is nothing in literature but change and change is mockery. I'll write whatever I damn please, whenever I damn please and as I damn please and it'll be good if the authentic spirit of change is on it.

But in any case H. D. misses the entire intent of what I am doing no matter how just her remarks concerning that particular poem happen to have been. The hey-ding-ding touch *was* derivative, but it filled a gap that I did not know how better to fill at the time. It might be said that that touch is the prototype of the improvisations.

It is to the inventive imagination we look for deliverance from every other misfortune as from the desolation of a flat Hellenic perfection of style. What good then to turn to art from the atavistic religionists, from a science doing slavery service upon gas engines, from a philosophy tangled in a miserable sort of dialect that means nothing if the full power of initiative be denied at the beginning by a lot of baying and snapping scholiasts? If the inventive imagination must look, as I think, to the field of art for its richest discoveries today it will best make its way by compass and follow no path.

But before any material progress can be accomplished there must be someone to draw a discriminating line between true and false values.

The true value is that peculiarity which gives an object a character by itself. The associational or sentimental value is the false. Its imposition is due to lack of

From *Kora in Hell: Improvisations* (San Francisco: City Lights Books, 1973), pp. 10–14.

imagination, to an easy lateral sliding. The attention has been held too rigid on the one plane instead of following a more flexible, jagged resort. It is to loosen the attention, my attention since I occupy part of the field, that I write these improvisations. Here I clash with Wallace Stevens.

The imagination goes from one thing to another. Given many things of nearly totally divergent natures but possessing one-thousandth part of a quality in common, provided that be new, distinguished, these things belong in an imaginative category and not in a gross natural array. To me this is the gist of the whole matter. It is easy to fall under the spell of a certain mode, especially if it be remote of origin, leaving thus certain of its members essential to a reconstruction of its significance permanently lost in an impenetrable mist of time. But the thing that stands eternally in the way of really good writing is always one: the virtual impossibility of lifting to the imagination those things which lie under the direct scrutiny of the senses, close to the nose. It is this difficulty that sets a value upon all works of art and makes them a necessity. The senses witnessing what is immediately before them in detail see a finality which they cling to in despair, not knowing which way to turn. Thus the so-called natural or scientific array becomes fixed, the walking devil of modern life. He who even nicks the solidity of this apparition does a piece of work superior to that of Hercules when he cleaned the Augean stables.

Stevens' letter applies really to my book of poems, *Al Que Quiere* (which means, by the way, "To Him Who Wants It") but the criticism he makes of that holds good for each of the improvisations if not for the *oeuvre* as a whole.

It begins with a postscript in the upper left hand corner: "I think, after all, I should rather send this than not, although it is quarrelsomely full of my own ideas of discipline."

April 9

My dear Williams:

. . .

What strikes me most about the poems themselves is their casual character.... Personally I have a distaste for miscellany. It is one of the reasons I do not bother about a book myself.

[*Wallace Stevens is a fine gentleman whom Cannell likened to a Pennsylvania Dutchman who has suddenly become aware of his habits and taken to "society" in self-defense. He is always immaculately dressed. I don't know why I should always associate him in my mind with an imaginary image I have of Ford Madox Hueffer.*]

...My idea is that in order to carry a thing to the extreme necessity to convey it one has to stick to it;...Given a fixed point of view, realistic, imagistic or what you will, everything adjusts itself to that point of view; the process of adjustment is a world in flux, as it should be for a poet. But to fidget with points of view leads always to new beginnings and incessant new beginnings lead to sterility.

(This sounds like Sir Roger de Coverly)

A single manner
or mood thoroughly matured and exploited is that fresh thing...etc.

One has to keep looking for poetry as Renoir looked for colors in old walls, woodwork and so on.

Your place is

– among children
Leaping around a dead dog.

A book of that would feed the hungry...

Well a book of poems is a damned serious affair. I am only objecting that a book that contains your particular quality should contain anything else and suggesting that if the quality were carried to a communicable extreme, in intensity and volume, etc.... I see it all over the book, in your landscapes and portraits, but dissipated and obscured. Bouquets for brides and Spencerian compliments for poets... There are a very few men who have anything native in them or for whose work I'd give a Bolshevik ruble.... But I think your tantrums not half mad enough.

[*I am not quite clear about the last sentence but I presume he means that I do not push my advantage through to an overwhelming decision. What would you have me do with my Circe, Stevens, now that I have double-crossed her game, marry her? It is not what Odysseus did.*]

I return Pound's letter... observe how in everything he does he proceeds with the greatest positiveness, etc.

Wallace Stevens

... I thought at first to adjoin to each improvisation a more or less opaque commentary. But the mechanical interference that would result makes this inadvisable. Instead I have placed some of them in the preface where without losing their original intention (see reference numerals at the beginning of each) they relieve the later text and also add their weight to my present fragmentary argument.

V. No. 2. By the brokenness of his composition the poet makes himself master of a certain weapon which he could possess himself of in no other way. The speed of the emotions is sometimes such that thrashing about in a thin exaltation or despair many matters are touched but not held, more often broken by the contact.

II. No. 3. The instability of these improvisations would seem such that they must inevitably crumble under the attention and become particles of a wind that falters. It would appear to the unready that the fiber of the thing is a thin jelly. It would be these same fools who would deny touch cords to the wind because they cannot split a storm endwise and wrap it upon spools. The virtue of strength lies not in the grossness of the fiber but in the fiber itself. Thus a poem is tough by no quality it borrows from a logical recital of events nor from the events themselves but solely from that attenuated power which draws perhaps many broken things into a dance giving them thus a full being.

It is seldom that anything but the most elementary communications can be exchanged one with another. There are in reality only two or three reasons generally accepted as the causes of action. No matter what the motive it will seldom happen that true knowledge of it will be anything more than vaguely divined by some one person, some half a person whose intimacy has perhaps been cultivated over the whole of a lifetime. We live in bags. This is due to the gross fiber of all action. By action itself almost nothing can be imparted. The world of action is a world of stones....

XII. No. 2B. It is chuckleheaded to desire a way through every difficulty. Surely one might even communicate with the dead – and lose his taste for truffles. Because snails are slimy when alive and because slime is associated (erroneously) with filth, the fool is convinced that snails are detestable when, as it is proven every day, fried in butter with chopped parsley upon them, they are delicious. This is both sides of the question: the slave and the despoiled of his senses are one. But to weigh a difficulty and to turn it aside without being wrecked upon a destructive solution bespeaks an imagination of force sufficient to transcend action. The difficulty has thus been solved by ascent to a higher plane. It is energy of the imagination alone that cannot be laid aside.

Rich as are the gifts of the imagination, bitterness of world's loss is not replaced thereby. On the contrary it is intensified, resembling thus possession itself. But he who has no power of the imagination cannot even know the full of his injury....

Chapter 16
Ernest Fenollosa

Ernest Fenollosa (1853–1908) was a scholar and aesthete who devoted his working life to teaching western philosophy, literature, and political economy in Japan while interpreting Japanese and Chinese art and poetry for audiences in the United States and Europe. He studied at both Harvard and Cambridge universities, and then benefited from Japan's new policy of openness to the West when in 1878 he was appointed to teach political economy and philosophy at the Imperial University in Tokyo. In 1888 he was appointed manager of the newly opened Tokyo Fine Arts Academy and Imperial Museum. By this time, Fenollosa had become a Buddhist. He became a man with three names: the one given him at birth, the one given to him by Buddhism, Tai-Shin, and his Japanese name, Keito Yeitan Masanobu, given to him as a result of his apprenticeship in the Kano School of Art. In 1890 he returned to the United States where he became Curator of Oriental Art at the Boston Museum of Fine Arts. In 1897 he returned to Japan as a Professor of English Literature at the Imperial Normal School in Tokyo. But his second stay was shorter than his first. In 1900 he was back in the United States. He continued to lecture on Chinese and Japanese art and poetry in the United States and Europe until his sudden death in London in 1908.

Mary Fenollosa, his widow, was left with the problem of what to do with his unpublished manuscripts. One solution came in the form of a meeting with Ezra Pound in a London Hotel in 1913. Pound became Fenollosa's literary executor. He drew on Fenollosa's notes when he prepared his first volume of translations from Chinese poetry, Cathay, *in 1915. Pound published an edited version of "The Chinese Written Character" in 1920 as an addition to* Instigations, *a collection of his own criticism. In a prefatory note Pound described the essay as "a study of the fundamentals of aesthetics" and he clearly regarded it as a key text for understanding the true nature of poetry, publishing it again as a separate work in 1936. Fenollosa's interpretation of the Chinese written character gave further authority to Pound's poetics of Imagism. According to Fenellosa, the Chinese ideograph was shaped by its affinity to fundamental natural processes. It had not been corrupted by western concerns with abstraction and grammatical classification. Instead, the Chinese written character presented word pictures that showed the origins of the word in an act of perception. It combined visual immediacy with a sense of movement, act, and process. It exemplified the ideal of a concrete poetic language.*

Fenollosa's essay became an important source for a number of modern poets. Transforming English into imaginary Chinese became one of the dreams of twentieth-century poetic language and helps explain why one version of the poetic is characterized by the omission of definite and indefinite articles. Scholars who came after Fenollosa have dismissed his claims about the Chinese ideograph. They argued that in actual use the Chinese ideograph was not more or less abstract than western alphabetic script. But these dismissals did not diminish the essay's attraction for Pound and the poets who followed him.

The Chinese Written Character as the Medium for Poetry

. . . My subject is poetry, not language, yet the roots of poetry are in language. In the study of a language so alien in form to ours as is Chinese in its written character, it is necessary to inquire how these universal elements of form which constitute poetics can derive appropriate nutriment.

In what sense can verse, written in terms of visible hieroglyphics, be reckoned true poetry? It might seem that poetry, which like music is a *time art*, weaving its unities out of successive impressions of sound, could with difficulty assimilate a verbal medium consisting largely of semi-pictorial appeals to the eye.

Contrast, for example, Gray's line:

The curfew tolls the knell of parting day

with the Chinese line:

Unless the sound of the latter be given, what have they in common? It is not enough to adduce that each contains a certain body of prosaic meaning; for the question is, how can the Chinese line imply, *as form*, the very element that distinguishes poetry from prose?

On second glance, it is seen that the Chinese words, though visible, occur in just as necessary an order as the phonetic symbols of Gray. All that poetic form requires is a regular and flexible sequence, as plastic as thought itself. The characters may be seen and read, silently by the eye, one after the other:

From *Instigations of Ezra Pound, together with an Essay on the Chinese Written Character by Ernest Fenollosa*, by Ezra Pound (San Francisco: City Lights Books, 1969), pp. 6–26, 27–9, 31–2.

Moon rays like pure snow.

Perhaps we do not always sufficiently consider that thought is successive, not through some accident or weakness of our subjective operations but because the operations of nature are successive. The transferences of force from agent to object, which constitute natural phenomena, occupy time. Therefore, a reproduction of them in imagination requires the same temporal order.

Suppose that we look out of a window and watch a man. Suddenly he turns his head and actively fixes his attention upon something. We look ourselves and see that his vision has been focused upon a horse. We saw, first, the man before he acted; second, while he acted; third, the object toward which his action was directed. In speech we split up the rapid continuity of this action and of its picture into its three essential parts or joints in the right order, and say:

Man sees horse.

It is clear that these three joints, or words, are only three phonetic symbols, which stand for the three terms of a natural process. But we could quite as easily denote these three stages of our thought by symbols equally arbitrary, *which had no basis in sound*; for example, by three Chinese characters:

Man *Sees* *Horse*

If we all knew *what division* of this mental horse-picture each of these signs stood for, we could communicate continuous thought to one another as easily by drawing them as by speaking words. We habitually employ the visible language of gesture in much this same manner.

But Chinese notation is something much more than arbitrary symbols. It is based upon a vivid shorthand picture of the operations of nature. In the algebraic figure and in the spoken word there is no natural connection between thing and sign: all depends upon sheer convention. But the Chinese method follows natural suggestion. First stands the man on his two legs. Second, his eye moves through space: a bold figure represented by running legs under an eye, a modified picture of an eye, a modified picture of running legs, but unforgettable once you have seen it. Third stands the horse on his four legs.

The thought-picture is not only called up by these signs as well as by words, but far more vividly and concretely. Legs belong to all three characters: they are *alive*. The group holds something of the quality of a continuous moving picture.

The untruth of a painting or a photograph is that, in spite of its concreteness, it drops the element of natural succession.

Contrast the Laocoön statue with Browning's lines:

"I sprang to the stirrup, and Joris, and he
...
And into the midnight we galloped abreast."

One superiority of verbal poetry as an art rests in its getting back to the fundamental reality of *time*. Chinese poetry has the unique advantage of combining both elements. It speaks at once with the vividness of painting, and with the mobility of sounds. It is, in some sense, more objective than either, more dramatic. In reading Chinese we do not seem to be juggling mental counters, but to be watching *things* work out their own fate.

Leaving for a moment the form of the sentence, let us look more closely at this quality of vividness in the structure of detached Chinese words. The earlier forms of these characters were pictorial, and their hold upon the imagination is little shaken, even in later conventional modifications. It is not so well known, perhaps, that the great number of these ideographic roots carry in them a *verbal idea of action*. It might be thought that a picture is naturally the picture of a *thing*, and that therefore the root ideas of Chinese are what grammar calls nouns.

But examination shows that a large number of the primitive Chinese characters, even the so-called radicals, are shorthand pictures of actions or processes.

For example, the ideograph meaning "to speak" is a mouth with two words and a flame coming out of it. The sign meaning "to grow up with difficulty" is grass with a twisted root. But this concrete *verb* quality, both in nature and in the Chinese signs, becomes far more striking and poetic when we pass from such simple, original pictures to compounds. In this process of compounding, two things added together do not produce a third thing but suggest some fundamental relation between them. For example, the ideograph for a "messmate" is a man and a fire.

A true noun, an isolated thing, does not exist in nature. Things are only the terminal points, or rather the meeting points, of actions, cross-sections cut through actions, snapshots. Neither can a pure verb, an abstract motion, be possible in nature. The eye sees noun and verb as one: things in motion, motion in things, and so the Chinese conception tends to represent them.

The sun underlying the bursting forth of plants = spring.

The sun sign tangled in the branches of the tree sign = east.

"Rice-field" plus "struggle" = male.

"Boat" plus "water" = boat-water, a ripple.

Let us return to the form of the sentence and see what power it adds to the verbal units from which it builds. I wonder how many people have asked themselves why the sentence form exists at all, why it seems so universally necessary *in all languages*? Why must all possess it, and what is the normal type of it? If it be so universal, it ought to correspond to some primary law of nature.

I fancy the professional grammarians have given but a lame response to this inquiry. Their definitions fall into two types: one, that a sentence expresses a "complete thought"; the other, that in it we bring about a union of subject and predicate.

The former has the advantage of trying for some natural objective standard, since it is evident that a thought can not be the test of its own completeness. But in nature there is *no* completeness. On the one hand, practical completeness may be expressed by a mere interjection, as "Hi! there!", or "Scat!", or even by shaking one's fist. No sentence is needed to make one's meaning more clear. On the other hand, no full sentence really completes a thought. The man who sees and the horse which is seen will not stand still. The man was planning a ride before he looked. The horse kicked when the man tried to catch him. The truth is that acts are successive, even continuous; one causes or passes into another. And though we may string ever so many clauses into a single compound sentence, motion leaks everywhere, like electricity from an exposed wire. All processes in nature are interrelated; and thus there could be no complete sentence (according to this definition) save one which it would take all time to pronounce.

In the second definition of the sentence, as "uniting a subject and a predicate," the grammarian falls back on pure subjectivity. *We* do it all; it is a little private juggling between our right and left hands. The subject is that about which *I* am going to talk; the predicate is that which *I* am going to say about it. The sentence according to this definition is not an attribute of nature but an accident of man as a conversational animal.

If it were really so, then there could be no possible test of the truth of a sentence. Falsehood would be as specious as verity. Speech would carry no conviction.

Of course this view of the grammarians springs from the discredited, or rather the useless, logic of the Middle Ages. According to this logic, thought deals with abstractions, concepts drawn out of things by a sifting process. These logicians never inquired how the "qualities" which they pulled out of things came to be there. The truth of all their little checker-board juggling depended upon the natural order by which these powers or properties or qualities were folded in concrete things, yet they despised the "thing" as a mere "particular," or pawn. It was as if Botany should reason from the leaf-patterns woven into our table-cloths. Valid scientific thought consists in following as closely as may be the actual and entangled lines of forces as they pulse through things. Thought deals with no bloodless concepts but watches *things move* under its microscope.

The sentence form was forced upon primitive men by nature itself. It was not we who made it; it was a reflection of the temporal order in causation. All truth has to be expressed in sentences because all truth is the *transference of power.* The type of sentence in nature is a flash of lightning. It passes between two terms, a cloud and the earth. No unit of natural process can be less than this. All natural processes are, in their units, as much as this. Light, heat, gravity, chemical affinity, human will, have this in common, that they redistribute force. Their unit of process can be represented as:

term	*transference*	*term*
from	*of*	*to*
which	*force*	*which*

If we regard this transference as the conscious or unconscious act of an agent we can translate the diagram into:

agent *act* *object*

In this the act is the very substance of the fact denoted. The agent and the object are only limiting terms.

It seems to me that the normal and typical sentence in English as well as in Chinese expresses just this unit of natural process. It consists of three necessary words: the first denoting the agent or subject from which the act starts, the second embodying the very stroke of the act, the third pointing to the object, the receiver of the impact. Thus:

Farmer *pounds* *rice*

The form of the Chinese transitive sentence, and of the English (omitting particles), exactly corresponds to this universal form of action in nature. This brings language close to *things*, and in its strong reliance upon verbs it erects all speech into a kind of dramatic poetry.

A different sentence order is frequent in inflected languages like Latin, German or Japanese. This is because they are inflected, i.e. they have little tags and word-endings, or labels, to show which is the agent, the object, etc. In uninflected languages, like English and Chinese, there is nothing but the order of the words to distinguish their functions. And this order would be no sufficient indication, were it not the *natural order* – that is, the order of cause and effect.

It is true that there are, in language, intransitive and passive forms, sentences built out of the verb "to be," and, finally, negative forms. To grammarians and logicians these have seemed more primitive than the transitive, or at least exceptions to the transitive. I had long suspected that these apparently exceptional forms had grown from the transitive or worn away from it by alteration, or modification. This view is confirmed by Chinese examples, wherein it is still possible to watch the transformation going on.

The intransitive form derives from the transitive by dropping a generalised, customary, reflexive or cognate object: "He runs (a race)." "The sky reddens (itself)." "We breathe (air)." Thus we get weak and incomplete sentences which suspend the picture and lead us to think of some verbs as denoting states rather than acts. Outside grammar the word "state" would hardly be recognised as scientific. Who can doubt that when we say "The wall shines," we mean that it actively reflects light to our eye?

The beauty of Chinese verbs is that they are all transitive or intransitive at pleasure. There is no such thing as a naturally intransitive verb. The passive form is evidently a correlative sentence, which turns about and makes the object into a subject. That the object is not in itself passive, but contributes some positive force of its own to the action, is in harmony both with scientific law and with ordinary experience. The English passive voice with "is" seemed at first an obstacle to this hypothesis, but one suspected that the true form was a generalised transitive verb meaning something like "receive," which had degenerated into an auxiliary. It was a delight to find this the case in Chinese.

In nature there are no negations, no possible transfers of negative force. The presence of negative sentences in language would seem to corroborate the logicians' view that assertion is an arbitrary subjective act. *We* can assert a negation, though nature can not. But here again science comes to our aid against the logician: all apparently negative or disruptive movements bring into play other positive forces. It requires great effort to annihilate. Therefore we should suspect that, if we could follow back the history of all negative particles, we should find that they also are sprung from transitive verbs. It is too late to demonstrate such derivations in the Aryan languages, the clue has been lost; but in Chinese we can still watch positive verbal conceptions passing over into so-called negatives. Thus in Chinese the sign meaning "to be lost in the forest" relates to a state of non-existence. English "not" = the Sanskrit *na*, which may come from the root *na*, to be lost, to perish.

Lastly comes the infinitive which substitutes for a specific colored verb the universal copula "is," followed by a noun or an adjective. We do not say a tree "greens itself," but "the tree is green"; not that 'monkeys bring forth live young," but that "the monkey is a mammal." This is an ultimate weakness of language. It has come from generalising all intransitive words into one. As "live," "see," "walk," "breathe," are generalised into states by dropping their objects, so these weak verbs are in turn reduced to the abstractest state of all, namely bare existence.

There is in reality no such verb as a pure copula, no such original conception: our very word *exist* means "to stand forth," to show oneself by a definite act. "Is" comes from the Aryan root *as*, to breathe. "Be" is from *bhu*, to grow.

In Chinese the chief verb for "is" not only means actively "to have," but shows by its derivation that it expresses something even more concrete, namely "to snatch from the moon with the hand." 有 Here the baldest symbol of prosaic analysis is transformed by magic into a splendid flash of concrete poetry.

I shall not have entered vainly into this long analysis of the sentence if I have succeeded in showing how poetical is the Chinese form and how close to nature. In translating Chinese, verse especially, we must hold as closely as possible to the concrete force of the original, eschewing adjectives, nouns and intransitive forms wherever we can, and seeking instead strong and individual verbs.

Lastly we notice that the likeness of form between Chinese and English sentences renders translation from one to the other exceptionally easy. The genius of the two is much the same. Frequently it is possible by omitting English particles to make a literal word-for-word translation which will be not only intelligible in English, but even the strongest and most poetical English. Here, however, one must follow closely what is said, not merely what is abstractly meant.

Let us go back from the Chinese sentence to the individual written word. How are such words to be classified? Are some of them nouns by nature, some verbs and some adjectives? Are there pronouns and prepositions and conjunctions in Chinese as in good Christian languages?

One is led to suspect from an analysis of the Aryan languages that such differences are not natural, and that they have been unfortunately invented by grammarians to confuse the simple poetic outlook on life. All nations have written their strongest and most vivid literature before they invented a grammar. Moreover, all Aryan etymology points back to roots which are the equivalents of simple Sanskrit verbs, such as we find tabulated at the back of our Skeat. Nature herself has no grammar. Fancy picking up a man and telling him that he is a noun, a dead thing rather than a bundle of functions! A "part of speech" is only *what it does*. Frequently our lines of cleavage fail, one part of speech acts for another. They *act for* one another because they were originally one and the same.

Few of us realise that in our own language these very differences once grew up in living articulation; that they still retain life. It is only when the difficulty of placing some odd term arises, or when we are forced to translate into some very different language, that we attain for a moment the inner heat of thought, a heat which melts down the parts of speech to recast them at will.

One of the most interesting facts about the Chinese language is that in it we can see, not only the forms of sentences, but literally the parts of speech growing up, budding forth one from another. Like nature, the Chinese words are alive and plastic, because *thing* and *action* are not formally separated. The Chinese language naturally knows no grammar. It is only lately that foreigners, European and Japanese, have begun to torture this vital speech by forcing it to fit the bed of their definitions. We import into our reading of Chinese all the weakness of our own formalisms. This is especially sad in poetry, because the one necessity, even in our own poetry, is to keep words as flexible as possible, as full of the sap of nature.

Let us go further with our example. In English we call "to shine" a *verb in the infinitive*, because it gives the abstract meaning of the verb without conditions. If we want a corresponding adjective we take a different word, "bright." If we need a noun we say "luminosity," which is abstract, being derived from an adjective. To get a tolerably concrete noun, we have to leave behind the verb and adjective roots, and light upon a thing arbitrarily cut off from its power of action, say "the sun" or "the moon." Of course there is nothing in nature so cut off, and therefore this nounising is itself an abstraction. Even if we did have a common word underlying at once the verb "shine," the adjective "bright" and the noun "sun" we should probably call it an "infinitive of the infinitive." According to our ideas, it should be something extremely abstract, too intangible for use.

The Chinese have one word, *ming* or *mei*. Its ideograph is the sign of the sun together with the sign of the moon. It serves as verb, noun, adjective. Thus you write literally, "the sun and moon of the cup" for "the cup's brightness." Placed as a verb, you write "the cup sun-and-moons," actually "cup sun-and-moon," or in a weakened thought, "is like sun," i.e. shines. "Sun-and-moon cup" is naturally a bright cup. There is no possible confusion of the real meaning, though a stupid scholar may spend a week trying to decide what "part of speech" he should use in translating a very simple and direct thought from Chinese to English.

The fact is that almost every written Chinese word is properly just such an underlying word, and yet it is *not* abstract. It is not exclusive of parts of speech, but comprehensive; not something which is neither a noun, verb, nor adjective, but something which is all of them at once and at all times. Usage may incline the full meaning now a little more to one side, now to another, according to the point of view, but through all cases the poet is free to deal with it richly and concretely, as does nature.

In the derivation of nouns from verbs, the Chinese language is forestalled by the Aryan. Almost all the Sanskrit roots, which seem to underlie European languages, are primitive verbs, which express characteristic actions of visible nature. The verb must be the primary fact of nature, since motion and change are all that we can recognise in her. In the primitive transitive sentence, such as "Farmer pounds rice," the agent and the object are nouns only in so far as they limit a unit of action. "Farmer" and "rice" are mere hard terms which define the extremes of the pounding. But in themselves, apart from this sentence-function, they are naturally verbs. The farmer is one who tills the ground, and the rice is a plant which grows in a special way. This is indicated in the Chinese characters. And this probably exemplifies the ordinary derivation of nouns from verbs. In all languages, Chinese included, a noun is originally "that which does something," that which performs the verbal action. Thus the moon comes from the root *ma*, and means, "the measurer." The sun means that which begets.

The derivation of adjectives from the verb need hardly be exemplified. Even with us, today, we can still watch participles passing over into adjectives. In Japanese the adjective is frankly part of the inflection of the verb, a special mood, so that every verb is also an adjective. This brings us close to nature, because everywhere the quality is only a power of action regarded as having an abstract inherence. Green is only a certain rapidity of vibration, hardness a degree of tenseness in cohering. In Chinese the adjective always retains a substratum of verbal meaning. We should try to render this in translation, not be content with some bloodless adjectival abstraction plus "is."

Still more interesting are the Chinese "prepositions" – they are often post-positions. Prepositions are so important, so pivotal in European speech only because we have weakly yielded up the force of our intransitive verbs. We have to add small supernumerary words to bring back the original power. We still say "I see a horse," but with the weak verb "look" we have to add the directive particle "at" before we can restore the natural transitiveness.

Prepositions represent a few simple ways in which incomplete verbs complete themselves. Pointing toward nouns as a limit, they bring force to bear upon them. That is to say, they are naturally verbs, of generalised or condensed use. In Aryan languages it is often difficult to trace the verbal origins of simple prepositions. Only in "*off*" do we see a fragment of the thought "to throw off." In Chinese the preposition is frankly a verb, specially used in a generalised sense. These verbs are often used in their special verbal sense, and it greatly weakens an English translation if they are systematically rendered by colorless prepositions.

Thus in Chinese, by = to cause; to = to fall toward; in = to remain, to dwell; from = to follow; and so on.

Conjunctions are similarly derivative; they usually serve to mediate actions between verbs, and therefore they are necessarily themselves actions. Thus in Chinese, because = to use; and = to be included under one; another form of "and" = to be parallel; or = to partake; if = to let one do, to permit. The same is true of a host of other particles, no longer traceable in the Aryan tongues.

Pronouns appear a thorn in our evolution theory, since they have been taken as unanalysable expressions of personality. In Chinese, even they yield up their striking secrets of verbal metaphor. They are a constant source of weakness if colorlessly translated. Take, for example, the five forms of "I." There is the sign of a "spear in the hand" = a very emphatic I; five and a mouth = a weak and defensive I, holding off a crowd by speaking; to conceal = a selfish and private I; self (the cocoon sign) and a mouth = an egoistic I, one who takes pleasure in his own speaking; the self presented is used only when one is speaking to one's self.

I trust that this digression concerning parts of speech may have justified itself. It proves, first, the enormous interest of the Chinese language in throwing light upon our forgotten mental processes, and thus furnishes a new chapter in the philosophy of language. Secondly, it is indispensable for understanding the poetical raw material which the Chinese language affords. Poetry differs from prose in the concrete colors of its diction. It is not enough for it to furnish a meaning to philosophers. It must appeal to emotions with the charm of direct impression, flashing through regions where the intellect can only grope. Poetry must render what is said, not what is merely meant. Abstract meaning gives little vividness, and fullness of imagination gives all. Chinese poetry demands that we abandon our narrow grammatical categories, that we follow the original text with a wealth of concrete verbs.

But this is only the beginning of the matter. So far we have exhibited the Chinese characters and the Chinese sentence chiefly as vivid shorthand pictures of actions and processes in nature. These embody true poetry as far as they go. Such actions are *seen*, but Chinese would be a poor language, and Chinese poetry but a narrow art, could they not go on to represent also what is unseen. The best poetry deals not only with natural images but with lofty thoughts, spiritual suggestions and obscure relations. The greater part of natural truth is hidden in processes too minute for vision and in harmonies too large, in vibrations, cohesions and in affinities. The Chinese compass these also, and with great power and beauty.

You will ask, how could the Chinese have built up a great intellectual fabric from mere picture writing? To the ordinary Western mind, which believes that thought is concerned with logical categories and which rather condemns the faculty of direct imagination, this feat seems quite impossible. Yet the Chinese language with its peculiar materials has passed over from the seen to the unseen by exactly the same process which all ancient races employed. This process is metaphor, the use of material images to suggest immaterial relations.

The whole delicate substance of speech is built upon substrata of metaphor. Abstract terms, pressed by etymology, reveal their ancient roots still embedded in direct action. But the primitive metaphors do not spring from arbitrary *subjective* processes. They are possible only because they follow objective lines of relations in nature herself. Relations are more real and more important than the things which they relate. The forces which produce the branch-angles of an oak lay potent in the acorn. Similar lines of resistance, half-curbing the out-pressing vitalities, govern the branching of rivers and of nations. Thus a nerve, a wire, a roadway, and a clearing-house are only varying channels which communication forces for itself. This is more than analogy, it is identity of structure. Nature furnishes her own clues. Had the world not been full of homologies, sympathies, and identities, thought would have been starved and language chained to the obvious. There would have been no bridge whereby to cross from the minor truth of the seen to the major truth of the unseen. Not more than a few hundred roots out of our large vocabularies could have dealt directly with physical processes. These we can fairly well identify in primitive Sanskrit. They are, almost without exception, vivid verbs. The wealth of European speech grew, following slowly the intricate maze of nature's suggestions and affinities. Metaphor was piled upon metaphor in quasi-geological strata.

Metaphor, the revealer of nature, is the very substance of poetry. The known interprets the obscure, the universe is alive with myth. The beauty and freedom of the observed world furnish a model, and life is pregnant with art. It is a mistake to suppose, with some philosophers of aesthetics, that art and poetry aim to deal with the general and the abstract. This misconception has been foisted upon us by mediaeval logic. Art and poetry deal with the concrete of nature, not with rows of separate "particulars," for such rows do not exist. Poetry is finer than prose because it gives us more concrete truth in the same compass of words. Metaphor, its chief device, is at once the substance of nature and of language. Poetry only does consciously what the primitive races did unconsciously. The chief work of literary men in dealing with language, and of poets especially, lies in feeling back along the ancient lines of advance. He must do this so that he may keep his words enriched by all their subtle undertones of meaning. The original metaphors stand as a kind of luminous background, giving color and vitality, forcing them closer to the concreteness of natural processes. Shakespeare everywhere teems with examples. For these reasons poetry was the earliest of the world arts; poetry, language and the care of myth grew up together.

I have alleged all this because it enables me to show clearly why I believe that the Chinese written language has not only absorbed the poetic substance of nature and built with it a second work of metaphor, but has, through its very pictorial visibility, been able to retain its original creative poetry with far more vigor and vividness than any phonetic tongue. Let us first see how near it is to the heart of nature in its metaphors. We can watch it passing from the seen to the unseen, as we saw it passing from verb to pronoun. It retains the primitive sap, it is not cut and dried like a walking-stick. We have been told that these people are cold, practical, mechanical, literal, and without a trace of imaginative genius. That is nonsense.

Our ancestors built the accumulations of metaphor into structures of language and into systems of thought. Languages today are thin and cold because we think less and less into them. We are forced, for the sake of quickness and sharpness, to file down each word to its narrowest edge of meaning. Nature would seem to have become less like a paradise and more and more like a factory. We are content to accept the vulgar misuse of the moment.

A late stage of decay is arrested and embalmed in the dictionary.

Only scholars and poets feel painfully back along the thread of our etymologies and piece together our diction, as best they may, from forgotten fragments. This anaemia of modern speech is only too well encouraged by the feeble cohesive force of our phonetic symbols. There is little or nothing in a phonetic word to exhibit the embryonic stages of its growth. It does not bear its metaphor on its face. We forget that personality once meant, not the soul, but the soul's mask. This is the sort of thing one can not possibly forget in using the Chinese symbols.

In this Chinese shows its advantage. Its etymology is constantly visible. It retains the creative impulse and process, visible and at work. After thousands of years the lines of metaphoric advance are still shown, and in many cases actually retained in the meaning. Thus a word, instead of growing gradually poorer and poorer as with us, becomes richer and still more rich from age to age, almost consciously luminous. Its uses in national philosophy and history, in biography and in poetry, throw about it a nimbus of meanings. These centre about the graphic symbol. The memory can hold them and use them. The very soil of Chinese life seems entangled in the roots of its speech. The manifold illustrations which crowd its annals of personal experience, the lines of tendency which converge upon a tragic climax, moral character as the very core of the principle – all these are flashed at once on the mind as reinforcing values with accumulation of meaning which a phonetic language can hardly hope to attain. Their ideographs are like bloodstained battle-flags to an old campaigner. With us, the poet is the only one for whom the accumulated treasures of the race-words are real and active. Poetic language is always vibrant with fold on fold of overtones and with natural affinities, but in Chinese the visibility of the metaphor tends to raise this quality to its intensest power.

I have mentioned the tyranny of mediaeval logic. According to this European logic thought is a kind of brickyard. It is baked into little hard units or concepts. These are piled in rows according to size and then labeled with words for future use. This use consists in picking out a few bricks, each by its convenient label, and sticking them together into a sort of wall called a sentence by the use either of white mortar for the positive copula "is," or of black mortar for the negative copula "is not." In this way we produce such admirable propositions as "A ring-tailed baboon is not a constitutional assembly."

Let us consider a row of cherry trees. From each of these in turn we proceed to take an "abstract," as the phrase is, a certain common lump of qualities which we may express together by the name cherry or cherry-ness. Next we place in a second table several such characteristic concepts: cherry, rose, sunset, iron-rust, flamingo. From these we abstract some further common quality, dilutation or mediocrity, and label it "red" or "redness." It is evident that this process of abstraction may be carried on indefinitely and with all sorts of material. We may go on for ever building pyramids of attenuated concept until we reach the apex "being."

But we have done enough to illustrate the characteristic process. At the base of the pyramid lie *things*, but stunned, as it were. They can never know themselves for things until they pass up and down among the layers of the pyramids. The way of passing up and down the pyramid may be exemplified as follows: We take a concept of lower attenuation, such as "cherry"; we see that it is contained under one higher, such as "redness." Then we are permitted to say in sentence form, "Cherryness is contained under redness," or for short, "(The) cherry is red." If, on the other hand, we do not find our chosen subject under a given predicate we use the black copula and say, for example, "(The) cherry is not liquid."...

Science fought till she got at the things.

All her work has been done from the base of the pyramids, not from the apex. She has discovered how functions cohere in things. She expresses her results in grouped sentences which embody no nouns or adjectives but verbs of special character. The true formula for thought is: The cherry tree is all that it does. Its correlated verbs compose it. At bottom these verbs are transitive. Such verbs may be almost infinite in number.

In diction and in grammatical form science is utterly opposed to logic. Primitive men who created language agreed with science and not with logic. Logic has abused the language which they left to her mercy.

Poetry agrees with science and not with logic.

The moment we use the copula, the moment we express subjective inclusions, poetry evaporates. The more concretely and vividly we express the interactions of things the better the poetry. We need in poetry thousands of active words, each doing its utmost to show forth the motive and vital forces. We can not exhibit the wealth of nature by mere summation, by the piling of sentences. Poetic thought works by suggestion, crowding maximum meaning into the single phrase pregnant, charged, and luminous from within.

In Chinese character each word accumulated this sort of energy in itself.

Should we pass formally to the study of Chinese poetry, we should warn ourselves against logicianised pitfalls. We should be ware of modern narrow utilitarian meanings ascribed to the words in commercial dictionaries. We should try to preserve the metaphoric overtones. We should be ware of English grammar, its hard parts of speech, and its lazy satisfaction with nouns and adjectives. We should seek and at least bear in mind the verbal undertone of each noun. We should avoid "is" and bring in a wealth of neglected English verbs. Most of the existing translations violate all of these rules.

The development of the normal transitive sentence rests upon the fact that one action in nature promotes another; thus the agent and the object are secretly verbs. For example, our sentence, "Reading promotes writing," would be expressed in Chinese by three full verbs. Such a form is the equivalent of three expanded clauses and can be drawn out into adjectival, participal, infinitive, relative or conditional members. One of many possible examples is, "If one reads it teaches him how to write." Another is, "One who reads becomes one who writes." But in the first condensed form a Chinese would write, "Read promote write." The dominance of the verb and its power to obliterate all other parts of speech give us the model of terse fine style....

Still, is it not enough to show that Chinese poetry gets back near to the processes of nature by means of its vivid figure, its wealth of such figure? If we attempt to follow it in English we must use words highly charged, words whose vital suggestion shall interplay as nature interplays. Sentences must be like the mingling of the fringes of feathered banners, or as the colors of many flowers blended into the single sheen of a meadow.

The poet can never see too much or feel too much. His metaphors are only ways of getting rid of the dead white plaster of the copula. He resolves its indifference into a thousand tints of verb. His figures flood things with jets of various light, like the sudden up-blaze of fountains. The prehistoric poets who created language discovered the whole harmonious framework of nature, they sang out her processes in their hymns. And this diffused poetry which they created, Shakespeare has condensed into a more tangible substance. Thus in all poetry a word is like a sun, with its corona and chromosphere; words crowd upon words, and enwrap each other in their luminous envelopes until sentences become clear, continuous light-bands....

Part II
1920–1940

Chapter 17
Mina Loy

Mina Loy (1882–1966) initially trained to be a painter, an education that took her away from an oppressive but comfortable Victorian English home to work in Munich, London, and Paris. During her stay in Florence she encountered the work of the Italian Futurists and it was shortly after this that she began to publish her poetry in small avant-garde magazines of the period. In 1916 she visited the United States, the country where she eventually settled. In 1917 her work appeared alongside that of Eliot, Moore, Stevens, and William Carlos Williams in Others: An Anthology of the New Verse. *Pound praised this anthology for its "first adequate presentation of the work of Mina Loy and Marianne Moore," and, despite Loy's English origins, hailed their work as a "distinctly national product" of the USA. But Loy's poetry was more outspoken and more obviously experimental than Moore's. She had adapted both Futurism and feminism to her own artistic purposes. Her poems dealt with awkward topics like sex and childbirth in a manner that disconcerted some of her critics. But she also deployed the techniques of Futurism for the purposes of satire. A number of her poems mock masculine self-satisfaction and feminine passivity. Some of her work begins in lyric, occasions that are then subverted by a sardonic voice. Her work brought her an intense but brief reputation. She published only two books in her lifetime,* Lunar Baedeker, *in 1923 and* Lunar Baedeker and Time-Tables *in 1958. Loy wrote in different forms – novels, plays, and stories as well as poetry – and practiced different arts – dress-designing as well as painting – but she chose not to make a career out of any of them. She claimed that she was "never a poet," and argued that "it is necessary to stay very unknown." She settled in New York in 1936 and then moved to Aspen, Colorado in 1954 where she lived until her death. Roger Conover edited her work posthumously and she has become the subject of renewed critical attention. Conover's* The Lost Lunar Baedeker, *published in 1996, provides a comprehensive selection of her poetry from 1914 to 1949, and some of the prose she wrote between 1914 and 1925.*

Loy's recently discovered review essay, "Modern Poetry," was first published in a woman's fashion magazine, Charm, *in 1925. It is reprinted in the Conover edition mentioned above. Loy firmly places modern poetry as a distinctively American expression. But, unlike some other modernist poets, she declares its affinity with a popular form,*

American jazz. Both respond to the new rhythms of modern American life, and both invent new rhythmic forms. Like Marianne Moore, Loy believed that "Poetic rhythm... is the chart of a temperament." It followed that the freedoms offered by the revolt against tradition enabled poetry to express a diversity of temperaments. But Loy's sense of modern poetry as an individual emancipation is matched by her understanding of the collective sources of poetry. The variety of languages and idioms that go into the making of American English give it an unparalleled vitality: "on the baser avenues of Manhattan every voice swings to the triple rhythm of its race, its citizenship and its personality."

Modern Poetry

Poetry is prose bewitched, a music made of visual thoughts, the sound of an idea.

The new poetry of the English language has proceeded out of America. Of things American it attains the aristocratic situation of vitality. This unexpectedly realized valuation of American jazz and American poetry is endorsed by two publics; the one universal, the other infinitesimal in comparison.

And why has the collective spirit of the modern world, of which both are the reflection, recognized itself unanimously in the new music of unprecedented instruments, and so rarely in the new poetry of unprecedented verse? It is because the sound of music capturing our involuntary attention is so easy to get in touch with, while the silent sound of poetry requires our voluntary attention to obliterate the cold barrier of print with the whole "intelligence of our senses." And many of us who have no habit of reading not alone with the eye but also with the ear, have – especially at a superficial first reading – overlooked the beauty of it.

More than to read poetry we must listen to poetry. All reading is the evocation of speech; the difference in our approach, then, in reading a poem or a newspaper is that our attitude in reading a poem must be rather that of listening to and looking at a pictured song. Modern poetry, like music, has received a fresh impetus from contemporary life; they have both gained in precipitance of movement. The structure of all poetry is the movement that an active individuality makes in expressing itself. Poetic rhythm, of which we have all spoken so much, is the chart of a temperament.

The variety and felicity of these structural movements in modern verse has more than vindicated the rebellion against tradition. It will be found that one can recognize each of the modern poets' work by the gait of their mentality. Or rather that the formation of their verses is determined by the spontaneous tempo of their response to life. And if at first it appears irksome to adjust pleasure to unaccustomed meters, let us reflect in time that hexameters and alexandrines, before they became poetic laws, originated as the spontaneous structure of a poet's inspiration.

Imagine a tennis champion who became inspired to write poetry, would not his verse be likely to embody the rhythmic transit of skimming balls? Would not his meter depend on his way of life, would it not form itself, without having recourse

From *The Lost Lunar Baedeker: Poems of Mina Loy*, ed. Roger Conover (New York: Farrar, Straus and Giroux/ Manchester: Carcanet, 1997), pp. 157–61.

to traditional, remembered, or accepted forms? This, then, is the secret of the new poetry. It is the direct response of the poet's mind to the modern world of varieties in which he finds himself. In each one we can discover his particular inheritance of that world's beauty.

Close as this relationship of poetry to music is, I think only once has the logical transition from verse to music, on which I had so often speculated, been made, and that by the American, Ezra Pound. To speak of the modern movement is to speak of him; the masterly impresario of modern poets, for without the discoveries he made with his poet's instinct for poetry, this modern movement would still be rather a nebula than the constellation it has become. Not only a famous poet, but a man of action, he gave the public the required push on to modern poetry at the psychological moment. Pound, the purveyor of geniuses, to such journals as the "Little Review," on which he conferred immortality by procuring for its pages the manuscript of Joyce's "Ulysses." Almost together with the publication of his magnificent Cantos, his music was played in Paris; it utters the communings of a poet's mind with itself making decisions on harmony.

It was inevitable that the renaissance of poetry should proceed out of America, where latterly a thousand languages have been born, and each one, for purposes of communication at least, English – English enriched and variegated with the grammatical structure and voice-inflection of many races, in novel alloy with the fundamental time-is-money idiom of the United States, discovered by the newspaper cartoonists.

This composite language is a very living language, it grows as you speak. For the true American appears to be ashamed to say anything in the way it has been said before. Every moment he ingeniously coins new words for old ideas, to keep good humor warm. And on the baser avenues of Manhattan every voice swings to the triple rhythm of its race, its citizenship and its personality.

Out of the welter of this unclassifiable speech, while professors of Harvard and Oxford labored to preserve "God's English" the muse of modern literature arose, and her tongue had been loosened in the melting-pot.

You may think it impossible to conjure up the relationship of expression between the high browest modern poets and an adolescent Slav who has speculated in a wholesale job-lot of mandarines and its trying to sell them in a retail market on First Avenue. But it lies simply in this: both have had to become adapted to a country where the mind has to put on its verbal clothes at terrific speed if it would speak in time; where no one will listen if you attack him twice with the same missile of argument. And, that the ear that has listened to the greatest number of sounds will have the most to choose from when it comes to self-expression, each has been liberally educated in the flexibility of phrases.

So in the American poet wherever he may wander, however he may engage himself with an older culture, there has occurred no Europeanization of his fundamental advantage, the acuter shock of the New World consciousness upon life. His is still poetry that has proceeded out of America.

The harvest from this recent fertiliser is the poetry of E. E. Cummings. Where other poets have failed for being too modern he is more modern still, and altogether successful; where others were entirely anti-human in their fear of sentimentality, he keeps that rich compassion that poets have for common things leads them to deck them [*sic*] with their own conception; for surely if there were a heaven it would be where this horrible ugliness of human life would arise self-consciously as that which the poet has made of it.

Cummings has united free verse and rhyme which so urgently needed to be married. His rhymes are quite fresh – "radish-red" and "hazarded," and the freeness of his verse gives them a totally new metric relationship.

But fundamentally he is a great poet because his verse wells up abundantly from the foundations of his soul; a sonorous dynamo. And as I believe that the quality of genius must be largely unconscious, I can understand how Cummings can turn out such gabble when he is not being sublime. He is very often sublime.

In reading modern poetry one should beware of allowing mere technical eccentricities or grammatical disturbances to turn us from the main issue which is to get at the poem's reality. We should remember that this seeming strangeness is inevitable when any writer has come into an independent contact with nature: to each she must show herself in a new manner, for each has a different organic personality for perceiving her.

When the little controversies over what is permissible in art evaporate, we will always find that the seeming strangeness has disappeared with them in the larger aspect of the work which has the eternal quality that is common to all true art.

Out of the past most poets, after all, call to us with one or two perfect poems. And we have not complained of being too poor. You will find that the moderns have already done as much.

H. D., who is an interesting example of my claims for the American poet who engages with an older culture, has written at least two perfect poems: one about a swan.

Marianne Moore, whose writing so often amusingly suggests the soliloquies of a library clock, has written at least one perfect poem, "The Fish."

Lawrence Vail has written one perfect poem, the second "Cannibalistic Love Song," a snatch of primitive ideation with a rhythm as essential as daylight. Maxwell Bodenheim, I think, had one among his early work, and perfect also is a poem of Carlos Williams about the wind on a window-pane.

Williams brings me to a distinction that is necessary to make in speaking of modern poets. Those I have spoken of are poets according to the old as well as the new reckoning; there are others who are poets only according to the new reckoning. They are headed by the doctor, Carlos Williams. Here is the poet whose expression derives from his life. He is a doctor. He loves bare facts. He is also a poet, he must recreate everything to suit himself. How can he reconcile these two selves?

Williams will make a poem of a bare fact – just show you something he noticed. The doctor wishes you to know just how uncompromisingly itself that fact is. But the poet would like you to realize all that it means to him, and he throws that bare fact onto a paper in such a way that it becomes a part of Williams' own nature as well as the thing itself. That is the new rhythm.

Chapter 18
Hart Crane

Hart Crane (1899–1932) published two volumes of poetry, White Buildings *in 1926 and* The Bridge *in 1930, before he killed himself by jumping from a boat* en route *from Mexico to the United States. Crane's ambition was to invent a poetic language that would realize a visionary promise in American experience. His long poem* The Bridge *was his most sustained attempt to achieve this ambition. Crane's work influenced a number of American poets who came after him, including Robert Lowell and John Berryman. More recently, his work has been reinterpreted for its rhetorically complex presentation and invention of gay experience.*

"General Aims and Theories" was first published posthumously in 1937 in Philip Horton's Hart Crane: The Life of an American Poet. *It was written in 1925 to help Eugene O'Neill write a projected but finally unpublished foreword to* White Buildings. *There are apparent similarities between Eliot's concept of tradition and Crane's idea of the poet as "building a bridge between so-called classic experience and many divergent realities of our seething, confused cosmos of today." But the contrast between the two is emphatic: Crane's modern poet is immersed in the machine energies of the city, searching out the rhythms of modern experience. Eliot's "impersonal" poet is a more detached figure, living amongst the monuments of tradition.*

General Aims and Theories

When I started writing Faustus & Helen it was my intention to embody in modern terms (words, symbols, metaphors) a contemporary approximation to an ancient human culture or mythology that seems to have been obscured rather than illumined with the frequency of poetic allusions made to it during the last century. The name of

From *The Complete Poems and Selected Letters and Prose of Hart Crane*, ed. Brom Weber (New York: W. W. Norton, 1937), pp. 217–23.

Helen, for instance, has become an all-too-easily employed crutch for evocation whenever a poet felt a stitch in his side. The real evocation of this (to me) very real and absolute conception of beauty seemed to consist in a reconstruction in these modern terms of the basic emotional attitude toward beauty that the Greeks had. And in so doing I found that I was really building a bridge between so-called classic experience and many divergent realities of our seething, confused cosmos of today, which has no formulated mythology yet for classic poetic reference or for religious exploitation.

So I found "Helen" sitting in a street car; the Dionysian revels of her court and her seduction were transferred to a Metropolitan roof garden with a jazz orchestra; and the *katharsis* of the fall of Troy I saw approximated in the recent World War. The importance of this scaffolding may easily be exaggerated, but it gave me a series of correspondences between two widely separated worlds on which to sound some major themes of human speculation – love, beauty, death, renascence. It was a kind of grafting process that I shall doubtless not be interested in repeating, but which is consistent with subsequent theories of mine on the relation of tradition to the contemporary creating imagination.

It is a terrific problem that faces the poet today – a world that is so in transition from a decayed culture towards a reorganization of human evaluations that there are few common terms, general denominators of speech that are solid enough or that ring with any vibration or spiritual conviction. The great mythologies of the past (including the Church) are deprived of enough façade to even launch good raillery against. Yet much of their traditions are operative still – in millions of chance combinations of related and unrelated detail, psychological references, figures of speech, precepts, etc. These are all a part of our common experience and the terms, at least partially, of that very experience when it defines or extends itself.

The deliberate program, then, of a "break" with the past or tradition seems to me to be a sentimental fallacy.... The poet has a right to draw on whatever practical resources he finds in books or otherwise about him. He must take his sensibility and his touchstone of experience for the proper selections of these themes and details, however—and that is where he either stands, or falls into useless archeology.

I put no particular value on the simple objective of "modernity." The element of the temporal location of an artist's creation is of very secondary importance; it can be left to the impressionist or historian just as well. It seems to me that a poet will accidentally define his time well enough simply by reacting honestly and to the full extent of his sensibilities to the states of passion, experience and rumination that fate forces on him, first hand. He must, of course, have a sufficiently universal basis of experience to make his imagination selective and valuable. His picture of the "period," then, will simply be a by-product of his curiosity and the relation of his experience to a postulated "eternity."

I am concerned with the future of America, but not because I think that America has any so-called par value as a state or as a group of people.... It is only because I feel persuaded that here are destined to be discovered certain as yet undefined spiritual quantities, perhaps a new hierarchy of faith not to be developed so completely elsewhere. And in this process I like to feel myself as a potential factor; certainly

I must speak in its terms and what discoveries I may make are situated in its experience.

But to fool one's self that definitions are being reached by merely referring frequently to skyscrapers, radio antennae, steam whistles, or other surface phenomena of our time is merely to paint a photograph. I think that what is interesting and significant will emerge only under the conditions of our submission to, and examination and assimilation of, the organic effects on us of these and other fundamental factors of our experience. It can certainly not be an organic expression otherwise. And the expression of such values may often be as well accomplished with the vocabulary and blank verse of the Elizabethans as with the calligraphic tricks and slang used so brilliantly at times by an impressionist like Cummings.

It may not be possible to say that there is, strictly speaking, any "absolute" experience. But it seems evident that certain aesthetic experience (and this may for a time engross the total faculties of the spectator) can be called absolute, inasmuch as it approximates a formally convincing statement of a conception or apprehension of life that gains our unquestioning assent, and under the conditions of which our imagination is unable to suggest a further detail consistent with the design of the aesthetic whole.

I have been called an "absolutist" in poetry, and if I am to welcome such a label it should be under the terms of the above definition. It is really only a *modus operandi*, however, and as such has been used organically before by at least a dozen poets such as Donne, Blake, Baudelaire, Rimbaud, etc. I may succeed in defining it better by contrasting it with the impressionistic method. The impressionist is interesting as far as he goes – but his goal has been reached when he has succeeded in projecting certain selected factual details into his reader's consciousness. He is really not interested in the *causes* (metaphysical) of his materials, their emotional derivations or their utmost spiritual consequences. A kind of retinal registration is enough, along with a certain psychological stimulation. And this is also true of your realist (of the Zola type), and to a certain extent of the classicist, like Horace, Ovid, Pope, etc.

Blake meant these differences when he wrote;

> We are led to believe in a lie
> When we see *with* not *through* the eye.

The impressionist creates only with the eye and for the readiest surface of the consciousness, at least relatively so. If the effect has been harmonious or even stimulating, he can stop there, relinquishing entirely to his audience the problematic synthesis of the details into terms of their own personal consciousness.

It is my hope to go *through* the combined materials of the poem, using our "real" world somewhat as a spring-board and to give the poem *as a whole* an orbit or predetermined direction of its own. I would like to establish it as free from my own personality as from any chance evaluation on the reader's part. (This is, of course, an impossibility, but it is a characteristic worth mentioning.) Such a poem is at least a stab at a truth, and to such an extent may be differentiated from other kinds of poetry and called "absolute." Its evocation will not be toward decoration or amusement, but rather toward a state of consciousness, an "innocence" (Blake) or absolute beauty. In this condition there may be discoverable under new forms certain spiritual illuminations, shining with a morality essentialized from experience directly, and not from previous precepts or preconceptions. It is as though a poem gave the reader as he left it a single, new *word*, never before spoken and impossible to actually enunciate, but self-evident as an active principle in the reader's consciousness henceforward.

As to technical considerations: the motivation of the poem must be derived from the implicit emotional dynamics of the materials used, and the terms of expression employed are often selected less for their logical (literal) significance than for their associational meanings. Via this and their metaphorical inter-relationships, the entire construction of the poem is raised on the organic principle of a "logic of metaphor," which antedates our so-called pure logic, and which is the genetic basis of all speech, hence consciousness and thought-extension.

These dynamics often result, I'm told, in certain initial difficulties in understanding my poems. But on the other hand I find them at times the only means possible for expressing certain concepts in any forceful or direct way whatever. To cite two examples: – when, in Voyages (II), I speak of "adagios of islands," the reference is to the motion of a boat through islands clustered thickly, the rhythm of the motion, etc. And it seems a much more direct and creative statement than any more logical employment of words such as "coasting slowly through the islands," besides ushering in a whole world of music. Similarly in Faustus and Helen (III) the speed and tense altitude of an aeroplane are much better suggested by the idea of "nimble blue plateaus" – *implying* the aeroplane and its speed against a contrast of stationary elevated earth. Although the statement is pseudo in relation to formal logic – it is completely logical in relation to the truth of the imagination, and there is expressed a concept of speed and space that could not be handled so well in other terms.

In manipulating the more imponderable phenomena of psychic motives, pure emotional crystallizations, etc. I have had to rely even more on these dynamics of inferential mention, and I am doubtless still very unconscious of having committed myself to what seems nothing but obscurities to some minds. A poem like Possessions really cannot be technically explained. It must rely (even to a large extent with myself) on its organic impact on the imagination to successfully imply its meaning. This seems to me to present an exceptionally difficult problem, however, considering the real clarity and consistent logic of many of the other poems.

I know that I run the risk of much criticism by defending such theories as I have, but as it is part of a poet's business to risk not only criticism – but folly – in the conquest of consciousness I can only say that I attach no intrinsic value to what means I use beyond their practical service in giving form to the living stuff of the imagination.

New conditions of life germinate new forms of spiritual articulation. And while I feel that my work includes a more consistent extension of traditional literary elements than many contemporary poets are capable of appraising, I realize that I am utilizing the gifts of the past as instruments principally; and that the voice of the present, if it is to be known, must be caught at the risk of speaking in idioms and circumlocutions sometimes shocking to the scholar and historians of logic. Language has built towers and bridges, but itself is inevitably as fluid as always.

Chapter 19
Langston Hughes

Langston Hughes (1902–67) was one of the leading figures in the Harlem Renaissance. He worked in a variety of genres including poetry, fiction, drama, and autobiography. His early poetry drew on blues and jazz in an attempt to create a style informed by black American culture. The deliberate attempt to create a literature that would be black, American and popular informed much of his subsequent work. In the 1930s he worked increasingly in the theater and throughout the 1940s and 1950s wrote prolifically as a journalist, autobiographer, and lyricist. At the time of his death, Hughes's reputation was uncertain. His later work met with mixed reviews and his version of racial pride was rejected by the generation of radical politicians and intellectuals associated with the Black Panthers.

"The Negro Artist and the Racial Mountain" was first published in The Nation *in June 1926 and presented one side of a debate about the necessity for an ethnically self-conscious "negro" art. Hughes takes the situation of the "young Negro poet" as typical of the problem confronting all black artists: that acceptance by white audiences in the United States would require an unacceptable sacrifice of black American culture and the historical experience it represented. He sketches the conditions for a black American culture that could celebrate and learn from its origins.*

The Negro Artist and the Racial Mountain

One of the most promising of the young Negro poets said to me once, "I want to be a poet – not a Negro poet," meaning, I believe, "I want to write like a white poet"; meaning subconsciously, "I would like to be a white poet"; meaning behind that, "I would like to be white." And I was sorry the young man said that, for no great poet

From *Voices from the Harlem Renaissance*, ed. N. I. Higgins (Oxford: Oxford University Press, 1976), pp. 305–9.

has ever been afraid of being himself. And I doubted then that, with his desire to run away spiritually from his race, this boy would ever be a great poet. But this is the mountain standing in the way of any true Negro art in America – this urge within the race toward whiteness, the desire to pour racial individuality into the mold of American standardization, and to be as little Negro and as much American as possible.

But let us look at the immediate background of this young poet. His family is of what I suppose one would call the Negro middle class: people who are by no means rich yet never uncomfortable nor hungry – smug, contented, respectable folk, members of the Baptist church. The father goes to work every morning. He is a chief steward at a large white club. The mother sometimes does fancy sewing or supervises parties for the rich families of the town. The children go to a mixed school. In the home they read white papers and magazines. And the mother often says "Don't be like niggers" when the children are bad. A frequent phrase from the father is, "Look how well a white man does things." And so the word white comes to be unconsciously a symbol of all virtues. It holds for the children beauty, morality, and money. The whisper of "I want to be white" runs silently through their minds. This young poet's home is, I believe, a fairly typical home of the colored middle class. One sees immediately how difficult it would be for an artist born in such a home to interest himself in interpreting the beauty of his own people. He is never taught to see that beauty. He is taught rather not to see it, or if he does, to be ashamed of it when it is not according to Caucasian patterns.

For racial culture the home of a self-styled "high-class" Negro has nothing better to offer. Instead there will perhaps be more aping of things white than in a less cultured or less wealthy home. The father is perhaps a doctor, lawyer, landowner, or policitican. The mother may be a social worker, or a teacher, or she may do nothing and have a maid. Father is often dark but he has usually married the lightest woman he could find. The family attend a fashionable church where few really colored faces are to be found. And they themselves draw a color line. In the North they go to white theatres and white movies. And in the South they have at least two cars and house "like white folks." Nordic manners, Nordic faces, Nordic hair, Nordic art (if any), and an Episcopal heaven. A very high mountain indeed for the would-be racial artist to climb in order to discover himself and his people.

But then there are the low-down folks, the so-called common element, and they are the majority – may the Lord be praised! The people who have their hip of gin on Saturday nights and are not too important to themselves or the community, or too well fed, or too learned to watch the lazy world go round. They live on Seventh Street in Washington or State Street in Chicago and they do not particularly care whether they are like white folks or anybody else. Their joy runs, bang! into ecstasy. Their religion soars to a shout. Work maybe a little today, rest a little tomorrow. Play awhile. Sing awhile. O, let's dance! These common people are not afraid of spirituals, as for a long time their more intellectual brethren were, and jazz is their child. They furnish a wealth of colorful, distinctive material for any artist because they still hold their own individuality in the face of American standardizations. And perhaps these common people will give to the world its truly great Negro artist, the one who is not afraid to be himself. Whereas the better-class Negro would tell the artist what to do, the people at least let him alone when he does appear. And they are not ashamed of him – if they know he exists at all. And they accept what beauty is their own without question.

Certainly there is, for the American Negro artist who can escape the restrictions the more advanced among his own group would put upon him, a great field of unused material ready for his art. Without going outside his race, and even among the better classes with their "white" culture and conscious American manners, but still Negro enough to be different, there is sufficient matter to furnish a black artist with a lifetime of creative work. And when he chooses to touch on the relations between Negroes and whites in this country with their innumerable overtones and undertones surely, and especially for literature and the drama, there is an inexhaustible supply of themes at hand. To these the Negro artist can give his racial individuality, his heritage of rhythm and warmth, and his incongruous humor that so often, as in the Blues, becomes ironic laughter mixed with tears. But let us look again at the mountain.

A prominent Negro clubwoman in Philadelphia paid eleven dollars to hear Raquel Meller sing Andalusian popular songs. But she told me a few weeks before she would not think of going to hear "that woman," Clara Smith, a great black artist, sing Negro folksongs. And many an upper-class Negro church, even now, would not dream of employing a spiritual in its services. The drab melodies in white folks' hymnbooks are much to be preferred. "We want to worship the Lord correctly and quietly. We don't believe in 'shouting.' Let's be dull like the Nordics," they say, in effect.

The road for the serious black artist, then, who would produce a racial art is most certainly rocky and the mountain is high. Until recently he received almost no encouragement for his work from either white or colored people. The fine novels of Chesnutt go out of print with neither race noticing their passing. The quaint charm and humor of Dunbar's dialect verse brought to him, in his day, largely the same kind of encouragement one would give a sideshow freak (A colored man writing poetry! How odd!) or a clown (How amusing!).

The present vogue in things Negro, although it may do as much harm as good for the budding colored artist, has at least done this: it has brought him forcibly to the attention of his own people among whom for so long, unless the other race had noticed him beforehand, he was a prophet with little honor. I understand that Charles Gilpin acted for years in Negro theatres without any special acclaim from his own, but when Broadway gave him eight curtain calls, Negroes, too, began to beat a tin pan in his honor. I know a young colored writer, a manual worker by day, who had been writing well for the colored magazines for some years, but it was not until he recently broke into the white publications and his first book was accepted by a prominent New York publisher that the "best" Negroes in his city took the trouble to discover that he lived there. Then almost immediately they decided to give a grand dinner for him. But the society ladies were careful to whisper to his mother that perhaps she'd better not come. They were not sure she would have an evening gown.

The Negro artist works against an undertow of sharp criticism and misunderstanding from his own group and unintentional bribes from the whites. "Oh, be respectable, write about nice people, show how good we are," say the Negroes. "Be stereotyped, don't go too far, don't shatter our illusions about you, don't amuse us too seriously. We will pay you," say the whites. Both would have told Jean Toomer not to write *Cane*. The colored people did not praise it. The white people did not buy it. Most of the colored people who did read *Cane* hate it. They are afraid of it. Although the critics gave it good reviews the public remained indifferent. Yet (excepting the work of Du Bois) *Cane* contains the finest prose written by a Negro in America. And like the singing of Robeson, it is truly racial.

But in spite of the Nordicized Negro intelligentsia and the desires of some white editors we have an honest American Negro literature already with us. Now I await the rise of the Negro theatre. Our folk music, having achieved world-wide fame, offers itself to the genius of the great individual American composer who is to come. And within the next decade I expect to see the work of a growing school of colored artists who paint and model the beauty of dark faces and create with new technique the expressions of their own soul-world. And the Negro dancers who will dance like flame and the singers who will continue to carry our songs to all who listen – they will be with us in even greater numbers tomorrow.

Most of my own poems are racial in theme and treatment, derived from the life I know. In many of them I try to grasp and hold some of the meanings and rhythms of jazz. I am as sincere as I know how to be in these poems and yet after every reading I answer questions like these from my own people: Do you think Negroes should always write about Negroes? I wish you wouldn't read some of your poems to white folks. How do you find anything interesting in a place like a cabaret? Why do you write about black people? You aren't black. What makes you do so many jazz poems?

But jazz to me is one of the inherent expressions of Negro life in America; the eternal tom-tom beating in the Negro soul – the tom-tom of revolt against weariness in a white world, a world of subway trains, and work, work, work; the tom-tom of joy and laughter, and pain swallowed in a smile. Yet the Philadelphia clubwoman is ashamed to say that her race created it and she does not like me to write about it. The old subconscious "white is best" runs through her mind. Years of study under white teachers, a lifetime of white books, pictures, and papers, and white manners, morals, and Puritan standards made her dislike the spirituals. And now she turns up her nose at jazz and all its manifestations – likewise almost everything else distinctly racial. She doesn't care for the Winold Reiss portraits of Negroes because they are "too Negro." She does not want a true picture of herself from anybody. She wants the artist to flatter her, to make the white world believe that all Negroes are as smug and as near white in soul as she wants to be. But, to my mind, it is the duty of the younger Negro artist, if he accepts any duties at all from outsiders, to change through the force of his art that old whispering "I want to be white," hidden in the aspirations of his people, to "Why should I want to be white? I am a Negro – and beautiful!"

So I am ashamed for the black poet who says, "I want to be a poet, not a Negro poet," as though his own racial world were not as interesting as any other world. I am ashamed, too, for the colored artist who runs from the painting of Negro faces to the painting of sunsets after the manner of the academicians because he fears the strange un-whiteness of his own features. An artist must be free to choose what he does, certainly, but he must also never be afraid to do what he might choose.

Let the blare of Negro jazz bands and the bellowing voice of Bessie Smith singing Blues penetrate the closed ears of the colored near-intellectuals until they listen and perhaps understand. Let Paul Robeson singing "Water Boy," and Rudolph Fisher writing about the streets of Harlem, and Jean Toomer holding the heart of Georgia in his hands, and Aaron Douglas drawing strange black fantasies cause the smug Negro middle class to turn from their white, respectable, ordinary books and papers to catch a glimmer of their own beauty. We younger Negro artists who create now intend to express our individual dark-skinned selves without fear or shame. If white people are pleased we are glad. If they are not, it doesn't matter. We know we are beautiful. And ugly too. The tom-tom cries and the tom-tom laughs. If colored people are pleased we are glad. If they are not, their displeasure doesn't matter either. We build our temples for tomorrow, strong as we know how, and we stand on top of the mountain, free within ourselves.

Chapter 20
Vladimir Mayakovsky

Vladimir Mayakovsky (1893–1930) joined the Bolshevik wing of the Russian Social Democratic party in 1906. He was imprisoned on a number of occasions for his political activities. Shortly after his release from prison in 1910 he met in Moscow the avant-garde painter, David Buryluck, who introduced him to the work of the Futurist group of poets and painters. Politics and poetry, often in heady and volatile mixtures, were to dominate the rest of his life. In 1915 Mayakovsky published A Cloud in Trousers, *a long poem that he described as "four cries" against "your" love, art, order, and religion. He continued to write lyric poetry preoccupied with the equivalence between failure in love and alienation from the world of bourgeois respectability. Mayakovsky welcomed the Russian Revolution and in the years after 1917 he devoted himself to agit-prop poetry that attempted to be both popular and formally innovative. He committed suicide in 1930.*

How Are Verses Made? *was first published in 1926. In the following excerpts, Mayakovsky presents his guidebook for poets who are working in a revolutionary society that has done away with the mystique of poetic creativity or inspiration. Poets are workers in words, and words are a material that can be prepared according to certain techniques. Their obligations are no longer to a tradition but to the desires of a social class. Mayakovsky's revolutionary poetics draw on the preoccupations of Russian Futurism and of modernist arguments about free verse and the poetic image. But his account of the poet as worker carries its own self-parodying energy. Mayakovsky writes his prescriptions in the awareness that they may soon be out of date.*

From *How Are Verses Made?*

. . . Neologisms are obligatory in writing poetry. The material of words and phrases that falls to the poet must be reworked. If old scraps of words present themselves in the

From *How Are Verses Made?*, trans. G. M. Hyde (Bristol: Bristol Classical Press, 1990), pp. 48–51, 68–70, 78–81, 88–90.

composition of a poem, they must be used in strict proportion to the quantities of new material. Alloys of this kind are useful or not according to the quantity and quality of the new material in them.

Innovation, of course, doesn't imply the constant utterance of undreamed-of truths. The iambus, free verse, alliteration, assonance aren't invented every day. Work can be done on them, too, extending, going deeper, spreading wider in application.

'Twice two is four' – it doesn't live on its own, and it can't. You must know how to apply this truth (rules of application). You must make it memorable (more rules). You must show that it is irrefutable with a wealth of illustrative facts (example, content, theme).

From this it is clear that the depletion and representation of reality have no place in poetry on their own account. Work of that kind is necessary, but it must be evaluated as if it were the work of the secretary of a mass-meeting. It's just a matter of 'They listened, they made resolutions'. That's the tragedy of the fellow-travellers: they heard five years ago and made their proposals a bit late – when all the rest had already implemented them.

Poetry is at its very roots tendentious.

In my opinion, the line: 'I walk alone into the road' constitutes agitation: the poet agitates for girls to walk with him. It's boring, you see, on your own! Ah, if only there were poetry as powerful as this calling people together into co-operatives!

The old textbooks on writing poetry, of course, weren't like that. They describe only a historical and already accepted mode of writing. Actually these books shouldn't be called 'how to write' but 'how they used to write'.

I'll be honest with you. I know nothing of iambuses or trochees, I've never differentiated between them and I never will. Not because it's hard work, but because in my work I've had no occasion to concern myself with such things. And if snatches of such metres can be found, they've been written entirely by ear, because these time-worn patterns are encountered extraordinarily frequently... like 'Down mother Volga's mighty stream'.

I've several times got down to studying this, understood the mechanics of it, and then forgotten again. Things like this, which take up ninety per cent of poetry textbooks, are about three per cent of my practical work!

In poetical work there are only a few general rules about how to begin. And these rules are a pure convention. Like in chess. The opening gambits are almost identical. But already from the next move you begin to think up a new attack. The most inspired move can't be repeated in any given situation in your next game. Only its unexpectedness defeats the opponent.

Just like the unexpected rhymes in poetry.

What basic propositions are indispensable, when one begins poetical work?

First thing. The presence of a problem society, the solution of which is conceivable only in poetical terms. A social command. (An interesting theme for special study would be the disparity between the social command and actual commissions.)

Second thing. An exact knowledge, or rather sense, of the desires of your class (or the group you represent) on a given question, i.e. an orientation towards an objective.

Third thing. Materials. Words. Fill your storehouse constantly, fill the granaries of your skull with all kinds of words, necessary, expressive, rare, invented, renovated and manufactured.

Fourth thing. Equipment for the plant and tools for the assembly line. A pen, a pencil, a typewriter, a telephone, an outfit for your visits to the doss-house, a bicycle for your trips to the publishers, a table in good order, an umbrella for writing in the rain, a room measuring the exact number of paces you have to take when you're working, connection with a press agency to send you information on questions of concern to the provinces and so on and so forth, and even a pipe and cigarettes.

Fifth thing. Skills and techniques of handling words, extremely personal things, which come only with years of daily work: rhymes, metres, alliteration, images, lowering of style, pathos, closure, finding a title, layout, and so on and so forth.

For example: the social task may be to provide the words for a song for the Red Army men on their way to the Petersburg front. The objective is to defeat Yudenich. The material is words from the vocabulary of soldiers. The tools of production – a pencil stub. The device – the rhymed *chastushka.*

The result:

My darling gave me a long felt cloak
And a pair of woolly socks.
Yudenich scurries from Petersburg
Fast as a smoked-out fox.

The originality of the quatrain, warranting the production of this *chastushka*, lies in the rhyming of 'woolly socks' and 'smoked-out fox'. It's this novelty that makes the thing relevant, poetical, and typical.

The effect of the *chastushka* depends on the device of unexpected rhymes where there is disharmony between the first pair of lines and the second. Thus the first two lines can be called subsidiary, or auxiliary.

Even these general and basic rules of poetic practice offer greater possibilities than we now have for labelling and classifying poetic works.

Aspects of the material used, the means of production and the technical skills can simply be regarded as quantifiable on a points system.

Did society demand this? It did. Two points. An objective? Two points. Is it rhymed? Another point. Is there alliteration? Another half-point. And another point for the rhythm – since its strange movement necessitated bus journeys.

Let the critics smile, but I would rate the poetry of any Alaskan poet (other things being equal of course) higher than, let's say, the work of a poet from Yalta.

Well of course! The Alaskan must freeze, and buy a fur coat, and his ink solidifies in his fountain-pen. Whereas the Yalta poet writes against a background of palm trees, in surroundings which are nice even without poems.

Clear-sightedness about such matters is a component of a writer's qualifications. . . .

I walk along, waving my arms and mumbling almost wordlessly, now shortening my steps so as not to interrupt my mumbling, now mumbling more rapidly in time with my steps.

So the rhythm is established and takes shape – and rhythm is the basis of any poetic work, resounding through the whole thing. Gradually you ease individual words free of this dull roar.

Several words just jump away and never come back, others hold on, wriggle and squirm a dozen times over, until you can't imagine how any word will ever stay in its place (this sensation, developing with experience, is called talent). More often than not the most important word emerges first: the word that most completely conveys the meaning of the poem, or the word that underpins the rhyme. The other words come forward and take up dependent positions in relation to the most important word. When the fundamentals are already there, one has a sudden sensation that the rhythm is strained: there's some little syllable or sound missing. You begin to shape all the words anew, and the work drives you to distraction. It's like having a tooth crowned. A hundred times (or so it seems) the dentist tries a crown on the tooth, and it's the wrong size; but at last, after a hundred attempts, he presses one down, and it fits. The analogy is all the more apposite in my case, because when at last the crown fits, I (quite literally) have tears in my eyes, from pain and relief.

Where this basic dull roar of a rhythm comes from is a mystery. In my case it's all kinds of repetitions in my mind of sounds, noises, rocking motions, or in fact of any perceptible repetition which comes to me as a sound shape. The sound of the sea, endlessly repeated, can provide my rhythm, or a servant who slams the door every morning, recurring and intertwining with itself, trailing through my consciousness; or even the rotation of the earth, which in my case, as in a shop full of visual aids, gives way to, and inextricably connects with, the whistle of a high wind.

This struggle to organize movement, to organize sounds around oneself, discovering their intrinsic nature, their peculiarities, is one of the most important constants of the work of the poet: laying in rhythmic supplies. I don't know if the rhythm exists outside me or only inside me – more probably inside. But there must be a jolt to awaken it; in the same way as the sound of a violin, any violin, provokes a buzz in the guts of the piano, in the same way as a bridge sways to and fro and threatens to collapse under the synchronized tread of ants.

Rhythm is the fundamental force, the fundamental energy of verse. You can't explain it, you can only talk about it as you do about magnetism or electricity. Magnetism and electricity are manifestations of energy. The rhythm can be the same in a lot of poems, even in the whole oeuvre of the poet, and still not make his work monotonous, because a rhythm can be so complex, so intricately shaped, that even several long poems won't exhaust its possibilities.

A poet must develop just this feeling for rhythm in himself, and not go learning up other people's measurements: iambus, trochee or even this much-vaunted free verse: rhythm accommodating itself to some concrete situation, and of use only for that concrete situation. Like, for example, magnetic energy discharged on to a horseshoe, which will attract iron filings, but which you can't use for anything else.

I know nothing of metre. Only I'm convinced, on my own account, that to communicate heroic or majestic sentiments, you must choose long measures with a large collection of syllables, and for cheerful sentiments, short ones. For some reason or other I have associated the former since childhood (from the age of nine) with:

As a sacrifice you fell in that fateful struggle...

and the latter with:

Let's bid the old world farewell...

Curious. But, word of honour, that's how it is.

I get my metre by covering this rhythmical roar with words, words suggested by the objective (all the time you ask yourself: is this the word I want? Who must I read it to? Will it be understood in the right way? and so on.) – and with words that are regulated by a highly developed sense of appropriateness, by one's abilities, and one's talent....

You have to bring the poem to the highest pitch of expressiveness. One of the most noteworthy vehicles of this expressiveness is the image. Not that essential visionary image which rises up at the beginning of one's work as a first, dim response to the social command. No, I'm talking about the auxiliary images which help this central image to take shape. These images are one of the contemporary methods of poetry, and a movement like Imaginism, for instance, making them instead the goal, has in essence condemned itself to working on just one of poetry's technical components.

There are endless ways of fabricating images.

One of the most primitive ways of making an image is by comparison. My first things, 'A Cloud in Trousers' for example, were entirely based on similes – 'like, like and like' all the time. Isn't it just this primitive quality that makes later critics consider my 'Cloud' my 'ultimate synthesis' in poetry? In my most recent things and in my 'Esenin', of course, I've got rid of this primitivism. I've discovered only one comparison:

'Drawn-out and droning like Doronin's attempts.'

Why like Doronin, and not like the distance to the moon, for example? In the first place, a comparison is drawn from literary life because my whole subject is literary. And in the second place, 'The Ploughman of Steel' (is that what it's called?) is longer than the journey to the moon, because that journey is unreal, and 'The Ploughman of Steel' is, alas, real; then the journey to the moon would seem shorter because of its novelty, while Doronin's four thousand lines afflict you with the monotony of a verbal and metrical landscape you've seen sixteen thousand times before. And then of course the image must be tendentious, that is, elaborating a large subject, and you must use separate little images that you come across along the way to help in the struggle, in your literary agitation.

The most commonly accepted way of making images is by the use of a metaphor, that is, by transferring attributes, which up to the present have been associated with certain things only, to other words, things, phenomena and notions.

For instance the metaphorical line:

And they bear funereal scraps of verse.

We've heard of scrap-iron, and of table-scraps. But how are we to describe those odds and ends of poetry, left over otiosely, which can't be made use of anywhere else when they've been part of other poems already? These, of course, are scrap verse, or verse-scraps. And in this case, the scrap is all of one kind – funereal, these are funereal verse-scraps. We can't leave the line like that, because we get 'verse-scraps', which, when you read it, sounds like 'verse-crap', and there's what the Formalists call a 'shift', which ruins the line from the point of view of the sense. That kind of carelessness is very common.

For example in a lyrical poem of Utkin's printed not long ago in the journal *Projector* there are the lines:

> He comes again no more, ah
> So the swan comes not when lakes freeze hard as glass.

You can distinctly hear the word 'arse'.

The first line of a poem published by Bryusov in the early days of the war, in the journal *Our Times*, is particularly effective:

> We were a regiment who learnt what pain meant.

The 'shift' is neutralised if you give a simpler, more telling order to the words –

> funereal scraps of verse

One way of making an image, the one I've most often adopted recently, is by describing the most fantastic events and facts, reinforced by exaggeration.

> So that Kogan scattered that way and this
> Impaling passers-by on his moustache's bayonets.

In this way Kogan becomes a collectivity, which allows him to run in all directions, his moustaches turn into bayonets, and to intensify the idea of bayonets people lie around, run through by his moustaches.

Ways of forming images vary, like all the other devices of poetry, according to how familiar or over-familiar the reader is with one form or another.

You can have imagery on the opposite principle, such that it not only doesn't enlarge the scope of what's said, by means of the imagination, but on the contrary tries to squeeze the impression made by the words into a deliberately limited framework. For example, in my old poem 'War and the Universe':

> In the rotting waggon were forty men –
> And four legs.

Many of Selvinsky's things are based on numerical images of this kind.

After that comes the work of selecting your verbal material. You have to take accurate stock of the milieu in which your poetical work is being carried on, so that no word foreign to these conditions can get in by accident.

For example, I had the line:

> What things, my dear friend, you knew of.

'My dear friend' is false, firstly because it goes clean against the stern, accusatory development of the poem; secondly because we have never used this locution in our poetic circles. Thirdly, it's petty, and often employed in meaningless conversations, and used more often to suppress feelings than to show them more clearly. Fourthly, a man who is truly grief-stricken will find a much harsher word to take refuge behind. In any case, this word doesn't specify *what* the man knew of – *what* did you know of, Esenin? . . .

Some conclusions:

1. Poetry is a manufacture. A very difficult, very complex kind, but a manufacture.
2. Instruction in poetical work doesn't consist in the study of already fixed and delimited models of poetical works, but a study of the procedures of manufacture, a study that helps us to make new things.
3. Innovation, innovation in materials and devices, is a *sine qua non* of every poetical composition.
4. The work of the verse-maker must be carried on daily, to perfect his craft, and to lay in poetical supplies.
5. A good notebook and an understanding of how to make use of it are more important than knowing how to write faultlessly in worn-out metres.
6. Don't set in motion a huge poetry factory just to make poetic cigarette lighters. You must renounce the uneconomical production of poetical trifles. Reach for your pen only when there is no other way of saying something except verse. You must work up things you've prepared only when you feel a clear social command.
7. To understand the social command accurately, a poet must be in the middle of things and events. A knowledge of theoretical economics, a knowledge of the realities of everyday life, an immersion in the scientific study of history are for the poet, in the very fundamentals of his work, more important than scholarly textbooks by idealist professors who worship the past.
8. To fulfil the social command as well as possible you must be in the vanguard of your class, and carry on the struggle, along with your class, on all fronts. You must smash to smithereens the myth of an apolitical art. This old myth is appearing again now in a new form under cover of twaddle about 'broad epic canvases' (first epic, then objective, and in the end politically uncommitted), or about the 'grand style' (first grand, then elevated, and in the end celestial) and so on and so forth.
9. Only by approaching art as a manufacture can you eliminate chance, arbitrariness of taste and subjectivity of values. Only by regarding it as part of the productive process can you get the different aspects of literary work in perspective: poems, and reports by workers' and peasants' journalists. Instead of mystically pondering a poetic

theme you will have the power to tackle a pressing problem with accuracy, according to the poetic tariffs and standards.

10. You mustn't make the manufacturing, the so-called technical process, an end in itself. But it *is* this process of manufacture that makes the poetic work fit for use. It's the difference just in these methods of production that marks the difference between poets, and only a knowledge, a mastery, an accumulation of the widest possible range of varied literary devices makes a man a professional writer.

11. The everyday circumstances of poetry have as much influence on the composition of a real work of art as other factors do. The word 'Bohemian' has become a term of opprobrium describing every artistic-Philistine way of life. Unfortunately war has often been waged on the *word* 'Bohemian', and only on the word. But what remains actively with us is the individualist and careerist atmosphere of the old literary world, the petty interests of malevolent coteries, mutual back-scratching; and the word 'poetical' has come to mean 'lax', 'a bit drunk', 'debauched' and so on. Even the way a poet dresses and the way he talks to his wife at home has to be different, and entirely dictated by the kind of poetry he writes.

12. We, the poets of the Left Front never claim that we alone possess the secrets of poetical creativity. But we are the only ones who want to lay these secrets open, the only ones who don't want to surround the creative process with a catchpenny religio-artistic aura of sanctity....

Chapter 21
I. A. Richards

Ivor Armstrong Richards (1893–1979) was a literary critic and theorist who played a formative role in the invention of literary study as a modern academic discipline. Richards rejected the idea of a criticism based upon judgments of taste alone and in three works, The Principles of Literary Criticism *(1924),* Science and Poetry *(1926), and* Practical Criticism *(1929), he set out the concepts and procedures for the study of literature as a discipline that could only be understood in the context of a general theory of communication. He was one of the pioneers of the method of "close reading" that has since become a standard practice in school and university classrooms in Britain and the United States. In 1931 he began working at Harvard University and was a professor there from 1943 to 1963.*

The two excerpts included here come from Science and Poetry. *In the first excerpt Richards sets out a twentieth-century defence of poetry by drawing on his work as a psychologist to explain the mental processes involved in reading a poem. He puts forward his central claim that reading poetry is valuable because it brings into balance competing "interests" or impulses seeking satisfaction. In the second excerpt he argues that poetry does not have to meet scientific criteria for truthfulness. Instead, poetry makes "pseudo-statements" which have a therapeutic value that is independent of their truth or falsity.*

The Poetic Experience

Extraordinary claims have often been made for poetry... claims which very many people are inclined to view with astonishment or with the smile which tolerance gives to the enthusiast. Indeed a more representative modern view would be that the future of poetry is *nil.* Peacock's conclusion in his *The Four Ages of Poetry* finds a

From *Selected Works of I. A. Richards,* vol. 3: *Principles of Literary Criticism,* ed. John Constable (London: Routledge, 2001), Appendix 3.

more general acceptance. 'A poet in our times is a semi-barbarian in a civilized community. He lives in the days that are past...In whatever degree poetry is cultivated, it must necessarily be to the neglect of some branch of useful study... Poetry was the mental rattle that awakened the attention of intellect in the infancy of civil society: but for the maturity of mind to make a serious business of the playthings of its childhood, is as absurd as for a grown man to rub his gums with coral, and cry to be charmed asleep by the jingle of silver bells.' And with more regret many others... have thought that the inevitable effect of the advance of science would be to destroy the possibility of poetry.

What is the truth in this matter? How is our estimate of poetry going to be affected by science? And how will poetry itself be influenced? The extreme importance which has in the past been assigned to poetry is a fact which must be accounted for whether we conclude that it was rightly assigned or not, and whether we consider that poetry will continue to be held in such esteem or not. It indicates that the case for poetry, whether right or wrong, is one which turns on momentous issues. We shall not have dealt adequately with it unless we have raised questions of great significance.

Very much toil has gone to the endeavour to explain the high place of poetry in human affairs, with, on the whole, few satisfactory or convincing results. This is not surprising. For in order to show how poetry is important it is first necessary to discover to some extent what it is. Until recently this preliminary task could only be very incompletely carried out; the psychology of instinct and emotion was too little advanced; and, moreover, the wild speculations natural in pre-scientific enquiry definitely stood in the way. Neither the professional psychologist, whose interest in poetry is frequently not intense, nor the man of letters, who as a rule has no adequate ideas of the mind as a whole, has been equipped for the investigation. Both a passionate knowledge of poetry and a capacity for dispassionate psychological analysis are required if it is to be satisfactorily prosecuted.

It will be best to begin by asking 'What *kind of a thing*, in the widest sense, is poetry?' When we have answered this we shall be ready to ask 'How can we use and misuse it?' and 'What reasons are there for thinking it valuable?'

Let us take an experience, ten minutes of a person's life, and describe it in broad outline. It is now possible to indicate its general structure, to point out what is important in it, what trivial and accessory, which features depend upon which, how it has arisen, and how it is probably going to influence his future experience. There are, of course, wide gaps in this description, none the less it *is* at last possible to understand in general how the mind works in an experience, and what sort of stream of events experience is.

A poem, let us say Wordsworth's *Westminster Bridge* sonnet, is such an experience, it is the experience the right kind of reader has when he peruses the verses. And the first step to an understanding of the place and future of poetry in human affairs is to see what the general structure of such an experience is. Let us begin by reading it very slowly, preferably aloud, giving every syllable time to make its full effect upon us. And let us read it experimentally, repeating it, varying our tone of voice until we are satisfied that we have caught its rhythm as well as we are able, and – whether our reading is such as to please other people or not – we ourselves at least are certain how it should "go."

Earth has not anything to show more fair:
Dull would he be of soul who could pass by
A sight so touching in its majesty:
This City now doth like a garment wear
The beauty of the morning: silent, bare,
Ships, towers, domes, theatres and temples lie
Open to the fields, and to the sky;
All bright and glittering in the smokeless air.
Never did sun more beautifully steep
In his first splendour valley, rock or hill;
Ne'er saw I, never felt, a calm so deep!
The river glideth at its own sweet will:
Dear God! the very houses seem asleep
And all that mighty heart is lying still!

We may best make our analysis of the experience that arises through reading these lines from the surface inwards, to speak metaphorically. The surface is the impression of the printed words on the retina. This sets up an agitation which we must follow as it goes deeper and deeper.

The first things to occur (if they do not, the rest of the experience will be gravely inadequate) are the sound of the words 'in the mind's ear' and the feel of the words imaginarily spoken. These together give the *full body*, as it were, to the words, and it is with the full bodies of words that the poet works, not with their printed signs. But many people lose nearly everything in poetry through these indispensable parts escaping them.

Next arise various pictures 'in the mind's eye'; not of words but of things for which the words stand; perhaps of ships, perhaps of hills; and together with them, it may be, other images of various sorts. Images of what it feels like to stand leaning on the parapet of Westminster Bridge. Perhaps that odd thing an image of 'silence'. But, unlike the image-bodies of the words themselves, those other images of things are not vitally important. Those who have them may very well think them indispensable, and *for them* they may be necessary; but other people may not require them at all. This is a point at which differences between individual minds are very marked.

Thence onwards the agitation which is the experience divides into a major and a minor branch, though the two streams have innumerable interconnections and influence one another intimately. Indeed it is only as an expositor's artifice that we may speak of them as two streams.

The minor branch we may call the intellectual stream; the other, which we may call the active, or emotional, stream, is made up of the play of our interests.

The intellectual stream is fairly easy to follow; it follows itself, so to speak; but it is the less important of the two. In poetry it matters only *as a means*; it directs and excites the active stream. It is made up of thoughts, which are not static little entities that bob up into consciousness and down again out of it, but fluent happenings, events, which reflect or point to the things the thoughts are 'of'. Exactly how they do this is a matter which is still much disputed.

This pointing to or reflecting things is all that thoughts do. They appear to do much more; which is our chief illusion. The realm of thought is never a sovereign state. Our thoughts are the servants of our interests, and even when they seem to rebel it is usually our interests that are in disorder. Our thoughts are pointers and it is the other, the active, stream which deals with the things which thoughts reflect or point to.

Some people who read verse (they do not often read much of it), are so constituted that very little more happens than this intellectual stream of thoughts. It is perhaps superfluous to point out that they miss the real poem. To exaggerate this part of the experience, and give it too much importance on its own account, is a notable current tendency, and for many people explains why they do not read poetry.

The active branch is what really matters; for from it all the energy of the whole agitation comes. The thinking which goes on is somewhat like the play of an ingenious and invaluable 'governor' run by but controlling the main machine. Every experience is essentially some interest or group of interests swinging back to rest.

To understand what an interest is we should picture the mind as a system of very delicately poised balances, a system which so long as we are in health is constantly growing. Every situation we come into disturbs some of these balances to some degree. The ways in which they swing back to a new equipoise are the impulses with which we respond to the situation. And the chief balances in the system are our chief interests.

Suppose that we carry a magnetic compass about in the neighbourhood of powerful magnets. The needle waggles as we move and comes to rest pointing in a new direction whenever we stand still in a new position. Suppose that instead of a single compass we carry an arrangement of many magnetic needles, large and small, swung so that they influence one another, some able only to swing horizontally, others vertically, others hung freely. As we move, the perturbations in this system will be very complicated. But for every position in which we place it there will be a final position of rest for all the needles into which they will in the end settle down, a general poise for the whole system. But even a slight displacement may set the whole assemblage of needles busily readjusting themselves.

One further complication. Suppose that while all the needles influence one another, some of them respond only to some of the outer magnets among which the system is moving. The reader can easily draw a diagram if his imagination needs a visual support.

The mind is not unlike such a system if we imagine it to be incredibly complex. The needles are our interests, varying in their importance, that is in the degree to which any movement they make involves movement in the other needles. Each new disequilibrium, which a shift of position, a fresh situation, entails, corresponds to a need; and the wagglings which ensue as the system rearranges itself are our responses, the impulses through which we seek to meet the need. Often the new poise is not found until long after the original disturbance. Thus states of strain can arise which last for years. . . .

We must picture then the stream of the poetic experience as the swinging back into equilibrium of these disturbed interests. We are reading the poem in the first place only because we are in some way interested in doing so, only because some interest is attempting to regain its poise thereby. And whatever happens as we read happens only for a similar reason. We understand the words (the intellectual branch of the stream goes on its way successfully) only because an interest is reacting through that means, and all the rest of the experience is equally but more evidently our adaptation working itself out.

The rest of the experience is made up of emotions and attitudes. Emotions are what the reaction, with its reverberation in bodily changes, feels like. Attitudes are the impulses towards one kind of behaviour or another which are set ready by the response. They are, as it were, its outward going part. Sometimes, as here in *Westminster Bridge*, they are very easily overlooked. But consider a simpler case – a fit of laughter which it is absolutely essential to conceal, in Church or during a solemn interview, for example. You contrive not to laugh; but there is no doubt about the activity of the impulses in their restricted form. The much more subtle and elaborate impulses which a poem excites are not different in principle. They do not show themselves as a rule, they do not come out into the open, largely because they are so complex. When they have adjusted themselves to one another and become organized into a coherent whole, the needs concerned may be satisfied. *In a fully developed man a state of readiness for action will take the place of action when the full appropriate situation for action is not present.* The essential peculiarity of poetry as of all the arts is that the full appropriate situation is *not* present. It is an *actor* we are seeing upon the stage, not Hamlet. So readiness for action takes the place of actual behaviour. . . .

. . . [W]hy is it essential in reading poetry to give the words their full imagined sound and body? What is meant by saying that the poet works with this sound and body? The answer is that even before the words have been intellectually understood and the thoughts they occasion formed and followed, the movement and sound of the words is playing deeply and intimately upon the interests. How this happens is a matter which has yet to be successfully investigated, but that it happens no sensitive reader of poetry doubts. A good deal of poetry and even some great poetry exists . . . in which the sense of the words can be *almost* entirely missed or neglected without loss. Never perhaps entirely without effort however; though sometimes with advantage. But the plain fact that the relative importance of grasping the sense of the words may vary . . . is enough for our purpose here.

In nearly all poetry the sound and feel of the words, what is often called the *form* of the poem in opposition to its *content*, get to work first, and the sense in which the words are taken is subtly influenced by this fact. Most words are ambiguous as regards their plain sense, especially in poetry. We can take them as we please in a variety of senses. The sense we are pleased to choose is the one which most suits the impulses already stirred through the form of the verse. The same thing can be noticed in conversation. Not the strict logical sense of what is said, but the tone of voice and the occasion are the primary factors by which we interpret. Science, it is worth noting, endeavours with increasing success to bar out these factors. We believe a scientist because he can substantiate his remarks, not because he is eloquent or forcible in his enunciation. In fact, we distrust him when he seems to be influencing us by his manner.

In its use of words poetry is just the reverse of science. Very definite thoughts do occur, but not because the words are so chosen as logically to bar out all possibilities but one. No. But because the manner, the tone of voice, the cadence and the rhythm play upon our interests and make *them* pick out from among an indefinite number of possibilities the precise particular thought which they need. This is why poetical descriptions often seem so much more accurate than prose descriptions. Language logically and scientifically used cannot describe a landscape or a face. To do so it would need a prodigious apparatus of names for shades and nuances, for precise particular qualities. These names do not exist, so other means have to be used. The poet, even when, like Ruskin or De Quincey, he writes in prose, makes the reader pick out the precise particular sense required from an indefinite number of possible senses which a word, phrase or sentence may carry. The means by which he does this are many and varied. Some of them have been mentioned above, but the way in which he uses them is the poet's own secret, something which cannot be taught. He knows how to do it, but he does not himself know how it is done.

Misunderstanding and under-estimation of poetry is mainly due to over-estimation of the thought in it. We can see still more clearly that thought is not the prime factor if we consider for a moment not the experience of the reader but that of the poet. Why does the poet use these words and no others? Not because they stand for a series of thoughts which in themselves are what he is concerned to communicate. It is never what a poem *says* which matters, but what it *is*. The poet is not writing as a scientist. He uses these words because the interests which the situation calls into play combine to bring them, just in this form, into his consciousness *as a means of ordering, controlling and consolidating* the whole experience. The experience itself, the tide of impulses sweeping through the mind, is the source and the sanction of the words. They represent this experience itself, not any set of perceptions or reflections, though often to a reader who approaches the poem wrongly they will seem to be only a series of remarks about other things. But to a suitable reader the words – if they actually spring from experience and are not due to verbal habits, to the desire to be effective, to factitious excogitation, to imitation, to irrelevant contrivances, or to any other of the failings which prevent most people from writing poetry – the words will reproduce in his mind a similar play of interests putting him for the while into a similar situation and leading to the same response....

Poetry and Beliefs

...Roughly and inadequately, even in the light of our present knowledge, we can say that words work in the poem in two main fashions. As sensory stimuli and as (in the *widest* sense) symbols. We must refrain from considering the sensory side of the poem, remarking only that it is *not* in the least independent of the other side, and that it has for definite reasons prior importance in most poetry. We must confine ourselves to the other function of words in the poem, or rather, omitting much that is of secondary relevance, to one form of that function, let me call it *pseudo-statement.*

It will be admitted – by those who distinguish between scientific statement, where truth is ultimately a matter of verification as this is understood in the laboratory, and emotive utterance, where 'truth' is primarily acceptability *by* some attitude, and more remotely is the acceptability *of* this attitude itself – that it is *not* the poet's business to make true statements. Yet poetry has constantly the air of making statements, and important ones; which is one reason why some mathematicians cannot read it. They find the alleged statements to be *false*. It will be agreed that their approach to poetry and their expectations from it are mistaken. But what exactly is the other, the right, the poetic, approach and how does it differ from the mathematical?

The poetic approach evidently limits the framework of possible consequences into which the pseudo-statement is taken. For the scientific approach this framework is unlimited. Any and every consequence is relevant. If any of the consequences of a statement conflicts with acknowledged fact then so much the worse for the statement. Not so with the pseudo-statement when poetically approached. The problem is – just how does the limitation work? The usual account is in terms of a supposed universe of discourse, a world of make-believe, of imagination, of recognised fictions common to the poet and his readers. A pseudo-statement which fits into this system of assumptions would be regarded as 'poetically true'; one which does not, as 'poetically false'. This attempt to treat 'poetic truth' on the model of general 'coherence theories' is very natural for certain schools of logicians: but is inadequate, on the wrong lines from the outset. To mention two objections out of many; there is no means of discovering what the 'universe of discourse' is on any occasion, and the kind of coherence which must hold within it, supposing it to be discoverable, is not an affair of logical relations. Attempt to define the system of propositions into which

'O Rose, thou art sick!'

must fit, and the logical relations which must hold between them if it is to be 'poetically true'; the absurdity of the theory becomes evident.

We must look further. In the poetic approach the relevant consequences are not logical or to be arrived at by a partial relaxation of logic. Except occasionally and by accident logic does not enter at all. They are the consequences which arise through our emotional organisation. The acceptance which a pseudo-statement receives is entirely governed by its effects upon our feelings and attitudes. Logic only comes in, if at all, in subordination, as a servant to our emotional response. It is an unruly servant, however, as poets and readers are constantly discovering. A pseudo-statement is 'true' if it suits and serves some attitude or links together attitudes which on other grounds are desirable. This kind of truth is so opposed to scientific 'truth' that it is a pity to use so similar a word, but at present it is difficult to avoid the malpractice.

This brief analysis may be sufficient to indicate the fundamental disparity and opposition between pseudo-statements as they occur in poetry and statements as they occur in science. A pseudo-statement is a form of words which is justified entirely by its effect in releasing or organizing our impulses and attitudes (due regard being had for the better or worse organizations of these *inter se*); a statement, on the other hand, is justified by its truth, *i.e.* its correspondence, in a highly technical sense, with the fact to which it points.

Statements true and false alike do of course constantly touch off attitudes and action. Our daily practical existence is largely guided by them. On the whole true statements are of more service to us than false ones. None the less we do not and, at present, cannot order our emotions and attitudes by true statements alone. Nor is there any probability that we ever shall contrive to do so. This is one of the great new dangers to which civilisation is exposed. Countless pseudo-statements – about God, about the universe, about human nature, the relations of mind to mind, about the soul, its rank and destiny – pseudo-statements which are pivotal points in the organization of the mind, vital to its well-being, have suddenly become, for sincere, honest and informal minds, impossible to believe. For centuries they have been believed; now they are gone, irrecoverably; and the knowledge which has killed them is not of a kind upon which an equally fine organization of the mind can be based.

This is the contemporary situation. The remedy, since there is no prospect of our gaining adequate knowledge, and since indeed it is fairly clear that genuine knowledge cannot serve us here and can only increase our practical control of Nature, is to cut our pseudo-statements free from belief, and yet retain them, in this released state, as the main instruments by which we order our attitudes to one another and to the world. Not so desperate a remedy as may appear, for poetry conclusively shows that even the most important among our attitudes can be aroused and maintained without any belief entering in at all. Those of Tragedy, for example. We need no beliefs, and indeed we must have none, if we are to read *King Lear.* Pseudo-statements to which we attach no belief and statements proper such as science provides cannot conflict. It is only when we introduce illicit beliefs into poetry that danger arises. To do so is from this point of view a profanation of poetry....

Chapter 22
Robert Graves and Laura Riding

Robert Graves (1895–1985) and Laura Riding (1901–91) first met in 1926 when Riding moved from the United States to work as Graves's secretary. Their emotionally charged and turbulent relationship lasted until 1938, when Riding returned to the United States. For much of that time they lived in Deya, Majorca, where they founded a press, wrote poetry, and, in Graves's case, some commercially successful historical fiction. Riding had a formative influence on Graves's career, introducing him to the work of modernist poets such as E. E. Cummings and instilling in him a belief in the necessity of an absolute devotion to a female muse. Riding's influence led in 1948 to the publication by Graves of The White Goddess, *a learned and question-begging "historical grammar of poetic myth." Riding gave up writing poetry on her return to the States and devoted her time to work in the philosophy of language. One result of that work was the posthumous publication in 1997 of* Rational Meaning, *a book co-authored with her husband, Schuyler Jackson.*

Graves and Riding first published A Survey of Modernist Poetry *in 1927. It is one of the earliest critical assessments of modernist poetry and its analytic method influenced William Empson's thinking about ambiguity in poetry. In the first excerpt, from chapter 1 of the book, Graves and Riding test the claims of modernist poetry on the "plain reader" through a close analysis and rewriting of E. E. Cummings's poem, "Sunset." In the second, from chapter 7, they explore the cultural meanings of the term "modernism," and attempt to distinguish authentic from inauthentic forms of modern poetry.*

Modernist Poetry and the Plain Reader's Rights

It must be assumed for the moment that poetry not characteristically "modernist" presents no difficulty to the plain reader; for the complaint against modernist poetry turns on its differences from traditional poetry. These differences would seem to justify themselves if their effect was to bring poetry any nearer the plain reader; even traditional poetry, it is sometimes charged, has a tendency to withdraw itself from

From *A Survey of Modernist Poetry* (New York: Haskell House, 1969), pp. 9–21, 22–6, 155–8, 160–3.

the plain reader. But the sophistications of advanced modern poetry seem only to make the breach wider. In the poetry of E. E. Cummings, for example, who may be considered conveniently to illustrate the divorce of advanced contemporary poetry from the common-sense standards of ordinary intelligence, is to be found apparently not only a disregard of this intelligence, but an insult to it. Such poetry seems to say: "Keep out. This is a private performance."

What we have to do, then, is to discover whether or not the poet means to keep the public out. If, after a careful examination of poems that seem to be only part of the game of high-brow baiting low-brow, they still resist all reasonable efforts, then we must conclude that such work is, after all, merely a joke at the plain reader's expense and let him return to his newspapers and to his Shakespeare (who we are for the moment assuming is understood without difficulty). But if, on the other hand, we are able to get out of these poems the experiences we are accustomed to expect of poetry, or at least see that the poet originally wrote them as poetry and not as literary tricks, then the plain reader must make certain important alterations in his critical attitude. In the first place, he must admit that what is called our common intelligence is the mind in its least active state: that poetry obviously demands a more vigorous imaginative effort than the plain reader has been willing to apply to it; and that, if anthologies compiled to refresh tired minds have indulged his lazy reading habits, the poet can be excused for using exceptional means to make him do justice to his poems, even for inventing a new kind of poem in this end. Next he must wonder whether such innovations have not a real place in the normal course of poetry-writing. Finally, if these things are so, he must question the depth of his understanding of the poetry which, like Shakespeare's, is taken for granted and ask whether a poet like E. E. Cummings must not be accepted, if not for his own sake, at least for his effect on the future reading of poetry of any age or style.

To begin with, we shall choose one of E. E. Cummings' earlier and simpler poems, one which will nevertheless excite much the same hostility as his later work. It is unusually suitable for analysis, because it is on just the kind of subject that the plain reader looks for in poetry. . . .

Sunset

stinging
gold swarms
upon the spires
silver

        chants the litanies the
great bells are ringing with rose
the lewd fat bells
                and a tall

wind
is dragging
the

sea
with

dream

-S

With so promising a title, what barriers does the poem raise between itself and the plain reader? In what respects does it seem to sin against the common intelligence? To begin with, the lines do not begin with capitals. The spacing does not suggest any regular verse-form, though it seems to be systematic. No punctuation marks are used. There is no obvious grammar either of the prose or of the poetic kind. But even overlooking these technical oddities, it still seems impossible to read the poem as a logical sequence. A great many words essential to the coherence of the ideas suggested have been deliberately omitted; and the entire effect is so sketchy that the poem might be made to mean almost anything or nothing. If the author once had a precise meaning it was lost in the writing of the poem. Let us, however, assume for the sake of this argument that it is possible to discover the original poem at the back of the poet's mind; or at least to gather enough material from the poem as it stands from which to make a poem that would satisfy all formal requirements, the poem that Cummings perhaps meant to hint at with these fragments. Just as the naturalist Cuvier could reconstruct an extinct animal in full anatomical detail from a single tooth, let us restore this extinct poem from what Cummings has permitted to survive.

First we must decide if there are not positive features in the poem which make it possible to judge it in these respects as a formal poem and which should occur in any rewriting of the poem with much the same emphasis. The title might undergo some amplification because of a veiled literary reference in lines five and six to Rémy De Gourmont's *Litanies De La Rose*: it might reasonably include some acknowledgement of the poet's debt to French influences, and read "Sunset Piece: After Reading Rémy De Gourmont"; although the original title *Sunset* would be no less literary. The heavy alliteration in *s* in the first seven lines, confirmed in the last by the solitary capitalized *S*, cannot be discarded. The context demands it – certain inevitable associations are connected with the words as they stand. The first word, *stinging*, taken alone suggests merely a sharp feeling; its purpose is only to prepare for the poem and supply an emotional source from which the other *s* ideas may derive. In the second line *swarms* develops the alliteration, at the same time colouring *stinging* with the association of golden bees and softening it with the suppressed idea of buzzing. We are now ready for the more tender *s* word, *spires*, in the third line. *Silver*, the single word of the fourth line, brings us back to the contrast between cold and warm in the first and second lines (*stinging* suggests cold in contrast with the various suggestions of warmth in the *gold swarms*) because *silver* reminds one of cold water as *gold* does of warm light. Two suppressed *s* words play behind the scenes in this first part of the poem, both disguised in *silver* and *gold*, namely, *sea* and *sun*. *Sea* itself does not actually occur until the twelfth line, when the *s* alliteration has flagged: separated from alliterative associations, it becomes the definite image *sea* and the centre around which the poem is to be built up. But once it has appeared there is little more to be said; the poem trails off, closing with the large *S* echo of the last line. The hyphen before this *S* detaches it from *dream* and sets it apart as the alliterative summary of the poem; in a realistic sense -*S* might stand for the alternation of quiet and hiss in wave movement. As a formal closing it leaves us with a feeling like the one we started with, but less acute, because the *z* sound has prevailed over the *s* sound with which the poem was begun. The sunset is over, the final impression is darkness and sleep, though the *-S* vaguely returns to the two large *S*'s of the title.

Another feature which would recur in the rewriting is the slowing down of the rhythm in the last half of the poem, indicated by the shortening of the line and by the double spacing. In regular verse this would naturally mean line lengthening, the closing of a ten-syllabled line series with a twelve-syllabled couplet, for example. Though no end-rhymes occur in the poem as it stands, the rhyme element is undoubtedly strong. The only obvious rhyme sympathy is between *stinging* and *ringing*, but many suppressed rhymes are present: not only *swinging* accompanying the idea of bells but other new rhyme suggestions such as *bees* and *seas, bells* and *swells, spires* and *fires.* In the rewritten poem a definite metrical scheme would have to be employed, but the choice would be governed by the character of the original poem. The rhythm would be gentle and simple, with few marked emphases. Monosyllables would prevail, with a noticeable recurrence of *ing* words; and *bells* would have to be repeated. Here, then, is a poem embodying the important elements of E. E. Cummings' poem, but with each line starting with a capital, with normal spacing and punctuation, and with a regular verse-form. It contains no images not directly suggested by him, but links up grammatically what appeared to be an arrangement based on caprice.

Sunset Piece

After reading Rémy De Gourmont

White foam and vesper wind embrace.
The salt air stings my dazzled face
And sunset flecks the silvery seas
With glints of gold like swarms of bees
And lifts tall dreaming spires of light
To the imaginary sight,
So that I hear loud mellow bells
Swinging as each great wave swells,
Wafting God's perfumes on the breeze,
And chanting of sweet litanies
Where jovial monks are on their knees,
Bell-paunched and lifting glutton eyes
To windows rosy as these skies.

And this slow wind – how can my dreams forget –
Dragging the waters like a fishing-net.

This version shows that Cummings was bound to write the poem as he did in order to prevent it from becoming what we have made it. To write a new poem on an old subject like sunset and avoid all the obvious poetical formulas the poet must write in a new way if he is to evoke any fresh response in his readers at all. Not only does the rewritten poem demand much less attention than the first poem; but it is difficult to feel respect for a poem that is full of reminiscences not only of Rémy de Gourmont, but of Wordsworth ("To the imaginary sight"), Milton (in the metrical variations taken from L'Allegro), Messrs. Belloc and Chesterton ("Where jovial monks..." etc.) and

Tagore in English translation ("Dragging the waters like a fishing net"). Stale phrases such as "vesper wind" and "silver seas" have come to mean so little that they scarcely do their work in the poem. And yet we shall see that such phrases cannot be avoided if we are to revise the poem for the plain man. "White foam" is understood from the sea setting, the movement of the poem, the cold hissing implied in the sequence of *s*'s, "Vesper wind" is suggested by *sunset, spires, monks, bells, tall wind.* "Salt air", as well as resulting from the embrace of "white foam" and "vesper wind", is built up, from *stinging, sea,* and *wind....*

The conclusion to be drawn from this exercise might be that poems must in the future be written in the Cummings way if poetry is not to fall to pieces altogether. But the poetry of E. E. Cummings is clearly more important as a sign of local irritation in the poetic body than as the model for a new tradition. The important thing to recognize, in a time of popular though superficial education, is the necessity of emphasizing to the reading public the differences between good and bad poems, just such differences as we have been pointing out here. Poems in such a time, indeed, may forget that they have any function other than to teach the proper approach; to poetry there is an exaggerated though excusable tendency to suspend the writing of all poetry not intentionally critical. (There are, of course, always exceptions: poets whose writing is so self-contained that it is not affected by stalenesses in traditional poetry or obliged to attack them or escape from them.) Cummings in this poem was really rewriting the other poem which we gave into a good poem. But for the rarer poet there is no "other poem"; there is only the poem which he writes. Cummings' technique, indeed, if further and more systematically developed, would become so complicated that poetry would be no more than mechanical craftsmanship, the verse patterns growing so elaborate that the principal interest in them would be mathematical. In their present experimental stage, and only in their experimental stage, these patterns are undoubtedly suggestive. Poets, however, do not pursue innovations for their own sake. They are on the whole conservative in their methods so long as these ensure the proper security and delivery of the poem.

For the virtue of the poem is not in its being set down on paper, as a picture's is in the way it is set down on canvas. Genius in the poet is a sympathy between different parts of his own mind, in the painter between his paint-brush and his canvas. Method in poetry is therefore not anything that can be talked about in terms of physical form. The poem is not the paper, not the type, not the spoken syllables. It is as invisible and as inaudible as thought; and the only method that the real poet is interested in using is one that will present the poem without making it either visible or audible, without turning it into a substitute for a picture or for music. But when conservatism of method, through its abuse by slack-minded poets, has come to mean the supplanting of the poem by an exercise in poet-craft, then there is a reasonable place for innovation, if the new method defeats the old method and brings up the important question: how should poetry be written? Once this question is asked, the new method has accomplished its end. Further than this it should not be allowed to go, for poems cannot be written from a formula....

Turning back for a more direct comparison of these two versions, we perceive how much of the force of the original has been lost in the second. We have used capitals throughout as in formal verse, but have thus eliminated the large final *S*, which was one of the most important properties of the original, and given a look of unnecessary importance to words like *And, To*, and *So*. By substituting normal spacing and verse-form we have had to disregard the significance of the double spacing and indentation, and of the variation in the length of the lines. Formal indentation can either be a guide to rhyming pairs or a sign that the first part of a line is missing, but it cannot denote musical rests of varying value as with Cummings. We have also expanded the suggested ideas by grammatic means and supplemented them with the words that seemed to have been omitted. But in so doing we have sacrificed the compactness of the previous poem and introduced a definiteness which is false to its carefully devised dreaminess. So by correcting the poem in those poetic features in which it seemed deficient we have not added anything to it but on the contrary detracted from it.

What, now, has happened to the formal features of the Cummings' poem when reproduced in the rewritten poem? The expansion of the poem by the addition of the suppressed words has necessarily multiplied the number of *s*'s in the poem, because these suppressed words show a high proportion of *s*'s. This alliteration, sustained over several couplets, does not match the alliteration of the shorter poem, especially since we have been obliged to use many *s*'s that have no alliterative significance ("To windows rosy as the skies"). Neither has the gradual slowing down of the rhythm in the last half of the poem been effectively reproduced. In the actual poem the slowing down extends over the sestet of this fragmentary sonnet (the fragmentary line, -*S*, being an alliterative hang-over). But as in the formal treatment Cummings' simple octave develops a prolixity which destroys the proper balance between it and its sestet, we have had to abandon the sonnet form and pack into two lines words which should have had the time-value of six. The best we have been able to do is to keep fourteen lines (or rather seven rhyming couplets, one of which has an extra line). The rhymes, too, in the new poem have mutilated the sense: they express the remoteness of the scene by a series of echoes instead of by silences: for Cummings' lines can definitely be regarded as sonnet-lines filled out with musical rests. So by putting the poem into a form in which a definite metrical scheme could be recognized we have entirely altered the character of the poem. We have not even been able to save the scraps of quite regular iambic rhythm with which we started.

Certain admissions must, therefore, be made. We have not only rejected the formal poem in favour of the Cummings poem: we have seen that the Cummings poem itself was an intensely formal poem. Indeed, its very technicalities caused it to be mistaken for a mere assemblage of words, a literary trick. But as it is apparently capable of yielding the kind of experiences customarily expected from poetry, in fact the most ordinary of such experiences, our conclusion must be that the plain reader's approach to poetry is adequate only for poems as weak as the critical effort that he is ready to apply to them; and that Cummings, to disregard the satiric hilarity in which many of his poems are written, really means to write serious poetry and to have his poetry taken seriously, that is, read with the critical sympathy it deserves. The importance of any new technical methods that he makes use of to bring this about lies not in their ultimate permanence or impermanence, but in their establishment of what the poet's rights are in his poem: how free he is to proceed without regard to the inferior critical efforts to which the poem will probably be submitted. What, then, of the plain reader's rights? They are, presumably, like the poet's, whatever his intelligence is able to make them.

It must be admitted that excessive interest in the mere technique of the poem can become morbid both in the poet and the reader, like the composing and solving of cross-word puzzles. Once the sense of a poem with a technical soul, so to speak, is unriddled and its patterns plainly seen, it is not fit for re-reading; as with the Sphinx in the fable, allowing its riddle to be guessed is equivalent to suicide. A poem of this kind is nevertheless able to stave off death by continually revealing, under examination, an unexpected reserve of new riddles; and as long as it is able to supply these it can continue to live as a poem. Yet at some stage or other the end must come. If it is asked: "Is this really a poem?" the answer must be: "Yes, as long as one can go on discovering new surprises in it." But clearly the surprises cannot last for ever; nor can we, as in the indestructible poem whose soul is not technical, go back to the beginning and start all over again as with a new poem. The obvious weakness in the surprise-poem is that it encourages the reader to discover many things not consciously intended by the poem. But, while there is no way of being absolutely sure that the steps taken in unravelling the poem are the same as those involved in inventing the poem, the strength of such a poem is proved by the room it allows for surprises thus improvised by the reader, by the extent to which it is tactically disposed to resist critical attacks. As long as a poem is so disposed, it justifies itself. . . .

Modernist Poetry and Civilization

The vulgar meaning of modernism, especially when the word is employed as a term of critical condemnation or by poets themselves as a literary affectation, is modern-ness, a keeping-up in poetry with the pace of civilization and intellectual history. It is thus used by the reader or critic who makes a sentimental association of poetry with the past, and perhaps with a particular period of the past, as an epithet for "new" poetry which seems irreverent of the general tradition; and, in the other extreme, it is deliberately adopted by individual poets and movements as a contemporary programme. Poetry in this light becomes a matter of temperamental politics, with a conservative flank opposed to a radical flank; and an imaginary battle ensues in which the main issue is lost sight of: may a poet write as a poet or must he write as a period? For modernism, in this perverted sense, likewise becomes a critical tyranny, increasing contemporary mannerisms in poetry instead of freeing the poet of obligation to conform to any particular set of literary theories. There is, indeed, a genuine modernism, which is not a part of a "modernist" programme but a natural personal manner and attitude in the poet to his work, and which accepts the denomination "modernist" because it prefers this to other denominations; also because there is a conspicuous force operating at great odds to free the *poem* of many of the traditional habits which prevented it from achieving its full significance. Keeping in mind this conspicuous force, more excuse can be found for "modernist" as applied to the poem than to the poet; as *poems* is a more accurate, less prejudiced term for *poetry* (a vague and sentimental idea in relation to which *poet* is a more vague and sentimental idea still). But even into this more genuine aspect of poetic modernism creep some of the prejudices of perverted modernism – into its criticism especially. It has, for example, an intolerance toward contemporary poetry which confesses no programme, a suspicion, more properly, of poetry which does not seem to profess a literary cause; and a self-protective sympathy for manifestations of modernism in the past – the present vogue of eighteenth-century poetry is largely inspired by its quaintness, which, however affected, was in its day an up-to-dateness.

For no matter how restrained, how impersonal a literary attitude may be, it is difficult for it to resist the temptation to convert and to receive converts; and modernist poetry, whatever its purity, is especially in danger of succumbing to this temptation to convert, because it is much attacked, and to receive converts, because there are always literary loose-ends anxious to acquire character and standing by attaching themselves to a cause.

The sense of modernism is further perverted by the existence of a middle position between the conservative flank and the radical flank – the intelligent, plain-man point of view. This middle view, this middle population, we might say, is the prop and advocate of civilization; and the idea of civilization as a steady human progress does not exclude the idea of a modernist, *historically* forward poetry. A possible rapprochement exists, therefore, between this middle population, to whom poetry is just one of the many instruments of progress, and that type of contemporary poetical writing which advertises itself by its historical progressiveness. It is difficult, in attempting to make clear some of the aspects of genuine poetic modernism, to avoid appealing to the progressiveness of this middle population, that is, making poetry a historical branch of civilization, and to avoid likewise the appearance of condoning that perverted modernism which takes advantage of a false idea of "advance" to justify feeble eccentricity. The real task is, in fact, not to explain modernism in poetry but to separate false modernism, or faith in history, from genuine modernism, or faith in the immediate, the *new* doings of poems (or poets or poetry) as not necessarily derived from history. Modernist poetry as such should mean no more than fresh poetry, more poetry, poetry based on honest invention rather than on conscientious imitation of the time-spirit.

But honest invention and affectation of originality can both be confused in the single term "modernism." Francis Thompson, in his essay on Coleridge, complained that "the charge of affectation has been buried in turn at the outset of their careers against Coleridge, Wordsworth, Shelley, Keats, Tennyson and Browning. Wordsworth wrote simple diction and his simplicity was termed affected; Shelley gorgeous diction and his gorgeousness was affected; Keats rich diction and his richness was affected; Tennyson cunning diction and his cunning was affected; Browning rugged diction and his ruggedness was affected...."...

The history of these affectations is the history of the various social requirements made of poetry by the middle position, by the intelligent plain man who is religiously devoted to the idea of human uplift; and of the conforming by poets themselves to popular notions held about the place of poetry in this uplift. Poetry is seen first of all as supplying an elegance and refinement which must of necessity be neglected in practical experience. Common affairs are not genteel; and so poetry has generally been expected to feed an upper class hunger in man for nobility: poetry is the high polish of civilization. The next general demand thus made on poetry is that it should be romantically imbued with progressiveness, that it should act as a superior touter for civilization.... Following this is the demand for poetry as a sign of intellectual advancement, as distinct from social or political advancement: poetry as deep and deeper thinking. Browning is an excellent example of the poet who appreciated the popular weakness for profundity. He fed this vanity successfully, without bringing it low; seeming to be profound without really being profound, keeping the necessary illusion by various technical devices such as unnecessarily protracted sentences and an over-clipped grammar.

Poetry, consequently, is made into a constantly expanding institution, embodying from period to period all the rapidly developing specialized forms of knowledge, enlarging itself by broadening the definition of poetry to include psychology, applied theories of music and painting, philosophy, physical science and so on. The poet himself feels obliged to appear as a sage... Not only is the nature of the poet, in this view, expected to change in a scheme of constant and minute adjustment to history, but the nature of poetry itself is supposed to undergo historical evolution: keeping up with the times is a sign of its good behaviour and its worthiness to be incorporated among the material evidences of progress.

Such an opinion of poetry is based on a view of civilization as modernist, as continuously developing in the direction of an absolute and perfect end – which it obviously is not.... A strong distinction must be drawn between poetry as something developing through civilization and as something developing organically by itself – not a minor branch of human endeavour but a complete and separate form of energy which is neither more nor less in the twentieth century A.D. than in the tenth century B.C., nor a different kind of energy now from what it was in Homeric times, but merely lodged in different, or *other*, persons. Civilization develops only in the sense that one thing follows another, not in the sense that things get progressively better or more harmonious because they follow. Poetry does develop in the sense that it is contemporaneous with civilization; but for this reason it has even to protect itself from civilization, to resist, to a certain extent, contemporaneous influences, since there is no merit in modernism for the sake of modernism, and since civilization must, in self-defence, believe in modernism for the sake of modernism. It is therefore always important to distinguish between what is historically new in poetry because the poet is contemporary with a civilization of a certain kind, and what is intrinsically new in poetry because the poet is a new and original individual, something more than a mere servant and interpreter of civilization.

Chapter 23
William Empson

William Empson (1906–84) was a critic and poet whose account of ambiguity in literature became a major force in twentieth-century debates about the nature of literary language. Empson wrote the first draft of what was to become Seven Types of Ambiguity *while he was an undergraduate student working under the supervision of I. A. Richards. He developed his understanding of ambiguity in two further pioneering works of criticism.* Some Versions of Pastoral *published in 1935 drew on Freudian and Marxist ideas to engage with the social and unconscious forces at work in literature.* The Structure of Complex Words *(1951) drew on work in linguistics and the philosophy of language to establish a historical grammar of certain key words in English, and attempted to show how literary works were acutely attuned to the changing meanings of words over time. Empson worked in universities in Japan and China during the 1930s and for a brief period after the Second World War. He finally returned to England in 1952, where he devoted much of the rest of his career to resisting the influence of Christianity on the study of literature.*

The following excerpt comes from the first chapter of Seven Types of Ambiguity, *first published in 1930. It gives one example of Empson's brilliance as a close reader of poetry, but it also shows his style as a literary theorist. He raises a fundamental question: how does poetic language work? His answer is open-ended and exploratory. The theory is invented as the argument proceeds rather than being determined in advance and then demonstrated. As a result his concept of ambiguity does not settle into a single definition, but accumulates different uses and applications as Empson's argument unfolds.*

Seven Types of Ambiguity

An ambiguity, in ordinary speech, means something very pronounced, and as a rule witty or deceitful. I propose to use the word in an extended sense, and shall think

From *Seven Types of Ambiguity* (London: Chatto & Windus, 1930), pp. 1–8.

relevant to my subject any verbal nuance, however slight, which gives room for alternative reactions to the same piece of language. Sometimes, especially in this first chapter, the word may be stretched absurdly far, but it is descriptive because it suggests the analytical mode of approach, and with that I am concerned.

In a sufficiently extended sense any prose statement could be called ambiguous. In the first place it can be analysed. Thus, "The brown cat sat on the red mat" may be split up into a series: "This is a statement about a cat. The cat the statement is about is brown," and so forth. Each such simple statement may be translated into a complicated statement which employs other terms; thus you are now faced with the task of explaining what a "cat" is; and each such complexity may again be analysed into a simple series; thus each of the things that go to make up a "cat" will stand in some spatial relation to the "mat." "Explanation," by choice of terms, may be carried in any direction the explainer wishes; thus to translate and analyse the notion of "sat" might involve a course of anatomy; the notion of "on" a theory of gravitation. Such a course, however, would be irrelevant not only to my object in this essay but to the context implied by the statement, the person to whom it seems to be addressed, and the purpose for which it seems to be addressed to him; nor would you be finding out anything very fundamental about the sentence by analysing it in this way; you would merely be making another sentence, stating the same fact, but designed for a different purpose, context, and person. Evidently, the literary critic is much concerned with implications of this last sort, and must regard them as a main part of the meaning. There is a difference (you may say that between thought and feeling) between the fact stated and the circumstance of the statement, but very often you cannot know one without knowing the other, and an apprehension of the sentence involves both without distinguishing between them. Thus I should consider as on the same footing the two facts about this sentence, that it is about a cat and that it is suited to a child. And I should only isolate two of its "meanings," to form an ambiguity worth notice; it has contradictory associations, which might cause some conflict in the child who heard it, in that it might come out of a fairy story and might come out of *Reading without Tears*.

In analysing the statement made by a sentence (having, no doubt, fixed on the statement by an apprehension of the implications of the sentence), one would continually be dealing with a sort of ambiguity due to metaphors, made clear by Mr. Herbert Read in *English Prose Style*; because metaphor, more or less far-fetched, more or less complicated, more or less taken for granted (so as to be unconscious), is the normal mode of development of a language. "Words used as epithets are words used to *analyse* a direct statement," whereas "metaphor is the synthesis of several units of observation into one commanding image; it is the expression of a complex idea, not by analysis, nor by direct statement, but by a sudden perception of an objective relation." One thing is said to be like another, and they have several different properties in virtue of which they are alike. Evidently this, as a verbal matter, yields more readily to analysis than the social ambiguities I have just considered; and I shall take it as normal to the simplest type of ambiguity, which I am considering in this chapter. The fundamental situation, whether it deserves to be called ambiguous or not, is that a word or a grammatical structure is effective in several ways at once. To take a famous example, there is no pun, double syntax, or dubiety of feeling, in

Bare ruined choirs, where late the sweet birds sang,

but the comparison holds for many reasons; because ruined monastery choirs are places in which to sing, because they involve sitting in a row, because they are made of wood, are carved into knots and so forth, because they used to be surrounded by a sheltering building crystallised out of the likeness of a forest, and coloured with stained glass and painting like flowers and leaves, because they are now abandoned by all but the grey walls coloured like the skies of winter, because the cold and Narcissistic charm suggested by choir-boys suits well with Shakespeare's feeling for the object of the Sonnets, and for various sociological and historical reasons (the protestant destruction of monasteries; fear of puritanism), which it would be hard now to trace out in their proportions; these reasons, and many more relating the simile to its place in the Sonnet, must all combine to give the line its beauty, and there is a sort of ambiguity in not knowing which of them to hold most clearly in mind. Clearly this is involved in all such richness and heightening of effect, and the machinations of ambiguity are among the very roots of poetry.

Such a definition of the first type of ambiguity covers almost everything of literary importance, and this chapter ought to be my longest and most illuminating, but it is the most difficult. The important meanings of this sort, as may be seen from the example about the cat, are hard to isolate, or to be sure of when you have done so; and there is a sort of meaning, the sort that people are thinking of when they say "this poet will mean more to you when you have had more experience of life," which is hardly in reach of the analyst at all. They mean by this not so much that you will have more information (which could be given at once) as that the information will have been digested; that you will be more experienced in the apprehension of verbal subtleties or of the poet's social tone; that you will have become the sort of person that can feel at home in, or imagine, or extract experience from, what is described by the poetry; that you will have included it among the things you are prepared to apprehend. There is a distinction here of the implied meanings of a sentence into what is to be assimilated at the moment and what must already be part of your habits; in arriving at the second of these the educator (that mysterious figure) rather than the analyst would be helpful. In a sense it cannot be explained in language, because to a person who does not understand it any statement of it is as difficult as the original one, while to a person who does understand it a statement of it has no meaning because no purpose.

Meanings of this kind, indeed, are conveyed, but they are conveyed much more by poets than by analysts; that is what poets are for, and why they are important. For poetry has powerful means of imposing its own assumptions, and is very independent of the mental habits of the reader; one might trace its independence to the ease with which it can pass from the one to the other of these two sorts of meaning. A single word, dropped where it comes most easily, without being stressed, and as if to fill out the sentence, may signal to the reader what he is meant to be taking for granted; if it is already in his mind the word will seem natural enough and will not act as an unnecessary signal. Once it has gained its point, on further readings, it will take for granted that you always took it for granted; only very delicate people are as tactful in this matter as the printed page. Nearly all statements assume in this way that you know something but not everything about the matter in hand, and would tell you something different if you knew more; but printed commonly differ from spoken ones in being intended for a greater variety of people, and poetical from prosaic ones in imposing the system of habits they imply more firmly or more quickly.

As examples of the things that are taken for granted in this way, and assume a habit, rather than a piece of information, in the reader, one might give the fact that a particular section of the English language is being used; the fact that English is being used, which you can be conscious of if you can use French; the fact that a European language is used, which you can be conscious of if you can use Chinese. The first of these "facts" is more definite than it sounds; a word in a speech which falls outside the expected vocabulary will cause an uneasy stir in all but the soundest sleepers; many sermons use this with painful frankness. Evidently such a section is defined by its properties rather than by enumeration, and so alters the character of the words it includes; for instance, one would bear it in mind when considering whether the use of a word demands that one should consider its derivation. Regional or dialect poets are likely to use words flatly from that point of view. No single example of so delicate and continuous a matter can be striking; I shall take one at random out of the Synge *Deirdre*, to make clear that a word need not be unpoetical merely because its meaning has been limited:

DEIRDRE: ... It should be a sweet thing to have what is best and richest, if it's for a short space only.
NAISI: And we've a short space only to be triumphant and brave.

The language here seems rich in implications; it certainly carries much feeling and conveys a delicate sense of style. But if one thinks of the Roman or medieval associations of *triumphant*, even of its normal use in English, one feels a sort of unexplained warning that these are irrelevant; the word here is a thin counter standing for a notion not fully translated out of Irish; it is used to eke out that alien and sliding speech-rhythm, which puts no weight upon its single words.

The process of becoming accustomed to a new author is very much that of learning what to exclude in this way, and this first of the three "facts," hard as it may be to explain in detail, is one with which appreciative critics are accustomed to deal very effectively. But the other two are more baffling; one can say little about the quality of a language, if only because the process of describing it in its own language is so top-heavy, and the words of another language will not describe it. The English prepositions, for example, from being used in so many ways and in combination with so many verbs, have acquired not so much a number of meanings as a body of meaning continuous in several dimensions; a tool-like quality, at once thin, easy to the hand, and weighty, which a mere statement of their variety does not convey. In a sense all words have a body of this sort; none can be reduced to a finite number of points, and if they could the points could not be conveyed by words.

Thus a word may have several distinct meanings; several meanings connected with one another; several meanings which need one another to complete their meaning; or several meanings which unite together so that the word means one relation or one process. This is a scale which might be followed continuously. "Ambiguity" itself can mean an indecision as to what you mean, an intention to mean several things, a probability that one or other or both of two things has been meant, and the fact that a statement has several meanings. It is useful to be able to separate these if you wish, but it is not obvious that in separating them at any particular point you will not be raising more problems than you solve. Thus I shall often use the ambiguity of "ambiguity," and pronouns like "one," to make statements covering both reader and author of a poem, when I want to avoid raising irrelevant problems as to communication. To be less ambiguous would be like analysing the sentence about the cat into a course of anatomy. In the same way the words of the poet will, as a rule, be more justly words, what they represent will be more effectively a unit in the mind, than the more numerous words with which I shall imitate their meaning so as to show how it is conveyed.

And behind this notion of the word itself, as a solid tool rather than as a collection of meanings, must be placed a notion of the way such a word is regarded as a member of the language; this seems still darker and less communicable in any terms but its own. For one may know what has been put into the pot, and recognise the objects in the stew, but the juice in which they are sustained must be regarded with a peculiar respect because they are all in there too, somehow, and one does not know how they are combined or held in suspension. One must feel the respect due to a profound lack of understanding for the notion of a potential, and for the poet's sense of the nature of a language.

These examples of the "meanings" of an English sentence should make clear that no explanation, certainly no explanation written in English, can be conceived to list them completely; and that there may be implications (such as I should call meanings) of which a statement would be no use. Neither of these are objections to my purpose, because I can assume that my readers already understand and enjoy the examples I shall consider, and I am concerned only to conduct a sufficient analysis of their enjoyment to make it seem more understandable.

It is possible that there are some writers who write very largely with this sense of a language as such, so that their effects would be almost out of reach of analysis. Racine always seems to me to write with the whole weight of the French language, to remind one always of the latent assumptions of French, in a way that I am not competent to analyse in any case, but that very possibly could not be explained in intelligible terms. Dryden is a corresponding English figure in this matter; Miss Gertrude Stein, too, at this point, implores the passing tribute of a sigh. To understand their methods one might have to learn a great deal about the mode of action of language which is not yet known, and it might always be quicker to use habit than analysis, to learn the language than to follow the explanation.

I propose, then, to consider a series of definite and detachable ambiguities, in which several large and crude meanings can be separated out, and to arrange them in order of increasing distance from simple statement and logical exposition. There is much danger of triviality in this, because it requires a display of ingenuity such as can easily be used to escape from the consciousness of one's ignorance; because it ignores the fact that the selection of meanings is more important to the poet than their multitude, and harder to understand; and because it gives no means of telling how much has been done by meanings latent in the mode of action of the language, which may be far more elaborate and fundamental than those that can be written up. My methods can only be applied at intervals; I shall frequently pounce on the least interesting aspect of a poem, as being large enough for my forceps; and the atoms which build up the compounds I analyse will always be more complex than they. But in so far as anything can be said about this mysterious and important matter, to say it ought not to require apology.

I shall almost always take poems that I admire, and write with pleasure about their merits; you might say that, from the scientific point of view, this is a self-indulgence, and that as much is to be learnt from saying why bad poems are bad. This would be true if the field were of a known size; if you knew the ways in which a poem *might* be good, there would be a chance of seeing why it had failed. But, in fact, you must rely on each particular poem to show you the way in which it is trying to be good; if it fails you cannot know its object; and it would be trivial to explain why it had failed at something it was not trying to achieve. Of course, it may succeed in doing something that you understand and hate, and you may then explain your hatred; but all you can explain about the poem is its success. And even then, you can only have understood the poem by a stirring of the imagination, by something like an enjoyment of it from which you afterwards revolt in your own mind. It is more self-centred, therefore, and so less reliable, to write about the poems you have thought bad than about the poems you have thought good. . . .

Chapter 24
Kenneth Burke

Kenneth Burke (1897–1993) argued that human cultures were fundamentally dramatic in character: "the social sphere" was to be considered in terms of "situations and acts," and not in terms of the operations of physical laws. The role of rhetoric in coordinating "situations and acts" was a continuing intellectual preoccupation, and Burke elaborated a rich analytic terminology for understanding different modes of persuasion or conversion in politics, philosophy, science, and the arts. Rhetoric provided repetitive genres of speech and writing, but logical argument was only one of its kinds. Narrative and symbol were equally important as methods of creating what Burke described as "the mental equipment... by which one handles the significant factors of his time."

"The Poetic Process," first published in 1931 as part of Counter-Statement, *traces the creation of a symbol from the writer's experience to the structure of the symbol itself to its effects upon an audience. The following excerpt illustrates a number of Burke's basic methods and assumptions. Form in art is understood as a response to a fundamental human need for pattern in experience. The process that creates a symbol transforms the experience on which the symbol is based. Symbolic effects depend upon the need for identification in an audience at particular times, but their appeal can also be the result of artistic technique. The poetic symbol has both an emotional and a logical order, each supporting the other.*

The Poetic Process

If we wish to indicate a gradual rise to a crisis, and speak of this as a climax, or a crescendo, we are talking in intellectualistic terms of a mechanism which can often be highly emotive. There is in reality no such general thing as a crescendo. What does exist is a multiplicity of individual art-works each of which may be arranged as a whole, or

From *Counter-Statement* (Berkeley: University of California Press, 1968), pp. 34–48.

in some parts, in a manner which we distinguish as climactic. And there is also in the human brain the potentiality for reacting favorably to such a climactic arrangement. Over and over again in the history of art, different material has been arranged to embody the principle of the crescendo; and this must be so because we "think" in a crescendo, because it parallels certain psychic and physical processes which are at the roots of our experience. The accelerated motion of a falling body, the cycle of a storm, the procedure of the sexual act, the ripening of crops – growth here is not merely a linear progression, but a fruition. Indeed, natural processes are, inevitably, "formally" correct, and by merely recording the symptoms of some physical development we can obtain an artistic development. Thomas Mann's work has many such natural forms converted into art forms, as, in *Death in Venice*, his charting of a sunrise and of the progressive stages in a cholera epidemic. And surely, we may say without much fear of startling anyone, that the work of art utilizes climactic arrangement because the human brain has a pronounced potentiality for being arrested, or entertained, by such an arrangement.

But the concept "crescendo" does not have the emotive value of a crescendo. To arouse the human potentiality for being moved by the crescendo, I must produce some particular experience embodying a crescendo, a story, say, about A and B, where A becomes more and more involved in difficulties with B and finally shoots him. Here I have replaced the concept by a work of art illustrating it, and now for the first time I have an opportunity of making the crescendo play upon the human emotions.

In this way the work of art is seen to involve a principle of individuation. A shoots B in a crescendo, X weathers a flood and rescues Y in a crescendo – the artist may particularize, or individuate, the crescendo in any of the myriad aspects possible to human experience, localizing or channelizing it according to the chance details of his own life and vision. And similarly, throughout the permutations of history, art has always appealed, by the changing individuations of changing subject matter, to certain potentialities of appreciation which would seem to be inherent in the very germ plasm of man, and which, since they are constant, we might call innate forms of the mind. These forms are the "potentiality for being interested by certain processes or arrangements," or the "feeling for such arrangements of subject matter as produce crescendo, contrast, comparison, balance, repetition, disclosure, reversal, contraction, expansion, magnification, series, and so on." Such "forms of the mind" might be listed at greater length. But I shall stop at the ones given, as I believe they illustrate to the extent of being a definition of my meaning. At bottom these "forms" may be looked upon as minor divisions of the two major "forms," unity and diversity. In any case, both unity and diversity will be found intermingling in any example of such forms. Contrast, for instance, is the use of elements which conflict in themselves but are both allied to a broader unity (as laughter on one page, tears on the next, but each involving an incident which furthers the growth of the plot). But the emotions cannot enjoy these forms, or laws (naturally, since they are merely the *conditions of emotional response*) except in their concreteness, in their... material incorporation, in their specification or individuation....

... [R]eturning to the Poetic Process, let us suppose that while a person is sleeping some disorder of the digestion takes place, and he is physically depressed. Such depression in the sleeper immediately calls forth a corresponding psychic depression, while this psychic depression in turn translates itself into the invention of details which will more or less adequately symbolize this depression. If the sleeper has had some set of experiences strongly marked by the feeling of depression, his mind may summon details from this experience to symbolize his depression. If he fears financial ruin, his depression may very reasonably seize upon the cluster of facts associated with this fear in which to individuate itself. On the other hand, if there is no strong set of associations in his mind clustered about the mood of depression, he may invent details which, on waking, seem inadequate to the mood. This fact accounts for the incommunicable wonder of a dream, as when at times we look back on the dream and are mystified at the seemingly unwarranted emotional responses which the details "aroused" in us. Trying to convey to others the emotional overtones of this dream, we laboriously recite the details, and are compelled at every turn to put in such confessions of defeat as "There was something strange about the room," or "For some reason or other I was afraid of this boat, although there doesn't seem to be any good reason now." But the details were not the cause of the emotion; the emotion, rather, dictated the selection of the details. Especially when the emotion was one of marvel or mystery, the invented details seem inadequate – the dream becoming, from the standpoint of communication, a flat failure, since the emotion failed to individuate itself into adequate symbols. And the sleeper himself, approaching his dream from the side of consciousness after the mood is gone, feels how inadequate are the details for conveying the emotion that caused them, and is aware that even for him the wonder of the dream exists only in so far as he still remembers the quality pervading it. . . .

The analogy between these instances and the procedure of the poet is apparent. In this way the poet's moods dictate the selection of details and thus individuate themselves into one specific work of art.

However, it may have been noticed that in discussing the crescendo and the dream I have been dealing with two different aspects of the art process. When art externalizes the human sense of crescendo by inventing one specific crescendo, this is much different from the dream externalizing depression by inventing a combination of details associated with depression. If the artist were to externalize his mood of horror by imagining the facts of a murder, he would still have to externalize his sense of crescendo by the arrangement of these facts. In the former case he is individuating an "emotional form," in the latter a "technical form." And if the emotion makes for the consistency of his details, by determining their selection, technique makes for the vigor, or saliency, or power of the art-work by determining its arrangement.

We now have the poet with his moods to be individuated into subject matter, and his feeling for technical forms to be individuated by the arrangement of this subject matter. And as our poet is about to express himself, we must now examine the nature of self-expression.

First, we must recognize the element of self-expression which is in all activity. In both metaphysics and the sphere of human passions, the attraction of two objects has been called will, love, gravitation. Does water express itself when it seeks its level? Does the formation of a snow crystal satisfy some spiritual hunger awakened by the encroachment of chill upon dormant clouds? Forgoing these remoter implications, avoiding what need not here be solved, we may be content with recognizing the element of self-expression in all human activities. There is the expression of racial properties, types of self-expression common to all mankind, as the development from puberty to adolescence, the defense of oneself when in danger, the seeking of relaxation after labor. And there is the self-expression of personal characteristics: the development from puberty to adolescence manifesting itself in heightened religiosity, cruelty, sentimentality, or cynicism; the defense of oneself being procured by weapons, speech, law, or business; the relaxation after labor being sought in books rather than alcohol, alcohol rather than books, woman rather than either – or perhaps by a long walk in the country. One man attains self-expression by becoming a sailor, another by becoming a poet.

Self-expression today is too often confused with pure utterance, the spontaneous cry of distress, the almost reflex vociferation of triumph, the clucking of the pheasant as he is startled into flight. Yet such utterance is obviously but one small aspect of self-expression. And, if it is a form of self-expression to utter our emotions, it is just as truly a form of self-expression to provoke emotion in others, if we happen to prefer such a practice, even though the emotions aimed at were not the predominant emotions of our own lives. The maniac attains self-expression when he tells us that he is Napoleon; but Napoleon attained self-expression by commanding an army. And, transferring the analogy, the self-expression of the artist, *qua* artist, is not distinguished by the uttering of emotion, but by the evocation of emotion. If, as humans, we cry out that we are Napoleon, as artists we seek to command an army.

Mark Twain, before setting pen to paper, again and again transformed the bitterness that he *wanted* to utter into the humor that he *could* evoke. This would indicate that his desire to evoke was a powerful one; and an event which is taken by Mr. Van Wyck Brooks as an evidence of frustration can just as easily be looked upon as the struggle between two kinds of self-expression. We might say that Mark Twain, as artist, placed so much greater emphasis upon evocation than utterance that he would even change the burden of his message, evoking what he best could, rather than utter more and evoke less. Certain channels of expression will block others. To become an athlete, for instance, I must curb my appetite for food and drink; or I may glut and carouse, and regret to the end of my days the flabbiness of my muscles. Perhaps those critics, then, who would see us emancipated, who would show us a possible world of expression without frustration, mean simply that we are now free to go and storm a kingdom, to go and become Napoleons? In this they provide us with a philosophy of action rather than a method, and in the last analysis I fear that their theories are the self-expression of utterance, not a rigid system for compelling conviction, but a kind of standard for those of their own mind to rally about.

Thus, we will suppose that the artist, whom we have left for some time at the agonizing point of expressing himself, discovers himself not only with a message, but also with a desire to produce effects upon his audience. He will, if fortunate, attempt to evoke the feelings with which he himself is big; or else these feelings will undergo transformations (as in the case of Twain) before reaching their fruition in the art-work. Indeed, it is inevitable that all initial feelings undergo some transformation when being converted into the mechanism of art, and Mark Twain differs from less unhappy artists not in kind, but in degree. Art is a translation, and every translation is a compromise (although, be it noted, a compromise which may have new virtues of its own, virtues not part of the original). The mechanism invented to reproduce the original mood of the artist in turn develops independent requirements. A certain theme of itself calls up a counter-theme; a certain significant moment must be prepared for. The artist will add some new detail of execution because other details of his mechanism have created the need for it; hence while the originating emotion is still in ferment, the artist is concerned with impersonal mechanical processes.

This leads to another set of considerations: *the artist's means are always tending to become ends in themselves.* The artist begins with his emotion, he translates this emotion into a mechanism for arousing emotion in others, and thus his interest in his own emotion transcends into his interest in the treatment....

The poet steps forth, and his first step is the translation of his original mood into a symbol. So quickly has the mood become something else, no longer occupying the whole of the artist's attention, but serving rather as a mere indicator of direction, a principle of ferment. We may imagine the poet to suffer under a feeling of inferiority, to suffer sullenly and mutely until, being an artist, he spontaneously generates a symbol to externalize this suffering. He will write, say, of the King and the Peasant. This means simply that he has attained articulacy by linking his emotion to a technical form, and it is precisely this junction of emotion and technical form which we designate as the "germ of a plot," or "an idea for a poem." For such themes are merely the conversion of one's mood into a relationship, and the consistent observance of a relationship is the conscious or unconscious observance of a technical form. To illustrate:

In "The King and the Peasant" the technical form is one of contrast: the Humble and the Exalted. We might be shown the King and the Peasant, each in his sphere, each as a human being; but the "big scene" comes when the King is convoyed through the streets, and the Peasant bows speechless to the passing of the royal cortège. The Peasant, that is, despite all the intensity and subtlety of his personal experiences, becomes at this moment Peasant in the abstract – and the vestiture of sheer kingliness moves by...This basic relationship may be carried by variation into a new episode. The poet may arrange some incidents, the outcome of which is that the King and the Peasant find themselves in a common calamity, fleeing from some vast impersonal danger, a plague or an earthquake, which, like lightning, strikes regardless of prestige. Here King and Peasant are leveled as in death: both are Humble before the Exalted of unseen forces...The basic relationship may now be inverted. The King and the Peasant, say, are beset by brigands. There is a test of personal ingenuity or courage, it is the Peasant who saves the day, and lo! the Peasant is proved to be a true King and the King a Peasant.

Our suppositional poet is now producing furiously, which prompts us to realize that his discovery of the symbol is no guaranty of good writing. If we may believe Jules Gaultier, Flaubert possessed genius in that he so ardently desired to be a genius; and we might say that this ratio was re-individuated into the symbol of Madame Bovary, a person trying to live beyond her station. This symbol in turn had to be carried down into a myriad details. But the symbol itself made for neither good writing nor bad. George Sand's symbols, which seemed equally adequate to encompass certain emotional and ideological complexities of her day, did not produce writing of such beauty. While as for Byron, we approach him less through the beauty of his workmanship than through our interest in, sympathy with, or aversion to, Byronism – Byronism being the quality behind such symbols as Manfred, Cain, and Childe Harold: the "man against the sky."

This brings up the matter of relationship between the symbol and the beautiful.

This symbol, I should say, attracts us by its power of formula, exactly as a theory of history or science. If we are enmeshed in some nodus of events and the nodus of emotions surrounding those events, and someone meets us with a diagnosis (simplification) of our partially conscious, partially unconscious situation, we are charmed by the sudden illumination which this formula throws upon our own lives. Mute Byrons (potential Byrons) were waiting in more or less avowed discomfiture for the formulation of Byronism, and when it came they were enchanted. Again and again through Byron's pages they came upon the minutiae of their Byronism (the ramifications of the symbol) and continued enchanted. And thus, the symbol being so effective, they called the work of Byron beautiful. By which they meant that it was successful in winning their emotions.

But suppose that I am not Byronic, or rather that the Byronic element in me is subordinated to other much stronger leanings. In proportion as this is so, I shall approach Byron, not through his Byronism, but through his workmanship (not by the ramifications of the symbol, but by the manner in which these ramifications are presented). Byronism will not lead me to accept the workmanship; I may be led, rather, by the workmanship to accept Byronism. Calling only those parts of Byron beautiful which lead me to accept Byronism, I shall find less of such beauty than will all readers who are potential Byrons. Here technical elements mark the angle of my approach, and it will be the technical, rather than the symbolic, elements of the poet's mechanism that I shall find effective in evoking my emotions, and thus it will be in these that I shall find beauty. For beauty is the term we apply to the poet's success in evoking our emotions.

Falstaff may, I think, be cited as an almost perfect symbol from the standpoint of approach through workmanship, for nearly all readers are led to Falstaff solely through the brilliancy of his presentation. The prince's first speech, immediately before Falstaff himself has entered, strikes a theme and a pace which startles us into attention. Thereafter, again and again the enormous obligations which the poet has set himself are met with, until the character of this boisterous "bedpresser" becomes for us one of the keenest experiences in all literature. If one needs in himself the itch of Byronism to meet Byron halfway, for the enjoyment of Falstaff he needs purely the sense of literary values. . . .

Yet we must not consider the symbol, in opposition to style, as outside of technical form. The technical appeal of the symbol lies in the fact that it is a principle of logical guidance, and makes for the repetition of itself in changing detail, which preserve as a constant the original ratio. A study of evolution, for instance, may be said to repeat again and again, under new aspects, the original proposition of evolution. And in the same way the symbol of art demands a continual restatement of itself in all the ramifications possible to the artist's imagination.

In closing: We have the original emotion, which is channelized into a symbol. This symbol becomes a generative force, a relationship to be repeated in varying details, and thus makes for one aspect of technical form. From a few speeches of Falstaff, for instance, we advance unconsciously to a synthesis of Falstaff; and thereafter, each time he appears on the stage, we know what to expect of him in essence, or quality, and we enjoy the poet's translation of this essence, or quality, into particulars, or quantity. The originating emotion makes for *emotional* consistency within the parts; the symbol demands a *logical* consistency within this emotional consistency. In a horror story about a murder, for instance, the emotion of horror will suggest details associated with horror, but the specific symbol of murder will limit the details of horror to those adapted to murder....

Chapter 25
Paul Éluard and André Breton

Paul Éluard (1895–1952) and André Breton (1896–1966) were both leading figures in the Surrealist movement. They first met in 1919, and in 1930 published one result of their collaboration, Immaculate Conception, *a work that simulated the verbal symptoms of mental disorder. In 1938 Éluard broke with Breton as a result of a political disagreement over their affiliation to communism. During the period of their collaboration they helped define the techniques and values of Surrealism. Both were deeply influenced by Freud's theory of the unconscious mind as an entity formed by repressed desires and wishes. The aim of Surrealist art was to engage with these repressed contents and create an art that would liberate desire. A direct engagement with the logic and imagery of dreams was central to this project. The technique of automatic writing provided the method of accessing unconscious images and processes. According to Breton, automatic writing followed "the actual functioning of thought freed from any control of the reason and any aesthetic or moral preoccupations."*

The excerpts printed here come from two works published in the 1930s. "Poetry's Evidence" by Éluard was first published in an English translation that appeared in the journal This Quarter: Surrealist Number *in September 1932. The excerpt from Breton comes from his text, "The Automatic Message", first published in French in the journal* Minotaure *in 1933. Éluard's aphoristic presentation moves between meditations on the nature of poetry and the Surrealist image to visions of a dead world brought back to life by the hazardous liberation of imagination. Breton is more briskly scientific, in his analysis of the psychological conditions for automatic writing and its difference from hypnotic states or the trances of spiritualist mediums.*

Poetry's Evidence, Paul Éluard

I

Nothing is more effortless than falling asleep. But once we are sleeping there begins a mental activity so great that the body, for all its real physical inertia, may be found on waking utterly exhausted.

The practice of automatic writing takes place in the opposite way. For the mind to become completely detached a considerable effort is required, but however lengthy the production which thereupon follows, it does not and should not involve any effort or fatigue.

If dreams often interfere with the sleeper's rest, the mind's dictation, *occurring apart from all control by the intellect, and free of either aesthetic or moral preoccupation*, confers fresh strength upon him who lends himself to it.

The sleeper's feelings invariably tend to harmonize more or less easily or strenuously with the real world of his dreams. Hence the belief that reason is joining in behind the curtain of memory. The sleeping dreamer is almost never surprised by the contradictions among which his mind moves naturally. Once, however, he is back in ordinary life, it is only with difficulty that he realizes how, for example, he has been loving or hating things or persons to which he now feels indifferent. If he does not shrink from *self-knowledge*, if he analyses his dreams, he will find reasons for hoping or fearing. On the other hand, it is hope or fear which in the waking dreamer – the poet – shapes the imaginative activity. Let the poet express this hope or fear, and his relations to the world immediately change. For him, everything is an object for sensation, and, consequently, for feeling. Then all concrete things are his imagination's natural food, and, become motor, hope and fear pass, with his sensations and feelings, into the concrete.

Hallucination, innocence, rage, memory (that insane Proteus), old tales, unexpected recollections, conflagrations of ideas, feelings and things, systematic undertakings for idle ends, and idle ends which turn into immediately useful ends, the disorder of logic to absurdity, the use of the absurd to the point of sense – all that, and not a more or less felicitous assembling of vowels and consonants, of syllables and words, is what produces harmony in a poem. It is a matter of uttering a musical thought. And such music has no use for the drums and fiddles, the rhythms and rhymes employed in concerts for asses' ears.

I have known a woman singer who squinted and a dumb woman whose eyes said "I love you" in every known tongue, not to mention the tongues she had invented.

Bread is more useful than poetry. But love, in the full, human sense of the word, is not more useful than poetry. Since man puts himself at the top of the scale of living things, he cannot deny value to his feelings, however non-productive and anti-social they may be. "Man," says Feuerbach, "has the same senses as animals have, but in man sensation

From *This Quarter: Surrealist Number* (New York: Arno and the New York Times, 1969), pp. 139–48.

is not relative and subordinated to life's lower needs; it is an absolute being, its own end, and its own enjoyment." This brings us back to necessity. Man has constantly to be aware of his supremacy over nature in order to guard himself against, and subdue, it.

Elsewhere Feuerbach says: "Belief in a future life is an altogether unpoetic belief. Poetry springs out of pain. . . . Belief in a future life makes of all pain a lie, and hence it cannot be the source of real inspiration."

In adolescence man longs for childhood, in maturity for youth; in old age he feels the bitterness of having lived. The poet's images grow out of something to be forgotten and something to be remembered. He wearily projects his prophecies into the past. Everything he makes vanishes with the man he was yesterday. Tomorrow there will be novelties. But there is no today in his universal present.

Caprice, contradiction, violence – they are poetry; in other words, poetry is a perpetual struggle, life's very principle, the queen of unrest.

Imagination lacks the imitative instinct. It is the spring and the torrent no vessel ever goes up. Out of and back into this living sleep, day is ever arising and dying. It is the universe without association, the universe which is not part of a greater universe, the godless universe, since it never lies, since it never confuses "witty women with time's remembrance and the amusements of savages."

Truth, the whole truth, is the wandering castle of the imagination. Truth gets told very quickly, unreflectingly, steadily, and sadness, rage, gravity and joy are, for truth, but changes in time and skies which have been won.

Above everything – yes, I know, there have always been some to talk such twaddle, but as they were not there they have not been able to tell us that it was raining there, that it was dark and shivery, and that one was still aware there of man and his deplorable appearance, that one was still and must go on being still aware there of vile stupidity, and still hear muddy laughter and dead man's chatter. Above everything, "O, you, who are my brothers because I have enemies," and it is there alone that wretchedness undoes and sets up again incessantly a world, drab, common, unbearable and impossible.

Mind can only triumph in its most perilous activities. No daring is fatal.

Order is prudence: the preservation of food; and man is stupidly dying of hunger beside spoiled treasures.

Every man who pauses loses caste. Every satisfied man is a beast. The most common specimen is the warrior resting on his laurels.

Size does not exist for whoever wishes to grow. He has no model who seeks what he has never seen.

We shall annihilate the masters with their servants. Men will be equal.

Our brothers are setting themselves free. We are all on the same level. Let us blot out the others.

Jacques Vaché, while with the colours, wrote to André Breton on November 14, 1918: "How, my poor friend, am I going to stand this final period in uniform? (I have been assured that the war was over.) I am absolutely up against it . . . and then THEY are suspicious . . . THEY smell a rat. So long as they do not draw out my brains while THEY have me in their power?"

Two months later he killed himself.

Sade's twenty-seven years in prison, Hölderlin's madness, and Nerval's and Baudelaire's, Rimbaud's return to nothingness, Lautréamont's loneliness and death, Nouveau's poverty, Jarry's despair. Nothing that they made has perished. The evil principle which they represented in opposition to bourgeois good, the insurance-of-property good, is certain to win.

Employing contradictions purely with an equalizing purpose, and sorry to please provided it is self-satisfied, poetry has always *applied itself*, in spite of all kinds of persecutions, to refusing to work for an order not its own, for unwanted fame, and the various advantages given to obedience and weakness.

Pure poetry? Poetry's absolute power will purify men, all men. "Poetry must be made by all. Not by one" (Lautréamont). All the ivory towers will be pulled down, all speech will be holy, and, having at last overthrown reality, man will only have to shut his eyes to see opening the gates of Faerie.

II

"*Your tongue, that goldfish in the bowl of your voice.*"

The beauty of this image of Apollinaire's results from its apparent accuracy. It falsely flatters in us our sense of the familiar. It is the same with:

"*Brook, the silver in the dell's canteen,*"

of Saint-Pol Roux's. As in the case of the hardy metaphors, "marble breasts" and "coral lips," we accept their evidence. A few simple relations lead us to overlook the strange terms of comparison. We understand "hard as marble" and "red as coral" without objecting that marble and coral are cold. We are dazzled, and so take as an absolute truth a wholly relative resemblance.

To the mobility of the tongue and the fish, Apollinaire adds their colour. The brook is table silver because we have often said or heard, "the silvery brook" – a commonplace. And thanks to these identities of form, colour and relation, new images are accepted although made up in a more arbitrary because purely formal manner—"the bowl of your voice" and "the dell's canteen." For, primarily, each image is nothing but a comparison – "that goldfish in the bowl" for "your voice's tongue" and "the silver in the canteen" for "the dell's brook." And yet what delights us is "the bowl of your voice" and "the dell's canteen" – what is unfathomable, what is true.

If I go to the extreme of giving such an elementary explanation of these two admirable images, it is in order to insist more strongly then ever on the supreme attraction I feel for unfathomable images, of the altogether novel relations of which the poetry called surrealist gives us a glimpse. Here are some among the many images which obsess me, lightning images which disturb and comfort me, and make me feel that nothing is incomprehensible and that for the mind nothing is lost:

"*... Beautiful like the chance meeting on a dissecting-table of a sewing-machine and an umbrella*" (Lautréamont).

"*The champagne's ruby*" (Lautréamont).

"*Old ocean, O noble celibate*" (Lautréamont).

"*I have seen a fig eat an onager*" (Lautréamont).

"*Doubt's duck with the vermouth lips*" (Lautréamont).

"*I am the saint at prayer on the terrace, as the cattle graze as far as the Sea of Palestine*" (Rimbaud).

"*The vigil's sea, like Amelia's breasts*" (Rimbaud).

"*Find flowers that are chairs*" (Rimbaud).

"*The genius, 'I am the Stilton! It'll be our death...'*" (Rimbaud).

"*His heart, amber and spunsk*" (Rimbaud).

"*In eating the sound of moths*" (Jarry).

"*Near a gentleman swallowing himself*" (Apollinaire).

"*A charming mantelpiece holding its bitch on a lead*" (Apollinaire).

"*I shall laugh like a waterfall and like a blaze*" (Tzara).

"*In the stunted clay of mimes*" (Tzara).

"*The lock of hair digs a tunnel under Paris*" (Breton).

"*Night's pedals move uninterruptedly*" (Breton).

"*On the hill only inspired by the painted lip*" (Péret).

"*The earth was shaped like a horseshoe*" (Péret).

"*The lazy suns which fed on meningitis*" (Char).

"*The lonely poet*

Great wheelbarrow of the swamps" (Char).

"*The numerous species of animals on heat upon the backs of which were painted famous lakes and other kinds of twilight*" (Dali).

"*To sail ship is the bird of the latitudes*" (Unik).

Images are, images live, and everything becomes image. They were long mistaken for illusions because they were restricted, were made to undergo the test of reality, an insensitive and dead reality, when reality should have been made to undergo the test of its own interdependence which makes it alive, active, and perpetually moving.

"Nothing is incomprehensible." Everything can be compared to everything, everything has its echo, its reason, its resemblance, its opposition and its becoming, everywhere. And this becoming is infinite.

It was between 1866 and 1875 that poets dared to bring together what had seemed to be permanently apart. Lautréamont did this more deliberately than any one else. A wonderful medium, he realized that here was a true intellectual phenomenon ("At the moment I write, new thrills are shaking the intellectual atmosphere: it is only necessary to have the courage to look them in the face"). He was unaware of Rimbaud and Rimbaud was unaware of him, and yet it was the same voice which made them write down:

"*My hunger is the black air's bits*" (Rimbaud).
"*... In the air beautiful and black*" (Lautréamont).

That was the time when, before unfortunately sinking to the most sinister of formal preoccupations, Mallarmé was writing *Igitur*, the last moonless night of a phantom; the time when Lewis Carroll went hunting the Snark "with a railway-share," "with smiles and soap," with the authentic poetic sense which, being a humorist, he nicknamed nonsense.

At last the poetic intelligence was seeing its frontiers destroyed and was restoring unity to the world.

Reduced to the level of scribblers, painters were copying apples and displaying virtuosity. Surrealist painters have copied an elephant which had an apple where its head should have been, an elephant of which the shadow was an umbrella. They copied it scrupulously, their eyes wide open, studying the least oddities of this apple pierced, like a heart, by an arrow.

They have scrupulously traced the irrational shapes beside which there could no longer be the mediocrity of a landscape or portrait it was beyond the capillary powers of comprehension of so many mediocre painters to embellish. They have made objective, they will go on making objective, what it has not been and is not yet possible to make objective – everything.

"*One no longer sits at the tables*
Of the blessed, for one is dead" (Charles Cros).

Only the living sit at tables. Blessed are the living, say the dead. And wretched the dead. And dead the wretched. Why refuse to sit at the tables of the blessed? Because one is dead. Better to admit one is dead than wretched. It is thus possible to get the better of the blessed, of the living. In any case, death in the context of the poem is only moral death, deadness to the world.

When applied to such a statement of sentiment, how logic becomes precarious and ridiculous!

But ask a pure logician to expound these two lines of verse and you will find that he too is unable to reproduce their tone, which is so unexpected and thereby so deeply moving...

In opposition to Balzac, who claimed to be the loser by the sexual act ("It costs me," he was in the habit of saying, "a page of my work each time"), I have always felt fitter, more fluent, more inventive, and especially surer of myself, after making love.

The Automatic Message, André Breton

...We are aware that the term "automatic writing" as used in surrealism, lends itself to disputation. If I may be held partly responsible for this impropriety, it is because "automatic" writing (or "mechanical" writing, as Flournoy would have it, or better still "unconscious" writing, as Mr René Sudre prefers) has always seemed to me the limit towards which the surrealist poet must tend, but without losing sight of the fact that, contrary to what spiritualism proposes – that is, the dissociation of the subject's psychological personality – surrealism proposes nothing less than the *unification* of that personality. For us, obviously, the question of the externality of the "voice" (to repeat for the sake of simplification) could not even be raised.

From the beginning it has appeared to us quite difficult and almost superfluous, considering what there could be of the extra-psychological in the goal we pursue, to burden ourselves with a division of the writing currently called "inspired" (which we would oppose to calculated literature) into "mechanical," "semimechanical" and "intuitive," these three adjectives describing merely differences of degree.

It has been a case, once more, of going as far as possible along a road opened by Lautréamont and Rimbaud (one clear proof of this in the latter is the first phrase of his poem "Promontoire") – a road made particularly appealing by the application of certain processes of psychoanalytic investigation. In the twentieth century, immediately after World War I, this road necessarily had to pass through our small group of poets. As we began to follow it, there seemed an infinite murmuring behind and before us. We know that in addition to the procedure of obtaining the written automatic message there is a procedure by which one attempts to obtain this message in its spoken form. But our experience on this point has fully verified Myers's affirmation that automatic *speech* is a less developed form of the motor message than automatic *writing* and is

From *André Breton: What is Surrealism?*, ed. and trans. Franklin Rosemont (London: Pluto Press, 1978), pp. 105–9.

made dubious, moreover, by the profound modifications of memory and personality involved.

It is to the credit of surrealism that it has proclaimed the total equality of all ordinary human beings before the subliminal message; that it has constantly insisted that this message is the heritage of all, too precious to remain the patrimony of a few and that nothing remains but for each to claim his share. I say all men, all women, deserve to be convinced of the absolute possibility of their own appeal to that language which, having nothing to do with the supernatural, is for each and every one the very vehicle of revelation. For this it is indispensable that they avoid any narrow, erroneous conception of it as a vocation in itself, artistic or mediumistic. If we look carefully we can see that all such vocations began with a fortuitous circumstance whose effect was to weaken certain resistances of the individual. For whoever preoccupies himself with something other than his prosaic immediate interests, the weakening of these resistances is essential. As Professor Lipps observed in his studies of the automatist dances of the medium Magdeleine, around 1908, "hypnosis is only the negative rationalisation of talents that manifest themselves under its influence; their real source is to be found in previously existing tendencies, faculties and predispositions, which have been prevented from their natural exercise by contrary factors, and the role of hypnotism remains the liberation of the first by paralysing these latter factors."

Automatic writing, which is facile and attractive, and which we hope to put once again at the disposal of *all* in freeing it from the imposing and cumbrous apparatus of hypnosis, seems to realise, despite all obstacles, what von Schrenck-Notzing wished to see in hypnosis itself: "an assured means of favouring the development of psychic faculties, and particularly of artistic talent, in concentrating consciousness on the task at hand and in freeing the individual from inhibitory factors which restrain and trouble him, sometimes to the point of completely choking off the exercise of his latent gifts."

This viewpoint of artistic talent, with the incredible vanity that is attached to it, is naturally not foreign to the internal and external causes of mistrust which, in surrealism, have prevented automatic writing from fulfilling all its promises. Originally the aim was simply to grasp involuntary verbal representation and fix it on the page without imposing on it any kind of qualitative judgment. However, critical comparisons have not failed to raise questions regarding the degree of richness or elegance, in this or that person, of the interior language. In this game an execrable poetic rivalry soon demanded its due.

On the other hand an inevitable delectation (after the fact) in the very terms of the texts obtained, and particularly in the images and symbolic figurations abounding in them, has had a secondary effect of diverting most of their authors from the inattention and indifference which, at least during the production of such texts, must be maintained. This attitude, instinctive in those who are used to appreciating poetic value, has had the vexing consequence of giving the participant an immediate awareness of each part of the message received. Thus we find broken the cycle called by Dr Georges Petit, in a remarkable work, "apperceptive autorepresentation," *on which,* by definition, *we still propose to operate by linking it, without any possible ambiguity, to the ego.* There has resulted for us, even as we listen, an almost uninterrupted succession of visual images which have disrupted the murmur and which, to its detriment, we have not always escaped the temptation to set down.

Let me explain: It is not merely that I think there is almost always a complexity in imaginary sounds. (The question of the unity and speed of dictation remains on the order of the day.) I am also certain that visual or tactile images (primitive, unpreceded or unaccompanied by words, like the representation of blankness or elasticity without intervention previous, concomitant or even subsequent to the words that express them or derive from them) give free access to the unmeasurable region between the conscious and the unconscious. But if automatic dictation can be obtained with a certain continuity, the process of unravelling and linking these images is extremely difficult to grasp, presenting, to the best of our knowledge, an eruptive character. So it was on the very evening (27 September) when I took down the two phrases beginning this article. When my endeavour to produce a verbal equivalent proved unavailing, at the very moment that I completely abandoned this endeavour I saw a representation of myself (of my hand?) with a sort of scallop shell, folding its edges, as one must do in preparing a paper filter, and smoothing its ribs. This to me was indubitably a different kind of automatism. But was it obtained as compensation for the other, which was too closely scrutinised? I do not know. But I do believe, and this is the essential point, that verbal inspiration is infinitely richer in visual meaning, infinitely more resistant to the eye, than visual images properly so called. This belief is the source of my unceasing protest against the presumed "visionary" power of the poet. No, Lautréamont and Rimbaud did not see what they described, they never were confronted by it *a priori.* That is to say, they never *described* anything. They threw themselves into the dark recesses of being; they heard indistinctly, and with no more comprehension than any of us had the first time we read them, certain realised and realisable works. "Illumination" comes afterwards.

It always has seemed to me that verbo-auditive automatism creates for the reader the most exalting visual images. Verbo-visual automatism never has seemed to create for the reader visual images that are from any viewpoint comparable. It is enough to say that I believe as fully today as I did ten years ago – I believe blindly... blindly, with a blindness that covers all visible things – in the triumph *auditorily* of what is unverifiable visually.

This much having been said, the painters obviously are now the ones to speak, whether to contradict or not.

To my very great regret, I can do no more here than outline the problem that surely will be imposed on purely speculative thought by the surrealist attitude concerning the degree of reality to be accorded the *object.* Poets and artists, theologians and psychologists, patients and psychiatrists, always are seeking a line of demarcation by which one might isolate the imaginary from the real object – always granting, pending further developments, that the real may easily disappear from the field of consciousness and the imaginary appear there; that subjectively their properties are demonstrably interchangeable.

Automatic writing, practised with some fervour, leads directly to visual hallucination. I have experienced this myself, and by recalling "Alchemy of the Word" it can be observed that Rimbaud experienced it before me. But the reason for the "terror" of his renunciation is unclear to me. I know few psychological texts as guileless and at the same time as pathetic as the closing sentence of the excellent two-volume work recently published by Pierre Quercy, *L'Hallucination*, which, by a most pessimistic verification of fact, puts an end to the continual debates between mystics and non-mystics, between the mentally ill and doctors, between (fanatical) partisans of "objectless perception" and those of "the image we call perception". Quercy says: "One can affirm the presence or perception of an object when it is present and perceived, when it is absent and perceived, when it is neither present nor perceived." The degree of spontaneity which individuals, taken in isolation, are capable of – this alone decides for them which pan of the scale will go up or down. The "derangement" of the senses, of all the senses, remains to be achieved. Or, putting it another way, the education (actually the diseducation) of all the senses is yet to be accomplished.

In this regard we must give particular attention to the recent work of the Marburg School, notwithstanding the sharp controversies it continues to provoke. According to the teachers of that school (Kiesow, Jaensch) one may cultivate in the child remarkable dispositions consisting in the ability to change a given object into *anything* by focusing on it. In the experimenters' experience, if a child is invited to gaze at an object for fifteen seconds and the object is then withdrawn, the effect will be to form not a weakening nebulous afterimage, of a colour complementing that of the object considered, but a pure *eidetic* image with great complexity of detail and the same colour as the object. The object may be infinitely changeable, it would immediately be distinguished from the model by particular variations. "If we show the child the silhouette of a horse, with its head high and a rider in the saddle, the eidetic image may very well show the horse grazing and the rider turned, in the saddle, towards the horse's tail. If we show the child an F, he sees an ꟻ, an Ⅎ, or even an ⅎ, and the horse perceived earlier may reappear with four hoofs in the air."

All the experimentation here would be of a nature to demonstrate that perception and representation (which to the ordinary adult seem radically opposed) are merely products of the dissociation of *one original faculty*, of which the eidetic image gives us an idea and of which one still finds a trace among primitives and children. All who have striven to define the true human condition have aspired, more or less confusedly, to regain that state of grace. I say automatism alone provides access to it. Systematically, without frenzy, one can work from this point where the distinction between subjective and objective ceases to be necessary or useful.

"There is," says Myers, "a form of internal hearing [how strange] . . . It exists in powerful and complex clusters of conceptions that are formulated outside [some would say beyond] articulated language and reasoned thought. There is a path, an ascension through ideal spaces, that some consider the only true ascension; there is an architecture that certain individuals consider the only abode . . ."

From the single fact that she saw her wooden cross transform itself into a crucifix of precious stones, and accepted this vision as both *imaginative and sensory*, Teresa of Avila could be credited with having ordained this line on which mediums and poets are situated. Unfortunately she is still no more than a saint.

Chapter 26
F. R. Leavis

Frank Raymond Leavis (1895–1978) dedicated his career as a critic to the argument that literary criticism was the central mode of humanist inquiry and should therefore be a major discipline in any university. Literary works could present experience with a subtlety and detail that eluded the concepts of philosophy or the social sciences. Moreover, this capacity for presentation was also a mode of evaluation. Rightly read, literature could provide its readers with a moral education based not upon dogmas but a capacity for fine discrimination. However, not all literature could do this. Leavis devoted a number of critical books to establishing his canon of English literature, and exemplified in his work on particular authors the kind of attentive reading necessary to discern the value of great literature. Leavis had a polemical awareness that others did not share his judgments. He defined literary criticism as a discipline at odds with the main trends and values of modern culture. His version of criticism had a considerable influence on the teaching of literature in schools and universities, not least because of the arguments it provoked.

Leavis was one of the first critics to assess modernist poetry as a significant event in the history of literature and culture. New Bearings in English Poetry *was first published in 1932. The excerpts from the book that follow show how Leavis argued for the value of one modernist poet, T. S. Eliot. Typically, he begins by identifying what is bad: a trend in poetry starting in the eighteenth century and reaching its height in the nineteenth. By the end of the nineteenth century this kind of poetry has, according to Leavis, become dissociated from the complexities of modern culture. Against this background, Eliot emerges as one amongst a small number of poets who exemplify Leavis's Romantic conviction that the poet can be "the point at which the growth of the mind shows itself." In his account of Eliot's poem* The Waste Land, *Leavis argues that the poem is unified by the consciousness it exhibits, not by lyric, dramatic, or narrative form.*

Poetry and the Modern World

Poetry matters little to the modern world. That is, very little of contemporary intelligence concerns itself with poetry. It is true that a very great deal of verse has come from the press in the last twenty years, and the uninterested might take this as proving the existence both of a great deal of interest in poetry and of a great deal of talent. Indeed, anthologists do. They make, modestly, the most extravagant claims on behalf of the age. 'It is of no use asking a poetical renascence to conform to type,' writes Mr J. C. Squire in his *Prefatory Note to Selections from Modern Poets.* 'There are marked differences in the features of all those English poetical movements which have chiefly contributed to the body of our "immortal" poetry.... Should our literary age be remembered by posterity solely as an age during which fifty men had written lyrics of some durability for their truth and beauty, it would not be remembered with contempt. It is in that conviction that I have compiled this anthology.' Mr Harold Monro, introducing *Twentieth Century Poetry,* is more modest and more extravagant: 'Is it a great big period, or a minutely small? Reply who can! Somebody with whom I was talking said: "They are all of them only poetical persons – *not* poets. Who will be reading them a century hence?" To which I answered: 'There are so many of them that, a century hence, they may appear a kind of Composite Poet; there may be 500 excellent poems proceeding from 100 poets mostly not so very great, but well worth remembering a century hence."'

Such claims are symptoms of the very weakness that they deny: they could have been made only in an age in which there were no serious standards current, no live tradition of poetry, and no public capable of informed and serious interest. No one *could* be seriously interested in the great bulk of the verse that is culled and offered to us as the fine flower of modern poetry. For the most part it is not so much bad as dead – it was never alive. The words that lie there arranged on the page have no roots: the writer himself can never have been more than superficially interested in them. Even such genuine poetry as the anthologies of modern verse do contain is apt, by its kind and quality, to suggest that the present age does not favour the growth of poets. A study of the latter end of *The Oxford Book of Victorian Verse* leads to the conclusion that something has been wrong for forty or fifty years at the least.

For it seems unlikely that the number of potential poets born varies as much from age to age as literary history might lead one to suppose. What varies is the use made of talent. And the use each age makes of its crop of talent is determined largely by the preconceptions of 'the poetical' that are current, and the corresponding habits, conventions and techniques. There are, of course, other very important conditions, social, economic, philosophical and so on; but my province is that of literary criticism, and I am confining myself as far as possible to those conditions which it rests with the poet and the critic to modify – those which are their immediate concern.

Every age, then, has its preconceptions and assumptions regarding poetry: these are the essentially poetical subjects, these the poetical materials, these the poetical modes. The most influential are apt to be those of which we are least aware. The

From *New Bearings in English Poetry* (London: Chatto & Windus, 1950), pp. 5–10, 12–15, 21–4, 25–6.

preconceptions coming down to us from the last century were established in the period of the great Romantics, Wordsworth, Coleridge, Byron, Shelley and Keats. To attempt to define them is to risk misrepresenting them, for it is largely in their being vague and undefined that their power has lain. Their earliest formulation is to be found, perhaps, in the *Dedication* (dated 1756) of Joseph Warton's *Essay on the Genius and Writings of Pope.* What Warton, consciously challenging the prevailing ideas, puts explicitly, afterwards came to be implicitly assumed.

> We do not, it should seem, sufficiently attend to the difference there is between a MAN OF WIT, a MAN OF SENSE, and a TRUE POET. Donne and Swift were undoubtedly men of wit, and men of sense: but what traces have they left of PURE POETRY?

The question would seem to determine the spirit of the affirmation: any doubt that may remain, both affirmation and question in the following combine to settle:

> The sublime and the pathetic are the two chief nerves of all genuine poesy. What is there transcendently sublime or pathetic in Pope?

Warton goes on to classify the English Poets:

> In the first class I would place our only three sublime and pathetic poets; SPENSER, SHAKESPEARE, MILTON.

The collocation is decisive: it defines with sufficient precision the nineteenth-century idea of the poetical. Donne, we may note, Warton places in the third class. The reign of the idea is challenged when Donne comes to be associated with Shakespeare in contrast to Spenser and Milton. How universal and unquestioned it had become in the Victorian Age Matthew Arnold may be cited to prove. His evidence is the more significant in that it was unwitting, for he regarded himself as a critic of the ideas about poetry current in his day.

> Though they may write in verse, though they may in a certain sense be masters of the art of versification, Dryden and Pope are not classics of our poetry, they are classics of our prose.
>
> The difference between genuine poetry and the poetry of Dryden, Pope, and all their school, is briefly this: their poetry is conceived and composed in their wits, genuine poetry is conceived and composed in the soul.

– Arnold, that is, shares with his age a prejudice against recognizing as poetry anything that is not, in the obvious sense of Milton's formula, 'simple, sensuous, and passionate'. Poetry, it was assumed, must be the direct expression of simple emotions, and these of a limited class: the tender, the exalted, the poignant, and, in general, the sympathetic. (It is still quite common to come to the University from school doubting whether satire can be poetry.) Wit, play of intellect, stress of cerebral muscle had no place: they could only hinder the reader's being 'moved' – the correct poetical response.

There is something further to be noted of 'the poetical' in the nineteenth century. It comes out if one considers these half-a-dozen well-known and representative poems: *La Belle Dame Sans Merci, Mariana, The Lady of Shalott, The Blessed Damozel,* Morris's *The Nymph's Song to Hylas, A Forsaken Garden,* O'Shaughnessy's *Ode.* Nineteenth-century poetry, we realize, was characteristically preoccupied with the creation of a dream-world. Not all of the poetry, or all of the poets: but the preoccupation was characteristic. So that when a poetaster like O'Shaughnessy, with nothing personal to communicate, was moved by the desire to write poetry he produced this:

> We are the music-makers,
>   And we are the dreamers of dreams,
> Wandering by lone sea-breakers,
>   And sitting by desolate streams;
> World-losers and world forsakers,
>   On whom the pale moon gleams....

The preoccupation, the habit, then, became a dominant element in the set of ideas, attitudes and sentiments constituting 'the poetical' for the nineteenth century, and may often be seen to be present and potent when it is not avowed or even wittingly entertained....

It is not only in the practice of poetasters that such preconceptions, habits and conventions assert themselves: they exercise a decisive influence over the use of genuine talent. Poetry tends in every age to confine itself by ideas of the essentially poetical which, when the conditions which gave rise to them have changed, bar the poet from his most valuable material, the material that is most significant to sensitive and adequate minds in his own day; or else sensitive and adequate minds are barred out of poetry. Poetry matters because of the kind of poet who is more alive than other people, more alive in his own age. He is, as it were, at the most conscious point of the race in his time. ('He is the point at which the growth of the mind shows itself', says Mr I. A. Richards.) The potentialities of human experience in any age are realized only by a tiny minority, and the important poet is important because he belongs to this (and has also, of course, the power of communication). Indeed, his capacity for experiencing and his power of communicating are indistinguishable; not merely because we should not know of the one without the other, but because his power of making words express what he feels is indistinguishable from his awareness of what he feels. He is unusually sensitive, unusually aware, more sincere and more himself than the ordinary man can be. He knows what he feels and knows what he is interested in. He is a poet because his interest in his experience is not separable from his interest in words; because, that is, of his habit of seeking by the evocative use of words to sharpen his awareness of his ways of feeling, so making these communicable. And poetry can communicate the actual quality of experience with a subtlety and precision unapproachable by any other means. But if the poetry and the intelligence of the age lose touch with each other, poetry will cease to matter much, and the age will be lacking in finer awareness. What this last prognostication means it is perhaps impossible to bring home to any one who is not already convinced of the importance of poetry. So that it is indeed deplorable that poetry should so widely have ceased to interest the intelligent.

The mischievousness of the nineteenth-century conventions of 'the poetical' should by now be plain. They had behind them the prestige of the Romantic achievement and found their sanction in undoubted poetic successes. But as the situation changed and the incidence of stress for the adult sensitive mind shifted, more and more did they tend to get between such a mind and its main concerns. It clearly could not take the day-dream habit seriously, though to cut free from the accompanying conventions and techniques would not be so easy as one might think. The other habits and conventions that have been indicated would be still harder to escape. But they would be equally disabling. For a sensitive adult in the nineteenth century could not fail to be preoccupied with the changed intellectual background, and to find his main interests inseparable from the modern world. Tennyson did his best. But, in spite of a great deal of allusion to scientific ideas ('If that hypothesis of theirs be sound'), and in spite of the approval of contemporary savants, his intellectual interests (of which, therefore, we need not discuss the quality) have little to do with his successful poetry, which answers to the account of 'the poetical' given above. Indeed, there could be no better illustration. To justify his ambition would have taken a much finer intelligence and a much more robust original genius than Tennyson's – much greater strength and courage. He might wrestle solemnly with the 'problems of the age', but the habits, conventions and techniques that he found congenial are not those of a poet who could have exposed himself freely to the rigours of the contemporary climate. And in this he is representative. It was possible for the poets of the Romantic period to believe that the interests animating their poetry were the forces moving the world, or that might move it. But Victorian poetry admits implicitly that the actual world is alien, recalcitrant and unpoetical, and that no protest is worth making except the protest of withdrawal. . . .

And if we look through any anthologies covering the last fifty years, it becomes impossible to doubt that distinguished minds that should have gone into poetry have gone elsewhere. It is hard to explain otherwise the dearth of original talent in any form or degree. When original talent of a minor order does manifest itself, as, for instance, in Mr A. E. Housman, or, though the collocation is unfair to Mr Housman, Rupert Brooke, it is apt to exert a disproportionate influence. The books of 'Georgian' verse abound with tributes, more or less unconscious, to these two poets (not to insist on R. L. Stevenson's part): indeed it was largely in terms of them that the Victorian bequest of habits and conventions was brought up to date. But these remained essentially the same, as a perusal of the representative anthology, Mr J. C. Squire's *Selections from Modern Poets*, will show. The modernity manifests itself, for the most part, in a complacent debility; the robust, full-blooded emotional confidence of the Victorians is lacking, a modest quietness being the Georgian study; and technical liberation, accordingly, takes the form of loose, careless, unconvinced craftsmanship.

To make a fresh start in poetry under such conditions is a desperate matter. It is easy enough to say that poetry must be adequate to modern life, and it has often been said. But nothing has been done until such generalities have been realized in particulars, that is, in the invention of new techniques, and this, in an age when the current conventions will not serve even to provide a start, is something beyond any but a very unusually powerful and original talent. The established habits form a kind of atmosphere from which it is supremely difficult to escape. Mr J. C. Squire, for instance, reviewing in *The Observer* the late Poet Laureate's *The Testament of Beauty*, wrote:

> ... the old poet has done triumphantly what none of his juniors have managed to do – he has, assisted by courage, a natural sincerity, a belief in the function of poetry, contrived to bring within the borders of a poem, and avoiding flatness, all his feelings, knowledge, speculations, interests, hopes and fears. For generations, owing to the reaction of the aesthetic against the new scientific, industrial and largely materialistic world, we have become accustomed to the idea that certain things are "not poetical," that a poet can mention a rose, but not a Rolls-Royce, that poetry is a refuge and not an attack, that a poet is a sensitive refugee and not a man facing life, the whole of it, and sounding a clarion call to his more speechless and encumbered fellows.

The first sentence might seem to be in the spirit of this essay, though the phrase 'bring within the borders of a poem' should put us on our guard. On the next sentence – 'we have become accustomed to the idea that certain things are not poetical' – our commentary runs: worse, we have become accustomed to the idea that certain things *are* poetical, e.g. flowers, dawn, dew, birds, love, archaisms and country place-names; 'that a poet can mention a rose, but not a Rolls-Royce' – suspicious; 'that poetry is a refuge and not an attack, that a poet is a sensitive refugee and not a man facing life, the whole of it, and sounding a clarion call' – this will not do: it is plain by now that the critic is trying to put a misconception right by turning it upside-down. For we are no more justified in demanding that poetry shall be an attack than in demanding that it shall be a refuge. Indeed, it is very unlikely that a significant modern poem will be anything in the nature of a clarion call. The passage betrays a total misconception of the way in which such a poem will exhibit modernity. It will not be by mentioning modern things, the apparatus of modern civilization, or by being about modern subjects or topics. If the Rolls-Royce enters significantly into poetry it will be, perhaps, in some such way as Mr T. S. Eliot suggests when he says that probably the modern's perception of rhythm has been affected by the internal combustion engine. All that we can fairly ask of the poet is that he shall show himself to have been fully alive in our time. The evidence will be in the very texture of his poetry.

... To invent techniques that shall be adequate to the ways of feeling, or modes of experience, of adult, sensitive moderns is difficult in the extreme. Until it has been once done it is so difficult as to seem impossible. One success makes others more probable because less difficult.

That is the peculiar importance of Mr T. S. Eliot. For, though there is, inevitably, a great deal of snobbism in the cult he suffers from, mere snobbism will not account for his prestige among the young. Having a mind unquestionably of rare distinction he has solved his own problem as a poet, and so done more than solve the problem for himself. His influence has been the more effective in that he is a critic as well as a poet, and his criticism and his poetry reinforce each other. It is mainly due to him that no serious poet or critic to-day can fail to realize that English poetry in the future must develop (if at all) along some other line than that running from the Romantics through Tennyson, Swinburne, *A Shropshire Lad*, and Rupert Brooke. He has made a new start, and established new bearings....

T. S. Eliot

...The poem [*The Waste Land*] appeared first in the opening numbers of *The Criterion* (October 1922 and January 1923). The title, we know, comes from Miss J. L. Weston's book, *From Ritual to Romance*, the theme of which is anthropological: the Waste Land there has a significance in terms of Fertility Ritual. What is the significance of the modern Waste Land? The answer may be read in what appears as the rich disorganization of the poem. The seeming disjointedness is intimately related to the erudition that has annoyed so many readers and to the wealth of literary borrowings and allusions. These characteristics reflect the present state of civilization. The traditions and cultures have mingled, and the historical imagination makes the past contemporary; no one tradition can digest so great a variety of materials, and the result is a break-down of forms and the irrevocable loss of that sense of absoluteness which seems necessary to a robust culture. The bearing of this on the technique developed in *Burbank* and *A Cooking Egg* does not need enlarging upon.

In considering our present plight we have also to take account of the incessant rapid change that characterizes the Machine Age. The result is breach of continuity and the uprooting of life. This last metaphor has a peculiar aptness, for what we are witnessing to-day is the final uprooting of the immemorial ways of life, of life rooted in the soil....

The remoteness of the civilization celebrated in *The Waste Land* from the natural rhythms is brought out, in ironical contrast, by the anthropological theme. Vegetation cults, fertility ritual, with their sympathetic magic, represent a harmony of human culture with the natural environment, and express an extreme sense of the unity of life. In the modern Waste Land

> April is the cruellest month, breeding
> Lilacs out of the dead land,

but bringing no quickening to the human spirit. Sex here is sterile, breeding not life and fulfilment but disgust, accidia and unanswerable questions. It is not easy to-day to accept the perpetuation and multiplication of life as ultimate ends.

But the anthropological background has positive functions. It plays an obvious part in evoking that particular sense of the unity of life which is essential to the poem. It helps to establish the level of experience at which the poem works, the mode of consciousness to which it belongs. In *The Waste Land* the development of impersonality that *Gerontion* shows in comparison with *Prufrock* reaches an extreme limit: it would be difficult to imagine a completer transcendence of the individual self, a completer projection of awareness. We have, in the introductory chapter, considered the poet as being at the conscious point of his age. There are ways in which it is possible to be too conscious; and to be so is, as a result of the break-up of forms and the loss of axioms noted above, one of the troubles of the present age (if the abstraction may be permitted, consciousness being in any case a minority affair). We recognize in modern literature the accompanying sense of futility.

The part that science in general has played in the process of disintegration is matter of commonplace: anthropology is, in the present context, a peculiarly significant expression of the scientific spirit. To the anthropological eye beliefs, religions and moralities are human habits – in their odd variety too human. Where the anthropological outlook prevails, sanctions wither. In a contemporary consciousness there is inevitably a great deal of the anthropological, and the background of *The Waste Land* is thus seen to have a further significance.

To be, then, too much conscious and conscious of too much – that is the plight:

> After such knowledge, what forgivenness?

At this point Mr Eliot's note on Tiresias deserves attention:

> Tiresias, although a mere spectator and not indeed a 'character,' is yet the most important personage in the poem, uniting all the rest. Just as the one-eyed merchant, seller of currants, melts into the Phoenician Sailor, and the latter is not wholly distinct from Ferdinand Prince of Naples, so all the women are one woman, and the two sexes meet in Tiresias. What Tiresias *sees*, in fact, is the substance of the poem.

If Mr Eliot's readers have a right to a grievance, is it that he has not given this note more salience; for it provides the clue to *The Waste Land*. It indicates plainly enough what the poem is: an effort to focus an inclusive human consciousness. The effort, in ways suggested above, is characteristic of the age; and in an age of psycho-analysis, an age that has produced the last section of *Ulysses*, Tiresias ... presents himself as the appropriate impersonation. A cultivated modern is (or feels himself to be) intimately aware of the experience of the opposite sex.

Such an undertaking offers a difficult problem of organization, a distinguishing character of the mode of consciousness that promotes it being a lack of organizing principle, the absence of any inherent direction. A poem that is to contain all myths cannot construct itself upon one. It is here that *From Ritual to Romance* comes in. It provides a background of reference that makes possible something in the nature of a musical organization. . . .

Not that the *poem* lacks organization and unity. The frequent judgments that it does betray a wrong approach. The author of *The Lyric Impulse in the Poetry of T. S. Eliot*, for instance, speaks of 'a definitely willed attempt to weld various fine fragments into a metaphysical whole.' But the unity of *The Waste Land* is no more 'metaphysical' than it is narrative or dramatic, and to try to elucidate it metaphysically reveals complete misunderstanding. The unity the poem aims at is that of an inclusive consciousness: the organization it achieves as a work of art is of the kind that has been illustrated, an organization that may, by analogy, be called musical. It exhibits no progression:

> I sat upon the shore
> Fishing, with the arid plain behind me

– the thunder brings no rain to revive the Waste Land, and the poem ends where it began.

At this point the criticism has to be met that . . . the poem in any case exists, and can exist, only for an extremely limited public equipped with special knowledge. The criticism must be admitted. But that the public for it is limited is one of the symptoms of the state of culture that produced the poem. Works expressing the finest consciousness of the age in which the word 'high-brow' has become current are almost inevitably such as to appeal only to a tiny minority. It is still more serious that this minority should be more and more cut off from the world around it – should, indeed, be aware of a hostile and overwhelming environment. This amounts to an admission that there must be something limited about the kind of artistic achievement possible in our time: even Shakespeare in such conditions could hardly have been the 'universal' genius. And *The Waste Land*, clearly, is not of the order of *The Divine Comedy* or of *Lear*. The important admission, then, is not that *The Waste Land* can be appreciated only by a very small minority (how large in any age has the minority been that has really comprehended the masterpieces?), but that this limitation carries with it limitations in self-sufficiency. . . .

Chapter 27
Federico García Lorca

Federico García Lorca (1898–1936) is a writer who achieved mythic status through the circumstances of his death. He was executed in 1936 by troops of the Spanish fascist dictator, Franco, and became an emblem of the authoritarian state's murderous rage against art. During his lifetime Lorca dedicated himself to poetry and drama, two art forms that for him existed on a single continuum. In his work as a poet and dramatist Lorca drew on the traditions of Andalucian folk culture, but his interest was not that of an antiquarian. His collection Gypsy Ballads, *published in 1928, was a critical and popular success in the Spanish-speaking world. It showed Lorca's ability to give a modern edge and inflection to a traditional form. In 1929 he visited New York. One result of his trip was a remarkable sequence of poems,* The Poet in New York, *published posthumously in 1940. Lorca's continuing experiments with verse forms as well as his own development of Surrealist imagery are evident in the poem that develops a powerful vision of the modern city as a place of small ecstasies, large horrors, and racial tensions. During the 1930s Lorca wrote some of his best-known plays, including* Blood Wedding, Yerma, *and* The House of Bernarda Alba.

"Play and Theory of the Duende" was first given as a lecture in Buenos Aires in 1933. The following excerpt shows Lorca creating a bridge between popular traditions of performance and the practice of modern poetry. Lorca identifies duende *– the word in Spanish is usually translated as "demon" – as a primitive sacrificial energy that can be realized in different forms of Spanish art, but especially in "music, dance and spoken poetry." But* duende *is not confined by tradition. In Lorca's thinking it becomes a kind of modernist intensity, comparable to Lawrence's poetry of the instant or Pound's image, but one with a Spanish location and genealogy.*

Play and Theory of the Duende

...As simply as possible, in the register of my poetic voice that has neither the glow of woodwinds nor bends of hemlocks, nor sheep who suddenly turn into knives of irony, I shall try to give you a simple lesson in the hidden spirit of disconsolate Spain.

Whoever finds himself on the bull's hide stretched between the Júcar, Guadalfeo, Sil, and Pisuerga rivers – not to mention the great streams that meet the tawny waves churned by the Plata – often hears people say, "This has much duende." Manuel Torre, great artist of the Andalusian people, once told a singer, "You have a voice, you know the styles, but you will never triumph, because you have no duende."

All over Andalusia, from the rock of Jaén to the whorled shell of Cádiz, the people speak constantly of the "duende," and identify it accurately and instinctively whenever it appears. The marvelous singer El Lebrijano, creator of the debla, used to say, "On days when I sing with duende, no one can touch me." The old Gypsy dancer La Malena once heard Brailowsky play a fragment of Bach and exclaimed, "Olé! That has duende!" but was bored by Gluck, Brahms, and Darius Milhaud. Manuel Torre, who had more culture in the blood than any man I have ever known, pronounced this splendid sentence on hearing Falla play his own *Nocturno del Generalife*: "All that has black sounds has duende." And there is no greater truth.

These black sounds are the mystery, the roots fastened in the mire that we all know and all ignore, the mire that gives us the very substance of art. "Black sounds," said that man of the Spanish people, concurring with Goethe, who defined the duende while speaking of Paganini: "A mysterious power which everyone senses and no philosopher explains."

The duende, then, is a power, not a work; it is a struggle, not a thought. I have heard an old maestro of the guitar say, "The duende is not in the throat; the duende climbs up inside you, from the soles of the feet." Meaning this: it is not a question of ability, but of true, living style, of blood, of the most ancient culture, of spontaneous creation.

This "mysterious power which everyone senses and no philosopher explains" is, in sum, the spirit of the earth, the same duende that scorched the heart of Nietzsche, who looked for its external forms on the Rialto Bridge and in the music of Bizet, without ever finding it and without knowing that the duende he was pursuing had leaped straight from the Greek mysteries to the dancers of Cádiz or the beheaded, Dionysian scream of Silverio's siguiriya.

But I do not want anyone to confuse the duende with the theological demon of doubt at whom Luther, with bacchic feeling, hurled a pot of ink in [Eisenach] nor with the destructive and rather stupid Catholic devil who disguises himself as a bitch to get into convents, nor with the talking monkey carried by Cervantes' Malgesi in his *Comedy of Jealousy and the Forest of Ardenia.*

No. The duende I am talking about is the dark, shuddering descendant of the happy marble-and-salt demon of Socrates, ... on the day Socrates swallowed the hemlock, and of that melancholy demon of Descartes, a demon who was small as a green almond

From *In Search of Duende*, trans. Christopher Maurer (New York: New Directions, 1980), pp. 42–6, 47, 49–50, 51, 52–3.

and who sickened of circles and lines and escaped down the canals to listen to the songs of blurry sailors.

Every man and every artist, whether he is Nietzsche or Cézanne, climbs each step in the tower of his perfection by fighting his duende, not his angel, as has been said, nor his muse. This distinction is fundamental, at the very root of the work.

The angel guides and gives like Saint Raphael, defends and avoids like Saint Michael, announces and forewarns like Saint Gabriel.

The angel dazzles, but he flies high over a man's head, shedding his grace, and the man effortlessly realizes his work or his charm or his dance. The angel on the road to Damascus and the one that came through the crack of the little balcony at Assisi, and the one who tracked Heinrich Suso are all *ordering*, and it is no use resisting their lights, for they beat their steel wings in an atmosphere of predestination.

The muse dictates and sometimes prompts. She can do relatively little, for she is distant and so tired (I saw her twice) that one would have to give her half a heart of marble. Poets who have muses hear voices and do not know where they are coming from. They come from the muse that encourages them and sometimes snacks on them, as happened to Apollinaire, a great poet destroyed by the horrible muse the divine, angelic Rousseau painted him with. The muse awakens the intelligence, bringing a landscape of columns and a false taste of laurels. But intelligence is often the enemy of poetry, because it limits too much, and it elevates the poet to a sharp-edged throne where he forgets that ants could eat him or that a great arsenic lobster could fall on his head – things against which the muses that live in monocles and in the lukewarm lacquered roses of tiny salons are quite helpless.

The muse and angel come from without; the angel gives lights, and the muse gives forms (Hesiod learned from her). Loaf of gold or tunic fold: the poet receives norms in his bosk of laurels. But one must awaken the duende in the remotest mansions of the blood.

And reject the angel, and give the muse a kick in the seat of the pants, and conquer our fear of the smile of violets exhaled by eighteenth-century poetry and of the great telescope in whose lens the muse, sickened by limits, is sleeping.

The true fight is with the duende.

We know the roads where we can search for God, from the barbarous way of the hermit to the subtle one of the mystic. With a tower like Saint Theresa or with the three ways of Saint John of the Cross. And though we may have to cry out in the voice of Isaiah, "Truly thou art a hidden God," in the end God sends each seeker his first fiery thorns.

But there are neither maps nor disciplines to help us find the duende. We only know that he burns the blood like a poultice of broken glass, that he exhausts, that he rejects all the sweet geometry we have learned, that he smashes styles and makes Goya (master of the grays, silvers, and pinks of the best English painting) work with his fists and knees in horrible bitumins. He strips Mossèn Cinto Verdaguer in the cold of the Pyrenees, or takes Jorge Manrique to watch for death in the wasteland of Ocaña, or dresses Rimbaud's delicate body in the green suit of a saltimbanque, or puts the eyes of a dead fish on the Comte de Lautréamont in the early morning of the boulevard.

The great artists of the south of Spain, whether Gypsy or flamenco, whether they sing, dance, or play, know that no emotion is possible unless the duende comes. They may be able to fool people into thinking they have duende – authors and painters and literary fashionmongers do so every day – but we have only to pay a little attention and not surrender to our own indifference in order to discover their fraud and chase away their clumsy artifice.

The Andalusian singer Pastora Pavón, "La Niña de los Peines," dark Hispanic genius whose powers of fantasy are equal to those of Goya or Rafael el Gallo, was once singing in a little tavern in Cádiz. For a while she played with her voice of shadow, of beaten tin, her moss-covered voice, braiding it into her hair or soaking it in wine or letting it wander away to the farthest, darkest bramble patches. No use. Nothing. The audience remained silent.

In the same room was Ignacio Espeleta, handsome as a Roman tortoise, who had once been asked, "How come you don't work?" and had answered, with a smile worthy of Argantonius, "Work? I'm from Cádiz!" And there was Hot Elvira, aristocrat, Sevillian whore, direct descendant of Soledad Vargas, who in 1930 refused to marry a Rothschild because he was not of equal blood. And the Floridas, whom the people take to be butchers but who are really millennial priests who still sacrifice bulls to Geryon. And in one corner sat the formidable bull rancher Don Pablo Murube, with the air of a Cretan mask. When Pastora Pavón finished singing there was total silence, until a tiny man, one of those dancing manikins that rise suddenly out of brandy bottles, sarcastically murmured "¡Viva Paris!" as if to say: "Here we care nothing about ability, technique, skill. Here we are after something else."

As though crazy, torn like a medieval weeper, La Niña de los Peines got to her feet, tossed off a big glass of firewater and began to sing with a scorched throat, without voice, without breath or color, but with duende. She was able to kill all the scaffolding of the song and leave way for a furious, enslaving duende, friend of sand winds, who made the listeners rip their clothes with the same rhythm as do the blacks of the Antilles when, in the "lucumí" rite, they huddle in heaps before the statue of Santa Bárbara.

La Niña de los Peines had to tear her voice because she knew she had an exquisite audience, one which demanded not forms but the marrow of forms, pure music with a body so lean it could stay in the air. She had to rob herself of skill and security, send away her muse and become helpless, that her duende might come and deign to fight her hand to hand. And how she sang! Her voice was no longer playing, it was a jet of blood worthy of her pain and her sincerity, and it opened like a ten-fingered hand around the nailed but stormy feet of a Christ by Juan de Juni.

The duende's arrival always means a radical change in forms. It brings to old planes unknown feelings of freshness, with the quality of something newly created, like a miracle, and it produces an almost religious enthusiasm. . . .

All arts are capable of duende, but where it finds greatest range, naturally, is in music, dance, and spoken poetry, for these arts require a living body to interpret them, being forms that are born, die, and open their contours against an exact present.

Often the duende of the composer passes into the duende of the interpreter, and at other times, when a composer or poet is no such thing, the interpreter's duende – this is interesting – creates a new marvel that looks like, but is not, the primitive form. This was the case of the duende-ridden Eleanora Duse, who looked for plays that had failed so she could make them triumph thanks to her own inventions, and the case of Paganini, as explained by Goethe, who made one hear deep melodies in vulgar trifles, and the case of a delightful little girl I saw in Port St. Marys singing and dancing that horrible, corny Italian song "O Marí!" with such rhythms, silences, and intention that she turned the Neopolitan gewgaw into a hard serpent of raised gold. All three of these people had found something new and totally unprecedented that could give lifeblood and art to bodies devoid of expressiveness.

Every art and in fact every country is capable of duende, angel, and muse. And just as Germany has, with few exceptions, muse, and Italy shall always have angel, so in all ages Spain is moved by the duende, for it is a country of ancient music and dance where the duende squeezes the lemons of dawn – a country of death. A country open to death.

Everywhere else, death is an end. Death comes, and they draw the curtains. Not in Spain. In Spain they open them. Many Spaniards live indoors until the day they die and are taken out into the sunlight. A dead man in Spain is more alive as a dead man than any place else in the world. His profile wounds like the edge of a barber's razor. . . .

The moon-frozen heads that Zurbarán painted, the butter yellow and lightning yellow of El Greco, the narrative of Father Sigüenza, the whole work of Goya, the apse of the church of the Escorial, all polychromed sculpture, the crypt of the house of the Duke of Osuna, the "Death with a guitar" in the Chapel of the Benaventes at Medina de Rioseco – all these mean the same, culturally, as the processions of San Andrés de Teixido, where the dead play a role, the dirges sung by Asturian women with flame-filled torches in the November night, the chant and dance of the Sibyl in the cathedrals of Mallorca and Toledo, the dark "In Recort" of Tortosa, and the innumerable rites of Good Friday which, along with the supremely civilized festival of the bullfight, are the popular triumph of Spanish death. In all the world, only Mexico can take my country's hand.

When the muse sees death arrive, she closes the door or raises a plinth or promenades an urn and writes an epitaph with waxen hand, but soon she is watering her laurel again in a silence that wavers between two breezes. Beneath the broken arch of the ode, she joins with funereal feeling the limpid flowers of fifteenth-century Italian painters, and asks Lucretius' trusty rooster to frighten away unforeseen shades.

When the angel sees death come, he flies in slow circles and weaves, from tears of narcissus and ice, the elegy we have seen tremble in the hands of Keats, Villasandino, Herrera, Bécquer, and Juan Ramón Jiménez. But how it horrifies him to feel even the tiniest spider on his tender, rosy foot!

And the duende? The duende does not come at all unless he sees that death is possible. The duende must know beforehand that he can serenade death's house and rock those branches we all wear, branches that do not have, will never have, any consolation.

With idea, sound, or gesture, the duende enjoys fighting the creator on the very rim of the well. Angel and muse escape with violin and compass; the duende wounds. In the healing of that wound, which never closes, lies the invented, strange qualities of a man's work.

The magical property of a poem is to remain possessed by duende that can baptize in dark water all who look at it, for with duende it is easier to love and understand, and one can be *sure* of being loved and understood. In poetry this struggle for expression and the communication of expression is sometimes fatal.

Think of the case of Saint Theresa, that supremely "flamenco" woman who was so filled with duende. "Flamenco" not because she caught a bull and gave it three magnificent passes (which she did!) and not because she thought herself very lovely in the presence of Fray Juan de Miseria, nor because she slapped the papal nuncio, but because she was one of the few creatures whose duende – not angel, for the angel never attacks – pierced her with a dart and wanted to kill her for having stolen his deepest secret, the subtle bridge that unites the fives senses with the raw wound, that living cloud, that stormy ocean of Love freed from Time....

We have said that the duende loves the rim of the wound, and that he draws near places where forms fuse together into a yearning superior to their visible expression....

The duende works on the body of the dancer as the wind works on sand. With magical power he changes a girl into a lunar paralytic, or fills with adolescent blushes the broken old man begging in the wineshop, or make's woman's hair smell like a nocturnal port, and he works continuously on the arms with expressions that are the mothers of the dances of every age.

But he can never repeat himself. This is interesting to emphasize: the duende does not repeat himself, any more than do the forms of the sea during a squall.

The duende is at his most impressive in the bullfight, for he must fight both death, which can destroy him, and geometry – measurement, the very basis of the festival.

The bull has his orbit and the bullfighter has his, and between these orbits is a point of danger, the vertex of the terrible play.

You can have muse with the muleta and angel with the banderillas and pass for a good bullfighter, but in the capework, when the bull is still clean of wounds, and at the moment of the kill, you need the duende's help to achieve artistic truth.

The bullfighter who scares the audience with his bravery is not bullfighting, but has ridiculously lowered himself to doing what anyone can do – gambling his life. But the torero who is bitten by duende gives a lesson in Pythagorean music and makes us forget he is always tossing his heart over the bull's horns.

From the crepuscule of the ring, Lagartijo with his Roman duende, Joselito with his Jewish duende, Belmonte with his baroque duende, and Cagancho with his Gypsy duende show poets, painters, musicians, and composers the four great roads of Spanish tradition.

Spain is the only country where death is a national spectade, the only one where death sounds long trumpet blasts at the coming of spring, and Spanish art is always ruled by a shrewd duende who makes it different and inventive....

Each art has a duende different in form and style, but their roots all meet in the place where the black sounds of Manuel Torre come from – the essence, the uncontrollable, quivering, common base of wood, sound, canvas, and word.

Behind those black sounds, tenderly and intimately, live zephyrs, ants, volcanoes, and the huge night, straining its waist against the Milky Way.

Ladies and gentlemen, I have raised three arches and with clumsy hand have placed in them the angel, the muse, and the duende.

The muse stays still; she can have a minutely folded tunic or cow eyes like the ones that stare at us in Pompeii or the huge, four-faced nose her great friend Picasso has given her. The angel can shake the hair of Antonello da Messina, the tunic of Lippi, and the violin of Masolino or Rousseau.

The duende... Where is the duende? Through the empty arch comes a wind, a mental wind blowing relentlessly over the heads of the dead, in search of new landscapes and unknown accents; a wind that smells of baby's spittle, crushed grass, and jellyfish veil, announcing the constant baptism of newly created things.

Chapter 28
Gertrude Stein

Gertrude Stein (1874–1946) was an experimental writer whose subtle and subversive adjustments of literary form and language have influenced subsequent generations of writers, including Ernest Hemingway, William Gass, and the Language Poets. She left the United States in 1902 and settled in France, only returning once again for a lecture tour in 1934–5. In Paris she and her brother Leo became early collectors of the work of Matisse and Picasso. But Stein's interest in modern art was more than that of a connoisseur. The example of Cézanne, Matisse, and Picasso showed how the reality of a painting's model could be transformed by composition. Cubism's abstraction and disruption of perspective found their verbal equivalents in her own work in fiction, poetry, and autobiography.

"Poetry and Grammar" was originally one of the lectures Stein gave when she revisited the United States in the mid-1930s. It was first published in 1935 as part of a collection, Lectures in America. *In the following excerpt Stein takes up a traditional critical debate about the distinction between poetry and prose, and decides the difference in terms of grammatical distinctions: prose gravitates towards work on verbs while poetry is attracted to nouns. But grammar in Stein's world is a matter of personal experience, not of abstract classification. It identifies a passion for language and for the world that language can both obscure and reveal.*

Poetry and Grammar

...Poetry is concerned with using with abusing, with losing with wanting, with denying with avoiding with adoring with replacing the noun. It is doing that always doing that, doing that and doing nothing but that. Poetry is doing nothing but using losing refusing and pleasing and betraying and caressing nouns. That is what poetry does, that is what poetry has to do no matter what kind of poetry it is. And there are a great many kinds of poetry.

From *Lectures in America* (New York: Random House, 1935), pp. 136–43, 144–5.

When I said.

A rose is a rose is a rose is a rose.

And then later made that into a ring I made poetry and what did I do I caressed completely caressed and addressed a noun.

Now let us think of poetry any poetry all poetry and let us see if this is not so. Of course it is so anybody can know that.

I have said that a noun is a name of anything by definition that is what it is and a name of anything is not interesting because once you know its name the enjoyment of naming it is over and therefore in writing prose names that is nouns are completely uninteresting. But and that is a thing to be remembered you can love a name and if you love a name then saying that name any number of times only makes you love it more, more violently more persistently more tormentedly. Anybody knows how anybody calls out the name of anybody one loves. And so that is poetry really loving the name of anything and that is not prose. Yes any of you can know that.

Poetry like prose has lived through a good deal. Anybody or anything lives through a good deal. Sometimes it included everything and sometimes it includes only itself and there can be any amount of less and more at any time of its existence.

Of course when poetry really began it practically included everything it included narrative and feelings and excitements and nouns so many nouns and all emotions. It included narrative but now it does not include narrative.

I often wonder how I am ever to come to know all that I am to know about narrative. Narrative is a problem to me. I worry about it a good deal these days and I will not write or lecture about it yet, because I am still too worried about it worried about knowing what it is and how it is and where it is and how it is and how it will be what it is. However as I say now and at this time I do not I will not go into that. Suffice it to say that for the purpose of poetry it has now for a long time not had anything to do with being there.

Perhaps it is a mistake perhaps not that it is no longer there.

I myself think that something else is going to happen about narrative and I work at it a great deal at this time not work but bother about it. Bother is perhaps the better word for what I am doing just now about narrative. But anyway to go back to poetry.

Poetry did then in beginning include everything and it was natural that it should because then everything including what was happening could be made real to anyone by just naming what was happening in other words by doing what poetry always must do by living in nouns.

Nouns are the name of anything. Think of all that early poetry, think of Homer, think of Chaucer, think of the Bible and you will see what I mean you will really realize that they were drunk with nouns, to name to know how to name earth sea and sky and all that was in them was enough to make them live and love in names, and that is what poetry is it is a state of knowing and feeling a name. I know that now but I have only come to that knowledge by long writing.

So then as I say that is what poetry was and slowly as everybody knew the names of everything poetry had less and less to do with everything. Poetry did not change, poetry never changed, from the beginning until now and always in the future poetry will concern itself with the names of things. The names may be repeated in different ways and very soon I will go into that matter but now and always poetry is created by naming names the names of something the names of somebody the names of anything. Nouns are the names of things and so nouns are the basis of poetry.

Before we go any further there is another matter. Why are the lines of poetry short, so much shorter than prose, why do they rhyme, why in order to complete themselves do they have to end with what they began, why are all these things the things that are in the essence of poetry even when the poetry was long even when now the poetry has changed its form.

Once more the answer is the same and that is that such a way to express oneself is the natural way when one expresses oneself in loving the name of anything. Think what you do when you do do that when you love the name of anything really love its name. Inevitably you express yourself in that way, in the way poetry expresses itself that is in short lines in repeating what you began in order to do it again. Think of how you talk to anything whose name is new to you a lover a baby or a dog or a new land or any part of it. Do you not inevitably repeat what you call out and is that calling out not of necessity in short lines. Think about it and you will see what I mean by what you feel.

So as I say poetry is essentially the discovery, the love, the passion for the name of anything.

Now to come back to how I know what I know about poetry.

I was writing *The Making of Americans*, I was completely obsessed by the inner life of everything including generations of everybody's living and I was writing prose, prose that had to do with the balancing the inner balancing of everything. I have already told you all about that.

And then, something happened and I began to discover the names of things, that is not discover the names but discover the things the things to see the things to look at and in so doing I had of course to name them not to give them new names but to see that I could find out how to know that they were there by their names or by replacing their names. And how was I to do so. They had their names and naturally I called them by the names they had and in doing so having begun looking at them I called them by their names with passion and that made poetry, I did not mean it to make poetry but it did, it made the *Tender Buttons*, and the *Tender Buttons* was very good poetry it made a lot more poetry, and I will now more and more tell about that and how it happened.

I discovered everything then and its name, discovered it and its name. I had always known it and its name but all the same I did discover it.

I remember very well when I was a little girl and I and my brother found as children will the love poems of their very very much older brother. This older brother had just written one and it said that he had often sat and looked at any little square of grass and it had been just a square of grass as grass is, but now he was in love and so the little square of grass was all filled with birds and bees and butterflies, the difference was what love was. The poem was funny we and he knew the poem was funny but he was right, being in love made him make poetry, and poetry made him feel the things and their names, and so I repeat nouns are poetry.

So then in *Tender Buttons* I was making poetry but and it seriously troubled me, dimly I knew that nouns made poetry but in prose I no longer needed the help of nouns and in poetry did I need the help of nouns. Was there not a way of naming things that would not invent names, but mean names without naming them.

I had always been very impressed from the time that I was very young by having had it told me and then afterwards feeling it myself that Shakespeare in the forest of Arden had created a forest without mentioning the things that make a forest. You feel it all but he does not name its names.

Now that was a thing that I too felt in me the need of making it be a thing that could be named without using its name. After all one had known its name anything's name for so long, and so the name was not new but the thing being alive was always new.

What was there to do.

I commenced trying to do something in *Tender Buttons* about this thing. I went on and on trying to do this thing. I remember in writing *An Acquaintance With Description* looking at anything until something that was not the name of that thing but was in a way that actual thing would come to be written.

Naturally, and one may say that is what made Walt Whitman naturally that made the change in the form of poetry, that we who had known the names so long did not get a thrill from just knowing them. We that is any human being living has inevitably to feel the thing anything being existing, but the name of that thing of that anything is no longer anything to thrill any one except children. So as everybody has to be a poet, what was there to do. This that I have just described, the creating it without naming it, was what broke the rigid form of the noun the simple noun poetry which now was broken.

Of course you all do know that when I speak of naming anything, I include emotions as well as things.

So then there we were and what were we to do about it. Go on, of course go on what else does anybody do, so I did, I went on.

Of course you might say why not invent new names new languages but that cannot be done. It takes a tremendous amount of inner necessity to invent even one word, one can invent imitating movements and emotions in sounds, and in the poetical language of some languages you have that, the german language as a language suffers from this what the words mean sound too much like what they do, and children do these things by one sort or another of invention but this has really nothing to do with language. Language as a real thing is not imitation either of sounds or colors or emotions it is an intellectual recreation and there is no possible doubt about it and it is going to go on being that as long as humanity is anything. So every one must stay with the language their language that has come to be spoken and written and which has in it all the history of its intellectual recreation.

And so for me the problem of poetry was and it began with *Tender Buttons* to constantly realize the thing anything so that I could recreate that thing. I struggled I struggled desperately with the recreation and the avoidance of nouns as nouns and yet poetry being poetry nouns are nouns. Let me read you bits of the *Portrait of Sherwood Anderson* and *The Birthplace of Bonnes* to show you what I mean.

Can anybody tell by looking which was the towel used for cooking.

A VERY VALENTINE

Very fine is my valentine.
Very fine and very mine.
Very mine is my valentine very mine and very fine.
Very fine is my valentine and mine, very fine very mine and mine is my valentine.

BUNDLES FOR THEM

A HISTORY OF GIVING BUNDLES

We were able to notice that each one in a way carried a bundle, they were not a trouble to them nor were they all bundles as some of them were chickens some of them pheasants some of them sheep and some of them bundles, they were not a trouble to them and then indeed we learned that it was the principal recreation and they were so arranged that they were not given away, and today they were given away.

I will not look at them again.
They will not look for them again.
They have not seen them here again.
They are in there and we hear them again.
In which way are stars brighter than they are. When we have come to this decision. We mention many thousands of buds. And when I close my eyes I see them.
If you hear her snore
It is not before you love her
You love her so that to be her beau is very lovely
She is sweetly there and her curly hair is very lovely.
She is sweetly here and I am very near and that is very lovely.
She is my tender sweet and her little feet are stretched out well which is a treat and very lovely.
Her little tender nose is between her little eyes which close and are very lovely.
She is very lovely and mine which is very lovely.

I found in longer things like Operas and Plays and Portraits and *Lucy Church Amiably* and *An Acquaintance With Description* that I could come nearer to avoiding names in recreating something.

That brings us to the question will poetry continue to be necessarily short as it has been as really good poetry has been for a very long time. Perhaps not and why not.

If enough is new to you to name or not name, and these two things come to the same thing, can you go on long enough. Yes I think so.

So then poetry up to the present time has been a poetry of nouns a poetry of naming something of really naming that thing passionately completely passionately naming that thing by its name.

Slowly and particularly during the nineteenth century the English nineteenth century everybody had come to know too well very much too well the name anything had when you called it by its name.

That is something that inevitably happened. And what else could they do. They had to go on doing what they did, that is calling anything by its name passionately but if as

I say they really knew its name too well could they call it its name simply in that way. Slowly they could not.

And then Walt Whitman came. He wanted really wanted to express the thing and not call it by its name. He worked very hard at that, and he called it *Leaves of Grass* because he wanted it to be as little a well known name to be called upon passionately as possible. I do not at all know whether Whitman knew that he wanted to do this but there is no doubt at all but that is what he did want to do.

You have the complete other end of this thing in a poet like Longfellow, I cite him because a commonplace poet shows you more readily and clearly just what the basis of poetry is than a better one. And Longfellow knew all about calling out names, he on the whole did it without passion but he did it very well.

Of course in the history of poetry there have been many who have also tried to name the thing without naming its names, but this is not a history of poets it is a telling what I know about poetry.

And so knowing all this about poetry I struggled more and more with this thing. I say I knew all this about poetry but I did not really know all this then about poetry, I was coming to know then then when I was writing commencing to know what I do now know about prose but I did not then know anything really to know it of what I now know about poetry.

And so in *Tender Buttons* and then on and on I struggled with the ridding myself of nouns, I knew nouns must go in poetry as they had gone in prose if anything that is everything was to go on meaning something.

And so I went on with this exceeding struggle of knowing really knowing what a thing was really knowing it knowing anything I was seeing anything I was feeling so that its name could be something, by its name coming to be a thing in itself as it was but would not be anything just and only as a name.

I wonder if you do see what I mean.

What I mean by what I have just said is this. I had to feel anything and everything that for me was existing so intensely that I could put it down in writing as a thing in itself without at all necessarily using its name. The name of a thing might be something in itself if it could come to be real enough but just as a name it was not enough something. At any rate that is the way I felt and still do feel about it.

And so I went through a very long struggle and in this struggle I began to be troubled about narrative a narrative of anything that was or might be happening.

The newspapers tell us about it but they tell it to us as nouns tell it to us that is they name it, and in naming it, it as a telling of it is no longer anything. That is what a newspaper is by definition just as a noun is a name by definition.

And so I was slowly beginning to know something about what poetry was. And here was the question if in poetry one could lose the noun as I had really and truly lost it in prose would there be any difference between poetry and prose. As this thing came once more to be a doubt inside me I began to work very hard at poetry.

At that time I wrote *Before the Flowers of Friendship Faded Friendship Faded* and there I went back again to a more or less regular form to see whether inside that regular form I could do what I was sure needed to be done and also to find out if eventually prose and poetry were one or not one.

In writing this poem I found I could be very gay I could be very lively in poetry, I could use very few nouns in poetry and call out practically no names in poetry and yet make poetry really feel and sound as poetry, but was it what I wanted that should be done. But it did not decide anything for me but it did help me in my way. . . .

I decided . . . I decided that if one definitely completely replaced the noun by the thing in itself, it was eventually to be poetry and not prose which would have to deal with everything that was not movement in space. There could no longer be form to decide anything, narrative that is not newspaper narrative but real narrative must of necessity be told by any one having come to the realization that the noun must be replaced not by inner balance but by the thing in itself and that will eventually lead to everything. I am working at this thing and what will it do this I do not know but I hope that I will know. In the Four In America I have gone on beginning but I am sure that there is in this what there is that it is necessary to do if one is to do anything or everything. Do you see what I mean. Well anyway that is the way that I do know feel about it, and this is all that I do know, and I do believe in knowing all I do know, about prose and poetry. The rest will come considerably later.

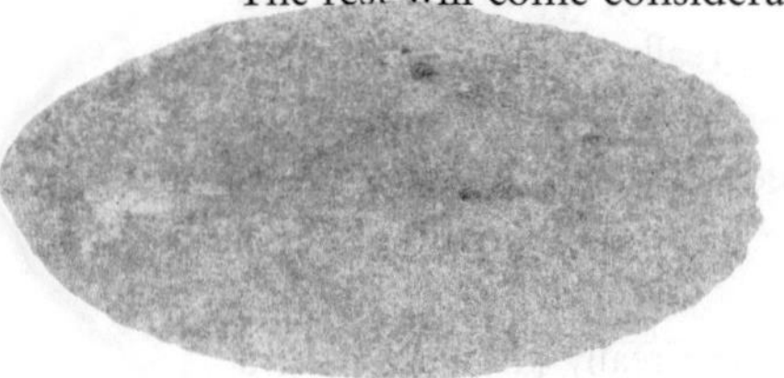

Chapter 29
Marina Tsvetaeva

Marina Tsvetaeva (1892–1941) was one of a generation of Russian poets whose lives and careers were profoundly affected by the Russian Revolution and its aftermath. Her first two books, published in 1910 and 1912, established her reputation as a lyric poet. In her next two books, published in 1921 and 1922, she experimented with lyric sequences organized chronologically and thematically. By 1922 she had gone into exile first in Berlin and Prague, before settling in Paris in 1925. In the 1930s she published her work in émigré presses and from 1928 to 1939 wrote both prose essays and semi-autobiographical works. During the same period she published verse-plays as well as satirical narrative poems, the satire directed against what, in another context, the economist J. K. Galbraith has called the "culture of contentment." She returned to the Soviet Union in 1939. By this time many of her friends and family had been lost in Stalin's purges. Tsvetaeva committed suicide in 1941, shortly after the German invasion of the Soviet Union.

The following excerpt is from "Poets with History and Poets without History," one of Tsvetaeva's most sustained meditations on lyric form. First published in 1935, the essay begins by distinguishing the special impersonality of the lyric first-person voice. Tsvetaeva then defines the difference between two kinds of poet: those like Goethe and Pushkin whose careers are organized around a definite and evolving project, and lyric poets, whose work does not vary or evolve. According to Tsvetaeva, the material of lyric poetry is a feeling that "doesn't need experience, it knows in advance that it is doomed."

Poets with History and Poets without History

...What is the 'I' of a poet? It is – to all appearances – the human 'I' expressed in poetic speech. But only to appearances, for often poems give us something that

From *Art in the Light of Conscience*, trans. Angela Livingstone (Cambridge, Mass.: Harvard University Press, 1992), pp. 136–7, 138–41, 143–4, 145–6.

had been hidden, obscured, even quite stifled, something the person hadn't known was in him, and would never have recognised had it not been for poetry, the poetic gift. Action of forces which are unknown to the one who acts, and which he only becomes conscious of in the instant of action. An almost complete analogy to dreaming. If it were possible to direct one's own dreams – and for some it is, especially children – the analogy would be complete. That which is hidden and buried in you is revealed and exposed in your poems: this is the poetic 'I', your dream-self.

The 'I' of the poet, in other words, is his soul's devotion to certain dreams, his being visited by certain dreams, the secret source – not of his will, but of his whole nature.

The poet's self is a dream-self and a language-self; it is the 'I' of a dreamer awakened by inspired speech and realised only in that speech.

This is the sum of the poet's personality. This is the law of his idiosyncrasy. This is why poets are all so alike and so unalike. Like, because all without exception have dreams. Unlike, in what dreams they have. Like – in their ability to dream; unlike – in the dreams.

All poets can be divided into poets with development and poets without development. Into poets with history and poets without history. The first could be depicted graphically as an arrow shot into infinity, the second – as a circle.

Above the first (the image of the arrow) stands the law of gradual self-discovery. These poets discover themselves through all the phenomena they meet along their way, at every step and in every new object.

Mine or others', the vital or the superfluous, the accidental and the eternal; everything is for them a touchstone. Of their power, which increases with each new obstacle. Their self-discovery is their coming to self-knowledge through the world, self-knowledge of the soul through the visible world. Their path is the path of experience. As they walk, we physically sense a wind, the air they cleave with their brows. A wind blows from them.

They walk without turning round. Their experience accumulates as if by itself, and piles up somewhere behind, like a load on the back which never makes the back hunch. One doesn't look round at the sack on one's back. The walker knows nothing of his rucksack until the moment he needs it: at the stopping-place. The Goethe of *Götz von Berlichingen* and the Goethe of the *Metamorphosis of Plants* are not acquainted with each other. Goethe put in his sack everything he needed from *himself of that time*, left himself in the wondrous forests of young Germany and of his own youth, and went – onward. Had the mature Goethe met the young Goethe at a crossroads, he might actually have failed to recognise him and might have sought to make his acquaintance. I'm not talking of Goethe the person, but of Goethe the creator, and I take this great example as an especially evident one.

Poets with history (like people with history in general and like history itself) do not even renounce themselves: they simply don't turn round to themselves – no time for it, only onward! Such is the law of movement and of pressing forward....

Poets with history are, above all, poets of a theme. We always know what they are writing about. And, if we don't learn where they were going to, we do at least realise, when their journey is completed, that they had always been going somewhere (the existence of a goal). Rarely are they pure lyricists. Too large in size and scope, their own 'I' is too small for them – even the biggest is too small – or they spread it out till nothing is left and it merges with the rim of the horizon (Goethe, Pushkin). The human 'I' becomes the 'I' of a country – a people – a given continent – a century – a millennium – the heavenly vault (Goethe's geological 'I': 'I live in the millennia'). For such a poet a theme is the occasion for a new self, and not necessarily a human one. Their whole earthly path is a sequence of reincarnations, not necessarily into a human being. From a human to a stone, a flower, a constellation. They seem to incarnate in themselves all the days of creation.

Poets with history are, above all, poets of will. I don't mean the will to fulfil, which is taken for granted: no one will doubt that a physically huge bulk like *Faust*, or indeed any poem of a thousand lines, cannot come into being by itself. Eight, sixteen or, rarely, twenty lines may come about by themselves – the lyric tide most often lays fragments at our feet, albeit the most precious ones. I mean the will to choose, the will to have choice. To decide not merely to become another, but – this particular other. To decide to part with oneself. To decide – like the hero in the fairy tale – between right, left and straight on (but, like that same hero, never backward!). Waking up one morning, Pushkin makes a decision: 'Today I shall write Mozart!' This Mozart is his refusal to a multitude of other visions and subjects; it is total choice – that is, a sacrifice. To use contemporary vocabulary, I'd say that the poet with history rejects everything that lies outside his general line – the line of his personality, his gift, his history. The choice is made by his infallible instinct for the most important. And yet, at the end of Pushkin's path, we have the sense that Pushkin could not have done otherwise than create what he did create, could not have written anything he did not write... And no one regrets that in Gogol's favour he refused the *Dead Souls* project, something that lay on Gogol's general line. (The poet with history also has a clear view of others – Pushkin had, especially.) The main feature of poets of this sort is the striving towards a goal. A poet without history cannot have a striving towards a goal. He himself doesn't know what the lyric flood will bring him.

Pure lyric poetry has no project. You can't make yourself have a particular dream or feel a particular feeling. Pure lyricism is the sheer condition of going through something, suffering something through, and in the intervals (when the poet is not being summoned by Apollo to holy sacrifice), in the ebbs of inspiration, it is a condition of infinite poverty. The sea has departed, carried everything away, and won't return *before its own time.* A continual, awful hanging in the air, on the word of honour of perfidious inspiration. And suppose one day it lets you go?

Pure lyric poetry is solely the record of our dreams and feelings, along with the entreaty that these dreams and feelings should never run dry... To demand more from lyricism... But what more could be demanded from it?

The lyric poet has nothing to grasp hold of: he has neither the skeleton of a theme nor obligatory hours of work at a desk; no material he can dip into, which he's preoccupied with or even immersed in, at the ebb times: he is wholly suspended on a thread of trust.

Don't expect sacrifices: the pure lyricist sacrifices nothing – he is glad when anything comes at all. Don't expect moral choice from him either – whatever comes, 'bad' or 'good', he is so happy it has come at all that to you (society, morality, God) he won't yield a thing.

The lyric poet is given only the will to fulfil his task, just enough for sorting out the tide's offerings.

Pure lyricism is nothing but the recording of our dreams and sensations. The greater the poet, the purer the record.

A walker and a stylite. For the poet without history is a stylite or – same thing – a sleeper. Whatever may happen around his pillar, whatever the waves of history may create (or destroy), he sees, hears and knows only what is his. (Whatever may be going on around him, he sees only his own dreams.) Sometimes he seems to be really great, like Boris Pasternak, but the small and the great draw us equally irresistibly into the enchanted circle of dream. We too turn into stone.

To exactly the extent that other people's dreams, when they tell us them, are inexpressive and uninfectious, these lyric dreams are irresistible, affecting us more than our own!

> Now beyond the slumbering mountain
> the evening ray has faded.
> In a resounding stream the hot
> spring faintly sparkles...

These lines by the young Lermontov are more powerful than all my childhood dreams – and not only childhood, and not only mine.

It could be said of poets without history that their soul and their personality are formed in their mother's womb. The don't need to learn or acquire or fathom anything at all – they know everything from the start. They don't ask about anything – they make manifest. Evidence, experience are nothing to them.

Sometimes the range of their knowledge is very narrow. They don't go beyond it. Sometimes the range of their knowledge is very wide. They never narrow it to oblige experience.

They came into the world not to learn, but to say. To say what they already know: everything they know (if it is a lot) or the only thing they know (if it is just one thing).

They came into the world to make themselves known. Pure lyricists, only-lyricists, don't allow anything alien into themselves, and they have an instinct for this just as poets with history have an instinct for their own general line. The whole empirical world is to them a foreign body. In this sense they have the power to choose, or more exactly, the power to select, or more exactly still, the power to reject. But the rejection is done by the whole of their nature, not by their will alone. And is usually unconscious. In this, as in much, maybe in everything, they are children. Here is how the world is for them: 'That's the wrong way.' – 'No, it's the right way! I know! I know better!' What does he know? That any other way is impossible. They are the absolute opposite: I am the world (meaning the human world – society, family, morality, ruling church, science, commonsense, any form of power – human organisation in general, including our much-famed 'progress'). Enter into the poems and the biography too, which are always a single whole.

For poets with history there are no foreign bodies, they are conscious participants in the world. Their 'I' is equal to the world. From the human to the cosmic.

Here lies the distinction between the genius and the lyric genius. There do exist purely lyric geniuses. But we never call them 'geniuses'. The way this kind of genius is closed upon himself, and doomed to himself, is expressed in the adjective 'lyrical'. Just as the boundlessness of the genius, his impersonality even, is expressed by the absence, even impossibility, of any adjective whatever. (Every adjective, since it gives an exact meaning, is limiting.)

The 'I' cannot be a genius. A genius may call itself 'I', dress itself in a certain name, make use of certain earthly tokens. We must not forget that among ancient peoples 'genius' signified quite factually a good higher being, a divinity from *above*, not the person himself. Goethe was a genius because above him there hovered a genius. This genius distracted and sustained him up to the end of his eighty-third year, up to the last page of *Faust* Part Two. That same genius is shown in his immortal face.

A last, and perhaps the simplest, explanation. Pure lyric poetry lives on feelings. Feelings are always the same. Feelings are not regular or consistent. They are all given to us at once, all the feelings we are ever to experience; like the flames of a torch, they are squeezed into our breast from birth. Feeling (the childhood of a person, a nation, the planet) always starts at a maximum, and in strong people and in poets it remains at that maximum. Feeling doesn't need a cause, it itself is the cause of everything. Feeling doesn't need experience, it knows everything earlier and better. (Every sentiment is also a presentiment.) Someone in whom there is love, loves; someone in whom there is anger, gets angry; and someone in whom there is a sense of hurt, is hurt, from the day he is born. Sensitivity to hurt gives rise to hurt. Feeling doesn't need experience, it knows in advance that it is doomed. There's nothing for feeling to do on the periphery of the visible, it is in the centre, is itself the centre. There's nothing for feeling to seek along any roads, it knows that it will come – will lead – into itself.

An enchanted circle. A dream circle. A magic circle.

Thus once again:

> Thought is an arrow.
> Feeling is a circle.

This is the essence of the purely lyrical sort of poet, the nature of pure lyricism. And if they sometimes seem to develop and change – it is not *they* that develop and change, but only their vocabulary, their linguistic equipment. . . .

Of our contemporaries I will name three exceptional cases of perfection in the innate lyrical quality: Anna Akhmatova, Osip Mandelstam and Boris Pasternak, poets born already equipped with their own vocabulary and with maximum expressiveness.

When in the first poem of her first book, the young Akhmatova conveys the confusion of love in the lines:

> I drew my left-hand glove
> onto my right hand –

she conveys at one blow all feminine and all lyric confusion (all the confusion of the empirical!), immortalising with one flourish of the pen that ancient nervous gesture of woman and of poet who at life's great moments forget right and left – not only of glove, but of hand, and of country of the world, suddenly losing all their certainty. Through a patent and even penetrating precision of detail, something bigger than an emotional state is affirmed and symbolised – a whole structure of the mind. (A poet lets go the pen, a woman lets go her lover's hand, and immediately they can't tell the left hand from the right.) In brief, from these two lines of Akhmatova's, a broad, abundant flow of associations comes into being, associations which spread like the circles from a flung pebble. The whole woman, the whole poet is in these two lines; the whole Akhmatova, unique, unrepeatable, inimitable. Before Akhmatova none of us portrayed a gesture like this. And no one did after her. (Of course, Akhmatova is not only this gesture; I'm giving just one of her main characteristics.) 'Again or still?' was what I asked in 1916, about Akhmatova who in 1912 had begun by dipping the same jug into the same sea. Now, seventeen years later, I can see that then, without suspecting it, she had provided the formula for a lyric constant. Listen to the image: it has a depth. Look at its movement: it conveys roundness. The roundness of the dipping gesture, essentially deep. A jug. A sea. Together they constitute volume. Thinking about it today, seventeen years later, I might say: 'the same bucket into the same well', preferring an accurate image to a beautiful one. But the essence of the image would be the same. I offer this as yet another instance of lyric constancy.

I've never heard anyone say, about Akhmatova or Pasternak: 'Same thing over and over again – boring!' Just as you cannot say 'Same thing over and over again – boring!' about the sea, of which Pasternak wrote the following:

> All becomes dull, only you never grow familiar –
> days pass, years pass, thousands and thousands of years...

For, both Akhmatova and Pasternak scoop not from the surface of the sea (the heart), but from its depth (the fathomless). They can't become boring, just as sleep can't be boring – which is always the same, but with always different dreams. Just as dreaming can't be boring....

Lyricism, for all that it is doomed to itself, is itself inexhaustible. (Perhaps the best formula for the lyrical and for the lyric essence is this: being doomed to inexhaustibility!) The more you draw out, the more there remains. This is why it never disappears. This is why we fling ourselves with such avidity on every new lyric poet: maybe he'll succeed in drawing out all that essence which is the soul, thereby slaking our own? It's as if they were all trying to get us drunk on bitter, salty, green sea-water and each time we believe it is drinking-water. And once again it turns out bitter! (We must not forget that the structure of the sea, of the blood, and of lyricism – is one and the same.)

What's true of dull people is true of dull poets: what's dull is not the monotony, but the fact that the thing repeated – though it may be very varied – is insignificant. How murderously identical are the newspapers on the table, with all their various dissonances; how murderously identical are the Parisian women in the streets with all their variety! As if these things – advertisements, newspapers, Parisian women – were not varied, but were all the same. At all the crossroads, in all the shops and trams, at all auctions, in all concert-halls – innumerable, and yet, however many, they all amount to one thing! And this one thing is: everyone!

It is boring when, instead of a human face, you see something worse than a mask: a mould for the mass production of facelessness: paper money with no security in gold! When, instead of a person's own words, no matter how clumsy, you hear someone else's, no matter how brilliant (which, by the way, straightaway lose their brilliance – like the fur on a dead animal). It is boring when you hear from the person you're talking to not his own words, but somebody else's. Moreover, if a repetition has bored you, you can be pretty sure it's a case of someone else's words – words not created, but repeated. For one cannot repeat oneself in words: even the slightest change in the speech means it is not a repetition but a transformation with another essence behind it. Even if one tries to repeat a thought of one's own, already caressed, one will involuntarily do it differently every time; the slightest change and something new is said. Unless one learns it by heart. When a poet is obviously 'repeating himself', it means he has abandoned his creative self and is robbing himself just as if he were robbing someone else.

In calling renewal the pivot of lyricism, I don't mean the renewal of my own or others' dreams and images, I only mean the return of the lyric wave in which the composition of the lyrical is constant.

The wave always returns, and always returns as a different wave.

The same water – a different wave.

What matters is that it is a *wave.*

What matters is that the wave *will return.*

What matters is that it will *always* return *different.*

What matters most of all: however different the returning wave, it will always return as a wave of the *sea.*

What is a wave? Composition and muscle. The same goes for lyric poetry.

Similarity, variation on the same, is not repetition. Similarity is in the nature of things, at the basis of nature itself. In the renewing (the constant developing) of the given forms of trees, not one oak repeats its neighbour, and on one and the same oak not one leaf repeats a preceding one. Similarity in nature: creation of the similar, not of the same; the like, not the identical; new, not old; creation, not repetition.

Each new leaf is the next variation on the eternal theme of the oak. Renewal in nature: infinite variation on a single theme.

Repetition does not happen in nature, it is outside nature, thus outside creativity too. That is the way it is. Only machines repeat. In 'poets who repeat', the machine of memory, separated from the springs of creativity, has become a mere mechanism.

Repetition is the purely mechanical reproduction of something which inevitably turns into someone else's, even when it is one's own. For, if I've learnt my own thought by heart, I repeat it as though it were someone else's, without the participation of anything creative. It may be that only the intonation is creative, is mine, the feeling, that is, with which I utter it and change its form, the linguistic and semantic vicinity in which I place it. But when, for example, I write on a blank page the bare formula I once found: 'Etre vaut mieux qu'avoir' ('it's better to be than to have'), I repeat a formula which doesn't belong to me any more than an algebraic one does. A thing can only be created once. . . .

Chapter 30
Walter Benjamin

Walter Benjamin (1892–1940) was a philosopher, cultural theorist, and critic, who wrote in a variety of genres: short newspaper articles, critical and philosophical essays, and longer works based on historical research and philosophical critique such as his rejected doctoral thesis, The Origins of the German Mourning Play. *Benjamin's survival was threatened by the rise of fascism in Germany and in 1933 he moved to Paris. Here he dedicated himself to his unfinished work, an encyclopedic study of nineteenth-century Paris, now known as* The Arcades Project. *Benjamin was forced to flee once again when the Germans invaded France. He committed suicide in 1940 after he failed to cross the border between France and Spain. The collection and translation of his work from the 1960s onwards has had a profound impact on literary criticism, cultural theory, film studies, and philosophy.*

Nineteenth-century Paris was for Benjamin the first city of modernity. He studied its architecture, its commodities and fashions, its politics, and its entertainment industry. A central figure in this study is the poet Charles Baudelaire. According to Benjamin, Baudelaire incorporated modern urban experience into the form and language as well as the content of his poetry. His work produced a double perspective: at once within and outside the crowds and the shocks of the city. The following excerpt is from The Paris of the Second Empire in Baudelaire, *first published in German in 1969, but written by Benjamin in 1938. Characteristically detailed and digressive, it traces the defeated heroism Benjamin discerned at the heart of both Baudelaire's poetry and modernism.*

Modernism

Baudelaire patterned his image of the artist after an image of the hero. From the beginning, each is an advocate of the other. In the 'Salon de 1845' he wrote: 'Will-

From *Charles Baudelaire: A Lyric Poet in the Era of High Capitalism*, trans. Harry Zohn (London: NLB, 1973), pp. 67–8, 69, 70, 71–2, 74–6, 79–87, 94–6, 99–100.

power has to be well developed and always very fruitful, to be able to give the stamp of uniqueness even to second-rate works. The viewer enjoys the effort and his eye drinks the sweat'... Baudelaire knows the '*indolence naturelle des inspirés*'; Musset – so he says – never understood how much work it takes 'to let a work of art emerge from a daydream'. He, on the other hand, comes before the public from the very first moment with his own code, precepts, and taboos. Barrès claimed that he could recognize 'in every little word of Baudelaire a trace of the toil that helped him achieve such great things'. 'Even in his nervous crises,' writes Gourmont, 'Baudelaire retains something healthy.' The most felicitous formulation is given by the symbolist Gustave Kahn when he says that 'with Baudelaire, poetic work resembled a physical effort'. Proof of this may be found in his work – in a metaphor worth closer inspection.

It is the metaphor of the fencer. Baudelaire was fond of using it to present martial elements as artistic elements. When he describes Constantin Guys, to whom he was attached, he catches him at a time when others are asleep. How he stands there 'bent over his table, scrutinizing the sheet of paper just as intently as he does the objects around him by day; how he *stabs away* with his pencil, his pen, his brush, spurts water from his glass to the ceiling and tries his pen on his shirt; how he pursues his work swiftly and intensely, as though afraid that his images might escape him; thus he is combative, even when alone, and parries his own blows'. In the opening stanza of his poem 'Le Soleil', Baudelaire portrayed himself in the throes of such 'curious exercise', and this is probably the only place in the *Fleurs du mal* where he is shown at his poetic labours. The duel in which every artist is engaged and in which he 'screams with fright before he is vanquished' is given the framework of an idyll; its violence recedes into the background and its charm may be recognized.

> Le long du vieux faubourg, où pendent aux masures
> Les persiennes, abri des secrètes luxures,
> Quand le soleil cruel frappe à traits redoublés
> Sur la ville et les champs, sur les toits et les blés,
> Je vais m'exercer seul à ma fantasque escrime,
> Flairant dans tous les coins les hasards de la rime,
> Trébuchant sur les mots comme sur les pavés,
> Heurtant parfois des vers depuis longtemps rêvés.

(Through the old suburb, where the Persian blinds hang at the windows of tumbledown houses, hiding furtive pleasures; when the cruel sun strikes blow upon blow on the city and the meadows, the roofs and the cornfields, I go practising my fantastic fencing all alone, scenting a chance rhyme in every corner, stumbling against words as against cobblestones, sometimes striking on verses I had long dreamt of.)

(translated by Francis Scarfe)

...

If one tries to picture this rhythm and investigate this mode of work, it turns out that Baudelaire's *flâneur* was not a self-portrait of the poet to the extent that this might be assumed. An important trait of the real-life Baudelaire – that is, of the man committed to his work – is not part of this portrayal: his absentmindedness. In the *flâneur*, the joy of watching is triumphant. It can concentrate on observation, the result is the amateur detective. Or it can stagnate in the gaper; then the *flâneur* has turned into a *badaud*. The revealing presentations of the big city have come from neither. They are the work of those who have traversed the city absently, as it were, lost in thought or worry. The image of *fantasque escrime* does justice to them; Baudelaire has in mind their condition which is anything but the condition of the observer....

In his later years Baudelaire was not often able to move through the streets of Paris as a stroller. His creditors pursued him, his illness made itself felt, and there was strife between him and his mistress. The shocks which his worries caused him and the hundred ideas with which he parried them were reproduced by Baudelaire the poet in the feints of his prosody. To recognize the labour that Baudelaire bestowed upon his poems under the image of fencing means to learn to comprehend them as a continuous series of tiny improvisations. The variants of his poems indicate how constantly he was at work and how much he was concerned with the least of them....

...The stereotypes in Baudelaire's experiences, the lack of mediation between his ideas, and the congealed uneasiness in his features indicate that he did not have at his disposal the reserves which great knowledge and a comprehensive view of history give a person. 'Baudelaire had what is a great defect in a writer, a defect of which he was not aware: he was ignorant. What he knew, he knew thoroughly; but he knew little. He remained unacquainted with history, physiology, archaeology, and philosophy.... He had little interest in the outside world; he may have been aware of it, but he certainly did not study it.' In the face of this and similar criticisms, it may be natural and legitimate to point to the necessary and useful inaccessibility of a working poet and to the idiosyncratic touches which are essential to all productivity. But there is another side to the situation, and it promotes the overtaxing of the productive person in the name of a principle, the principle of 'creativity'. This overtaxing is all the more dangerous because as it flatters the self-esteem of the productive person, it effectively guards the interests of a social order that is hostile to him. The life-style of the bohemian has contributed to creating a superstition about creativeness which Marx has countered with an observation that applies equally to intellectual and to manual labour. To the opening sentence of the draft of the Gotha programme, 'Labour is the source of all wealth and all culture', he appends this critical note: 'The bourgeois have very good reasons for imputing supernatural creative power to labour, since it follows precisely from the fact that labour depends on nature, that a man who has no other property than his labour must be in all societies and civilizations the slave of other people who have become proprietors of the material working conditions.' Baudelaire owned few of the material conditions of intellectual labour. From a library to an apartment there was nothing that he did not have to do without in the course of his life, which was equally unsteady in Paris and outside the city....

The hero is the true subject of modernism. In other words, it takes a heroic constitution to live modernism. That was also Balzac's opinion. With their belief, Balzac and Baudelaire are in opposition to Romanticism. They transfigure passions and resolution; the Romanticists transfigured renunciation and surrender. But the new way of looking at things is far more variegated and richer in reservations in a poet than in a storyteller. Two figures of speech will demonstrate how this is so. Both introduce the hero in his modern manifestation to the reader. In Balzac the gladiator becomes a *commis voyageur.* The great travelling salesman Gaudissart is getting ready to work the Touraine. Balzac describes his preparations and interrupts himself to exclaim: 'What an athlete! What an arena! And what weapons: he, the world, and his glib tongue!' Baudelaire on the other hand, recognizes the fencing slave in the proletarian. Of the promises which the wine gives the disinherited, the fifth stanza of the poem 'L'Ame du vin' names the following:

> J'allumerai les yeux de ta femme ravie;
> À ton fils je rendrai sa force et ses couleurs
> Et serai pour ce frêle athlète de la vie
> L'huile qui raffermit les muscles des lutteurs.
>
> (I'll light the eyes of your enraptured wife;
> Give your son strength and make his pale cheeks ruddy
> And for this frail athlete of life
> Will be the oil that toughens the wrestler's body.)
> (translated by C. F. MacIntyre)

What the man working for wages achieves in his daily work is no less than what in ancient times helped a gladiator win applause and fame. This image is one of the best insights that Baudelaire had; it derives from his reflection about his own situation. A passage from the 'Salon de 1859' indicates how he wanted to have it viewed. 'When I hear how a Raphael or a Veronese are glorified with the veiled intention of depreciating what came after them, . . . I ask myself whether an achievement which must be rated *at least* equal to theirs . . . is not infinitely *more meritorious*, because it triumphed in a hostile atmosphere and place.'. . .

The resistance which modernism offers to the natural, productive élan of a person is out of proportion to his strength. It is understandable if a person grows tired and takes refuge in death. Modernism must be under the sign of suicide, an act which seals a heroic will that makes no concessions to a mentality inimical towards this will. This suicide is not a resignation but a heroic passion. It is *the* achievement of modernism in the realm of passions. In this form, as the *passion particulière de la vie moderne*, suicide appears in the classical passage that is devoted to the theory of modernism. The suicide of ancient heroes is an exception. 'Apart from Heracles on Mount Oeta, Cato of Utica, and Cleopatra . . . where does one find suicides in the ancient accounts?' Not that Baudelaire could find them in modern accounts, the reference to Rousseau and Balzac which follows this sentence is a meagre one. But modernism does keep the raw material for such presentations in readiness, and it waits for the man who will master it. This raw material has deposited itself in those very strata that have turned out to be the foundation of modernism. The first notes on the theory of modernism were made in 1845. Around that time the idea of suicide became familiar to the working masses. 'People are scrambling for copies of a lithograph depicting an English worker who is taking his life because he despairs of earning a livelihood. One worker even goes to

Eugène Sue's apartment and hangs himself there. In his hand there is a slip of paper with this note; "I thought dying would be easier for me if I die under the roof of a man who stands up for us and loves us".' In 1841 Adolphe Boyer, a printer, published a small book entitled *De l'état des ouvriers et de son amélioration par l'organisation du travail.* It was a moderate presentation that sought to recruit the old corporations of itinerant journeymen which stuck to guild practices for the workers' associations. His work was unsuccessful. The author took his own life and in an open letter invited his companions in misfortune to follow suit. Someone like Baudelaire could very well have viewed suicide as the only heroic act that had remained for the *multitudes maladives* of the cities in reactionary times. Perhaps he saw [Alfred] Rethel's 'Death', which he greatly admired, as the work of a subtle artist in front of an easel sketching on a canvas the ways in which suicides died....

The poets find the refuse of society on their street and derive their heroic subject from this very refuse. This means that a common type is, as it were, superimposed upon their illustrious type. This new type is permeated by the features of the ragpicker with whom Baudelaire repeatedly concerned himself. One year before he wrote 'Le Vin des chiffonniers' he published a prose presentation of the figure: 'Here we have a man who has to gather the day's refuse in the capital city. Everything that the big city threw away, everything it lost, everything it despised, everything it crushed underfoot, he catalogues and collects. He collates the annals of intemperance, the *capharnaüm* (stockpile) of waste. He sorts things out and makes a wise choice; he collects, like a miser guarding a treasure, the refuse which will assume the shape of useful or gratifying objects between the jaws of the goddess of Industry.' This description is one extended metaphor for the procedure of the poet in Baudelaire's spirit. Ragpicker or poet – the refuse concerns both, and both go about their business in solitude at times when the citizens indulge in sleeping; even the gesture is the same with both. Nadar speaks of Baudelaire's 'jerky gait' ('*pas saccadé*'). This is the gait of the poet who roams the city in search of rhyme-booty; it must also be the gait of the ragpicker who stops on his path every few moments to pick up the refuse he encounters. There is much to indicate that Baudelaire secretly wished to bring this relationship out. It contains a prophecy in any case. Sixty years later a brother of the poet who has deteriorated into a ragpicker appears in Apollinaire. It is Croniamantal, the *poète assassiné*, the first victim of the pogrom that is intended to end the species of the lyric poets in the entire world.

...Do the dregs of society supply the heroes of the big city? Or is the hero the poet who fashions his work from such material? The theory of modernism admits both. But in a late poem, 'Les Plaintes d'un Icare', the ageing Baudelaire indicates that he no longer feels with the kind of people among whom he sought heroes in his youth.

> Les amants des prostituées
> Sont heureux, dispos et repus;
> Quant à moi, mes bras sont rompus
> Pour avoir étreint des nuées.

(Who gives a prostitute his love
Is happy, satisfied and free;
My arms are broken utterly
For having clasped the clouds above.)
(translated by Lewis Piaget Shanks)

The poet, who, as the poem's title indicates is the stand-in for the ancient hero, has had to give way to the modern hero whose deeds are reported by the *Gazette des Tribunaux.* In actuality this resignation is already inherent in the concept of the modern hero. He is predestined for doom, and no tragedian need come forward to set forth the necessary for this downfall. But once modernism has received its due, its time has run out. Then it will be put to the test. After its end it will become apparent whether it will ever be able to become antiquity.

Baudelaire always remained aware of this question. He experienced the ancient claim to immortality as his claim to being read as an ancient writer some day. 'That all *modernism* is worthy of becoming antiquity some day'.... What made him indifferent towards opportunities and occasions was the consciousness of that mission. In the epoch to which he belonged, nothing came closer to the 'task' of the ancient hero, to the 'labours' of a Hercules than the task imposed upon him as his very own; to give shape to modernity.

Among all relationships into which modernity entered, its relationship to classical antiquity stands out. For Baudelaire this could be seen in the works of Victor Hugo. 'Fate led him...to remodel the classical ode and classical tragedy...into the poems and the dramas which we know by him.' Modernity designates an epoch, and it also denotes the energies which are at work in this epoch to bring it close to antiquity. Baudelaire conceded such energies to Hugo reluctantly and in only a few cases. Wagner, on the other hand, appeared to him as an unbounded, unadulterated effusion of this energy. 'If in the choice of his subjects and his dramatic method Wagner approaches classical antiquity, his passionate power of expression makes him the most important representative of modernity at the present time.' This sentence contains Baudelaire's theory of modern art in a nutshell. In his view, the quality of antiquity is limited to the construction; the substance and the inspiration of a work are the concern of modernism. 'Woe to him who studies other aspects of antiquity than pure art, logic, the general method. He who becomes excessively absorbed in antiquity, divests himself of the privileges opportunity offers him.' And in the final passage of his essay on Guys he says 'Everywhere he sought the transitory, fleeting beauty of our present life, the character of what the reader has permitted us to call *modernism.*' In summary form, his doctrine reads as follows: 'A constant, unchangeable element...and a relative, limited element cooperates to produce beauty.... The latter element is supplied by the epoch, by fashion, by morality, and the passions. Without this second element...the first would not be assimilable.' One cannot say that this is a profound analysis.

In Baudelaire's view of modernism, the theory of modern art is the weakest point. His general view brings out the modern themes; his theory of art should probably have concerned itself with classical art, but Baudelaire never attempted anything of the kind. His theory did not cope with the resignation which in his work appears as a loss of nature and naïveté. Its dependence on Poe down to its formulation is one expression of its constraint. Its polemical orientation is another; it stands out against the grey background of historicism, against the academic Alexandrinism which was in vogue with Villemain and Cousin. None of the aesthetic reflections in Baudelaire's theory of art presented modernism in its interpenetration with classical antiquity, something that was done in certain poems of the *Fleurs du mal.*

Among these the poem 'Le Cygne' is paramount. It is no accident that it is an allegory. The city which is in constant flux grows rigid. It becomes as brittle and as transparent as glass – that is, as far as its meaning is concerned – 'The form of a city, alas, changes more quickly than a mortal's heart' ('*La forme d'une ville/Change plus vite, hélas! que le coeur d'un mortel*'). The stature of Paris is fragile; it is surrounded by symbols of fragility – living creatures (the negress and the swan) and historical figures (Andromache, 'widow of Hector and wife of Helenus'). Their common feature is sadness about what was and lack of hope for what is to come. In the final analysis, this decrepitude constitutes the closest connection between modernism and antiquity. Wherever Paris occurs in the *Fleurs du mal,* it bears the signs of this decrepitude. 'Le Crépuscule du matin' is the sobbing of an awakening person reproduced through the material of a city. 'Le Soleil' shows the city threadbare, like an old fabric in the sunlight. The old man who resignedly reaches for his tools day after day because even in his old age he has not been freed from want is the allegory of the city, and among its inhabitants old women – 'Les Petites vieilles' – are the only spiritualized ones. That these poems have travelled through the decades unchallenged, they owe to a reservation which guards them. It is the reservation against the big city, and it differentiates them from almost all later big-city poetry. A stanza by Verhaeren suffices to understand what is involved here.

> Et qu'importent les maux et les heures démentes
> Et les cuves de vice où la cité fermente
> Si quelque jour, du fond des brouillards et des voiles
> Surgit un nouveau Christ, en lumière sculpté
> Qui soulève vers lui l'humanité
> Et la baptise au feu de nouvelles étoiles.

(And of what consequence are the evils and the lunatic hours and the vats of vice in which the city ferments, if some day a new Christ arises from the fog and the veils in a sculpted light, lifts humanity toward himself and baptizes it by the fire of new stars?)

Baudelaire knows no such perspectives. His idea of the decrepitude of the big city is the basis of the permanence of the poems which he has written about Paris.

The poem 'Le Cygne', too, is dedicated to Hugo, one of the few men whose work, it seemed to Baudelaire, produced a new antiquity. To the extent that one can speak of a source of inspiration in Hugo's case, it was fundamentally different from Baudelaire's. Hugo did not know the capacity to become rigid which – if a biological term may be used – manifests itself a hundredfold in Baudelaire's writings as a kind of mimesis of death. On the other hand, it is possible to speak of Hugo's chthonian bent. Although it is not specifically mentioned, it is brought out in the following remarks by Charles

Péguy which reveal where the difference between Hugo's and Baudelaire's conceptions of classical antiquity lies. 'One thing one may be sure of: when Hugo saw a beggar by the road, he saw him the way he is, really saw him the way he really is . . . saw him, the ancient beggar, the ancient supplicant, on the ancient road. When he saw the marble inlay of one of our fireplaces or the cemented bricks on one of our modern fireplaces, he saw them as what they are – namely, the stones from the hearth, the stones from the ancient hearth. When he saw the door of a house and the threshold, which is usually a squared stone, he recognized in this squared stone the antique line, the line of the sacred threshold which it is.' There is no better commentary on the following passage of *Les Misérables*: 'The taverns of the Faubourg Saint-Antoine resembled the taverns of the Aventine which are built over the sibyl's cave and are connected with the sacred inspirations; the tables of these taverns were almost tripods, and Ennius speaks of the sibylline wine that was drunk there.' The same way of viewing things gave birth to the work in which the first image of a 'Parisian antiquity' appears, Hugo's poetic cycle *A l'Arc de Triomphe*. The glorification of this architectural monument proceeds from the vision of a Paris Campagna, an '*immense campagne*' in which only three monuments of the vanished city have survived: the Sainte-Chapelle, the Vendôme column, and the Arc de Triomphe. The great significance which this cycle has in the work of Victor Hugo corresponds to the position that it occupies in the genesis of a picture of Paris in the nineteenth century which is modelled upon classical antiquity. Baudelaire undoubtedly knew this cycle which was written in 1837.

Seven years earlier the historian Friedrich von Raumer wrote in his letters from Paris and France in the year 1830: 'Yesterday I surveyed the enormous city from the Notre Dame tower. Who built the first house, when will the last one collapse and the ground of Paris look like the ground of Thebes and Babylon?' Hugo has described this soil as it will be one day when 'this bank where the water surges against resounding bridge-arches will have been restored to the murmuring, bending rushes':

> Mais non, tout sera mort. Plus rien dans cette plaine
> Qu'un peuple évanoui dont elle est encore pleine.

(But no, everything will be dead. Nothing more in this plain than a vanished people with which it is still pregnant.)

A hundred years after Raumer, Léon Daudet took a look at Paris from the Sacré-Coeur, another elevated place in the city. In his eyes the history of 'modernism' up to that time was mirrored in a frightening contraction: 'From above one looks down on this agglomeration of palaces, monuments, houses, and barracks, and one gets the feeling that they are predestined for a catastrophe or several, meteorological or social. . . . I have spent hours on Fourvières with a view of Lyons, on Notre-Dame de la Garde with a view of Marseille, on the Sacré Coeur with a view of Paris. . . . What becomes most clearly recognizable from these heights is a threat. The agglomerations of human beings are threatening. . . . A man needs work, that is correct, but he has other needs, too. . . . Among his other needs there is suicide, something that is inherent in him and in the society which forms him, and it is stronger than his drive of self-preservation. Thus, when one stands on Sacré-Coeur, Fourvières, and Notre-Dame de la Garde and looks down, one is surprised that Paris, Lyons, and Marseille are still there.' This is the face that the *passion modern* which Baudelaire recognized in suicide has received in this century.

The city of Paris entered this century in the form which Haussmann gave it. He had revolutionized the physiognomy of the city with the most modest means imaginable: spades, pickaxes, crowbars, and the like. What measure of destruction had been caused by even these limited instruments! And along with the growth of the big cities there developed the means of razing them to the ground. What visions of the future are evoked by this! Haussmann's activity was at its height and entire sections were being torn down when Maxime Du Camp found himself on the Pont Neuf one afternoon in 1862. He was waiting for his eyeglasses near an optician's shop. 'The author, who was at the threshold of old age, experienced one of those moments in which a man who thinks about his past life finds his own melancholy reflected in everything. The slight deterioration of his eyesight which had been demonstrated on his visit to the optician reminded him of the law of the inevitable infirmity of all human things.... It suddenly occurred to the man who had travelled widely in the Orient, who was acquainted with the deserts whose sand is the dust of the dead, that this city, too, whose bustle was all around him, would have to die some day, the way so many capitals had died. It occurred to him how extraordinarily interesting an accurate description of Athens at the time of Pericles, Carthage at the time of Barca, Alexandria at the time of the Ptolemies, and Rome at the time of the Caesars would be to us today.... In a flash of inspiration, of the kind that occasionally brings one an extraordinary subject, he resolved to write the kind of book about Paris that the historians of antiquity failed to write about their cities.... In his mind's eye he could see the work of his mature old age.' In Hugo's *A l'Arc de Triomphe* and in Du Camp's great presentation of his city from the administrative point of view, the same inspiration is discernable that became decisive for Baudelaire's idea of modernism.

...At the beginning of the fifties the population of Paris began to accommodate itself to the idea that a great face-cleaning of the city was inevitable. It may be assumed that in its incubation period this clean-up could have at least as great an effect upon a good imagination as the work of urban renewal itself. 'Poets are more inspired by the image than by the actual presence of objects' ('*Les poètes sont plus inspirés par les images que par la présence même des objets*'), said Joubert. The same is true of artists. Anything about which one knows that one soon will not have it around becomes an image. Presumably this is what happened to the streets of Paris at that time. In any case, the work whose subterranean connection with the great remodelling of Paris is least to be doubted, was finished a few years before this remodelling was undertaken. It was Meryon's engraved views of Paris. No one was more impressed with them than Baudelaire. To him the archaeological view of the catastrophe, the basis of Hugo's dreams, was not the really moving one. For him antiquity was to spring suddenly like an Athena from the head of an unhurt Zeus, from an intact modernism. Meryon brought out the ancient face of the city without abandoning one cobblestone. It was this view of the matter that Baudelaire had unceasingly pursued in the idea of modernism....

...In 1895 Jules Lemaître wrote: 'One confronts a work full of artifice and intentional contradictions....Even as he gives the crassest descriptions of the bleakest details of reality, he indulges in a spiritualism which greatly distracts us from the immediate impression that things make upon us.... Baudelaire regards a woman as a slave or animal, but he renders her the same homage as he does to the Holy Virgin.... He curses "progress", he loathes the industry of the century, and yet he enjoys the special flavour which this industry has given today's life.... I believe the specifically Baudelairean is the constant combination of two opposite modes of reaction ... one could call it a past and a present mode. A masterpiece of the will ... the latest innovation, in the sphere of emotional life.' To present this attitude as a great achievement of the will was in Baudelaire's spirit. But the other side of the coin is a lack of conviction, insight, and steadiness. In all his stirrings Baudelaire was subject to an abrupt, shock-like change, so his vision of another way of living in the extremes was all the more alluring. This way takes shape in the incantations which emanate from many of his perfect verses; in some of them it names itself.

Vois sur ces canaux
Dormir ces vaisseaux
Dont l'humeur est vagabonde;
C'est pour assouvir
Ton moindre désir
Qu'ils viennent du bout du monde.

(See, sheltered from the swells
There in the still canals
Those drowsy ships that dream of sailing forth;
It is to satisfy
Your least desire, they ply
Hither through all the waters of the earth.)
(translated by Richard Wilbur)

This famous stanza has a rocking rhythm; its movement seizes the ships which lie fast in the canals. To be rocked between the extremes, as is the privilege of ships – that is what Baudelaire longed for. The ships emerge where the profound, secret, and paradoxical image of his dreams is involved: being supported and sheltered by greatness. 'These beautiful big ships that lie on the still water imperceptibly rocking, these strong ships that look so idle and so nostalgic – are they not asking us in a mute language: when are we setting out for happiness?' In the ships, nonchalance is combined with readiness for the utmost exertion of energy. This gives them a secret significance. There is a special constellation in which greatness and indolence meet in human beings, too. This constellation governed Baudelaire's life. He deciphered it and called it 'modernism'. When he loses himself to the spectacle of the ships lying at anchor, he does so in order to derive an allegory from them. The hero is as strong, as ingenious, as harmonious, and as well-built as those boats. But the high seas beckon to him in vain, for his life is under an ill star. Modernism turns out to be his doom. The hero was not provided for in it; it has no use for this type....

The division of words into those that seemed suitable for elevated speech, and those that were to be excluded from it, influenced poetic production generally and from the beginning applied to tragedy no less than to lyric poetry. In the first decades of the nineteenth century this convention was in undisputed force. When Lebrun's *Cid* was performed, the word *chambre* evoked mutterings of disapproval. *Othello*, in Alfred de Vigny's translation, failed because of the word *mouchoir* whose mention seemed unbearable in a tragedy. Victor Hugo had begun smoothing out the difference in literature between the words of colloquial language and those of elevated speech. Sainte-Beuve had proceeded in a similar fashion. In his life of Joseph Delorme he explained: "I have tried to be original in my own way, in a modest, homely way. I called the things of intimate life by their names, but in doing so a hut was closer to me than a boudoir." Baudelaire transcended both Victor Hugo's linguistic Jacobinism and Sainte-Beuve's bucolic liberties. His images are original by virtue of the inferiority of the objects of comparison. He is on the lookout for banal incidents in order to approximate them to poetic events. He speaks of the 'vague terrors of those frightful nights which compress the heart the way a piece of paper is crumpled' ('*vagues terreurs de ces affreuses nuits/ Qui compriment le coeur comme un papier qu'on froisse*'). This linguistic gesture, characteristic of the artist in Baudelaire, becomes truly significant only in the allegorist. It gives his allegory the confusing quality that distinguishes it from the ordinary kind. Lemercier had been the last to populate the Parnassus of the Empire with such allegories, and the nadir of neoclassical literature had thus been reached. Baudelaire was unconcerned about that. He took up a profusion of allegories and altered their character fundamentally by virtue of the linguistic environment in which he placed them. The *Fleurs da mal* is the first book that used in poetry not only words of ordinary provenance but words of urban origin as well. Yet Baudelaire by no means avoided locutions which, free from poetic patina, strike one with the brilliance of their coinage. He uses *quinquet, wagon*, or *omnibus*, and does not shrink from *bilan, réverbère*, or *voirie*. This is the nature of the lyric vocabulary in which an allegory appears suddenly and without prior preparation. If Baudelaire's linguistic spirit can be apprehended anywhere, it may be captured in this brusque coincidence. Claudel gave it its definitive formulation when he said that Baudelaire combined the style of Racine with the style of a journalist of the Second Empire. Not a word of his vocabulary is predestined for allegory. A word is given this assignment in a particular case, depending on what is involved, what subject's turn it is to be reconnoitred, besieged, and occupied. For the *coup de main* which Baudelaire calls writing poetry, he takes allegories into his confidence. They are the only ones that have been let in on the secret. Where *la Mort* or *le Souvenir, le Repentir* or *le Mal* appear, centres of poetic strategy are located. The flash-like appearance of these figures, recognizable by their majuscule, in a text which does not disdain the most banal word betrays Baudelaire's hand. His technique is the technique of the *putsch*....

Chapter 31
Robert Frost

Robert Frost (1874–1963) had by the time of his death established a reputation as the national poet of the United States. Regarded as more accessible and home-spun than that of some of his modernist contemporaries, Frost's poetry is nonetheless metaphorically complex and rhythmically subtle. Frost worked for much of his life as a farmer or a teacher in New England. He stayed in England from 1912 to 1915, where he met Edward Thomas and discovered with him a common interest in making poetry close to the sounds of vernacular speech. The publication of North of Boston *in 1914 confirmed Frost's reputation as a poet and he went on to win four Pulitzer prizes and numerous other awards. Although his hostility to the politics and social policies of the New Deal upset part of his readership in the 1930s, Frost's image as the grand old man of American poetry became ever more firmly established, as did the sense that he represented a traditional alternative to the modernism of Eliot and Pound. More recently, critics such as Richard Poirier have demonstrated Frost's distinctive modernity and rescued him from an image that was always in danger of being misleading.*

"The Figure a Poem Makes" was first published in 1939 as the preface to an edition of Frost's Collected Poems. *It measures Frost's distance from various forms of poetic experiment with sound, rhythm, or the free play of verbal associations. Yet Frost's defence of subject matter and its development in poetry is not as straightforwardly conservative as it might sound. The essay's ambiguous title, the fascination with wildness in poetry, the analogy between poetry and erotic love, all indicate that Frost's poetics acknowledge the force of desire in language: the poem as something that "makes" as well as the poem as something "made."*

The Figure a Poem Makes

Abstraction is an old story with the philosophers, but it has been like a new toy in the hands of the artists of our day. Why can't we have any one quality of poetry we choose

From *Modern Poets on Modern Poetry*, ed. James Scully (London: Collins, 1966), pp. 54–7.

by itself? We can have in thought. Then it will go hard if we can't in practice. Our lives for it.

Granted no one but a humanist much cares how sound a poem is if it is only *a* sound. The sound is the gold in the ore. Then we will have the sound out alone and dispense with the inessential. We do till we make the discovery that the object in writing poetry is to make all poems sound as different as possible from each other, and the resources for that of vowels, consonants, punctuation, syntax, words, sentences, meter are not enough. We need the help of context – meaning – subject matter. That is the greatest help towards variety. All that can be done with words is soon told. So also with meters – particularly in our language where there are virtually but two, strict iambic and loose iambic. The ancients with many were still poor if they depended on meters for all tune. It is painful to watch our sprung-rhythmists straining at the point of omitting one short from a foot for relief from monotony. The possibilities for tune from the dramatic tones of meaning struck across the rigidity of a limited meter are endless. And we are back in poetry as merely one more art of having something to say, sound or unsound. Probably better if sound, because deeper and from wider experience.

Then there is this wildness where of it is spoken. Granted again that it has an equal claim with sound to being a poem's better half. If it is a wild tune, it is a poem. Our problem then is, as modern abstractionists, to have the wildness pure; to be wild with nothing to be wild about. We bring up as abstractionists, giving way to undirected associations and kicking ourselves from one chance suggestion to another in all directions as of a hot afternoon in the life of a grasshopper. Theme alone can steady us down. Just as the first mystery was how a poem could have a tune in such a straightness as meter, so the second mystery is how a poem can have wildness and at the same time a subject that shall be fulfilled.

It should be of the pleasure of a poem itself to tell how it can. The figure a poem makes. It begins in delight and ends in wisdom. The figure is the same as for love. No one can really hold that the ecstasy should be static and stand still in one place. It begins in delight, it inclines to the impulse, it assumes direction with the first line laid down, it runs a course of lucky events, and ends in a clarification of life – not necessarily a great clarification, such as sects and cults are founded on, but in a momentary stay against confusion. It has denouement. It has an outcome that though unforeseen was predestined from the first image of the original mood – and indeed from the very mood. It is but a trick poem and no poem at all if the best of it was thought of first and saved for the last. It finds its own name as it goes and discovers the best waiting for it in some final phrase at once wise and sad – the happy-sad blend of the drinking song.

No tears in the writer, no tears in the reader. No surprise for the writer, no surprise for the reader. For me the initial delight is in the surprise of remembering something I didn't know I knew. I am in a place, in a situation, as if I had materialized from cloud or risen out of the ground. There is a glad recognition of the long lost and the rest follows. Step by step the wonder of unexpected supply keeps growing. The impressions most useful to my purpose seem always those I was unaware of and made no note of at the time when taken, and the conclusion is come to that like giants we are always hurling experience ahead of us to pave the future with against the day when we may want to strike a line of purpose across it for somewhere. The line will have the more charm for not being mechanically straight. We enjoy the straight crookedness of a good walking stick. Modern instruments of precision are being used to make things crooked as if by eye and hand in the old days.

I tell how there may be a better wildness of logic than of inconsequence. But the logic is backward, in retrospect, after the act. It must be more felt than seen ahead like prophecy. It must be a revelation, or a series of revelations, as much for the poet as for the reader. For it to be that there must have been the greatest freedom of the material to move about in it and to establish relations in it regardless of time and space, previous relation, and everything but affinity. We prate of freedom. We call our schools free because we are not free to stay away from them till we are sixteen years of age. I have given up my democratic prejudices and now willingly set the lower classes free to be completely taken care of by the upper classes. Political freedom is nothing to me. I bestow it right and left. All I would keep for myself is the freedom of my material – the condition of body and mind now and then to summons aptly from the vast chaos of all I have lived through.

Scholars and artists thrown together are often annoyed at the puzzle of where they differ. Both work from knowledge; but I suspect they differ most importantly in the way their knowledge is come by. Scholars get theirs with conscientious thoroughness along projected lines of logic; poets theirs cavalierly and as it happens in and out of books. They stick to nothing deliberately, but let what will stick to them like burrs where they walk in the fields. No acquirement is on assignment, or even self-assignment. Knowledge of the second kind is much more available in the wild free ways of wit and art. A schoolboy may be defined as one who can tell you what he knows in the order in which he learned it. The artist must value himself as he snatches a thing from some previous order in time and space into a new order with not so much as a ligature clinging to it of the old place where it was organic.

More than once I should have lost my soul to radicalism if it had been the originality it was mistaken for by its young converts. Originality and initiative are what I ask for my country. For myself the originality need be no more than the freshness of a poem run in the way I have described: from delight to wisdom. The figure is the same as for love. Like a piece of ice on a hot stove the poem must ride on its own melting. A poem may be worked over once it is in being, but may not be worried into being. Its most precious quality will remain its having run itself and carried away the poet with it. Read it a hundred times: it will forever keep its freshness as a metal keeps its fragrance. It can never lose its sense of a meaning that once unfolded by surprise as it went.

Chapter 32
Paul Valéry

Paul Valéry (1871–1945) was one of the poets who established the work of the French symbolist poet, Stephan Mallarmé, as a tradition in French writing. Mallarmé praised Valéry's first published poem, "Narcisse parle," and in 1891, the year of the poem's publication, the two men met in Paris. Mallarmé's preoccupations with a poetry of suggestion rather than direct statement and his ambition to create a poetic language where linguistic form and meaning would be united are recurrent concerns in Valéry's poetry. But he was more than just a disciple. Increasingly Valéry came to regard poetry as part of a larger intellectual project: the investigation and analysis of the operations of the human mind by the human mind. Valéry pursued this project by way of science, mathematics, philosophy, and poetry in the thirty volumes of his notebooks, not published until after his death. After the publication of Charmes *in 1922, a collection that included Valéry's best known poem, "Le Cimitière marin," he was widely acknowledged as a major French poet and intellectual.*

"Poetry and Abstract Thought" was initially given as a lecture at Oxford University in 1939. Valéry addresses the ostensible subject of his lecture only intermittently, although he hints that his own career exemplifies an ability to engage with both terms of his title. In the following excerpt, Valéry explains the difference, as he sees it, between language in poetry and language used in an everyday context. This difference is a starting point for his account of the "poetic universe" and he returns to it again in his analogy of prose to walking and poetry to dance. This translation is by Denise Follet.

Poetry and Abstract Thought

. . . Poetry is an art of language. But language is a practical creation. It may be observed that in all communication between men, certainty comes only from practical acts and

From *The Collected Works of Paul Valéry*, vol. 7, ed. Jackson Matthews (London: Routledge & Kegan Paul, 1958), pp. 64–72, 74–5, 79–80.

from the verification which practical acts give us. *I ask you for a light. You give me a light*: you have understood me.

But in asking me for a light, you were able to speak those few unimportant words with a certain intonation, a certain tone of voice, a certain inflection, a certain languor or briskness perceptible to me. I have understood your words, since without even thinking I handed you what you asked for – a light. But the matter does not end there. The strange thing: the sound and as it were the features of your little sentence come back to me, echo within me, as though they were pleased to be there; I, too, like to hear myself repeat this little phrase, which has almost lost its meaning, which has stopped being of use, and which can yet go on living, though with quite another life. It has acquired a value; and has acquired it *at the expense of its finite significance.* It has created the need to be heard again.... Here we are on the very threshold of the poetic state. This tiny experience will help us to the discovery of more than one truth.

It has shown us that language can produce effects of two quite different kinds. One of them tends to bring about the complete negation of language itself. I speak to you, and if you have understood my words, those very words are abolished. If you have understood, it means that the words have vanished from your minds and are replaced by their counterpart, by images, relationships, impulses; so that you have within you the means to retransmit these ideas and images in a language that may be very different from the one you received. *Understanding* consists in the more or less rapid replacement of a system of sounds, intervals, and signs by something quite different, which is, in short, a modification or interior reorganization of the person to whom one is speaking. And here is the counterproof of this proposition: the person who does not understand *repeats* the words, or *has them repeated* to him.

Consequently, the perfection of a discourse whose sole aim is comprehension obviously consists in the ease with which the words forming it are transformed into something quite different: the *language* is transformed first into *non-language* and then, if we wish, into a form of language differing from the original form.

In other terms, in practical or abstract uses of language, the form – that is the physical, the concrete part, the very act of speech – does not last; it does not outlive understanding; it dissolves in the light; it has acted; it has done its work; it has brought about understanding; it has lived.

But on the other hand, the moment this concrete form takes on, by an effect of its own, such importance that it asserts itself and makes itself, as it were, respected; and not only remarked and respected, but desired and therefore repeated – then something new happens: we are insensibly transformed and ready to live, breathe, and think in accordance with a rule and under laws which are no longer of the practical order – that is, nothing that may occur in this state will be resolved, finished, or abolished by a specific act. We are entering the poetic universe.

Permit me to support this notion of a *poetic universe* by referring to a similar notion that, being much simpler, is easier to explain: the notion of a *musical universe.* I would ask you to make a small sacrifice: limit yourselves for a moment to your faculty of hearing. One simple sense, like that of hearing, will offer us all we need for our definition and will absolve us from entering into all the difficulties and subtleties to which the conventional structure and historical complexities of ordinary language would lead us. We live by ear in the world of noises. Taken as a whole, it is generally incoherent and irregularly supplied by all the mechanical incidents which the ear may interpret as it can. But the same ear isolates from this chaos a group of noises particularly remarkable and simple – that is, easily recognizable by our sense of hearing and furnishing it with points of reference. These elements have relations with one another which we sense as we do the elements themselves. The interval between two of these privileged noises is as clear to us as each of them. These are the *sounds*, and these units of sonority tend to form clear combinations, successive or simultaneous implications, series, and intersections which one may term *intelligible*: this is why abstract possibilities exist in music. But I must return to my subject.

I will confine myself to saying that the contrast between noise and sound is the contrast between pure and impure, order and disorder; that this differentiation between pure sensations and others has permitted the constitution of music; that it has been possible to control, unify, and codify this constitution, thanks to the intervention of physical science, which knows how to adjust measure to sensation so as to obtain the important result of teaching us to produce this sonorous sensation consistently, and in a continuous and identical fashion, by instruments that are, in reality, *measuring instruments.*

The musician is thus in possession of a perfect system of well-defined means which exactly match sensations with acts. From this it results that music has formed a domain absolutely its own. The world of the art of music, a world of sounds, is distinct from the world of noises. Whereas a *noise* merely rouses in us some isolated event – a dog, a door, a motor car – *a sound evokes, of itself, the musical universe.* If, in this hall where I am speaking to you and where you hear the noise of my voice, a tuning fork or a well-tempered instrument began to vibrate, you would at once, as soon as you were affected by this pure and exceptional noise that cannot be confused with others, have the feeling of a beginning, the beginning of a world; a quite different atmosphere would immediately be created, a new order would arise, and you yourselves would unconsciously *organize* yourselves to receive it. The musical universe, therefore, was within you, with all its associations and proportions – as in a saturated salt solution a crystalline universe awaits the molecular shock of a minute crystal in order *to declare itself.* I dare not say: the crystalline idea of such a system awaits....

And here is the counter proof of our little experiment: if, in a concert hall dominated by a resounding symphony, a chair happens to fall, someone coughs, or a door shuts, we immediately have the impression of a kind of rupture. Something indefinable, something like a spell or a Venetian glass, has been broken or cracked....

The poetic universe is not created so powerfully or so easily. It exists, but the poet is deprived of the immense advantages possessed by the musician. He does not have before him, ready for the uses of beauty, a body of resources expressly made for his art. He has to borrow *language* – the voice of the public, that collection of traditional and irrational terms and rules, oddly created and transformed, oddly codified, and very variedly understood and pronounced. Here there is no physicist who has determined the relations between these elements; no tuning forks, no metronomes, no inventors of scales or theoreticians of harmony. Rather, on the contrary, the phonetic and semantic fluctuations of vocabulary. Nothing pure; but a mixture of completely incoherent auditive and psychic stimuli. Each word is an instantaneous coupling of a *sound* and a *sense* that have no connection with each other. Each sentence is an act so complex that I doubt whether anyone has yet been able to provide a tolerable definition of it. As for the use of the resources of language and the modes of this action, you know what diversity there is, and what confusion sometimes results. A discourse can be logical, packed with sense, but devoid of rhythm and measure. It can be pleasing to the ear, yet completely absurd or insignificant; it can be clear, yet useless; vague, yet delightful. But to grasp its strange multiplicity, which is no more than the multiplicity of life itself, it suffices to name all the sciences which have been created to deal with this diversity, each to study one of its aspects. One can analyze a text in many different ways, for it falls successively under the jurisdiction of phonetics, semantics, syntax, logic, rhetoric, philology, not to mention metrics, prosody, and etymology....

So the poet is at grips with this verbal matter, obliged to speculate on sound and sense at once, and to satisfy not only harmony and musical timing but all the various intellectual and aesthetic conditions, not to mention the conventional rules....

You can see what an effort the poet's undertaking would require if he had *consciously* to solve all these problems....

It is always interesting to try to reconstruct one of our complex activities, one of those complete actions which demand a specialization at once mental, sensuous, and motor, supposing that in order to accomplish this act we were obliged to understand and organize all the functions that we know play their part in it. Even if this attempt, at once imaginative and analytical, is clumsy, it will always teach us something. As for myself, who am, I admit, much more attentive to the formation or fabrication of works than to the works themselves, I have a habit, or obsession, of appreciating works only as actions. In my eyes a poet is a man who, as a result of a certain incident, undergoes a hidden transformation. He leaves his ordinary condition of general disposability, and I see taking shape in him an agent, a living system for producing verses. As among animals one suddenly sees emerging a capable hunter, a nest maker, a bridge builder, a digger of tunnels and galleries, so in a man one sees a composite organization declare itself, bending its functions to a specific piece of work. Think of a very small child: the child we have all been bore many possibilities within him. After a few months of life he has learned, at the same or almost the same time, to speak and to walk. He has acquired two types of action. That is to say that he now possesses two kinds of potentiality from which the accidental circumstances of each moment will draw what they can, in answer to his varying needs and imaginings.

Having learned to use his legs, he will discover that he can not only walk, but run; and not only walk and run, but dance. This is a great event. He has at that moment both invented and discovered a kind of *secondary use* for his limbs, a generalization of his formula of movement. In fact, whereas walking is after all a rather dull and not easily perfectible action, this new form of action, the Dance, admits of an infinite number of creations and variations or *figures.*

But will he not find an analogous development in speech? He will explore the possibilities of his faculty of speech; he will discover that more can be done with it than to ask for jam and deny his little sins. He will grasp the power of reasoning; he will invent stories to amuse himself when he is alone; he will repeat to himself words that he loves for their strangeness and mystery.

So, parallel with *Walking* and *Dancing*, he will acquire and distinguish the divergent types. *Prose and Poetry....*

Walking, like prose, has a definite aim. It is an act directed at something we wish to reach. Actual circumstances, such as the need for some object, the impulse of my desire, the state of my body, my sight, the terrain, etc., which order the manner of walking, prescribe its direction and its speed, and give it a *definite end.* All the characteristics of walking derive from these instantaneous conditions, which combine in a *novel way* each time. There are no movements in walking that are not special adaptations, but, each time, they are abolished and, as it were, absorbed by the accomplishment of the act, by the attainment of the goal.

The dance is quite another matter. It is, of course, a system of actions; but of actions whose end is in themselves. It goes nowhere. If it pursues an object, it is only an ideal object, a state, an enchantment, the phantom of a flower, an extreme of life, a smile – which forms at last on the face of the one who summoned it from empty space.

It is therefore not a question of carrying out a limited operation whose end is situated somewhere in our surroundings, but rather of creating, maintaining, and exalting a certain *state*, by a periodic movement that can be executed on the spot; a movement which is almost entirely dissociated from sight, but which is stimulated and regulated by auditive rhythms.

But please note this very simple observation, that however different the dance may be from walking and utilitarian movements, it uses the same organs, the same bones, the same muscles, only differently co-ordinated and aroused.

Here we come again to the contrast between prose and poetry. Prose and poetry use the same words, the same syntax, the same forms, and the same sounds or tones, but differently co-ordinated and differently aroused. Prose and poetry are therefore distinguished by the difference between certain links and associations which form and dissolve in our psychic and nervous organism, whereas the components of these modes of functioning are identical. This is why one should guard against reasoning about poetry as one does about prose. What is true of one very often has no meaning when it is sought in the other. But here is the great and decisive difference. When the man who is walking has reached his goal – as I said – when he has reached the place, book, fruit, the object of his desire (which desire drew him from his repose), this possession at once entirely annuls his whole act; the effect swallows up the cause, the end absorbs the means; and, whatever the act, only the result remains. It is the same with utilitarian language: the language I use to express my design, my desire, my command, my opinion; this language, when it has served its purpose, evaporates almost as it is heard. I have given it forth to perish, to be radically transformed into something else in your mind; and I shall know that I was *understood* by the remarkable fact that my speech no longer exists: it has been completely replaced, by its *meaning* – that is, by images, impulses, reactions, or acts that belong to you: in short, by an interior modification in you....

The poem, on the other hand, does not die for having lived: it is expressly designed to be born again from its ashes and to become endlessly what it has just been. Poetry can be recognized by this property, that it tends to get itself reproduced in its own form: it stimulates us to reconstruct it identically....

I should like to give you a simple illustration. Think of a pendulum oscillating between two symmetrical points. Suppose that one of these extremes represents *form*: the concrete characteristics of the language, sound, rhythm, accent, tone, movement – in a word, the *Voice* in action. Then associate with the other point, the acnode of the first, all significant values, images and ideas, stimuli of feeling and memory, virtual impulses and structures of understanding – in short, everything that makes the *content*, the meaning of a discourse. Now observe the effect of poetry on yourselves. You will find that at each line the meaning produced within you, far from destroying the musical form communicated to you, recalls it. The living pendulum that has swung from *sound* to *sense* swings back to its felt point of departure, as though the very sense which is present to your mind can find no other outlet expression, no other answer, than the very music which gave it birth....

The result of this analysis is to show that the value of a poem resides in the indissolubility of sound and sense. Now this is a condition that seems to demand the impossible. There is no relation between the sound and the meaning of a word. The same thing is called HORSE in English, HIPPOS in Greek, EQUUS in Latin, and CHEVAL in French; but no manipulation of any of these terms will give me an idea of the animal in question; and no manipulation of the idea will yield me any of these words – otherwise, we should easily know all languages, beginning with our own.

Yet it is the poet's business to give us the feeling of an intimate union between the word and the mind.

This must be considered, strictly speaking, a marvelous result. I say *marvelous*, although it is not exceptionally rare. I use *marvelous* in the sense we give that word when we think of the miracles and prodigies of ancient magic. It must not be forgotten that for centuries poetry was used for purposes of enchantment. Those who took part in these strange operations had to believe in the power of the word, and far more in the efficacy of its sound than in its significance. Magic formulas are often without meaning; but it was never thought that their power depended on their intellectual content.

Let us listen to lines like these:

> Mère des souvenirs, maîtresse des maîtresses...

or

> Sois sage, ô ma Douleur, et tiens-toi plus tranquille....

These words work on us (or at least on some of us) without telling us very much. They tell us, perhaps, that they have nothing to tell us; that, by the very means which usually tell us something, they are exercising a quite different function. They act on us like a chord of music. The impression produced depends largely on resonance, rhythm, and the number of syllables; but it is also the result of the simple bringing together of meanings. In the second of these lines the accord between the vague ideas of Wisdom and Grief, and the tender solemnity of the tone produce the inestimable value of a spell: the *momentary being* who made that line could not have done so had he been in a state where the form and the content occurred separately to his mind. On the contrary, he was in a special phase in the domain of his psychic existence, a phase in which the sound and the meaning of the word acquire or keep an equal importance – which is excluded from the habits of practical language, as from the needs of abstract language. The state in which the inseparability of sound and sense, in which the desire, the expectation, the possibility of their intimate and indissoluble fusion are required and sought or given, and sometimes anxiously awaited, is a comparatively rare state. It is rare, firstly because all the exigencies of life are against it; secondly because it is opposed to the crude simplifying and specializing of verbal notations. . . .

A poem is really a kind of machine for producing the poetic state of mind by means of words. The effect of this machine is uncertain, for nothing is certain about action on other minds. But whatever may be the result, in its uncertainty, the construction of the machine demands the solution of many problems. If the term *machine* shocks you, if my mechanical comparison seems crude, please notice that while the composition of even a very short poem may absorb years, the action of the poem on the reader will take only a few minutes. In a few minutes the reader will receive his shock from discoveries, connections, glimmers of expression that have been accumulated during months of research, waiting, patience, and impatience. He may attribute much more to inspiration than it can give. He will imagine the kind of person it would take to create, without pause, hesitation, or revision, this powerful and perfect work which transports him into a world where things and people, passions and thoughts, sonorities and meanings proceed from the same energy, are transformed one into another, and correspond according to exceptional laws of harmony, for it can only be an exceptional form of stimulus that simultaneously produces the exaltation of our sensibility, our intellect, our memory, and our powers of verbal action, so rarely granted to us in the ordinary course of life.

Perhaps I should remark here that the execution of a poetic work – if one considers it as the engineer just mentioned would consider the conception and construction of his locomotive, that is, making explicit the problems to be solved – would appear impossible. In no other art is the number of conditions and independent functions to be co-ordinated so large. I will not inflict on you a detailed demonstration of this proposition. It is enough for me to remind you of what I said regarding sound and sense, which are linked only by pure convention, but which must be made to collaborate as effectively as possible. From their double nature words often make me think of those complex quantities which geometricians take such pleasure in manipulating.

Fortunately, some strange virtue resides in certain moments in certain people's lives which simplifies things and reduces the insurmountable difficulties I spoke of to the scale of human energies. . . .

Part III
1940–1960

Chapter 33
Martin Heidegger

Martin Heidegger (1889–1976) was a German philosopher whose work has informed a number of tendencies in twentieth-century thought, including existentialism, hermeneutics, and post-structuralism. His major philosophical work, Being and Time, *was published in 1927. In it he challenged the dominant western tradition in philosophy and its preoccupation with questions about how we know the world. He proposed a return to what he regarded as philosophy's original concern in ancient Greek thought: the question of being, of what it is for something to take on existence in the world. Rejecting the idea that being consists in the possession of an essence or substance that endures through time, Heidegger argued that being only ever arises in a context or against a background of everyday life and practice. Heidegger elaborated and qualified his thinking in his writing after* Being and Time *but it remains the groundwork of his philosophy. The reception of Heidegger's philosophy has been the subject of controversy: in the 1930s he was clearly sympathetic to fascism and his thinking can lapse back into dogmas about the importance of German blood and soil.*

Heidegger's thinking was immersed in questions about language insofar as language was a fundamental feature of the being that is characteristic of humans. Language was never a transparent or unproblematic medium for Heidegger, and his thinking often returned to the histories and associations that gather around particular words. In his thinking about language in general, the question of poetry and poetic language figured prominently.

The following excerpts all start with lines drawn from the work of Hölderlin, the German Romantic poet whose work defines the condition of modern poetry for Heidegger. "The Metaphysical Interpretation of Art" comes from a lecture given in 1941 and discovers in Hölderlin's poetry a form of symbolism that is no longer framed by the traditional metaphysical distinction between the sensuous and spiritual meanings of the poetic image. "What Are Poets For?" was written in 1944 and sets out Heidegger's interpretation of the obligations of poetry in modernity. "Poetically Man Dwells" from 1946 continues this theme but identifies the special relation of the poet to language: an attentive passivity that "listens to the appeal of language," a condition that Heidegger firmly distinguishes from any masterful use of language for expression.

The Ister Hymn

The metaphysical interpretation of art

In our attempt to heed what Hölderlin poetizes when he names the rivers, we will often have occasion to test a form of representation that for centuries has secured itself a validity in poetry, as well as in the interpretation of poetic works and in the way poetizing in general is determined.

According to this form of representation, the rivers and waters that are sung in a poetic work, for example, are grasped as perceivable events of "nature." Which indeed they are. In the poetic work, however, these things of nature assume the role of appearances that can be grasped as something sensuous [*sinnlich*], as something that offers a view and thus provides an "image." Yet in the poetic work such images present not only themselves, but also a nonsensuous meaning. They "mean" something. The sensuous image points toward a "spiritual" content, a "sense" ["*Sinn*"]. The river that is named and that appears in the image [*Bild*] is a "symbolic image" ["*Sinnbild*"]. Under the broadly conceived concept of a symbolic image, we also include what is called "allegory." This word, which stems from the Greek, aptly says what is at issue: ἄλλο-ἀγορεύειν, ἀγορεύειν (ἀγορά, the open, public place for a gathering of the people): to openly and publicly proclaim in a manner that everyone can understand. ἄλλο, something other, namely, to proclaim something other than what the image by itself allows to appear. ἀλληγορία is a proclamation of something else by way of something, namely, by way of something familiar that can be experienced sensuously. Legends and fairy tales, for example, count as "allegories." Another kind of symbolic image alongside "allegories" are "similes"; yet another kind are "symbols." σύμβολον derives from συμβάλλειν, which means, to bring together, to hold the halves of a ring against one another and to test whether they fit and belong to one another so that one can then recognize that the possessors of the pieces of the ring themselves belong to one another. The "symbol" is a sign of recognition that demonstrates and thereby legitimizes a belonging together. In the symbol too there lies the reference of something sensuous, the ring, to something nonsensuous – something pertaining to the soul – something spiritual, in the first instance, the belonging together of friends, friendship. The "symbol," too, is a symbolic image.

We can also count as symbolic images in the broadest sense what we call "examples," something that, as an instance that can be sensuously intuited, exemplifies and furnishes us with a rule that cannot be grasped sensuously. "Metaphors" likewise belong to symbolic images – μεταφορά, transference. Every "in-signia" is also a

From *Hölderlin's Hymn "The Ister" / Martin Heidegger*, trans. William McNeill and Julie Davis (Bloomington, Ind.: Indiana University Press, 1966), pp. 16–19.

symbolic image in a certain way. The distinctions between allegory and symbol, simile and metaphor, example and insignia are fluid, and have not been firmly established with unequivocal validity. More important than the distinctions is the pervasive framework wherein these variations of "symbolic images," and the symbolic image in general, have their ground. That framework is the distinction that is made between a sensuous and a nonsensuous realm. In every employment of symbolic images we presuppose that this distinction has been made. The decisive drawing of this distinction, its unfolding and its structuring, which are normative for the Western world, occurred in Plato's thought. What emerges as essential in that thought is that the nonsensuous, the realm of the soul and of the spiritual, is the true actuality, and that the sensuous realm is a preliminary and subordinate stage. And if one designates the realm of the sensuous, taken in the broadest sense, as the "physical" realm, then the nonsensuous and suprasensuous realm is that which lies over and beyond the physical.

Going over and beyond something is called μετά in Greek. In relation to the physical, the suprasensuous realm is the metaphysical. The distinction made between the sensuous and the suprasensuous is a transition from the physical and from "physics," taken in the broadest sense, to the metaphysical and to metaphysics. The distinction between the sensuous (αἰσθητόν) and the nonsensuous (νοητόν) is the fundamental configuration of what has long since been called metaphysics. If we name "world" the entirety of what is actual, including its ground and cause, then we may say that, since Plato, all Western conceptions and interpretations of the world have been "metaphysical." Since that same period, the essence of art (τέχνη, *ars*), and thus the essence of poetic art also, has been determined in accordance with metaphysics. In all metaphysics, the work of art counts as something sensuous that does not exist just for itself; rather, what is sensuous about the artwork is as it is in the artwork: it exists for the nonsensuous and suprasensuous, for that which is also named the spiritual or spirit. Given this, we can understand a statement made by that thinker who, in the first half of the previous century, created the most comprehensive metaphysics of art. Hegel says in his Lectures on Aesthetics (*Werke* X, 1, 48): "What is sensuous in the work of art is meant to have existence only insofar as it exists for the human spirit, and not insofar as it itself exists for itself as something sensuous." As Hegel understands it, an example of something sensuous existing for itself is a piece of material painted over in many colors; such a thing, however, is not a painting by Rembrandt. Yet the painting is not merely placed onto this material thing either; rather, this material thing is sublated into the painting and now is what it is only *through* the latter. With respect to the metaphysical essence of art, we can also say that all art has to do with symbolic images [*ist sinnbildlich*]. "Image" ["*Bild*"] then stands for what can be perceived sensuously in general, as can sound. The symbolic "sense" ["*Sinn*"] is the nonsensuous [*das Nichtsinnliche*], which is understood and given meaning and has been determined in manifold ways in the course of metaphysics: the nonsensuous and suprasensuous are the spiritual; ideals and "values" are the ideational. The superior and the true are what is sensuously represented in the symbolic image. The essence of art stands or falls in accordance with the essence and truth of metaphysics.

Hölderlin's poetry is not concerned with images in a symbolic or metaphysical sense. The concealed essence of the river

Hölderlin's poetry too appears in the course of the history of Western metaphysics and art. We can even classify it accurately in terms of its temporal relation to this history. The genesis of the hymns lies between the years 1800 and 1806. Precisely this same time span covers the genesis of the principle work in Hegel's thought, the *Phenomenology of Spirit* (1807). Hegel, the thinker, was the friend of the poet Hölderlin while they were both students in Tübingen and also later during their years together in Frankfurt until 1799. Thus Hölderlin's poetry, if it is art, will also be metaphysical and will therefore be concerned with "symbolic images." The German rivers that are sung in Hölderlin's poems, the Main, the Neckar, the Donau, and the Rhine, are "symbolic images" of German essence and life. Nothing prevents us from interpreting Hölderlin's river poetry according to this perspective or in such a way.

Perhaps the sense that Hölderlin gives these images of rivers is more difficult to discern than the content of other poetic works written by other poets who also sing of rivers, streams, and brooks, the ocean and the seas. This greater interpretive difficulty may have its grounds in the fact that Hölderlin poetizes more mysteriously than these other poets and perhaps also in the fact that his poetry remains incomplete in many ways, and is indeed occasionally overshadowed and confused by his impending madness.

The rivers in Hölderlin's poetry are, however, in no way symbolic images that are merely more difficult to interpret in terms of degree. If that were the case, they would still remain essentially "symbolic images." Yet this is precisely what they are not. The "rivers" are therefore not to count as symbols of a higher level or of "deeper," "religious" content. Hölderlin's hymnal poetry, which is the vocation of the poet after 1799, is not concerned with symbolic images at all.

Yet what we have said then means that this poetry must stand entirely outside of metaphysics, and thus outside of the essential realm of Western art. Then all the usual readings and interpretations of these poems would be in vain, because all such interpretation borrows its tools and its effort indiscriminately from metaphysics and from the metaphysical doctrine of art, that is, from aesthetics.

But if the rivers in Hölderlin's poetry are in truth not "symbolic images," then what else can they be? How are we supposed to be able to know anything about them, when all our knowledge, and especially scientific knowledge, has its grounds and hold in metaphysics? It almost seems as though the poet himself were saying that we can know nothing of the rivers. The Ister hymn closes, or more precisely, it comes to a halt, with the words:

Was aber jener thuet der Strom,
Weis niemand.

Yet what that one does, that river,
No one knows.

Does this mean that the slightest effort to call attention to this river poem thus already infringes the poet's own word? No. The lines just cited tell us that the flow of the river that is named here is an activity that takes its own time, and that such activity is concealed. The concealment of its activity signifies that this river has a distinction. The poet knows of this concealment. How else could he tell us that no one knows what this river does? (Moreover, we must ponder the fact that these words, with which the Ister hymn breaks off, tell in their own specific way of that river that is referred to as "the Rhine," as distinct ("Yet") from the "Ister." All the same, the "poetic" essence of the river in general remains concealed in the knowledge of the poet and conditions that intimative telling: "he appears. . . .")

The poetic word unveils this concealment of the river's activity, and indeed unveils it as such an activity. This unveiling is poetic. Whatever song is capable of here, and how much it is capable of, given that it is to tell of the rivers and especially of their "youth" and their origin, this poet knows full well. . . .

What Are Poets For?

". . . and what are poets for in a destitute time?" asks Hölderlin's elegy "Bread and Wine." We hardly understand the question today. How, then, shall we grasp the answer that Hölderlin gives?

". . . and what are poets for in a destitute time?" The word "time" here means the era to which we ourselves still belong. For Hölderlin's historical experience, the appearance and sacrificial death of Christ mark the beginning of the end of the day of the gods. Night is falling. Ever since the "united three" – Herakles, Dionysos, and Christ – have left the world, the evening of the world's age has been declining toward its night. The world's night is spreading its darkness. The era is defined by the god's failure to arrive, by the "default of God." But the default of God which Hölderlin experienced does not deny that the Christian relationship with God lives on in individuals and in the churches; still less does it assess this relationship negatively. The default of God means that no god any longer gathers men and things unto himself, visibly and unequivocally, and by such gathering disposes the world's history and man's sojourn in it. The default of God forebodes something even grimmer, however. Not only have the gods and the god fled, but the divine radiance has become extinguished in the world's history. The time of the world's night is the destitute time, because it becomes ever more destitute. It has already grown so destitute, it can no longer discern the default of God as a default.

Because of this default, there fails to appear for the world the ground that grounds it. The word for abyss – *Abgrund* – originally means the soil and ground toward which, because it is undermost, a thing tends downward. But in what follows we shall think of the *Ab-* as the complete absence of the ground. The ground is the soil in which to strike root and to stand. The age for which the ground fails to come, hangs in the abyss.

From *Poetry, Language and Thought*, trans. Albert Hofstadter (New York: Harper and Row, 1971), pp. 91–4.

Assuming that a turn still remains open for this destitute time at all, it can come some day only if the world turns about fundamentally – and that now means, unequivocally: if it turns away from the abyss. In the age of the world's night, the abyss of the world must be experienced and endured. But for this it is necessary that there be those who reach into the abyss.

The turning of the age does not take place by some new god, or the old one renewed, bursting into the world from ambush at some time or other. Where would he turn on his return if men had not first prepared an abode for him? How could there ever be for the god an abode fit for a god, if a divine radiance did not first begin to shine in everything that is?

The gods who "were once there," "return" only at the "right time" – that is, when there has been a turn among men in the right place, in the right way. For this reason Hölderlin, in the unfinished hymn "Mnemosyne," written soon after the elegy "Bread and Wine," writes (IV, 225):

> ... The heavenly powers
> Cannot do all things. It is the mortals
> Who reach sooner into the abyss. So the turn is
> With these. Long is
> The time, but the true comes into
> Its own.

Long is the destitute time of the world's night. To begin with, this requires a long time to reach to its middle. At this night's midnight, the destitution of the time is greatest. Then the destitute time is no longer able even to experience its own destitution. That inability, by which even the destitution of the destitute state is obscured, is the time's absolutely destitute character. The destitution is wholly obscured, in that it now appears as nothing more than the need that wants to be met. Yet we must think of the world's night as a destiny that takes place this side of pessimism and optimism. Perhaps the world's night is now approaching its midnight. Perhaps the world's time is now becoming the completely destitute time. But also perhaps not, not yet, not even yet, despite the immeasurable need, despite all suffering, despite nameless sorrow, despite the growing and spreading peacelessness, despite the mounting confusion. Long is the time because even terror, taken by itself as a ground for turning, is powerless as long as there is no turn with mortal men. But there is a turn with mortals when these find the way to their own nature. That nature lies in this, that mortals reach into the abyss sooner than the heavenly powers. Mortals, when we think of their nature, remain closer to that absence because they are touched by presence, the ancient name of Being. But because presence conceals itself at the same time, it is itself already absence. Thus the abyss holds and remarks everything. In his hymn "The Titans" Hölderlin says of the "abyss" that it is "all-perceiving." He among mortals who must, sooner than other mortals and otherwise than they, reach into the abyss, comes to know the marks that the abyss remarks. For the poet, these are the traces of the fugitive gods. In Hölderlin's experience, Dionysos the wine-god brings this trace down to the god-less amidst the darkness of their world's night. For in the vine and in its fruit, the god of wine guards the being toward one another of earth and sky as the site of the wedding feast of men and gods. Only within reach of this site, if anywhere, can traces of the fugitive gods still remain for god-less men.

"... and what are poets for in a destitute time?"

Hölderlin shyly puts the answer into the mouth of his poet-friend Heinse, whom he addresses in the elegy:

"But they are, you say, like the wine-god's holy priests,
Who fared from land to land in holy night."

Poets are the mortals who, singing earnestly of the wine-god, sense the trace of the fugitive gods, stay on the gods' tracks, and so trace for their kindred mortals the way toward the turning. The ether, however, in which alone the gods are gods, is their godhead. The element of this ether, that within which even the godhead itself is still present, is the holy. The element of the ether for the coming of the fugitive gods, the holy, is the track of the fugitive gods. But who has the power to sense, to trace such a track? Traces are often inconspicuous, and are always the legacy of a directive that is barely divined. To be a poet in a destitute time means: to attend, singing, to the trace of the fugitive gods. This is why the poet in the time of the world's night utters the holy. This is why, in Hölderlin's language, the world's night is the holy night.

It is a necessary part of the poet's nature that, before he can be truly a poet in such an age, the time's destitution must have made the whole being and vocation of the poet a poetic question for him. Hence "poets in a destitute time" must especially gather in poetry the nature of poetry. Where that happens we may assume poets to exist who are on the way to the destiny of the world's age. We others must learn to listen to what *these* poets say – assuming that, in regard to the time that conceals Being because it shelters it, we do not deceive ourselves through reckoning time merely in terms of that which is by dissecting that which is....

"... Poetically Man Dwells ..."

The phrase is taken from a late poem by Hölderlin, which comes to us by a curious route. It begins: "In lovely blueness blooms the steeple with metal roof" (Stuttgart edition 2, 1, pp. 372 ff.; Hellingrath VI, pp. 24 ff.) If we are to hear the phrase "poetically man dwells" rightly, we must restore it thoughtfully to the poem. For that reason let us give thought to the phrase. Let us clear up the doubts it immediately arouses. For otherwise we should lack the free readiness to respond to the phrase by following it.

"... poetically man dwells ..." If need be, we can imagine that poets do on occasion dwell poetically. But how is "man" – and this means every man and all the time –

From *Poetry, Language and Thought*, trans. Albert Hofstadter (New York: Harper and Row, 1971), p. 213–16.

supposed to dwell poetically? Does not all dwelling remain incompatible with the poetic? Our dwelling is harassed by the housing shortage. Even if that were not so, our dwelling today is harassed by work, made insecure by the hunt for gain and success, bewitched by the entertainment and recreation industry. But when there is still room left in today's dwelling for the poetic, and time is still set aside, what comes to pass is at best a preoccupation with aestheticizing, whether in writing or on the air. Poetry is either rejected as a frivolous mooning and vaporizing into the unknown, and a flight into dreamland, or is counted as a part of literature. And the validity of literature is assessed by the latest prevailing standard. The prevailing standard, in turn, is made and controlled by the organs for making public civilized opinions. One of its functionaries – at once driver and driven – is the literature industry. In such a setting poetry cannot appear otherwise than as literature. Where it is studied entirely in educational and scientific terms, it is the object of literary history. Western poetry goes under the general heading of "European literature."

But if the sole form in which poetry exists is literary to start with, then how can human dwelling be understood as based on the poetic? The phrase, "man dwells poetically," comes indeed from a mere poet, and in fact from one who, we are told, could not cope with life. It is the way of poets to shut their eyes to actuality. Instead of acting, they dream. What they make is merely imagined. The things of imagination are merely made. Making is, in Greek, *poiesis.* And man's dwelling is supposed to be poetry and poetic? This can be assumed, surely, only by someone who stands aside from actuality and does not want to see the existent condition of man's historical-social life today – the sociologists call it the collective.

But before we so bluntly pronounce dwelling and poetry incompatible, it may be well to attend soberly to the poet's statement. It speaks of man's dwelling. It does not describe today's dwelling conditions. Above all, it does not assert that to dwell means to occupy a house, a dwelling place. Nor does it say that the poetic exhausts itself in an unreal play of poetic imagination. What thoughtful man, therefore, would presume to declare, unhesitatingly and from a somewhat dubious elevation, that dwelling and the poetic are incompatible? Perhaps the two can bear with each other. This is not all. Perhaps one even bears the other in such a way that dwelling rests on the poetic. If this is indeed what we suppose, then we are required to think of dwelling and poetry in terms of their essential nature. If we do not balk at this demand, we think of what is usually called the existence of man in terms of dwelling. In doing so, we do of course give up the customary notion of dwelling. According to that idea, dwelling remains merely one form of human behavior alongside many others. We work in the city, but dwell outside it. We travel, and dwell now here, now there. Dwelling so understood is always merely the occupying of a lodging.

When Hölderlin speaks of dwelling, he has before his eyes the basic character of human existence. He sees the "poetic," moreover, by way of its relation to this dwelling, thus understood essentially.

This does not mean, though, that the poetic is merely an ornament and bonus added to dwelling. Nor does the poetic character of dwelling mean merely that the poetic turns up in some way or other in all dwelling. Rather, the phrase "poetically man dwells" says: poetry first causes dwelling to be dwelling. Poetry is what really lets us dwell. But through what do we attain to a dwelling place? Through building. Poetic creation, which lets us dwell, is a kind of building.

Thus we confront a double demand: for one thing, we are to think of what is called man's existence by way of the nature of dwelling; for another, we are to think of the nature of poetry as a letting-dwell, as a – perhaps even *the* – distinctive kind of building. If we search out the nature of poetry according to this viewpoint, then we arrive at the nature of dwelling.

But where do we humans get our information about the nature of dwelling and poetry? Where does man generally get the claim to arrive at the nature of something? Man can make such a claim only where he receives it. He receives it from the telling of language. Of course, only when and only as long as he respects language's own nature. Meanwhile, there rages round the earth an unbridled yet clever talking, writing, and broadcasting of spoken words. Man acts as though he were the shaper and master of language, while in fact language remains the master of man. When this relation of dominance gets inverted, man hits upon strange maneuvers. Language becomes the means of expression. As expression, language can decay into a mere medium for the printed word. That even in such employment of language we retain a concern for care in speaking is all to the good. But this alone will never help us to escape from the inversion of the true relation of dominance between language and man. For, strictly, it is language that speaks. Man first speaks when, and only when, he responds to language by listening to its appeal. Among all the appeals that we human beings, on our part, may help to be voiced, language is the highest and everywhere the first. Language beckons us, at first and then again at the end, toward a thing's nature. But that is not to say, ever, that in any word-meaning picked up at will language supplies us, straight away and definitively, with the transparent nature of the matter as if it were an object ready for use. But the responding in which man authentically listens to the appeal of language is that which speaks in the element of poetry. The more poetic a poet is – the freer (that is, the more open and ready for the unforeseen) his saying – the greater is the purity with which he submits what he says to an ever more painstaking listening, and the further what he says is from the mere prepositional statement that is dealt with solely in regard to its correctness or incorrectness....

Chapter 34
Wallace Stevens

Wallace Stevens (1879–1955) led a double life as an insurance executive and a poet. By the time he published his first volume of poetry, Harmonium, *in 1923 Stevens had completed his training as a lawyer and joined the Hartford Accident and Indemnity Company, whose vice president he became in 1934.* Harmonium *shows Stevens giving a distinctive voice and inflection to the poetics of Imagism. But his ambitions as a poet went well beyond the small, beautifully crafted poem. Stevens was the American inheritor of European Romanticism and he repeatedly explored the relations between imagination and reality in long and philosophically resonant poems such as "The Idea of Order in Key West" or "An Ordinary Evening in New Haven." Stevens developed a powerful ethos for his poetry, one that affirmed the capacity of the imagination to create fictions that did not flee or corrupt reality but informed our perception of the world.*

Poetry and the theory of poetry are constantly crossing over in Stevens's work. He wrote a number of essays on poetry, including the one excerpted here, "The Noble Rider and the Sound of Words," first given as a paper in 1941 at a symposium on the language of poetry, and published the following year in a collection called The Language of Poetry. *The complete text can be found in a collection of Stevens's essays,* The Necessary Angel: Essays on Reality and Imagination, *first published in 1951. The essay is a meditation on the historically changing relation between imagination and reality, and how these changes affect our capacity to respond to poetic figures and the values they imply. He goes on to consider the role of the poet in modern culture and affirms that the poet has no particular social or political obligations, only the requirement to create works that embody "the imagination pressing back against the pressure of reality."*

The Noble Rider and the Sound of Words

In the *Phaedrus*, Plato speaks of the soul in a figure. He says:

> Let our figure be of a composite nature – a pair of winged horses and a charioteer. Now the winged horses and the charioteer of the gods are all of them noble, and of noble breed, while ours are mixed; and we have a charioteer who drives them in a pair, and one of them is noble and of noble origin, and the other is ignoble and of ignoble origin; and, as might be expected, there is a great deal of trouble in managing them. I will endeavor to explain to you in what way the mortal differs from the immortal creature. The soul or animate being has the care of the inanimate, and traverses the whole heaven in divers forms appearing; – when perfect and fully winged she soars upwards, and is the ruler of the universe; while the imperfect soul loses her feathers, and drooping in her flight at last settles on the solid ground.

We recognize at once, in this figure, Plato's pure poetry; and at the same time we recognize what Coleridge called Plato's dear, gorgeous nonsense. The truth is that we have scarcely read the passage before we have identified ourselves with the charioteer, have, in fact, taken his place and, driving his winged horses, are traversing the whole heaven. Then suddenly we remember, it may be, that the soul no longer exists and we droop in our flight and at last settle on the solid ground. The figure becomes antiquated and rustic.

1

What really happens in this brief experience? Why does this figure, potent for so long, become merely the emblem of a mythology, the rustic memorial of a belief in the soul and in a distinction between good and evil? The answer to these questions is, I think, a simple one.

I said that suddenly we remember that the soul no longer exists and we droop in our flight. For that matter, neither charioteers nor chariots any longer exist. Consequently, the figure does not become unreal because we are troubled about the soul. Besides, unreal things have a reality of their own, in poetry as elsewhere. We do not hesitate, in poetry, to yield ourselves to the unreal, when it is possible to yield ourselves. The existence of the soul, of charioteers and chariots and of winged horses is immaterial. They did not exist for Plato, not even the charioteer and chariot; for certainly a charioteer driving his chariot across the whole heaven was for Plato precisely what he is for us. He was unreal for Plato as he is for us. Plato, however, could yield himself, was free to yield himself, to this gorgeous nonsense. We cannot yield ourselves. We are not free to yield ourselves.

Just as the difficulty is not a difficulty about unreal things, since the imagination accepts them, and since the poetry of the passage is, for us, wholly the poetry of the unreal, so it is not an emotional difficulty. Something else than the imagination is

From *Modern Poets on Modern Poetry*, ed. James Scully (London: Collins, 1966), pp. 128–31, 135–7, 138–9, 140–3, 144–50, 151–2.

moved by the statement that the horses of the gods are all of them noble, and of noble breed or origin. The statement is a moving statement and is intended to be so. It is insistent and its insistence moves us. Its insistence is the insistence of a speaker, in this case Socrates, who, for the moment, feels delight, even if a casual delight, in the nobility and noble breed. Those images of nobility instantly become nobility itself and determine the emotional level at which the next page or two are to be read. The figure does not lose its vitality because of any failure of feeling on Plato's part. He does not communicate nobility coldly. His horses are not marble horses, the reference to their breed saves them from being that. The fact that the horses are not marble horses helps, moreover, to save the charioteer from being, say, a creature of cloud. The result is that we recognize, even if we cannot realize, the feelings of the robust poet clearly and fluently noting the images in his mind and by means of his robustness, clearness and fluency communicating much more than the images themselves. Yet we do not quite yield. We cannot. We do not feel free.

In trying to find out what it is that stands between Plato's figure and ourselves, we have to accept the idea that, however legendary it appears to be, it has had its vicissitudes. The history of a figure of speech or the history of an idea, such as the idea of nobility, cannot be very different from the history of anything else. It is the episodes that are of interest, and here the episode is that of our diffidence. By us and ourselves, I mean you and me; and yet not you and me as individuals but as representatives of a state of mind. Adams in his work on Vico makes the remark that the true history of the human race is a history of its progressive mental states. It is a remark of interest in this relation. We may assume that in the history of Plato's figure there have been incessant changes of response; that these changes have been psychological changes, and that our own diffidence is simply one more state of mind due to such a change.

The specific question is partly as to the nature of the change and partly as to the cause of it. In nature, the change is as follows: The imagination loses vitality as it ceases to adhere to what is real. When it adheres to the unreal and intensifies what is unreal, while its first effect may be extraordinary, that effect is the maximum effect that it will ever have. In Plato's figure, his imagination does not adhere to what is real. On the contrary, having created something unreal, it adheres to it and intensifies its unreality. Its first effect, its effect at first reading, is its maximum effect, when the imagination, being moved, puts us in the place of the charioteer, before the reason checks us. The case is, then, that we concede that the figure is all imagination. At the same time, we say that it has not the slightest meaning for us, except for its nobility. As to that, while we are moved by it, we are moved as observers. We recognize it perfectly. We do not realize it. We understand the feeling of it, the robust feeling, clearly and fluently communicated. Yet we understand it rather than participate in it.

As to the cause of the change, it is the loss of the figure's vitality. The reason why this particular figure has lost its vitality is that, in it, the imagination adheres to what is unreal. What happened, as we were traversing the whole heaven, is that the imagination lost its power to sustain us. It has the strength of reality or none at all.

[Section 2 omitted]

3

...A variation between the sound of words in one age and the sound of words in another age is an instance of the pressure of reality. Take the statement by Bateson that a language, considered semantically, evolves through a series of conflicts between the denotative and the connotative forces in words; between an asceticism tending to kill language by stripping words of all association and a hedonism tending to kill language by dissipating their sense in a multiplicity of associations. These conflicts are nothing more than changes in the relation between the imagination and reality. Bateson describes the seventeenth century in England as predominantly a connotative period. The use of words in connotative senses was denounced by Locke and Hobbes, who desired a mathematical plainness; in short, perspicuous words. There followed in the eighteenth century an era of poetic diction. This was not the language of the age but a language of poetry peculiar to itself. In time, Wordsworth came to write the preface to the second edition of the *Lyrical Ballads* (1800), in which he said that the first volume had been published, "as an experiment, which, I hoped, might be of some use to ascertain how far, by fitting to metrical arrangement a selection of the real language of a man in a state of vivid sensation, that sort of pleasure and that quantity of pleasure may be imparted, which a Poet may rationally endeavor to impart."

As the nineteenth century progressed, language once more became connotative. While there have been intermediate reactions, this tendency toward the connotative is the tendency today. The interest in semantics is evidence of this. In the case of some of our prose writers, as, for example, Joyce, the language, in quite different ways, is wholly connotative. When we say that Locke and Hobbes denounced the connotative use of words as an abuse, and when we speak of reactions and reforms, we are speaking, on the one hand, of a failure of the imagination to adhere to reality, and, on the other, of a use of language favorable to reality. The statement that the tendency toward the connotative is the tendency today is disputable. The general movement in the arts, that is to say, in painting and in music, has been the other way. It is hard to say that the tendency is toward the connotative in the use of words without also saying that the tendency is toward the imagination in other directions. The interest in the subconscious and in surrealism shows the tendency toward the imaginative. Boileau's remark that Descartes had cut poetry's throat is a remark that could have been made respecting a great many people during the last hundred years, and of no one more aptly than of Freud, who, as it happens, was familiar with it and repeats it in his *Future of an Illusion*. The object of that essay was to suggest a surrender to reality. His premise was that it is the unmistakable character of the present situation not that the promises of religion have become smaller but that they appear less credible to people. He notes the decline of religious belief and disagrees with the argument that man cannot in general do without the consolation of what he calls the religious illusion and that without it he would not endure the cruelty of reality. His conclusion is that man must venture at last into the hostile world and that this may be called education to reality. There is much more in that essay inimical to poetry and not least the observation in one of the final pages that "The voice of the intellect is a soft one, but it does not rest until it has gained a hearing." This, I fear, is intended to be the voice of the realist.

A tendency in language toward the connotative might very well parallel a tendency in other arts toward the denotative. We have just seen that that is in fact the situation. I suppose that the present always appears to be an illogical complication. The language of Joyce goes along with the dilapidations of Braque and Picasso and the music of the Austrians. To the extent that this painting and this music are the work of men who regard it as part of the science of painting and the science of music it is the work of realists. Actually its effect is that of the imagination, just as the effect of abstract painting is so often that of the imagination, although that may be different. Busoni said, in a letter to his wife, "I have made the painful discovery that nobody loves and feels music." Very likely, the reason there is a tendency in language toward the connotative today is that there are many who love it and feel it. It may be that Braque and Picasso love and feel painting and that Schönberg loves and feels music, although it seems that what they love and feel is something else.

A tendency toward the connotative, whether in language or elsewhere, cannot continue against the pressure of reality. If it is the pressure of reality that controls poetry, then the immediacy of various theories of poetry is not what it was. For instance, when Rostrevor Hamilton says, "The object of contemplation is the highly complex and unified content of consciousness, which comes into being through the developing subjective attitude of the percipient," he has in mind no such "content of consciousness" as every newspaper reader experiences today. . . .

Quite apart from the abnormal aspect of everyday life today, there is the normal aspect of it. The spirit of negation has been so active, so confident and so intolerant that the commonplaces about the romantic provoke us to wonder if our salvation, if the way out, is not the romantic. All the great things have been denied and we live in an intricacy of new and local mythologies, political, economic, poetic, which are asserted with an ever-enlarging incoherence. This is accompanied by an absence of any authority except force, operative or imminent. What has been called the disparagement of reason is an instance of the absence of authority. We pick up the radio and find that comedians regard the public use of words of more than two syllables as funny. We read of the opening of the National Gallery at Washington and we are convinced, in the end, that the pictures are counterfeit, that museums are impositions and that Mr Mellon was a monster. We turn to a recent translation of Kierkegaard and we find him saying: "A great deal has been said about poetry reconciling one with existence; rather it might be said that it arouses one against existence; for poetry is unjust to men . . . it has use only for the elect, but that is a poor sort of reconciliation. I will take the case of sickness. Aesthetics replies proudly and quite consistently, 'That cannot be employed, poetry must not become a hospital.' Aesthetics culminates . . . by regarding sickness in accordance with the principle enunciated by Friedrich Schlegel: 'Nur Gesundheit ist liebens würdig.' (Health alone is lovable.)"

The enormous influence of education in giving everyone a little learning, and in giving large groups considerably more: something of history, something of philosophy, something of literature, the expansion of the middle class with its common preference for realistic satisfactions; the penetration of the masses of people by the ideas of liberal thinkers, even when that penetration is indirect, as by the reporting of the reasons why people oppose the ideas that they oppose, – these are normal aspects of everyday life. The way we live and the way we work alike cast us out on reality. If fifty private houses were to be built in New York this year, it would be a phenomenon. We no longer live in homes but in housing projects and this is so whether the project is literally a project or a club, a dormitory, a camp or an apartment in River House. It is not only that there are more of us and that we are actually close together. We are close together in every way. We lie in bed and listen to a broadcast from Cairo, and so on. There is no distance. We are intimate with people we have never seen and, unhappily, they are intimate with us....

These, nevertheless, are not the things that I had in mind when I spoke of the pressure of reality. These constitute the drift of incidents, to which we accustom ourselves as to the weather. Materialism is an old story and an indifferent one. Robert Wolseley said: "True genius... will enter into the hardest and dryest thing, enrich the most barren Soyl, and inform the meanest and most uncomely matter... the baser, the emptier, the obscurer, the fouler, and the less susceptible of Ornament the subject appears to be, the more is the Poet's Praise... who, as Horace says of Homer, can fetch Light out of Smoak, Roses out of Dunghills, and give a kind of Life to the Inanimate..." (Preface to Rochester's *Valentinian*, 1685, *English Association Essays and Studies* 1939). By the pressure of reality, I mean the pressure of an external event or events on the consciousness to the exclusion of any power of contemplation. The definition ought to be exact and, as it is, may be merely pretentious. But when one is trying to think of a whole generation and of a world at war, and trying at the same time to see what is happening to the imagination, particularly if one believes that that is what matters most, the plainest statement of what is happening can easily appear to be an affectation.

For more than ten years now, there has been an extraordinary pressure of news – let us say, news incomparably more pretentious than any description of it, news, at first, of the collapse of our system, or, call it, of life; then of news of a new world, but of a new world so uncertain that one did not know anything whatever of its nature, and does not know now, and could not tell whether it was to be all-English, all-German, all-Russian, all-Japanese, or all-American, and cannot tell now; and finally news of a war, which was a renewal of what, if it was not the greatest war, became such by this continuation. And for more than ten years, the consciousness of the world has concentrated on events which have made the ordinary movement of life seem to be the movement of people in the intervals of a storm. The disclosures of the impermanence of the past suggested, and suggest, an impermanence of the future. Little of what we have believed has been true. Only the prophecies are true. The present is an opportunity to repent. This is familiar enough. The war is only a part of a war-like whole. It is not possible to look backward and to see that the same thing was true in the past. It is a question of pressure, and pressure is incalculable and eludes the historian. The Napoleonic era is regarded as having had little or no effect on the poets and the novelists who lived in it. But Coleridge and Wordsworth and Sir Walter Scott and Jane Austen did not have to put up with Napoleon and Marx and Europe, Asia and Africa all at one time. It seems possible to say that they knew of the events of their day much as we know of the bombings in the interior of China and not at all as we know of the bombings of London, or, rather, as we should know of the bombings of Toronto or Montreal. Another part of the war-like whole to which we do not respond quite as we do to the news of war is the income tax. The blanks are specimens of mathematical prose. They titillate the instinct of self-preservation in a class in which that instinct has been forgotten. Virginia Woolf thought that the income tax, if continued, would benefit poets by enlarging their vocabularies and I dare say that she was right.

If it is not possible to assert that the Napoleonic era was the end of one era in the history of the imagination and the beginning of another, one comes closer to the truth by making that assertion in respect to the French Revolution. The defeat or triumph of Hitler are parts of a war-like whole but the fate of an individual is different from the fate of a society. Rightly or wrongly, we feel that the fate of a society is involved in the orderly disorders of the present time. We are confronting, therefore, a set of events, not only beyond our power to tranquillize them in the mind, beyond our power to reduce them and metamorphose them, but events that stir the emotions to violence, that engage us in what is direct and immediate and real, and events that involve the concepts and sanctions that are the order of our lives and may involve our very lives; and these events are occurring persistently with increasing omen, in what may be called our presence. These are the things that I had in mind when I spoke of the pressure of reality, a pressure great enough and prolonged enough to bring about the end of one era in the history of the imagination and, if so, then great enough to bring about the beginning of another. It is one of the peculiarities of the imagination that it is always at the end of an era. What happens is that it is always attaching itself to a new reality, and adhering to it. It is not that there is a new imagination but that there is a new reality. The pressure of reality may, of course, be less than the general pressure that I have described. It exists for individuals according to the circumstances of their lives or according to the characteristics of their minds. To sum it up, the pressure of reality is, I think, the determining factor in the artistic character of an individual. The resistance to this pressure or its evasion in the case of individuals of extraordinary imagination cancels the pressure so far as those individuals are concerned.

4

Suppose we try, now, to construct the figure of a poet, a possible poet. He cannot be a charioteer traversing vacant space, however ethereal. He must have lived all of the last two thousand years, and longer, and he must have instructed himself, as best he could, as he went along. He will have thought that Virgil, Dante, Shakespeare, Milton placed themselves in remote lands and in remote ages; that their men and women were the dead – and not the dead lying in the earth, but the dead still living in their remote lands and in their remote ages, and living in the earth or under it, or in the heavens – and he will wonder at those huge imaginations, in which what is remote becomes near, and what is dead lives with an intensity beyond any experience of life. He will consider that although he has himself witnessed, during the long period of his life, a general transition to reality, his own measure as a poet, in spite of all the passions of all the lovers of the truth, is the measure of his power to abstract himself, and to withdraw with him into his abstraction the reality on which the lovers of truth insist. He must be able to abstract himself and also to abstract reality, which he does by placing it in his imagination. . . .

The poet has his own meaning for reality, and the painter has, and the musician has; and besides what it means to the intelligence and to the senses, it means something to everyone, so to speak. Notwithstanding this, the word in its general sense, which is the sense in which I have used it, adapts itself instantly. The subject-matter of poetry is not that "collection of solid, static objects extended in space" but the life that is lived in the scene that it composes; and so reality is not that external scene but the life that is lived in it. Reality is things as they are. The general sense of the word proliferates its special senses. It is a jungle in itself. As in the case of a jungle, everything that makes it up is pretty much of one color. First, then, there is the reality that is taken for granted, that is latent and, on the whole, ignored. It is the comfortable American state of life of the eighties, the nineties and the first ten years of the present century. Next, there is the reality that has ceased to be indifferent, the years when the Victorians had been disposed of and intellectual minorities and social minorities began to take their place and to convert our state of life to something that might not be final. This much more vital reality made the life that had preceded it look like a volume of Ackermann's colored plates or one of Topfer's books of sketches in Switzerland. I am trying to give the feel of it. It was the reality of twenty or thirty years ago. I say that it was a vital reality. The phrase gives a false impression. It was vital in the sense of being tense, of being instinct with the fatal or with what might be the fatal. The minorities began to convince us that the Victorians had left nothing behind. The Russians followed the Victorians, and the Germans, in their way, followed the Russians. The British Empire, directly or indirectly, was what was left and as to that one could not be sure whether it was a shield or a target. Reality then became violent and so remains. This much ought to be said to make it a little clearer that in speaking of the pressure of reality, I am thinking of life in a state of violence, not physically violent, as yet, for us in America, but physically violent for millions of our friends and for still more millions of our enemies and spiritually violent, it may be said, for everyone alive.

A possible poet must be a poet capable of resisting or evading the pressure of the reality of this last degree, with the knowledge that the degree of today may become a deadlier degree tomorrow. There is, however, no point in dramatizing the future in advance of the fact. I confine myself to the outline of a possible poet, with only the slightest sketch of his background.

5

Here I am, well-advanced in my paper, with everything of interest that I started out to say remaining to be said. I am interested in the nature of poetry and I have stated its nature, from one of the many points of view from which it is possible to state it. It is an interdependence of the imagination and reality as equals. This is not a definition, since it is incomplete. But it states the nature of poetry. Then I am interested in the role of the poet and this is paramount. In this area of my subject I might be expected to speak of the social, that is to say sociological or political, obligation of the poet. He has none. That he must be contemporaneous is as old as Longinus and I dare say older. But that he *is* contemporaneous is almost inevitable. How contemporaneous in the direct sense in which being contemporaneous is intended were the four great poets of whom I spoke a moment ago? I do not think that a poet owes any more as a social obligation than he owes as a moral obligation, and if there is anything concerning poetry about which people agree it is that the role of the poet is not to be found in morals. I cannot say what that wide agreement amounts to because the agreement (in which I do not join) that the poet is under a social obligation is equally wide. Reality is life and life is society and the imagination and reality; that is to say, the imagination and society are inseparable. That is pre-eminently true in the case of the poetic drama. The poetic drama needs a terrible genius before it is anything more than a literary relic. Besides the theater has forgotten that it could ever be terrible. It is not one of the instruments of fate, decidedly. Yes: the all-commanding subject-matter of poetry is life, the never-ceasing source. But it is not a social obligation. One does not love and go back to one's ancient mother as a social obligation. One goes back out of a suasion not to be denied. Unquestionably if a social movement moved one deeply enough, its moving poems would follow. No politician can command the imagination, directing it to do this or that. Stalin might grind his teeth the whole of a Russian winter and yet all the poets in the Soviets might remain silent the following spring. He might excite their imaginations by something he said or did. He would not command them. He is singularly free from that "cult of pomp," which is the comic side of the European disaster; and that means as much as anything to us. The truth is that the social obligation so closely urged is a phase of the pressure of reality which a poet (in the absence of dramatic poets) is bound to resist or evade today. Dante in Purgatory and Paradise was still the voice of the Middle Ages but not through fulfilling any social obligation. Since that is the role most frequently urged, if that role is eliminated, and if a possible poet is left facing life without any categorical exactions upon him, what then? What is his function? Certainly it is not to lead people out of the confusion in which they find themselves. Nor is it, I think, to comfort them while they follow their readers to and fro. I think that his function is to make his imagination theirs and that he fulfills himself only as he sees his imagination become the light in the minds of others. His role, in short, is to help people to live their lives. Time and time again it has been said that he may not address himself to an élite. I think he may. There is not a poet whom we prize living today that does not address himself to an élite. The poet will continue to do this: to address himself to an élite even in a classless society, unless, perhaps, this exposes him to imprisonment or exile. In that event he is likely not to address himself to anyone at all. He may, like Shostakovich, content himself with pretence. He will, nevertheless, still be addressing himself to an élite, for all poets address themselves to someone and it is of the essence of that instinct, and it seems to amount to an instinct, that it should be to an élite, not to a drab but to a woman with the hair of a pythoness, not to a chamber of commerce but to a gallery of one's own, if there are enough of one's own to fill a gallery. And that élite, if it responds, not out of complaisance, but because the poet has quickened it, because he has educed from it that for which it was searching in itself and in the life around it, and which it had not yet quite found, will thereafter do for the poet what he cannot do for himself, that is to say, receive his poetry.

I repeat that his role is to help people to live their lives. He has had immensely to do with giving life whatever savor it possesses. He has had to do with whatever the imagination and the senses have made of the world. He has, in fact, had to do with life except as the intellect has had to do with it and, as to that, no one is needed to tell us that poetry and philosophy are akin. I want to repeat for two reasons a number of observations made by Charles Mauron. The first reason is that these observations tell us what it is that a poet does to help people to live their lives and the second is that they prepare the way for a word concerning escapism. They are: that the artist transforms us into epicures; that he has to discover the possible work of art in the real world, then to extract it, when he does not himself compose it entirely; that he is *un amoureux perpétuel* of the world that he contemplates and thereby enriches; that art sets out to express the human soul; and finally that everything like a firm grasp of reality is eliminated from the aesthetic field. With these aphorisms in mind, how is it possible to condemn escapism? The poetic process is psychologically an escapist process. The chatter about escapism is, to my way of thinking, merely common cant. My own remarks about resisting or evading the pressure of reality mean escapism, if analyzed. Escapism has a pejorative sense, which it cannot be supposed that I include in the sense in which I use the word. The pejorative sense applies where the poet is not attached to reality, where the imagination does not adhere to reality, which, for my part, I regard as fundamental. If we go back to the collection of solid, static objects extended in space, which Dr. Joad posited, and if we say that the space is blank space, nowhere, without color, and that the objects, though solid, have no shadows and, though static, exert a mournful power, and, without elaborating this complete poverty, if suddenly we hear a different and familiar description of the place:

> This City now doth, like a garment, wear
> The beauty of the morning, silent bare,
> Ships, towers, domes, theatres, and temples lie
> Open unto the fields, and to the sky;
> All bright and glittering in the smokeless air;

If we have this experience, we know how poets help people to live their lives. This illustration must serve for all the rest. There is, in fact, a world of poetry indistinguishable from the world in which we live, or, I ought to say, no doubt, from the world in which we shall come to live, since what makes the poet the potent figure that he is, or was, or ought to be, is that he creates the world to which we turn incessantly and without knowing it and that he gives to life the supreme fictions without which we are unable to conceive of it.

And what about the sound of words? What about nobility, of which the fortunes were to be a kind of test of the value of the poet? I do not know of anything that will appear to have suffered more from the passage of time than the music of poetry and that has suffered less. The deepening need for words to express our thoughts and feelings which, we are sure, are all the truth that we shall ever experience, having no illusions, makes us listen to words when we hear them, loving them and feeling them, makes us search the sound of them, for a finality, a perfection, an unalterable vibration, which it is only within the power of the acutest poet to give them. Those of us who may have been thinking of the path of poetry, those who understand that words are thoughts and not only our own thoughts but the thoughts of men and women ignorant of what it is that they are thinking, must be conscious of this: that, above everything else, poetry is words; and that words, above everything else, are, in poetry, sounds. This being so, my time and yours might have been better spent if I had been less interested in trying to give our possible poet an identity and less interested in trying to appoint him to his place. But unless I had done these things, it might have been thought that I was rhetorical, when I was speaking in the simplest way about things of such importance that nothing is more so. A poet's words are of things that do not exist without the words.... Poetry is a revelation in words by means of the words. Croce was not speaking of poetry in particular when he said that language is perpetual creation. About nobility I cannot be sure that the decline, not to say the disappearance of nobility is anything more than a maladjustment between the imagination and reality. We have been a little insane about the truth. We have had an obsession. In its ultimate extension, the truth about which we have been insane will lead us to look beyond the truth to something in which the imagination will be the dominant complement. It is not only that the imagination adheres to reality, but, also, that reality adheres to the imagination and that the interdependence is essential. We may emerge from our *bassesse* and, if we do, how would it happen if not by the intervention of some fortune of the mind? And what would that fortune of the mind happen to be? It might be only commonsense but even that, a commonsense beyond the truth, would be a nobility of long descent.

The poet refuses to allow his task to be set for him. He denies that he has a task and considers that the organization of materia poetica is a contradiction in terms. Yet the imagination gives to everything that it touches a peculiarity, and it seems to me that the peculiarity of the imagination is nobility, of which there are many degrees. This inherent nobility is the natural source of another, which our extremely headstrong generation regards as false and decadent. I mean that nobility which is our spiritual height and depth; and while I know how difficult it is to express it, nevertheless I am bound to give a sense of it. Nothing could be more evasive and inaccessible. Nothing distorts itself and seeks disguise more quickly. There is a shame of disclosing it and in its definite presentations a horror of it. But there it is. The fact that it is there is what makes it possible to invite to the reading and writing of poetry men of intelligence and desire for life. I am not thinking of the ethical or the sonorous or at all of the manner of it. The manner of it is, in fact, its difficulty, which each man must feel each day differently, for himself. I am not thinking of the solemn, the portentous or demoded. On the other hand, I am evading a definition. If it is defined, it will be fixed and it must not be fixed. As in the case of an external thing, nobility resolves itself into an enormous number of vibrations, movements, changes. To fix it is to put an end to it. . . .

. . . There is no element more conspicuously absent from contemporary poetry than nobility. There is no element that poets have sought after, more curiously and more piously, certain of its obscure existence. Its voice is one of the inarticulate voices which it is their business to overhear and to record. The nobility of rhetoric is, of course, a lifeless nobility. Pareto's epigram that history is a cemetery of aristocracies easily becomes another: that poetry is a cemetery of nobilities. For the sensitive poet, conscious of negations, nothing is more difficult than the affirmations of nobility and yet there is nothing that he requires of himself more persistently, since in them and in their kind, alone, are to be found those sanctions that are the reasons for his being and for that occasional ecstasy, or ecstatic freedom of the mind, which is his special privilege.

It is hard to think of a thing more out of time than nobility. Looked at plainly it seems false and dead and ugly. To look at it at all makes us realize sharply that in our present, in the presence of our reality, the past looks false and is, therefore, dead and is, therefore, ugly; and we turn away from it as from something repulsive and particularly from the characteristic that it has a way of assuming: something that was noble in its day, grandeur that was, the rhetorical once. But as a wave is a force and not the water of which it is composed, which is never the same, so nobility is a force and not the manifestations of which it is composed, which are never the same. Possibly this description of it as a force will do more than anything else I can have said about it to reconcile you to it. It is not an artifice that the mind has added to human nature. The mind has added nothing to human nature. It is a violence from within that protects us from a violence without. It is the imagination pressing back against the pressure of reality. It seems, in the last analysis, to have something to do with our self-preservation; and that, no doubt, is why the expression of it, the sound of its words, helps us to live our lives.

Chapter 35
Randall Jarrell

Randall Jarrell (1914–1965) was, like Ezra Pound, a promoter of other poets' work as well as his own. His correspondence with Robert Lowell played a formative role in shaping Lowell's first book, Lord Weary's Castle. *Jarrell's criticism in the late 1940s and 1950s celebrated the work of a number of twentieth-century American poets, including Elizabeth Bishop, William Carlos Williams, Wallace Stevens, Marianne Moore, and Robert Frost. Jarrell was born and educated in Tennessee. He studied at Vanderbilt University, where his thinking about poetry was strongly shaped by his teachers, John Crowe Ransom and Robert Penn Warren. His first book of poems,* Blood for a Stranger, *published in 1942, was strongly influenced by their and W. H. Auden's example. The cultural pessimism evident in his first book was carried over into his next two,* Little Friend, Little Friend *(1945) and* Losses *(1948). Both draw on his experience of the Second World War and both show his fascination with writing from a child's perspective. Jarrell had by this time moved away from the experiments with traditional verse forms that characterized his first book. He was increasingly drawn to a poetry of narration, often in the form of dramatic monologues that echoed the work of Robert Frost. But Jarrell was read as much for his criticism as for his poetry. From 1949 to 1953 he was poetry critic for the influential journal,* The Partisan Review. *His criticism combined intellectual subtlety with an accessible style. Poetry was not a marginal art for Jarrell. His criticism showed why the work of certain poets could have a public significance for American culture. His own work as a poet gave him an acute sense of the potentials and limits of particular poetic idioms. In addition to an important collection of essays,* Poetry and the Age, *published in 1953, and various selections of his poetry, Jarrell published another three books of poetry:* The Seven League Crutches *in 1951,* The Woman at Washington Zoo *in 1960, and* The Lost World *in 1965. Jarrell taught at the University of North Carolina from 1947 until his death as a result of a car accident in 1965.*

"The End of the Line" was first published in The Nation *in 1942. It was subsequently published in a posthumous collection of Jarrell's essays,* Kipling, Auden and Co. *in 1980. Like Graves and Riding before him, Jarrell starts with the ordinary reader's suspicion of modernist poetry's "differentness." But, unlike them, he does not approach this phenom-*

enon by way of a close verbal analysis. Instead he provides a synoptic cultural history of the evolution of modernist poetry, arguing that it is an extension of and not a break from romanticism. Although not engaged in a specific polemic with the work of T. E. Hulme, his interpretation of modernist poetry is antithetical to Hulme's claims in Romanticism and Classicism. *Jarrell's argument is characterized by an ambivalence of tone. Modernist poetry has exhausted its possibilities and marks the end of the line for a cultural form of poetry that began with Romanticism. He claims that he wants to celebrate the achievements of the modernists, but he also shows a marked impatience with modernism's complicity with "late capitalist society." At the end of the essay, Jarrell puts forward what was to become a repeated claim about the superiority of twentieth-century American poetry to the work of English poets.*

The End of the Line

What has impressed everyone about modernist poetry is its *differentness.* The familiar and rather touching "I like poetry – but not modern poetry" is only another way of noticing what almost all criticism has emphasized: that modernist poetry is a revolutionary departure from the romantic poetry of the preceding century. Less far-reaching changes would have seemed a revolutionary disaster to "conventional" poets, critics, and readers, who were satisfied with romantic poetry; a revolutionary improvement to more "advanced" poets and critics, who disliked romanticism with the fervor of converts. *Romantic* once again, after almost two centuries, became a term of simple derogation; correspondingly, there grew up a rather blank cult of the "classical," and poets like Eliot hinted that poets like Pound might be the new classicism for which all had been waiting.

All this seems to me partially true, essentially false. The change from romantic poetry was evolutionary, not revolutionary: the modernists were a universe away from the great-grandfathers they admired; they *were* their fathers, only more so. I want to sketch this evolution. But if the reader understands me to be using *romantic* as an unfavorably weighted term, most of what I say will be distorted. Some of the tendencies of romanticism are bad; some of the better tendencies, exaggerated enough, are bad; but a great deal of the best poetry I know is romantic. Of course, one can say almost that about any of the larger movements into which critics divide English poetry; and one might say even better things about the "classical tradition" in English poetry, if there were one. (It is not strange that any real movement, compared to this wax monster, comes off nowhere; but it is strange that anyone should take the comparison for a real one.) If I pay more attention to unfortunate or exaggerated romantic tendencies, it is because these are the most characteristic: the "good" tendencies of movements are far more alike than the "bad" ones, and a proof that two movements are essentially similar needs to show that they share each other's vices.

From *Kipling, Auden and Co.: Essays and Reviews, 1935–1964* (New York: Farrar, Straus and Giroux, 1980), pp. 76–83.

Modernist poetry – the poetry of Pound, Eliot, Crane, Tate, Stevens, Cummings, MacLeish, et cetera – appears to be and is generally considered to be a violent break with romanticism; it is actually, I believe, an extension of romanticism, an end product in which most of the tendencies of romanticism have been carried to their limits. Romanticism – whether considered as the product of a whole culture or, in isolation, as a purely literary phenomenon – is necessarily a process of extension, a vector; it presupposes a constant experimentalism, the indefinite attainment of "originality," generation after generation, primarily by the novel extrapolation of previously exploited processes. (Neoclassicism, in theory at least, is a static system.) All these romantic tendencies are exploited to their limits; and the movement which carries out this final exploitation, apparently so different from earlier stages of the same process, is what we call modernism. Then, at last, romanticism is confronted with an impasse, a critical point, a genuinely novel situation that it can meet successfully only by contriving genuinely novel means – that is, means which are not romantic; the romantic means have already been exhausted. Until these new means are found, romanticism operates by repeating its last modernist successes or by reverting to its earlier stages; but its normal development has ended, and – the momentum that gave it most of its attraction gone – it becomes a relatively eclectic system, much closer to neoclassicism than it has hitherto been. (A few of these last romanticists resort to odd varieties of neoclassicism.) If this account seems unlikely to the reader, let me remind him that a similar course of development is extremely plain in modern music.

A good many factors combine to conceal the essentially romantic character of modernist poetry. (1) A great quantitative change looks like a qualitative one: for instance, the attenuation or breaking up of form characteristic of romanticism will not be recognized or tolerated by the average romantic when it reaches its limit in modernist poetry. (2) The violent contrast between the modernist limits of romantic tendencies and the earlier stages of these tendencies, practiced belatedly and eclectically by "conventional" poets, is an important source of confusion. (3) Most of the best modern criticism of poetry is extremely anti-romantic – a poet's criticism is frequently not a reflection of but a compensation for his own poetry; and this change in theory has helped to hide the lack of any essential change in practice. (4) Modernist poems, while possessing some romantic tendencies in hypertrophied forms, often lack others so spectacularly that the reader disregards those they still possess; and these remaining tendencies may be too common for him to be conscious of them as specifically romantic. (Most of the romantic qualities that poetry has specialized in since 1800 seem to the average reader "normal" or "poetic," what poetry inescapably is.) (5) Romanticism holds in solution contradictory tendencies which, isolated and exaggerated in modernism, look startlingly opposed both to each other and to the earlier stages of romanticism. (6) Both modernist and conventional critics have been unable to see the fundamental similarities between modernist and romantic poetry because they were unwilling to see anything but differences: these were to the former a final recommendation, and to the latter a final condemnation.

We can understand modernist poetry better by noticing where and how it began. The English poetry that we call *fin de siècle* – the most important tendency of its time – was a limit of one easily recognizable extension of romanticism. These "decadent" poets were strongly influenced by Baudelaire, Verlaine, and similar French poets. Rimbaud, Laforgue, and Corbière – who had already written "modern" poetry – had no influence on them. Why? Because a section of French poetry was developing a third of a century ahead of English poetry: Rimbaud wrote typically modernist poetry in the 1870s; in the nineties a surrealist play, Jarry's *Ubu Roi*, scared the young Yeats into crying: "After us the Savage God!" France, without England's industrial advantages and enormous colonial profits, had had little of the Victorian prosperity which slowed up the economic and political rate of change in England – had still less of that complacent mercantile Christianity the French dismissed as "English hypocrisy." And – if we stick to a part of the culture, literature – the rate of change could be greater in France because romanticism was more of a surface phenomenon there. English poetry was not *ready* to be influenced by French modernism for many years. Meanwhile, there were two movements particularly suited to criticism. Accompanying the triumph of prose naturalism there was a prosy, realistic, rather limited reaction against "decadent" poetry (it included Robinson, Frost, Masters, Masefield, some of the Georgians, etc.). The other movement, imagism, carried three or four romantic tendencies to their limits with the perfection of a mathematical demonstration.

French modernist poetry first influenced poetry in English through Americans who, lacking a determining or confining tradition of their own, were particularly accessible and susceptible: Pound and Eliot (like Picasso, Stravinsky, and Joyce) were in some sense expatriates in both space and time. They imported modernism into English rather more deliberately and openly than Wordsworth and Coleridge had imported romanticism; but all Pound's early advice to poets could be summed up in a sentence half of which is pure Wordsworth: Write like prose, like speech – and *read French poetry!* The work of this most influential of modern poets, Ezra Pound, is a recapitulation of the development of our poetry from late romanticism to modernism. His early work is a sort of anthology of romantic sources: Browning, early Yeats, the *fin de siècle* poets, Villon and the troubadours (in translations or imitations that remind one of Swinburne's and Rossetti's), Heine. *His* variety of imagism is partly a return to the fresh beginnings of romantic practices, from their diluted and perfunctory ends; partly an extension to their limits of some of the most characteristic obsessions of romanticism – for instance, its passion for "pure" poetry, for putting everything in terms of sensation and emotion, with logic and generalizations excluded; and partly an adaptation of the exotic procedures of Chinese poetry, those silks that swathe a homely heart. When Pound first wrote poems that are modernist in every sense of the word, their general "feel" is reminiscent of what one might call a lowest common denominator of Corbière, Laforgue, and Rimbaud; but Heine had by no means disappeared; and the original Cantos I and II, gone now, were still full of Browning. But if Eliot was willing to base his form on Browning's (the dramatic monologue is primarily a departure from the norm of ordinary poetry; but in modernist poetry this departure *itself becomes the norm*), he had no interest in Browning's content and manner; in even his earliest poems one is seeing romanticism through Laforgue, and one can reconstruct this romanticism, in the pure form in which it had once existed, only from Eliot's remarks about his early feelings for Rossetti and Swinburne . . . All during this time the Irish expatriate Joyce was making his way from late-romantic lyrics (in verse, though there is much that is similar in his early prose) to the modernist poetry (in prose) that crops up here and there in *Ulysses*, and that is everywhere in *Finnegans Wake*.

But it would take fifty or a hundred pages to write about this development in terms of specific poets. One can indicate the resemblances of romanticism and modernism more briefly, by making a list of some of the general characteristics of modernist poetry:

(1) A pronounced experimentalism: "originality" is everyone's aim, and novel techniques are as much prized as new scientific discoveries. Eliot states it with surprising naïveté: "It is exactly as wasteful for a poet to do what has been done already as for a biologist to re-discover Mendel's discoveries." (2) External formlessness, internal disorganization: these are justified either as the disorganization necessary to express a disorganized age or as new and more complex forms of organization. Language is deliberately disorganized, meter becomes irregular or disappears; the rhythmical flow of verse is broken up into a jerky half-prose *collage* or *montage*. (3) Heightened emotional intensity; violence of every sort. (4) Obscurity, inaccessibility: logic, both for structure and for texture, is neglected; without this for a ground the masses of the illogical or alogical lose much of their effectiveness. The poet's peculiar erudition and allusiveness (compare the Alexandrian poet Lycophron) consciously restrict his audience to a small, highly specialized group; the poet is a specialist like everyone else. He intimidates or overawes the public by an attitude one may paraphrase as: "The poet's cultivation and sensibility are of a different order from those of his readers; even if he tried to talk down to them – and why should he try? – he would talk about things they have never heard of, in ways they will never understand." But he did not despair of their understanding a slap in the face. (5) A lack of restraint or proportion: all tendencies are forced to their limits, even contradictory tendencies – and not merely in the same movement but, frequently, in the same poet or the same poem. Some modernist poetry puts an unparalleled emphasis on texture, connotation, violently "interesting" language (attained partly by an extension of romantic principles, partly by a more violent rhetoric based on sixteenth- and seventeenth-century practices); but there has never before been such prosaic poetry – conversational-colloquial verse without even a pretense at meter. (6) A great emphasis on details – on parts, not wholes. Poetry is essentially lyric: the rare narrative or expository poem is a half-fortuitous collocation of lyric details. Poetry exploits particulars and voids and condemns generalizations. (7) A typically romantic preoccupation with sensation, perceptual nuances. (8) A preoccupation with the unconscious, dreams, the stream of consciousness, the irrational: this *surréaliste* emphasis might better have been called *sousréaliste*. (9) Irony of every type: Byronic, Laforguian, dryly metaphysical, or helplessly sentimental. Poetry rejects a great deal, accepts a little, and is embarrassed by that little, (10) *Fauve* or neo-primitive elements, (11) Modernist poets, though they may write about the ordinary life of the time, are removed from it, have highly specialized relations with it. The poet's naturalism is employed as indictment, as justification for his own isolation; prosaic and sordid details become important as what writers like Wallace Stevens and William Carlos Williams somewhat primitively think of as the *anti-poetic*. Contemporary life is condemned, patronized, or treated as a disgraceful aberration or special case, compared to the past; the poet hangs out the

window of the Ivory Tower making severe but obscure remarks about what is happening below – he accepts the universe with several (thin) volumes of reservations. What was happening below was bad enough; the poet could characterize it, truthfully enough, with comparative forms of all those adjectives that Goethe and Arnold had applied to their ages. But its disasters, at least, were of unprecedented grandeur; it was, after all, "the very world, which is the world / Of all of us, – the place where, in the end, / We find our happiness or not at all"; and the poet's rejection or patronizing acceptance of it on his own terms – and, sometimes, what terms they were! – hurt his poetry more than he would have believed. (12) Individualism, isolation, alienation. The poet is not only different from society, he is as different as possible from other poets; all this differentness is exploited to the limit – is used as subject matter, even. Each poet develops an elaborate, "personalized," bureaucratized machinery of effect; *refine your singularities* is everybody's maxim. (13) These poets, typically, dislike and condemn science, industrialism, humanitarianism, "progress," the main tendencies of Western development; they want to trade the present for a somewhat idealized past, to turn from a scientific, commercial, and political world view to one that is literary, theological, and personal.

This complex of qualities is essentially romantic, and the poetry that exhibits it is the culminating point of romanticism.

It is the end of the line. Poets can go back and repeat the ride; they can settle in attractive, atavistic colonies along the railroad; they can repudiate the whole system, à la Yvor Winters, for some neoclassical donkey caravan of their own. But Modernism As We Knew It – the most successful and influential body of poetry of this century – is dead. Compare a 1940 issue of *Poetry* with a 1930 issue. Who could have believed that modernism would collapse so fast? Only someone who realized that modernism is a limit which it is impossible to exceed. How can poems be written that are more violent, more disorganized, more obscure, more – supply your own adjective – than those that have already been written? But if modernism could go no further, it was equally difficult for it to stay where it was: how could a movement completely dynamic in character, as "progressive" as the science and industrialism it accompanied, manage to become static or retrogressive without going to pieces? Among modernist poets, from 1910 to 1925, there was the same feeling of confident excitement, of an individual but irregularly cooperative experimentalism, of revolutionary discoveries just around the corner, that one regularly sees at certain stages in the development of a science; they had ahead of them the same Manifest Destiny that poets have behind them today. Today, for the poet, there is an embarrassment of choices: young poets can choose – do choose – to write anything from surrealism to imitations of Robert Bridges; the only thing they have no choice about is making their own choice. The Muse, forsaking her sterner laws, says to everyone: "Do what you will." Originality can no longer be recognized by, and condemned or applauded for, its obvious experimentalism; the age offers to the poet a fairly heartless eclecticism or a fairly solitary individuality. He can avoid being swept along by the current – there is no current; he can congratulate himself on this, and see behind him, glittering in the distance of time, all those bright streams sweeping people on to the wildest of excesses, the unlikeliest of triumphs.

For a long time society and poetry have been developing in the same direction, have been carrying certain tendencies to their limits: how could anyone fail to realize that the excesses of modernist poetry are the necessary concomitants of the excesses of late-capitalist society? (An example too pure and too absurd even for allegory is Robinson Jeffers, who must prefer a hawk to a man, a stone to a hawk, because of an individualism so exaggerated that it contemptuously rejects affections, obligations, relations of any kind whatsoever, and sets up as a nostalgically awaited goal the war of all against all. Old Rocky Face, perched on his sea crag, is the last of *laissez faire*; Free Economic Man at the end of his rope.) How much the modernist poets disliked their society, and how much they resembled it! How often they contradicted its letter and duplicated its spirit! They rushed, side by side with their society, to the limits of all tendencies. When, at the beginning of the thirties, these limits were reached, what became of these individualists? They turned toward anything collective: toward Catholicism, communism, distributism, social credit, agrarianism; they wrote neoclassical criticism or verse; they wrote political (Marxist or fellow traveler) criticism or verse; they stopped writing; and when they read the verse of someone like E. E. Cummings, as it pushed on into the heart of that last undiscovered continent, *e. e. cummings*, they thought of this moral impossibility, this living fossil, with a sort of awed and incredulous revulsion.

I have no space to write of later developments. Auden was so influential because his poetry was the only novel and successful reaction away from modernism; and a few years later Dylan Thomas was so influential – in England – because his poetry was the only novel and successful reaction away from Auden. But his semi-surrealist experimentalism could be as good as it was, and as influential as it was, only in a country whose poets had never carried modernism to the limits of its possibilities. No one can understand these English developments if he forgets that, while we were having the modernism of Pound, Stevens, Williams, Moore, Eliot, Tate, Crane, Cummings, and all the rest, England was having the modernism of the Sitwells.

I am afraid that my hypothesis about romanticism and modernism, without the mass of evidence that can make a theory plausible, or the tangle of extensions and incidental insights that can make it charming, may seem improbable or unpleasant to some of my readers. It is intended to be partial: I have not written about the hard or dry or "classical" tendencies of some modern verse – what Empson and Marianne Moore have in common, for instance; and I have not listed the differences between modernism and romanticism that everybody has seen and stated. But I hope that nobody will dislike my article because he thinks it an attack on romanticism or modernism. This has been description, not indictment. Burke said that you can't indict a whole people, and I hope I am not such a fool as to indict a century and a half of a world. Besides, so far as its poetry is concerned, it was wonderful. Wordsworth and Blake and Heine, Baudelaire and Corbière, Hardy and Yeats and Rilke – the names crowd in; and there are dozens more. That some of these poets were, sometimes, as strange as they were wonderful; that some of their successors were, alas, rather stranger: all this is as true as it is obvious. But the "classical" prejudice which hints that these poets were somehow deceived and misguided as (say) Dryden and Valéry were not seems every year more grotesque. One repeats to oneself, *Whom God deceives is well deceived*, and concludes that if these poets were not classical, so much the worse for classicism.

Chapter 36
Aimé Césaire

Aimé Césaire (1913–) is a poet, cultural theorist, and politician who played a central role in debates about black cultural identity. Césaire moved from Martinique to Paris in 1931, where after further study at the Lycée Louis Le Grand he attended the École Normale Supérieure. During the 1930s Paris was a meeting point for black intellectuals from Africa, the Caribbean, and the United States. The Harlem Renaissance provided one example for the assertion of black cultural identity. Working with his colleague, Leopold Senghor, Césaire developed another "negritude," described by Senghor as an affirmation of "the cultural inheritance, the values, above all the spirit of the black African civilization." On this basis Césaire found the terms to reject the values of French colonialism, which assumed that all races and creeds could be assimilated to the ideal of French republican citizenship. By 1935 Césaire had begun work on his remarkable long poem, Cahier d'un retour au pays natal. *The poem was completed in 1939 when Césaire returned to Martinique. It was during this period that Césaire's career as a politician began. In 1945 he was elected as Martinique's deputy to the French National Assembly and appointed Mayor of Fort-de-France, two positions he held until 1993. In 1947 the publication of his* Cahier *in an American edition with an English translation brought him international recognition as a poet, and throughout the 1950s and 1960s he published poetry, analyses of colonialism, and work for the theater. Césaire has had the difficult experience of becoming a figure of classic stature in his own lifetime. Subsequent generations of francophone Caribbean writers have rejected "negritude" because it links race to culture too strongly.*

"Poetry and Knowledge" was first given as an address at a conference held in Haiti in 1941. It was subsequently published in January 1945 in Tropiques, *a journal editied by Césaire and his wife, the Martinician poet, Suzanne Roussy. In its rhythms, images, and shifts in perspective, "Poetry and Knowledge" echoes the form of Césaire's* Cahier. *Although it is not an explicit statement of the principles and values of "negritude" it shows Césaire's identification of modern poetry both as a revolt against a technological culture and as the basis for a new universal culture. Its exalted claims for poetry echo those of the Surrealists, Breton and Éluard. Césaire's affirmation of a distinctive form of poetic knowledge,*

separate from the knowledge of science, is central to his philosophy of liberation. Unless otherwise indicated in the text, this translation is by the editor and is published here for the first time.

Poetry and Knowledge

Poetic knowledge is born in the silence of scientific knowledge.

By reflection, observation, and experience, man, disoriented by the world of fact, comes to dominate it. From that moment he knows how to find his way in the forest of phenomena. He knows how to use the world.

But, for all that, he is not the king of the world.

A perspective on the world. Yes. Science offers him a perspective on the world. But of a summary and superficial kind.

Physics classifies and explains, but the essence of things escapes it. The natural sciences classify, but the quid proprium of things escapes them.

As for mathematics, what escapes its logical and abstract activity is the real, reality.

All in all, scientific knowledge counts, measures, classifies and kills.

But it is not enough to say that scientific knowledge is summary. We must add that it is impoverished and half-starved.

To acquire it man has sacrificed everything: desires, fears, feelings, psychological complexes.

To acquire this impersonal knowledge that is scientific knowledge, man has *depersonalized* himself, has deprived himself of individuality.

An impoverished knowledge, I say, because at its origin, whatever may be its riches beside, stands an impoverished man.

In Aldous Huxley's *The Angel and the Animal* there is a very amusing passage: "We all think we know what a lion is. A lion is an animal of a desert colour, that possesses a mane and claws, and an expression like Garibaldi's. But it's also, in Africa, amid all the surrounding antelopes and zebras, and, as a consequence, all the surrounding grassland. If there weren't antelopes and zebras there wouldn't be any lions. When the supply of prey becomes scarce, the king of beasts becomes thin and mangy. If it ceases completely, he dies."

The same is true for knowledge. Scientific knowledge is a lion without antelopes and zebras. It is gnawed at from within. Gnawed at by hunger, the hunger of feeling, the hunger of life.

So, unsatisfied, man looked elsewhere for his salvation, which is here a plenitude.

And, little by little, man became aware that, besides the scientific, half-starved knowledge, there was another kind of knowledge. A satisfying knowledge.

Through this discovery, an Ariadne's thread: some very simple remarks on the faculty which has allowed what we must call primitive men of learning to discover, by intuition and without either deduction or induction, the most substantial truths.

And this is what leads us to humanity's earliest period. The error is to believe that knowledge awaited, in order to be born, the methodical exercise of thought or the scruples of experimentation. In fact, I believe that man has never been closer to certain truths than in the earliest days of the species. The time when man discovered through emotion the first sun, the first rain, the first breath of wind, the first moon. A time when man discovered, in fear and delight, the palpitating freshness of the world.

Attraction and terror. Trembling and rapture. Estrangement and intimacy. Only the sacred phenomenon of love can still give us an idea of what this solemn encounter might have been like.

It is in this state of fear and love, in this climate of feeling and imagination, that man made his first, most decisive and fundamental discoveries.

It was fatal and desirable that humanity should attain powers of mental precision.

It was fatal and desirable that humanity should regret what was most keenly felt.

It is this nostalgia for a mild season of fruitfulness that, at the zenith of scientific knowledge, threw man back on to the nocturnal forces of poetry.

In every period poets have known this. All the legends of antiquity testify to it. But in modern times it is only in the nineteenth century, at the moment when the Apollonian era began to come to an end, that poets dared to affirm what they knew.

1850 The revenge of Dionysus on Apollo.

1850 The great leap into the poetic void.

An extraordinary phenomenon... Until then the French attitude had been made of prudence, circumspection and mistrust. France was dying of prose. And then, there was a great nervous trembling before the great adventure. The most prosaic nation, and amongst its most eminent members, by the steepest, abruptest, loftiest, most breatheless routes, the only ones that are to me worth calling sacred and royal – with arms and supplies – went over to the enemy. I mean to the army with a skull-and-crossbones made from liberty and imagination.

Prosaic France passed over to poetry. And everything changed.

Poetry stopped being a game, even a serious one. Poetry stopped being a profession, however honourable.

Poetry became an adventure. The finest of human adventures.... Its goal: vision and knowledge.

And so we come to Baudelaire.

It is significant that so much of Baudelaire's poetry relates itself to the idea of penetrating the universe.

...

As for Rimbaud, literature is still feeling the after shocks of the incredible earthquake produced by the famous "letter of a visionary":

> I say we must be visionaries, make ourselves visionaries.

Memorable words of victory and distress.

From now on, the field is open for the greatest dreams of humanity.

There can no longer be any doubt allowed about Mallarmé's project. The daring lucidity of what he wrote to Verlaine made Mallarmé an engineer of the mind of special importance, even more than the poet of whom Paul Valéry is the reflection.

> Apart from the fragments of youthful prose and verse and what followed it by way of an echo... I have always dreamt of and attempted to do something else... A book, quite simply, a book which is premeditated and architectural, not a gathering of random inspirations, however marvellous. I shall go further still, I shall say the Book, persuaded that fundamentally there is only one... The orphic explanation of the Earth, which is the only duty of the poet. And the literary gamble without equal... Here is the confession of my vice.

To move from Mallarmé to Apollinaire is to pass from the cold calculator, the strategist of poetry to the enthusiastic adventurer, the leader of the pack.

Apollinaire was great because between a popular song and a war poem he knew how still to be, fundamentally, one of those horrifying workers whose advent Rimbaud celebrated:

> You whose mouth is made in the image of God's
> Mouth that is order itself
> Be indulgent when you compare us
> To those who were the perfection of order
> Us who seek everywhere for adventure
> . . .
> (Apollinaire, *The Pretty Redhead*, translated by Robert Chandler)

I now come, not without having jumped a few stops, to André Breton. It will be the glory of surrealism to have created against itself a block of all the avowed and unavowed enemies of poetry. To have distilled several centuries of poetic experience. To have purged the past, given direction to the present, prepared the future.

It is André Breton who writes:

> Despite everything it is from poets, in the sequence of the centuries, that it is possible both to receive and be permitted to await the impulses likely to restore man at the heart of the universe, to abstract him for a moment from his debilitating fate, to remind him that there is for every sadness and joy outside him an infinitely perfectible place of resolution and echo.

And still more significantly:

> Everything points to the belief that a certain spiritual state exists where life and death, the real and the imaginary, the past and the future, the communicable and the incommunicable, the high and the low cease to be perceived as contradictory. And it is in vain that people might look to surrealist activity for any other motive than the hope of determining this state.

Never in the course of time has a more exalted ambition been expressed so calmly.

This lofty ambition is the ambition of poetry itself.

Nothing more remains to us than to examine the conditions for satisfying this ambition and by what means.

At the basis of poetic knowledge, an astonishing mobilization of all cosmic and human forces.

It is not with his entire soul but with his entire being that the poet approaches the poem. What governs the poem is not the most lucid intelligence nor the most acute sensibility, but the entirety of experience, every woman loved, every desire tested, every dream dreamt, every image received or seized, the whole weight of the body and the spirit. Everything that has been lived, every possibility. Around the emerging poem the precious vortex: myself, itself, the world. And the most surprising encounters, all pasts, all futures, the anticyclone creates its stable levee, the amoeba loses its pseudopods, vegetable forms are gathered together. Every flux, every ray of light. The body is no longer deaf or blind. Everything has the right to life. Everything is summoned. Everything waits. I mean everything. The whole individual experience reconfigured by poetic inspiration. And, in a more disturbing way, the entire cosmos too.

Now is the moment to remember that the unconscious which all true poetry appeals to is the receptacle of the kinship that, originally, united us with nature.

In us the man of all times. In us every man. In us animal, vegetable, mineral. Man is not only man. He is *universe.*

It is all as if before the secondary scattering of life there had been an intricate primary unity whose dazzling, marvellous quality would be protected by poets.

Distracted by action, possessed by utility, man lost the sense of this bond. Here (we discover, see) the superiority of the animal. And of the tree still more than the animal, because the tree is fixity, attachment and perseverance in what is essential. . . .

And because the tree is stability, the tree is also surrender.

Abandonment to the dynamic life, the creative impulse. Joyous abandonment.

And the flower is the sign of this recognition.

Superiority of the tree over man, of the tree which says "yes" over man who says "no". Superiority of the tree which is acceptance over man who is evasiveness; superiority of the tree, which is rooted and going down deeper, over man who is anxious and in grave error.

And the result is that man does not flourish.

He is not in the least a tree. His arms imitate branches, but they are withered branches which, having misunderstood their function which is to embrace life, have fallen back on the trunk – dried up, man does not flourish.

But one man saves humanity, one man restores it to universal harmony, one man weds human flourishing to the universal flourishing; this man is the poet.

What has he done to achieve this?

Very little, but the little that he did only he could do. Like the tree, like the animal, he has abandoned himself to life in its first principles, he said yes, he accepted the immense life that exceeded him. He rooted himself in the earth, he spread his arms, he played with the sun, he became tree; he flourished, he sang.

To put it another way, poetry is a blossoming.

Blossoming of man to the measure of the world – a dizzying opening out. And one can say that all great poetry, without ever renouncing its humanity, at a very mysterious moment ceases to be strictly human to begin being truly cosmic.

So here – by means of the poetic state – is a resolution of two of the most painful antinomies that there can be: the antinomy between one and another, the antinomy between Self and World.

> "Finally, o happiness, o reason, I listened to the blue of the sky, the blue that is black, and I lived, a sparkle of gold in nature's light."

So big with the world, the poet speaks.

> In the beginning was the verb....
> ...Never has any man believed this more strongly than the poet.

And it is on the word, that shaving of the world, the modest, secret lick of the world, that he gambles everything for us... first and last.

More and more, the word risks looking like an algebraic notation that makes the world intelligible. In the same way that the new Cartesian algebra made possible the construction of a theoretical physics, so an original handling of the word can give to every possible moment a new theoretical undercurrent of which poetry would already give a fairly good idea. Then the new time will come when the study of language will condition the study of nature. But for now we are still in the shadows...

Let's return to the poet... Big with the world, the poet speaks.

He speaks and his tongue returns language to its pure state.

A pure state. I mean by this a state subordinated neither to habit nor to thought, but only to the sole pulse of the cosmos. The poet's word, the primitive word: a design on rock in a matter made of sound.

The poet's utterance: the primitive utterance: a universe performed and undermined.

And because in every authentic poem, the poet plays the world's game, the true poet wants to abandon the word to its free associations, in the assurance that to do so is, in the last analysis, to abandon it to the will of the universe.

Everything I have just said risks making you think of the poet as a disempowered figure. However it is nothing like that. If I specify that in the poetic emotion, nothing is closer to anything than to its contrary, you will understand that never was a man of the depths of things more rebellious and pugnacious.

It is to poetry itself that the old idea of the irritable poet must be transferred to poetry. It is in this particular sense that it is admissible to talk of poetic violence, poetic aggression, poetic instability. In the climate of fire and fury which is the climate of poetry, money ceases to have value, tribunals cease to pass judgement, judges cease to condemn and juries to acquit. Only the execution squads still know what their work is. The further forward one goes, the more evident become the signs of a rout. The police choke themselves. Conventions lose all their force. The Grammont laws for the protection of men, the Locarno conventions for the protection of animals abruptly and magically renounce their authority. A wind of disarray... An anxiety which disturbs the most secure foundations. At the bloodied end of deathly avenues a huge perfidious sun sneers and sniggers. It is the sun of humour. And in the dust of clouds the crows write one name over and over again: ISIDORE DUCASSE COMTE DE LAUTRÉAMONT.

Effectively the first to do so, Lautréamont integrated humour into poetry. He was the first to discover the functional role of humour. He was the first to make us aware that what love had started, humour had the power to continue.

Not the least role of humour is to cleanse the spaces of the mind. To dissolve with a blow-torch the connections which, in passing, are in danger of encrusting themselves on the mind's tender stuff and hardening it. First it is humour which, contrary to Pascal, la Rochefoucauld and so many other moralists assures Lautréamont that if Cleopatra's nose had been shorter, the face of the world would not have been changed; that the sun and death can look each other in the face; that man is a subject without illusions... that nothing is less strange than the contraries discovered in man. It is humour first of all that assures me that it is as true to say the thief makes the opportunity as "opportunity makes the thief..."

Only humour assures me that the most prodigious inversions are legitimate. Only humour alerts me to the other side of things.

But here we find ourselves brought to the lively spaces of metaphor.

It is impossible to think about the richness of the image without dreaming as a result of the poverty of judgement.

Judgement is impoverished by all the reason of the world.
The image is rich with all the world's absurdity.
Judgement is rich with all the "thought" of the world.
The image is rich with all the life of the universe.
Judgement is impoverished by all that is rational in existence.

The image is rich with all the irrationality of life.
Judgement is impoverished by all immanence.
The image is rich with all transcendence.

Let me explain...

Try though you might to identify analytic judgement with synthetic judgement; to say that judgement presupposes making a connection between two different concepts; to insist on the idea that there is no judgement without X; that every judgement is moving towards the unknown; that every judgement is transcendent, it is still no less true that in every valid judgement the space of transcendence is limited.

The safety railings are there: the law of identity, the law of contradiction, the principle of the excluded middle.

Precious safety railings. But also singular limitations.

It's through the image, the revolutionary image, the remote image, the image which overturns all laws of thought, that man at last breaks through the barrier.

In the image A is no longer A:

> You whose so many raspberry scented smiles
> Are a flock of tame lambs
> (translated by Clive Scott)

In the image A is perhaps not-A:

> The backplate of the blackened heath, real suns on strands; ah! well of many magics...
> (Rimbaud, "Illuminations", translated by Martin Sorrell)

In the image any object of thought is not necessarily A or not-A.

The image preserves the possibility of the "juste milieu":

Rimbaud again:

> Silver chariots, and copper –
> Steel prows, and silver –
> Smack the foam –
> Heave the thorn stumps out
> (Rimbaud, "Illuminations", translated by Martin Sorrell)

Without reckoning on the heartening complicities of the world as found and the world as invented which mean that we can say *motor* for *sun*, *dynamo* for *mountain*, *carburettor* for *Caribbean* etc.... and lyrically celebrate the shining crank-arm of moons and the airless (breathless) piston of stars...

Because the image immeasurably extends the space of transcendence and the right to transcendence, poetry is always on the road to truth. And because the image ceaselessly goes beyond what is perceived, because the dialectic of the image transcends antinomies, taken in its entirety modern science is perhaps only the cumbersome verification of some lively images launched by poets....

When the sun of the image reaches its zenith, everything again becomes possible... The complexes created by curses disappear in the moment of emergences...

What emerges is individual depth. Intimate conflicts, obsessions, phobias, fixations. All the codes of the personal message.

It's not a matter as in a former lyric mode of immortalizing a moment of joy and pain. Here we are well beyond anecdotal forms, in the very heart of man, in the seething hollow of his destiny. My past is there revealing myself to me and concealing from me its face. My future is there giving me its beckoning hand. Rockets go up in the sky. It's my childhood that burns. It's my childhood that speaks and seeks me out. And in who I am who I will be rises up on tiptoe.

What also emerges is the old ancestral depth.

Ancestral images which only the poetic atmosphere can bring up- to- date for the purposes of decipherment. The buried millenarian knowledge. Knowledge's engulfed cities of Ys.

In this sense all the mythologies the poet happens upon, all the symbols he gathers and gilds are true. And only poetry takes them seriously. This contributes to making poetry into something serious.

The German philosopher Jung discovers the idea of energy and its conservation in Heraclitus' metaphor of eternal fire, in medieval legends concerning the haloes of saints, in the theory of metempsychosis. And on his side, Pierre Mabille regrets that the biologist thinks himself "dishonoured by depicting the evolution of the blood cell through the story of the phoenix, or the functioning of the spleen through the myth of Saturn giving birth to children only then to devour them."

To put it another way, science rejects myth where poetry accepts it. This is not to say that science is superior to poetry. In truth myth is at one and the same time inferior and superior to the law. Myth is inferior in precision. But it is superior in richness and sincerity. Only myth satisfies man in his entirety: his heart, his reason, his taste for the part and the whole, for the false and the true, because myth is all these things at once. A foggy and emotional apprehension more than a means of poetic expression . . .

Hence love and humour.
Hence the word, the image and myth.

Relying on these great powers of synthesis we are at last in a position to understand the words of André Breton

> Columbus had to leave with madmen in order to discover America.
> And see how this madness came into being.
> It is not the fear of madness that will force us to leave the banner of imagination at half-mast
> . . .

And the poet Lucretius discovered the indestructibility of matter, the plurality of worlds, and the existence of the infinitely small.

And the poet Seneca in Medea launched ships in search of worlds:

> Epochs will come when the Ocean will burst the bounds by which it surrounds us. An infinite land will open out. The steersman will discover new lands and Thule will no longer be the world's end.
>
> It is not the fear of madness that will force us to leave the banner of imagination at half-mast . . . And the painter Rousseau *invents* tropical vegetation. And the painter Chirico as prophetically paints his future wound on Apollinaire's brow. And the poet André Breton in about 1924 prophetically connects the word "war" with the number "1939".
>
> It is not the fear of madness that will force us to leave the banner of imagination at half-mast. And the poet Rimbaud writes "Illuminations".

You know the result: strange cities, extraordinary countrysides, twisted, crushed, dismembered worlds, cosmos returned to chaos, order to disorder, being to becoming, absurdity everywhere, incoherence everywhere, insanity everywhere. And at the end of all this! What is there? Not failure but the dazzling vision of his own destiny. And the most authentic vision of the world, if, as I persist in believing, Rimbaud is the first man to have experienced to the innermost depths of his feeling, and to the point of anguish, modern idea, of energetic forces which, concealed in matter, cunningly lie in stealthy wait for our tranquillity . . .

No: "It is not the fear of madness that will force us to leave the banner of imagination at half-mast."

Now some propositions which are as much a résumé as a clarification.

First proposition

Poetry is that process which by way of the word, the image, myth, love and humour establishes me in the living heart of myself and the world.

Second proposition

The poetic process is a naturing force which takes place under the lunatic impulse of imagination.

Third proposition

Poetic knowledge occurs when a man showers an object with all his activated riches.

Fourth proposition

If affective energy can be endowed with causal powers as Freud has shown, it is paradoxical to deny it the power of penetration. It is permissible to think that nothing is able to resist the unheard of mobilization of force that poetry requires, and the multiplied impetus of each of these forces.

Fifth proposition

From the marvellous contact between the interior and exterior totalities perceived imaginatively and simultaneously by the poet, better within the poet, remarkable discoveries can be made.

Sixth proposition

Scientific truth operates under the sign of coherence and efficiency. Poetic truth operates under the sign of beauty.

Seventh and final proposition

Poetic beauty is not only beauty of expression or muscular well-being. Too Apollonian or gymnastic a conception of beauty paradoxically risks padding out or stiffening what is beautiful.

Corollary

The music of poetry could never be external. The only acceptable music comes from somewhere deeper than sound. The search for music is a crime against the music of poetry which can only be the beating of the mind's wave against the rock of the world. The poet is this being at once very old and very new, very complex and very simple who at the lived limits of dream and reality, day and night, between absence and presence, seeks and receives in the sudden release of inner cataclysms the password to hidden understanding and to power.

Chapter 37
Charles Olson

Charles Olson (1910–70) worked for the Democratic Party and the Office of War Information before he began seriously writing poetry in the late 1940s. In 1951 he became rector of Black Mountain College in North Carolina and in 1953 he published his first collection, In Cold Hell, In Thicket. *During his time in charge of the College it became a gathering point for a number of poets, including Edward Dorn and Robert Creeley, who regularly published in two journals,* Origin *and* Black Mountain Review. *In 1956 Black Mountain College closed and Olson moved to Gloucester, Massachusetts. Here he continued to dedicate himself to the composition of* The Maximus Poems, *a long experimental work, influenced by Pound's* Cantos, *written from 1950 until shortly before Olson's death in 1970, and published in three volumes in 1960, 1968, and 1975.*

"Projective Verse" was first published in 1950 as a pamphlet in the Poetry New York *series. In the following extract Olson presents Projective or Open Field poetics as the next step in the developments in poetry inaugurated by Pound and Williams. But the next step is also a return to the fundamental elements of poetry – the syllable and the line rather than the image or symbol – that Olson argues were lost from the time of the late Elizabethans to Ezra Pound. Olson's idiom is assertively American. Working in the Open Field the poet is a literary frontiersman, endlessly exploring new territories of perception, with a body attuned to the movement of the syllable by way of the ear and to the line by way of breath. "Projective Verse" became a significant reference point for experimental poetry in both the United States and Britain during the 1960s and 70s. More recently its influence can be traced in the work of the Language poets.*

Projective Verse

1

First, some simplicities that a man learns, if he works in OPEN, or what can also be called COMPOSITION BY FIELD, as opposed to inherited line, stanza, over-all form, what is the "old" base of the non-projective.

(1) the *kinetics* of the thing. A poem is energy transferred from where the poet got it (he will have some several causations), by way of the poem itself to, all the way over to, the reader. Okay. Then the poem itself must, at all points, be a high energy-construct and, at all points, an energy-discharge. So: how is the poet to accomplish same energy, how is he, what is the process by which a poet gets in, at all points energy at least the equivalent of the energy which propelled him in the first place, yet an energy which is peculiar to verse alone and which will be, obviously, also different from the energy which the reader, because he is a third term, will take away?

This is the problem which any poet who departs from closed form is specially confronted by. And it involves a whole series of new recognitions. From the moment he ventures into FIELD COMPOSITION – puts himself in the open – he can go by no track other than the one the poem under hand declares, for itself. Thus he has to behave, and be, instant by instant, aware of some several forces just now beginning to be examined. (It is much more, for example, this push, than simply such a one as Pound put, so wisely, to get us started: "the musical phrase," go by it, boys, rather than by the metronome.)

(2) is the *principle*, the law which presides conspicuously over such compositions, and, when obeyed, is the reason why a projective poem can come into being. It is this: FORM IS NEVER MORE THAN AN EXTENSION OF CONTENT. (Or so it got phrased by one, R. Creeley, and it makes absolute sense to me, with this possible corollary, that right form, in any given poem, is the only and exclusively possible extension of content under hand.) There it is, brothers, sitting there, for USE.

Now (3) the process of the thing, how the principle can be made so to shape the energies that the form is accomplished. And I think it can be boiled down to one statement (first pounded into my head by Edward Dahlberg): ONE PERCEPTION MUST IMMEDIATELY AND DIRECTLY LEAD TO A FURTHER PERCEPTION. It means exactly what it says, is a matter of, at *all* points (even, I should say, of our management of daily reality as of the daily work) get on with it, keep moving, keep in, speed, the nerves, their speed, the perceptions, theirs, the acts, the split second acts, the whole business, keep it moving as fast as you can, citizen. And if you also set up as a poet, USE USE USE the process at all points, in any given poem always, always one perception must must must MOVE, INSTANTER, ON ANOTHER!

So there we are, fast, there's the dogma. And its excuse, its usableness, in practice. Which gets us, it ought to get us, inside the machinery, now, 1950, of how projective verse is made.

From *Modern Poets on Modern Poetry*, ed. James Scully (London: Collins, 1966), pp. 272–81.

If I hammer, if I recall in, and keep calling in, the breath, the breathing as distinguished from the hearing, it is for cause, it is to insist upon a part that breath plays in verse which has not (due, I think, to the smothering of the power of the line by too set a concept of foot) has not been sufficiently observed or practiced, but which has to be if verse is to advance to its proper force and place in the day, now, and ahead. I take it that PROJECTIVE VERSE teaches, is, this lesson, that that verse will only do in which a poet manages to register both the acquisitions of his ear *and* the pressures of his breath.

Let's start from the smallest particle of all, the syllable. It is the king and pin of versification, what rules and holds together the lines, the larger forms, of a poem. I would suggest that verse here and in England dropped this secret from the late Elizabethans to Ezra Pound, lost it, in the sweetness of meter and rime, in a honey-head. (The syllable is one way to distinguish the original success of blank verse, and its falling off, with Milton.)

It is by their syllables that words juxtapose in beauty, by these articles of sound as clearly as by the sense of the words which they compose. In any given instance, because there is a choice of words, the choice, if a man is in there, will be, sponaneously, the obedience of his ear to the syllables. The fineness, and the practice, lie here, at the minimum and source of speech.

> O western wynd, when wilt thou blow
> And the small rain down shall rain
> O Christ that my love were in my arms
> And I in my bed again

It would do no harm, as an act of correction to both prose and verse as now written, if both rime and meter, and, in the quantity words, both sense and sound, were less in the forefront of the mind than the syllable, if the syllable, that fine creature, were more allowed to lead the harmony on. With this warning, to those who would try: to step back here to this place of the elements and minims of language, is to engage speech where it is least careless – and least logical. Listening for the syllables must be so constant and so scrupulous, the exacting must be so complete, that the assurance of the ear is purchased at the highest – 40 hours a day – price. For from the root out, from all over the place, the syllable comes, the figures of, the dance:

> "Is" comes from the Aryan root, *as*, to breathe. The English "not" equals the Sanscrit *na*, which may come from the root *na*, to be lost, to perish. "Be" is from *bhu*, to grow.

I say the syllable, king, and that it is spontaneous, this way: the ear, the ear which has collected, which has listened, the ear, which is so close to the mind that it is the mind's, that it has the mind's speed...

it is close, another way: the mind is brother to this sister and is, because it is so close, is the drying force, the incest, the sharpener...

it is from the union of the mind and the ear that the syllable is born.

But the syllable is only the first child of the incest of verse (always, that Egyptian thing, it produces twins!). The other child is the LINE. And together, these two, the syllable *and* the line, they make a poem, they make that thing, the – what shall we call it, the Boss of all, the "Single Intelligence." And the line comes (I swear it) from the breath, from the breathing of the man who writes, at the moment that he writes, and thus is, it is here that, the daily work, the WORK, gets in, for only he, the man who writes, can declare, at every moment, the line its metric and its ending – where its breathing, shall come to, termination.

The trouble with most work, to my taking, since the breaking away from traditional lines and stanzas, and from such wholes as, say, Chaucer's *Troilus* or S's *Lear*, is: contemporary workers go lazy RIGHT HERE WHERE THE LINE IS BORN.

Let me put it baldly. The two halves are:

the HEAD, by way of the EAR, to the SYLLABLE
the HEART, by way of the BREATH, to the LINE

And the joker? that it is in the 1st half of the proposition that, in composing, one lets-it-rip; and that it is in the 2nd half, surprise, it is the LINE that's the baby that gets, as the poem is getting made, the attention, the control, that it is right here, in the line, that the shaping takes place, each moment of the going.

I am dogmatic, that the head shows in the syllable. The dance of the intellect is there, among them, prose or verse. Consider the best minds you know in this here business: where does the head show, is it not, precise, here, in the swift currents of the syllable? can't you tell a brain when you see what it does, just there? It is true, what the master says he picked up from Confusion: all the thots men are capable of can lie entered on the back of a postage stamp. So, is it not the PLAY of a mind we are after, is not that that shows whether a mind is there at all?

And the threshing floor for the dance? Is it anything but the LINE? And when the line has, is, a deadness, is it not a heart which has gone lazy, is it not, suddenly, slow things, similes, say, adjectives, or such, that we are bored by?

For there is a whole flock of rhetorical devices which have now to be brought under a new bead, now that we sight with the line. Simile is only one bird who comes down, too easily. The descriptive functions generally have to be watched, every second, in projective verse, because of their easiness, and thus their drain on the energy which composition by field allows into a poem. *Any* slackness takes off attention, that crucial thing, from the job in hand, from the *push* of the line under hand at the moment, under the reader's eye, in his moment. Observation of any kind is, like argument in prose, properly previous to the act of the poem, and, if allowed in, must be so juxtaposed, apposed, set in, that it does not, for an instant, sap the going energy of the content toward its form.

It comes to this, this whole aspect of the newer problems. (We now enter, actually, the large area of the whole poem, into the FIELD, if you like, where all the syllables and all the lines must be managed in their relations to each other.) It is a matter, finally, of OBJECTS, what they are, what they are inside a poem, how they got there, and, once there, how they are to be used. This is something I want to get to in another way in Part II, but, for the moment, let me indicate this, that every element in an open poem (the syllable, the line, as well as the image, the sound, the sense) must be taken up as participants in the kinetic of the poem just as solidly as we are accustomed to take what we call the objects of reality; and that these elements are to be seen as creating the tensions of a poem just as totally as do those other objects create what we know as the world.

The objects which occur at every given moment of composition (of recognition, we can call it) are, can be, must be treated exactly as they do occur therein and not by any ideas or preconceptions from outside the poem, must be handled as a series of objects in field in such a way that a series of tensions (which they also are) are made to *hold*, and to hold exactly inside the content and the context of the poem which has forced itself, through the poet and them, into being.

Because breath allows *all* the speech-force of language back in (speech is the "solid" of verse, is the secret of a poem's energy), because, now, a poem has, by speech, solidity, everything in it can now be treated as solids, objects, things; and, though insisting upon the absolute difference of the reality of verse from that other dispersed and distributed thing, yet each of these elements of a poem can be allowed to have the play of their separate energies and can be allowed, once the poem is well composed, to keep, as those other objects do, their proper confusions.

Which brings us up, immediately, bang, against tenses, in fact against syntax, in fact against grammar generally, that is, as we have inherited it. Do not tenses, must they not also be kicked around anew, in order that time, that other governing absolute, may be kept, as must the space-tensions of a poem, immediate, contemporary to the acting-on-you of the poem? I would argue that here, too, the LAW OF THE LINE, which projective verse creates, must be hewn to, obeyed, and that the conventions which logic has forced on syntax must be broken open as quietly as must the too set feet of the old line. But an analysis of how far a new poet can stretch the very conventions on which communication by language rests, is too big for these notes, which are meant, I hope it is obvious, merely to get things started.

Let me just throw in this. It is my impression that *all* parts of speech suddenly, in composition by field, are fresh for both sound and percussive use, spring up like unknown, unnamed vegetables in the patch, when you work it, come spring. Now take Halt Crane. What strikes me in him is the singleness of the push to the nominative, his push along that one arc of freshness, the attempt to get back to word as handle. (If logos is word as thought, what is word as noun, as, pass me that, as Newman Shea used to ask, at the galley table, put a jib on the blood, will ya.) But there is a loss in Crane of what Fenollosa is so right about, in syntax, the sentence as first act of nature, as lightning, as passage of force from subject to object, quick, in this case, from Hart to me, in every case, from me to you, the VERB, between two nouns. Does not Hart miss the advantages, by such an isolated push, miss the point of the whole front of syllable, line, field, and what happened to all language, and to the poem, as a result?

I return you now to London, to beginnings, to the syllable, for the pleasures of it, to intermit:

> If music be the food of love, play on,
> give me excess of it, that, surfeiting,

the appetite may sicken, and so die.
That strain again. It had a dying fall,
o, it came over my ear like the sweet sound
that breathes upon a bank of violets,
stealing and giving odour.

What we have suffered from, is manuscript, press, the removal of verse from its producer and its reproducer, the voice, a removal by one, by two removes from its place of origin *and* its destination. For the breath has a double meaning which Latin had not yet lost.

The irony is, from the machine has come one gain not yet sufficiently observed or used, but which leads directly on toward projective verse and its consequences. It is the advantage of the typewriter that, due to its rigidity and its space precisions, it can, for a poet, indicate exactly the breath, the pauses, the suspensions even of syllables, the juxtapositions even of parts of phrases, which he intends. For the first time the poet has the stave and the bar a musician has had. For the first time he can, without the convention of rime and meter, record the listening he has done to his own speech and by that one act indicate how he would want any reader, silently or otherwise, to voice his work.

It is time we picked the fruits of the experiments of Cummings, Pound, Williams, each of whom has, after his way, already used the machine as a scoring to his composing, as a script to its vocalization. It is now only a matter of the recognition of the conventions of composition by field for us to bring into being an open verse as formal as the closed, with all its traditional advantages.

If a contemporary poet leaves a space as long as the phrase before it, he means that space to be held, by the breath, an equal length of time. If he suspends a word or syllable at the end of a line (this was most Cummings' addition) he means that time to pass that it takes the eye – that hair of time suspended – to pick up the next line. If he wishes a pause so light it hardly separates the words, yet does not want a comma – which is an interruption of the meaning rather than the sounding of the line – follow him when he uses a symbol the typewriter has ready to hand:

"What does not change / is the will to change"

Observe him, when he takes advantage of the machine's multiple margins, to juxtapose:

"Sd he:
   to dream takes no effort
      to think is easy
         to act is more difficult
   but for a man to act after he has taken thought, this!
is the most difficult thing of all"

Each of these lines is a progressing of both the meaning and the breathing forward, and then a backing up, without a progress or any kind of movement outside the unit of time local to the idea.

There is more to be said in order that this convention be recognized, especially in order that the revolution out of which it came may be so forwarded that work will get published to offset the reaction now afoot to return verse to inherited forms of cadence and rime. But what I want to emphasize here, by this emphasis on the typewriter as the personal and instantaneous recorder of the poet's work, is the already projective nature of verse as the sons of Pound and Williams are practicing it. Already they are composing as though verse was to have the reading its writing involved, as though not the eye but the ear was to be its measurer, as though the intervals of its composition could be so carefully put down as to be precisely the intervals of its registration. For the ear, which once had the burden of memory to quicken it (rime & regular cadence were its aids and have merely lived on in print after the oral necessities were ended) can now again, that the poet has his means, be the threshold of projective verse.

2

Which gets us to what I promised, the degree to which the projective involves a stance toward reality outside a poem as well as a new stance towards the reality of a poem itself. It is a matter of content, the content of Homer or of Euripides or of Seami as distinct from that which I might call the more "literary" masters. From the moment the projective purpose of the act of verse is recognized, the content does – it will – change. If the beginning and the end is breath, voice in its largest sense, then the material of verse shifts. It has to. It starts with the composer. The dimension of his line itself changes, not to speak of the change in his conceiving, of the matter he will turn to, of the scale in which he imagines that matter's use. I myself would pose the difference by a physical image. It is no accident that Pound and Williams both were involved variously in a movement which got called "objectivism." But that word was then used in some sort of a necessary quarrel, I take it, with "subjectivism." It is now too late to be bothered with the latter. It has excellently done itself to death, even though we are all caught in its dying. What seems to me a more valid formulation for present use is "objectism," a word to be taken to stand for the kind of relation of man to experience which a poet might state as the necessity of a line or a work to be as wood is, to be as clean as wood is as it issues from the hand of nature, to be shaped as wood can be when a man has had his hand to it. Objectism is the getting rid of the lyrical interference of the individual as ego, of the "subject" and his soul, that peculiar presumption by which western man has interposed himself between what he is as a creature of nature (with certain instructions to carry out) and those other creations of nature which we may, with no derogation, call objects. For a man is himself an object, whatever he may take to be his advantages, the more likely to recognize himself as such the greater his advantages, particularly at that moment that he achieves an humilitas sufficient to make him of use.

It comes to this: the use of a man, by himself and thus by others, lies in how he conceives his relation to nature, that force to which he owes his somewhat small existence. If he sprawl, he shall find little to sing but himself, and shall sing, nature has such paradoxical ways, by way of artificial forms outside himself. But if he stays inside himself, if he is contained within his nature as he is participant in the larger force, he will be able to listen, and his hearing through himself will give him secrets objects share. And by an inverse law his shapes will make their own way. It is in this sense that the projective act, which is the artist's act in the larger field of objects, leads to dimensions larger than the man. For a man's problem, the moment he takes speech up in all its fullness, is to give his work his seriousness, a seriousness sufficient to cause the thing he makes to try to take its place alongside the things of nature. This is not easy. Nature works from reverence, even in her destruction (species go down with a crash). But breath is man's special qualification as animal. Sound is a dimension he has extended. Language is one of his proudest acts. And when a poet rests in these as they are in himself (in his physiology, if you like, but the life in him, for all that) then he, if he chooses to speak from these roots, works in that area where nature has given him size, projective size. . . .

Chapter 38
Louis Zukofsky

Louis Zukofsky (1904–78) was a precociously talented poet and critic whose early work was admired by the triumvirate of early modernist poetry: Eliot, Pound, and Williams. In February 1931, with Pound's support, Zukofsky edited the Objectivist issue of Poetry Chicago. *Objectivism was an early attempt to establish a canon of modernist poetry that included the work of Williams, Stevens, Eliot, Pound, and Moore. It also proposed a modern poetics that would succeed Imagism, although it shared some of Imagism's assumptions about the importance of precision of language and observation in poetry. What Objectivism emphasized was the importance of formal structure in poetry. In his* Autobiography, *first published in 1951, William Carlos Williams gave an account of Objectivism's aims: "The poem being an object (like a symphony or a cubist painting) it must be the purpose of the poet to make of his words a new form: to invent that is an object consonant with his day." Objectivism also supplied a rationale for Zukofsky's own verbally playful and intellectually demanding poetry. He is probably best known for "A," a long poetic sequence, that displays both the range of Zukofsky's learning and his microscopic attention to words and their multiple associations. For Zukofsky, all words, however grammatically humble, could take on a resonant life once they entered a poem.*

Zukofsky wrote "A Statement for Poetry" in 1950. It was first published in mimeograph form in 1958 at San Francisco State College and in 1967 it was published in book form in his collection of essays, Prepositions. *Like other modernist statements and manifestos, its aim is to set out as concisely as possible the basic building blocks of poetry and by doing so reveal its stature as a fundamental human tradition. Zukofsky revisits the concerns of Objectivism with his affirmation of the poem as a "design or construction," and provides his own more technical version of the French symbolists' belief that poetry should aspire to the condition of music. But Zukofsky seeks to balance the claims of poetry as a technical art with its origins in "everyday existence."*

A Statement for Poetry

Any definition of poetry is difficult because the implications of poetry are complex – and that despite the natural, physical simplicity of its best examples. Thus poetry may be defined as an order of words that as movement and tone (rhythm and pitch) approaches in varying degrees the wordless art of music as a kind of mathematical limit. Poetry is derived obviously from everyday existence (real, or ideal).

Whoever makes it may very well consider a poem as a design or construction. A contemporary American poet says: "A poem is a small (or large) machine made of words." The British mathematician George Hardy has envied poetry its fineness of immediate logic. A scientist may envy its bottomless perception of relations which, for all its intricacies, keeps a world of things tangible and whole. Perhaps poetry is what Hideki Yukawa is looking for when, with reference to his latest theory of particles that possess not only charge and mass but also dimensions in space, he says: "This problem of infinity is a disease that must be cured. I am very eager to be healthy."

"Poetry is something more philosophic and of graver import than history" (Aristotle, *Poetics* 9.) True or not this statement recalls that poetry has contributed intense records to history. The rhythmic or intoned utterance that punctuates the movement of a body in a dance or ritual, aware of dead things as alive, as it fights animals and earth; Homer's heavenly singer who gave pleasure at a feast in a society accomplished in husbandry and craft, whose group beliefs *saw* the Muses presiding over the harmony that moved the words; the dry passages of Lucretius forced by his measures to sing despite their regard for abstract patterns of thought, beginnings of atomic speculation: the stages of culture are concretely delineated in these three examples.

Poetry has always been considered more literary than music, though so-called pure music may be literary in a communicative sense. The parts of a fugue, Bach said, should behave like reasonable men in an orderly discussion. But music does not depend mainly on the human voice, as poetry does, for rendition. And it is possible in imagination to divorce speech of all graphic elements, to let it become a movement of sounds. It is this musical horizon of poetry (which incidentally poems perhaps never reach) that permits anybody who does not know Greek to listen and get something out of the poetry of Homer: to "tune in" to the human tradition, to its voice which has developed among the sounds of natural things, and thus escape the confines of a time and place, as one hardly ever escapes them in studying Homer's grammar. In this sense poetry is international.

The foregoing definition of poetry has been, for the most part, cultural in its bearings. But what specifically is good poetry? It is precise information on existence out of which it grows, and information of its own existence, that is, the movement (and tone) of words. Rhythm, pulse, keeping time with existence, is the distinction of its technique. This integrates any human emotion, any discourse, into an order of words that exists as another created thing in the world, to affect it and be judged by it. Condensed speech is most of the method of poetry (as distinguished from the

From *Prepositions: The Collected Critical Essays of Louis Zukofsky* (Berkeley, Calif.: University of California Press, 1981), pp. 19–23.

essentially discursive art of prose). The rest is ease, pause, grace. If read properly, good poetry does not argue its attitudes or beliefs; it exists independently of the reader's preferences for one kind of "subject" or another. Its conviction is in its mastery or technique. The length of a poem has nothing to do with its merits as composition in which each sound of a word is weighed, though obviously it is possible to have more of a good thing – a wider range of things felt, known, and conveyed.

The oldest recorded poems go back to the Egyptian *Chapters of Coming Forth by Day*, some of whose hieroglyphs were old by 3000 B.C. The human tradition that survives the esoteric significance of these poems remains, as in these lines praising the sun:

> Millions of years have passed, we cannot count their number,
> Millions of years shall come. You are above the years.

It is quite safe to say that the *means* and *objects* of poetry (cf. Aristotle's *Poetics*) have been constant, that is, recognizably human, since ca. 3000 B.C.

I. The Means of Poetry: *Words* – consisting of *syllables*, in turn made up of *phones* that are denoted by *letters* that were once graphic symbols or pictures. Words grow out of affects of

A. Sight, touch, taste, smell
B. Hearing
G. Thought with respect to other words, the interplay of concepts.

II. The Objects of Poetry: *Poems* – rhythmic compositions of words whose components are

A. Image
B. Sound
C. Interplay of Concepts (judgments of other words either abstract or sensible, or both at once).

Some poems make use of – i.e. resolve – all three components. Most poems use only A and B. Poems that use B and C are less frequent, though C is a poetic device (invention) at least as old as Homer's puns on the name of Odysseus: "the man of all odds," "how odd I see you Od-ysseus." (cf. also the earlier, homophonic devices of syllabaries.)

A. *Image*. Composed groups of words used as symbols for things and states of sight, touch, taste and smell present an image. For example: Homer's "a dark purple wave made an arch over them like a mountain cave"; the image of Hades evoked by the eleventh book of *The Odyssey*; or the landscape and journey which is all of *The Odyssey* – the home-coming of Odysseus.

> cf. Weight, grandeur, and energy in writing are very largely produced, dear pupil, by the use of "images." (That at least is what some people call the actual mental pictures.) For the term Imagination is applied in general to an idea which enters the mind from any source and engenders speech, but the word has now come to be used of passages where,

> inspired by strong emotion, you seem to see what you describe and bring it vividly before the eyes of your audience. That imagination means one thing in oratory and another in poetry you will yourself detect, and also that the object of poetry is to enthral, of prose writing to present ideas clearly, though both indeed aim at this latter and at excited feeling. (Longinus (213–273), *On the Sublime* XV, 2)

B. *Sound.* Besides the imitation in words of natural sound (the sound of the sea in Homer, the sound of birds in "Bare ruined choirs where late the sweet birds sang"), the component of sound in poetry, as conveyed by rendition, comprises sound that is

1. Spoken (e.g.

   "and we'll talk with them too,
   Who loses and who wins, who's in,
   who's out," – *King Lear*)
2. Declaimed (e.g. Milton's *Paradise Lost*)
3. Intoned or Chanted (e.g. words used in a liturgical monotone)
4. Sung (to a melody, i.e. a musical phrase or idea. Some of the best examples in English are Campion's poems, Shakespeare's songs – which have been set to music by Purcell, Johnson, Arne – and Burns' songs written to folk tunes.)

C. *Interplay of Concepts.* This component effects compositions in which words involve other words in common or contrasting logical implications, and to this end it employs sound, and sometimes image, as an accessory. The elements of grammar and rhetorical balance (v.s., Shakespeare's "who's *in*, who's *out*") contribute to this type of poetry. (Examples: most of Donne's poems, Andrew Marvell's *The Definition of Love*, George Herbert's *Heaven*, Lord Rochester's *Ode to Nothing*, Fitzgerald's translation of *Rubaiyat*, Eliot's *The Hollow Men.*)

From the preceding analysis of the components of poems it is clear that their forms are achieved as a dynamics of speech and sound, that is, as a resolution of their interacting rhythms – with no loss of value to any word at the expense of the movement. In actual practice, this dynamics works out standards of measure – or metres. The good poems of the past have developed the "science" of prosody in the same way that the effective use of words has developed the logic of grammar. But poetry, though it has its constants, is made in every age.

Prosody analyses poems according to line lengths and groups of lines or verses as vehicles of rhythm, varieties of poetic feet or units of rhythm (analogous to a measure in music) *and* their variants (e.g. unexpected inversions of accent, unexpected "extra" syllables), rhymes *and* their variants (e.g. consonance, assonance, perfect rhyme – i.e. the same sound rhymes with itself, etc.), rhyming patterns, stanzas or strophes, fixed forms and free verse. No verse is "free," however, if its rhythms inevitably carry the words in contexts that do not falsify the function of words as speech probing the possibilities and attractions of existence. This being the practice of poetry, prosody as such is of secondary interest to the poet. He looks, so to speak, into his ear as he does at the same time into his heart and intellect. His ear is sincere, if his words convey his awareness of the range of differences and subtleties of duration. He does not measure with handbook, and is not a pendulum. He may find it right to count syllables, or their relative lengths and stresses, or to be sensitive to all these metrical factors. As a matter of fact, the good poets do all these things. But they do not impose their count on what is said or made – as may be judged from the impact of their poems.

Symmetry occurs in all the arts as they develop. It is usually present in some form in most good poetry. The stanza was perhaps invented in an attempt to fit a tune to more words than it had notes: the words were grouped into stanzas permitting the tune to be repeated. But existence does not foster this technique in all times indiscriminately. The least unit of a poem must support the stanza; it should never be inflicted on the least unit. As Sidney wrote in his *Apology* (1595): "One may be a poet without versing, and a versifier without poetry."

The best way to find out about poetry is to read the poems. That way the reader becomes something of a poet himself: not because he "contributes" to the poetry, but because he finds himself subject of its energy.

Chapter 39
Roland Barthes

Roland Barthes (1915–1980) developed an intellectual idiom that enabled him to write about cars, film stars' faces, and wrestling, as well as works of literature. What connected these and his many other subjects was a passion for signs and their different cultural manifestations. Barthes inherited the research project proposed by the Swiss linguist, Ferdinand de Saussure, a general semiology that would study not just verbal language but the whole life of signs in society. But Barthes was not simply Saussure's disciple. He drew on other intellectual traditions: Sartre's existentialism and its preoccupation with the nature of freedom; the Marxist critique of ideology; and Lacan's psychoanalytic approach to the workings of the unconscious in language. Two of Barthes's earliest publications, Writing Degree Zero *and* Elements of Semiology, *indicate the direction of his subsequent thought. On the one hand was a recurrent concern with the identity of literature as a semiotic system, one that would take Barthes from a structural analysis of the different levels of narrative and their integration to a post-structuralist understanding of the text as a mobile and boundless weave of codes or "voices"; on the other was an expansive project that took different forms of sign and discourse as its subject: advertisements, film, photography, music, fashion, and love. In all these intellectual adventures Barthes combined academic rigor with a personal investment in his subjects.*

"Is There Any Poetic Writing?" was published in 1953 as part of Writing Degree Zero. *Its starting point is a long-standing question in criticism: what is the difference between poetry and prose? Barthes argues that our understanding of this question has to change because the nature of the poetic text changed as a result of the work of Rimbaud and others. The old distinction was quantitative: poetry was prose with additional ornamentation. The new distinction must be qualitative. Modern poetry is a poetry of the Word that destroys customary relations of grammar, syntax, and ideology. It is, in effect, the invention of a new language within a language, an alien, radical, and disturbing force.*

Is There Any Poetic Writing?

In the classical period, prose and poetry are quantities, their difference can be measured; they are neither more nor less separated than two different numbers, contiguous like them, but dissimilar because of the very difference in their magnitudes. If I use the word prose for a minimal form of speech, the most economical vehicle for thought, and if I use the letters a, b, c for certain attributes of language, which are useless but decorative, such as metre, rhyme or the ritual of images, all the linguistic surface will be accounted for in M. Jourdain's[1] double equation:

Poetry = Prose + a + b + c
Prose = Poetry − a − b − c

whence it clearly follows that Poetry is always different from Prose. But this difference is not one of essence, it is one of quantity. It does not, therefore, jeopardize the unity of language, which is an article of classical dogma. One may effect a different dosage in manner of speech, according to the social occasion: here, prose or rhetoric, there, poetry or precocity, in accordance with a whole ritual of expression laid down by good society, but there remains everywhere a single language, which reflects the eternal categories of the mind. Classical poetry is felt to be merely an ornamental variation of prose, the fruit of an *art* (that is, a technique), never a different language, or the product of a particular sensibility. Any poetry is then only the decorative equation, whether allusive or forced, of a possible prose which is latent, virtually and potentially, in any conceivable manner of expression. 'Poetic', in the days of classicism, never evokes any particular domain, any particular depth of feeling, any special coherence, or separate universe, but only an individual handling of a verbal technique, that of 'expressing oneself' according to rules more artistic, therefore more sociable, than those of conversation, in other terms, the technique of projecting out an inner thought, springing fully armed from the Mind, a speech which is made more socially acceptable by virtue of the very conspicuousness of its conventions.

We know that nothing of this structure remains in modern poetry, which springs not from Baudelaire but from Rimbaud, unless it is in cases where one takes up again, in a revised traditional mode, the formal imperatives of classical poetry: henceforth, poets give to their speech the status of a closed Nature, which covers both the function and the structure of language. Poetry is then no longer a Prose either ornamental or shorn of liberties. It is a quality *sui generis* and without antecedents. It is no longer an attribute but a substance, and therefore it can very well renounce signs, since it carries its own nature within itself, and does not need to signal its identity outwardly: poetic language and prosaic language are sufficiently separate to be able to dispense with the very signs of their difference.

Furthermore, the alleged relations between thought and language are reversed; in classical art, a ready-made thought generates an utterance which 'expresses' or 'translates' it. Classical thought is devoid of duration, classical poetry has it only in

From *Writing Degree Zero*, trans. Annette Lavers and Colin Smith (London: Jonathan Cape, 1984), pp. 35–43.

such degree as is necessary to its technical arrangement. In modern poetics, on the contrary, words produce a kind of formal continuum from which there gradually emanates an intellectual or emotional density which would have been impossible without them; speech is then the solidified time of a more spiritual gestation, during which the 'thought' is prepared, installed little by little by the contingency of words. This verbal luck, which will bring down the ripe fruit of a meaning, presupposes therefore a poetic time which is no longer that of a 'fabrication', but that of a possible adventure, the meeting-point of a sign and an intention. Modern poetry is opposed to classical art by a difference which involves the whole structure of language, without leaving between those two types of poetry anything in common except the same sociological intention.

The economy of classical language (Prose and Poetry) is relational, which means that in it words are abstracted as much as possible in the interest of relationships. In it, no word has a density by itself, it is hardly the sign of a thing, but rather the means of conveying a connection. Far from plunging into an inner reality consubstantial to its outer configuration, it extends, as soon as it is uttered, towards other words, so as to form a superficial chain of intentions. A glance at the language of mathematics will perhaps enable us to grasp the relational nature of classical prose and poetry: we know that in mathematical language, not only is each quantity provided with a sign, but also that the relations between these quantities are themselves transcribed, by means of a sign expressing operative equality or difference. It may be said that the whole movement of mathematical flow derives from an explicit reading of its relations. The language of classicism is animated by an analogous, although of course less rigid, movement: its 'words', neutralized, made absent by rigorous recourse to a tradition which dessicates their freshness, avoid the phonetic or semantic accident which would concentrate the flavour of language at one point and halt its intellectual momentum in the interest of an unequally distributed enjoyment. The classical flow is a succession of elements whose density is even, it is exposed to the same emotional pressure, and relieves those elements of any tendency towards an individual meaning appearing at all invented. The poetic vocabulary itself is one of usage, not of invention: images in it are recognizable in a body; they do not exist in isolation; they are due to long custom, not to individual creation. The function of the classical poet is not therefore to find new words, with more body or more brilliance, but to follow the order of an ancient ritual, to perfect the symmetry or the conciseness of a relation, to bring a thought exactly within the compass of a metre. Classical conceits involve relations, not words: they belong to an art of expression, not of invention. The words, here, do not, as they later do, thanks to a kind of violent and unexpected abruptness, reproduce the depth and singularity of an individual experience; they are spread out to form a surface, according to the exigencies of an elegant or decorative purpose. They delight us because of the formulation which brings them together, not because of their own power or beauty.

True, classical language does not reach the functional perfection of the relational network of mathematics: relations are not signified, in it, by any special signs, but only by accidents of form and disposition. It is the restraint of the words in itself, their alignment, which achieves the relational nature of classical discourse. Overworked in a restricted number of ever-similar relations, classical words are on the way to becoming an algebra where rhetorical figures of speech, clichés, function as virtual linking devices; they have lost their density and gained a more interrelated state of speech; they operate in the manner of chemical valences, outlining a verbal area full of symmetrical connections, junctions and networks from which arise, without the respite afforded by wonder, fresh intentions towards signification. Hardly have the fragments of classical discourse yielded their meaning than they become messengers or harbingers, carrying ever further a meaning which refuses to settle within the depths of a word, but tries instead to spread widely enough to become a total gesture of intellection, that is, of communication.

Now the distortion to which Hugo tried to subject the alexandrine, which is of all meters the most interrelational, already contains the whole future of modern poetry, since what is attempted is to eliminate the intention to establish relationships and to produce instead an explosion of words. For modern poetry, since it must be distinguished from classical poetry and from any type of prose, destroys the spontaneously functional nature of language, and leaves standing only its lexical basis. It retains only the outward shape of relationships, their music, but not their reality. The Word shines forth above a line of relationships emptied of their content, grammar is bereft of its purpose, it becomes prosody and is no longer anything but an inflexion which lasts only to present the Word. Connections are not properly speaking abolished, they are merely reserved areas, a parody of themselves, and this void is necessary for the density of the Word to rise out of a magic vacuum, like a sound and a sign devoid of background, like 'fury and mystery'.

In classical speech, connections lead the word on, and at once carry it towards a meaning which is an ever-deferred project; in modern poetry, connections are only an extension of the word, it is the Word which is "the dwelling place", it is rooted like a *fons et origo* in the prosody of functions, which are perceived but unreal. Here, connections only fascinate, and it is the Word which gratifies and fulfils the sudden revelation of a truth. To say that this truth is of a poetic order is merely to say that the Word in poetry can never be untrue, because it is a whole; it shines with an infinite freedom and prepares to radiate towards innumerable uncertain and possible connections. Fixed connections being abolished, the word is left only with a vertical project, it is like a monolith, or a pillar which plunges into a totality of meanings, reflexes and recollections: it is a sign which stands. The poetic word is here an act without immediate past, without environment, and which holds forth only the dense shadow of reflexes from all sources which are associated with it. Thus under each Word in modern poetry there lies a sort of existential geology, in which is gathered the total content of the Name, instead of a chosen content as in classical prose and poetry. The Word is no longer guided *in advance* by the general intention of a socialized discourse; the consumer of poetry, deprived of the guide of selective connections, encounters the Word frontally, and receives it as an absolute quantity, accompanied by all its possible associations. The Word, here, is encyclopaedic, it contains simultaneously all the acceptations from which a relational discourse might have required it to choose. It therefore achieves a state which is possible only in the dictionary or in poetry – places where the noun can live without its article – and is reduced to a sort of zero degree, pregnant with all past and future specifications. The word here has a generic form; it is a category. Each poetic word is thus an unexpected object, a Pandora's box from which fly out all the potentialities of language; it is therefore produced and consumed with a peculiar curiosity, a kind of sacred relish. This Hunger of the Word, common to the whole of modern poetry, makes poetic speech terrible and inhuman. It initiates a discourse full of gaps and full of lights, filled with absences and overnourishing signs, without foresight or stability of intention, and thereby so opposed to the social function of language that merely to have recourse to a discontinuous speech is to open the door to all that stands above Nature.

For what does the rational economy of classical language mean, if not that Nature is a plenum, that it can be possessed, that it does not shy away or cover itself in shadows, but is in its entirety subjected to the toils of language? Classical language is always reducible to a persuasive continuum, it postulates the possibility of dialogue, it establishes a universe in which men are not alone, where words never have the terrible weight of things, where speech is always a meeting with the others. Classical language is a bringer of euphoria because it is immediately social. There is no genre, no written work of classicism which does not suppose a collective consumption, akin to speech; classical literary art is an object which circulates among several persons brought together on a class basis; it is a product conceived for oral transmission, for a consumption regulated by the contingencies of society: it is essentially a spoken language, in spite of its strict codification.

We have seen that on the contrary modern poetry destroyed relationships in language and reduced discourse to words as static things. This implies a reversal in our knowledge of Nature. The interrupted flow of the new poetic language initiates a discontinuous Nature, which is revealed only piecemeal. At the very moment when the withdrawal of functions obscures the relations existing in the world, the object in discourse assumes an exalted place: modern poetry is a poetry of the object. In it Nature becomes a fragmented space, made of objects solitary and terrible, because the links between them are only potential. Nobody chooses for them a privileged meaning, or a particular use, or some service; nobody imposes a hierarchy on them, nobody reduces them to the manifestation of a mental behaviour, or of an intention, of some evidence of tenderness, in short. The bursting upon us of the poetic word then institutes an absolute object; Nature becomes a succession of verticalities, of objects, suddenly standing erect, and filled with all their possibilities: one of these can be only a landmark in an unfulfilled, and thereby terrible, world. These unrelated objects – words adorned with all the violence of their irruption, the vibration of which, though wholly mechanical, strangely affects the next word, only to die out immediately – these poetic words exclude men: there is no humanism of modern poetry. This erect discourse is full of terror, that is to say, it relates man not to other men, but to the most inhuman images in Nature: heaven, hell, holiness, childhood, madness, pure matter, etc.

At such a point, it is hardly possible to speak of a poetic mode of writing, for this is a language in which a violent drive towards autonomy destroys any ethical scope. The verbal gesture here aims at modifying Nature, it is the approach of a demiurge; it is not an attitude of the conscience but an act of coercion. Such, at least, is the language of those modern poets who carry their intention to the limit, and assume Poetry not as a spiritual exercise, a state of the soul or a placing of oneself in a situation, but as the splendour and freshness of a dream language. For such poets, it is as vain to speak about a mode of writing as of poetic feeling. Modern Poetry, in Char, for instance, is beyond this diffuse tone, this precious *aura*, which *are*, indeed, a mode of writing, usually termed poetic feeling. There is no objection to speaking of a poetic mode of writing concerning the classical writers and their epigones, or even concerning poetic prose in the manner of Gide's *Fruits of the Earth*, in which Poetry is in fact a certain linguistic ethos. In both cases, the mode of writing soaks up the style, and we can imagine that for people living in the seventeenth century, it was not easy to perceive an *immediate* difference between Racine and Pradon (and even less a difference of a poetic kind), just as it is not easy for a modern reader to pass judgment on those contemporary poets who use the same uniform and indecisive poetic mode of writing, because for them Poetry is a *climate* which means, essentially, a linguistic convention. But when the poetic language radically questions Nature by virtue of its very structure, without any resort to the content of the discourse and without falling back on some ideology, there is no mode of writing left, there are only styles, thanks to which man turns his back on society and confronts the world of objects without going through any of the forms of History or of social life.

Note

1 Molière's *Bourgeois Gentilhomme.*

Chapter 40
W. K. Wimsatt

W. K. Wimsatt (1907–75) was a leading figure in a group of writers and teachers known as the "New Critics." Wimsatt wanted to rid criticism of what he regarded as a number of fallacies, including the intentional fallacy (understanding a work in terms of the intentions of its author) and the affective fallacy (understanding a work in terms of reader response). Both in Wimsatt's view diverted attention from the work itself, its distinctive structure and its agency. These were best approached by regarding the work as "tensional." Literature held together, but did not necessarily reconcile, divisions in human thought and experience between good and evil, thought and feeling, the general and the particular, and so on. Its success or failure in achieving this difficult balancing act was a primary criterion of its value.

The following extracts from "The Concrete Universal" come from Wimsatt's best-known book, The Verbal Icon, *first published in 1954. In it Wimsatt explores a long-standing claim in poetics: that it is a feature of literature that it can be both particular and universal at the same time. Metaphor is the central example of how literature, and poetry in particular, achieves this effect. Creating a resemblance between two classes of poetic metaphor implies the existence of a third, more abstract, category. The process of moving from particular to universal is produced rhetorically. Wimsatt goes on to argue that the idea of the concrete universal can combine the descriptive analysis of poetry with its evaluation.*

The Concrete Universal

I

The central argument of this essay, concerning what I shall call the "concrete universal," proceeds from the observation that literary theorists have from early times to the

From *The Verbal Icon: Studies in the Meaning of Poetry* (Lexington, Ky.: University of Kentucky Press, 1954), pp. 69–72, 75–7, 79–83.

present persisted in making statements which in their contexts seem to mean that a work of literary art is in some peculiar sense a very individual thing or a very universal thing or both. What that paradox can mean, or what important fact behind the paradox has been discerned by such various critics as Aristotle, Plotinus, Hegel, and Ransom, it will be the purpose of the essay to inquire, and by the inquiry to discuss not only a significant feature of metaphysical poetics from Aristotle to the present day but the relation between metaphysical poetics and more practical and specific rhetorical analysis. In the brief historical survey which forms one part of this essay it will not be my purpose to suggest that any of these writers meant exactly what I shall mean in later parts where I describe the structure of poetry. Yet throughout the essay I shall proceed on the theory not only that men have at different times used the same terms and have meant differently, but that they have sometimes used different terms and have meant the same or somewhat the same. In other words, I assume that there is continuity in the problems of criticism, and that a person who studies poetry today has a legitimate interest in what Plato said about poetry.

The view of common terms and their relations to classes of things from which I shall start is roughly that which one may read in the logic of J. S. Mill, a view which is not much different from the semantic view of today and for most purposes not much different from the Aristotelian and scholastic view. Mill speaks of the word and its denotation and connotation (the term, referent and reference, the sign, denotatum and designatum of more recent terminologies). The denotation is the *it*, the individual thing or the aggregate of things to which the term may refer; the connotation is the *what*, the quality or classification inferred for the it, or implicitly predicated by the application of the term or the giving of the name.[1] One main difference between all modern positivistic, nominalistic, and semantic systems and the scholastic and classical systems is that the older ones stress the similarity of the individuals denoted by the common term and hence the real universality of meaning, while the modern systems stress the differences in the individuals, the constant flux even of each individual in time and space and its kinetic structure, and hence infer only an approximate or nominal universality of meaning and a convenience rather than a truth in the use of general terms. A further difference lies in the view of how the individual is related to the various connotations of terms which may be applied to it. That is, to the question: What is it? the older writers seem to hold there is but one (essentially right) answer, while the moderns accept as many answers as there are classes to which the individual may be assigned (an indefinite number). The older writers speak of a proper essence or whatness of the individual, a quality which in some cases at least is that designated by the class name most commonly applied to the individual: a bench is a bench, essentially a bench, accidentally a heavy wooden object or something covered with green paint. "When we say *what* it is," observes Aristotle, "we do not say 'white,' or 'hot,' or 'three cubits long,' but 'a man' or 'a god.'" And this view is also a habit scarcely avoidable in our own daily thinking, especially when we think of living things or of artifacts, things made by us or our fellows for a purpose. What is it? Bench, we think, is an adequate answer. An assemblage of sticks painted green, we consider freakish.

II

Whether or not one believes in universals, one may see the persistence in literary criticism of a theory that poetry presents the concrete and the universal, or the individual and the universal, or an object which in a mysterious and special way is both highly general and highly particular. The doctrine is implicit in Aristotle's two statements that poetry imitates action and that poetry tends to express the universal. It is implicit again at the end of the classic period in the mystic doctrine of Plotinus, who in his later writing on beauty reverses the Platonic objection that art does not know the ultimate reality of the forms. Plotinus arrives at the view that the artist by a kind of bypass of the inferior natural productions of the world soul reaches straight to the forms that lie behind in the divine intelligence. Another version of the classic theory, with affinities for Plotinus, lies in the scholastic phrase *resplendentia formae.*

Cicero's account of how Zeuxis painted an ideal Helen from the five most beautiful virgins of Crotona is a typical development of Aristotelian theory, in effect the familiar neoclassic theory found in Du Fresnoy's *Art of Painting*, in the writings of Johnson, especially in the tulip passage in *Rasselas*, and in the *Discourses* and *Idlers* of Reynolds. The business of the poet is not to number the streaks of the tulip; it is to give us not the individual, but the species. The same thing is stated in a more complicated way by Kant in telling how the imagination constructs the "aesthetical normal Idea":

> It is the image for the whole race, which floats among all the variously different intuitions of individuals, which nature takes as archetype in her productions of the same species, but which seems not to be fully reached in any individual case.

And Hegel's account is as follows:

> The work of art is not only for the sensuous apprehension as sensuous object, but its position is of such a kind that as sensuous it is at the same time essentially addressed to the mind.
>
> In comparison with the show or semblance of immediate sensuous existence or of historical narrative, the artistic semblance has the advantage that in itself it points beyond self, and refers us away from itself to something spiritual which it is meant to bring before the mind's eye.... The hard rind of nature and the common world give the mind more trouble in breaking through to the idea than do the products of art.

The excellence of Shakespeare, says Coleridge, consists in a "union and interpenetration of the universal and particular." In one terminology or another this idea of a concrete universal is found in most metaphysical aesthetics of the eighteenth and nineteenth centuries....

III

. . . The question is how a work of literature can be either more individual (unique) or more universal than other kinds of writing, or how it can combine the individual and the universal more than other kinds. Every description in words, so far as it is a direct description (The barn is red and square) is a generalization. That is the nature of words. There are no individuals conveyed in words but only more or less specific generalizations, so that Johnson is right, though we have to ask him what degree of verbal generality makes art, and whether "tulip" is a better or more important generality than "tulip with ten streaks," or whether "beauty" is not in fact a much more impressive generality than "tulip." On the other hand, one cannot deny that in some sense there are more tulips in poetry than pure abstracted beauty. So that Bergson is right too; only we shall have to ask him what degree of specificity in verbal description makes art. And he can never claim complete verbal specificity or individuality, even for Hamlet.

If he could, if a work of literary art could be looked on as an artifact or concrete physical work, the paradox for the student of universals would return from the opposite direction even more forcibly – as it does in fact for theorists of graphic art. If Reynolds' picture "The Age of Innocence" presents a species or universal, what species does it present? Not an Aristotelian essence – "man," or "humanity," nor even a more specific kind of being such as "womanhood." For then the picture would present the same universal as Reynolds' portrait of Mrs. Siddons as "The Tragic Muse," and all differences between "The Age of Innocence" and "The Tragic Muse" would be aesthetically irrelevant. Does the picture then present girlhood, or barefoot girlhood, or barefoot girlhood in a white dress against a gloomy background? All three are equally valid universals (despite the fact that makeshift phrases are required to express two of them), and all three are presented by the picture. Or is it the title which tells us what universal is presented, "The Age of Innocence," and without the title should we not know the universal? The question will be: What in the individual work of art demands that we attribute to it one universal rather than another?

We may answer that for poetry it is the generalizing power of words already mentioned, and go on to decide that what distinguishes poetry from scientific or logical discourse is a degree of irrelevant concreteness in descriptive details. This is in effect what Ransom says in his doctrine of argument and local irrelevance, but it seems doubtful if the doctrine is not a version of the theory of ornamental metaphor. The argument, says Ransom, is the prose or scientific meaning, what the poem has in common with other kinds of writing. The irrelevance is a texture of concreteness which does not contribute anything to the argument but is somehow enjoyable or valuable for its own sake, the vehicle of a metaphor which one boards heedless of where it runs, whether crosstown or downtown – just for the ride. So Ransom nurses and refines the argument, and on one page he makes the remark that the poet searches for "suitability" in his particular phrases, and by suitability Ransom means "the propriety which consists in their denoting the particularity which really belongs to the logical object." But the difference between "propriety" and relevance in such a context is not easy to see. And relevance is logic. The fact is that all concrete illustration has about it something of the irrelevant. An apple falling from a tree illustrates gravity, but apple and tree are irrelevant to the pure theory of gravity. It may be that what happens in a poem is that the apple and the tree are somehow made more than usually relevant.

Such a theory, not that of Johnson and Reynolds, not that of Warton and Bergson, not quite that of Ransom, is what I would suggest – yet less as a novelty than as something already widely implicit in recent poetical analyses and exegeses, in those of Empson, for instance, Tate, Blackmur, or Brooks. If a work of literature is not in a simple sense either more individual or more universal than other kinds of writing, it may yet be such an individual or such a complex of meaning that it has a special relation to the world of universals. Some acute remarks on this subject were made by Ruskin in a chapter of *Modern Painters* neglected today perhaps because of its distasteful ingredient of "noble emotion." Poetry, says Ruskin in criticizing Reynolds' *Idlers*, is not distinguished from history by the omission of details, nor for that matter by the mere addition of details. "There must be something either in the nature of the details themselves, or the method of using them, which invests them with poetical power." Their nature, one may add, as assumed through their relation to one another, a relation which may also be called the method of using them. The poetic character of details consists not in what they say directly and explicitly (as if roses and moonlight were poetic) but in what by their arrangement they *show* implicitly.

IV

"One," observes Ben Jonson, thinking of literature, "is considerable two waies: either, as it is only separate, and by it self: or as being compos'd of many parts it beginnes to be one as those parts grow or are wrought together." A literary work of art is a complex of detail (an artifact, if we may be allowed that metaphor for what is only a verbal object), a composition so complicated of human values that its interpretation is dictated by the understanding of it, and so complicated as to seem in the highest degree individual – a concrete universal....

...[M]ost can be learned [about the concrete universal] by examination of metaphor – the structure most characteristic of concentrated poetry. The language of poets, said Shelley, "is vitally metaphorical: that is, it marks the before unapprehended relations of things and perpetuates their apprehension." Wordsworth spoke of the abstracting and modifying powers of the imagination. Aristotle said that the greatest thing was the use of metaphor, because it meant an eye for resemblances. Even the simplest form of metaphor or simile ("My love is like a red, red rose") presents us with a special and creative, in fact a concrete, kind of abstraction different from that of science. For behind a metaphor lies a resemblance between two classes, and hence a more general third class. This class is unnamed and most likely remains unnamed and is apprehended only through the metaphor. It is a new conception for which there is no other expression. Keats discovering Homer is like a traveler in the realms of gold, like an astronomer who discovers a planet, like Cortez gazing at the Pacific. The title of the sonnet, "On First Looking into Chapman's Homer," seems to furnish not so much the subject of the poem as a fourth member of a central metaphor, the real subject of the poem being an abstraction, a certain kind of thrill in discovering, for which there is no name and no other description, only the four members of the metaphor pointing, as to the center of their pattern. The point of the poem seems to lie outside both vehicle and tenor.

To take a more complicated instance, Wordsworth's "Solitary Reaper" has the same basic metaphorical structure, the girl alone reaping and singing, and the two bird images, the nightingale in Arabian sands and the cuckoo among the Hebrides, the three figures serving the parallel or metaphorical function of bringing out the abstraction of loneliness, remoteness, mysterious charm in the singing. But there is also a kind of third-dimensional significance, in the fact that one bird is far out in the northern sea, the other far off in southern sands, a fact which is not part of the comparison between the birds and the girl. By an implication cutting across the plane of logic of the metaphor, the girl and the two birds suggest extension in space, universality, and world communion – an effect supported by other details of the poem such as the overflowing of the vale profound, the mystery of the Erse song, the bearing of the song away in the witness' heart, the past and future themes which the girl may be singing. Thus a central abstraction is created, of communion, telepathy in solitude, the prophetic soul of the wide world dreaming on things to come – an abstraction which is the effect not wholly of the metaphor elaborated logically (in a metaphysical way) but of a working on two axes, by association rather than by logic, by a three-dimensional complexity of structure.

To take yet a third instance, metaphoric structure may appear where we are less likely to realize it explicitly – in poetic narratives, for example, elliptically concealed in the more obvious narrative outlines. "I can bring you," writes Max Eastman, "examples of diction that is metrical but not metaphoric – a great part of the popular ballads, for example – and you can hardly deny that they too are poetic." But the best story poems may be analyzed, I believe, as metaphors without expressed tenors, as symbols which speak for themselves. "La Belle Dame Sans Merci," for example (if a literary ballad may be taken), is about a knight, by profession a man of action, but sensitive, like the lily and the rose, and about a faery lady with wild, wild eyes. At a more abstract level, it is about the loss of self in the mysterious lure of beauty – whether woman, poetry, or poppy. It sings the irretrievable departure from practical normality (the squirrel's granary is full), the wan isolation after ecstasy. Each reader will experience the poem at his own level of experience or at several. A good story poem is like a stone thrown into a pond, into our minds, where ever widening concentric circles of meaning go out – and this because of the structure of the story.

"A poem should not mean but be." It is an epigram worth quoting in every essay on poetry. And the poet "nothing affirmeth, and therefore never lieth." "Sit quidvis," said Horace, "simplex dumtaxat et unum." It seems almost the reverse of the truth. "Complex dumtaxat et unum" would be better. Every real poem is a complex poem, and only in virtue of its complexity does it have artistic unity. A newspaper poem by Edgar Guest does not have this kind of unity, but only the unity of an abstractly stated sentiment.

The principle is expressed by Aristotle when he says that beauty is based on unity in variety, and by Coleridge when he says that "The Beautiful, contemplated in its essentials, that is, in *kind* and not in *degree*, is that in which the *many*, still seen as many becomes one," and that a work of art is "rich in proportion to the variety of parts which it holds in unity."

V

It is usually easier to show how poetry works than to show why anyone should want it to work in a given way. Rhetorical analysis of poetry has always tended to separate from evaluation, technique from worth. The structure of poems as concrete and universal is the principle by which the critic can try to keep the two together. If it be granted that the "subject matter" of poetry is in a broad sense the moral realm, human actions as good or bad, with all their associated feelings, all the thought and imagination that goes with happiness and suffering (if poetry submits "the shews of things to the desires of the Mind"), then the rhetorical structure of the concrete universal, the complexity and unity of the poem, is also its maturity or sophistication or richness or depth, and hence its value. Complexity of form is sophistication of content. The unity and maturity of good poems are two sides of the same thing. The kind of unity which we look for and find in poetry is attained only through a degree of complexity in design which itself involves maturity and richness. For a visual diagram of the metaphysics of poetry one might write vertically the word complexity, a column, and give it a head with Janus faces, one looking in the rhetorical direction, unity, and the other in the axiological, maturity.

A final point to be made is that a criticism of structure and of value is an objective criticism. It rests on facts of human psychology (as that a man may love a woman so well as to give up empires), facts, which though psychological, yet are so well acknowledged as to lie in the realm of what may be called public psychology – a realm which one should distinguish from the private realm of the author's psychology and from the equally private realm of the individual reader's psychology (the vivid pictures which poetry or stories are supposed to create in the imagination, or the venerable action of catharsis – all that poetry is said to *do* rather than to *be*). Such a criticism, again, is objective and absolute, as distinguished from the relative criticism of idiom and period. I mean that this criticism will notice that Pope is different from Shakespeare, but will notice even more attentively that Shakespeare is different from Taylor the Water Poet and Pope different from Sir Richard Blackmore. Such a criticism will be interested to analyze the latter two differences and see what these differences have in common and what Shakespeare and Pope have in common, and it will not despair of describing that similarity (that formula or character of great poetry) even though the terms be abstract and difficult. Or, if we are told that there is no universal agreement about what is good – that Pope has not been steadily held in esteem, that Shakespeare has been considered a barbarian, the objective analyst of structures can at least say (and it seems much to say) that he is describing a class of poems, those which through a peculiar complexity possess unity and maturity and in a special way can be called both individual and universal. Among all recorded "poems," this class is of a relative rarity, and further this class will be found in an impressive way to coincide with those poems which have by some body of critics, some age of educated readers, been called great.

The function of the objective critic is by approximate descriptions of poems, or multiple restatements of their meaning, to aid other readers to come to an intuitive and full realization of poems themselves and hence to know good poems and distinguish them from bad ones. It is of course impossible to tell all about a poem in other words. Croce tells us, as we should expect him to, of the "impossibility of ever rendering in logical terms the full effect of any poetry or of other artistic work." "Criticism, nevertheless," he tells us, "performs its own office, which is to discern and to point out exactly where lies the poetical motive and to formulate the divisions which aid in distinguishing what is proper to every work."...

Editor's Note

1 Wimsatt refers here to two contrasting theories of art and literature that are summarized in a part of his essay omitted from this text. In a passage in his philosophical novel *Rasselas*, first published in 1759, Samuel Johnson used a character called Imlac, "a man of learning," to provide a dissertation on poetry. Imlac argued that a poet's work should "examine not the individual but the species; to remark general properties and large appearances: he does not number the streaks of the tulip...". Writing nearly 150 years later, the French philosopher, Henri Bergson, put forward a very different view. In his long essay "Laughter," first published in French in 1900, he proposed that art "always aims at the *individual*... What the poet sings of is a certain mood, which was his, and his alone, and which will never return."

Chapter 41
Jacques Lacan

Jacques Lacan (1901–81) reinvented Freud's psychoanalysis, and claimed to discover a truth that Freud had not fully realized, by proposing in a memorable slogan that the "unconscious is structured like a language." The version of language that Lacan drew on came from Saussure. If the unconscious is structured like a language it is so in terms of the relation between signifiers (for example, an acoustic image) and signifieds (usually equated with concepts). Lacan insisted that in this relationship it was the signifier that predominated: meaning was the result of the interaction of signifiers; every signified could only be resolved into a signifier and so on. Another central theme of Lacan's psychoanalysis was its concern with the subject. Freud's ego, mediating between desires and the requirements of reality, was replaced by Lacan's notion of the subject as a necessary illusion created out of a relation to an image, as in a mirror, and by its place in language. Lacan's theories have been influential. Some have followed him like disciples, others have derided him as a charlatan. His ideas have been widely applied in the study of literature, film, and the visual arts since the 1960s.

Lacan was a deliberately provocative and controversial thinker. Three of the following extracts come from the celebrated seminars Lacan conducted in Paris from the early 1950s until 1980. Lacan used these occasions to develop his ideas about language, the unconscious, and the role of psychoanalysis. Sometimes, as in the first extract from a seminar held in 1954, he could use members of his audience as intellectual fall guys. This passage provides a succinct account of Lacan's theory of the subject as finding "its unity in the image of the other," a theory that has been applied to the reader's relation to poetic texts. In the next two extracts, drawn from seminars in 1955–6, Lacan develops his thinking about metaphor in relation to an example drawn from Victor Hugo's poem, "Booz Endormi". He insists that metaphor, which he regards as the central trope of poetic language, is based upon identification, not comparison; that it presents an example of creativity in language; and that it could not exist without the grammatical structure of subjects and predicates. In the final extract, taken from his 1957 paper, "The Agency of the Letter in the Unconscious," Lacan further develops his thinking about metaphor, initially by juxtaposing it with the trope of metonymy, and then by way of a critique of Surrealist poetics. Lacan explores the unconscious process at work in metaphor as one signifier is displaced by another.

The Subject from Homeostasis and Insistence

If I wanted to find an image for whatever it is we are investigating here, I would begin by rejoicing in the fact that given the accessibility of Freud's work I do not find myself forced, save by some unexpected intervention of the deity, to go and seek them on some Sinai, in other words to leave you by yourselves too soon. In actual fact, what we always see being reproduced in the most tightly argued parts of Freud's text is something which, while it isn't quite the adoration of the Golden Calf, is still an idolatry. What I am trying to do here is tear you away from it once and for all. I hope that I will do enough so that one day your tendency to use highly imagistic formulations will disappear.

In his presentation yesterday evening, our dear Leclaire did not quite prostrate himself before the calf, but there was a bit of that in it. You all felt it, the tenor of some of his terms of reference is of that order. The need to give an image certainly has its merits in scientific presentation no less than in other domains – but maybe not as much as one thinks. And nowhere does it offer more traps than in the domain we find ourselves in, which is that of subjectivity. When one speaks of subjectivity, the problem is not to turn the subject into an entity.

I think that, with the aim of making his constructions hold up – and it is indeed this aim which accounts for the fact that he presented his model to us as a pyramid, firmly seated on its bottom, and not on its tip – Leclaire made the subject into some sort of idol. There was no other way he could do it than represent it for us.

This remark comes up at the right moment in the course of our demonstration here, which is centred on the question – *What is the subject?* – raised both by a naive understanding and by the scientific, or philosophical, formulation of the subject.

Let us take up the discussion at the point where I left you last time, that is at the moment when the subject grasps his unity.

The body in pieces finds its unity in the image of the other, which is its own anticipated image – a dual situation in which a polar, but non-symmetrical relation, is sketched out. This asymmetry already tells us that the theory of the ego in psychoanalysis has nothing in common with the learned conception of the ego, which on the contrary partakes of a kind of naive understanding which I told you was peculiar to the historically datable psychology of modern man.

I brought you up short at the moment when I was showing you that this subject, really, is no one.

From *The Seminar of Jacques Lacan, Book II*, trans. Sylvania Tomaselli (New York: W. W. Norton, 1988), pp. 53–5.

The subject is no one. It is decomposed, in pieces. And it is jammed, sucked in by the image, the deceiving and realised image, of the other, or equally by its own specular image. That is where it finds its unity. Laying hold of a reference taken from the most modern of these mechanistic problems, which have such importance in the development of science and of thought, I'll show you this stage of development of the subject by using a model whose utility is that it doesn't in any way idolise the subject.

At the point where I left you, the subject was nowhere. We had our two little mechanical tortoises, one of which was stuck on the image of the other. We were in effect supposing that, through a regulative part of its mechanism – the photoelectric cell, for instance, but let's leave that, I'm not here to tell you about cybernetics, even an imaginary variety – the first machine was dependent on the image of the second, hanging on its unitary functioning, and consequently captivated by its procedures. Hence a circle, which can be vast, but whose essential set-up is given by this imaginary dual relation.

I showed you the consequences of this circle regarding desire. Let us be clear – what could the desire of a machine be, except to restock on energy sources? A machine can scarcely do anything other than feed itself, and that is indeed what Grey Walter's courageous little animals do. Machines which reproduce themselves have yet to be built, and have yet even to be conceived of – the schema of their symbolic has not even been established. The sole object of desire which we can presume of a machine is therefore its source of nourishment. Well then, if each machine is intent on the point to which the other is going, somewhere there will necessarily be a collision.

That is where we had got to.

Now let us suppose our machines to have some sound recording equipment, and let us suppose that a loud voice – we can easily imagine that someone supervises their operation, the legislator – intervenes so as to regulate the ballet which up until now was only a round which might lead to a disastrous end. What's being introduced is a symbolic regulation, of which the unconscious mathematical subjacency of the exchanges of the elementary structures gives us the schema. The comparison ends there, for we aren't going to make an entity of the legislator – that would be yet another idol.

Dr Leclaire: I'm sorry, but I'd like to reply. If I have a tendency to idolise the subject, it's because I think it necessary – you can't do otherwise.

Well, then, you are a little idolater. I come down from Sinai and break the Tables of the Law.

Dr Leclaire: Let me finish. I have the impression that in refusing this deliberate identification, the subject, we have a tendency, and you have a tendency, to carry this idolisation over to another point. At that moment, it won't be the subject, it will be the other, the image, the mirror.

I realise this. You aren't the only one. You and your transcendental preoccupations lead you to a specifically substantialist idea of the unconscious. Others have an idealist conception, in the sense of critical idealism, but they also think that I reintroduce what I am chasing away. There is more than one person here whose formation is in, let us say, traditional philosophy, and for whom consciousness's awareness of itself is one of the pillars of his conception of the world. That is doubtless something which shouldn't be treated lightly, and last time I did warn you that I was taking the step of cutting the Gordian knot, by deliberately being partial and radically neglecting one entire point of view. Someone here, whose identity I have no need to disclose, said to me after my last lecture – *This consciousness, it seems to me that after having badly maltreated it you bring it back in with this voice which reintroduces order, and which regulates the ballet of the machines.*

Our deduction of the subject however demands that we locate this voice somewhere in the interhuman game. To say that it is the legislator's voice would doubtless be an idolification, albeit of a high, though characterised, order. Isn't it rather the voice *Which knows itself when it resounds/No longer to be no one's voice/But that of the waves and the woods?*

It's language Valéry is speaking of here. And shouldn't we perhaps in the end recognise it, this voice, *as the voice of no one....*

Metaphor and Metonymy 1

...Metaphor is not the easiest thing in the world to speak about. Bossuet says it's an abridged simile [*comparaison*]. Everyone is aware that this is not entirely satisfactory, and I believe that in fact no poet would accept it. I say *no poet* because a definition of poetical style could be to say that it begins with metaphor, and that where metaphor ceases poetry ceases also.

His sheaf was neither miserly nor spiteful – Victor Hugo. That's a metaphor. It's certainly not a latent simile, it's not – *just as* the sheaf was willingly dispersed among the needy, *so* our character was neither miserly nor spiteful. There's not a comparison but an identification. The dimension of metaphor must be less difficult for us to enter than for anyone else, provided that we recognize that what we usually call it is identification. But that's not all – our use of the term *symbolic* in fact leads us to restrict its sense, to designate only the metaphorical dimension of the symbol.

Metaphor presupposes that a meaning is the dominant datum and that it deflects, commands, the use of the signifier to such an extent that the entire species of pre-established, I should say lexical, connections comes undone. Nothing in any dictionary usage can suggest for one instant that a sheaf is capable of being miserly, and even less of being spiteful. And yet it's clear that the use of a language is only susceptible to meaning once it's possible to say, *His sheaf was neither miserly nor spiteful*, that is to say, once the meaning has ripped the signifier from its lexical connections.

Here we have the ambiguity of the signifier and the signified. Without the signifying structure, that is, without predicative articulation, without the distance maintained between the subject and its attributes, the sheaf cannot be qualified as miserly or

From *The Seminar of Jacques Lacan, Book III*, trans. Russell Grigg (New York: W. W. Norton, 1993), pp. 218–19, 226–7.

spiteful. It's because there is a syntax, a primordial order of the signifier, that the subject is maintained as separate, as different from its qualities. It's completely out of the question that an animal could create a metaphor, even though we have no reason to think that it doesn't also have an intuition of what is generous and what can easily and abundantly grant it what it desires. But insofar as it doesn't possess the articulation, the discursive – which is not just meaning, with all that this entails about attraction and repulsion, but an alignment of signifiers – metaphor is unthinkable within the animal psychology of attraction, appetite, and desire.

This phase of symbolism that is expressed in metaphor presupposes similarity, which is exhibited uniquely by position. It's by virtue of being the subject of *miserly* and *spiteful* that the sheaf can be identified with Booz in his lack of avarice and in his generosity. It's by virtue of the similarity of position that the sheaf is literally identical to the subject Booz. This dimension of similarity is, surely, the most striking thing about the significant use of language, which so dominates the apprehension of the workings of symbolism as to mask from us the existence of the other dimension, the syntactic. However, this sentence would lose all sense if we disturbed the word order.

This is what gets neglected when symbolism is discussed – the dimension linked to the signifier's existence, its organization.

Metaphor and Metonymy 2

. . . Let's move to the limit of poetic metaphor, which you wouldn't hesitate to describe as surrealist, even though we didn't have to wait for the surrealists to make metaphors. You are unable to say whether it makes sense or not. I won't say that this is the best way of putting things, but, in any case, it's near enough.

Take an expression that we can agree is indeed a metaphor. You will see whether it's the sense that sustains it.

Love is a pebble laughing in the sun.

What does this mean? It's indisputably a metaphor. It's likely enough that if it was born, it's because it contains a sense. As for finding one . . . I could do a whole seminar on it. This seems to me to be an indisputable definition of love, and I shall say that it's the last I paused at, because to me it appears indispensable if one wants to avoid falling endlessly into irremediable confusions.

In short, a metaphor is above all sustained by a positional articulation. This can be demonstrated even in its most paradoxical forms.

None of you has, I believe, failed to hear of the exercise that a poet of our day has carried out under the rubric of *Un mot pour un autre* [one word for another]. It's a little comedy in one act by Jean Tardieu. It concerns a dialogue between two women. One is announced, the other goes up to her and says:

My dear, my dearest, how many pebbles is it since I have had the apprentice to sugar you?

Alas, my dear, answers the other, *I myself have been extremely unvitreous, my three littlest oil-cakes, etc.*

This is confirmation that, even if it's in a paradoxical form, not only is the sense maintained, but that it tends to manifest itself in a particularly fortunate and metaphorical manner. It may be said that the sense is in some way renewed. Whatever effort the poet may have made to push it in the direction of a demonstration, one is at every instant a hair's breadth from a poetic metaphor. It belongs to a register that is no different from what arises as natural poetry as soon as a powerful meaning is involved.

The important thing isn't that the similarity should be sustained by the signified – we make this mistake all the time – it's that the transference of the signified is possible only by virtue of the structure of language. All language implies a metalanguage, it's already a metalanguage of its own register. It's because potentially all language is to be translated that it implies metaphrase and metalanguage, language speaking of language. The transference of the signified, so essential to human life, is possible only by virtue of the structure of the signifier.

Do get it into your heads that language is a system of positional coherence, and secondly that this system reproduces itself within itself with an extraordinary, and frightful, fecundity. . . .

The Agency of the Letter in the Unconscious

The properly signifying function thus depicted in language has a name. We learned this name in some grammar of our childhood, on the last page, where the shade of Quintilian, relegated to some phantom chapter concerning 'final considerations on style', seemed suddenly to speed up his voice in an attempt to get in all he had to say before the end.

It is among the figures of style, or tropes – from which the verb 'to find' (*trouver*) comes to us – that this name is found. This name is *metonymy.*

I shall refer only to the example given there: 'thirty sails'. For the disquietude I felt over the fact that the word 'ship', concealed in this expression, seemed, by taking on its figurative sense, through the endless repetition of the same old example, only to increase its presence, obsured (*voilait*) not so much those illustrious sails (*voiles*) as the definition they were supposed to illustrate.

The part taken for the whole, we said to ourselves, and if the thing is to be taken seriously, we are left with very little idea of the importance of this fleet, which 'thirty sails' is precisely supposed to give us: for each ship to have just one sail is in fact the least likely possibility.

By which we see that the connexion between ship and sail is nowhere but in the signifier, and that it is in the *word-to-word* connexion that metonymy is based.

I shall designate as metonymy, then, the one side (*versant*) of the effective field constituted by the signifier, so that meaning can emerge there.

The other side is *metaphor.* Let us immediately find an illustration; Quillet's dictionary seemed an appropriate place to find a sample that would not seem to be chosen

From *Ecrits: A Selection,* trans. Alan Sheridan (London: Tavistock Publications, 1977), pp. 156–8.

for my own purposes, and I didn't have to go any further than the well known line of Victor Hugo:

His sheaf was neither miserly nor spiteful...

under which aspect I presented metaphor in my seminar on the psychoses.

It should be said that modern poetry and especially the Surrealist school have taken us a long way in this direction by showing that any conjunction of two signifiers would be equally sufficient to constitute a metaphor, except for the additional requirement of the greatest possible disparity of the images signified, needed for the production of the poetic spark, or in other words for metaphoric creation to take place.

It is true this radical position is based on the experiment known as automatic writing, which would not have been attempted if its pioneers had not been reassured by the Freudian discovery. But it remains a confused position because the doctrine behind it is false.

The creative spark of the metaphor does not spring from the presentation of two images, that is, of two signifiers equally actualized. It flashes between two signifiers one of which has taken the place of the other in the signifying chain, the occulted signifier remaining present through its (metonymic) connexion with the rest of the chain.

One word for another: that is the formula for the metaphor and if you are a poet you will produce for your own delight a continuous stream, a dazzling tissue of metaphors. If the result is the sort of intoxication of the dialogue that Jean Tardieu wrote under this title, that is only because he was giving us a demonstration of the radical superfluousness of all signification in a perfectly convincing representation of a bourgeois comedy.

It is obvious that in the line of Hugo cited above, not the slightest spark of light springs from the proposition that the sheaf was neither miserly nor spiteful, for the reason that there is no question of the sheaf's having either the merit or demerit of these attributes, since the attributes, like the sheaf, belong to Booz, who exercises the former in disposing of the latter and without informing the latter of his sentiments in the case.

If, however, his sheaf does refer us to Booz, and this is indeed the case, it is because it has replaced him in the signifying chain at the very place where he was to be exalted by the sweeping away of greed and spite. But now Booz himself has been swept away by the sheaf, and hurled into the outer darkness where greed and spite harbour him in the hollow of their negation.

But once *his* sheaf has thus usurped his place, Booz can no longer return there; the slender thread of the little word *his* that binds him to it is only one more obstacle to his return in that it links him to the notion of possession that retains him at the heart of greed and spite. So *his* generosity, affirmed in the passage, is yet reduced to *less than nothing* by the munificence of the sheaf which, coming from nature, knows neither our reserve nor our rejections, and even in its accumulation remains prodigal by our standards.

But if in this profusion the giver has disappeared along with his gift, it is only in order to rise again in what surrounds the figure of speech in which he was annihilated. For it is the figure of the burgeoning of fecundity, and it is this that announces the surprise that the poem celebrates, namely, the promise that the old man will receive in the sacred context of his accession to paternity.

So, it is between the signifier in the form of the proper name of a man and the signifier that metaphorically abolishes him that the poetic spark is produced, and it is in this case all the more effective in realizing the signification of paternity in that it reproduces the mythical event in terms of which Freud reconstructed the progress, in the unconscious of all men, of the paternal mystery.

Modern metaphor has the same structure. So the line *Love is a pebble laughing in the sunlight*, recreates love in a dimension that seems to me most tenable in the face of its imminent lapse into the mirage of narcissistic altruism.

We see, then that, metaphor occurs at the precise point at which sense emerges from non-sense, that is, at that frontier which, as Freud discovered, when crossed the other way produces the word that in French is *the* word *par excellence*, the word that is simply the signifier '*esprit*'; it is at this frontier that we realize that man defies his very destiny when he derides the signifier. . . .

Chapter 42
Donald Davie

Donald Davie (1922–95) was a poet and critic who rejected what he identified as a new orthodoxy about poetry created by the modernism of Eliot, Pound, and Valéry. In the 1950s he was one of the group of British poets known as the Movement who believed in a poetry of formal restraint and disillusioned common sense. Yet unlike some of the Movement poets, Davie did not become a cultural chauvinist. His rejection of modernist poetics was based upon a deep and informed reading of Pound's poetry, exemplified in his book Ezra Pound, Poet as Sculptor, *published in 1965. Nor did his skepticism about Olson's development of Pound's poetics prevent him from writing sympathetically about the work of Olson's followers. The same cosmopolitan range was evident in his work on Polish and Russian poetry.*

Davie wrote a number of influential works of criticism, including Purity of Diction in English Verse *(1952) and* Articulate Energy *(1955). In the following excerpts from two chapters of* Articulate Energy, *Davie provides a definition of modern poetry that is linguistic rather than historical. A poetry that is self-consciously modern is dominated by the logic of images and their juxtaposition in sequences that are not ordered grammatically or syntactically. Where syntax is evident in modern poetry its purpose is "musical," not grammatical. Davie argues that this becomes a limitation on the expressive resources of poetry, inhibiting the kinds of direct statement and reflective commentary that can open the poem to shared human experience.*

What is Modern Poetry?

What is modern poetry? We cannot say, simply, that all poets who have written since a specific date are thereby modern poets. Or rather, we can talk of "modern poetry" in this sense, but more often we do not. Mr. Walter De La Mare is presumably a modern

From *Articulate Energy* (London: Routledge & Kegan Paul, 1955), pp. 147–54, 161–3, 164–5.

poet in this sense, but his is not the poetry we have in mind when we speak of "modern" poetry. Usually when we use the term, we have in mind poetry which has broken with the poetry of our grandfathers in a way that Mr. De La Mare's exquisite poetry has not. "Modern", in fact, has taken over the functions of the now outmoded adjective "modernist"; modern poetry, as we usually understand it, is something that appears aggressively and consciously different, in important ways, from the poetry of the past. In this sense of "modern", the modern poet is standing on the near side of a gulf. Very often, indeed, the poet is at some pains to show us that the gulf can be bridged, and he points to the bridges he has crossed. But at any rate the bridges are thrown over in unlikely places; they are not broad and obvious like the bridge that leads back from Mr. De La Mare to Keats.

All the same, the bridges are easier to find than is the gulf beneath them. Or rather, the gulf is plain when we are "on the spot", and very deep and wide; but it is hard to find it on the map or to instruct the stranger where to look out for it. There is a distinct break with the past, that we know; there is a gulf to be crossed if we want to move from Tennyson to T. S. Eliot; but when we try to define that break, to chart the gulf, we fall out among ourselves. We have all negotiated the passage, yet it seems we have come by different routes. One party of poets and critics finds the decisive innovation in one place, another in quite another, and so on. And though we feel, viewing the matter from a distance, that all modern poetry hangs together, when we come closer this impression vanishes and we see only a bewildering diversity. Somehow, we acknowledge, modern poetry begins with symbolism. Modern poetry, we say, is post-symbolist poetry. *Post hoc*, certainly, but *propter hoc*? And there we begin to wrangle. It is just there, when we try to explain just *how* symbolism "started it all", that we fall out.

If the foregoing pages have tended to any one conclusion it is this: the break with the past is at bottom a change of attitude towards poetic syntax. It is from that point of view, in respect of syntax, that modern poetry, so diverse in all other ways, is seen as one. And we can define it thus: *What is common to all modern poetry is the assertion or the assumption (most often the latter) that syntax in poetry is wholly different from syntax as understood by logicians and grammarians.* When the poet retains syntactical forms acceptable to the grammarian, this is merely a convention which he chooses to observe. We may acknowledge that such emptied forms are to be found (and frequently too) in Shakespeare and in Milton. But never before the modern period has it been taken for granted that all poetic syntax is necessarily of this sort.

This is, surely, the one symbolist innovation that is at the root of all the other technical novelties that the symbolist poets introduced. Later poets could refuse to countenance all the other symbolist methods and still, by sharing, consciously or not, the symbolist attitude to syntax, they stand out as patently "post-symbolist". This aspect of the symbolist doctrine – and, as I have pointed out, it is more than just one aspect, it is at the core – has been obscured by the fact that Mallarmé and Valéry talk of syntax, and appear to lay great store by it, in a way that earlier poets did not. But this arises from the use of one word "syntax" to mean two things which are really widely different. In fact I think we shall find that we need, not just two terms, but several, instead of the one. At any rate, Mallarmé and Valéry, when they speak of "syntax", do not mean by it what is meant by the common reader.

Here only blunt common sense will serve:

> The point was not that the emotions of, say, Jules Laforgue were necessarily more complicated than those of, say, Catullus in his sequence of poems about Lesbia, but rather that the symbolist poet – instead of disentangling a complex emotion into a series of varying moods or at least, when the mood of a single poem is allowed to change abruptly (as in Catullus's *Illa Lesbia*...), of subduing the disordered feeling to the logic of consecutive statement – is in the habit of telescoping the whole thing by a few stenographic strokes. Nor are his feelings necessarily more difficult to render than those, say, of Wordsworth in the most mysterious of his visions of the natural world; but the symbolist – instead of attempting to reduce an unearthly elusive sensation to the lucidity of simple language – invents for it a vocabulary and a syntax as unfamiliar as the sensation itself.[1]

The symbolist poet, we realize, has a choice of two alternatives: either he telescopes his feeling "by a few stenographic strokes" – that is, he abandons even the appearance of syntactical arrangement and merely juxtaposes images; or else he "invents... a syntax as unfamiliar as the sensation itself" – that is, something that may look like normal syntax but fulfils a quite different function.

As H. M. McLuhan has pointed out, Wordsworth comes nearest to symbolist poetry in such a poem as "The Solitary Reaper", where he leaves the reader to gather from the poem the feeling, never overtly described, which inspired the poet to write it. This is the poetry of "the objective correlative", which describes, not the emotion itself, but a symbolic landscape or action which may stand as its equivalent. It is sometimes maintained that the discovery how to do this was the decisive innovation of the symbolists, and the starting-point for the symbolist movement. But this is not the case, as the reference to Wordsworth serves to show. What is novel in symbolist technique is the way of organizing the items inside the symbolic landscape or the train of symbolic events.

When Edmund Wilson points out that Tennyson "was nearer to the school of Verlaine than it is likely to occur to us to notice", he is enforcing this point, that the objective correlative is not peculiar to symbolism but can be found in pre-symbolist writing. Tennyson indeed is a crucial case, and H. M. McLuhan has treated him at some length from this point of view, arguing that he anticipates the symbolist expedient of "*le paysage intérieur* or the psychological landscape":

> This landscape, by means of discontinuity, which was first developed in picturesque painting, effected the apposition of widely diverse objects as a means of establishing what Mr. Eliot has called "an objective correlative" for a state of mind... Whereas in external landscape diverse things lie side by side, so in psychological landscape the juxtaposition of various things and experiences becomes a precise musical means of orchestrating that which could never be rendered by systematic discourse. Landscape is the means of presenting, without the copula of logical enunciation, experiences which are united in existence but not in conceptual thought. Syntax becomes music, as in Tennyson's "Mariana".[2]

"Syntax becomes music"; and this is plainly the "music" of St.-John Perse, which is best fitted for "joining without binding, and gathering together without fettering". It is the music of Suzanne Langer, in which "The actual function of meaning, which calls for permanent contents, is not fulfilled; for the *assignment* of one rather than another possible meaning to each form is never explicitly made." And if our earlier analysis was correct, this means a syntax that is a shadow-play, a lifting of non-existent weights, a dance that ends where it began.

It will have been noticed that Wilson and McLuhan differ at one point, radically. For the latter the symbolist sort of syntax is justified because by it the poet may communicate or embody "that which could never be rendered by systematic discourse". And this is something that Wilson goes out of his way to deny. Laforgue, he insists, could have been as systematic as Catullus; he chose not to be:

> Symbolism, at its most successful, contrives to communicate emotions by images whose connection with the subject and whose relevance to one another we may not always understand... These images could probably have been conveyed in a perfectly conventional manner – as Dante, describing a state of mind surely not less unusual and difficult, would write in the *Paradiso* of the fading from his memory of the divine vision, "so the snow is unsealed by the sun, so the light leaves of the Sybil's message are scattered by the wind."[3]

If Wilson is right, then McLuhan's case for symbolism comes out of a loss of faith in conceptual thought. It testifies to a loss of nerve, as with Hofmannsthal's Lord Chandos. And this was general. As Richard Ellmann says, Yeats stands almost alone in the post-symbolist generations as "stubbornly loyal in his art to the conscious mind's intelligible structure." For that, we see again, is what it amounts to: where there is authentic syntax in poetry (syntax, that is, not wholly different from the syntax of logician and grammarian), the poet retains hope of the conscious mind's activity; when he has lost that hope, his syntax is either dislocated altogether, or else turns into music.

H. M. McLuhan distinguishes between "picturesque" and "symbolist" poetry, though only as phases in the development of one tradition. He distinguishes between them as follows:

> The picturesque artists saw the wider range of experience that could be managed by discontinuity and planned irregularity, but they kept to the picture-like single perspective. The interior landscape, however, moves naturally towards the principle of multiple perspectives as in the first two lines of *The Waste Land* where the Christian Chaucer, Sir James Frazer and Jessie Weston are simultaneously present. This is "cubist perspective" which renders, at once, a diversity of views with the spectator always in the centre of the picture, whereas in picturesque art the spectator is always outside. The cubist perspective of interior landscape typically permits an immediacy, a variety and solidity of experience denied to the picturesque and to Tennyson.[4]

Now this, too, immediately recalls Yeats, speaking of Joyce, of Pound, and of Proust:

> This new art which has arisen in different countries simultaneously seems related... to that form of the new realist philosophy which thinks that the secondary and primary qualities alike are independent of consciousness, that an object can at the same moment

> have contradictory qualities. This philosophy seems about to follow the analogy of an art that has more rapidly completed itself, and after deciding that a penny is bright and dark, oblong and round, hot and cold, dumb and ringing in its own right; to think of the calculations it incites, our distaste and pleasure at its sight, the decision that made us pitch it, our preference for head or tail, as independent of a consciousness that has shrunk back, grown intermittent and accidental, into the looking-glass...
>
> If you ask me why I do not accept a doctrine so respectable and convenient, its cruder forms so obviously resurrected to get science down from Berkeley's roasting-spit, I can but answer like Zarathustra, "Am I a barrel of memories that I should give you my reasons?", somewhere among those memories something compels me to reject whatever – to borrow a metaphor of Coleridge's – drives mind into the quicksilver.[5]

There is an obvious relation between McLuhan's cubist perspective offering "at once, a diversity of views", and the new realist philosophy indicated by Yeats, according to which "an object can at the same moment have contradictory qualities". Where McLuhan speaks of "the spectator always in the centre of the picture", Yeats talks, here and elsewhere, of a consciousness withdrawn into the quicksilver at the back of the mirror. The critic and the poet are speaking of the same thing, and in very similar imagery, though from different points of view.

Yeats's appeal to Coleridge is just:

> In disciplining the mind one of the first rules should be, to lose no opportunity of tracing words to their origin; one good consequence of which will be, that he will be able to use the *language* of sight without being enslaved by its affections. He will at least save himself from the delusive notion, that what is not *imageable* is likewise not *conceivable.* To emancipate the mind from the despotism of the eye is the first step towards its emancipation from the influences and intrusions of the senses, sensations and passions generally. Thus most effectively is the power of abstraction to be called forth....[6]

This is the Coleridge who admonished Wordsworth that the best part of human language comes from the allocation of fixed symbols to internal acts of the mind. All this side of Coleridge's thought flies in the face of modern poetic theory, symbolist or imagist. And from his point of view, such modern theory is grounded upon the delusion that what cannot be imaged cannot be conceived. According to Coleridge, conceptual thinking outstrips thinking in images; for H. M. McLuhan, as for most symbolist and post-symbolist theorists, the truth is just the other way round – images, if cunningly arranged, can get beyond concepts. At this point, the alignment of forces, for and against authentic syntax in poetry, is particularly clear.

...

The Reek of the Human

...The tendency of all symbolist theories is to make the world of poetry more autonomous. Most of them, like Mrs. Langer's, stop short of making the world of poetry wholly self-sufficient, and keep open some avenue, however narrow and winding, by which the world of poetry can communicate with the outside world, through mimesis. But some theorists – those, perhaps, who see poetic syntax as mathematics rather than music – seem prepared to cut poetry loose altogether. And here I will use Mr. Northrop Frye, once again, as whipping-boy:

> The assumption in the word "universe", whether applied to physics or to literature, is not that these subjects are descriptive of total existence, but simply that they are in themselves totally intelligible. No one can know the whole of physics at once, but physics would not be a coherent subject unless this were theoretically possible. The argument of Aristotle's *Physics,* which treats physics as the study of motion in nature, leads inexorably to the conception of an unmoved mover at the circumference of the world. In itself this is merely the postulate that the total form of physics is the physical universe. If Christian theology takes physics to be descriptive of an ultra-physical reality or activity, and proceeds to identify this unmoved first mover with an existent God, that is the business of Christian theology: physics as physics will be unaffected by it. The assumption of a verbal universe similarly leads to the conception of an unspeakable first word at its circumference. This in itself is merely the postulate that literature is totally intelligible. If Christian theology identifies this first word with the Word of God or person of Christ, and says that the vision of total human creative power is divine as well as human, the literary critic, as such, is not concerned either to support or to refute the identification.[7]

I go so far as I can in understanding this passage by setting it beside Elizabeth Sewell's very suggestive notion of systems in the mind, some "open" and some "closed", an idea which comes by analogy from mechanics.

Miss Sewell observes that "The mind has a choice of systems within which it can work." She quotes, "The primary control of the concepts of mathematics is that contradiction should not be involved." And she goes on:

> Nightmare works in reverse, including all that is disorder and excluding all that is order. In the one system there is the certainty of the expected, in the other the certainty of the unexpected, but in neither system is there any room for probability or uncertainty.[8]

It should now be plain that Mr. Frye's rhetoric converts language from an open system into a closed one. In literature, on his view, there is the certainty of the intelligible, and there is therefore no room in it for probability or uncertainty. Literature is certain to find what it seeks because its conclusions are implicit in its postulate. But then, our mistake is in thinking that it seeks anything. It does not seek, it constructs...

It is quite natural, therefore, for Mr. Frye to pronounce:

> The relation of literature to factual verbal structures has to be established from within one of the latter. Literature must be approached centrifugally, from the outside, if we are to get any factual significance out of it.... One begins talking about "Lycidas", for instance, by itemizing all the things that "Lycidas" illustrates in the non-literary verbal world: English history in 1637, the Church and Milton's view of it, the position of Milton as a young poet planning an epic and a political career, the literary convention of the pastoral elegy, Christian teachings on the subject of death and resurrection, and so on. It would be

> quite possible to spend a whole critical life in this allegorical limbo of background, without ever getting to the poem at all, or even feeling the need of doing so.[9]

"Lycidas" is an apt example, of course. But take Wordsworth's "Complaint of a Forsaken Indian Woman". The whole point of this poem lies in its truth to human nature, and is it really true that, to get its factual significance, as presenting the feelings of a woman separated from her child, we need to come at it from within a "factual verbal structure", that is, presumably, through a treatise on the psychology of mother and child? We need, it is true, to have some humanity ourselves; but is that searching of our own hearts an "allegorical limbo of background"? And when we come out of that limbo and get to the poem, what is left for us to get to? Once we have taken the truth of the poem to a human predicament, there is nothing left; for diction, metre, rhyme, imagery, all are made transparent for the truth to shine out through them. This poem is not a world, like the world of a symbolist poem, "closed and self-sufficient, being the pure system of the ornaments and the chances of language". It takes on meaning only as it is open to another world; unless it refers to that other "real" world, it is meaningless. Its syntax articulates not just itself, not only its own world, but the world of common experience.

The appeal of theories such as Mr. Frye's is manifest in the loaded words that their promoters use, in recommending them. A poetry in which the syntax articulates only "the world of the poem" is said to be "pure", "absolute", "sheer", "self-sufficient". Wordsworth's poems are "impure" because they have about them the smell of soil and soiled flesh, the reek of humanity. Their syntax is not "pure" syntax because it refers to, it mimes, something outside itself and outside the world of its poem, something that smells of the human, of generation and hence of corruption. It is my case against the symbolist theorists that, in trying to remove the human smell from poetry, they are only doing harm. For poetry to be great, it must reek of the human, as Wordsworth's poetry does. This is not a novel contention; but perhaps it is one of those things that cannot be said too often.

Notes

1 Edmund Wilson, *The Shores of Light* (London: W. H. Allen, 1953), pp. 55–6.
2 H. M. McLuhan, "Tennyson and Picturesque Poetry", *Essays in Criticism*, vol. 1, no. 3, pp. 270–1.
3 Wilson, *Shores of Light*, pp. 55–6.
4 McLuhan, "Tennyson and Picturesque Poetry", pp. 281–2.
5 Davie quotes from Yeats's Introduction to J. M. Hone and H. M. Rossi's *Bishop Berkeley: His Life, Writings and Philosophy*, first published by Faber and Faber in 1931. For a more accessible source see W. B. Yeats, *Essays and Introductions* (London: Macmillan, 1969), pp. 405–7. [JC]
6 Quoted by Herbert Read, *The True Voice of Feeling* (London: Faber and Faber, 1948), p. 179.
7 Northrop Frye, "Levels of Meaning in Literature", *Kenyon Review*, vol. 12, no. 2, pp. 260–1.
8 Elizabeth Sewell, *The Structure of Poetry* (London: Routledge and Kegan Paul, 1951), p. 64.
9 Frye, "Levels of Meaning", pp. 260–1.

Chapter 43
Maurice Blanchot

Maurice Blanchot (1907–2003) was a theorist and writer whose work became an important reference point for a younger and better-known generation of French writers, including Derrida and Foucault. Blanchot's publishing career began in the early 1930s and since then he published works of fiction, including Thomas the Obscure *and* Death Sentence; *intricate and exacting meditations on literature, notably* The Gaze of Orpheus *and* The Sirens' Song; *and, more recently, works on ethics and politics such as* The Unavowable Community. *Blanchot's thinking about literature refuses any gesture of consolation or redemptive possibility. Literature deals with what is opaque, anonymous, and strange in experience, a negativity that cannot be resolved into something positive or definite. At its extreme, when literature is most itself, it does not use language to represent the world. Literature's experience is composed of language, but in a condition that moves language away from a familiar world of objects. In this poetic estrangement words are deprived of all use. They become ends in themselves, but in becoming ends in themselves, they also, Blanchot argues, become nothing.*

These issues are developed in the following excerpt from "Mallarmé's Experience," published in France in 1955 in L'Espace litteraire. *Blanchot traces the logic of Mallarmé's experience as a poet through a series of distinctions: first between poetic language and ordinary or "crude" language; then between poetic language and the language of thought; finally, between the "finished work of the poem" and "the vision of the pure work." Blanchot finds in Mallarmé's work a radical modern poetics in which "the word itself is no longer anything but the appearance of what has disappeared."*

Mallarmé's Experience

Here we must appeal to references that are well known today and that hint at the transformation to which Mallarmé was exposed as soon as he took writing to heart. These references are by no means anecdotal in character. When Mallarmé affirms, "I felt the very disquieting symptoms caused by the sole act of writing," it is the last words which matter. With them an essential situation is brought to light. Something extreme is grasped, something which has for its context and substance "the sole act of writing." Writing appears as an extreme situation which presupposes a radical reversal. Mallarmé alludes briefly to this reversal when he says: "Unfortunately, by digging this thoroughly into verse, I have encountered two abysses which make me despair. One is Nothingness" (the absence of God; the other is his own death). Here too it is the flattest expression that is rich with sense: the one which, in the most unpretentious fashion, seems simply to remind us of a craftsmanly procedure. "By digging into verse," the poet enters that time of distress which is caused by the gods' absence. Mallarmé's phrase is startling. Whoever goes deeply into poetry escapes from being as certitude, meets with the absence of the gods, lives in the intimacy of this absence, becomes responsible for it, assumes its risk, and endures its favor. Whoever digs at verse must renounce all idols; he has to break with everything. He cannot have truth for his horizon, or the future as his element, for he has no right to hope. He has, on the contrary, to despair. Whoever delves into verse dies; he encounters his death as an abyss.

The crude word and the essential word

When he seeks to define the aspect of language which "the sole act of writing" disclosed to him, Mallarmé acknowledges a "double condition of the word, crude or immediate on the one hand, essential on the other." This distinction itself is crude, yet difficult to grasp, for Mallarmé attributes the same substance to the two aspects of language which he distinguishes so absolutely. In order to characterize each, he lights on the same term, which is "silence." The crude word is pure silence: "It would, perhaps, be enough for anyone who wants to exchange human speech, silently to take or put in someone else's hand a coin." Silent, therefore, because meaningless, crude language is an absence of words, a pure exchange where nothing is exchanged, where there is nothing real except the movement of exchange, which is nothing. But it turns out the same for the word confided to the questing poet – that language whose whole force lies in its not being, whose very glory is to evoke, in its own absence, the absence of everything. This language of the unreal, this fictive language which delivers us to fiction, comes from silence and returns to silence.

Crude speech "has a bearing upon the reality of things." "Narration, instruction, even description" give us the presence of things, "represent" them. The essential word moves them away, makes them disappear. It is always allusive; it suggests, evokes. But

From *The Space of Literature*, trans. Ann Smock (Lincoln, Nebr.: University of Nebraska Press, 1982), pp. 38–45.

what is it, then, to remove "a fact of nature," to grasp it through this absence, to "transpose it into its vibratory, almost-disappearance"? To speak, but also to think, essentially. Thought is the pure word. In thought we must recognize the supreme language, whose lack is all that the extreme variety of different tongues permits us to grasp. "Since to think is to write without appurtenances or whispers, but with the immortal word still tacit, the world's diversity of idioms keeps anyone from proffering expressions which otherwise would be, in one stroke, the truth itself materially." (This is Cratylus's ideal, but also the definition of automatic writing.) One is thus tempted to say that the language of thought is poetic language par excellence, and that sense – the pure notion, the idea – must become the poet's concern, since it alone frees us from the weight of things, the amorphous natural plenitude. "Poetry, close to the idea."

However, the crude word is by no means crude. What it represents is not present. Mallarmé does not want "to include, upon the subtle paper... the intrinsic and dense wood of trees." But nothing is more foreign to the tree than the word *tree*, as it is used nonetheless by everyday language. A word which does not name anything, which does not represent anything, which does not outlast itself in any way, a word which is not even a word and which disappears marvelously altogether and at once in its usage: what could be more worthy of the essential and closer to silence? True, it "serves." Apparently that makes all the difference. We are used to it, it is usual, useful. Through it we are in the world: it refers us back to the life of the world where goals speak and the concern to achieve them once and for all is the rule. Granted, this crude word is a pure nothing, nothingness itself. But it is nothingness in action: that which acts, labors, constructs. It is the pure silence of the negative which culminates in the noisy feverishness of tasks.

In this respect, the essential word is exactly the opposite. It is a rule unto itself; it is imposing, but it imposes nothing. It is also well removed from thought which always pushes back the elemental obscurity, for verse "attracts no less than it disengages," "polishes all the scattered ore, unknown and floating." In verse, words become "elements" again, and the word *nuit*, despite its brilliance, becomes night's intimacy.

In crude or immediate speech, language as language is silent. But beings speak in it. And, as a consequence of the *use* which is its purpose – because, that is, it serves primarily to put us in connection with objects, because it is a tool in a world of tools where what speaks is utility and value – beings speak in it as values. They take on the stable appearance of objects existing one by one and assume the certainty of the immutable.

The crude word is neither crude nor immediate. But it gives the illusion of being so. It is extremely reflective; it is laden with history. But, most often – and as if we were unable in the ordinary course of events to know that we are the organ of time, the guardians of becoming – language seems to be the locus of an immediately granted revelation. It seems to be the sign that truth is immediate, always the same and always at our disposal. Immediate language is perhaps in fact a relation with the immediate world, with what is immediately close to us, our environs. But the immediacy which common language communicates to us is only veiled distance, the absolutely foreign passing for the habitual, the unfamiliar which we take for the customary, thanks to the veil which is language and because we have grown accustomed to words' illusion.

Language has within itself the moment that hides it. It has within itself, through this power to hide itself, the force by which mediation (that which destroys immediacy) seems to have the spontaneity, the freshness, and the innocence of the origin. Moreover, this power, which language exercises by communicating to us the illusion of immediacy when in fact it gives us only the habitual, makes us believe that the immediate is familiar; and thus language's power consists in making the immediate appear to us not as the most terrible thing, which ought to overwhelm us – the error of the essential solitude – but as the pleasant reassurance of natural harmonies or the familiarity of a native habitat.

In the language of the world, language as the being of language and as the language of being keeps still. Thanks to this silence, beings speak, and in it they also find oblivion and rest. When Mallarmé speaks of the essential language, part of the time he opposes it only to this ordinary language which gives us the reassuring illusion of an immediacy which is actually only the customary. At these junctures he takes up and attributes to literature the language of thought, that silent movement which affirms in man his decision not to be, to separate himself from being, and, by making this separation real, to build the world. This silence is the production and the expression of signification itself. But this language of thought is, all the same, "ordinary" language as well. It always refers us back to the world, sometimes showing it to us in the infinite qualities of a task and the risk of an undertaking, sometimes as a stable position where we are allowed to believe ourselves secure.

The poetic word, then, is no longer opposed only to ordinary language, but also to the language of thought. In poetry we are no longer referred back to the world, neither to the world as shelter nor to the world as goals. In this language the world recedes and goals cease; the world falls silent; beings with their preoccupations, their projects, their activity are no longer ultimately what speaks. Poetry expresses the fact that beings are quiet. But how does this happen? Beings fall silent, but then it is being that tends to speak and speech that wants to be. The poetic word is no longer someone's word. In it no one speaks, and what speaks is not anyone. It seems rather that the word alone declares itself. Then language takes on all of its importance. It becomes essential. Language speaks as the essential, and that is why the word entrusted to the poet can be called the essential word. This means primarily that words, having the initiative, are not obliged to serve to designate anything or give voice to anyone, but that they have their ends in themselves. From here on, it is not Mallarmé who speaks, but language which speaks itself: language as the work and the work as language.

From this perspective, we rediscover poetry as a powerful universe of words where relations, configurations, forces are affirmed through sound, figure, rhythmic mobility, in a unified and sovereignly autonomous space. Thus the poet produces a work of pure language, and language in this work is its return to its essence. He creates an object made of language just as the painter, rather than using colors to reproduce what is, seeks the point at which his colors produce being. Or again, the poet strives – as Rilke did during his Expressionist period, or as today perhaps Ponge does – to create the "poem-thing," which would be, so to speak, the language of mute being. He wants to make of the poem something which all by itself will be form, existence, and being: that is, the work.

We call this powerful linguistic construction – this structure calculated to exclude chance, which subsists by itself and rests upon itself – the work. And we call it being. But it is from this perspective neither one nor the other. It is a work, since it is constructed, composed, calculated; but in this sense it is a work like any work, like any object formed by professional intelligence and skillful know-how. It is not a work of art, a work which has art for its origin, through which art is lifted from time's absence where nothing is accomplished to the unique, dazzling affirmation of the beginning. Likewise, the poem, understood as an independent object sufficing to itself – an object made out of language and created for itself alone, a monad of words where nothing is reflected but the nature of words – is perhaps in this respect a reality, a particular being, having exceptional dignity and importance; but it is *a* being, and for this reason it is by no means close to being, to that which escapes all determination and every form of existence.

Mallarmé's experience proper

It seems that the specifically Mallarméan experience begins at the moment when he moves from consideration of the finished work which is always one particular poem or another, or a certain picture, to the concern through which the work becomes the search for its origin and wants to identify itself with its origin – "horrible vision of a pure work." Here lies Mallarmé's profundity; here lies the concern which, for Mallarmé, "the sole act of writing" encompasses. What is the work? What is language in the work? When Mallarmé asks himself, "Does something like Literature exist?," this question is literature itself. It is literature when literature has become concern for its own essence. Such a question cannot be relegated. What is the result of the fact that we have literature? What is implied about being if one states that "something like Literature exists"?

Mallarmé had the most profoundly tormented awareness of the particular nature of literary creation. The work of art reduces itself to being. That is its task: to be, to make present "those very words: *it is*... There lies all the mystery." But at the same time it cannot be said that the work belongs to being, that it exists. On the contrary, what must be said is that it never exists in the manner of a thing or a being in general. What must be said, in answer to our question, is that literature does not exist or again that if it takes place, it does so as something "not taking place in the form of any object that exists." Granted, language is present – "made evident" – in it: language is affirmed in literature with more authority than in any other form of human activity. But it is wholly realized in literature, which is to say that it has only the reality of the whole; it is all – and nothing else, always on the verge of passing from all to nothing. This passage is essential; it belongs to the essence of language because, precisely, nothing operates in words. Words, we know, have the power to make things disappear, to make them appear as things that have vanished. This appearance is only that of disappearance; this presence too returns to absence through the movement of wear and erosion which is the soul and the life of words, which draws light from their dimming, clarity from the dark. But words, having the power to make things "arise" at the heart of their absence – words which are masters of this absence – also have the power to disappear in it themselves, to absent themselves marvelously in the midst of the totality which they realize, which they proclaim as they annihilate themselves therein, which they accomplish eternally by destroying themselves there endlessly. This act of self-destruction is in every respect similar to the ever so strange event of suicide which, precisely, gives to the supreme instant of *Igitur* all its truth.

The central point

Such is the central point. Mallarmé always comes back to it as though he were returning to the intimacy of the risk to which the literary experience exposes us. This point is the one at which complete realization of language coincides with its disappearance. Everything is pronounced ("Nothing," as Mallarmé says, "will remain unproffered"); everything is word, yet the word is itself no longer anything but the appearance of what has disappeared – the imaginary, the incessant, and the interminable. This point is ambiguity itself.

On the one hand, in the work, it is what the work realizes, how it affirms itself, the place where the work must "allow no luminous evidence except of existing." In this sense, the central point is the presence of the work, and the work alone makes it present. But at the same time, this point is "the presence of Midnight," the point anterior to all starting points, from which nothing ever begins, the empty profundity of being's inertia, that region without issue and without reserve, in which the work, through the artist, becomes the concern, the endless search for its origin.

Yes, the center, the concentration of ambiguity. It is very true that only the work – if we come toward this point through the movement and strength of the work – only the accomplishment of the work makes it possible. Let us look again at the poem: what could be more real, more evident? And language itself is "luminous evidence" within it. This evidence, however, shows nothing, rests upon nothing; it is the ungraspable in action. There are neither terms nor moments. Where we think we have words, "a virtual trail of fires" shoots through us – a swiftness, a scintillating exaltation. A reciprocity: for what is not is revealed in this flight; what there isn't is reflected in the pure grace of reflections that do not reflect anything. Then, "everything becomes suspense, fragmentary disposition with alternations and oppositions." Then, just as the tremor of the unreal turned into language gleams only to go out, simultaneously the unfamiliar presence is affirmed of real things turned into pure absence, pure fiction: a glorious realm where "willed and solitary celebrations" shine forth their splendor. One would like to say that the poem, like the pendulum that marks the time of time's abolition in *Igitur*, oscillates marvelously between its presence as language and the absence of the things of the world. But this presence is itself oscillating perpetuity: oscillation between the successive unreality of terms that terminate nothing, and the total realization of this movement – language, that is, become the whole of language, where the power of departing from and coming back to nothing, affirmed in each word and annulled in all, realizes itself as a whole, "total rhythm," "with which, silence."

In the poem, language is never real at any of the moments through which it passes, for in the poem language is affirmed in its totality. Yet in this totality, where it constitutes its own essence and where it is essential, it is also supremely unreal. It is the total realization of this unreality, an absolute fiction which says "being" when, having "worn away," "used up" all existing things, having suspended all possible beings, it comes up against an indelible, irreducible residue. What is left? "Those very words, *it is*." Those words sustain all others by letting themselves be hidden by all the others, and hidden thus, they are the presence of all words, language's entire possibility held in reserve. But when all words cease ("the instant they shimmer and die in a swift bloom upon some transparency like ether's"), "those very words, *it is*," present themselves, "lightning moment," "dazzling burst of light."...

Chapter 44
Philip Larkin

Philip Larkin (1922–1985) was one of England's major poets in the period after the Second World War. His first book of poems, The North Ship, *published in 1945, was written under the spell of W. B. Yeats. Larkin later reacted against what he came to regard as its overly rhetorical style. As an antidote he published two novels,* Jill *(1946) and* Girl in Winter *(1947), both set amidst the constraints and deprivations of an English culture affected by war. Although Larkin planned to continue writing fiction, it was a book of poems,* The Less Deceived, *published in 1955, that firmly established his literary reputation. Larkin's earlier preoccupations with solitude, mortality, and the loss of hope were given voice in a poetry that had the power to transform negativity into lyric grace. Larkin's distinctive tone came out of his attunement to an English poetic tradition, notably the work of the Elizabethan lyric, but it was also created out of his incorporation of the work of his most powerful and immediate precursors, T. S. Eliot and W. H. Auden. Larkin published two further books of poetry in his lifetime,* Whitsun Weddings *in 1964 and* High Windows *in 1974. Both of these continued the style and the persona established in* The Less Deceived. *For much of his life Larkin worked as a librarian at the universities of Belfast, Leicester, and Hull.*

Larkin made a point of being an "anti-modernist" in literature, music, and art. Like Donald Davie, he was identified as part of the Movement group of poets in postwar Britain. Unlike Davie, Larkin could be assertively chauvinist in his tastes. He preferred John Betjeman to Ezra Pound and had no time for poetry in translation. As with other aspects of Larkin's public personality, these assertions can be deceptive. A reading of his poetry shows how much he learned from the work of the French symbolists as well as Eliot and Auden. The two pieces that follow show Larkin's distaste for what he regarded as gratuitous modernist complexity, although the title of the first is effectively a quotation from Freud, one of the great modernist complicators. "The Pleasure Principle" was first published in 1957 in Listen 11: New Fiction. *It rehearses a basically Wordsworthian account of the poetic process and deplores the modern academy's creation of a conspiracy between poet, critic, and reader, one that has alienated the traditional audience for poetry. The second piece, "Writing Poems," was first published in 1964 in the* Poetry Book Society

Bulletin. *It begins in a characteristically deadpan fashion, but goes on to qualify the account of poetic composition given in* The Pleasure Principle *and discusses the role of the will in the making of poetry.*

The Pleasure Principle

It is sometimes useful to remind ourselves of the simpler aspects of things normally regarded as complicated. Take, for instance, the writing of a poem. It consists of three stages: the first is when a man becomes obsessed with an emotional concept to such a degree that he is compelled to do something about it. What he does is the second stage, namely, construct a verbal device that will reproduce this emotional concept in anyone who cares to read it, anywhere, any time. The third stage is the recurrent situation of people in different times and places setting off the device and re-creating in themselves what the poet felt when he wrote it. The stages are interdependent and all necessary. If there has been no preliminary feeling, the device has nothing to reproduce and the reader will experience nothing. If the second stage has not been well done, the device will not deliver the goods, or will deliver only a few goods to a few people, or will stop delivering them after an absurdly short while. And if there is no third stage, no successful reading, the poem can hardly be said to exist in a practical sense at all.

What a description of this basic tripartite structure shows is that poetry is emotional in nature and theatrical in operation, a skilled re-creation of emotion in other people, and that, conversely, a bad poem is one that never succeeds in doing this. All modes of critical derogation are no more than different ways of saying this, whatever literary, philosophical or moral terminology they employ, and it would not be necessary to point out anything so obvious if present-day poetry did not suggest that it had been forgotten. We seem to be producing a new kind of bad poetry, not the old kind that tries to move the reader and fails, but one that does not even try. Repeatedly he is confronted with pieces that cannot be understood without reference beyond their own limits or whose contented insipidity argues that their authors are merely reminding themselves of what they know already, rather than re-creating it for a third party. The reader, in fact, seems no longer present in the poet's mind as he used to be, as someone who must understand and enjoy the finished product if it is to be a success at all; the assumption now is that no one will read it, and wouldn't understand or enjoy it if they did. Why should this be so? It is not sufficient to say that poetry has lost its audience, and so need no longer consider it: lots of people still read and even buy poetry. More accurately, poetry has lost its old audience, and gained a new one. This has been caused by the consequences of a cunning merger between poet, literary critic and academic critic (three classes now notoriously indistinguishable): it is hardly an exaggeration to say that the poet has gained the happy position wherein he can praise his own poetry in the press and explain it in the class-room, and the reader has been bullied into giving up the consumer's power to say 'I don't like this, bring me something different.' Let

From *Required Writing* (London: Faber and Faber, 1983), pp. 80–4.

him now so much as breathe a word about not liking a poem, and he is in the dock before he can say Edwin Arlington Robinson. And the charge is a grave one: flabby sensibility, insufficient or inadequate critical tools, and inability to meet new verbal and emotional situations. Verdict: guilty, plus a few riders on the prisoner's mental upbringing, addiction to mass amusements, and enfeebled responses. It is time some of you playboys realized, says the judge, that reading a poem is hard work. Fourteen days in stir. Next case.

The cash customers of poetry, therefore, who used to put down their money in the sure and certain hope of enjoyment as if at a theatre or concert hall, were quick to move elsewhere. Poetry was no longer a pleasure. They have been replaced by a humbler squad, whose aim is not pleasure but self-improvement, and who have uncritically accepted the contention that they cannot appreciate poetry without preliminary investment in the intellectual equipment which, by the merest chance, their tutor happens to have about him. In short, the modern poetic audience, when it is not taking in its own washing, is a *student* audience, pure and simple. At first sight this may not seem a bad thing. The poet has at last a moral ascendancy, and his new clientele not only pay for the poetry but pay to have it explained afterwards. Again, if the poet has only himself to please, he is no longer handicapped by the limitations of his audience. And in any case nobody nowadays believes that a worthwhile artist can rely on anything but his own judgement: public taste is always twenty-five years behind, and picks up a style only when it is exploited by the second-rate. All this is true enough. But at bottom poetry, like all art, is inextricably bound up with giving pleasure, and if a poet loses his pleasure-seeking audience he has lost the only audience worth having, for which the dutiful mob that signs on every September is no substitute. And the effect will be felt throughout his work. He will forget that even if he finds what he has to say interesting, others may not. He will concentrate on moral worth or semantic intricacy. Worst of all, his poems will no longer be born of the tension between what he non-verbally feels and what can be got over in common word-usage to someone who hasn't had his experience or education or travel grant, and once the other end of the rope is dropped what results will not be so much obscure or piffling (though it may be both) as an unrealized, "undramatized" slackness, because he will have lost the habit of testing what he writes by this particular standard. Hence, no pleasure. Hence, no poetry.

What can be done about this? Who wants anything done about it? Certainly not the poet, who is in the unprecedented position of peddling both his work and the standard by which it is judged. Certainly not the new reader, who, like a partner of some unconsummated marriage, has no idea of anything better. Certainly not the old reader, who has simply replaced one pleasure with another. Only the romantic loiterer who recalls the days when poetry was condemned as sinful might wish things different. But if the medium is in fact to be rescued from among our duties and restored to our pleasures, I can only think that a large-scale revulsion has got to set in against present notions, and that it will have to start with poetry readers asking themselves more frequently whether they do in fact enjoy what they read, and, if not, what the point is of carrying on. And I use 'enjoy' in the commonest of senses, the sense in which we leave a radio on or off. Those interested might like to read David Daiches's essay 'The New

Criticism: Some Qualifications' (in *Literary Essays*, 1956); in the meantime, the following note by Samuel Butler may reawaken a furtive itch for freedom: 'I should like to like Schumann's music better than I do; I dare say I could make myself like it better if I tried; but I do not like having to try to make myself like things; I like things that make me like them at once and no trying at all' (*Notebooks*, 1919).

Writing Poems

It would, perhaps, be fitting for me to return the heartening compliment paid by the Selectors to *The Whitsun Weddings* with a detailed annotation of its contents. Unfortunately, however, once I have said that the poems were written in or near Hull, Yorkshire, with a succession of Royal Sovereign 2B pencils during the years 1955 to 1963, there seems little to add. I think in every instance the effect I was trying to get is clear enough. If sometimes I have failed, no marginal annotation will help now. Henceforth the poems belong to their readers, who will in due course pass judgement by either forgetting or remembering them.

If something must be said, it should be about the poems one writes not necessarily being the poems one wants to write. Some years ago I came to the conclusion that to write a poem was to construct a verbal device that would preserve an experience indefinitely by reproducing it in whoever read the poem. As a working definition, this satisfied me sufficiently to enable individual poems to be written. In so far as it suggested that all one had to do was pick an experience and preserve it, however, it was much oversimplified. Nowadays nobody believes in 'poetic' subjects, any more than they believe in poetic diction. The longer one goes on, though, the more one feels that some subjects *are* more poetic than others, if only that poems about them get written whereas poems about other subjects don't. At first one tries to write poems about everything. Later on, one learns to distinguish somewhat, though one can still make enormously time-wasting mistakes. The fact is that my working definition defines very little: it makes no reference to this necessary element of distinction, and it leaves the precise nature of the verbal pickling unexplained.

This means that most of the time one is engaged in doing, or trying to do, something of which the value is doubtful and the mode of operation unclear. Can one feel entirely happy about this? The days when one could claim to be the priest of a mystery are gone: today mystery means either ignorance or hokum, neither fashionable qualities. Yet writing a poem is still not an act of the will. The distinction between subjects is not an act of the will. Whatever makes a poem successful is not an act of the will. In consequence, the poems that actually get written may seem trivial or unedifying, compared with those that don't. But the poems that get written, even if they do not please the will, evidently please that mysterious something that has to be pleased.

This is not to say that one is forever writing poems of which the will disapproves. What it does mean, however, is that there must be among the ingredients that go towards the writing of a poem a streak of curious self-gratification, almost impossible to describe except in some such terms, the presence of which tends to nullify any satisfaction the will might be feeling at a finished job. Without this element of self-interest, the theme, however worthy, can drift away and be forgotten. The situation is full of ambiguities. To write a poem is a pleasure: sometimes I deliberately let it compete in the open market, so to speak, with other spare-time activities, ostensibly on the grounds that if a poem isn't more entertaining to write than listening to records or going out it won't be entertaining to read. Yet doesn't this perhaps conceal a subconscious objection to writing? After all, how many of our pleasures really bear thinking about? Or is it just concealed laziness?

Whether one worries about this depends, really, on whether one is more interested in writing or in finding how poems are written. If the former, then such considerations become just another technical difficulty, like noisy neighbours or one's own character, parallel to a clergyman's doubts: one has to go on in spite of them. I suppose in raising them one is seeking some justification in the finished product for the sacrifices made on its behalf. Since it is the will that is the seeker, satisfaction is unlikely to be forthcoming. The only consolation in the whole business, as in just about every other, is that in all probability there was really no choice.

Chapter 45
Theodor Adorno

Theodor Weisgrund Adorno (1903–69) was a philosopher, cultural theorist, and leading member of the Frankfurt School of critical theory. Adorno's thinking about art and culture was deeply affected by the rise of fascism, not least because it posed a central question for him about the sources and the attractions of authoritarianism in modern culture. One answer to the question came in one of his best known works, The Dialectic of Enlightenment, *co-authored with his colleague, Max Horkheimer. They argued that, from a standpoint in the mid-twentieth century, the form of reason associated with the Enlightenment and social progress came at a heavy price. Reason had become instrumental, a force of domination rather than a means of achieving freedom. Modern societies were governed by a mode of thinking that was unreflective, that ignored the specific characteristics of what it sought to understand, and denied reality or value to whatever was deemed irrational. The result was the creation of "total" or "administered" societies that left no room for sensuous or instinctual life. One further result was a division between the mimetic languages of art and literature and the conceptual languages of science.*

Elements of this gloomy diagnosis are evident in "On Lyric Poetry and Society," first given as a lecture and subsequently published by Adorno in the German journal, Akzente, *in 1957. But so are the more affirmative aspects of his thought. In the following excerpt Adorno argues that the lyric poem is the central kind of modern poetry; that as a modern form its history goes back to the mid-eighteenth century, roughly coterminous with the rise of bourgeois societies and capitalism; that lyric form bears the imprint of instrumental reason insofar as it implies a world in which human beings are treated as things; that lyric language is both affective and conceptual; and that it contains a utopian moment, evoking "an image of life free from the coercion of reigning practice." However, the poetic mediation at the heart of the lyric poem, one that brings the expression of individual feeling into relation with the "voice of humankind," may no longer be possible.*

On Lyric Poetry and Society

The announcement of a lecture on lyric poetry and society will make many of you uncomfortable. You will expect a sociological analysis of the kind that can be made of any object, just as fifty years ago people came up with psychologies, and thirty years ago with phenomenologies, of everything conceivable. You will suspect that examination of the conditions under which works are created and their effect will try to usurp the place of experience of the works as they are and that the process of categorizing and relating will suppress insight into the truth or falsity of the object itself. You will suspect that an intellectual will be guilty of what Hegel accused the "formal understanding" of doing, namely that in surveying the whole it stands above the individual existence it is talking about, that is, it does not see it at all but only labels it. This approach will seem especially distressing to you in the case of lyric poetry. The most delicate, the most fragile thing that exists is to be encroached upon and brought into conjunction with bustle and commotion, when part of the ideal of lyric poetry, at least in its traditional sense, is to remain unaffected by bustle and commotion. A sphere of expression whose very essence lies in either not acknowledging the power of socialization or overcoming it through the pathos of detachment, as in Baudelaire or Nietzsche, is to be arrogantly turned into the opposite of what it conceives itself to be through the way it is examined. Can anyone, you will ask, but a man who is insensitive to the Muse talk about lyric poetry and society?

Clearly your suspicions will be allayed only if lyric works are not abused by being made objects with which to demonstrate sociological theses but if instead the social element in them is shown to reveal something essential about the basis of their quality. This relationship should lead not away from the work of art but deeper into it. But the most elementary reflection shows that this is to be expected. For the substance of a poem is not merely an expression of individual impulses and experiences. Those become a matter of art only when they come to participate in something universal by virtue of the specificity they acquire in being given aesthetic form. Not that what the lyric poem expresses must be immediately equivalent to what everyone experiences. Its universality is no *volonté de tous*, not the universality of simply communicating what others are unable to communicate. Rather, immersion in what has taken individual form elevates the lyric poem to the status of something universal by making manifest something not distorted, not grasped, not yet subsumed. It thereby anticipates, spiritually, a situation in which no false universality, that is, nothing profoundly particular, continues to fetter what is other than itself, the human. The lyric work hopes to attain universality through unrestrained individuation. The danger peculiar to the lyric, however, lies in the fact that its principle of individuation never guarantees that something binding and authentic will be produced. It has no say over whether the poem remains within the contingency of mere separate existence.

The universality of the lyric's substance, however, is social in nature. Only one who hears the voice of humankind in the poem's solitude can understand what the poem is saying; indeed, even the solitariness of lyrical language itself is prescribed by an

From *Notes on Literature*, vol. 1, ed. Rolf Tiedmann, trans. Shierry Weber Nicholsen (New York: Columbia University Press, 1991), pp. 37–46.

individualistic and ultimately atomistic society, just as conversely its general cogency depends on the intensity of its individuation. For that reason, however, reflection on the work of art is justified in inquiring, and obligated to inquire concretely into its social content and not content itself with a vague feeling of something universal and inclusive. This kind of specification through thought is not some external reflection alien to art; on the contrary, all linguistic works of art demand it. The material proper to them, concepts, does not exhaust itself in mere contemplation. In order to be susceptible of aesthetic contemplation, works of art must always be thought through as well, and once thought has been called into play by the poem it does not let itself be stopped at the poem's behest.

Such thought, however – the social interpretation of lyric poetry as of all works of art – may not focus directly on the so-called social perspective or the social interests of the works or their authors. Instead, it must discover how the entirety of a society, conceived as an internally contradictory unity, is manifested in the work of art, in what way the work of art remains subject to society and in what way it transcends it. In philosophical terms, the approach must be an immanent one. Social concepts should not be applied to the works from without but rather drawn from an exacting examination of the works themselves. Goethe's statement in his *Maxims and Reflections* that what you do not understand you do not possess holds not only for the aesthetic attitude to works of art but for aesthetic theory as well; nothing that is not in the works, not part of their own form, can legitimate a determination of what their substance, that which has entered into their poetry, represents in social terms. To determine that, of course, requires both knowledge of the interior of the works of art and knowledge of the society outside. But this knowledge is binding only if it is rediscovered through complete submission to the matter at hand. Special vigilance is required when it comes to the concept of ideology, which these days is belabored to the point of intolerability. For ideology is untruth, false consciousness, deceit. It manifests itself in the failure of works of art, in their inherent falseness, and it is countered by criticism. To repeat mechanically, however, that great works of art, whose essence consists in giving form to the crucial contradictions in real existence, and only in that sense in a tendency to reconcile them, are ideology, not only does an injustice to their truth content but also misrepresents the concept of ideology. That concept does not maintain that all spirit serves only for some human beings to falsely present some particular values as general ones; rather, it is intended to unmask spirit that is specifically false and at the same time to grasp it in its necessity. The greatness of works of art, however, consists solely in the fact that they give voice to what ideology hides. Their very success moves beyond false consciousness, whether intentionally or not.

Let me take your own misgivings as a starting point. You experience lyric poetry as something opposed to society, something wholly individual. Your feelings insist that it remain so, that lyric expression, having escaped from the weight of material existence, evoke the image of a life free from the coercion of reigning practices, of utility, of the relentless pressures of self-preservation. This demand, however, the demand that the lyric word be virginal, is itself social in nature. It implies a protest against a social situation that every individual experiences as hostile, alien, cold, oppressive, and this situation is imprinted in reverse on the poetic work: the more heavily the situation weighs upon it, the more firmly the work resists it by refusing to submit to anything heteronomous and constituting itself solely in accordance with its own laws. The work's distance from mere existence becomes the measure of what is false and bad in the latter. In its protest the poem expresses the dream of a world in which things would be different. The lyric spirit's idiosyncratic opposition to the superior power of material things is a form of reaction to the reification of the world, to the domination of human beings by commodities that has developed since the beginning of the modern era, since the industrial revolution became the dominant force in life. Rilke's cult of the thing [as in his *Dinggedichte* or "thing poems"] is part of this idiosyncratic opposition; it attempts to assimilate even alien objects to pure subjective expression and to dissolve them, to give them metaphysical credit for their alienness. The aesthetic weakness of this cult of the thing, its obscurantist demeanor and its blending of religion with arts and crafts, reveals the real power of reification, which can no longer be gilded with a lyrical halo and brought back within the sphere of meaning.

To say that the concept of lyric poetry that is in some sense second nature to us is a completely modern one is only to express this insight into the social nature of the lyric in different form. Analogously, landscape painting and its idea of "nature" have had an autonomous development only in the modern period. I know that I exaggerate in saying this, that you could adduce many counterexamples. The most compelling would be Sappho. I will not discuss the Chinese, Japanese, and Arabic lyric, since I cannot read them in the original and I suspect that translation involves them in an adaptive mechanism that makes adequate understanding completely impossible. But the manifestations in earlier periods of the specifically lyric spirit familiar to us are only isolated flashes, just as the backgrounds in older painting occasionally anticipate the idea of landscape painting. They do not establish it as a form. The great poets of the distant past – Pindar and Alcaeus, for instance, but the greater part of Walther von der Vogelweide's work as well – whom literary history classifies as lyric poets are uncommonly far from our primary conception of the lyric. They lack the quality of immediacy, of immateriality, which we are accustomed, rightly or not, to consider the criterion of the lyric and which we transcend only through rigorous education.

Until we have either broadened it historically or turned it critically against the sphere of individualism, however, our conception of lyric poetry has a moment of discontinuity in it – all the more so, the more pure it claims to be. The "I" whose voice is heard in the lyric is an "I" that defines and expresses itself as something opposed to the collective, to objectivity; it is not immediately at one with the nature to which its expression refers. It has lost it, as it were, and attempts to restore it through animation, through immersion in the "I" itself. It is only through humanization that nature is to be restored the rights that human domination took from it. Even lyric works in which no trace of conventional and concrete existence, no crude materiality remains, the greatest lyric works in our language, owe their quality to the force with which the "I" creates the illusion of nature emerging from alienation. Their pure subjectivity, the aspect of them that appears seamless and harmonious, bears witness to its opposite, to suffering in an existence alien to the subject and to love for it as well – indeed, their harmoniousness is actually nothing but the mutual accord of this suffering and this love. Even the line from Goethe's "Wanderers Nachtlied" ["Wanderer's Night-Song"], "Warte nur, balde / ruhest du auch" ["Only wait, soon / you too shall rest"] has an air of consolation: its unfathomable beauty cannot be separated from something it makes no reference to, the notion of a world that withholds peace. Only in resonating with sadness about that withholding does the poem maintain that there is peace nevertheless. One is tempted to use the line "Ach, ich bin des Treibens müde" ["I am weary of restless activity"] from the companion poem of the same title to interpret the "Wanderers Nachtlied." To be sure, the greatness of the latter poem derives from the fact that it does not speak about what is alienated and disturbing, from the fact that within the poem the restlessness of the object is not opposed to the subject; instead, the subject's own restlessness echoes it. A second immediacy is promised: what is human, language itself, seems to become creation again, while everything external dies away in the echo of the soul. This becomes more than an illusion, however; it becomes full truth, because through the expression in language of a good kind of tiredness, the shadow of yearning and even of death continues to fall across the reconciliation. In the line "Warte nur, balde" the whole of life, with an enigmatic smile of sorrow, turns into the brief moment before one falls asleep. The note of peacefulness attests to the fact that peace cannot be achieved without the dream disintegrating. The shadow has no power over the image of life come back into its own, but as a last reminder of life's deformation it gives the dream its profound depths beneath the surface of the song. In the face of nature at rest, a nature from which all traces of anything resembling the human have been eradicated, the subject becomes aware of its own insignificance. Imperceptibly, silently, irony tinges the poem's consolation: the seconds before the bliss of sleep are the same seconds that separate our brief life from death. After Goethe, this sublime irony became a debased and spiteful irony. But it was always bourgeois: the shadow-side of the elevation of the liberated subject is its degradation to something exchangeable, to something that exists merely for something else; the shadow-side of personality is the "So who are you?" The authenticity of the "Nachtlied," however, lies in its moment in time: the background of that destructive force removes it from the sphere of play, while the destructive force has no power over the peaceable power of consolation. It is commonly said that a perfect lyric poem must possess totality or universality, must provide the whole within the bounds of the poem and the infinite within the poem's finitude. If that is to be more than a platitude of an aesthetics that is always ready to use the concept of the symbolic as a panacea, it indicates that in every lyric poem the historical relationship of the subject to objectivity, of the individual to society, must have found its precipitate in the medium of a subjective spirit thrown back upon itself. The less the work thematizes the relationship of "I" and society, the more spontaneously it crystallizes of its own accord in the poem, the more complete this process of precipitation will be.

You may accuse me of so sublimating the relationship of lyric and society in this definition out of fear of a crude sociologism that there is really nothing left of it; it is precisely what is not social in the lyric poem that is now to become its social aspect. You could call my attention to Gustav Doré's caricature of the arch-reactionary deputy whose praise of the *ancien régime* culminated in the exclamation, "And to whom, gentlemen, do we owe the revolution of 1789 if not to Louis XVI!" You could apply that to my view of lyric poetry and society: in my view, you could say, society plays the role of the executed king and the lyric the role of his opponents; but lyric poetry, you say, can no more be explained on the basis of society than the revolution can be made the achievement of the monarch it deposed and without whose inanities it might not have occurred at that time. We will leave it an open question whether Doré's deputy was truly only the stupid, cynical propagandist the artist derided him for being or whether there might be more truth in his unintentional joke than common sense admits; Hegel's philosophy of history would have a lot to say in his defense. In any case, the comparison does not really work. I am not trying to deduce lyric poetry from society; its social substance is precisely what is spontaneous in it, what does not simply follow from the existing conditions at the time. But philosophy – Hegel's again – is familiar with the speculative proposition that the individual is mediated by the universal and vice versa. That means that even resistance to social pressure is not something absolutely individual; the artistic forces in that resistance, which operate in and through the individual and his spontaneity, are objective forces that impel a constricted and constricting social condition to transcend itself and become worthy of human beings; forces, that is, that are part of the constitution of the whole and not at all merely forces of a rigid individuality blindly opposing society. If, by virtue of its own subjectivity, the substance of the lyric can in fact be addressed as an objective substance – and otherwise one could not explain the very simple fact that grounds the possibility of the lyric as an artistic genre, its effect on people other than the poet speaking his monologue – then it is only because the lyric work of art's withdrawal into itself, its self-absorption, its detachment from the social surface, is socially motivated behind the author's back. But the medium of this is language. The paradox specific to the lyric work, a subjectivity that turns into objectivity, is tied to the priority of linguistic form in the lyric; it is that priority from which the primacy of language in literature in general (even in prose forms) is derived. For language is itself something double. Through its configurations it assimilates itself completely into subjective impulses; one would almost think it had produced them. But at the same time language remains the medium of concepts, remains that which establishes an inescapable relationship to the universal and to society. Hence the highest lyric works are those in which the subject, with no remaining trace of mere matter, sounds forth in language until language itself acquires a voice. The unself-consciousness of the subject submitting itself to language as to something objective, and the immediacy and spontaneity of that subject's expression are one and the same: thus language mediates lyric poetry and society in their innermost core. This is why the lyric reveals itself to be most deeply grounded in society when it does not chime in with society, when it communicates nothing, when, instead, the subject whose expression is successful reaches an accord with language itself, with the inherent tendency of language.

On the other hand, however, language should also not be absolutized as the voice of Being as opposed to the lyric subject, as many of the current ontological theories of language would have it. The subject, whose expression – as opposed to mere signification of objective contents – is necessary to attain to that level of linguistic objectivity, is not something added to the contents proper to that layer, not something external to it. The moment of unself-consciousness in which the subject submerges itself in language is not a sacrifice of the subject to Being. It is a moment not of violence, nor of violence against the subject, but reconciliation: language itself speaks only when it speaks not as something alien to the subject but as the subject's own voice. When the "I" becomes oblivious to itself in language it is fully present nevertheless; if it were not, language would become a consecrated abracadabra and succumb to reification, as it does in communicative discourse. But that brings us back to the actual relationship between the individual and society. It is not only that the individual is inherently socially mediated, not only that its contents are always social as well. Conversely, society is formed and continues to live only by virtue of the individuals whose quintessence it is. Classical philosophy once formulated a truth now disdained by scientific logic: subject and object are not rigid and isolated poles but can be defined only in the process in which they distinguish themselves from one another and change. The lyric is the aesthetic test of that dialectical philosophical proposition. In the lyric poem the subject, through its identification with language, negates both its opposition to society as something merely monadological and its mere functioning within a wholly socialized society [*vergesellschaftete Gesellschaft*]. But the more the latter's ascendancy over the subject increases, the more precarious the situation of the lyric becomes. Baudelaire's work was the first to record this; his work, the ultimate consequence of European *Weltschmerz*, did not stop with the sufferings of the individual but chose the modern itself, as the antilyrical pure and simple, for its theme and struck a poetic spark in it by dint of a heroically stylized language. In Baudelaire a note of despair already makes itself felt, a note that barely maintains its balance on the tip of its own paradoxicalness. As the contradiction between poetic and communicative language reached an extreme, lyric poetry became a game in which one goes for broke; not, as philistine opinion would have it, because it had become incomprehensible but because in acquiring self-consciousness as a literary language, in striving for an absolute objectivity unrestricted by any considerations of communication, language both distances itself from the objectivity of spirit, of living language, and substitutes a poetic event for a language that is no longer present. The elevated, poeticizing, subjectively violent moment in weak later lyric poetry is the price it has to pay for its attempt to keep itself undisfigured, immaculate, objective; its false glitter is the complement to the disenchanted world from which it extricates itself.

Everything I have said needs to be qualified if it is to avoid misinterpretation. My thesis is that the lyric work is always the subjective expression of a social antagonism. But since the objective world that produces the lyric is an inherently antagonistic world, the concept of the lyric is not simply that of the expression of a subjectivity to which language grants objectivity. Not only does the lyric subject embody the whole all the more cogently, the more it expresses itself; in addition, poetic subjectivity is itself indebted to privilege: the pressures of the struggle for survival allow only a few human beings to grasp the universal through immersion in the self or to develop as autonomous subjects capable of freely expressing themselves. The others, however, those who not only stand alienated, as though they were objects, facing the disconcerted poetic subject but who have also literally been degraded to objects of history, have the same right, or a greater right, to grope for the sounds in which sufferings and dreams are welded. This inalienable right has asserted itself again and again, in forms however impure, mutilated, fragmentary, and intermittent – the only forms possible for those who have to bear the burden.

A collective undercurrent provides the foundation for all individual lyric poetry. When that poetry actually bears the whole in mind and is not simply an expression of the privilege, refinement, and gentility of those who can afford to be gentle, participation in this undercurrent is an essential part of the substantiality of the individual lyric as well: it is this undercurrent that makes language the medium in which the subject becomes more than a mere subject. Romanticism's link to the folksong is only the most obvious, certainly not the most compelling example of this. For Romanticism practices a kind of programmatic transfusion of the collective into the individual through which the individual lyric poem indulged in a technical illusion of universal cogency without that cogency characterizing it inherently. Often, in contrast, poets who abjure any borrowing from the collective language participate in that collective undercurrent by virtue of their historical experience. Let me mention Baudelaire again, whose lyric poetry is a slap in the face not only to the *juste milieu* but also to all bourgeois social sentiment, and who nevertheless, in poems like the "Petites vieilles" or the poem about the servant woman with the generous heart in the *Tableaux Parisiens*, was truer to the masses toward whom he turned his tragic, arrogant mask than any "poor people's" poetry. Today, when individual expression, which is the precondition for the conception of lyric poetry that is my point of departure, seems shaken to its very core in the crisis of the individual, the collective undercurrent in the lyric surfaces in the most diverse places: first merely as the ferment of individual expression and then perhaps also as an anticipation of a situation that transcends mere individuality in a positive way. If the translations can be trusted, García Lorca, whom Franco's henchmen murdered and whom no totalitarian regime could have tolerated, was the bearer of a force of this kind; and Brecht's name comes to mind as a lyric poet who was granted linguistic integrity without having to pay the price of esotericism. I will forgo making a judgment about whether the poetic principle of individuation was in fact sublated to a higher level here, or whether its basis lies in regression, a weakening of the ego. The collective power of contemporary lyric poetry may be largely due to the linguistic and psychic residues of a condition that is not yet fully individuated, a state of affairs that is prebourgeois in the broadest sense – dialect. Until now, however, the traditional lyric, as the most rigorous aesthetic negation of bourgeois convention, has by that very token been tied to bourgeois society. . . .

Chapter 46
Roman Jakobson

Roman Jakobson (1896–1982) was a linguistician, literary theorist, and scholar whose work has had an impact on a wide range of disciplines. From an early stage in his career, technical studies in linguistics combined with a profound interest in poetry. At the same time as he was a member of the Moscow Linguistics Circle he encountered the work of Mayakovsky and Khlebnikov. Their experiments in poetry were as important to his thinking about language as studies in phonology and semantics. By 1926 he had joined the Prague Linguistics Circle (form and function). With the rise of fascism Jakobson had to leave Europe for the United States where he met the French anthropologist, Claude Lévi-Strauss. Their intellectual collaboration produced some classic examples of the structural analysis of poetry, notably their work on Baudelaire's poem, Les Chats.

"Closing Statement: Linguistics and Poetics" was first given as a talk at a conference on style in language held at the University of Indiana in 1958, and then published in 1960 in the book that took its title from the conference, edited by Thomas Seboek. In the following extracts, Jakobson identifies what is for him the central question of poetics – what makes a verbal message into a work of art – and provides an answer by identifying the poetic as a form of language whose function can only be understood in the context of a general theory of communication. Moving between an analysis of the poetic function at work in all language and discussions of poetry as a literary genre, Jakobson established a method for understanding the distinctive complexity of the "poetic sign" and a powerful technique for the close analysis of poetry.

Closing Statement: Linguistics and Poetics

...I have been asked for summary remarks about poetics in its relation to linguistics. Poetics deals primarily with the question, *What makes a verbal message a work of art?*

From *Style in Language*, ed. Thomas A. Seboek (Cambridge, Mass.: MIT Press, 1960), pp. 350–4, 355–6, 357–9, 368–9, 370–1.

Because the main subject of poetics is the *differentia specifica* of verbal art in relation to other arts and in relation to other kinds of verbal behavior, poetics is entitled to the leading place in literary studies.

Poetics deals with problems of verbal structure, just as the analysis of painting is concerned with pictorial structure. Since linguistics is the global science of verbal structure, poetics may be regarded as an integral part of linguistics.

Arguments against such a claim must be thoroughly discussed. It is evident that many devices studied by poetics are not confined to verbal art. We can refer to the possibility of transposing *Wuthering Heights* into a motion picture, medieval legends into frescoes and miniatures, or *L'après-midi d'un faune* into music, ballet, and graphic art. However ludicrous may appear the idea of the *Iliad* and *Odyssey* in comics, certain structural features of their plot are preserved despite the disappearance of their verbal shape. The question whether Blake's illustrations to the *Divina Commedia* are or are not adequate is a proof that different arts are comparable. The problems of baroque or any other historical style transgress the frame of a single art. When handling the surrealistic metaphor, we could hardly pass by Max Ernst's pictures or Luis Buñuel's films, *An Andalusian Dog* and *The Golden Age*. In short, many poetic features belong not only to the science of language but to the whole theory of signs, that is, to general semiotics. This statement, however, is valid not only for verbal art but also for all varieties of language since language shares many properties with some other systems of signs or even with all of them (pansemiotic features).

Likewise a second objection contains nothing that would be specific for literature: the question of relations between the word and the world concerns not only verbal art but actually all kinds of discourse. Linguistics is likely to explore all possible problems of relation between discourse and the "universe of discourse": what of this universe is verbalized by a given discourse and how is it verbalized. The truth values, however, as far as they are – to say with the logicians – "extralinguistic entities," obviously exceed the bounds of poetics and of linguistics in general.

Sometimes we hear that poetics, in contradistinction to linguistics, is concerned with evaluation. This separation of the two fields from each other is based on a current but erroneous interpretation of the contrast between the structure of poetry and other types of verbal structure: the latter are said to be opposed by their "casual," designless nature to the "noncasual," purposeful character of poetic language. In point of fact, any verbal behavior is goal-directed, but the aims are different and the conformity of the means used to the effect aimed at is a problem that evermore preoccupies inquirers into the diverse kinds of verbal communication. There is a close correspondence, much closer than critics believe, between the question of linguistic phenomena expanding in space and time and the spatial and temporal spread of literary models. Even such discontinuous expansion as the resurrection of neglected or forgotten poets – for instance, the posthumous discovery and subsequent canonization of Gerard Manley Hopkins (d. 1889), the tardy fame of Lautréamont (d. 1870) among surrealist poets, and the salient influence of the hitherto ignored Cyprian Norwid (d. 1883) on Polish modern poetry – find a parallel in the history of standard languages which are prone to revive outdated models, sometimes long forgotten, as was the case in literary Czech which toward the beginning of the nineteenth century leaned to sixteenth-century models.

Unfortunately the terminological confusion of "literary studies" with "criticism" tempts the student of literature to replace the description of the intrinsic values of a literary work by a subjective, censorious verdict. The label "literary critic" applied to an investigator of literature is as erroneous as "grammatical (or lexical) critic" would be applied to a linguist. Syntactic and morphologic research cannot be supplanted by a normative grammar, and likewise no manifesto, foisting a critic's own tastes and opinions on creative literature, may act as substitute for an objective scholarly analysis of verbal art. This statement is not to be mistaken for the quietist principle of *laissez faire*; any verbal culture involves programmatic, planning, normative endeavors. Yet why is a clear-cut discrimination made between pure and applied linguistics or between phonetics and orthoëpy but not between literary studies and criticism?

Literary studies, with poetics as their focal portion, consist like linguistics of two sets of problems: synchrony and diachrony. The synchronic description envisages not only the literary production of any given stage but also that part of the literary tradition which for the stage in question has remained vital or has been revived. Thus, for instance, Shakespeare on the one hand and Donne, Marvell, Keats, and Emily Dickinson on the other are experienced by the present English poetic world, whereas the works of James Thomson and Longfellow, for the time being, do not belong to viable artistic values. The selection of classics and their reinterpretation by a novel trend is a substantial problem of synchronic literary studies. Synchronic poetics, like synchronic linguistics, is not to be confused with statistics; any stage discriminates between more conservative and more innovatory forms. Any contemporary stage is experienced in its temporal dynamics, and, on the other hand, the historical approach both in poetics and in linguistics is concerned not only with changes but also with continuous, enduring, static factors. A thoroughly comprehensive historical poetics or history of language is a superstructure to be built on a series of successive synchronic descriptions.

Insistence on keeping poetics apart from linguistics is warranted only when the field of linguistics appears to be illicitly restricted, for example, when the sentence is viewed by some linguists as the highest analyzable construction or when the scope of linguistics is confined to grammar alone or uniquely to nonsemantic questions of external form or to the inventory of denotative devices with no reference to free variations. Voegelin has clearly pointed out the two most important and related problems which face structural linguistics, namely, a revision of "the monolithic hypothesis of language" and a concern with "the interdependence of diverse structures within one language." No doubt, for any speech community, for any speaker, there exists a unity of language, but this over-all code represents a system of interconnected subcodes; each language encompasses several concurrent patterns which are each characterized by a different function.

Obviously we must agree with Sapir that, on the whole, "ideation reigns supreme in language...", but this supremacy does not authorize linguistics to disregard the "secondary factors." The emotive elements of speech which, as Joos is prone to believe, cannot be described "with a finite number of absolute categories," are classified by him "as non-linguistic elements of the real world." Hence, "for us they remain vague, protean, fluctuating phenomena," he concludes, "which we refuse to tolerate in our science". Joos is indeed a brilliant expert in reduction experiments, and his emphatic requirement for an "expulsion" of the emotive elements "from linguistic science" is a radical experiment in reduction – *reductio ad absurdum.*

Language must be investigated in all the variety of its functions. Before discussing the poetic function we must define its place among the other functions of language. An outline of these functions demands a concise survey of the constitutive factors in any speech event, in any act of verbal communication. The ADDRESSER sends a MESSAGE to the ADDRESSEE. To be operative the message requires a CONTEXT referred to ("referent" in another, somewhat ambiguous, nomenclature), seizable by the addressee, and either verbal or capable of being verbalized; a CODE fully, or at least partially, common to the addresser and addressee (or in other words, to the encoder and decoder of the message); and, finally, a CONTACT, a physical channel and psychological connection between the addresser and the addressee, enabling both of them to enter and stay in communication. All these factors inalienably involved in verbal communication may be schematized as follows:

CONTEXT

ADDRESSER .... MESSAGE .... ADDRESSEE

CONTACT

CODE

Each of these six factors determines a different function of language. Although we distinguish six basic aspects of language, we could, however, hardly find verbal messages that would fulfill only one function. The diversity lies not in a monopoly of some one of these several functions but in a different hierarchical order of functions. The verbal structure of a message depends primarily on the predominant function. But even though a set (*Einstellung*) toward the referent, an orientation toward the CONTEXT – briefly the so-called REFERENTIAL, "denotative," "cognitive" function – is the leading task of numerous messages, the accessory participation of the other functions in such messages must be taken into account by the observant linguist.

The so-called EMOTIVE or "expressive" function, focused on the ADDRESSER, aims a direct expression of the speaker's attitude toward what he is speaking about. It tends to produce an impression of a certain emotion whether true or feigned; therefore, the term "emotive," launched and advocated by Marty has proved to be preferable to "emotional." The purely emotive stratum in language is presented by the interjections. They differ from the means of referential language both by their sound pattern (peculiar sound sequences or even sounds elsewhere unusual) and by their syntactic role (they are not components but equivalents of sentences). "*Tut! Tut!* said McGinty": the complete utterance of Conan Doyle's character consists of two suction clicks. The emotive function, laid bare in the interjections, flavors to some extent all our utterances, on their phonic, grammatical, and lexical level. If we analyze language from the standpoint of the information it carries, we cannot restrict the notion of information to the cognitive aspect of language. A man, using expressive features to indicate his angry or ironic attitude, conveys ostensible information, and evidently this verbal behavior cannot be likened to such nonsemiotic, nutritive activities as "eating grapefruit" (despite Chatman's bold simile). The difference between [big] and the emphatic prolongation of the vowel [bi:g] is a conventional, coded linguistic feature like the difference between the short and long vowel in such Czech pairs as [vi] "you" and [vi:] "knows," but in the latter pair the differential information is phonemic and in the former emotive. As long as we are interested in phonemic invariants, the English /i/ and /i:/ appear to be mere variants of one and the same phoneme, but if we are concerned with emotive units, the relation between the invariant and variants is reversed: length and shortness are invariants implemented by variable phonemes. Saporta's surmise that emotive difference is a nonlinguistic feature, "attributable to the delivery of the message and not to the message," arbitrarily reduces the informational capacity of messages....

Orientation toward the ADDRESSEE, the CONATIVE function, finds its purest grammatical expression in the vocative and imperative, which syntactically, morphologically, and often even phonemically deviate from other nominal and verbal categories. The imperative sentences cardinally differ from declarative sentences: the latter are and the former are not liable to a truth test. When in O'Neill's play *The Fountain*, Nano, "(in a fierce tone of command)," says "Drink!" – the imperative cannot be challenged by the question "is it true or not?" which may be, however, perfectly well asked after such sentences as "one drank," "one will drink," "one would drink." In contradistinction to the imperative sentences, the declarative sentences are convertible into interrogative sentences: "did one drink?" "will one drink?" "would one drink?"

The traditional model of language as elucidated particularly by Bühler was confined to these three functions – emotive, conative, and referential – and the three apexes of this model – the first person of the addresser, the second person of the addressee, and the "third person," properly – someone or something spoken of. Certain additional verbal functions can be easily inferred from this triadic model. Thus the magic, incantatory function is chiefly some kind of conversion of an absent or inanimate "third person" into an addressee of a conative message. "May this sty dry up, *tfu, tfu, tfu, tfu*" (Lithuanian spell). "Water, queen river, daybreak! Send grief beyond the blue sea, to the sea-bottom, like a grey stone never to rise from the sea-bottom, may grief never come to burden the light heart of God's servant, may grief be removed and sink away." (North Russian incantation). "Sun, stand thou still upon Gibeon; and thou. Moon, in the valley of Aj-a-lon. And the sun stood still, and the moon stayed..." (Josh. 10.12). We observe, however, three further constitutive factors of verbal communication and three corresponding functions of language.

There are messages primarily serving to establish, to prolong, or to discontinue communication, to check whether the channel works ("Hello, do you hear me?"), to attract the attention of the interlocutor or to confirm his continued attention ("Are you listening?" or in Shakespearean diction, "Lend me your ears!" – and on the other – end of the wire "Um-hum!"). This set for CONTACT, or in Malinowski's terms PHATIC function, may be displayed by a profuse exchange of ritualized formulas, by entire dialogues with the mere purport of prolonging communication. Dorothy Parker caught eloquent examples: "'Well!' the young man said. 'Well!' she said. 'Well, here we are,' he said. 'Here we are,' she said, 'Aren't we?' 'I should say we were,' he said, 'Eeyop! Here we are.' 'Well!' she said. 'Well!' he said, 'well.'" The endeavor to start and sustain communication is typical of talking birds; thus the phatic function of language is the only one they share with human beings. It is also the first verbal function acquired by infants; they are prone to communicate before being able to send or receive informative communication.

A distinction has been made in modern logic between two levels of language, "object language" speaking of objects and "metalanguage" speaking of language. But metalanguage is not only a necessary scientific tool utilized by logicians and linguists; it plays also an important role in our everday language. Like Molière's Jourdain who used prose without knowing it, we practice metalanguage without realizing the metalingual character of our operations. Whenever the addresser and/or the addressee need to check up whether they use the same code, speech is focused on the CODE: it performs a METALINGUAL (i.e., glossing) function. "I don't follow you – what do you mean?" asks the addressee, or in Shakespearean diction, "What is't thou say'st?" And the addresser in anticipation of such recapturing questions inquires: "Do you know what I mean?" Imagine such an exasperating dialogue: "The sophomore was plucked." "But what is *plucked?*" "*Plucked* means the same as *flunked*." "And *flunked?*" "*To be flunked* is *to fail in an exam*." "And what is *sophomore?*" persists the interrogator innocent of school vocabulary. "*A sophomore* is (or means) a *second-year student*." All these equational sentences convey information merely about the lexical code of English; their function is strictly metalingual. Any process of language learning, in particular child acquisition of the mother tongue, makes wide use of such metalingual operations; and aphasia may often be defined as a loss of ability for metalingual operations.

We have brought up all the six factors involved in verbal communication except the message itself. The set (*Einstellung*) toward the MESSAGE as such, focus on the message for its own sake, is the POETIC function of language. This function cannot be productively studied out of touch with the general problems of language, and, on the other hand, the scrutiny of language requires a thorough consideration of its poetic function. Any attempt to reduce the sphere of poetic function to poetry or to confine poetry to poetic function would be a delusive oversimplification. Poetic function is not the sole function of verbal art but only its dominant, determining function, whereas in all other verbal activities it acts as a subsidiary, accessory constituent. This function, by promoting the palpability of signs, deepens the fundamental dichotomy of signs and objects. Hence, when dealing with poetic function, linguistics cannot limit itself to the field of poetry. . . .

The political slogan "I like Ike" /ay layk ayk/, succinctly structured, consists of three monosyllables and counts three diphthongs /ay/, each of them symmetrically followed by one consonantal phoneme, /. . l . . k . . k /. The make-up of the three words presents a variation: no consonantal phonemes in the first word, two around the diphthong in the second, and one final consonant in the third. A similar dominant nucleus /ay/ was noticed by Hymes in some of the sonnets of Keats. Both cola of the trisyllabic formula "I like / Ike" rhyme with each other, and the second of the two rhyming words is fully included in the first one (echo rhyme), /layk/—/ayk/, a paronomastic image of a feeling which totally envelops its object. Both cola alliterate with each other, and the first of the two alliterating words is included in the second: /ay/ – /ayk/, a paronomastic image of the loving subject enveloped by the beloved object. The secondary, poetic function of this electional catch phrase reinforces its impressiveness and efficacy.

As we said, the linguistic study of the poetic function must overstep the limits of poetry, and, on the other hand, the linguistic scrutiny of poetry cannot limit itself to the poetic function. The particularities of diverse poetic genres imply a differently ranked participation of the other verbal functions along with the dominant poetic function. Epic poetry, focused on the third person, strongly involves the referential function of language; the lyric, oriented toward the first person, is intimately linked with the emotive function; poetry of the second person is imbued with the conative function and is either supplicatory or exhortative, depending on whether the first person is subordinated to the second one or the second to the first.

Now that our cursory description of the six basic functions of verbal communication is more or less complete, we may complement our scheme of the fundamental factors by a corresponding scheme of the functions:

	REFERENTIAL	
EMOTIVE	POETIC PHATIC	CONATIVE
	METALINGUAL	

What is the empirical linguistic criterion of the poetic function? In particular, what is the indispensable feature inherent in any piece of poetry? To answer this question we must recall the two basic modes of arrangement used in verbal behavior, *selection* and *combination.* If "child" is the topic of the message, the speaker selects one among the extant, more or less similar, nouns like child, kid, youngster, tot, all of them equivalent in a certain respect, and then, to comment on this topic, he may select one of the semantically cognate verbs – sleeps, dozes, nods, naps. Both chosen words combine in the speech chain. The selection is produced on the base of equivalence, similarity and dissimilarity, synonymity and antonymity, while the combination, the build up of the sequence, is based on contiguity. *The poetic function projects the principle of equivalence from the axis of selection into the axis of combination.* Equivalence is promoted to the constitutive device of the sequence. In poetry one syllable is equalized with any other syllable of the same sequence; word stress is assumed to equal word stress, as unstress equals unstress; prosodic long is matched with long, and short with short; word boundary equals word boundary, no boundary equals no boundary; syntactic pause equals syntactic pause, no pause equals no pause. Syllables are converted into units of measure, and so are morae or stresses. . . .

Measure of sequences is a device which, outside of poetic function, finds no application in language. Only in poetry with its regular reiteration of equivalent units is the time of the speech flow experienced, as it is – to cite another semiotic pattern – with musical time. Gerard Manley Hopkins, an outstanding searcher in the science of poetic language, defined verse as "speech wholly or partially repeating the same figure of sound". Hopkins' subsequent question, "but is all verse poetry?" can be definitely answered as soon as poetic function ceases to be arbitrarily confined to the domain of poetry. Mnemonic lines cited by Hopkins (like "Thirty days hath September"), modern advertising jingles, and versified medieval laws, mentioned by Lotz, or finally Sanscrit scientific treatises in verse which in Indic tradition are strictly distinguished from true poetry (*kāvya*) – all these metrical texts make use of poetic function without, however, assigning to this function the coercing, determining role it carries in poetry. Thus verse actually exceeds the limits of poetry, but at the same time verse always implies poetic function. And apparently no human culture ignores versemaking, whereas there are many cultural patterns without "applied" verse; and even in such cultures which possess both pure and applied verses, the latter appear to be a secondary, unquestionably derived phenomenon. The adaptation of poetic means for some heterogeneous purpose does not conceal their primary essence, just as elements of emotive language, when utilized in poetry, still maintain their emotive tinge. A filibusterer may recite *Hiawatha* because it is long, yet poeticalness still remains the primary intent of this text itself. Self-evidently, the existence of versified, musical, and pictorial commercials does not separate the questions of verse or of musical and pictorial form from the study of poetry, music, and fine arts....

Rhyme is only a particular, condensed case of a much more general, we may even say the fundamental, problem of poetry, namely *parallelism*. Here again Hopkins, in his student papers of 1865, displayed a prodigious insight into the structure of poetry:

> The artificial part of poetry, perhaps we shall be right to say all artifice, reduces itself to the principle of parallelism. The structure of poetry is that of continuous parallelism, ranging from the technical so-called Parallelisms of Hebrew poetry and the antiphons of Church music up to the intricacy of Greek or Italian or English verse. But parallelism is of two kinds necessarily – where the opposition is clearly marked, and where it is transitional rather or chromatic. Only the first kind, that of marked parallelism, is concerned with the structure of verse – in rhythm, the recurrence of a certain sequence of syllables, in metre, the recurrence of a certain sequence of rhythm, in alliteration, in assonance and in rhyme. Now the force of this recurrence is to beget a recurrence or parallelism answering to it in the words or thought and, speaking roughly and rather for the tendency than the invariable result, the more marked parallelism in structure whether of elaboration or of emphasis begets more marked parallelism in the words and sense.... To the marked or abrupt kind of parallelism belong metaphor, simile, parable, and so on, where the effect is sought in likeness of things, and antithesis, contrast, and so on, where it is sought in unlikeness.

Briefly, equivalence in sound, projected into the sequence as its constitutive principle, inevitably involves semantic equivalence, and on any linguistic level any constituent of such a sequence prompts one of the two correlative experiences which Hopkins neatly defines as "comparison for likeness' sake" and "comparison for unlikeness' sake."...

In poetry not only the phonological sequence but in the same way any sequence of semantic units strives to build an equation. Similarity superimposed on contiguity imparts to poetry its throughgoing symbolic, multiplex, polysemantic essence which is beautifully suggested by Goethe's "Alles Vergängliche ist nur ein Gleichnis" (Anything transient is but a likeness). Said more technically, anything sequent is a simile. In poetry where similarity is superinduced upon contiguity, any metonymy is slightly metaphorical and any metaphor has a metonymical tint.

Ambiguity is an intrinsic, inalienable character of any self-focused message, briefly a corollary feature of poetry. Let us repeat with Empson: "The machinations of ambiguity are among the very roots of poetry". Not only the message itself but also its addresser and addressee become ambiguous. Besides the author and the reader, there is the "I" of the lyrical hero or of the fictitious storyteller and the "you" or "thou" of the alleged addressee of dramatic monologues, supplications, and epistles. For instance the poem "Wrestling Jacob" is addressed by its title hero to the Saviour and simultaneously acts as a subjective message of the poet Charles Wesley to his readers. Virtually any poetic message is a quasiquoted discourse with all those peculiar, intricate problems which "speech within speech" offers to the linguist.

The supremacy of poetic function over referential function does not obliterate the reference but makes it ambiguous. The double-sensed message finds correspondence in a split addresser, in a split addressee, and besides in a split reference, as it is cogently exposed in the preambles to fairy tales of various peoples, for instance, in the usual exordium of the Majorca storytellers: "Aixo era y no era" (It was and it was not). The repetitiveness effected by imparting the equivalence principle to the sequence makes reiterable not only the constituent sequences of the poetic message but the whole message as well. This capacity for reiteration whether immediate or delayed, this reification of a poetic message and its constituents, this conversion of a message into an enduring thing, indeed all this represents an inherent and effective property of poetry....

Part IV
1960–1980

Chapter 47
Edward Dorn

Edward Dorn (1929–99) was one of a group of poets who worked with Charles Olson at Black Mountain College, where Dorn was intermittently a student, first in 1951 and again in 1954. Dorn traveled extensively in the American West between his two periods at Black Mountain, and his early work, intent and serious in tone, develops in its attention to syllable and line his own version of Olson's theory of Projective Verse. Dorn's subject is the geography of the American West. He is fascinated by the close-up details of how people have come to inhabit a particular place and how they survive there, but his pioneer's interest in settlement is set in large vistas of historical and geological time. From 1965 to 1975 Dorn published a comic epic poem, Gunslinger. *This poem released an exuberant and subversive wit in his poetry. It was identified by its readers as a poem of the American counter-culture, ranging in its allusions and materials from Heidegger to cartoons to cocaine. In 1977 Dorn began his long association with the University of Colorado. His later work, often epigrammatic in style, shows his fierce dissent from the direction American culture took during the last twenty years of his life.*

"What I See in The Maximus Poems*" was first published in 1961 in* Kulchur 4. *The excerpt that follows is the first of a three-part meditation on the significance of Charles Olson's* Maximus Poems. *Olson's poems present Dorn with the possibility of a new poetics of place: the poem will not simply be about a place but emerge from it, drawing on local histories and idioms, and making those into a unique form that will compose what Dorn calls a "human inherited sense." Dorn's thinking about the relations between language, poetry, and place anticipate the later development of an ecological poetics.*

What I See in *The Maximus Poems*

Part I: There are places

There are a handful of places in America today where artists gather, in all their varieties, and some of them, New York, San Francisco, are large cities, with all the commitments to that size, i.e., streets that are busy over most of the day, traffic problems, buildings filled with other people, and generally, the so-called frenzy of specially concentrated peoples. Suburbs where it is said the really important people like computers live, and so on. Other towns, Santa Fe, Taos, Aspen, perhaps a place or two in Missouri, and the ones in New England, are much smaller, the buildings, streets, parties, private libraries and public, don't come on so fabulously. It is dangerous to imply that artists are either numerous or plentiful, no matter how true it is they are widespread. This doesn't at all depend on what one's *taste* is.

I find myself in one such particular place. Right now, this evening, there are some very nice bells coming from Christo Rey. Across the Santa Fe River. Perhaps a half-mile away. The sound fading into groves of cottonwood. There are departures like this that belie all the other grossnesses of this town, and for a brief period the sense is changed, and you feel as it is possible to feel about Santa Fe, not as the various literatures tell you you should. One really *is* New Mexico. One really *is* 7000 feet high. The threading Rio Grande really *is* off to the right, though many miles, down through what is to this day, a desolate and very breathtaking country. But the sweep-out of that land one can see standing here, where it runs down all the way more and more barren, away from the pine breaks of the mountains, to a moon-land, to Albuquerque, and below. And then at this time once in a while, I walk up to the ridge back of the house and can see the most standing thing on any of the horizons: the bulwark of the Sandias which is opposite Albuquerque. Or as Meline said, Albuquerque lies at the foot of... 60 miles south. For all of it is clearness, visibility, the sky itself is variation, accompanying the landscape.

Artists and skies, the range of the Sandias, later, the Indians and a few other things. This is perhaps a harsh way to talk, throwing the components of this place together, human and nonhuman, all together in the same bag. I certainly don't do this because I am impelled toward that basis from a wish to be modern and cold, "dehumanized." Not at all. In those terms, I know what I am doing. The reason is: it is not in my hands to do otherwise. As everyone knows, places vary widely. In spite of the fact the earth is reputed to be a ball, the formality stops there. And that man is of one species and can interbreed, endlessly, is not the same thing. Man makes his true hybrids manifest in the acts of men. Ultimately the general mass of men act the same from a desire, but as you come up, there is a smaller way of looking at It. For instance, Kemerer is not the same as Santa Fe, which is not the same as Biloxi. But all men try to act the same, there is the generality. "Nature is less indulgent. After the mule comes nothing." said Gauguin.

So that place has to shift for itself, largely. It is all *there*, certainly, and presumably, always was, but that isn't enough. Man, who is distinct from nature, will attempt almost anything. This has, unfortunately, a limited interest, for the rest of us. Because, though the direction, even stated intent, may differ, be a nuance, the place he comes back to, to

From *Poetics of the New American Poetry*, ed. Donald Allen and Warren Tallman (New York: Grove Press, 1974), pp. 293–300.

show the rest of us, the spot as a motivation, his very maligning reason, does not change, it officially is always the same. And when he takes off from the green and grey earth, from wherever, Kemerer or Santa Fe, he returns with the news, not surprising, that the planets are inhabited by the same creatures he is, with the same propensities for the half-cocked, the same deception in his well-stated motives. Finds, and brings back specimens we are already shy of, alas. But the trip out was ostentatious. That is not rewarding, either. Because place, as a nonhuman reality, is simply outside the presentments of human meaning. And not interesting. Although sometimes it may be. But I doubt it.

No. Where the depth, the strata are, that we as human beings require it, to be satisfied with the revelation, the recurring nouns that pronounce our lives, these are wilder places, not cast indefinitely upon the earth any more than gold is. Prose flounders now because it seeks to celebrate indiscriminately, out of a need for relief (we have gotten so far from catharsis the word can't be used), but the relief doesn't come on a continuing plane, and it is rather pitiful to see its aspects of commentary dwindle to the size of sociologist apprehensions. Invention is not the point. That Indians and artists and the mountains are the same here as the merchants the artists and the mountains, all lying in the strata of promotion I would never argue with. Because, having a flagging patience, I won't bring forth something which balks at coming. Not that it depends on me and my ability. It is that I refuse to be a party to any sort of obscurity.

Places, the geographic and oceanic tidal surgings which have been common ground for man since time, are built, not rebuilt (that refers to ruins, for which there is no hope) or they are birthed again. There is no loss implied although I can't seem to shake a term that implies *second* or *following*. . . . Anyway a beautiful thing is occurring in America, today. By the way, I don't use the term Place as a mannerism, as an indiscriminate word, covering the "doings of man," at all. Not in any of the senses of the usability of anything, there is no functionalism meant, we mustn't have anything to do with arrangements put into people's hands, with reports or accounts, at the same time not discounting it is a Place, where the din, of everything that happened there, and is, comes to the ear, and eye, the building front, the woman's smile influenced by the school she attended etc., but that man standing at the side of the street shouting in Navajo, at the police cars, shaking his first, going back and forth in a frenzy across the plaza to stand there, shaking his fist screaming in abrupt Navajo, at the passing cars.

The beautiful thing is the writing now of *The Maximus Poems*. This is all that I am saying Santa Fe would only hypocritically yield. I.e., one could force it out, carry it farther than Vestal would, but it would be a trick, and interesting as that might be, it wouldn't at all serve to spring immensities of reality, of art, because they were never here. I am aware that at any time such a statement can be "disproven." Men came into this area governed on the one hand by what they distinctly found – Indians & raw space in front of them, and carrying, a principle – Spanish Christianity, which produced at most some interesting carved doors and Santos. That's about it. That isn't good enough to support a structure of place. Indeed it propagates a condition for the effete, not the human art; the latter is dreadfully more deep and wide than the first. That is precisely why you found that the archaeologist, the anthropologist and the sociologist, take them all as one, flocked here. There was from the start a superabundance of the effete condition, surface, large thin space, and a principle just dead enough and known enough to make a likeable and easy complication in what they found. Which was *things*, which are effete. This is not a generality. It is awfully particular, it takes a very exacting registration, such as *Maximus* is capable of, to make *things* not effete, effects. The same thing, superficiality, probably explains too why opera is so popular here. And at the same time a predicament. Everyone wants an Art. But they want it too easily and casually, and they subscribe to very spurious people to get it sometimes. There is a series of letters in the local newspaper disputing the quality of reviews of the Opera. Naturally, when the local newspaper proceeded on its own account, for the first two or three performances it handled the thing as a social occasion. Which I comply with, opera has no possibility of art, it *is* a social occasion. But the ringer came when cultured people recognized this as a poor reflection on the *Place*, hence themselves, since they make up a disproportionate number. They wanted critical reviews, strictures, saying in effect, that this or that was or was not so etc., treating the thing seriously, analyzing, cribbing the procedures of art. Of course it is indisputable that these people are art lovers. But what is that? This is the point: you don't have a place just because you barge in on it as a literal physical reality, or want it to prosper because you live there. Instead go see the Grand Canyon, that's what it was made for. Place, you have to have a man bring it to you. You are *casual*. This is a really serious business, and *not* to be tampered with. You might just as well live in Buenos Aires or Newfoundland, it doesn't make a damn bit of difference. But being casual, you have to be patient and intelligent.

Now, once we have got our place, or hope for it, the fine relieving quality and discrimination, Gloucester, the thing is then art, and you can never go to it, by any other route. It is the complex instrument I at least never cease to carry with me and be kept alive by, live under, and feel myself very damn glad to be on this lovely earth, having been given this gift. This is probably the only sense in which I am a child. It seems to me the way Homer must have worked. Not to be underneath the writing, not to have to pay attention to that. Olson is a master in the normal sense, i.e., there is no trafficking possible with his means, so tied to the source is he with his art. Nor can we learn anything of use from him. When other poets, those who exchange terms, whose mechanisms in a sense overlap, or make sense in a functional procedural way to one another, address him "for Charles Olson" it isn't necessarily improper, who is to say that, but it is beautifully senseless. As a man he is in Gloucester, that is definitely something else. One takes uses from minor writers. This is their availability and to some extent their value, they are not deeply tied and the display of their talent is thinly spread, covered with bubbles, temporarily available to the eyes. They come to realizations late, and as an afterthought to their art. Wilde is an example. They never resurrect, theirs is a technology of the senses. It isn't that Olson doesn't manifest the same recognizable properties that mark writing. It is that the terms are not extractable from the whole art: there are no terms, but there is the term of the form. It isn't just a piece of logic to say that for the total art of Place to exist there has to be this coherent form, the range of implication isn't even calculable. I know *master* is a largish word. I don't mean my master. I mean Dostoevsky, Euripides. The power. It is a removal from the effete and at the same time the aesthetic. There was a certain fascism (not the political term) that existed in American writing for the last 35 years or more or less, in which the zeal for material effect was the cardinal quality, material effect being something that impresses itself by virtue of itself, per se, in which the springing is neither inward nor outward, but merely within. Images suffer. Technē is brought in.

Well, that is ended now, even though it is still practiced. Here in Santa Fe. The Indians are down in the plaza, some of them probably don't have a way home, but there seem to be many pick-up trucks. My man is probably there too, screaming in his off-reservation world. Haniel Long has been dead three years. Somewhere out there, I don't know where the cemetery is, the wind is blowing over his grave, blowing the grass and weeds, I must find out where he is buried.

Long was the only man concerned himself with art, here in the place, concerned with place. He never had one. He is a minor writer. A great minor writer, in America, and he had the radical mind it takes for that kind of art. He was involved with aesthetics, like minor art is, because the components themselves, the members that come together to make their art are always on the outside, as though the building were reversed in its construction, showing its structure first, enclosing its content, interiorly and arbitrarily. For want of the aspects of total place. The elements he brings forward would normally be those given elements that gracefully go together in an accordance which one could retain the mystery and buoyancy of and thus have the timelessness of the effect, which is what is lingering, and knows no tenses, the now, the then, the will be. Cabeza de Vaca and Haniel Long. And, his wandering Christ figure, who traversed the Southwest barefoot from Denver to the border, and cured, cast lovely spells, who had long hair, was a man full of grace and humility, a violent kind, who talked too much, walked, was lonely, and had meaning and cognizance, was followed, there was an awe. Would normally have been his elements, had, as I say, there been a concordance of place for him to work, but reality is not manysided like a prism here, here geology is, and the excavations will never cease. It was no loss to him probably. I love Long's writing for this abstraction of fulfillment. It *was* a loss to us. *Piñon Country* is the specimen of a radical mind with no home, no anchorage; as artist this is the one factor outside our control.

But when the Place is brought forward fully in form conceived entirely by the activation of a man who is under its spell it is a resurrection for us and the investigation even is not extractable. And it is then the only *real* thing. I am certain, without ever having been there, I would be bored to sickness walking through Gloucester. Buildings as such are not important. The wash of the sea is not interesting in itself, that is luxuria, a degrading thing, people as they stand, must be created, it doesn't matter at all they have reflexes of their own, they are casual, they do more than you could hope to know, it is useful, it is a part of industry. It has an arrogance of intention. This is the significance of Olson's distrust of Thucydides and his care for Herodotus. It is the significance of Blake's "the practice of art is anti-christ." Which further means that if you are not capable of the nonfunctional striking of a World, you are not practicing art. Description, letting things lay, was reserved for not necessarily the doubtful, but the slothful, or the merely busy.

The places still
half-dark, mud,
coal-dust.

There is no light
east
of the bridge

Only on the headland
toward the harbor
from Cressy's

have I seen it (once
when my daughter ran
out on a spit of sand

isn't even there). Where
is Bristow? when does I-A
get me home? I am caught

in Gloucester. (What's buried
behind Lufkin's
Diner? Who is

Frank Moore?

"The Librarian"

This is toward the most acute possible measurement. All the arrogance of intention that pervades Place is left out of "The Librarian" poem. The beginning of the poem, right down through the first two stanzas, is the key to this code of location, as of now. We can come home. From the Pacific or out west. And the ending fragment beginning, "The places still . . . ," is my reunion with the nouns and questionings, of my life, it makes me weep, there is no loss suffered, I am very much excited, what next, who is Frank Moore? When does I-A get me home?

The singular problem is difficult to come at. There is no contention that things, in the sense that one holds them, material things, but that is rather limiting, because utensils aren't only meant, or santos, or carved doors, or the "I" and all its predicament, its environment, inclement and unhappy, and in general the ranges upon ranges of materially disposed things that contain the mines of our lives, there is no contention that these things are really permanently deadening to us, they *are* grotesque in their deathly confrontation. I am perhaps a little suspicious about their strength, but that's all right. The important thing is that the only quarantine we have from them now is this new discovery of a total disposition of them in the human inherited sense. Coming all at once, and large, it is a morphology that up to now has been lacking. There is no aesthetic to bring us back into a social world of intention, delaying by way of modern functionalism our grasp, shortening our vision, putting us back outside again, where we spend so much time traveling the hall of distraction and apportionment, not ever coming to rest in cognizance and lingering mystery. Mystery, as it stands, is not a good word to apply to *Maximus*, because what I see in *The Maximus Poems* is the compelling casting of light over the compounds that make it up. I.e., regardless of their own distinct natures. There is a gain for me since there is nothing I detest so much as objectivity. So my sense of the mystery is: awelike, something unknown but more importantly, cognizant, a crest, by which our common histories are made human again, and thrilling, for *no* other motive than they are ours.

Chapter 48
Frank O'Hara

Frank O'Hara (1926–66) is a poet closely associated with a city, New York, and with a group of poets and painters who worked there during the 1950s and early 1960s. For much of this time O'Hara worked in the Museum of Modern Art, and his poems reflect his intense and witty engagement with abstract expressionism and other movements in modern painting. But his poetry is not imagistic or pictorial in any conventional sense. O'Hara's poems are full of echoes from many different sources: movies, television, the conversation of friends, love affairs, the work of other poets. He composes these into texts that can rapidly shift in tone and linguistic register, often deliberately careless of those pieties about the self that O'Hara associates with poetry in its academic and institutional forms. O'Hara was killed as a result of an accident with a beach buggy on Fire Island. His Collected Poems *were published posthumously in 1971.*

"Personism: A Manifesto" was first published in the journal, Yugen *7, in 1961. Seriously avoiding seriousness, it provides a camp parody of the conventions of the manifesto. All the hyperbolic claims of the typical manifesto – the sense of momentous discovery, the claim to revolutionize literature or transcend it, the significance attributed to poetic form – are rephrased as gossip. Nothing is to be taken straight in "Personism", but its ironies are exuberant, not cautious or guarded. Poetry is language dressed up to please and its rhetorical inventions evoke "overtones of love" that are not the soulful expressions of the poet.*

Personism: A Manifesto

Everything is in the poems, but at the risk of sounding like the poor wealthy man's Allen Ginsberg I will write to you because I just heard that one of my fellow poets

From *The Poetics of the New American Poetry*, ed. Donald Allen and Warren Tallman (New York: Grove Press, 1974), pp. 353–5.

thinks that a poem of mine that can't be got at one reading is because I was confused too. Now, come on. I don't believe in god, so I don't have to make elaborately sounded structures. I hate Vachel Lindsay, always have, I don't even like rhythm, assonance, all that stuff. You just go on your nerve. If someone's chasing you down the street with a knife you just run, you don't turn around and shout, "Give it up! I was a track star for Mineola Prep."

That's for the writing poems part. As for their reception, suppose you're in love and someone's mistreating (*mal aimé*) you, you don't say, "Hey, you can't hurt me this way, I *care*!" you just let all the different bodies fall where they may, and they always do may after a few months. But that's not why you fell in love in the first place, just to hang onto life, so you have to take your chances and try to avoid being logical. Pain always produces logic, which is very bad for you.

I'm not saying that I don't have practically the most lofty ideas of anyone writing today, but what difference does that make? they're just ideas. The only good thing about it is that when I get lofty enough I've stopped thinking and that's when refreshment arrives.

But how can you really care if anybody gets it, or gets what it means, or if it improves them. Improves them for what? For death? Why hurry them along? Too many poets act like a middle-aged mother trying to get her kids to eat too much cooked meat, and potatoes with drippings (tears). I don't give a damn whether they eat or not. Forced feeding leads to excessive thinness (effete). Nobody should experience anything they don't need to, if they don't need poetry bully for them, I like the movies too. And after all, only Whitman and Crane and Williams, of the American poets, are better than the movies. As for measure and other technical apparatus, that's just common sense: if you're going to buy a pair of pants you want them to be tight enough so everyone will want to go to bed with you. There's nothing metaphysical about it. Unless, of course, you flatter yourself into thinking that what you're experiencing is "yearning."

Abstraction in poetry, which Allen recently commented on in *It is*, is intriguing. I think it appears mostly in the minute particulars where decision is necessary. Abstraction (in poetry, not in painting) involves personal removal by the poet. For instance, the decision involved in the choice between "the nostalgia of the infinite" and "the nostalgia *for* the infinite" defines an attitude towards degree of abstraction. The nostalgia *of* the infinite representing the greater degree of abstraction, removal, and negative capability (as in Keats and Mallarmé). Personism, a movement which I recently founded and which nobody yet knows about, interests me a great deal, being so totally opposed to this kind of abstract removal that it is verging on a truer abstraction for the first time, really, in the history of poetry. Personism is to Wallace Stevens what *la poésie pure* was to Béranger. Personism has nothing to do with philosophy, it's all art. It does not have to do with personality or intimacy, far from it! But to give you a vague idea, one of its minimal aspects is to address itself to one person (other than the poet himself), thus evoking overtones of love without destroying love's life-giving vulgarity, and sustaining the poet's feelings towards the poem while preventing love from distracting him into feeling about the person. That's part of Personism. It was founded by me after lunch with LeRoi Jones on August 27, 1959, a day in which I was in love with someone (not Roi, by the way, a blond). I went back to work and wrote a poem for this person. While I was writing it I was realizing that if I wanted to I could use the telephone instead of writing the poem, and so Personism was born. It's a very exciting movement which will undoubtedly have lots of adherents. It puts the poem squarely between the poet and the person, Lucky Pierre style, and the poem is correspondingly gratified. The poem is at last between two persons instead of two pages. In all modesty, I confess that it may be the death of literature as we know it. While I have certain regrets, I am still glad I got there before Alain Robbe-Grillet did. Poetry being quicker and surer than prose, it is only just that poetry finish literature off. For a time people thought that Artaud was going to accomplish this, but actually, for all its magnificence, his polemical writings are not more outside literature than Bear Mountain is outside New York State. His relation is no more astounding than Dubuffet's to painting.

What can we expect of Personism? (This is getting good, isn't it?) Everything, but we won't get it. It is too new, too vital a movement to promise anything. But it, like Africa, is on the way. The recent propagandists for technique on the one hand, and for content on the other, had better watch out.

Chapter 49
Allen Ginsberg

Allen Ginsberg (1926–97) was, with his friends Jack Kerouac, William Burroughs, and Gregory Corso, amongst the leading figures in the Beat generation of writers. Like them, Ginsberg was committed to experiments in life as well as art. Howl and Other Poems, *published in 1956, was an expansive and rhythmically hypnotic declaration of his and his generation's rebellion against the "death culture" of the United States. These poems, like much of Ginsberg's subsequent work, refused to acknowledge customary distinctions between private and public subjects, yet his cultural radicalism did not renounce the past but drew on different writers and traditions for inspiration: the poetry of William Blake and Walt Whitman, Zen Buddhism, and Jewish mysticism amongst them. In 1961 he published one of his most compelling works,* Kaddish and Other Poems. *In the 1960s Ginsberg took an active part in the counter-culture he had helped invent. His poetry readings gathered large audiences and would include poems improvised for the occasion, often sung or chanted. Ginsberg encountered derision and mockery for his public refusal of a conventional life and the apparent naïveté of some of his work. But the rhythmic subtlety and the visionary power of his best work have been increasingly recognized since his death.*

"When the Mode of the Music Changes" was first published in Second Coming Magazine *in July 1961. In this excerpt Ginsberg takes up the familiar modernist preoccupation with poetic form and gives it his own distinctive inflection. Conventional form becomes a metaphor for the mind's imprisonment and stands in the way of the transfiguring expressions that come from the free, irrational, and improvised composition that Ginsberg advocates. He goes on to castigate the academic culture that fails to recognize the tradition of his work and its preoccupation with form, and finds a parallel but different threat from apparently sympathetic readers. "Abstraction in Poetry," first published in* Nomad *in Autumn 1962, bases its understanding of the nature of abstraction on a close-up view of some of the compositional techniques of the Beat writers. Ginsberg indicates some of the affiliations between their work and the New York School of poets.*

"When the Mode of the Music Changes, the Walls of the City Shake"

I

Trouble with conventional form (fixed line count and stanza form) is, it's too symmetrical, geometrical, numbered and pre-fixed – unlike to my own mind which has no beginning and end, nor fixed measure of thought (or speech – or writing) other than its own cornerless mystery – to transcribe the latter in a form most nearly representing its actual "occurrence" is my "method" – which requires the skill of freedom of composition – and which will lead poetry to the expression of the highest moments of the mindbody – mystical illumination – and its deepest emotion (through tears – love's all) – in the forms nearest to what it actually looks like (data of mystical imagery) and feels like (rhythm of actual speech and rhythm prompted by direct transcription of visual and other mental data) – plus not to forget the sudden genius-like imagination or fabulation of unreal and out of this world verbal constructions which express the true gaiety and excess of freedom – (and also by their nature express the first cause of the world) by means of spontaneous irrational juxtaposition of sublimely related fact, by the dentist drill singing against the piano music; or pure construction of imaginaries, hydrogen jukeboxes, in perhaps abstract images (made by putting together two things verbally concrete but disparate to begin with) – always bearing in mind, that one must verge on the unknown, write toward the truth hitherto unrecognizable of one's own sincerity, including the avoidable beauty of doom, shame and embarrassment, that very area of personal self-recognition (detailed individual is universal remember) which formal conventions, internalized, keep us from discovering in ourselves and others – For if we write with an eye to what the poem should be (has been), and do not get lost in it, we will never discover anything new about ourselves in the process of actually writing on the table, and we lose the chance to live in our works, and make habitable the new world which every man may discover in himself, if he lives – which is life itself, past present and future.

Thus the mind must be trained, i.e. let loose, freed – to deal with itself as it actually is, and not to impose on itself, or its poetic artifacts, an arbitrarily preconceived pattern (formal or subject) – and *all* patterns, unless discovered in the moment of composition – all remembered and *applied* patterns are by their very nature arbitrarily preconceived – no matter how wise and traditional – no matter what sum of inherited experience they represent – The only pattern of value or interest in poetry is the solitary, individual pattern peculiar to the poet's moment and the poem *discovered* in the mind and in the process of writing it out on the page, as notes, transcriptions, – reproduced in the fittest accurate form, at the time of composition. ("Time is the

From *Deliberate Prose: Selected Essays, 1952–1995*, ed. Bill Morgan (New York: HarperCollins, 2000), pp. 247–53, 243–5.

essence" says Kerouac.) It is this personal discovery which is of value to the poet and to the reader – and it is of course more, not less, communicable of actuality than a pattern chosen in advance, with matter poured into it arbitrarily to fit, which of course distorts and blurs the matter... Mind is shapely, art is shapely.

II

The amount of blather and built-in misunderstanding we've encountered – usually in the name of good taste, moral virtue or (at most presumptuous) civilized value – has been a revelation to me of the absolute bankruptcy of the academy in America today, or that which has set itself up as an academy for the conservation of literature. For the academy has been the enemy and Philistine host itself. For my works will be taught in the schools in 20 years, or sooner – it is already being taught for that matter – after the first screams of disgruntled mediocrity, screams which lasted 3 years before subsiding into a raped moan.

They should treat us, the poets, on whom they make their livings, more kindly while we're around to enjoy it. After all we are poets and novelists, not Martians in disguise trying to poison man's mind with anti-earth propaganda. Though to the more conformist of the lot this beat and Buddhist and mystic and poetic exploration may seem just that. And perhaps it is: "Any man who does not labor to make himself obsolete is not worth his salt." – Burroughs.

People take us too seriously and not seriously enough – nobody interested in what *we* mean – just a lot of bad journalism about beatniks parading itself as highclass criticism in what are taken by the mob to be the great journals of the intellect.

And the ignorance of the technical accomplishment and spiritual interests is disgusting. How often have I seen my own work related to Fearing and Sandburg, proletarian literature, the 1930s – by people who don't *connect* my long line with my own obvious reading: Crane's *Atlantis*, Lorca's *Poet in NY*, Biblical structures, psalms and lamentations, Shelley's high buildups, Apollinaire, Artaud, Mayakovsky, Pound, Williams and the American metrical tradition, the new tradition of measure. And Christopher Smart's *Rejoice in the Lamb*. And Melville's prose-poem *Pierre*. And finally the spirit and illumination of Rimbaud. Do I have to be stuck with Fearing (who's alright too) by phony critics whose only encounter with a long line has been anthology pieces in collections by Oscar Williams? By intellectual bastards and snobs and vulgarians and hypocrites who have never read Artaud's *Pour En Fini Avec Le Jugement de Dieu* and therefore wouldn't begin to know that this masterpiece which in 30 years will be as famous as *Anabasis* is the actual model of tone for my earlier writing? This is nothing but a raving back at the false Jews from Columbia who have lost memory of the *Shekinah* and are passing for middle class. Must I be attacked and condemned by these people, I who have heard Blake's own ancient voice recite me the "Sunflower" a decade ago in Harlem? and who say I don't know about "poetic tradition"?

The only poetic tradition is the voice out of the burning bush. The rest is trash, and will be consumed.

If anybody wants a statement of values – it is this, that I am ready to die for poetry and for the truth that inspires poetry – and will do so in any case – as all men, whether they like it or no – . I believe in the American Church of Poetry.

And men who wish to die for anything less or are unwilling to die for anything except their own temporary skins are foolish and bemused by illusion and had better shut their mouths and break their pens until they are taught better by death – and I am sick to death of prophesying to a nation that hath no ears to hear the thunder of the wrath and joy to come – among the "fabled damned" of nations – and the money voices of ignoramuses.

We are in American poetry and prose still continuing the venerable tradition of compositional self exploration and I would say the time has not come, historically, for any effort but the first sincere attempts at discovering those natural structures of which we have been dreaming and speaking. Generalizations about these natural patterns may yet be made – time for the academies to consider this in all technical detail – the data, the poetry and prose, the classics of original form, have already been written or are about to be – there is much to learn from them and there may be generalizations possible which, for the uninitiated, the non-poets, may be reduced to "rules and instructions" (to guide attention to what is being done) – but the path to freedom of composition goes through the eternal gateless gate which if it has "form" has an indescribable one – images of which are however innumerable.

There is nothing to agree or disagree with in Kerouac's method – there is a statement of fact (1953) of the method, the conditions of experiment, which he was pursuing, what he thought about it, how he went about it. He actually did extend composition in that mode, the results are apparent, he's learned a great deal from it and so has America. As a proposed method of experiment, as a completed accomplishment, there is nothing to agree or disagree with, it is a fact – that's what he was interested in doing, that's what he did – he's only describing his interest (his passion) for the curious craftsman or critic or friend – so be it. Why get mad and say he's in "error"? There's no more error here than someone learning how to build a unicorn table by building one. He's found out (rare for a writer) *how* he really wants to write and he is writing that way, courteously explaining his way.

Most criticism is semantically confused on this point – should and shouldn't and art is and isn't – trying to tell people to do something other than that which they basically and intelligently want to do, when they are experimenting with something new to them (and actually in this case to U.S. literature).

I've had trouble with this myself, everybody telling me or implying that I shouldn't really write the way I do. What do they want, that I should write some other way I'm not interested in? Which is the very thing which doesn't interest me in their prose and poetry and makes it a long confused bore? – all arty and by inherited rule and no surprises no new invention – corresponding inevitably to their own dreary characters – because anyway most of them have no character and are big draggy minds that don't *know* and just argue from abstract shallow moral principles in the void? These people are all too abstract, when it comes down to the poetry facts of poetry, – and I have learned in the past 2 years that argument, explanation, letters, expostulation are all vain – nobody listens anyway (not only to what I say, to what

I *mean*) they all have their own mental ax to grind. I've explained the prosodic structure of *Howl* as best I can, often, and I still read criticism, even favorable, that assumes that I am not interested in, have no, form – they just don't recognize any form but what they have heard about before and expect and what they want (they, most of them, being people who don't write poetry even and so have no idea what it involves and what beauty they're violating). – And it is also tiresome and annoying to hear Kerouac or myself or others "Beat" described because of our art as incoherent, we are anything but. After all.

But so far we have refused to make arbitrary abstract generalizations to satisfy a peculiar popular greed for banality. I perhaps lose some of this ground with this writing. I occasionally scream with exasperation (or giggles); this is usually an attempt to communicate with a blockhead. And Kerouac sometimes says "Wow" for joy. All this can hardly be called incoherence except by oververbal madmen who depend on longwinded defenses of their own bad prose for a livelihood.

The literary problems I wrote of above are explained at length in Dr. Suzuki's essay "Aspects of Japanese Culture" (*Evergreen Review*) and placed in their proper aesthetic context. Why should the art of spontaneity in the void be so, seem so, strange when applied in the U.S. prosepoetry context? Obviously a lack of intuitive spirit and/or classical experience on the part of these provincial frauds who have set themselves up as conservators of tradition and attack our work.

A sort of philistine brainwashing of the public has taken place. How long the actual sense of the new poetry will take to filter down, thru the actual writing and unprejudiced sympathetic reading of it, is beyond my power to guess and at this point beyond my immediate hope. More people take their ideas from reviews, newspapers and silly scholarly magazines than they do from the actual texts.

The worst I fear, considering the shallowness of opinion, is that some of the poetry and prose may be taken too familiarly, and the ideas accepted in some dopey sociological platitudinous form – as perfectly natural ideas and perceptions which they are – and be given the same shallow treatment, this time sympathetic, as, until recently, they were given shallow unsympathy. That would be the very we of fame. The problem has been to communicate the very spark of life, and not some opinion about that spark. Most negative criticism so far has been fearful overanxious obnoxious opinionation about this spark – and most later "criticism" will equally dully concern itself with favorable opinions about that spark. And that's not art, that's not even criticism, that's just more dreary sparkless blah blah blah – enough to turn a poet's guts. A sort of cancer of the mind that assails people whose loves are eaten by their opinions, whose tongues are incapable of wild lovely thought, which is poetry.

The brainwashing will continue, though the work be found acceptable, and people will talk as emptily about the void, hipness, the drug high, tenderness, comradeship, spontaneous creativity beat spiritual individuality and sacramentalism, as they have been talking about man's "moral destiny" (usually meaning a good job and full stomach and no guts and the necessity of heartless conformity and putting down your brother because of the inserviceability of love as against the legal discipline of tradition because of the unavailability of God's purity of vision and consequent souls angels – or anything else worthwhile). That these horrible monsters who do nothing but talk, teach, write crap and get in the way of poetry, have been accusing us, poets, of lack of "values" as they call it is enough to make me vow solemnly (for the second time) that pretty soon I'm going to stop even trying to communicate coherently to the majority of the academic, journalistic, mass media and publishing trade and leave them stew in their own juice of ridiculous messy ideas. SQUARES SHUT UP and LEARN OR GO HOME. But alas the square world will never and has never stopt bugging the hip muse.

That we have begun a revolution of literature in America, again, without meaning to, merely by the actual practice of poetry – this would be inevitable. No doubt we knew what we were doing....

Abstraction in Poetry

I said in the preface to Corso's *Gasoline*: "he gets pure abstract poetry, the inside sound of language itself." I didn't realize at the time that lots of things in Gregory's poetry which I took for sheer, flaming verbal construction – with no practical meaning – were really extremely complicated and poetic statements of real ideas – as for instance the ultimate lines of "Ode To Coit Tower": *hay-like universe / golden heap on a wall of fire / sprinting toward the gauzy eradication of / Swindleresque Ink* – which now strikes me, after the laughing gas experience, as one of the most perfect statements I've seen of the sensation of the self-elimination or disappearance of the universe and all being with the disappearance of the mind: when the mind is eliminated into unconsciousness either by yogic withdrawal or artificial knockout or possibly death.

No matter how crazy Corso sounds he usually makes great sense to me after a year or so. I have to catch up with his advanced methods of composition. I've seen him start a line on a typewriter – "I pump him full of" – (of what? he says to himself, having no idea in the world) – "of lost" – (lost what? his fingers circling magically over the keyboard, waiting for some incongruous inspiration which will alter the meaning of the whole sentence gone before) – "lost watches" – or fried shoes, or radiator soup, or flying owl cheese, or how to bring the dead back to life: carrots dipped in Kangarooian Weep for certain corpses. He has a whole poem made like that. He gets to "In ran the moonlight and grabbed the prunes," but all these are built on some kind of later explainable ellipse – the mind instinctively attracted to images coming from opposite ends of itself which, juxtaposed, present consciousness in all its irrational, un-figure-outable-in-advance completeness.

Kerouac has several examples of what might be called abstract prose. In *Visions of Cody* – after writing several hundred pages of sketch and narrative and copying actual recorded tape conversations of his hero and then imitating it in ideal dream-conversation prose – his mind breaks down during the book's composition (in which he has followed the rhythmic zigzag flow of his thinks thru all their a-syntactic forms) and for the next forty or fifty pages the book plunges into an organic prose bebop babble. The rhythm is continued, though, long, beautiful sentences, with variable base rhythms, an endless sound. The book slowly picks up from there, emerges from the mud of real prose and with the same endless rhythm (and slowly beginning to make sense again) into narrative, chronological accounts of a last voyage thru America. In a later example of his work, *Old Angel Midnight*, there is a sort of Joycean babble flow – a mixture of American sounds and styles predicated on the basic spontaneous rhythm that Kerouac has discovered in his speech, his mind, in other friends' speech, perhaps drunk old friends' explanatory bar room conversation. "All the sounds of the universe coming in through the window" at once – Kerouac hears that because he meditates a lot in silence. I find that he and Corso are usually right and make sense – which I miss at first, but catch later.

Without meaning to oppose abstraction to the making of sense, there are several other elements which might be considered (what is abstract in poetry?). Perhaps pure sound: Schwitters, Isou, etc. – though perhaps they too make sense in context, Artaud's "*tara bulla / rara bulla / ra para hutin*..." is, in context, a pure crucifixion cry. Certain elements can be abstracted – rhythm, as in Kerouac, or elliptical phraseology, as in Corso – carrying these out to logical conclusion (where the circle meets itself) they make common sense also.

Another interesting example of recent abstract composition – so might it be called – is W. S. Burroughs' *Word.* This consists of a sort of visual free-association abstract summary of all the images – linked together and passing into one another – that the author has conceived in the writing of the previous seven years. Burroughs has habituated himself (thru natural inclination and many years' addiction to opiates) to thinking visually rather than verbally, so that this was a noncommittal transcription into words of a succession of visual images passing in front of his mental eye. If a poet is concentrating on one specific thing – say, direct, spontaneous flow – anything he says is appreciable and makes sense once you know what he is doing. All you have to do is listen to what comes next if you are interested in the man's mind or in a general theory of actual mind.

Frank O'Hara (*Second Avenue*) and Kenneth Koch (*When the Sun Tries to Go On*) both wrote at the same time long meaningless poems to see what would happen – well maybe not meaningless, but they were just composing, bulling along page after page. The result, I guess, is that they learned how to write, learned the extent of their own imagination, learned how far out they could go, learned freedom of composition, and turned up some beautiful lines. Koch did many strange things. I heard a poem which I understood was composed of purely fixed (abstract) elements – each line to contain, I think I remember, the name of a city, a cold drink, an animal, maybe three other tough categories, and the word "bathtub." It sounded like an abstract Bach fugue; I came when I heard the phrase "mosquitoes squirting buttermilk, into (was it?) Wounded Knee bathtubs." That area of experiment is what attracted me – the freedom of composition and the sense it finally comes to – the final revelation of the irrational nonsense of Being....

Chapter 50
W. H. Auden

Wystan Hugh Auden (1907–73) was one of the leading poets to emerge in the generation after Eliot and Pound. In the 1930s he invented a poetic language, influenced by psychoanalysis and Marxism, that explored the relation between inner fantasies of violence and public events during a period dominated by the threat and the actuality of war. But Auden's poetry was not confined to the imagination of imminent disaster. Amidst the signs of disintegration and violence he discovered moments of lyric expression and revolutionary possibility. In 1939 Auden moved from England to the United States and in 1946 he became a US citizen. During this period he converted to Christianity and distanced himself from his earlier political radicalism. His increasing pessimism about the possibility of secular justice did not produce any reduction in the range and ambition of his poetry. In the 1940s and 1950s he continued to write poems, sometimes based on a single allegorical image, that compressed and commented on the long history of human violence and its relation to the achievements of civilization. The gravity of Auden's subjects found a counterpoint in his belief that poetry was an ironic and playful art. He enjoyed experimenting with a wide variety of poetic forms and often subverted the distinction between light verse and serious poetry. Auden was an energetic and prolific writer who saw no incompatibility between being a poet and being an intellectual. In addition to many volumes of poetry, he wrote verse plays, opera libretti, and numerous essays.

The following excerpt is from his essay "The Poet and the City" which was published in 1962, first in The Massachusetts Review *and then in Auden's collection of essays,* The Dyer's Hand. *He provides a typically synoptic and confident overview of modern culture's losses and how these restrict the poet's capacity. Ironically aware of the inflated claims made on behalf of poetry, he defines its distinctive contemporary value as a form of play and of human recognition in an increasingly managed society.*

The Poet and the City

. . . Being everything, let us admit that is to be something,
Or give ourselves the benefit of the doubt . . .
William Empson

There is little or nothing to be remembered written on the subject of getting an honest living. Neither the New Testament nor Poor Richard speaks to our condition. One would never think, from looking at literature, that this question had ever disturbed a solitary individual's musings.
H. D. Thoreau

It is astonishing how many young people of both sexes, when asked what they want to do in life, give neither a sensible answer like "I want to be a lawyer, an innkeeper, a farmer" nor a romantic answer like "I want to be an explorer, a racing motorist, a missionary, President of the United States." A surprisingly large number say "I want to be a writer," and by writing they mean "creative" writing. Even if they say "I want to be a journalist," this is because they are under the illusion that in that profession they will be able to create; even if their genuine desire is to make money, they will select some highly paid subliterary pursuit like Advertising.

Among these would-be writers, the majority have no marked literary gift. This in itself is not surprising; a marked gift for any occupation is not very common. What is surprising is that such a high percentage of those without any marked talent for any profession should think of writing as the solution. One would have expected that a certain number would imagine that they had a talent for medicine or engineering and so on, but this is not the case. In our age, if a young person is untalented, the odds are in favor of his imagining he wants to write. (There are, no doubt, a lot without any talent for acting who dream of becoming film stars but they have at least been endowed by nature with a fairly attractive face and figure.)

In accepting and defending the social institution of slavery, the Greeks were harder-hearted than we but clearer-headed; they knew that labor as such is slavery, and that no man can feel a personal pride in being a laborer. A man can be proud of being a worker – someone, that is, who fabricates enduring objects, but in our society, the process of fabrication has been so rationalized in the interests of speed, economy and quantity that the part played by the individual factory employee has become too small for it to be meaningful to him as work, and practically all workers have been reduced to laborers. It is only natural, therefore, that the arts which cannot be rationalized in this way – the artist still remains personally responsible for what he makes – should fascinate those who, because they have no marked talent, are afraid, with good reason, that all they have to look forward to is a lifetime of meaningless labor. This fascination is not due to the nature of art itself, but to the way in which an artist works; he, and in

From *The Dyer's Hand and Other Essays* (New York: Random House, 1962), pp. 72–4, 78–82, 83–5, 87–9.

our age, almost nobody else, is his own master. The idea of being one's own master appeals to most human beings, and this is apt to lead to the fantastic hope that the capacity for artistic creation is universal, something nearly all human beings, by virtue, not of some special talent, but of their humanity, could do if they tried. . . .

There are four aspects of our present *Weltanschauung* which have made an artistic vocation more difficult than it used to be.

(1) *The loss of belief in the eternity of the physical universe.* The possibility of becoming an artist, a maker of things which shall outlast the maker's life, might never have occurred to man, had he not had before his eyes, in contrast to the transitoriness of human life, a universe of things, earth, ocean, sky, sun, moon, stars, etc., which appeared to be everlasting and unchanging.

Physics, geology and biology have now replaced this everlasting universe with a picture of nature as a process in which nothing is now what it was or what it will be. Today, Christian and Atheist alike are eschatologically minded. It is difficult for a modern artist to believe he can make an enduring object when he has no model of endurance to go by; he is more tempted than his predecessors to abandon the search for perfection as a waste of time and be content with sketches and improvisations.

(2) *The loss of belief in the significance and reality of sensory phenomena.* This loss has been progressive since Luther, who denied any intelligible relation between subjective Faith and objective Works, and Descartes, with his doctrine of primary and secondary qualities. Hitherto, the traditional conception of the phenomenal world had been one of sacramental analogies; what the senses perceived was an outward and visible sign of the inward and invisible, but both were believed to be real and valuable. Modern science has destroyed our faith in the naïve observation of our senses: we cannot, it tells us, ever know what the physical universe is *really* like; we can only hold whatever subjective notion is appropriate to the particular human purpose we have in view.

This destroys the traditional conception of *art* as *mimesis*, for there is no longer a nature "out there" to be truly or falsely imitated; all an artist can be *true* to are his subjective sensations and feelings. The change in attitude is already to be seen in Blake's remark that some people see the sun as a round golden disc the size of a guinea but that he sees it as a host crying Holy, Holy, Holy. What is significant about this is that Blake, like the Newtonians he hated, accepts a division between the physical and the spiritual, but, in opposition to them, regards the material universe as the abode of Satan, and so attaches no value to what his physical eye sees.

(3) *The loss of belief in a norm of human nature which will always require the same kind of man-fabricated world to be at home in.* Until the Industrial Revolution, the way in which men lived changed so slowly that any man, thinking of his great-grandchildren, could imagine them as people living the same kind of life with the same kind of needs and satisfactions as himself. Technology, with its ever-accelerating transformation of man's way of living, has made it impossible for us to imagine what life will be like even twenty years from now.

Further, until recently, men knew and cared little about cultures far removed from their own in time or space; by human nature, they meant the kind of behavior exhibited in their own culture. Anthropology and archaeology have destroyed this provincial notion: we know that human nature is so plastic that it can exhibit varieties of behavior which, in the animal kingdom, could only be exhibited by different species.

The artist, therefore, no longer has any assurance, when he makes something, that even the next generation will find it enjoyable or comprehensible.

He cannot help desiring an immediate success, with all the danger to his integrity which that implies.

Further, the fact that we now have at our disposal the arts of all ages and cultures, has completely changed the meaning of the word tradition. It no longer means a way of working handed down from one generation to the next; a sense of tradition now means a consciousness of the whole of the past as present, yet at the same time as a structured whole the parts of which are related in terms of before and after. Originality no longer means a slight modification in the style of one's immediate predecessors; it means a capacity to find in any work of any date or place a clue to finding one's authentic voice. The burden of choice and selection is put squarely upon the shoulders of each individual poet and it is a heavy one.

(4) *The disappearance of the Public Realm as the sphere of revelatory personal deeds.* To the Greeks the Private Realm was the sphere of life ruled by the necessity of sustaining life, and the Public Realm the sphere of freedom where a man could disclose himself to others. Today, the significance of the terms private and public has been reversed; public life is the necessary impersonal life, the place where a man fulfills his social function, and it is in his private life that he is free to be his personal self.

In consequence the arts, literature in particular, have lost their traditional principal human subject, the man of action, the doer of public deeds.

The advent of the machine has destroyed the direct relation between a man's intention and his deed. If St. George meets the dragon face to face and plunges a spear into its heart, he may legitimately say "I slew the dragon," but, if he drops a bomb on the dragon from an altitude of twenty thousand feet, though his intention – to slay it – is the same, his act consists in pressing a lever and it is the bomb, not St. George, that does the killing.

If, at Pharaoh's command, ten thousand of his subjects toil for five years at draining the fens, this means that Pharaoh commands the personal loyalty of enough persons to see that his orders are carried out; if his army revolts, he is powerless. But if Pharaoh can have the fens drained in six months by a hundred men with bulldozers, the situation is changed. He still needs some authority, enough to persuade a hundred men to man the bulldozers, but that is all: the rest of the work is done by machines which know nothing of loyalty or fear, and if his enemy, Nebuchadnezzar, should get hold of them, they will work just as efficiently at filling up the canals as they have just worked at digging them out. It is now possible to imagine a world in which the only human work on such projects will be done by a mere handful of persons who operate computers.

It is extremely difficult today to use public figures as themes for poetry because the good or evil they do depends less upon their characters and intentions than upon the quantity of impersonal force at their disposal.

Every British or American poet will agree that Winston Churchill is a greater figure than Charles II, but he will also know that he could not write a good poem on Churchill while Dryden had no difficulty in writing a good poem on Charles. To write a good poem on Churchill, a poet would have to know Winston Churchill intimately, and his poem would be about the man, not about the Prime Minister. All attempts to write about persons or events, however important, to which the poet is not intimately related in a personal way are now doomed to failure. Yeats could write great poetry about the Troubles in Ireland, because most of the protagonists were known to him personally and the places where the events occurred had been familiar to him since childhood.

The true men of action in our time, those who transform the world, are not the politicians and statesmen, but the scientists. Unfortunately poetry cannot celebrate them because their deeds are concerned with things, not persons, and are, therefore, speechless.

When I find myself in the company of scientists, I feel like a shabby curate who has strayed by mistake into a drawing room full of dukes.

The growth in size of societies and the development of mass media of communication have created a social phenomenon which was unknown to the ancient world, that peculiar kind of crowd which Kierkegaard calls The Public.

> A public is neither a nation nor a generation, nor a community, nor a society, nor these particular men, for all these are only what they are through the concrete; no single person who belongs to the public makes a real commitment; for some hours of the day, perhaps, he belongs to the public – at moments when he is nothing else, since when he really is what he is, he does not form part of the public. Made up of such individuals at the moments when they are nothing, a public is a kind of gigantic something, an abstract and deserted void which is everything and nothing.

The ancient world knew the phenomenon of the crowd in the sense that Shakespeare uses the world, a visible congregation of a large number of human individuals in a limited physical space, who can, on occasions, be transformed by demagogic oratory into a mob which behaves in a way of which none of its members would be capable by himself, and this phenomenon is known, of course, to us, too. But the public is something else. A student in the subway during the rush hour whose thoughts are concentrated on a mathematical problem or his girl friend is a member of a crowd but not a member of the public. To join the public, it is not necessary for a man to go to some particular spot; he can sit at home, open a newspaper or turn on his TV set. . . .

The two characteristics of art which make it possible for an art historian to divide the history of art into periods, are, firstly, a common style of expression over a certain period and, secondly, a common notion, explicit or implicit, of the hero, the kind of human being who most deserves to be celebrated, remembered and, if possible, imitated. The characteristic style of "Modern" poetry is an intimate tone of voice, the speech of one person addressing one person, not a large audience; whenever a modern poet raises his voice he sounds phony. And its characteristic hero is neither the "Great Man" nor the romantic rebel, both doers of extraordinary deeds, but the man or woman in any walk of life who, despite all the impersonal pressures of modern society, manages to acquire and preserve a face of his own.

Poets are, by the nature of their interests and the nature of artistic fabrication, singularly ill-equipped to understand politics or economics. Their natural interest is in singular individuals and personal relations, while politics and economics are concerned with large numbers of people, hence with the human average (the poet is bored to death by the idea of the Common Man) and with impersonal, to a great extent involuntary, relations. The poet cannot understand the function of money in modern society because for him there is no relation between subjective value and market value; he may be paid ten pounds for a poem which he believes is very good and took him months to write, and a hundred pounds for a piece of journalism which costs him but a day's work. If he is a successful poet – though few poets make enough money to be called successful in the way that a novelist or playwright can – he is a member of the Manchester school and believes in absolute *laisser-faire*; if he is unsuccessful and embittered, he is liable to combine aggressive fantasies about the annihilation of the present order with impractical day-dreams of Utopia. Society has always to beware of the Utopias being planned by artists *manqués* over cafeteria tables late at night.

All poets adore explosions, thunderstorms, tornadoes, conflagrations, ruins, scenes of spectacular carnage. The poetic imagination is not at all a desirable quality in a statesman.

In a war or a revolution, a poet may do very well as a guerilla fighter or a spy, but it is unlikely that he will make a good regular soldier, or, in peace time, a conscientious member of a parliamentary committee.

All political theories which, like Plato's, are based on analogies drawn from artistic fabrication are bound, if put into practice, to turn into tyrannies. The whole aim of a poet, or any other kind of artist, is to produce something which is complete and will endure without change. A poetic city would always contain exactly the same number of inhabitants doing exactly the same jobs for ever.

Moreover, in the process of arriving at the finished work, the artist has continually to employ violence. A poet writes:

> The mast-high anchor dives through a cleft

changes it to

> The anchor dives through closing paths

changes it again to

> The anchor dives among hayricks

and finally to

> The anchor dives through the floors of a church.

A *cleft* and *closing paths* have been liquidated, and hayricks deported to another stanza.

A society which was really like a good poem, embodying the aesthetic virtues of beauty, order, economy and subordination of detail to the whole, would be a nightmare of horror for, given the historical reality of actual men, such a society could only come into being through selective breeding, extermination of the physically and mentally unfit, absolute obedience to its Director, and a large slave class kept out of sight in cellars.

Vice versa, a poem which was really like a political democracy – examples, unfortunately, exist – would be formless, windy, banal and utterly boring. . . .

What is peculiar and novel to our age is that the principal goal of politics in every advanced society is not, strictly speaking, a political one, that is to say, it is not concerned with human beings as persons and citizens but with human bodies, with the precultural, prepolitical human creature. It is, perhaps, inevitable that respect for the liberty of the individual should have so greatly diminished and the authoritarian powers of the State have so greatly increased from what they were fifty years ago, for the main political issue today is concerned not with human liberties but with human necessities.

As creatures we are all equally slaves to natural necessity; we are not free to vote how much food, sleep, light and air we need to keep in good health; we all need a certain quantity, and we all need the same quantity.

Every age is one-sided in its political and social preoccupation and in seeking to realize the particular value it esteems most highly, it neglects and even sacrifices other values. The relation of a poet, or any artist, to society and politics is, except in Africa or still backward semifeudal countries, more difficult than it has ever been because, while he cannot but approve of the importance of *everybody* getting enough food to eat and enough leisure, this problem has nothing whatever to do with art, which is concerned with *singular persons*, as they are alone and as they are in their personal relations. Since these interests are not the predominant ones in his society; indeed, in so far as it thinks about them at all, it is with suspicion and latent hostility – it secretly or openly thinks that the claim that one is a singular person, or a demand for privacy, is putting on airs, a claim to be superior to other folk – every artist feels himself at odds with modern civilization.

In our age, the mere making of a work of art is itself a political act. So long as artists exist, making what they please and think they ought to make, even if it is not terribly good, even if it appeals to only a handful of people, they remind the Management of something managers need to be reminded of, namely, that the managed are people with faces, not anonymous numbers, that *Homo Laborans* is also *Homo Ludens*.

If a poet meets an illiterate peasant, they may not be able to say much to each other, but if they both meet a public official, they share the same feeling of suspicion; neither will trust one further than he can throw a grand piano. If they enter a government building, both share the same feeling of apprehension; perhaps they will never get out again. Whatever the cultural differences between them, they both sniff in any official world the smell of an unreality in which persons are treated as statistics. The peasant may play cards in the evening while the poet writes verses, but there is one political principle to which they both subscribe, namely, that among the half dozen or so things for which a man of honor should be prepared, if necessary, to die, the right to play, the right to frivolity, is not the least.

Chapter 51
Imamu Baraka

Imamu Amiri Baraka (1934–) is a poet, dramatist, cultural critic, and political activist whose life and work have been deeply engaged in the struggle against racism. His early work, published under the name of Leroi Jones, marked an often tense convergence between the modernist poetics of Pound, Williams, and Olson and the complications of being a black writer in a racist society. Baraka's first books of poetry came out in the 1960s but he was probably better known for his work as a dramatist. In 1964 his play Dutchman *was produced in New York. Its ritualized and violent action presents Baraka's conviction that black identity is not possible in a white world and gives a clear indication of the separatist direction subsequently taken by his writing and his politics. He converted to the Kewaida sect of Islam in 1968, when he changed his name. In 1974 Baraka revised his commitment to black nationalism as a result of his adoption of a Marxist-Leninist politics. Throughout this period he continued to write poetry and drama dedicated to the creation of a black culture strong enough to resist the encroachments of racism. The publication of* Transbluency *in 1995 brought together poems written by Baraka between 1961 and the mid-1990s.*

"Hunting Is Not Those Heads on the Wall" and "State / Meant" were published in 1964 and 1965 and collected with other prose pieces in 1968, in Home: Social Essays. *The first piece takes over an aspect of Olson's poetics, its emphasis on the poem as a process not a product, and uses it as the basis for challenging the "academic Western mind" and its "artifact worship." It is this that produces a reverence for tradition and the pictures placed on a gallery wall. In pursuit of his poetics of process Baraka turns a familiar comparison between poetry and music in a new direction, that of the improvised modern jazz of Charlie Parker. Baraka's argument separates a strand of modernist poetics from its location in western culture and plays upon its resonances as a "non-Western concept" of an art that emerges from the world and returns to it. In "State/Meant" he gives an intransigent declaration of the creative destruction that he regards as the necessary work of the black artist in America.*

Hunting Is Not Those Heads on the Wall

Thought is more important than art. Without thought, art could certainly not exist. Art is one of many products of thought. An impressive one, perhaps the most impressive one, but to revere art, and have no understanding of the process that forces it into existence, is finally not even to understand what art is.

The artist is cursed with his artifact, which exists without and despite him. And even though the process, in good art, is everywhere perceptible, the risk of perfection corrupts the lazy public into accepting the material *in place of* what it is only the remains of.

The academic Western mind is the best example of the substitution of artifact worship for the lightning awareness of the art process. Even the artist is more valuable than his artifact, because the art process goes on in his mind. But the process itself is the most important quality because it can transform and create, and its only form is possibility. The artifact, because it assumes one form, is only that particular quality or idea. It is, in this sense, after the fact, and is only important because it remarks on its source.

The academician, the aesthete, are like deists whose specific corruption of mysticism is to worship things, thinking that they are God (thought, the process) too. But art is not capable of thought. Just as things are not capable of God, but the reverse is what we mean by the God function, the process I am talking about.

The Supermaker, is what the Greeks identified as "Gods." But here the emphasis is still muddled, since it is what the God can do that is really important, not the fact that he is the God. I speak of the *verb process*, the doing, the coming into being, the at-the-time-of. Which is why we think there is particular value in live music, contemplating the artifact as it arrives, listening to it emerge. *There* it is. And *There*.

But even this is after the fact. Music, the most valuable of artifacts, because it is the most abstract, is still not the activity that makes itself possible. Music is what is left after what? *That* is important.

A museum is a curious graveyard of thinking. But we can go through one hoping to get some inkling of what those various creators who made the creations were thinking. What was he thinking when he did That? is a common question. The answer is obvious, though: That.

Formal art, that is, artifacts made to cohere to preconceived forms, is almost devoid of this verb value. Usually a man playing Bach is only demonstrating his music lessons; the contemporary sonneteer, his ability to organize intellectual materials. But nothing that already exists is *that* valuable. The most valuable quality in life is the will to existence, the unconnected zoom, which finally becomes in anyone's hands whatever part of it he could collect. Like dipping cups of water from the falls. Which is what the artist does. Fools want to dictate what kind of dipper he uses.

Art is like speech, for instance, in that it is at the end, and a shadowy replica, of another operation, thought. And even to name something, is to wait for it in the place you think it will pass. Thought, "I've written" – understanding even this process is recording. Art-ing is what makes art, and is thereby more valuable. But we speak of the Muse, to make even the verb a thing.

From *Poetics of the New American Poetry*, ed. Donald Allen and Warren Tallman (New York: Grove Press, 1974), pp. 378–83.

If we describe a man by his life we are making him a verb, which is the only valid method since everything else is too arbitrary. The clearest description of now is the present participle, which if the activity described continues is always correct. Walking is not past or future. Be-ing, the most complex, since it goes on as itself, as adjective-verb, and at the moment of Art is not a be-ing, but a Being, the simple noun. It is not the verb, but its product. Worship the verb, if you need something. Then even God is after the fact, since He is the leavings of God-ing. The verb-God, is where it is, the container of all possibility. Art, like time, is the measurement of. Make no mistake.

Even "sense" is clearly a use some energy is put to. No one should fool around with art who is only trying to "make sense." We are all full of meaning and content, but to make that wild grab for more! To make words surprise themselves. Some more of the zoom trembling in its cage, where some fool will be impressed by its "perfection." This is what should be meant by a "primitive" mind, that which is satisfied with simple order. But "using" words denies the full possibility of expression, which is, we must suppose, impossible, since it could not be stopped and identified. Art is identification, and the slowing-down for it. But hunting is *not* those heads on the wall.

The imitator is the most pitiful phenomenon since he is like a man who eats garbage. A saxophonist who continues to "play like" Charlie Parker cannot understand that Charlie Parker wasn't certain that what had happened had to sound like that. But if a man tries to understand *why* Parker sounded like he did, the real value of his music begins to be understood.

Form is simply *how* a thing exists (or what a thing exists as). When we speak of man, we ask, "How does he make it?" Content is *why* a thing exists. Every thing has both these qualities; otherwise it could not (does not) exist. The art object has a special relationship between these two qualities, but they are not separable in any object.

The recent concern in the West for the found object and chance composition is an attempt to get closer to the non-Western concept of natural expression as an Art object, since of course such an object has form and content in special relationship like any thing a man made. Because a man cannot make a thing that is in this sense unnatural. The unnatural aspect of the man-made object is that it seems to exist only as a result of man, with no other real connection with the nonhuman world. *Artificial*, in this sense, is simply *made*. "Bad art" is usually unnatural, i.e., it seems as if it could not exist without being made by a man. It is strictly artificial.

Western men have always been more concerned with the artifact, the made thing, as "an art" separated from some natural use. Art as a separate category of concern is first seen when? Functional art is as old as man was when he made *anything*. To posit the idea that you will make a thing whose sole value and function is that you will make it, is a different emphasis.

God (which is separate, and before, A God) is in one sense an art object and was probably the first. In the secular West, God is a nonfunctional (literally) art object. But earlier, God was simply the naming of force, in the same sense I meant earlier of naming a thing by its life. God was "the force out of which the world (and life) issued." The *naming*, nominalization, of that force is finally a step at making it artificial. The arbitrary assignment of content (which means nothing in a strictly local context, i.e., Who will object?) based very likely on need, is the beginning of God as an art object.

But think about this, "the force out of which the world (and life) issued" exists everywhere, as we can see, and this is the basic form (and content) of God. Everything else is most likely to be nationalism. Nothing else exists. But again the confusing of process with artifact, or rather the substitution of process for artifact. When God gets to be a thing, it is an artifact. When the lightning was "the force out of which the world issued," the emphasis was on natural evidence, the natural thing. And lightning is curiously apt, since in its natural form, it is a process, a happening, as well as an artifact. Duplicating God signs was simple education.

When God started to *look like* a human being, men had gotten very sure of themselves. (That is, once the dog, the wolf, the fish, the bear, the leopard, etc., had all been God, and the fallacy of this reasoning, in whatever turn of environmental circumstance, became traditional. Some of the things we have seen are animals, possibly one of them is God. Men next.) But *naming* is the first appropriation, the earliest humanist trend. Jane Harrison says the Greeks took the fear away by not only making all the various qualities known in the world men, but understandable, knowable, men. They began to make lives for their Gods, so those Gods could only exist in that certain way. From the unknown verb, to the familiar artifact. Greek Gods are beautiful Greeks, which finally in social/political terms is the beginning of modern nationalism. What the Western white man calls the beginning of democracy was the positing of the sovereign state, wherein everyone was free. The rest of the world could be exploited. *Logos*, then, is not merely thought, but belief. Greeks were Greeks because they had the same beliefs. A Greek was a man who believed the Gods were Greeks.

Humanism is good in this sense, that it puts the emphasis on what we actually have, but there is a *loss* with the loss of the unspecific imagination because knowing man was all there was enabled the less imaginative to show up fully armed. Man's mind is revered and, in the ugliest emphasis, man's inventions. Again the hideous artifact, to replace the valuable process. The most stupid man ought to know he is more important than what he can make. But he will never understand that what moves him is even more important, because of the contemporary (post-Renaissance) loss of prestige for the unseen. When God had a rep, his curious "workings" were given deference. But now that everything is grounded or lodged in the sweaty palm, men only believe in what, as Auden inferred, "takes up space."

Thinking, in the most exalted humanist terms, is God, the force out of which the world issued. Nature, we make a "natural" process. Darwinian determinism provided the frame. From the Renaissance, the boost of the industrial revolution, and man surrounded by his artifacts. Machines, which are completely knowable.

State / Meant

The Black Artist's role in America is to aid in the destruction of America as he knows it. His role is to report and reflect so precisely the nature of the society, and of himself in that society, that other men will be moved by the exactness of his rendering and, if they are black men, grow strong through this moving, having seen their own strength, and weakness; and if they are white men, tremble, curse, and go mad, because they will be drenched with the filth of their evil.

The Black Artist must draw out of his soul the correct image of the world. He must use this image to band his brothers and sisters together in common understanding of the nature of the world (and the nature of America) and the nature of the human soul.

The Black Artist must demonstrate sweet life, how it differs from the deathly grip of the White Eyes. The Black Artist must teach the White Eyes their deaths, and teach the black man how to bring these deaths about.

We are unfair, and unfair.
We are black magicians, black art
s we make in black labs of the heart.

The fair are
fair, and death
ly white.

The day will not save them
and we own
the night.

Chapter 52
Robert Creeley

Robert Creeley (1926–) began his long correspondence with Charles Olson in 1950. Its effects can be seen in Olson's Manifesto for Projective Verse where one of the central axioms of the new poetic – "Form is never more than an extension of content" – is attributed to Creeley. Olson was an important poetic mentor for Creeley's early poetry, as was William Carlos Williams. But Creeley took the poetry of ordinary speech and projective verse in a distinctive direction. The poems of the 1950s gathered in the 1960 collection, For Love, *are spare and minimalist in form. They avoid images in favor of oblique and carefully measured utterances that indicate but never explicate emotional intensities and crises. They display what Creeley's later work also shows: an effort to compose poetry whose forms will be intimately connected to the circumstances that gave rise to them. This dedication to the discovery of rhythms and line lengths that will extend content into form has been a consistent principle in Creeley's poetic career.*

"A Sense of Measure" was first published in the Times Literary Supplement *in August 1964. Taking up William Carlos Williams's concern with "measure" as a music in poetry whose rhythm does not depend upon syllables and their alternation, Creeley finds in this one aspect of poetry an unwilled order, an order only discovered in the act of composition. The poem's order carries an intuiton of reality not available to intellectual analysis.*

A Sense of Measure

I am wary of any didactic program for the arts and yet I cannot ignore the fact that poetry, in my own terms of experience, obtains to an unequivocal order. What I deny, then, is any assumption that that order can be either acknowledged or gained by

From *The Collected Essays of Robert Creeley* (Berkeley, Los Angeles, London: University of California Press, 1989), pp. 486–8.

intellectual assertion, or will, or some like intention to shape language to a purpose which the literal act of writing does not itself discover. Such senses of pattern as I would admit are those having to do with a preparatory ritual, and however vague it may sound, I mean simply that character of invocation common to both prayer and children's games.

But it is more relevant here to make understood that I do not feel the usual sense of *subject* in poetry to be of much use. My generation has a particular qualification to make of this factor because it came of age at a time when a man's writing was either admitted or denied in point of its agreement with the then fashionable concerns of "poetic" comment. William Carlos Williams was, in this way, as much criticized for the things he said as for the way in which he said them. I feel that "subject" is at best a material of the poem, and that poems finally derive from some deeper complex of activity.

I am interested, for example, to find that "automatic or inspirational speech tends everywhere to fall into metrical patterns" as E. R. Dodds notes in *The Greeks and the Irrational.* Blake's "Hear the voice of the Bard" demands realization of a human phenomenon, not recognition of some social type. If we think of the orders of experience commonly now acknowledged, and of the incidence of what we call *chance*, it must be seen that no merely intellectual program can find reality, much less admit it, in a world so complexly various as ours has proved.

Recent studies in this country involved with defining the so-called creative personality have defined very little indeed and yet one of their proposals interests me. It is that men and women engaged in the arts have a much higher tolerance for disorder than is the usual case. This means, to me, that poets among others involved in comparable acts have an intuitive apprehension of a coherence which permits them a much greater admission of the real, the phenomenal world, than those otherwise placed can allow. Perhaps this is little more than what Otto Rank said some time ago in *Art and Artist* concerning the fact that an artist does die with each thing he does, insofar as he depends upon the conclusion of what possibilities do exist for him. Paradoxically, nothing can follow from that which is altogether successful. But again this risk is overcome – in the imagination – by trust of that coherence which no other means can discover. It would seem to me that occasional parallels between the arts and religion may well come from this coincidence of attitude, at least at times when neither philosophy nor psychology is the measure of either.

Lest I be misunderstood – by "religion" I mean a basic *visionary* experience, not a social order or commitment, still less a moral one. Gary Snyder tells me that the Indians consider the experience of visions a requisite for attaining manhood. So they felt their enemy, the whites, not men, simply that so few of the latter had ever gained this measure of their own phenomenality. In this sense I am more interested, at present, in what is *given* to me to write apart from what I might intend. I have never explicitly known – before writing – what it was that I would say. For myself, articulation is the intelligent ability to recognize the experience of what is so given, in words. I do not feel that such a sense of writing is "mindless" or "automatic" in a pejorative way. At the end of *Paterson V* Williams writes:

– Learning with age to sleep my life away:
saying
  The measure intervenes, to measure is all we know...

I am deeply interested in the act of such *measure*, and I feel it to involve much more than an academic sense of metric. There can no longer be a significant discussion of the meter of a poem in relation to iambs and like terms because linguistics has offered a much more detailed and sensitive register of this part of a poem's activity. Nor do I feel measure to involve the humanistic attempt to relate all phenomena to the scale of human appreciation thereof. And systems of language – the world of discourse which so contained Sartre et al. – are also for me a false situation if it is assumed they offer a modality for being, apart from description. I am not at all interested in describing anything.

I want to give witness not to the thought of myself – that specious concept of identity – but, rather, to what I am as simple agency, a thing evidently alive by virtue of such activity. I want, as Charles Olson says, to come into the world. Measure, then, is my testament. What uses me is what I use and in that complex measure is the issue. I cannot cut down trees with my bare hand, which is measure of both tree and hand. In that way I feel that poetry, in the very subtlety of its relation to image and rhythm, offers an intensely various record of such facts. It is equally one of them.

Chapter 53
John Ashbery

John Ashbery (1927–) is one of the most highly regarded American poets of his generation. His first book, Some Trees, *was published in 1956 and, while it showed his mastery of a range of traditional poetic forms, its subjects were elusive as was Ashbery's relation to his material. Like his friend, Frank O'Hara, Ashbery has taken over aspects of modern painting into his work, but his poems are not "imagist" in the sense of trying to create verbal equivalents for visual experience. Whether working in short or long forms, Ashbery's poetry takes an ironic stance towards the ambitious modernism of Pound and Eliot. But the challenge of his work is different from theirs, the result of a boundless eclecticism that mingles pastiche and parody with allusions to comic strips, movies, personal reminiscence, fantasy, and high art. Like the subject of one of his poems, Ashbery skates across the surfaces of language. He has invented a version of the democratic poem for late twentieth-century America in the linguistic variety and inclusiveness of his work. But democracy here is not the equivalent of accessibility. Ashbery does not write from a single perspective either within a poem or across a range of poems. His poems absorb interpretation, just as he deftly steps aside from what he takes to be a particular interpretation of his work or reputation. His 1976 volume,* Self Portrait in a Convex Mirror, *won the Pulitzer prize. Ashbery is a prolific poet. His inter work includes* Girls on the Run *(1999),* Your Name Here *(2000), and* Chinese Whispers *(2002).*

"The Invisible Avant-Garde" was first given as a lecture at the Yale Art School in 1968 and was published in the same year in Art News Annual. *Comparing the situation of poets, musicians, and painters, Ashbery gives an ironic review of the fate of twentieth-century avant-gardes. Where avant-garde art had once met with serious resistance from the public, and where it was a sign that it was working that it should do so, it now meets with almost instant acceptance. Ashbery contemplates the dilemma of sustaining artistic experiment and originality in the face of this acceptance world. His answer is not a version of impersonality, but the invisibility that will sustain "an attitude that neither accepts nor rejects acceptance, but is independent of it."*

The Invisible Avant-Garde

The fact that I, a poet, was invited by the Yale Art School to talk about the avant-garde, in one of a series of lectures under this general heading, is in itself such an eloquent characterization of the avant-garde today that no further comment seems necessary. It would appear then that this force in art which would be the very antithesis of tradition if it were to allow itself even so much of a relationship with tradition as an antithesis implies, is, on the contrary, a tradition of sorts. At any rate it can be discussed, attacked, praised, taught in seminars, just as a tradition can be. There may be a fine distinction to be made between "a" tradition and "the" tradition, but the point is that there is no longer any doubt in anyone's mind that the vanguard *is* – it's there, before you, solid, tangible, "alive and well," as the buttons say.

Things were very different twenty years ago when I was a student and was beginning to experiment with poetry. At that time it was the art and literature of the Establishment that were traditional. There was in fact almost no experimental poetry being written in this country, unless you counted the rather pale attempts of a handful of poets who were trying to imitate some of the effects of the French Surrealists. The situation was a little different in the other arts. Painters like Jackson Pollock had not yet been discovered by the mass magazines – this was to come a little later, though in fact *Life* did in 1949 print an article on Pollock, showing some of his large drip paintings and satirically asking whether he was the greatest living painter in America. This was still a long way from the decorous enthusiasm with which *Time* and *Life* today greet every new kink. But the situation was a bit better for the painters then, since there were a lot of them doing very important work and this fact was known to themselves and a few critics. Poetry could boast of no such good luck. As for music, the situation also was bleak but at least there was experimental music and a few people knew about it. It is hard to believe, however, that as late as 1945 such an acceptably experimental and posthumously successful composer as Bartók could die in total poverty, and that until a very few years ago such a respectable composer as Schönberg, was considered a madman. I remember that in the spring of 1949 there was a symposium on the arts at Harvard during which a number of new works were performed including Schönberg's Trio for Strings. My friend the poet Frank O'Hara, who was majoring in music at Harvard, went to hear it and was violently attacked for doing so by one of the young instructors in the music department, who maintained that Schönberg was literally insane. Today the same instructor would no doubt attack O'Hara for going to hear anything so academic. To paraphrase Bernard Shaw, it is the fate of some artists, and perhaps the best ones, to pass from unacceptability to acceptance without an intervening period of appreciation.

At that time I found the avant-garde very exciting, just as the young do today, but the difference was that in 1950 there was no sure proof of the existence of the avant-

From *Reported Sightings: Art Chronicles, 1957–1987*, ed. David Bergman (Manchester: Carcanet Press, 1989), pp. 389–95.

garde. To experiment was to have the feeling that one was poised on some outermost brink. In other words if one wanted to depart, even moderately, from the norm, one was taking one's life – one's life as an artist – into one's hands. A painter like Pollock for instance was gambling everything on the fact that he *was* the greatest painter in America, for if he wasn't, he was nothing, and the drips would turn out to be random splashes from the brush of a careless housepainter. It must often have occurred to Pollock that there was just a possibility that he wasn't an artist at all, that he had spent his life "toiling up the wrong road to art" as Flaubert said of Zola. But this very real possibility is paradoxically just what makes the tremendous excitement in his work. It is a gamble against terrific odds. Most reckless things are beautiful in some way, and recklessness is what makes experimental art beautiful, just as religions are beautiful because of the strong possibility that they are founded on nothing. We would all believe in God if we knew He existed, but would this be much fun?

The doubt element in Pollock – and I am using him as a convenient symbol for the avant-garde artist of the previous school – is what keeps his work alive for us. Even though he has been accepted now by practically everybody from *Life* on down, or on up, his work remains unresolved. It has not congealed into masterpieces. In spite of public acceptance the doubt is there – maybe the acceptance is there because of the doubt, the vulnerability which makes it possible to love the work.

It might be argued that traditional art is even riskier than experimental art; that it can offer no very real assurances to its acolytes, and since traditions are always going out of fashion it is more dangerous and therefore more worthwhile than experimental art. This could be true, and in fact certain great artists of our time have felt it necessary to renounce the experiments of their youth just in order to save them. The poet Ron Padgett has pointed out that the catalogue of the recent Museum of Modern Art exhibition of Dada and Surrealism praises Picabia's early work but ruefully assumes that with his later work he had "passed out of serious consideration as a painter." Padgett goes on to say:

> A parallel example is provided by de Chirico, who many feel betrayed his own best interests as a painter. Possibly so. But in Picabia's case, the curiosity that compelled him to go on to become a less "attractive" painter is the same that carried his adventure into Dada in the first place, and it is this spirit, as much as the paintings themselves, which is significant.

I think one could expand this argument to cover de Chirico and Duchamp as well. The former passed from being one of the greatest painters of this century to a crotchety fabricator of bad pictures who refuses to hear any good said of his early period, but he did so with such a vengeance that his act almost becomes exemplary. And Duchamp's silence is exemplary without question for a whole generation of young artists.

Therefore it is a question of distinguishing bad traditional art and bad avant-garde art from good traditional art and good avant-garde art. But after one has done this, one still has a problem with good traditional art. One can assume that good avant-garde art will go on living because the mere fact of its having been able to struggle into life at all will keep it alive. The doubt remains. But good traditional art may disappear at any moment when the tradition founders. It is a perilous business. I would class de Chirico's late paintings as good traditional art, though as bad art, because they embrace a tradition which everything in the artist's career seemed to point away from, and which he therefore accepted because, no doubt, he felt as an avant-garde artist that only the unacceptable is acceptable. On the other hand a painter like Thomas Hart Benton, who was Pollock's teacher, was at his best a better painter than de Chirico is now, but is a worse artist because he accepted the acceptable. *Life* used to have an article on Benton almost every month, showing his murals for some new post office or library. The fact that *Life* switched its affections from Benton to Pollock does not make either of them any worse, but it does illustrate that Benton's is the kind of art that cannot go on living without acceptance, while Pollock's is of the kind which cannot be destroyed by acceptance, since it is basically unacceptable.

What has happened since Pollock? The usual explanation is that "media" have multiplied to such an extent that it is no longer possible for secrets to remain secret very long, and that this has had the effect of turning the avant-garde from a small contingent of foolhardy warriors into a vast and well-equipped regiment. In fact the avant-garde has absorbed most of the army, or vice versa – in any case the result is that the avant-garde can now barely exist because of the immense amounts of attention and money that are focused on it, and that the only artists who have any privacy are the handful of decrepit stragglers behind the big booming avant-garde juggernaut. This does seem to be what has happened. I was amazed the other night while watching the news on television when the announcer took up a new book by the young experimental poet Aram Saroyan and read it aloud to the audience from beginning to end. It is true that this took only a couple of minutes and that it was done for purposes of a put-down – nevertheless we know that the way of the mass media is to pass from put-down to panegyric without going through a transitional phase of straight reportage, and it may be only a matter of weeks before Aram Saroyan has joined Andy Warhol and Viva and the rest of the avant-garde on *The Tonight Show.*

Looking back only as far as the beginning of this century we see that the period of neglect for an avant-garde artist has shrunk for each generation. Picasso was painting mature masterpieces for at least ten years before he became known even to a handful of collectors. Pollock's incubation period was a little shorter. But since then the period has grown shorter each year so that it now seems to be something like a minute. It is no longer possible, or it seems no longer possible, for an important avant-garde artist to go unrecognized. And, sadly enough, his creative life expectancy has dwindled correspondingly, since artists are no fun once they have been discovered. Dylan Thomas summed it up when he wrote that he had once been happy and unknown and that he was now miserable and acclaimed.

I am not convinced that it is "media" that are responsible for all this – there have always been mediums of one sort or another and they have taken up the cause of the avant-garde only recently. I am at a loss to say what it is, unless that it is that events during the first decades of this century eventually ended up proving that the avant-garde artist is a kind of hero, and that a hero is, of course, what everybody wants to be. We all have to be first, and it is now certain – as it was not, I think, before – that the experimenting artist does something first, even though it may be discarded later on. So that, paradoxically, it is safest to experiment. Only a few artists like de Chirico have realized the fallacy of this argument, and since his course was to reject his own genius and produce execrable art it is unlikely that many artists will follow him.

What then must the avant-garde artist do to remain avant-garde? For it has by now become a question of survival both of the artist and of the individual. In both art and life today we are in danger of substituting one conformity for another, or, to use a French expression, of trading one's one-eyed horse for a blind one. Protests against the mediocre values of our society such as the hippie movement seem to imply that one's only way out is to join a parallel society whose stereotyped manners, language, speech and dress are only reverse images of the one it is trying to reject. We feel in America that we have to join something, that our lives are directionless unless we are part of a group, a clan – an idea very different from the European one, where even friendships are considered not very important and life centers around oneself and one's partner, an extension of oneself. Is there nothing then between the extremes of Levittown and Haight-Ashbury, between an avant-garde which has become a tradition and a tradition which is no longer one? In other words, has tradition finally managed to absorb the individual talent?

On the other hand, perhaps these are the most exciting times for young artists, who must fight even harder to preserve their identity. Before they were fighting against general neglect, even hostility, but this seemed like a natural thing and therefore the fight could be carried on in good faith. Today one must fight acceptance which is much harder because it seems that one is fighting oneself.

If people like what I do, am I to assume that what I do is bad, since public opinion has always begun by rejecting what is original and new?

Perhaps the answer is not to reject what one has done, nor to be forced into a retrograde position, but merely to take into account that if one's work automatically finds acceptance, there may be a possibility that it could be improved. The Midas-like position into which our present acceptance-world forces the avant-garde is actually a disguised blessing which previous artists have not been able to enjoy, because it points the way out of the predicament it sets up – that is, toward an attitude which neither accepts nor rejects acceptance but is independent of it. Previously, vanguard artists never had to face the problems of integration into the art of their time because this usually happened at the end of a long career when the direction their art would take had long been fixed. When it took place earlier it could be dealt with by an explosion of bad temper, as in the possibly apocryphal story about Schönberg: when someone finally learned to play his violin concerto he stormed out of the concert hall, vowing to write another one that *nobody* would be able to play.

Today the avant-garde has come full circle – the artist who wants to experiment is again faced with what seems like a dead end, except that instead of creating in a vacuum he is now at the center of a cheering mob. Neither climate is exactly ideal for discovery, yet both are conducive to it because they force him to take steps that he hadn't envisaged. And today's young artist has the additional advantage of a fuller awareness of the hazards that lie in wait for him. He must now bear in mind that *he*, not *it*, is the avant-garde.

A few remarks by Busoni in his book *The Essence of Music* seem to apply to all the arts and also to the situation of the experimental artist today. Busoni's music has the unique quality of being excellent and of sounding like nobody else's; it has not even been successfully imitated. The essays that make up the book were written about the time of World War I when a crisis had developed in German music, involving on the one hand Expressionists like Schönberg, of whom he disapproved, and of conservative Neoclassicists like Reger, of whom he equally disapproved – a crisis which, without going into details, rather parallels that in the arts today. Somehow Busoni alone managed to avoid these extremes by taking what was valid in each and forging a totality.

He wrote:

> I am a worshipper of Form – I have remained sufficiently a Latin for that. But I demand – no! the organism of art demands – that every idea fashion its own form for itself; the organism – not I – revolts against having one single form for all ideas; today especially and how much more in the coming centuries.
>
> The creator really only strives for perfection. And as he brings this into harmony with his individuality a new law arises unintentionally.
>
> The "new" is included in the idea of "Creation" – for in that way creation is distinguished from imitation.
>
> One follows a great example most faithfully if one does not follow it, for it was through turning away from its predecessor that the example became great.

And finally, in an article addressed to his pupils he wrote, "Build up! But do not content yourself any longer with self-complacent experiments and the glory of the success of the season; but turn toward the perfection of the work seriously and joyfully. Only he who looks toward the future looks cheerfully."

Chapter 54
Barbara Herrnstein Smith

Barbara Herrnstein Smith (1932–) is a critic and theorist best known for two books, Poetic Closure: A Study of How Poems End *(1968) and* On The Margins of Discourse: The Relation of Literature to Language *(1978). In* Poetic Closure, *Herrnstein Smith offers a critical analysis not only of the different ways poems have ended, but explores the question of how it is that readers might feel that a poem has ended appropriately and satisfyingly. Drawing on concepts derived from gestalt psychology and other disciplines, Herrnstein Smith distinguishes between formal and thematic closure in poetry, and analyses how these two levels coincide in different kinds of poem. Our sense that a poem has ended in the right place depends upon both kinds of closure: the working through of a formal pattern and the sense that a subject has been adequately treated.* On The Margins of Discourse *addresses a fundamental critical question about the difference between literary and other contexts of language. Distinguishing between "natural utterance" and "fictive utterance," Herrnstein Smith argues that "fictive utterances" are representations of "natural utterances," but under the conditions of a literary form that supplies a context for understanding what is being said that does not apply in examples of everyday speech. Like William Empson, she believes that literary works have the capacity to carry their own contexts with them; these are taken up in the process of reading in ways that enable the reader to make sense of the literary work.*

In the following excerpts from Poetic Closure, *Herrnstein Smith explores the different styles of ending in modern poetry. Her basic assumption is that modern poetry is characterized by a multiplicity of viable traditions, so many in fact that talk of tradition is likely to become meaningless. Noting the persistence of traditional forms in modern poetry, Herrnstein Smith nonetheless develops an analysis of a distinctive kind of closure in modern poetry, one that is deliberately muted or indeterminate while still "securing in various ways the reader's sense of the poem's integrity."*

Closure and Anti-Closure in Modern Poetry

I suggested . . . that a study of poetic closure could probably be made on historical lines, in which one traced the styles of poem endings from one age to another and considered such matters as closural traditions, conventions, and revolutions. The broad outlines of such a study have been to some extent implied here, and we have on occasion touched upon some fairly specific historical points. Thus (although it was not my intention), the preponderance of examples drawn from sixteenth- and seventeenth-century poetry might have suggested that Renaissance closure was (or was being considered) normative, while the discussions of associative structure and free verse were obviously tending toward generalizations about closure in Romantic and post-Romantic poetry. If we add that epigrammatic closure, in both its techniques and its expressive effects, would naturally be associated with neoclassical verse, we can see what those broad outlines might come to: closure in Renaissance poetry tended to be strong and secure, in Augustan poetry to be maximal, in Romantic poetry to be weak, and in modern poetry it has become minimal. This formulation is neat, but the moment we have thus explicitly constructed it, we know it must crumble under the weight of all the exceptions and qualifications we should have to add. How does one delimit Renaissance poetry? What does one do with Milton? Are there not important distinctions to be made among genres in any age? Are Pope's satires and epistles really so well closed? Is Wordsworth like Keats in this respect? And is it possible to generalize at all about modern poetry?

It is because of such questions and all that would be required to answer them that the present study cannot be regarded as even a crude approach to a historical survey; nor is it offered as such. I recognize that the title of this section, especially since it is the last one of the study, may suggest that an implicit historical line here reaches its natural termination. But examples from modern poetry have appeared throughout the preceding chapters and without special comment on the fact. Indeed, one of my major points has been that whereas certain forms and devices of closure are more appropriate to, and effective for, particular styles and structures, their appearance is not otherwise confined to any particular period. This last section has, to be sure, a certain strategic propriety, but modern poetry is thus set apart primarily because certain stylistic and structural possibilities have been fully realized only or most notably in the poetry of this century, and some of these possibilities involve special forms or devices of closure, or unusual variations on and departures from those considered earlier. These innovations and variations are, moreover, quite radical in certain respects, and reflect developments common to all the arts, and developments in cultural and intellectual history as well. For these reasons it is revealing to consider the closural modes of modern poetry as such.

The term "modern poetry" is a literary historian's nightmare, not only because dates always imply definitions (and vice versa), but because the most striking characteristic of the poetry of our time is its stylistic multiplicity. Not only are the forms widely various, but also the modes and mannerisms, the implied aesthetics, and the allegiances – or

From *Poetic Closure: A Study of How Poems End* (Chicago: University of Chicago Press, 1968), pp. 234–41, 242–5, 247–9.

what we should ordinarily call the "traditions." The latter term is almost meaningless, however, in an era such as the present one, when almost every poetic tradition that has ever existed – native or foreign, Western or Oriental, classical or medieval – is to some extent viable, and the most characteristic feature of our poetic activity, broadly considered, is the apparent absence of any principle of *rejection.* It is an era in which we not only have free verse and syllabic verse, "Beat" poems and "academic" poems, poems inspired by drugs and poems created by electronic computers, but in which sonnets (a genre that both Pope and Whitman deplored) are printed side by side with epigrams (a genre that Keats would have regarded as subpoetical).

As this catalogue indicates, however, even if it is true that everything that has gone before still, in a way, goes, and that stylistic pluralism is more characteristic of twentieth-century poetry than any or all of its stylistic innovations, it is also true that some things now go in a very revolutionary way – and both facts are significant in an appreciation of closure in modern poetry.

First, we must recognize that modern poems exhibiting traditional formal and thematic structures are neither rare nor obviously anachronistic. We may observe, in fact, that contemporary poetry (of the past twenty years, let us say) is distinguished from contemporary music and art in just this respect. Although free verse, imagism, symbolism, and other stylistic developments have made their mark, none of them has created a break between modern and traditional poetry as radical as the break between nonobjective and representational painting, or between atonal and traditional music. Moreover, in art and music, *avant-garde* movements continue to occupy a significant and even dominant place, whereas in poetry, the very phrase "*avant-garde*" seems already dated. The point to be emphasized is that a large and entirely respectable part of contemporary poetry is simply indistinguishable from traditional poetry *in the ways that would affect closure*; and consequently, for much modern poetry there is little to add here – aside from that fact – that has not already been considered in earlier chapters.

Indeed, far from being revolutionary in this respect, much of the poetry that seems most characteristic of our time has struck several observers as being reactionary (commendably or not, as their positions incline them). John Press, for example, in a study subtitled "Trends in British Poetry Since the Second World War," writes:

> All these poets [he alludes to a large group including Elizabeth Jennings, Donald Davie, Philip Larkin, and A. Alvarez], mistrusting or ignoring the legacy of the Romantics . . . , are trying to bring back into the currency of the language the precision, the snap, the gravity, the decisive, clinching finality which have been lost since the late Augustan age.

And Karl Shapiro, from a quite different point of view, complains as follows:

> A poem, according to [William Carlos] Williams, should not be that closed, should not click like a box. . . . The "closed" poem – the poem that clicks like a box – is the type of poem which has lately become a standard in the twentieth century. . . .

The semiscriptural allusion to William Carlos Williams is, however, as "standard" as the alleged click, and the clear implication that strong closure is undesirable brings us to the second point.

In much modern poetry and in modern poems otherwise quite dissimilar in style, one may readily observe an apparent tendency toward anti-closure. To a considerable extent, this tendency reflects the proliferation and dominance of forms and modes such as free verse and interior monologue in which the structural resources of closure are minimal. More significantly, it seems to reflect a general preference for, and deliberate cultivation of, the expressive qualities of weak closure: even when the poem is firmly closed, it is not usually slammed shut – the lock may be secure, but the "click" has been muffled. Causality in these matters is, however, impossible to determine, for the forms and preferences not only reflect each other, but both reflect more general developments in literary history and ultimately in cultural history. Moreover, anti-closure is a recognizable impulse in all contemporary art, and at its furthest reaches it reflects changing presumptions concerning the nature of art itself.

I shall turn below to some of the broader considerations that may be involved in poetic anti-closure, but a relatively specific one will illustrate some of the points just raised... [O]ne of the functions or effects of poetic form is to "frame" the poetic utterance: to maintain its identity as distinct from that of ordinary discourse, to draw an enclosing line, in other words, that marks the boundary between "art" and "reality." Now, it is clear that to the extent that the propriety of that boundary line itself is questioned, so also will be the propriety of its closural effects. What one may think of here are certain current (though by no means exclusively modern) conceptions of poetry and art that value the "natural" or the illusion of naturalness while disdaining the artful, the obviously conventional or artificial. Anti-closure in modern poetry, then, may be referred to some extent to this effort toward poetic realism, where structural or other features that mark the work as a verbal artifact – rather than a direct transcription of personal utterance – are avoided. Free verse itself, of course, is often hailed as being closer than more fixed meters to the natural rhythms of speech, and other closurally weak forms of poetry – thematically diffuse and deliberately "unfinished" fragments, for example – might be cultivated for corresponding reasons. The conception of poetry referred to here should not, however, be consigned too quickly to literary history, viewed merely as a legacy of Romanticism or an extension of realism. For the challenge it delivers to traditional notions concerning the functions and effects of poetry, and the very nature of art, is not itself narrowly confined.

Some of the broader aspects and implications of anti-closure have been suggested by Leonard B. Meyer in an article published in 1963 in which he distinguishes traditional and contemporary music as, respectively, "teleological" and "anti-teleological." The latter, he writes, "directs us toward no points of culmination – establishes no goals toward which to move. It arouses no expectations, except presumably that it will stop." He suggests that anti-teleological art embraces not only the serial music of Stockhausen and John Cage's composition by random operations, but also the paintings of Tobey, Rothko, and Mathieu, and the writings of Beckett, Robbe-Grillet, and Jackson Mac Low. His major point, however, as the title of his article indicates, is that "underlying this new aesthetic is a conception of man and the universe, which is almost the opposite of the view that has dominated Western thought since its beginnings." Meyer associates this new conception, which he calls "radical empiricism," with Oriental philosophy and, to a lesser extent, with Existentialism and the philosophy of modern physics; but he points out that it is not so much a matter of the influence on one side as of the receptivity on the other.

The anti-teleological character of contemporary art has been observed by others and is, by one name or another, proclaimed by the spokesmen and leaders of *avant-garde* movements in painting, music, and fiction. The art critic, Doré Ashton, writes: "The feeling in much contemporary music that there is no beginning and no end but only 'aggregate units' corresponds to the feeling in certain abstractions [i.e., abstract paintings] that the heaving rhythms come to no formal conclusion but resume constantly. . . ." As for fiction, Meyer's observations are echoed by a reviewer in a recent issue of the *Times Literary Supplement.* Speaking of the French novelists, Nathalie Sarraute, Claude Simon, Michel Butor, and, again, Alain Robbe-Grillet, he writes:

> Two other features of the "New Novel" [i.e., in addition to the attempt to obliterate temporality] reinforce the sensation of unresolved movement in an abstract present where nothing is certain: the frequent recourse to labyrinthine patterns leading nowhere, and the use of detective-story suspense which remains suspended, or fizzles out in a non-solution.

This reviewer sees an obvious relation between the techniques of the new French novelists and the Existentialist theory of the "absurd." Meyer had made a similar connection between anti-teleological art and modern philosophy, while Miss Ashton remarked that one motive for "openness" in modern painting was part of a general reaction against the European tradition: "The general opinion that European art was too 'finished' led American artists to rationalize their own lack of finish. A positive value was placed on the 'unfinished' look." "Openness," the "anti-teleological," the positive value placed on the unfinished look or sound – anti-closure, in other words, is evidently a sign of the times in contemporary art; and whether one refers it specifically to a revolution in philosophy or in art history, one suspects that it is ultimately related to even more general developments and crises.

I do not propose to offer here a short history of modern times, nor do I think it necessary. The developments and crises I speak of are the commonplaces of our literature, sermons, political speeches, and lives. The stylistic pluralism of contemporary poetry reflects a broader pluralism of values in an age that is the heir to perhaps too many revolutions, what Nathalie Sarraute has called "the age of suspicion." We know too much and are sceptical of all that we know, feel, and say. All traditions are equally viable partly because all are equally suspect. Where conviction is seen as self-delusion and all last words are lies, the only resolution may be in the affirmation of irresolution, and conclusiveness may be seen as not only less honest but *less stable* than inconclusiveness.

What is particularly significant for poetry, as opposed here to art and music, is the suspicion of language. It is an age where linguistics is a branch of almost every discipline and almost every discipline is a branch of linguistics. Language is the badge of our suspect reason and humanity. It is the lethal trap sprung for truth; it is the reliquary of the mortmain of the past; it categorizes and codifies, obliterating the complexities, subtleties, and ambiguities of experience. Language is always making us mean more or less than what we want to mean. We look back upon our own self-betraying assertions not as the expressions of knowledge or conviction, but only as "a way of putting it," and upon the assertions of the past as "bequeathing us merely a receipt for deceit."...

The song of uncertainty in modern poetry expresses the temper (or distemper) of our times thematically; it also reflects it in its very structure. The relation between structure and closure is of considerable importance here, for "anti-closure" in all the arts is a matter not only of how the works terminate but how and whether they are organized throughout. The "openness" and "unfinished" look and sound of *avant-garde* poetry and music is not a quality of their endings only, but affect the audience's entire experience of such works. Also, when Charles Olson speaks of the new "OPEN verse" as opposed to the "'closed' verse... which is pretty much what we have had, in English & American, and have still got, despite the work of Pound & Williams," one gathers (though the openness of his rhetoric is often incoherent) that he refers to the over-all structure of both kinds of poetry. Whereas the weak closure of much modern poetry can be understood partly as the result of the prevalence of formal and thematic structures that offer minimal resources for closure, the reverse is also likely: the prevalence of free verse, for example, probably reflects, in part, the impulse to anti-closure, the reaction against poems that "click like a box." Thus, although a survey of the modifications of formal and thematic structure in modern poetry would take us far afield from our specific concerns here, it must be emphasized that anti-closure cannot be seen solely as a radical conception of how poems should *end*.

The relation of anti-structure to anti-closure is also important in view of the apparent backwardness of poetry in both respects as compared to modern painting and music. Although the *avant-gardism* to which Meyer was alluding is significant in these arts, it represents only a minor and tangential aspect of contemporary poetic activity. But if the anti-teleology of the modern poet is not so thoroughgoing as that of the painter or composer, it may be due more to the conservatism of the material of his art than to the conservatism of the poet himself. While he may share the general impulse to "radical empiricism," he is confined by the fact that if his empiricism is too radical, his art loses both its identity and, more important, the sources of its characteristic effects. For the material of poetry is not words, but *language* – a system of conventions previously determined and continuously mediated by usage in a community – and if the poem divorces itself utterly from the structure of discourse, it ceases to be poetry and ceases to affect us as such. Although traditional *formal* structures may yield to deliberate dissolution, the design of a poem is never wholly formal and a considerable degree of organization is built into it by virtue of its fundamental relation to the structure of discourse. Consequently, to the extent that anti-closure is a matter of anti-structure, the poet cannot go all the way.

Indeed, what we find as we look more closely at individual poems is that, while anti-closure in modern poetry is a recognizable tendency with interesting consequences, it is rarely realized as the total absence of closural effects. The tendency reveals itself primarily in what might be called "hidden closure," where the poet will avoid the expressive qualities of strong closure while securing, in various ways, the reader's sense of the poem's integrity.

The techniques of anti-closure and hidden closure are far too numerous and various to be adequately represented here, either in discussion or illustration. Some of the more significant possibilities can be considered, however, and we may begin by observing that any of the terminal features mentioned earlier as sources of weak closure can, of course, become anti-closural devices. Thus, even if a poem is otherwise well closed in terms of its structure, unwanted finality effects in the concluding lines can be weakened or obscured by metrical deviations, self-qualifying expressions, allusions to unstable events, and so forth. Also, some of the most interesting developments in modern modes of closure arise not so much from radical departures as from subtly effective variations upon traditional ones. Although the poems of Wallace Stevens, for example, frequently contain absolute pronouncements and epigrammatic aphorisms, they also illustrate extremely delicate kinds of terminal suspension, usually through a combination of strong and weak closural features. Thus, in the lines from "Sunday Morning" cited earlier as an example of closural allusion, we may also notice that the ultimate effect is far from a click, and more complex than even a settling:

> And, in the isolation of the sky,
> At evening, casual flocks of pigeons make
> Ambiguous undulations as they sink,
> Downward to darkness, on extended wings.

Frequently, as here, the sense of a lingering suspension results partly from the rhythm of the syntax, as a fairly long sequence of unresolved clauses is brought to syntactic completion, but concluded with a final qualification. The same sense of combined continuity and stability is achieved in different ways in the final stanza of "Thirteen Ways of Looking at a Blackbird":

> It was evening all afternoon.
> It was snowing
> And it was going to snow.
> The blackbird sat
> In the cedar limbs.

and in the concluding lines of "Debris of Life and Mind":

> ... she will listen
> And feel that her color is a meditation,
>
> The most gay and yet not so gay as it was.
> Stay here. Speak of familiar things a while.

...

The simplest way in which a poet can suggest a state of instability is to represent it directly – and here we approach one of the most interesting aspects of modern closure. As I remarked earlier, until the development of the Romantic lyric, a poem was likely to represent a dialectic process only when it could also be represented as ultimately resolved. In much modern poetry, however, the occasion for a poem is more likely to be the existence of an ultimately unresolvable process, and the conclusion is more likely to be a question than an answer. The following poem by Robert Graves is characteristic in this respect:

The Straw

Peace, the wild valley streaked with torrents,
A hoopoe perched on his warm rock. Then why
This tremor of the straw between my fingers?

What should I fear? Have I not testimony
In her own hand, signed with her own name
That my love fell as lightning on her heart?

These questions, bird, are not rhetorical.
Watch how the straw twitches and leaps
As though the earth quaked at a distance.

Requited love; but better unrequited
If this chance instrument gives warning
Of cataclysmic anguish far away.

Were she at ease, warmed by the thought of me
Would not my hand stay steady as this rock?
Have I undone her by my vehemence?

The questions are, indeed, not rhetorical, which is why they evade stability. Nevertheless, although closure here is not strong, it is secure; for if the central question remains unanswered, it has been, by the conclusion of the poem, explicitly *defined* – and we do know then why the straw trembles and what the speaker fears. The poem has developed toward a moment of self-recognition; although for the speaker it takes the form of self-doubt, for the reader it is transformed into a stable enough revelation of character and circumstance. The expressive effect of the concluding question is, again, that sense of a lingering suspension so typical of modern closure. But closure it is.

While it would be impossible to determine the specific origins of this particular closural mode, one of its most significant and probably influential realizations was in T. S. Eliot's early dramatic monologues. In these poems, Eliot depicted in a memorable style what would eventually become the most familiar representative *persona* of twentieth-century poetry and fiction. We encountered him earlier, with all his characteristic hesitations, qualifications, self-doubts, and self-questionings, in our discussion of "The Love Song of J. Alfred Prufrock," and, as we observed there, the representation of such a consciousness made irresolution the most and perhaps the only dramatically appropriate conclusion. In "Portrait of a Lady," Prufrock or another version of him once again enacts his internal dialectics and once again concludes in a quandary. His questions ring throughout the poem and, in one form or another, throughout the years that follow, unanswered and unanswerable: "Are these ideas right or wrong?" and, in the concluding passage:

> Well! and what if she should die some afternoon,
> Afternoon grey and smoky, evening yellow and rose;
> Should die and leave me sitting pen in hand
> With the smoke coming down above the housetops;
> Doubtful, for a while
> Not knowing what to feel or if I understand
> Or whether wise or foolish, tardy or too soon...
> Would she not have the advantage after all?
> This music is successful with a "dying fall"
> Now that we talk of dying –
> And should I have the right to smile?

The music that has accompanied the external and internal scenes ("attenuated tones of violins / Mingled with remote cornets," and "inside my brain a dull tom-tom..., / Absurdly hammering a prelude of its own") concludes, as does the poem itself, with a "dying fall" – just as, in "The Hollow Men," the poem ends in the same way the world does. The whimper, the question, the dying fall: with these, Eliot established a tone and style of poetic closure that has become as familiar and representative as the personality of Prufrock. What we must add, however, is that in "Portrait of a Lady," as in "Prufrock," "Gerontion," and "The Hollow Men," the inconclusiveness is only a thematic element, and that all these poems are, in terms of their respective structures, successfully closed. In "Portrait," for example, the concluding questions are not only appropriate to the consciousness that evolves them, but the passage in which they appear is clearly terminal: it is a retrospective summary, an evocation of death, of afternoon and evening "with the smoke coming down" – and the music is, indeed, "successful with a 'dying fall.' "...

Chapter 55
Gerard Genette

Gerard Genette (1930–) is a structuralist critic whose work has both extended and subtly questioned the taxonomic and classificatory ambitions of structuralism. He is probably best known in the English-speaking world for his work on narrative, published in translation in 1980 as Narrative Discourse. *In addition to his work on narrative, Genette has written on a wide range of critical and theoretical issues, including the relationship between texts and genres, the function of those numerous features such as prefaces and introductions that surround texts, and the devices such as imitation, parody, and pastiche, described by Genette as "transtextuality," that connect one text to another. More recently his work has turned to general questions in aesthetics about the identity and the reception of works of art.*

"Poetic Language, Poetics of Language" was first published in 1969 in Figures 2. *Genette starts with the same critical question about the relation between prose and poetry as does Roland Barthes in his essay, "Is There Any Poetic Writing?" For Genette the traditional distinction based upon the presence or absence of meter is no longer sustainable. But nor is the kind of analysis that insists upon defining poetic language as a deviation or disruption of a norm established by prose, thus establishing a "gap" between poetic and non-poetic language. Taking his lead from Mallarmé, Genette proposes another answer in the following excerpt, one that falls in the domain of what he calls "a poetics of language," or the study of all the dreams a culture has about language. Poetry's dream is to overcome the arbitrariness of the relation between signifier and signified, to invent a language in which form will be at one with meaning, and Genette sets out with characteristic clarity the different techniques that are at work in poetry's dreaming.*

Poetic Language, Poetics of Language

... [W]e should consider more closely a text by Mallarmé that seems to me to touch on what is essential in the poetic function:

> Languages, imperfect in that they are several, lack the supreme: to think being to write without accessories, nor whispering but immortal speech being still unspoken, the diversity, on earth, of idioms prevents anyone from uttering the words that, otherwise would find themselves, at a stroke, materially the truth itself. ... My meaning regrets that discourse fails to express objects by means of touches corresponding to them in coloring or tone, which exist in the instrument of the voice, among the various kinds of language and sometimes in one. Besides the opaque word *ombre, ténèbres* does not grow much darker; how disappointed one is by the perversity that confers on the word *jour* a suggestion of darkness and on *nuit*, contradictorily, a suggestion of light. The wish for a term of brilliant splendor, or, on the other hand, for one that dies out; as for the simple, luminous alternatives – *Only*, let it be known, *verse would not exist*: it philosophically makes up for the shortcomings of the languages, a superior complement.

The style of this passage should not conceal the firmness of the opinions expressed, or the soundness of their linguistic foundation: the "shortcomings" of language, demonstrated for Mallarmé, as, later for Saussure, by the *diversity of idioms*, and illustrated by the disparity between sounds and significations, is obviously what Saussure was to call the arbitrariness of the sign, the conventional character of the link between signifier and signified; but these very shortcomings are the raison d'être of poetry, which exists only through them: if languages were perfect, *verse would not exist*, because all speech would be poetry and, therefore, there would be no poetry. "If I follow you," Mallarmé said to Viélé-Griffin (according to the latter), "you attribute the creative privilege of the poet to the imperfection of the instrument on which he must play; a language hypothetically adequate to convey one's thought would eliminate the writer, who, by that very fact, would be called Mr. Average." For the poetic function lies precisely in this effort to "make up for," if only in an illusory way, the arbitrariness of the sign, that is to say, to motivate language. Valéry, who had thought long and deeply about the example and teaching of Mallarmé, often came back to this idea, contrasting the essentially transitive, prosaic function, in which we see the "form" eliminated in its meaning (to understand being to *translate*), with the poetic function, in which the form is united with the meaning and tends to be perpetuated indefinitely with it: we know that he compared the transitivity of prose with that of walking and the intransitivity of poetry with that of dancing. Speculation on the *sensuous properties* of speech, the indissolubility of form and meaning, the illusion of a resemblance between the "word" and the "thing" were for him, as for Mallarmé, the very essence of poetic language: "The power of a line of poetry stems from an indefinable harmony between what it *says*, and what it *is*." So we see the poetic activity closely bound up for certain thinkers, including Mallarmé himself (see his *Mots anglais*, and the interest he took in René Ghil's *Traité du verbe*), with a ceaseless *imagination of language* that is fundamentally a motivating daydream, a daydream of

From *Figures of Literary Discourse*, trans. Alan Sheridan (New York: Columbia University Press, 1982), pp. 91–7.

linguistic motivation, marked with a sort of semi-nostalgia for some hypothetical "primitive" state of language, when speech is supposed to have *been* what it said. "The poetic function, in the broadest sense of the term," says Barthes, "would thus be defined by a Cratylian awareness of signs, and the writer would be the reciter of that great age-old myth according to which language imitates ideas and, contrary to the lessons of linguistic science, signs are motivated."

The study of poetic language thus defined ought to be based on another study, which has still not yet been systematically undertaken, and which would concern the *poetics of language* (in the sense in which Gaston Bachelard spoke, for example, of a poetics of space), that is to say, the innumerable forms of linguistic imagination. For men dream not only with words, they also dream, even the least educated among them, about words, and about all the manifestations of language: there is on this subject, since Plato's *Cratylus* itself, what Claudel calls a "considerable file" – that should one day be opened. We should also analyze more closely all the methods and artifices to which poetic expression has recourse in order to motivate signs; we can do no more here than indicate its principal species.

The best-known, because the most immediately perceptible, groups together those procedures which, before tackling the "shortcomings" of language, apply themselves to reducing them, exploiting in a sense the shortcomings of the shortcomings, that is to say, the few bits of motivation, direct or indirect, which are to be found naturally in the language: onomatopoeia, forms of mimicry, imitative harmonies, effects of phonic or graphic expressivity, evocations by synesthesia, lexical associations. Valéry, who was as capable as anyone else of cracking his whip, had little regard for this kind of effect: harmony between being and saying "must not be definable," he wrote. "When it is, it is imitative harmony, and that is not good." What is certain at least is that these are the easiest means, since they are given in the language itself, and therefore are within reach of "Mr. Average," and above all that the mimicry that they set up is of the crudest kind. More subtlety is to be found in the artifices that (thus corresponding more directly to Mallarmé's statement) strive to correct the shortcomings by bringing more closely together, by adapting one to the other, the signifier and signified separated by the stern law of the arbitrary. Roughly speaking, this adaptation can be achieved in two different ways.

The first consists in bringing the signified closer to the signifier, that is to say, by bending the meaning, or, more exactly, perhaps, by choosing among the semic potentialities those that best suit the sensory form of the expression. Thus Roman Jakobson demonstrates how French poetry can exploit, and by that very fact justify, the inappropriateness noted by Mallarmé between the phonetisms of the words *jour* and *nuit*, and I have tried elsewhere to show in what way the effects of this inappropriateness and its exploitation may contribute to the particular nuance given by French poetry to the opposition of night and day; this is merely one example out of thousands of possible ones: we would need innumerable pre-poetic semantic studies, in every domain (and in every language) if we were so much as to begin to appreciate the effects of these phenomena and what is perhaps improperly called poetic "creation."

The second way consists, conversely, in bringing the signifier closer to the signified. This action on the signifier may be of two different kinds: of a morphological kind, if the poet, not satisfied with the expressive resources of his idiom, tries to modify the existing forms or even to forge new ones; the chapter of verbal invention has been, as we know, particularly illustrated in the twentieth century by such poets as Fargue and Michaux, but the method has remained unusual to this day, for obvious reasons. The most frequent, no doubt the most effective action on the signifier – in any case, the one most suited to the vocation of the poetic game, which is to situate oneself within natural language and not beside it – is of a semantic order: it consists not in deforming signifiers or inventing new ones, but in *displacing* them, that is to say, in substituting for the literal term another term that one diverts from its use and meaning by giving it a new use and a new meaning. This action of displacement, which Verlaine wittily called *méprise* (mistake), is obviously at the source of all those "figures of words taken outside their signification" that are the tropes of classical rhetoric. It is a function of the figure that has not been sufficiently elucidated, and which is of direct concern to our subject; unlike the literal term, which is usually arbitrary, the figurative term is essentially motivated, and motivated in two senses: first, quite simply, because it is *chosen* (even if it belongs to a traditional repertoire like that of the tropes of usage) instead of being imposed by the language; second, because the substitution of term always proceeds from a certain relation between the signifieds (a relation of analogy in the case of metaphor, of inclusion in the case of synecdoche, of contiguity in the case of metonymy, etc.) that remains present (connoted) in the displaced and substituted signifier, and because this signifier, though generally just as arbitrary, in its literal meaning, as the supplanted term, becomes motivated in its figurative use. To say *flame* to designate flame, *love* to designate love is to subject oneself to the language by accepting the arbitrary and transitive words it suggests to us; to say *flame* for *love* is to motivate one's language (I say *flame* because love burns), and by that very fact to give it the density, the relief, and the weight of existence which it lacks in general, *everyday circulation.*

However, it should be made quite clear that not every kind of motivation corresponds to the deep poetic wish, which is, in Eluard's words, to speak "a sensuous language." The "relative motivations," of an essentially morphological order: *vache/vacher* (cow/cowherd), *égal/inégal* (equal/unequal), *choix/choisir* (choice/to choose), etc., of which Saussure speaks, and which he sees at work in the most "grammatical" languages, are not among the more felicitous for poetic language, perhaps because their principle is too intellectual and their functioning too mechanical. The relation between *obscur* and *obscurité* is too abstract to give *obscurité* a real poetic motivation. An unanalyzable lexeme like *ombre* or *ténèbres*, with its immediate, sensory qualities and shortcomings and its network of indirect suggestions (*ombre-sombre, ténèbres-funèbre*) will no doubt give a pretext to a richer motivating action, despite its greater linguistic immotivation. And *obscurité* itself, in order to acquire some poetic density, will have to be given a sort of verbal freshness by drawing attention away from its derivation and by reactivating the sonorous and visual attributes of its lexical existence. This implies among other things that the presence of the morpheme is not stressed by a "categorial" rhyme of the *obscurité-vérité* kind, and one can imagine, let it be said in passing, that this reason, albeit unconsciously and among several others, has contributed to the the proscription of grammatical rhymes. On the other hand, observe how the word becomes regenerated and more sensory in the appropriate surroundings, as in these lines by Saint-Amant:

> J'écoute, à demi transporté,
> Le bruit des ailes du silence
> Qui vole dans l'obscurité.
>
> (I listen, half transported,
> To the sound of the wings of silence
> That beat in the darkness.)

"*Obscurité*" has found its poetic destiny here; it is no longer the abstract quality of that which is obscure or darkened, but has become a space, an element, a substance, and even (we can say, despite all logic and following the secret truth of the nocturnal) something luminous.

This digression has taken us away from *the procedures of motivation*, but it is not a matter for regret, for in fact the essence of poetic motivation is not to be found in these artifices, which perhaps serve it only as catalysts; more simply and more profoundly, it is to be found in the attitude of reading that the poem succeeds (or, more often, does not succeed) in imposing on the reader: a motivating attitude which, beyond or short of all the prosodic or semantic attributes, accords to all or part of the discourse the sort of intransitive presence and absolute existence that Eluard calls "poetic evidence."

Poetic language reveals here, it seems to me, its true "structure," which is not to be a particular *form*, defined by its specific accidents, but rather a *state*, a degree of presence and intensity to which any statement may be led, so to speak, on condition that there is established around it that *margin of silence* which isolates it from its surroundings (but not from the gap) of everyday speech. It is no doubt in this way that poetry is best distinguished from all sorts of style, with which it shares only a number of means. Style is certainly a gap in the sense that it moves away from neutral language by a certain effect of difference and eccentricity; poetry does not proceed in this way: it would be more correct to say that it withdraws from common language *from the inside*, by an action – no doubt largely illusory – of deepening and reverberation comparable to those exalted perceptions gained through drugs, which, according to Baudelaire, transform "grammar, arid grammar itself" into a sort of "evocative witchcraft: the words rise up in flesh and bones, the substantive, in its substantial majesty, the adjective, a transparent garment that clothes it and colors it like a glaze, and the verb, angel of movement, which sets the sentence in motion."

Of poetic language in this sense, which it might be better to call language in the poetic state, or the *poetic state of language*, one could say without pushing the metaphor too far, that it is language *in a state of dreaming*, and we know that the relation between dreaming and wakefulness is not one of gap, but on the contrary – but how can one *say* what the contrary of a gap is? In fact, what allows itself to be most accurately defined by the gap, as gap, is not poetic language, but prose, the *oratio soluta*, disjointed speech, language itself as gap and disjunction between signifiers and signifieds, signifier and signified. In which case, poetry would certainly be, as Cohen says (but in a different sense, or rather in the opposite direction), *antiprose* and *reduction of the gap*: gap from the gap, negation, rejection, oblivion, effacement of the gap, of the gap that *makes* language; illusion, dream, the necessary and absurd utopia of a language without gap, without hiatus – without shortcomings.

Chapter 56
Paul de Man

Paul de Man (1919–83) was one of a group of critics, including Harold Bloom, J. Hillis Miller, and Geoffrey Hartman, who worked in the English/ Comparative Literature faculty at Yale in the 1970s. They were, sometimes misleadingly, identified as establishing deconstruction as a powerful critical movement in the United States. During the 1970s and 1980s de Man published a series of influential books and essays, including Allegories of Reading *(1979),* Blindness and Insight *(1983), and* The Rhetoric of Romanticism *(1984). De Man developed his own style of deconstruction, one that constituted a sustained defence of the value of literature. Literary language, according to de Man, began in disillusionment and the illusion that it exposed was that there could ever be a coincidence between sign and meaning. Literature was "free from the fallacy of unmediated expression." Texts were composed of systems of tropes: metaphor, metonymy, synechdoche, and de Man's particular favorite, irony. Tropes formed experience and perception and conditioned the reading of texts. The task of criticism was to attempt to keep up with this elusive fact, to demonstrate, by way of a rigorous reading, how the play of tropes in a literary text always escaped the misguided attempt to make form and meaning coincide. This endless disjunction between what a text appears to say and the way it says it gives rise to the moment of deconstruction. For de Man deconstruction was not a critical method applied to literary texts from the outside. It was a constitutive fact of literature itself. "The poetic text is the most advanced and refined form of deconstruction" because it "simultaneously asserts and denies the authority of its rhetorical mode."*

"Intentional Structure of the Romantic Image" was first published in French in 1960, and then in de Man's own translation in 1970 in Romanticism and Consciousness, *edited by Harold Bloom. It was published again in 1984 in* The Rhetoric of Romanticism. *Historically, de Man locates the last significant mutation of the poetic image with the work of the Romantic poets. The deconstructive tension established in Romanticism between a poetics of the natural object and a poetics of the image persists in nineteenth- and twentieth-century poetry. The result is a poetic language torn between its desire to be at one with nature and an acknowledgment that words "remain essentially distinct from natural entities."*

Intentional Structure of the Romantic Image

In the history of Western literature, the importance of the image as a dimension of poetic language does not remain constant. One could conceive of an organization of this history in terms of the relative prominence and the changing structure of metaphor. French poetry of the sixteenth century is obviously richer and more varied in images than that of the seventeenth, and medieval poetry of the fifteenth century has a different kind of imagery than that of the thirteenth. The most recent change remote enough to be part of history takes place toward the end of the eighteenth century and coincides with the advent of romanticism. In a statement of which equivalences can be found in all European literatures, Wordsworth reproaches Pope for having abandoned the imaginative use of figural diction in favor of a merely decorative allegorization. Meanwhile the term *imagination* steadily grows in importance and complexity in the critical as well as in the poetic texts of the period. This evolution in poetic terminology – of which parallel instances could easily be found in France and in Germany – corresponds to a profound change in the texture of poetic diction. The change often takes the form of a return to a greater concreteness, a proliferation of natural objects that restores to the language the material substantiality which had been partially lost. At the same time, in accordance with a dialectic that is more paradoxical than may appear at first sight, the structure of the language becomes increasingly metaphorical and the image – be it under the name of symbol or even of myth – comes to be considered as the most prominent dimension of the style. This tendency is still prevalent today, among poets as well as among critics. We find it quite natural that theoretical studies such as, for example, those of Gaston Bachelard in France, of Northrop Frye in America, or of William Empson in England should take the metaphor as their starting point for an investigation of literature in general – an approach that would have been inconceivable for Boileau, for Pope, and even still for Diderot.

An abundant imagery coinciding with an equally abundant quantity of natural objects, the theme of imagination linked closely to the theme of nature, such is the fundamental ambiguity that characterizes the poetics of romanticism. The tension between the two polarities never ceases to be problematic. We shall try to illustrate the structure of this latent tension as it appears in some selected poetic passages.

In a famous poem, Hölderlin speaks of a time at which "the gods" will again be an actual presence to man:

> ...nun aber nennt er sein Liebstes,
> Nun, nun müssen dafür Worte, wie Blumen, entstehn.
> ("Brot und Wein," stanza 3)[1]

Taken by itself, this passage is not necessarily a statement about the image: Hölderlin merely speaks of words ("*Worte*"), not of images ("*Bilder*"). But the lines themselves

From *The Rhetoric of Romanticism* (New York: Columbia University Press, 1984), pp. 1–9.

contain the image of the flower in the simplest and most explicit of all metaphorical structures, as a straightforward simile introduced by the conjunction *wie*. That the words referred to are not those of ordinary speech is clear from the verb: to originate ("*entstehn*"). In everyday use words are exchanged and put to a variety of tasks, but they are not supposed to originate anew; on the contrary, one wants them to be as well known, as "common" as possible, to make certain that they will obtain for us what we want to obtain. They are used as established signs to confirm that something is recognized as being the same as before; and re-cognition excludes pure origination. But in poetic language words are not used as signs, not even as names, but in order to *name*: "Donner un sens plus pur aux mots de la tribu" (Mallarmé) or "erfand er für die Dinge eigene Namen" (Stefan George): poets know of the act of naming – "nun aber *nennt* er sein Liebstes" – as implying a return to the source, to the pure motion of experience at its beginning.

The word "entstehn" establishes another fundamental distinction. The two terms of the simile are not said to be identical with one another (the word = the flower), nor analogous in their general mode of being (the word is like the flower), but specifically in the way they originate (the word originates like the flower). The similarity between the two terms does not reside in their essence (identity), or in their appearance (analogy), but in the manner in which both originate. And Hölderlin is not speaking of any poetic word taken at random, but of an authentic word that fulfills its highest function in naming being as a presence. We could infer, then, that the fundamental intent of the poetic word is to originate in the same manner as what Hölderlin here calls "flowers." The image is essentially a kinetic process: it does not dwell in a static state where the two terms could be separated and reunited by analysis; the first term of the simile (here, "words") has no independent existence, poetically speaking, prior to the metaphorical statement. It originates with the statement, in the manner suggested by the flower image, and its way of being is determined by the manner in which it originates. The metaphor requires that we begin by forgetting all we have previously known about "words" – "donner un sens plus pur aux mots de la tribu" – and then informing the term with a dynamic existence similar to that which animates the "flowers." The metaphor is not a combination of two entities or experiences more or less deliberately linked together, but one single and particular experience: that of origination.

How do flowers originate? They rise out of the earth without the assistance of imitation or analogy. They do not follow a model other than themselves which they copy or from which they derive the pattern of their growth. By calling them *natural* objects, we mean that their origin is determined by nothing but their own being. Their becoming coincides at all times with the mode of their origination: it is as flowers that their history is what it is, totally defined by their identity. There is no wavering in the status of their existence: existence and essence coincide in them at all times. Unlike words, which originate like something else ("like flowers"), flowers originate like themselves: they are literally what they are, definable without the assistance of metaphor. It would follow then, since the intent of the poetic word is to originate like the flower, that it strives to banish all metaphor, to become entirely literal.

We can understand origin only in terms of difference: the source springs up because of the need to be somewhere or something else than what is now here. The word "entstehn," with its distancing prefix, equates origin with negation and difference. But the natural object, safe in its immediate being, seems to have no beginning and no end. Its permanence is carried by the stability of its being, whereas a beginning implies a negation of permanence, the discontinuity of a death in which an entity relinquishes its specificity and leaves it behind, like an empty shell. Entities engendered by consciousness originate in this fashion, but for natural entities like the flower, the process is entirely different. They originate out of a being which does not differ from them in essence but contains the totality of their individual manifestations within itself. All particular flowers can at all times establish an immediate identity with an original Flower, of which they are as many particular emanations. The original entity, which has to contain an infinity of manifestations of a common essence, in an infinity of places and at an infinity of moments, is necessarily transcendental. Trying to conceive of the natural object in terms of origin leads to a transcendental concept of the Idea: the quest for the Idea that takes the natural object for its starting point begins with the incarnated "minute particular" and works its way upward to a transcendental essence. Beyond the Idea, it searches for Being as the category which contains essences in the same manner that the Idea contains particulars. Because they are natural objects, flowers originate as incarnations of a transcendental principle. "Wie Blumen entstehn" is to become present as a natural emanation of a transcendental principle, as an epiphany.

Strictly speaking, an epiphany cannot be a beginning, since it reveals and unveils what, by definition, could never have ceased to be there. Rather, it is the rediscovery of a permanent presence which has chosen to hide itself from us – unless it is we who have the power to hide from it:

> So ist der Mensch; wenn da ist das Gut, und es sorget mit Gaaben
> Selber ein Gott für ihn, kennet und sieht er es nicht.
> ("Brot und Wein," stanza 3)

Since the presence of a transcendental principle, in fact conceived as omnipresence (parousia), can be hidden from man by man's own volition, the epiphany appears in the guise of a beginning rather than a discovery. Hölderlin's phrase: "Wie Blumen entstehn" is in fact a paradox, since origination is inconceivable on the ontological level; the ease with which we nevertheless accept it is indicative of our desire to forget. Our eagerness to accept the statement, the "beauty" of the line, stems from the fact that it combines the poetic seduction of beginnings contained in the word "entstehn" with the ontological stability of the natural object – but this combination is made possible only by a deliberate forgetting of the transcendental nature of the source.

That this forgetting, this ignorance, is also painful becomes apparent from the strategic choice of the word "flower," an object that seems intrinsically desirable. The effect of the line would have been thoroughly modified if Hölderlin had written, for instance, "Steinen" instead of "Blumen," although the relevance of the comparison would have remained intact as long as human language was being compared to a natural thing. The obviously desirable sensory aspects of the flower express the ambivalent aspiration toward a forgotten presence that gave rise to the image, for it is in experiencing the material presence of the particular flower that the desire arises to be reborn in the manner of a natural creation. The image is inspired by a nostalgia for the natural object, expanding to become nostalgia for the origin of this object. Such a nostalgia can only exist when the transcendental presence is forgotten, as in the "dürftiger Zeit" of Hölderlin's poem which we are all too eager to circumscribe as if it were a specific historical "time" and not Time in general. The existence of the poetic image is itself a sign of divine absence, and the conscious use of poetic imagery an admission of this absence.

It is clear that, in Hölderlin's own line, the words do *not* originate like flowers. They need to find the mode of their beginning in another entity; they originate out of nothing, in an attempt to be the first words that will arise as if they were natural objects, and, as such, they remain essentially distinct from natural entities. Hölderlin's statement is a perfect definition of what we call a natural image: the word that designates a desire for an epiphany but necessarily fails to be an epiphany, because it is pure origination. For it is in the essence of language to be capable of origination, but of never achieving the absolute identity with itself that exists in the natural object. Poetic language can do nothing but originate anew over and over again; it is always constitutive, able to posit regardless of presence but, by the same token, unable to give a foundation to what it posits except as an intent of consciousness. The word is always a free presence to the mind, the means by which the permanence of natural entities can be put into question and thus negated, time and again, in the endlessly widening spiral of the dialectic.

An image of this type is indeed the simplest and most fundamental we can conceive of, the metaphorical expression most apt to gain our immediate acquiescence. During the long development that takes place in the nineteenth century, the poetic image remains predominantly of the same kind that in the Hölderlin passage we took for our starting point – and which, be it said in passing, far from exhausts Hölderlin's own conception of the poetic image. This type of imagery is grounded in the intrinsic ontological primacy of the natural object. Poetic language seems to originate in the desire to draw closer and closer to the ontological status of the object, and its growth and development are determined by this inclination. We saw that this movement is essentially paradoxical and condemned in advance to failure. There can be flowers that "are" and poetic words that "originate," but no poetic words that "originate" as if they "were."

Nineteenth-century poetry reexperiences and represents the adventure of this failure in an infinite variety of forms and versions. It selects, for example, a variety of archetypal myths to serve as the dramatic pattern for the narration of this failure; a useful study could be made of the romantic and post-romantic versions of Hellenic myths such as the stories of Narcissus, of Prometheus, of the War of the Titans, of Adonis, Eros and Psyche, Proserpine, and many others; in each case, the tension and duality inherent in the mythological situation would be found to reflect the inherent tension that resides in the metaphorical language itself. At times, romantic thought and romantic poetry seem to come so close to giving in completely to the nostalgia for the object that it becomes difficult to distinguish between object and image, between imagination and perception, between an expressive or constitutive and a mimetic or literal language. This may well be the case in some passages of Wordsworth and Goethe, of Baudelaire and Rimbaud, where the vision almost seems to become a real landscape. Poetics of "unmediated vision," such as those implicit in Bergson and explicit in Bachelard, fuse matter and imagination by amalgamating perception and reverie, sacrificing, in fact, the demands of consciousness to the realities of the object. Critics who speak of a "happy relationship" between matter and consciousness fail to realize that the very fact that the relationship has to be established within the medium of language indicates that it does not exist in actuality.

At other times, the poet's loyalty toward his language appears so strongly that the object nearly vanishes under the impact of his words, in what Mallarmé called "sa presque disparition vibratoire." But even in as extreme a case as Mallarmé's, it would be a mistake to assume that the ontological priority of the object is being challenged. Mallarmé may well be the nineteenth-century poet who went further than any other in sacrificing the stability of the object to the demands of a lucid poetic awareness. Even some of his own disciples felt they had to react against him by reasserting the positivity of live and material substances against the annihilating power of his thought. Believing themselves to be in a situation where they had to begin their work at the point where Mallarmé had finished his, they took, like Claudel, the precise counterpart of his attitudes or, like Valéry, reversed systematically the meaning of some of his key images. Yet Mallarmé himself had always remained convinced of the essential priority of the natural object. The final image of his work, in *Un Coup de Dés*, is that of the poet drowned in the ubiquitous "sea" of natural substances against which his mind can only wage a meaningless battle, "tenter une chance oiseuse." It is true that, in Mallarmé's thought, the value emphasis of this priority has been reversed and the triumph of nature is being presented as the downfall of poetic defiance. But this does not alter the fundamental situation. The alternating feeling of attraction and repulsion that the romantic poet experiences toward nature becomes in Mallarmé the conscious dialectic of a reflective poetic consciousness. This dialectic, far from challenging the supremacy of the order of nature, in fact reasserts it at all times. "Nous savons, victimes d'une formule absolue, que certes n'est que ce qui est," writes Mallarmé, and this absolute identity is rooted, for him, in "la première en date, la nature. Idée tangible pour intimer quelque réalité aux sens frustes. . . ."

Mallarmé's conception and use of imagery is entirely in agreement with this principle. His key symbols – sea, winged bird, night, the sun, constellations, and many others – are not primarily literary emblems but are taken, as he says, "au répertoire de la nature"; they receive their meaning and function from the fact that they belong initially to the natural world. In the poetry, they may seem disincarnate to the point of abstraction, generalized to the point of becoming pure ideas, yet they never entirely lose contact with the concrete reality from which they spring. The sea, the bird, and the constellation act and seduce in Mallarmé's poetry, like any earthly sea, bird, or star in nature; even the Platonic "oiseau qu'on n'ouït jamais" still has about it some of the warmth of the nest in which it was born. Mallarmé does not linger over the concrete and material details of his images, but he never ceases to interrogate, by means of a conscious poetic language, the natural world of which they are originally a part – while knowing that he could never reduce any part of this world to his own, conscious mode of being. If this is true of Mallarmé, the most self-conscious and anti-natural poet of the nineteenth century, it seems safe to assert that the priority of the natural object remains unchallenged among the inheritors of romanticism. The detailed study of Mallarmé bears this out; the same is true, with various nuances and reservations, of most Victorian and post-Victorian poets. For most of them, as for Mallarmé, the priority of nature is experienced as a feeling of failure and sterility, but nevertheless asserted. A similar feeling of threatening paralysis prevails among our own contemporaries and seems to grow with the depth of their poetic commitment. It may be that this threat could only be overcome when the status of poetic language or, more restrictively, of the poetic image, is again brought into question....

Editor's Note

1 This is the first of two quotations in this extract that de Man makes from Hölderlin's poem "Brot und Wein" ("Bread and Wine"). Hölderlin wrote the poem in 1800. In the sequence of Hölderlin's poem, de Man's first quotation follows almost immediately after his second quotation from the concluding lines of stanza 3 of the poem. De Man's first quotation can be translated as follows:

> ... now what they love they name
> Now for it words must come into being like flowers.

The same translation for the second quotation reads:

> So humans are: when the good is there and with gifts a god
> Tends them himself, they neither know nor see it.

Both translations are taken from Friedrich Hölderlin, *Selected Poems*, translated by David Constantine (Newcastle upon Tyre: Bloodaxe Books, 1996).

Chapter 57
Derek Walcott

Derek Walcott (1930–) is a poet, playwright, and painter now widely recognized as one of the leading Caribbean writers of his generation. His work is born out of a learned engagement with the traditions of English and European poetry, but the echoes and transpositions that characterize his poetry are not occasions for nostalgia. The resources of tradition are reworked in an intense dialogue with the history and the present circumstances of the Caribbean. A central figure in Walcott's poetry is the wanderer or migrant, traveling from island to island or continent to continent. This produces a characteristic double movement in his poetry: forward into new experience and the exhilaration of discovery, combined with moments of retrospect and taking stock. He has tested the imaginative potential of a wide range of poetic forms, including sonnet sequences in his collection, Midsummer, *autobiography in his long poem,* Another Life, *and his transposition of Homeric epic to the Caribbean,* Omeros. *He was awarded the Nobel Prize for Literature in 1992.*

"The Muse of History" was first published in 1974 in Is Massa Day Dead?, *edited by Order Coombs and was later collected with other essays by Walcott in* What the Twilight Says. *It provides one of Walcott's most sustained statements on the situation of the postcolonial writer. In this essay, Walcott distinguishes between two stances towards colonial experience. One, which he rejects, is the creation of a literature of "recrimination and despair," trapped in an obligation to right the wrongs of past history. The other, which he embraces, absorbs rather than rejects the literary traditions of the colonizing nations, and uses these resources for the making of a literature of "elation which sees everything renewed." Walcott transforms Eliot's conception of tradition by putting it in the service of a "New World" writing.*

The Muse of History

> *History is the nightmare from which I am trying to awake.*
>
> Joyce

From *What the Twilight Says: Essays* (New York: Farrar, Straus and Giroux, 1998), pp. 36–64.

I

The common experience of the New World, even for its patrician writers whose veneration of the Old is read as the idolatry of the mestizo, is colonialism. They, too, are victims of tradition, but they remind us of our debt to the great dead, that those who break a tradition first hold it in awe. They perversely encourage disfavour, but because their sense of the past is of a timeless, yet habitable, moment, the New World owes them more than it does those who wrestle with that past, for their veneration subtilizes an arrogance which is tougher than violent rejection. They know that by openly fighting tradition we perpetuate it, that revolutionary literature is a filial impulse, and that maturity is the assimiliation of the features of every ancestor.

When these writers cunningly describe themselves as classicists and pretend an indifference to change, it is with an irony as true of the colonial anguish as the fury of the radical. If they appear to be phony aristocrats, it is because they have gone past the confrontation of history, that Medusa of the New World.

These writers reject the idea of history as time for its original concept as myth, the partial recall of the race. For them history is fiction, subject to a fitful muse, memory. Their philosophy, based on a contempt for historic time, is revolutionary, for what they repeat to the New World is its simultaneity with the Old. Their vision of man is elemental, a being inhabited by presences, not a creature chained to his past. Yet the method by which we are taught the past, the progress from motive to event, is the same by which we read narrative fiction. In time every event becomes an exertion of memory and is thus subject to invention. The further the facts, the more history petrifies into myth. Thus, as we grow older as a race, we grow aware that history is written, that it is a kind of literature without morality, that in its actuaries the ego of the race is indissoluble and that everything depends on whether we write this fiction through the memory of hero or of victim.

In the New World servitude to the muse of history has produced a literature of recrimination and despair, a literature of revenge written by the descendants of slaves or a literature of remorse written by the descendants of masters. Because this literature serves historical truth, it yellows into polemic or evaporates in pathos. The truly tough aesthetic of the New World neither explains nor forgives history. It refuses to recognize it as a creative or culpable force. This shame and awe of history possess poets of the Third World who think of language as enslavement and who, in a rage for identity, respect only incoherence or nostalgia.

II

The great poets of the New World, from Whitman to Neruda, reject this sense of history. Their vision of man in the New World is Adamic. In their exuberance he is still capable of enormous wonder. Yet he has paid his accounts to Greece and Rome and walks in a world without monuments and ruins. They exhort him against the fearful magnet of older civilizations. Even in Borges, where the genius seems secretive, immured from change, it celebrates an elation which is vulgar and abrupt, the life of the plains given an instant archaism by the hieratic style. Violence is felt with the simultaneity of history. So the death of a gaucho does not merely repeat, but is, the death of Caesar. Fact evaporates into myth. This is not the jaded cynicism which sees nothing new under the sun, it is an elation which sees everything as renewed. Like Borges, too, the poet St.-John Perse conducts us from the mythology of the past to the present without a tremor of adjustment. This is the revolutionary spirit at its deepest; it recalls the spirit to arms. In Perse there is the greatest width of elemental praise of winds, seas, rains. The revolutionary or cyclic vision is as deeply rooted as the patrician syntax. What Perse glorifies is not veneration but the perennial freedom; his hero remains the wanderer, the man who moves through the ruins of great civilizations with all his worldly goods by caravan or pack mule, the poet carrying entire cultures in his head, bitter perhaps, but unencumbered. His are poems of massive or solitary migrations through the elements. They are the same in spirit as the poems of Whitman or Neruda, for they seek spaces where praise of the earth is ancestral.

III

New World poets who see the "classic style" as stasis must see it also as historical degradation, rejecting it as the language of the master. This self-torture arises when the poet also sees history as language, when he limits his memory to the suffering of the victim. Their admirable wish to honour the degraded ancestor limits their language to phonetic pain, the groan of suffering, the curse of revenge. The tone of the past becomes an unbearable burden, for they must abuse the master or hero in his own language, and this implies self-deceit. Their view of Caliban is of the enraged pupil. They cannot separate the rage of Caliban from the beauty of his speech when the speeches of Caliban are equal in their elemental power to those of his tutor. The language of the torturer mastered by the victim. This is viewed as servitude, not as victory.

But who in the New World does not have a horror of the past, whether his ancestor was torturer or victim? Who, in the depth of conscience, is not silently screaming for pardon or for revenge? The pulse of New World history is the racing pulse beat of fear, the tiring cycles of stupidity and greed. The tongues above our prayers utter the pain of entire races to the darkness of a Manichean God: *Dominus illuminatio mea*, for what was brought to this New World under the guise of divine light, the light of the sword blade and the light of *dominus illuminatio mea*, was the same iridescent serpent brought by a contaminating Adam, the same tortured Christ exhibited with Christian exhaustion, but what was also brought in the seeded entrails of the slave was a new nothing, a darkness which intensified the old faith.

In time the slave surrendered to amnesia. That amnesia is the true history of the New World. That is our inheritance, but to try and understand why this happened, to condemn or justify is also the method of history, and these explanations are always the same: This happened because of that, this was understandable because, and in days men were such. These recriminations exchanged, the contrition of the master replaces the vengeance of the slave, and here colonial literature is most pietistic, for it can accuse great art of feudalism and excuse poor art as suffering. To radical poets poetry seems the homage of resignation, an essential fatalism. But it is not the pressure of the past which torments great poets but the weight of the present:

> there are so many dead,
> and so many dikes the red sun breached,
> and so many heads battering hulls
> and so many hands that have closed over kisses
> and so many things that I want to forget.
> (Pablo Neruda)

The sense of history in poets lives rawly along their nerves:

> My land without name, without America,
> equinoctial stamen, lance-like purple,
> your aroma rose through my roots
> into the cup I drained, into the most tenuous
> word not yet born in my mouth.
> (Pablo Neruda)

It is this awe of the numinous, this elemental privilege of naming the New World which annihilates history in our great poets, an elation common to all of them, whether they are aligned by heritage to Crusoe and Prospero or to Friday and Caliban. They reject ethnic ancestry for faith in elemental man. The vision, the "democratic vista," is not metaphorical, it is a social necessity. A political philosophy rooted in elation would have to accept belief in a second Adam, the re-creation of the entire order, from religion to the simplest domestic rituals. The myth of the noble savage would not be revived, for that myth never emanated from the savage but has always been the nostalgia of the Old World, its longing for innocence. The great poetry of the New World does not pretend to such innocence, its vision is not naïve. Rather, like its fruits, its savour is a mixture of the acid and the sweet, the apples of its second Eden have the tartness of experience. In such poetry there is a bitter memory and it is the bitterness that dries last on the tongue. It is the acidulous that supplies its energy. The golden apples of this sun are shot with acid. The taste of Neruda is citric, the *Pomme de Cythère* of Aimé Césaire sets the teeth on edge, the savour of Perse is of salt fruit at the sea's edge, the sea grape, the "fat poke," the sea almond. For us in the archipelago the tribal memory is salted with the bitter memory of migration.

To such survivors, to all the decimated tribes of the New World who did not suffer extinction, their degraded arrival must be seen as the beginning, not the end, of our history. The shipwrecks of Crusoe and of the crew in *The Tempest* are the end of an Old World. It should matter nothing to the New World if the Old is again determined to blow itself up, for an obsession with progress is not within the psyche of the recently enslaved. That is the bitter secret of the apple. The vision of progress is the rational madness of history seen as sequential time, of a dominated future. Its imagery is absurd. In the history books the discoverer sets a shod food on virgin sand, kneels, and the savage also kneels from his bushes in awe. Such images are stamped on the colonial memory, such heresy as the world's becoming holy from Crusoe's footprint or the imprint of Columbus's knee. These blasphemous images fade, because these hieroglyphs of progress are basically comic. And if the idea of the New and the Old becomes increasingly absurd, what must happen to our sense of time, what else can happen to history itself, but that it, too, is becoming absurd? This is not existentialism. Adamic, elemental man cannot be existential. His first impulse is not self-indulgence but awe, and existentialism is simply the myth of the noble savage gone baroque. Such philosophies of freedom are born in cities. Existentialism is as much nostalgia as in Rousseau's sophisticated primitivism, as sick as recurrence in French thought as the isle of Cythera, whether it is the tubercular, fevered imagery of Watteau or the same fever turned delirious in Rimbaud and Baudelaire. The poets of the "New Aegean," of the Isles of the Blest, the Fortunate Isles, of the remote Bermudas, of Prospero's isle, of Crusoe's Juan Fernandez, of Cythera, of all those rocks named like the beads of a chaplet, they know that the old vision of Paradise wrecks here.

> I want to hear a song in which the rainbow breaks
> and the curlew alights among forgotten shores
> I want the liana creeping on the palm-tree
> (on the trunk of the present 'tis our stubborn future)
> I want the conquistador with unsealed armour
> lying down in death of perfumed flowers,
> the foam censing a sword gone rusty
> in the pure blue flight of slow wild cactuses
>
> (Aimé Césaire)

But to most writers of the archipelago who contemplate only the shipwreck, the New World offers not elation but cynicism, a despair at the vices of the Old which they feel must be repeated. Their malaise is an oceanic nostalgia for the older culture and a melancholy at the new, and this can go as deep as a rejection of the untamed landscape, a yearning for ruins. To such writers the death of civilizations is architectural, not spiritual; seeded in their memories is an imagery of vines ascending broken columns, of dead terraces, of Europe as a nourishing museum. They believe in the responsibility of tradition, but what they are in awe of is not tradition, which is alert, alive, simultaneous, but history, and the same is true of the new magnifiers of Africa. For these their deepest loss is of the old gods, the fear that it is worship which has enslaved progress. Thus the humanism of politics replaces religion. They see such gods as part of the process of history, subjected like the tribe to cycles of achievement and despair. Because the Old World concept of God is anthropomorphic, the New World slave was forced to remake himself in His image, despite such phrases as "God is light, and in Him is no darkness," and at this point of intersecting faiths the enslaved poet and enslaved priest surrendered their power. But the tribe in bondage learned to fortify itself by cunning assimilation of the religion of the Old World. What seemed to be surrender was redemption. What seemed the loss of tradition was its renewal. What seemed the death of faith was its rebirth.

IV

Eliot speaks of the culture of a people as being the incarnation of its religion. If this is true, in the New World we have to ask this faceted question: (1) Whether the religion taught to the black slave has been absorbed as belief, (2) whether it has been altered by this absorption, and (3) whether wholly absorbed or absorbed and altered, it must now be rejected. In other terms, can an African culture exist, except on the level of polemical art or politics, without an African religion, and if so, which African religion?

The spectacle of mediocre talents raising old totems is more shameful than the faith of the convert which they ridicule, but the flare of a literary religion is brief, for faith needs more than style. At this stage the polemic poet, like the politician, will wish to produce epic work, to summon the grandeur of the past, not as myth but as history, and to prophesy in the way that Fascist architecture can be viewed as prophesy. Yet the more ambitious the zeal, the more diffuse and forced it becomes, the more it roots into research, until the imagination surrenders to the glorification of history, the ear becomes enslaved, the glorifiers of the tom-tom ignoring the dynamo. These epic poets create an artificial past, a defunct cosmology without the tribal faith.

What remains in the archipelago is the fragmentation into schisms, the private cosmology of the wayside preacher. Every day in these islands the sidewalk blossoms with such victims, minds disfigured by their attempt to comprehend both worlds unless they create a heaven of which they are the centre. Like the wayside prophets, the "epic" poet in the islands looks to anthropology, to a catalogue of forgotten gods, to midden fragments, artifacts, and the unfinished phrases of a dead speech. These engage in masochistic recollection. The epic-minded poet looks around these islands and finds no ruins, and because all epic is based on the visible presence of ruins, wind-bitten or sea-bitten, the poet celebrates what little there is, the rusted slave wheel of the sugar factory, cannon, chains, the crusted amphora of cutthroats, all the paraphernalia of degradation and cruelty which we exhibit as history, not as masochism, as if the ovens of Auschwitz and Hiroshima were the temples of the race. Morbidity is the inevitable result, and that is the tone of any literature which respects such a history and bases its truth on shame or on revenge.

And yet it is there that the epic poetry of the tribe originates, in its identification with Hebraic suffering, the migration, the hope of deliverance from bondage. There was this difference, that the passage over our Red Sea was not from bondage to freedom but its opposite, so that the tribes arrived at their New Canaan chained. There is this residual feeling in much of our literature, the wailing by strange waters for a lost home. It survives in our politics, the subdued search for a Moses. The epic concept was compressed in the folk lyric, the mass longing in chanter and chorus, couplet and refrain. The revivalist poems drew their strength from the self-hypnotic nature of their responses, interminable in monody as the tribal hope.

I know moonrise, I know star-rise,
Lay this body down,
I go to my Lord in the evening of the day,
Lay this body down.

But this monody is not only resigned but martial:

Joshua fit de battle of Jericho,
Jericho, Jericho,
Joshua fit de battle of Jericho,
And the walls come tumbling down.

The epic poem is not a literary project. It is already written; it was written in the mouths of the tribe, a tribe which had courageously yielded its history.

V

While the Old Testament epics of bondage and deliverance provided the slave with a political parallel, the ethics of Christianity tempered his vengeance and appeared to deepen his passivity. To his masters this world was not new but an extension of the old. Their vision of an earthly Paradise was denied him, and the reward offered in the name of Christian suffering would come after his death. All this we know, but the phenomenon is the zeal with which the slave accepted both the Christian and the Hebraic, resigned his gaze to the death of his pantheon, and yet deliberately began to invest a decaying faith with a political belief. Historians cannot chronicle this, except they go by the statistics of conversion. There is no moment of a mass tribal conversion equal to the light's unhorsing of Saul; what we were told to believe instead was a slow, massive groan of surrender, the immense laborious conversion of the defeated into good niggers, or true Christians; and certainly songs such as this one seem to be the most contemptible expression of the beaten:

I'm going to lay down my sword and shield,
Down by the riverside, down by the riverside...

I ain't going study war no more,
Study war no more...

How can we teach this as history? Aren't those the words of the whitewashed, the defeated, isn't this the Christian treachery that seduces revenge, that led the exhausted tribes to betray their gods? A new generation looks back on such conversion with contempt, for where are the songs of triumph, the defiance of the captured warrior, where are the nostalgic battle chants and the seasonal songs of harvest, the seeding of the great African pastoral? This generation sees in the epic poetry of the work song and the early blues self-contempt and inertia, but the deep truth is that pinioned and humiliated in body as the slave was, there is, beyond simple fortitude, a note of aggression, and what a later generation sees as defeat is really the willing of spiritual victory, for the captured warrior and the tribal poet had chosen the very battleground which the captor proposed, the soul:

I am a warrior, out in the field,
And I can sing, and I can shout,
And I can tell it all about that Jesus died for me,
When I get over yonder in the happy paradise,
When I get over yonder in the field.

What was captured from the captor was his God, for the subject African had come to the New World in an elemental intimacy with nature, with a profounder terror of blasphemy than the exhausted, hypocritical Christian. He understood too quickly the Christian rituals of a whipped, tortured, and murdered redeemer, though he may have recoiled at dividing and eating his flesh, for in primal cultures gods defeat each other like warriors, and for warriors there is no conversion in defeat. There are many such warriors in the history of the archipelago, but the true history is of the tribe's conversion, and it is this which is our concern. It returns us to Eliot's pronouncement, that a culture cannot exist without a religion, and to other pronouncements irradiating that idea, that an epic poetry cannot exist without a religion. It is the beginning of the poetry of the New World. And the language used is, like the religion, that of the conqueror of the God. But the slave had wrested God from his captor.

In tribal, elemental poetry, the epic experience of the race is compressed in metaphor. In an oral tradition the mode is simple, the response open-ended, so that each new poet can add his lines to the form, a process very much like weaving or the dance, based on the concept that the history of the tribe is endless. There is no dying fall, no egotistical signature of effect; in short, no pathos. The blues is not pathos, not the individual voice, it is a tribal mode, and each new oral poet can contribute his couplet, and this is based on the concept that the tribe, inured to despair, will also survive: there is no beginning but no end. The new poet enters a flux and withdraws, as the weaver continues the pattern, hand to hand and mouth to mouth, as the rockpile convict passes the sledge:

Many days of sorrow, many nights of woe,
Many days of sorrow, many nights of woe,
And a ball and chain, everywhere I go.

No history, but flux, and the only sustenance, myth:

Moses lived till he got old,
Where shall I be?

The difference is in the intensity of celebration. The pietistic rhythm of the missionary is speeded to a martial frenzy which the slave adapts to a triumphal tribal mode. Good, the missionary and merchant must have thought, once we've got them swinging and clapping, all will be peace, but their own God was being taken away from merchant and missionary by a submerged force that rose at ritual gatherings, where the subconscious rhythm rose and took possession and where, in fact, the Hebraic-European God was changing colour, for the names of the sub-deities did not matter, Saint Ursula or Saint Urzulie; the Catholic pantheon adapted easily to African pantheism. Catholic mystery adapted easily to African magic. Not all accepted the white man's God. As prologue to the Haitian revolution, Boukman was invoking Damballa in the Bois Cayman. Blood sacrifices, warrior initiations, tortures, escapes, revolts, even the despair of slaves who went mad and ate dirt, these are the historical evidence, but what is finally important is that the race or the tribes were converted, they became Christian. But no race is converted against its will. The slave master now encountered a massive pliability. The slave converted himself, he changed weapons, spiritual weapons, and as he adapted his master's religion, he also adapted his language, and it is here that what we can look at as our poetic tradition begins. Now began the new naming of things.

Epic was compressed in the folk legend. The act of imagination was the creative effort of the tribe. Later such legends may be written by individual poets, but their beginnings are oral, familial, the poetry of firelight which illuminates the faces of a tight, primal hierarchy. But even oral literature forces itself towards hieroglyph and alphabet. Today, still in many islands, the West Indian poet is faced with a language which he hears but cannot write because there are no symbols for such a language and because the closer he brings hand and word to the precise inflections of the inner language and to the subtlest accuracies of his ear, the more chaotic his symbols will appear on the page, the smaller the regional dialect, the more eccentric his representation of it will become, so his function remains the old one of being filter and purifier, never losing the tone and strength of the common speech as he uses the hieroglyphs, symbols, or alphabet of the official one. Now two of the greatest poets of this archipelago have come from French-patois-speaking islands. St.-John Perse, born and reared until late adolescence in Guadeloupe, and Aimé Césaire, the Martiniquan. Both have the colonial experience of language, one from privilege, the other from deprivation. Let it not be important for now that one is white, the other black. Both are Frenchmen, both are poets who write in French. Well, to begin with, it is Césaire's language which is the more abstruse, more difficult, more surrealist, while Perse's French is classic. Césaire has not written his great poem, *Cahier d'un retour au pays natal*, in dialect, but we must pay attention to its tone. For all the complexity of its surrealism, its sometimes invented words, it sounds, to at least one listener familiar with French patois, like a poem written tonally in Creole. Those tonal qualities are tartness and impatience, but the language of Césaire in this great revolutionary poem, or rather a poem partially appropriated by revolutionaries, is not proletarian. The tone of Perse is also majestic, it marches a path of inevitable conquest appropriating as it proceeds; and to the reader trying to listen purely to the language of either poet without prejudice, without subliminal whispers of history, they have at least one thing in common: authority. Their diction has other similarities, for instance, form. In *Cahier d'un retour au pays natal*, as well as in the prose poems of Perse from the Antillean *Eloges* to *Chronique* and beyond, there is a strict, synonymous armature shared within the tradition of the metropolitan language, and which both must have felt to be an inheritance despite their racial and social differences, despite the distance of Perse from the dialect of house servants and of fishermen, despite the fealty of Césaire to that dialect. The sources of that diction are both ancient and contemporary: the Bible and the tribal ode as well as French surrealist poetry, the proletarian hymns of Whitman, and the oral or written legends of other civilizations, for Perse the East and the Mediterranean, for Césaire the Hebraic Mediterranean and Africa. In visual structure the poetry of both shares the symmetry of the prose ode, the appearance of translation from an older epic which invests their poems with an air of legend. Now here are two colonials or, more precisely, two poets whose formative perceptions, whose apprehension of the visible worlds of their very different childhoods, were made numinous by their elation in the metropolitan language, and whose very different visions created indisputable masterpieces, and, here is the point, without doing violence to the language itself, in fact perpetuating its grandeur through opposite beliefs, Perse through prophesy and nostalgia, Césaire through nostalgia and polemic. Yet, as a translator, I would rather attempt an equivalent in English to Perse than to Césaire, for the simple reason that Perse is perhaps simpler, for where his language grows abstruse in the vocabularies of archaeology, marine biology, botany, and so forth, the language of Césaire skims the subtleties of modern surrealism. Yet as an Antillean, I feel more akin to Césaire's tone.

I do not know if one poet is indebted to the other, but whatever the bibliographical truth is, one acknowledges not an exchange of influences, not imitation, but the tidal advance of the metropolitan language, of its empire, if you like, which carries simultaneously, fed by such strong colonial tributaries, poets of such different beliefs as Rimbaud, Char, Claudel, Perse, and Césaire. It is the language which is the empire, and great poets are not its vassals but its princes. We continue to categorize these poets by the wrong process; that is, by history. We continue to fiddle with the obvious limitations of dialect because of chauvinism, but the great poem of Césaire's could not be written in a French Creole dialect because there are no words for some of its concepts; there are no equivalent nouns for its objects, and because even if these were suddenly found, they could not be visually expressed without the effort of an insane philologist. Both poets manipulate a supreme, visionary rhetoric that carries over into English. Sometimes they sound identical:

1. Narrow path of the surge in the blur of fables...

(Césaire)

2. Wandering, what did we know of our ancestral bed, all blazoned
though it were in that speckled wood of the Islands?...There
was no name for us in the ancient bronze gong of the old family house. There was no name
  for us in our mother's oratory
(jacaranda wood or cedar), nor in the golden antennae quivering
in the head-dresses of our guardians, women of colour. We were
not in the lute-maker's wood, in the spinet or the harp: nor...

(Perse)

3. I want to hear a song in which the rainbow breaks
and the curlew alights along forgotten shores

I want the liana creeping on the palm-tree
(on the trunk of the present 'tis our stubborn future)
I want the conquistador with unsealed armour
lying down in death of perfumed flowers,
the foam censing a sword gone rusty
in the pure blue flight of slow wild cactuses.

(Césaire)

4. Master of the three roads a man stands before you who walked much,
Master of the three roads a man stands before you who walked on hands who walked on feet who walked on the belly who walked on the behind.
Since Elam. Since Akkad. Since Sumer.
Master of the three roads a man stands before you who has carried much.
And truly, friends, I carried since Elam, since Akkad, since Sumer.

(Césaire)

Perse and Césaire, men of diametrically challenging backgrounds, racial opposites, to use the language of politics, one patrician and conservative, the other proletarian and revolutionary, classic and romantic, Prospero and Caliban, all such opposites balance easily, but they balance on the axis of a shared sensibility, and this sensibility, with or deprived of the presence of a visible tradition, is the sensibility of walking to a New World. Perse sees in this New World vestiges of the Old, of order and of hierarchy, Césaire sees in it evidence of past humiliations and the need for a new order, but the deeper truth is that both poets perceive this New World through mystery. Their language tempts us to endless quotation; there are moments when one hears both voices simultaneously, until the tone is one voice from these different men. If we think of one as poor and the other as privileged when we read their addresses to the New World, if we must see one as black and one as white, we are not only dividing this sensibility by the process of the sociologist, we are denying the range of either poet, the power of compassion and the power of fury. One is not making out a case for assimilation and for the common simplicity of all men; we are interested in their differences, openly, but what astonishes us in both poets is their elation, their staggering elation in possibility. And one is not talking of a possible ideal society, for you will find that only in the later work of Perse, a society which is inaccessible by its very grandeur, but of the elation in presences which exists in *Éloges* and in *Pour fêter une enfance*, the possibility of the individual Caribbean man, African, European, or Asian in ancestry, the enormous, gently opening morning of his possibility, his body touched with dew, his nerves as subtilized to sensation as the mimosa, his memory, whether of grandeur or of pain, gradually erasing itself as recurrent drizzles cleanse the ancestral or tribal markings from the coral skull, the possibility of a man and his language waking to wonder here. As the language of Perse later becomes hammered and artificial, so does the rhetoric of Césaire move towards the heraldic, but their first great work is as deeply rooted and supple as a vine.

But these poems are in French. The fact that they have now begun to influence English poetry from the archipelago is significant, because they are powerful works and all power attracts to itself, but their rhetoric is unmanageable for our minor "revolutionary" poets, who assume a grandeur without a language to create it, for these imitators see both poems through history, or through sociology; they are seduced by their subjects. Therefore, there is now a brood of thin, querulous fledglings who steal fragments of Césaire for their own nests, and yet these fledglings will condemn Perse as a different animal, a white poet. These convulsions of bad poetry appear when the society is screaming for change.

Because we think of tradition as history, one group of anatomists claims that this tradition is wholly African and that its responses are alerted through the nostalgia of one race, but that group must allow the Asian and the Mediterranean the same fiction, and then the desolate terraces of Perse's epic memory will be as West Indian to the Middle Easterners among us as the kingdoms of the Guinea coast are to Césaire or the poetry of China is to the Chinese grocer. If we can psychologize, divide, trace these degenerations easily, then we must accept the miracle of possibility which every poet demonstrates. The Caribbean sensibility is not marinated in the past. It is not exhausted. It is new. But it is its complexity, not its historically explained simplicities, which is new. Its traces of melancholy are the chemical survivals of the blood which remain after the slave's and the identured worker's convalescence. It will survive the malaria of nostalgia and the delirium of revenge, just as it survived its self-contempt.

Thus, while many critics of contemporary Commonwealth verse reject imitation, the basis of the tradition, for originality, the false basis of innovation, they represent eventually the old patronizing attitude adapted to contemporaneous politics, for their demand for naturalness, novelty, originality, or truth is again based on preconceptions of behaviour. They project reflexes as anticipated as the exuberance, spontaneity, and refreshing dialect of the tribe. Certain performances are called for, including the fashionable incoherence of revolutionary anger, and everyone is again appeased, the masochist critic by the required attack on his "values," the masochist poet by the approval of his victim. Minstrel postures, in their beginnings, are hard to identify from private truths, but their familiarity soon establishes the old formulae of entertainment. Basically, the anger of the black is entertainment or theater, if it makes an aesthetic out of anger, and this is no different in its "naturalness" than the legendary joy or spontaneous laughter of the minstrel. It is still nightclub and cabaret, professional fire-eating and dancing on broken bottles. The critic-tourist can only gasp at such naturalness. He wouldn't care to try it himself, really. We are back to Dr. Johnson's female preacher.

The liberal warms to the speech of the ghetto in a way quite contemptible to the poet, for the benignity of the liberal critic perpetuates the sociological conditions of that speech, despite his access to anger. What he really preaches again, but this time through criticism, is the old separate-but-equal argument. Blacks are different, and the pathos is that most blacks have been led to believe this, and into the tragedy of proclaiming their difference. The theories clash, for the radical seeks to equate the deprived up to the status of the privileged, while the liberal and his unconscious accomplices, the poets of the ghetto and of "revolutionary rhetoric," fear to lose "their own thing" if they let thought and education widen by materialist benefits. Often it is the educated and privileged poet who masks his education and privilege behind a fake exoticism of poverty and the pastoral. They write one way and speak another. There has been the treason of clerks, and now we have the treason of the intellectuals.

The degeneration of technique, when technique is an open question, hides itself in originality. Bad verse written by blacks is better than good verse written by whites, because, say the revolutionaries, the same standards do not apply. This is seen as pride, as the opposite of inferiority. So too, one can isolate in this writer's general demeanor of style that belligerent naïveté or a joy unqualified which characterizes a pubescent literature. One which accepts subconsciously a condition of being praised or corrected, which may resist, but also insinuates by resistance, the correctives of a "superior" or at least an older discipline or tradition. It is a flaw which also sees history as a ladder of achievement, but it is a competitive energy which either fails often from exhaustion or amazes by its prolixity. It is manic, it is inferior, but it is certain of its direction and challenges. It engages its peers. For purity, then, for pure black Afro-Aryanism, only the unsoiled black is valid, and West Indianism is a taint, and other strains adulterate him. The extremists, the purists, are beginning to exercise those infections, so that a writer of "mixed," hence "degenerate," blood can be nothing stronger than a liberal. This will develop a rich individualism through a deeper bitterness, it will increase egocentricity and isolation, because such writers and poets already have more complex values. They will seem more imperialistic, nostalgic, and out of the impetus of the West Indian proletariat, because they cannot simplify intricacies of race and the thought of the race. They will become hermits or rogue animals, increasingly exotic hybrids, broken bridges between two ancestries, Europe and the Third World of Africa and Asia; in other words, they will become islands. Because of this isolation their ironic fate will be to appear inaccessible, irrelevant, remote. The machinery of radicalism which makes culture heroes of more violent writers and which makes a virtue of immediacy will not include them. They are condemned to middle age.

And all of this has sprung, at the root, from a rejection of language. The new cult of incoherence, of manic repetition, glorifies the apprentice, and it also atrophies the young, who are warned against assimilation. It is as if the instinct of the black is still escape, escape to the labyrinth, escape to a special oblivion removed from the banalities of poverty and from the weight of a new industrial imperialism, that of absentee "power structures" which control the archipelago's economy. That there will always be abrupt eruptions of defiance is almost irrelevant itself, because the impulse of such eruptions, their political philosophy, remains simplistic and shallow. That all blacks are beautiful is an enervating statement, that all blacks are brothers more a reprimand than a charter, that the people must have power almost their death wish, for the real power of this time is silent. Art cannot last long in this shale. It crumbles like those slogans, fragments and shards of a historical fault. Power now becomes increasingly divided and tribal when it is based on genetics. It leads to the righteous secondary wars of the Third World, to the self-maiming of civil wars, the frontier divisions of third-rate, Third World powers, manipulated or encouraged by the first powers. Genocides increase, tribal wars increase and become increasingly hallucinatory and remote. Nigeria, Bangladesh, Vietnam, the Middle East, Greece, the Spains of our era. The provincial revolutions can only spare a general compassion because they know who manages or stages such things. They believe that the same manipulation is beneath them.

The revolution is here. It was always here. It does not need the decor of African tourism or the hip postures and speech of metropolitan ghettos. Change the old word "slum" for the new word "ghetto" and you have the psychology of funk, a market psychology that, within a year of the physical revolution, has been silently appropriated by Mediterranean and Asian merchants. Soul is a commodity. Soul is an outfit. The "metropolitan" emphasis of the "revolution" has clouded the condition of the peasant, of the inevitably rooted man, and the urban revolutionary is by imitation or by nature rootless and a drifter, fashionably so, and in time a potential exile. The peasant cannot spare himself these city changes. He is the true African who does not need to proclaim it.

On history as exile

Postures of metropolitan cynicism must be assumed by the colonial in exile if he is not to feel lost, unless he prefers utter isolation or the desperate, noisy nostalgia of fellow exiles. This cynicism is an attempt to enter the sense of history which is within every Englishman and European, but which he himself has never felt towards Africa or Asia. There develops the other sense, that the history of Africa or of Asia is inferior, and we see how close we draw to madness here, for this sense qualifies not the significance of an event but the event itself, the action of the event as second class. The exile will not be argued out of this. He has chosen to see history this way, and that is his vision. The simplifications of imperialism, of the colonial heritage, are more dignified, for these gave brutish tribes their own dignity. But even less honest than the colonial in exile is the generation after him, which wants to effect a eugenic leap from imperialism to independence by longing for the ancestral dignity of the wanderer-warrior. Mysterious customs. Defunct gods. Sacred rites. As much as the colonial, however, they are children of the nineteenth-century ideal, the romance of redcoat and savage warrior, their simplification of choosing to play Indian instead of cowboy, filtered through films and adolescent literature, is the hallucination of imperial romance; the posture is melodramatic, the language of its stances idealized from the literature of exploration remembered from Captain Marryat, Kipling, or Rider Haggard. It continues the juvenile romance of savage drums, tribal rites, barbarous but sacred sacrifices, golden journeys, lost cities. In the subconscious there is a black Atlantis buried in a sea of sand.

The colonial is tougher. He sees history for what it is in the world around him, an almost inexpressible banality. He sees the twentieth century without self-deceit and juvenile fantasy. The other curses the banality and chooses myth. Poets of the second group now begin to see poetry as a form of historical instruction. Their target is the officialized literature of the schools, the sociologists, their fellow historians, and, above all, the revolution. They become fascinated with the efficacy of poetry as an aspect of power not through its language but through its subject. Their poetry becomes a kind of musical accompaniment to certain theses, and as history it is forced to exclude certain contradictions, for history cannot be ambiguously recorded. Whatever its motive, either this happened or it did not. All piety is seen as villainy, all form as hypocrisy.

Inevitably, these poets grow obsessed with the innovation of forms, but this innovation is seen as critical strategy, for it will need to attack others as well as defend its position, if it is to be seen as spontaneous choice. Conservatively, it imitates what it believes to be the tribal mode, and it makes no distinction between the artificiality of the high style of tribal ceremony and the language which it employs to achieve this. It may even use fragments of the original language to adorn itself, even if such language is not its natural tongue. A new conservatism now appears, a new dignity more reactionary and pompous than the direction of the language used. It moves manically between the easy applause of dialect, the argot of the tribe and ceremonial speech, the "memory" of the tribe; that is, between the new dignity and the popular, and in between there is nothing. The normal voice of the poet, his own speaking voice is lost, and no language is writ.

No, if we look for the primal imagination in West Indian literature, its "revolutionary" aspect, we find it crucially evolving in West Indian fiction, the poetic principle is more alert in our best prose, and whatever ethnic impulse drives this imagination examines the roots of contemporary man with the same force as poets of a different race using English. In the Guyanese novelist Denis Williams's *Other Leopards* there is this passage:

> Now, having removed my body and the last traces of it, I am without context clear. Going up this new tree, picking the thorns bare, one by one, I am in a darkness nowhere at all, I am nothing, nowhere. This is something gained. Hughie has not found me; I have outwitted him. I have achieved a valuable state: a condition outside his method. Only remains now to remove my consciousness. This I can do whenever I wish. I am free of the earth. I do not need to go down there for anything.

In "Wodwo" by Ted Hughes there is:

> What am I? nosing here turning leaves over
> following a faint stain on the air to the river's edge
> I enter water...
>   I seem
> separate from the ground not rooted but dropped
> out of nothing casually I've not threads
> fastening me to anything I can go anywhere
> I seem to have been given the freedom
> of this place what am I then...

which, excuse the broken quotations, is the tone of the whole poem, language, tone, hesitation, and assurance, the deliberate picking out of names, the numinous process in Williams of a man reduced, in Hughes of a man evolving, the passage from the novel and the whole of Hughes's poem are the same. They are not merely the same in subject, anthropology; in fact, they are different in structure obviously, and there is absolutely no question of exchanged influences except Hughes had read Williams, whose book appeared some years before, but what is there is the displaced, searching psyche of modern man, the reversion of twentieth-century man, whether in Africa or in

Yorkshire, to his pre-Adamic beginning, to pre-history, and this shared contagion of madness exists universally in contemporary poetry, and particularly in a poet like Samuel Beckett.

The words jerk, the search is anguished, the pronouncing of chosen nouns, the cynical or violent rejection of the named thing itself, or the primal or the final elation of the power or of the decadence of the Word itself, the process is shared by three utterly different writers, one Guyanese-African, one English-Celtic, the third Irish-Celtic. What is shared is more than the language; it is the drilling, mining, molelike or mole-cricketlike burrowing into the origins of life or into its detritus. Logos as excrement, logos as engendering spasm. In the sense that these three are black writers, we can only use the term "black" to imply a malevolence towards historical system. The Old World, or visitors to the Old World, or those who exist in the Old World, whether it is Africa, or the Yorkshire submarine world deep as England, or Beckett's unnamed, unnameable gray world of a wrecked civilization, these who are embittered by those worlds write blackly, with a purging pessimism which goes beyond the morbid. In the New World there is the same process in writers with an optimistic or visionary force, there is the same slow naming. This exists wholly in Wilson Harris. But this blackness is luminous. The black in Williams returns in his madness to beginning again. He climbs his thorn tree, he reverts to the anthropological origins of all mankind, no doubt he will descend again, and like Hughes's medieval monster undergoing his thrilling metamorphosis from demon to man as he begins to name things, and he may wreck and destroy civilization and its languages again like those crawlers through primordial and post-atomic mud in Beckett, but these three elemental cycles are the common agony of three racially different writers. These crude cycles are the poet's knowledge of history. So what does this prove? It proves that the truest writers are those who see language not as linguistic process but as a living element; it more closely demonstrates the laziness of poets who confuse language with linguistics and with archaeology. It also annihilates provincial concepts of imitation and originality. Fear of imitation obsesses minor poets. But in any age a common genius almost indistinguishably will show itself, and the perpetuity of this genius is the only valid tradition, not the tradition which categorizes poetry by epochs and by schools. We know that the great poets have no wish to be different, no time to be original, that their originality emerges only when they have absorbed all the poetry which they have read, entire, that their first work appears to be the accumulation of other people's trash, but that they become bonfires, that it is only academics and frightened poets who talk of Beckett's debt to Joyce.

The tribe requires of its poets the highest language and more than predictable sentiment. Now pardon this excursion into autobiography. I knew, from childhood, that I wanted to become a poet, and like any colonial child I was taught English literature as my natural inheritance. Forget the snow and the daffodils. They were real, more real than the heat and the oleander, perhaps, because they lived on the page, in imagination, and therefore in memory. There is a memory of imagination in literature which has nothing to do with actual experience, which is, in fact, another life, and that experience of the imagination will continue to make actual the quest of a medieval knight or the bulk of a white whale, because of the power of a shared imagination. The world of poetry was natural and unlimited by what no child really accepts as the actual world, and of course, later disenchantment and alienation will come. But these are not altogether important, they become part of maturity. To simplify: once I had decided to make the writing of poetry my life, my actual, not my imaginative life, I felt both a rejection and a fear of Europe while I learned its poetry. I have remained this way, but the emotions have changed, they are subtler, more controlled, for I would no longer wish to visit Europe as if I could repossess it than I would wish to visit Africa for that purpose. What survives in the slave is nostalgia for imperial modes, Europe or Africa. I felt, I knew, that if I went to England I would never become a poet, far more a West Indian, and that was the only thing I could see myself becoming, a West Indian poet. The language I used did not bother me. I had given it, and it was irretrievably given; I could no more give it back than they could claim it. But I fear the cathedrals, the music, the weight of history, not because I was alien, but because I felt history to be the burden of others. I was not excited by continuation of its process but by discovery, by the plain burden of work, for there was too much to do here. Yet the older and more assured I grew, the stronger my isolation as a poet, the more I needed to become omnivorous about the art and literature of Europe to understand my own world. I write "my own world" because I had no doubt that it was mine, that it was given to me, by God, not by history, with my gift. At that time nobody anatomized the honesty of my commitment, nobody urged me to reject old values, but such people would have to go through an anguish of rejection and arrogant self-assertion later. These are qualifications of faith, but they are important. We are misled by new prophets of bitterness who warn us against experiences which we have never cared to have, but the mass of society has had neither the interest nor the opportunity which they chose. These preach not to the converted but to those who have never lost faith. I do not mean religious faith but reality. Fisherman and peasant know who they are and what they are and where they are, and when we show them our wounded sensibilities we are, most of us, displaying self-inflicted wounds.

I accept this archipelago of the Americas. I say to the ancestor who sold me, and to the ancestor who bought me, I have no father, I want no such father, although I can understand you, black ghost, white ghost, when you both whisper "history," for if I attempt to forgive you both I am falling into your idea of history which justifies and explains and expiates, and it is not mine to forgive, my memory cannot summon any filial love, since your features are anonymous and erased and I have no wish and no power to pardon. You were when you acted your roles, your given, historical roles of slave seller and slave buyer, men acting as men, and also you, father in the filth-ridden gut of the slave ship, to you they were also men, acting as men, with the cruelty of men, your fellowman and tribesman not moved or hovering with hesitation about your common race any longer than my other bastard ancestor hovered with his whip, but to you, inwardly forgiven grandfathers, I, like the more honest of my race, give a strange thanks. I give the strange and bitter and yet ennobling thanks for the monumental groaning and soldering of two great worlds, like the halves of a fruit seamed by its own bitter juice, that exiled from your own Edens you have placed me in the wonder of another, and that was my inheritance and your gift.

Chapter 58
Julia Kristeva

Julia Kristeva (1941–) is one of the leading writers and theorists associated with post-structuralism. The early phase of her work was mainly concerned with the critique of two related assumptions: that language was best understood as a formal system or rules, and one that took for granted the nature of the speaking subject. In books such as The Revolution in Poetic Language, *first published in 1974, Kristeva questioned these assumptions by providing an account, drawing on Lacan's psychoanalysis and Marxist and Hegelian ideas, of the conditions of the emergence of a language system. This account was guided by the relation between two concepts: one, the "semiotic," the mobile patterning of instinctual drives within the infant prior to the acquisition of language proper; the other, the "symbolic," the domain of articulate language, discriminating between subjects and objects, signifiers and signifieds, and concerned with propositions and judgments. Between the two stand the "thetic," or that moment in the acquisition of language when the speaking subject emerges as a distinct but unstable entity. In Kristeva's account, the "symbolic" arises through the repression of the "semiotic." Poetic language marks the return of the repressed elements of the semiotic within the realm of the symbolic, notably by way of rhythm, mimesis, intertextuality, and linguistic play. The dialectic between "symbolic" and "semiotic" in Kristeva's thought has political and gendered connotations. The "semiotic" is maternal and prior to law; the "symbolic" is paternal and associated with the law and judgment. In her later work, Kristeva's thinking has turned to the possibility of new forms of the symbolic order and the protection of a sphere of intimacy against media intrusions.*

"The Ethics of Linguistics" was first published in French in Critique *in March 1974. Drawing by implication on the concepts outlined above, in the following extract Kristeva aligns the work of a theorist, Roman Jakobson, with two Russian Futurist poets, Mayakovsky and Khlebnikov. Jakobson's theory comes out of the same historical moment as the poetry of Mayakovsky and Khlebnikov. In each case poetic language challenges the authority of the linguistic order that, in Kristeva's view, sustains a repressive political order. Out of this challenge a new ethics can emerge, one concerned not with the maintenance but the shattering of codes.*

The Ethics of Linguistics

Should a linguist, today, ever happen to pause and query the ethics of his own discourse, he might well respond by doing something else, e.g., engaging in political activity; or else, he might accommodate ethics to the ingenuousness of his good conscience – seeking socio-historical motives for the categories and relations involved in his model. One could thus account for the Janus-like behavior of a prominent modern grammarian; in his linguistic theories he sets forth a logical, normative basis for the speaking subject, while in politics he claims to be an anarchist. Then there are scholars, quite numerous but not so well known, who squeeze into modern linguistic theory a few additional considerations on the role of ideology; or who go no further than to lift their examples out of leftist newspapers when illustrating linguistic propositions.

Now, since the end of the nineteenth century, there have been intellectual, political, and, generally speaking, social ventures that have signaled the outbreak of something quite new within Western society and discourse, which is subsumed in the names of Marx, Nietzsche, and Freud, and their primary goal has been to reformulate an ethics. Ethics used to be a coercive, customary manner of ensuring the cohesiveness of a particular group through the repetition of a code – a more or less accepted apologue. Now, however, the issue of ethics crops up wherever a code (mores, social contract) must be shattered in order to give way to the free play of negativity, need, desire, pleasure, and jouissance, before being put together again, although temporarily and with full knowledge of what is involved. Fascism and Stalinism stand for the barriers that the new adjustment between a law and its transgression comes against.

Meanwhile, linguistics is still bathed in the aura of *systematics* that prevailed at the time of its inception. It is discovering the rules governing the coherence of our fundamental social code: language, either system of signs or strategy for the transformation of logical sequences. The ethical foundations for this belong to the past: in their work, contemporary linguists think like seventeenth-century men, while structuralist logic can be made to work only with primitive societies or their surviving elements. As wardens of repression and rationalizers of the social contract in its most solid substratum (discourse), linguists carry the Stoic tradition to its conclusion. The epistemology underlying linguistics and the ensuing cognitive processes (structuralism, for example), even though constituting a bulwark against irrational destruction and sociologizing dogmatism, seem helplessly anachronistic when faced with the contemporary mutations of subject and society. Even though "formalism" might have been right, contrary to Zhdanov, neither can think the rhythm of Mayakovsky through to his suicide or Khlebnikov's glossolalias to his disintegration – with the young Soviet state as backdrop.

From *Desire in Language: A Semiotic Approach to Literature and Art*, ed. Leon S. Roudiez, trans. Thomas Gora, Alice Jardine, and Leon S. Roudiez (New York: Columbia University Press, 1980), pp. 23–6, 27, 28–35.

For, as soon as linguistics was established as a science (through Saussure, for all intents and purposes) its field of study was thus hemmed in [*suturé*]; the problem of *truth* in linguistic discourse became dissociated from any notion of the *speaking subject*. Determining *truth* was reduced to a seeking out of the object-utterance's internal coherence, which was predetermined by the coherence of the particular metalinguistic theory within which the search was conducted. Any attempt at reinserting the "speaking subject," whether under the guise of a Cartesian subject or any other subject of enunciation more or less akin to the transcendental ego (as linguists make use of it), resolves nothing as long as that subject is not posited as the place, not only of structure and its regulated transformation, but especially, of its loss, its outlay.

It follows that formulating the problem of linguistic ethics means, above all, compelling linguistics to change its object of study. The speech practice that should be its object is one in which signified structure (sign, syntax, signification) is defined within boundaries that can be shifted by the advent of a semiotic rhythm that no system of linguistic communication has yet been able to assimilate. It would deflect linguistics toward a consideration of language as articulation of a heterogeneous process, with the speaking subject leaving its imprint on the dialectic between the articulation and its process. In short, this would establish *poetic language* as the object of linguistics' attention in its pursuit of truth in language. This does not necessarily mean, as is often said today, that poetic language is subject to *more* constraints than "ordinary language." It does mean that we must analyze those elements of the complex operation that I shall call poetic language (in which the dialectics of the subject is inscribed) that are screened out by ordinary language, i.e., *social constraint*. I shall then be talking about something other than language – a practice *for which any particular language is the margin*. The term "poetry" has meaning only insofar as it makes this kind of studies acceptable to various educational and cultural institutions. But the stakes it entails are totally different; what is implied is that language, and thus sociability, are defined by boundaries admitting of upheaval, dissolution, and transformation. Situating our discourse near such boundaries might enable us to endow it with a current ethical impact. In short, the ethics of a linguistic discourse may be gauged in proportion to the poetry that it presupposes.

A most eminent modern linguist believed that, in the last hundred years, there had been only two significant linguists in France: Mallarmé and Artaud. As to Heidegger, he retains currency, *in spite of everything*, because of his attentiveness to language and "poetic language" as an opening up of beings; as an openness that is checked but nonetheless occurs; as a struggle between world and earth; artistic creations are all conceived in the image of poetic language where the "Being" of "beings" is fulfilled and on which, as a consequence, "History" is grounded. If modern art, which is post-Hegelian, sounds a rhythm in language capable of stymieing any subjugated work or logic, this discredits only that closure in Heidegger's reflections that systematizes Being, beings and their historial veracity. But such discredit does not jeopardize poetry's logical stake, inasmuch as poetry is a practice of the speaking subject, consequently implying a dialectic between limits, both signified and signifying, and the setting of a pre- and trans-logical rhythm solely within this limit. Similarly, modern art's odyssey nevertheless remains the field where the possibility of History and dialectic struggle can be played out (before these become a particular history and a concrete struggle), since this artistic practice is the laboratory of a minimal signifying structure, its maximum dissolution, and the eternal return of both.

One might submit that Freud's discovery of the unconscious provided the necessary conditions for such a reading of poetic language. This would be true for the history of *thought*, but not for the history of *poetic practice*. Freud himself considered writers as his predecessors. Avant-garde movements of the twentieth century, more or less unaware of Freud's discovery, propounded a practice, and sometimes even a knowledge of language and its subject, that kept pace with, when they did not precede, Freudian breakthroughs. Thus, it was entirely possible to remain alert to this avant-garde laboratory, to perceive its experiments in a way that could be qualified only as a "love" relationship – and therefore, while bypassing Freud, to perceive the high stakes of any language as *always-already* poetic. Such, I believe, was the path taken by Roman Jakobson. It should not be surprising, then, that it is his discourse and his conception of linguistics, and those of no other linguist, that could contribute to the theory of the unconscious – allowing us to see it being made and unmade – *poiein* [ποιεῖν] – like the language of any subject....

It is quite an experience to listen to Harvard University's recording of Roman Jakobson's 1967 lecture, "Russian Poetry of my Generation" – he gave a reading of Mayakovsky and Khlebnikov, imitating their voices, with the lively, rhythmic accents, thrust out throat and fully militant tone of the first; and the softly whispered words, sustained swishing and whistling sounds, vocalizations of the disintegrating voyage toward the mother constituted by the "trans-mental" ("zaum") language of the second. To understand the real conditions needed for producing scientific models, one should listen to the story of their youth, of the aesthetic and always political battles of Russian society on the eve of the Revolution and during the first years of victory, of the friendships and sensitivities that coalesced into lives and life projects. From all this, one may perceive what initiates a science, what it stops, what deceptively ciphers its models. No longer will it be possible to read any treatise on phonology without deciphering within every phoneme the statement, "Here lies a poet." The linguistics professor doesn't know this, and that is another problem, allowing him blithely to put forward his models, never to invent any new notion of language, and to preserve the sterility of theory....

The struggle between poet and sun

Two tendencies seem to dominate Mayakovsky's poetic craft: *rhythmic* rapture and the simultaneous affirmation of the "*ego*."

Rhythm: "I walk along, waving my arms and mumbling almost wordlessly, now shortening my steps so as not to interrupt my mumbling, now mumbling more rapidly in time with my steps. So the rhythm is trimmed and takes shape – and rhythm is the basis of any poetic work, resounding through the whole thing. Gradually individual words begin to ease themselves free of this dull roar.... When the fundamentals are already there, one has a sudden sensation that the rhythm is strained: there's some little syllable or sound missing. You begin to shape all the words anew, and the work drives you to distraction. It's like having a tooth crowned. A hundred times (or so it seems) the dentist tries a crown on the tooth, and it's the wrong size; but at last, after a hundred attempts, he presses one down, and it fits. The analogy is all the more apposite in my case, because when at last the crown fits, I (quite literally) have tears in my eyes, from pain and relief. Where this basic dull roar of a rhythm comes from is a mystery. In my case, it's all kinds of repetitions in my mind of noises, rocking motions or in fact, of any phenomenon with which I can associate a sound. The sound of the sea, endlessly repeated, can provide my rhythm, or a servant who slams the door every morning, recurring and intertwining with itself, trailing through my consciousness; or even the rotation of the earth, which in my case, as in a shop full of visual aids, gives way to, and inextricably connects with, the whistle of a high wind."[1]

On the one hand, then, we have this rhythm; this repetitive sonority; this thrusting tooth pushing upwards before being capped with the crown of language; this struggle between word and force gushing with the pain and relief of a desperate delirium; the repetition of this growth, of this gushing forth around the crown-word, like the earth completing its revolution around the sun.

On the other hand, we have the "ego," situated within the space of language, crown, system: no longer rhythm, but sign, word, structure, contract, constraint; an "ego" declaring itself poetry's sole interest (cf. The poem "I Am Alone"), and comparing itself to Napoleon ("Napoleon and I": "Today, I am Napoleon / I am the chief of armies and more. / Compare / him and me!"). Trotsky called this erection of the poetic "I" a "Mayakomorphism," which he opposed to anthropomorphism (one can think of other word associations on the basis of *mayak* = "beacon").

Once the rhythm has been centered in the fixed position of an all powerful "ego", the poetic "I" thrusts at the sun – a paternal image that is coveted but also feared, murderous, and sentenced to die, a legislative seat which must be usurped. Thus: "one more minute / and you will meet / the monarch of the skies / if I want, I'll kill him for you, the sun!" ("Napoleon and I"); "Sun! / My father! / Won't you melt and stop torturing me! / My blood spilled by you runs along the road" ("A Few Words about Myself").

I could give many references, evoke Lautréamont, Bataille, Cyrano, or Schreber; the struggle between poet and sun, which Jakobson brought out, runs through such texts. We should understand it as a summary leading from the poet's condition to poetic formulation. Sun: agency of language since it is the "crown" of rhythmic thrust, limiting structure, paternal law abrading rhythm, destroying it to a large degree, but also bringing it to light, out of its earthy revolutions, to enunciate itself. Inasmuch as the "I" is poetic, inasmuch as it wants to enunciate rhythm, to socialize it, to channel it into linguistic structure if only to break the structure, this "I" is bound to the sun. It is a part of this agency because it must master rhythm, it is threatened by it because solar mastery cuts off rhythm. Thus, there is no choice but to struggle eternally against the sun; the "I" is successively the sun and its opponent, language and its rhythm, never one without the other, and poetic formulation will continue as long as the struggle does. The essential point to note is that there would be no struggle but for the sun's agency. Without it, rhythm incapable of formulation, would flow forth, growling, and in the end would dig itself in. Only by vying with the agency of limiting and structuring language does rhythm become a contestant – formulating and transforming.

Khlebnikov evokes another aspect of this solar contest; a mother, coming to the aid of her children in their fight against the sun. "The otter's children" are squared off against three suns, one white, one purple, the other dark green. In "The God of the Virgins," the protagonist is "the daughter of the sun prince." The poem "Ka" calls forth the "hairy-armed sun of Egypt." All of Khlebnikov's pagan mythology is underlain with a contest against the sun supported by a feminine figure, all-powerful mother or forbidden virgin, gathering into one representation and thus substantifying all that which, with Mayakovsky, hammered in sonorous thrusts within and against the system of language – that is, rhythm.

Here, pagan mythology is probably nothing more than rhythm become substantive: this *other* of the linguistic and/or social contract, this ultimate and primordial leash holding the body close to the mother before it can become a social speaking subject. In any case, what in Khlebnikov Tynanov called "infantilism" or "the poet's pagan attitude regarding words"[2] is essentially manifest in the *glossolalias* unique to Khlebnikov. He invented words by onomatopoeia, with a great deal of alliteration, demanding of him an acute awareness of the articulatory base and instinctual charge of that articulation. This entire strategy broke up the lexicon of the Russian language, drawing it closer to childhood soliloquy. But above all, it threaded through metaphor and metonymy a network of meaning supplementary to the normative signifying line, a network of phonemes or phonic groups charged with instinctual drives and meaning, constituting what for the author was a *numerical* code, a *ciphering*, underlying the verbal signs: for example, "Veterpenie / kogo i o chëm? / neterpenie – mecha stat' mjachom" (Wind-song / of whom and for what? / Impatience / of the sword to become a bullet). Jakobson notes the phonic displacement *mech-mjach* (sword-bullet) dominating several lines of Khlebnikov's poetry, where one notices also a tendency toward infantile regression and/or toward lessening of tension on the level of pronunciation as well as on the more general level of sexualized semantic areas. The vocalization of language thus becomes a way of deflecting the censorship that, for rhythm, is constituted by the structuring agency. Having become "trans-mental" Khlebnikov's instinctual, ciphered language projects itself as prophetic and seeks for homologues within this tradition: for example, "Through Zarathustra's golden mouth let us swear / Persia shall become a Soviet country, thus has the prophet spoken".[3]

Rhythm and death

"But how do we speak about the poetry of Mayakovsky, now that what prevails is not rhythm but the poet's death . . . ?" asks Jakobson in "The Generation That Wasted Its Poets."[4] We tend to read this article as if it were exclusively an indictment of a society founded on the murder of its poets. This is probably true; when the article first appeared in 1931, even psychoanalysts were not all convinced that "society was now based on complicity in the common crime," as Freud had written in *Totem and Taboo*.[5] On the basis of his work on Mayakovsky, Jakobson suggested that the crime was more concretely the murder of poetic language. By "society," he probably meant more than just Russian or Soviet society; there are frequent and more general allusions to the "stability of the unchanging present," to "life, hardened along narrow and rigid models," and to "daily existence." Consequently we have this Platonistic acknowledgment on the eve of Stalinism and fascism: a (any) society may be stabilized only if it excludes poetic language.

On the other hand, but simultaneously, poetic language alone carries on the struggle against such a death, and so harries, exorcises, and invokes it. Jakobson is fascinated by murder and suicide as themes with poets of his generation as well as of all time. The question is unavoidable: if we are not on the side of those whom society wastes in order to reproduce itself, where are we?

Murder, death, and unchanging society represent precisely the inability to hear and understand the signifier as such – as ciphering, as rhythm, as a presence that precedes the signification of object or emotion. The poet is put to death because he wants to turn rhythm into a dominant element; because he wants to make language perceive what it doesn't want to say, provide it with its matter independently of the sign, and free it from denotation. For it is this *eminently parodic* gesture that changes the system.

> The word is experienced as word and not as a simple substitute for a named object nor as the explosion of emotion [...] beside the immediate consciousness of the identity existing between the object and its sign (A is A), the immediate consciousness of the absence of this identity (A is not A) is necessary; this antinomy is inevitable, for, without contradiction, there is no interplay of concepts, no interplay of signs, the relationship between the concept and the sign becomes automatic, the progress of events comes to a halt, and all consciousness of reality dies [...] Poetry protects us from this automatization, from the rust that threatens our formulation of love, hate, revolt and reconciliation, faith and negation.[6]

Today, the analyst boasts of his ability to hear "pure signifiers." Can he hear them in what is known as "private life"? There is good reason to believe that these "wasted poets" are alone in meeting the challenge. Whoever understands them cannot "practice linguistics" without passing through whole geographic and discursive continents as an impertinent traveler, a "faun in the house" [*faune au logis* = *phonologie*, Ed.].

The futurists' future

According to Jakobson, Mayakovsky was interested in resurrection. It is easy, at that, to see that his poems, like those of Khlebnikov and other futurists, take up the theme of Messianic resurrection, a privileged one in Russian Medieval poetry. Such a theme is a very obvious and direct descendant of the contest against the sun myth that I mentioned earlier. The son assumes from his sun-father the task of completing the "self" and "rhythm" dialectic within the poem. But the irruption of semiotic rhythm within the signifying system of language will never be a Hegelian *Aufhebung*, that is, it will not truly be experienced in the present. The rigid, imperious, immediate present kills, puts aside, and fritters away the poem. Thus, the irruption within the order of language of the anteriority of language evokes a later time, that is, a forever. The poem's time frame is some "future anterior" that will never take place, never come about as such, but only as an upheaval of present place and meaning. Now, by thus suspending the present moment, by straddling rhythmic, meaningless, anterior memory with meaning intended for later or forever, poetic language structures itself as the very nucleus of a monumental historicity. Futurism succeeded in making this poetic law explicit solely because it extended further than anyone else the signifier's autonomy, restored its instinctual value, and aimed at a "trans-mental language." Consequently attuned to a scene preceding the logical systematicity of communication. Futurism managed to do so without withdrawing from its own historical period; instead, it paid strong attention to the explosion of the October Revolution. It heard and understood the Revolution only because its present was dependent on a future. Mayakovsky and Khlebnikov's pro-Soviet proposals and leaps into mythology came from a nonexistent place in the future. Anteriority and future join together to open that historical axis in relation to which concrete history will always be wrong: murderous, limiting, subject to regional imperatives (economic, tactical, political, familial . . .). Although, confronted with such regional necessities, poetic language's future anterior is an impossible, "aristocratic" and "elitist" demand, it is nonetheless the only signifying strategy allowing the speaking animal to shift the limits of its enclosure. In "As for the Self," Khebnikov writes:

> Short pieces are important when they serve as a break into the future, like a shooting star, leaving behind a trail of fire. They should move rapidly enough so that they pierce the present. While we wait, we cannot yet define the reason for this speech. But we know the piece is good when, in its role as a piece of the future, it sets the present ablaze. [. . .] the homeland of creation is the future. The wind of the gods of the word blows from that direction.[7]

Poetic discourse measures rhythm against the meaning of language structure and is thus always eluded by meaning in the present while continually postponing it to an impossible time-to-come. Consequently, it is assuredly the most appropriate *historical* discourse, if and only if we attribute to this word its new resonance; it is neither flight in the face of a supposed metaphysics of the notion of "history," nor mechanistic enclosure of this notion within a project oblivious to the violence of the social contract and evolution's being, above all, a refinement of the various forms of dissipating the tension we have been calling "poetic language."

It should come as no surprise that a movement such as the October Revolution, striving to remain antifeudal and antibourgeois, should call forth the same mythemes that dominated feudalism and were suppressed by the bourgeoisie, in order to exploit solely their dynamics producing exchange value. Beyond these mythemes, however, futurism stressed equally its participation in the anamnesis of a culture as well as a basic feature of Western discourse. "You have to bring the poem to the highest pitch of expressiveness" (Mayakovsky, "How are Verses Made"). At that point the code becomes receptive to the rhythmic body and it forms, in opposition to present meaning, another meaning, but a future, impossible meaning. The important element of this "future anterior" of language is "the word perceived as word," a phenomenon in turn induced by the contest between rhythm and sign system.

Mayakovsky's suicide, Khlebnikov's disintegration, and Artaud's incarceration prove that this contest can be prevented. Does this mean there is no future (no history) for this discourse, which found its own "anteriority" within the "poetic" experience of the twentieth century? Linguistic ethics, as it can be understood through Jakobson's practice, consists in following the resurgence of an "I" coming back to rebuild an ephemeral structure in which the constituting struggle of language and society would be spelled out.

Can contemporary linguistics hear this conception of language of which Jakobson's work is the major token?

The currently dominant course, generative grammar, surely rests on many of Jakobson's approaches, notably phonological, in the study of the linguistic system. Nonetheless, it is hard to see how notions of elision, metaphor, metonymy, and parallelism (cf. his study on biblical and Chinese verse) could fit into the generative apparatus, including generative semantics, except perhaps under the rubric of "additional rules," necessitating a cutoff point in the specific generation of a language. But the dramatic notion of language as a risky practice, allowing the speaking animal to sense the rhythm of the body as well as the upheavals of history, seems tied to a notion of signifying process that contemporary theories do not confront. Jakobson's linguistic ethics therefore unmistakably demands first a *historical epistemology of linguistics* (one wonders which Eastern or Western theories linked with what ideological corpus of Antiquity, the Middle Ages, or the Renaissance were able to formulate the problematic of language as a place of structure as well as of its bodily, subjective, and social outlay). Secondly, it demands a *semiology*, understood as moving beyond simple linguistic studies toward a typology of signifying systems composed of semiotic materials and varied social functions. Such an affirmation of Saussurian semiological exigencies in a period dominated by generative grammar is far from archaistic; rather, it is integrated into a tradition where linguistics is inseparable from concepts of subject and society. As it epitomizes the experiences of language and linguistics of our entire European century, it allows us to foresee what the discourse on the signifying process might be in times to come.

Notes

1 Vladimir Mayakovsky, *How Are Verses Made?*, trans. G. M. Hyde (London: Jonathan Cape, 1970), pp. 36–7. The other Mayakovsky quotations are from *Electric Iron*, trans. Jack Hirschman and Victor Erlich (Berkeley: Maya, 1971), p. 46.

2 From the preface of Velimir Khlebnikov, *Sobranie Sochinenij* (Moscow, 1927–33).

3 Velimir Khlebnikov, *Oeuvres*, trans. L. Schnitzer (Paris: Oswald, 1967).

4 In Tzvetan Todorov (ed.) *Questions de poétique* (Paris: Seuil, 1973). First appeared as "O pokolenii rastrativshem svoikh poetov," in *Smert' Vladimira Majakovskoga* (Berlin, 1931), pp. 7–45. This essay will appear in English translation in a future volume of Jakobson's *Selected Writings*, published by Mouton in The Hague.

5 *Totem and Taboo* in *The Standard Edition of the Complete Works of Sigmund Freud* (London: Hogarth and The Institute of Psycho-Analysis, 1953), 13: 146.
6 "Qu'est-ce que la poésie," in *Questions de poétique*, pp. 124–5.
7 Khlebnikov, *Oeuvres*.

Chapter 59
Hans Magnus Enzensberger

Hans Magnus Enzensberger (1929–) is one of Germany's leading public intellectuals and writers. His published work encompasses a wide range of genres: poetry, drama, fiction, essays in cultural and political criticism, as well as translations from a number of languages. The relation between politics and literature has been a central preoccupation of Enzensberger's writing life, whether in his response to the question of creating a postwar German literature, his engagement with Marxist critique, or his ironic sense of the obsolescence of literature in an age of electronic media. Enzensberger inherits from Bertolt Brecht a belief that the purpose of writing should be the exposure of illusions, and these include illusions about the cultural power of poetry. But Enzensberger's negations of received wisdom are energetic in their verbal inventiveness and formal sophistication. His writing is encyclopedic in its range of subjects and idioms. Much of Enzensberger's work has been translated into English, including the essay collections, Raids and Reconstructions *(1976) and* Mediocrity and Delusion *(1988), as well as Enzenzberger's own translation of his long poem,* The Sinking of the Titanic *(1981).*

The following excerpt comes from "A Modest Proposal for the Protection of Young People from the Products of Poetry," an essay first published in September 1976 in the Frankfurter Allgemeine Zeitung. *Its title, echoing the eighteenth-century satirist Swift's "Modest Proposal," is one indication of Enzensberger's intent. Accepting that poetry is an anachronism in contemporary culture despite political claims to the contrary, he finds in its persistence as an element in the education system the occasion for a satire on earnest attempts to teach poetry and its correct interpretation. What this does, apart from distressing the young, is destroy the very thing it claims to cherish. Enzensberger enters a comic plea for an end to such earnest endeavors and suggests that the young be protected from the compulsory reading of poems.*

A Modest Proposal for the Protection of Young People from the Products of Poetry

Our lives are full of anachronisms. In the words of a respected source, which has itself now become anachronistic, I understand by that "anything done or existing out of date; *hence* anything which was proper to a former age, but is, or, if it existed, would be, out of harmony with the present." One of the most curious phenomena of this kind is without doubt the writing and reading of poems and, even more so, every kind of discussion of these activities.

I see no reason to turn pale before such a thought. After all, measured by the standards which prevail in our societies most of our favourite occupations are anachronistic, and it's an open question whether suicide would not be preferable to a completely consistent, absolutely contemporary existence. Non-synchronicity is no disgrace. It's only disturbing, now and then. The occasional pleasure it can provide us will not suffer from our awareness of that.

Even more anachronistic than poetry itself appears to me the conviction that it is dangerous. In Europe people hit upon this idea quite some time ago. I only need to recall that famous philosopher from the Balkan peninsula, 427 to 347 BC, who, after he had himself composed a few verses which were evidently fairly amateurish, came to the conclusion that this was an activity which threatened the state. Strangely enough his point of view has survived into our own century, and so we can still register, here and there, attempts to put a stop to (anachronistic) so-called belles-lettres in general, and poetry in particular, by censorship, prosecution by the courts and the exile of its creators, and by all kinds of other unpleasantnesses. The vehemence of such responses is difficult to explain. An ancient justification refers to the tender minds of young people whose moral character has not yet been formed, and who must be protected from the creeping poison of the literary imagination.

One might think that the thesis of the corrupting character of poetry (and similar products) would meanwhile have died out. After all, the average sale of a volume of poetry today is around four to eight hundred copies. There is little to suggest that our school pupils and apprentices, gripped by a kind of mass hypnosis, might abandon their cassette recorders and motor cycles and flagrantly neglect their sport, consumption and copulation duties, in order recklessly to surrender themselves to the enjoyment of poetry.

The superstition which clings to the supposedly occult, therefore insidious, powers of poetry (as also to all other arts), is however so old and so deep rooted that it effortlessly resists the evidence. It is perhaps less at home today in conservative heads than in progressive ones, and that in two variants, which in addition might at first sight seem to exclude one another.

On the one hand the harmlessness of aesthetic productions is denied by reference to their hidden subversive potential. These fabulous critical energies which supposedly

From *Mediocrity and Delusion: Collected Diversions*, trans. Martin Chalmers (London and New York: Verso, 1992), pp. 3–15, 16–17.

slumber in sonatas and sonnets, this Utopian surplus points forever beyond the bad existing state of things and promises something Altogether Different. This discourse, which really intends a revolutionary vindication of poetry's honour, stands or falls of course with the belief in its dangerousness; and indeed its spokesmen have often gone as far as to utter the words "explosive force," just as if, for example, Brecht's *Household Breviary* were made not of paper but of dynamite.

No less critical are the theories, and no less vehemently expressed, which aim to slander poetry's revolutionary honour, instead of saving it. It serves, and this song too we all know by heart now, like all bourgeois art practices, only a single goal: the stabilization of capitalist relations of domination and ownership. Very far from releasing critical, emancipatory and revolutionary energies, it is an aesthetic drug that cripples the will to resist; it is superficial, elitist, parasitical, in a word: pernicious.

This song and response, which has been echoing over the heads of poets and readers for decades now, can, like the antiphony in the Catholic mass, be carried on indefinitely. The apparent conflict which it manifests, displays in reality only the two sides of one and the same coin. Both choruses are agreed at any rate that poems, like other art practices, are something extremely dangerous, whether they disrupt the system or maintain it; hence their excited manner. I believe one can listen to them with the greatest composure since they are even more harmless than what they sing and talk about, even if duller and more lacking in ideas than the latest tune in the charts.

They have, however, nothing to do with scholarship, and least of all with critical scholarship. Their contradictory assertions on the effects of poetry are completely unfounded. Not the faintest trace of evidence is advanced. At best, personal reading experiences are generalized, or meaningless statistics are strung together: the methodology limits itself in the one case to the sledgehammer, in the other it has amounted to projecting conclusions drawn from oneself on to others. It can all be called sociology of literature, aesthetics of reception and communications research; it sounds better and brings in research funding.

But no meaningful statements about the effects of poetry can be made using such methods. That is by no means necessary, since on the scale of society these effects are microscopic. Nevertheless should someone in all seriousness have the idea of carrying out research on them, then he would have to be prepared for a quite different endeavour. He would have to proceed just as confidently and just as modestly as a high-energy physicist. These scientists think nothing of tracing millions of minute natural occurrences in their fog, cloud and bubble chambers, always in the hope of discovering significant rules in the chaos of the minimal reactions which take place there. To this end they have created a fantastic theoretical and experimental apparatus, a giant intellectual toy, of which our aestheticians could not even dream, although the systems which they are concerned with are incomparably more complex, in terms of the quantity and variety of the elements and variables involved, than anything which can be observed in a bubble chamber. Nevertheless it was not they but the physicists who arrived at the obvious idea that there are micro-processes which in principle elude exact prognosis and about which only, if they occur frequently enough, probabilistic statements can be made. In the case of poetry this condition cannot be assumed. On this fact too I rest my supposition that its effects are not measurable. The assertion that it is dangerous, irrespective of whether it is intended positively or negatively, is therefore founded on prejudice.

If, after this unsophisticated introduction, I come to the principal question which I want to deal with here, namely how young people are to be protected from the products of poetry, it may perhaps seem that I am contradicting myself. In general I would prefer to confront the accusation of inconsistency directly rather than evade it; yet in this case it is unjustified. It is clear that even the most harmless object can become a public danger if, to mention only one example, it falls into criminal hands: there's the pacific onion knife in the fist of the man running amok, the benevolent pencil in the fingers of the bureaucrat, the helpful plug in the hand of the psychiatrist, who is once again administering an electric shock to a refractory patient – and, so I would like to continue, the harmless poem in the briefcase of the German teacher.

It's not as if I entertained prejudices or even simply reservations about a profession whose services stand in inverse proportion to the meagre recognition which an ungrateful world pays them. In contrast to the writer, the social influence of the German teacher is, if not weighty, then nevertheless of a macroscopic order. His work is correspondingly hard. He is the true Sisyphus. Completely dependent on his own resources, fighting for a lost cause, as it were, he is not only supposed to defend the ability to produce German sentences, but even to awaken it – an ability, which from the university to parliament, from the press to the progressive political organizations, has as good as died out in the public life of the country. The German teacher fights with his back to the wall for the categories of German grammar, and with them for cognitive possibilities of differentiation, like those between indicative and subjunctive or between perfect, imperfect and pluperfect, the ignorance of which is now demonstrated by the overwhelming majority of recent university dissertations. No – he should not have to expect rejection by the writer, but complete solidarity in his unequal struggle.

Anyway, quite recently I entered the butcher's shop at the corner – it's Friday afternoon – to buy a rump steak. The shop is crowded, but hardly has the butcher's wife caught sight of me than she drops her knife, pulls a piece of paper out of the drawer by the till and asks if that's by me. I look at the text and confess immediately. It's the first time that the butcher's wife gives me what might be described as a fiery glance. Accompanied by the grumbling of the other customers, this is what comes to light. Without suspecting a thing, I have interfered in the life of the butcher's daughter, who is about to sit her school-leaving certificate. Some old poem or other of mine was placed in front of her in the German lesson and she was requested to put something down on paper about it. The result: a plain four, tears, an argument in my butcher's bungalow, accusing glances which literally pierce me, a tough rump steak in my pan. My tentative reference to section 46, paragraph 1 of the Law on Copyright and Related Rights of 9 September 1965, Fed. Legal Gazette I, p. 1273 passim, according to which "reproduction and circulation," is permissible "if parts of works, spoken works, or works of music of limited length, individual works of the fine arts or individual photographic works are included after their publication in a collection which comprises the works of a larger number of authors and in this form is intended solely for church, school or educational purposes" – this reference which in any case is difficult to put forward in a crowded butcher's shop, met with a distinct lack of understanding and was reciprocated with the further inquiry, why on earth I wrote such peculiar things. My regard for the butcher's wife and the regard of the butcher's wife for me, which of course is far more important, has fortunately not suffered lasting damage from this incident. On the other hand, regrettably, my solidarity with German teachers was affected. "Would like," it says in a letter from 427 Dorsten, "briefly to ask a favour. Am about to sit final examination for teaching certificate and wanted to discuss your poem *Evening News* in the crit. German lesson. Would be very grateful to you, if you could poss. send me material on this poem. (Interpretation, intention etc.) And by return of post please, since otherwise it will arrive too late."

A warm-hearted teacher, who is "very concerned to maintain a feeling for poetry among her pupils or to awaken it in them," writes to me from 8543 Hiltpoltstein:

> During the German lesson with my 11th year class I discussed *To a Man in the Tramcar*, which means *wanted* to discuss. Intensive debate developed on content, addressee, conception of the world, style and various details. The pupils made a serious effort to understand the poem, have devoted time, intelligence and hard work to the defence of their interpretation which is certainly coherent, but in my opinion, is, despite that, not right. They have produced pages of work, to underpin their interpretation, nevertheless I stand by my opinion. I therefore proposed asking you as the only competent person.

Finally (the post brought all this in the course of three weeks) a scribbled plea for help from 504 Brühl:

> I am a schoolboy, 16 years of age and attend secondary school. Recently in German a class essay was set on your poem, *Birth Certificate*. I got into an argument with the teacher about my interpretation. I am aware of the linguistic inadequacy of my essay. I only find unfair the overall conclusion, that my interpretation in no way does justice to the poem. It would be very kind, if you could let me know, whether my interpretation of your poem really is completely wrong.

This letter is accompanied by a photocopy of the essay. The following marginal notes and comments in the teacher's handwriting can be deciphered: "Factually wrong!" – "That is much too narrow and shifts the problematic." – "At no point is there any mention of it." – "There is nothing about that in the text." – "It is not correct in that way." – "This situation does not exist in the poem." – "The sixth verse is completely ignored." – "That cannot be understood from the text like that." – "Factually wrong!" – "Repetition of what has already been said above." – "Factually wrong. This use of 'if' only occurs in the last verse. But then that would already need to have been mentioned." – "The interpretation in no way does justice to the poem." – "Inadequate (5)."

The teaching body which makes an appearance in these pieces of evidence is far from homogeneous: its methods extend from subtle intimidation to open brutality; its motives from purest benevolence to sheer sadism. Leaving these nuances aside, the teaching body as a whole gives the impression of a criminal association, which commits immoral acts against dependants and minors. Sometimes – I'm thinking above all of the marginal comments from Brühl – these acts can become cases of manifest child abuse. On each occasion the weapon used is an object whose harmless nature, in the abstract, I have already demonstrated: the poem. But how can such a fragile object become a dangerous criminal instrument? Special measures are necessary for that. After all, how many of us remember that it is possible to commit murder with the insignificant and little-used edge of one's hand? For that, however, a skilled teachnique is required. It's called karate, and in Germany there's a school at every third street corner where one can acquire it. The analogous skill, which permits a poem to be made into a club, is called interpretation.

The teachers of course, are innocent of the development of this techanique. In the first instance it is practised and refined at the universities where, for reasons unknown, academics are employed for this sole purpose. The "philistine refusal to leave the work of art alone" then spreads out over the whole cultural apparatus from these centres. The quotation comes from an essay, *Against Interpretation,* which Susan Sontag wrote in 1964. Since it has become famous, but has had no effect, I would like to quote a page from it:

> Of course, I don't mean interpretation in the broadest sense, the sense in which Nietzsche (righly) says "There are no facts, only interpretations." By interpretation, I mean where a conscious act of the mind which illustrates a certain code, certain "rules" of interpretation.
>
> Directed to art, interpretation means plucking a set of elements (the X, the Y, the Z, and so forth) from the whole work. The task of interpretation is virtually one of translation. The interpreter says, look, don't you see that X is really – or really means – A? That Y is really B? That Z is really C? . . . Interpretation in our own time is often prompted not by piety towards the troublesome text (which may conceal aggression), but by an open aggressiveness, an overt contempt for appearances. The old style of interpretation . . . erected another meaning on top of the literal one. The modern style of interpretation excavates, and as it excavates, destroys; it digs "behind" the text to find a sub-text which is the true one . . . Today the project of interpretation is largely reactionary, stifling. Like the fumes of the automobile and of heavy industry which befoul the atmosphere, the effusion of interpretation of art today poisons our sensibilities . . . To interpret is to impoverish, to deplete the world.

Drawing on the material which has come to hand I should like to add some observations to Sontag's brilliant polemic. On the interpretations market – perhaps because of the increasing pressure of competition, which suggests a permanent crisis of overproduction – an increasingly rapid change of the dominant "grids" and "models" can be observed. With a delay which can be calculated from the date of the teacher's training course, they are then deposited in the teaching of German, compressed together like the annual rings of a tree. The latest academic hit usually only surfaces in the schools when it has already been displaced by the subsequent one in the seminars. Yet there are certain constants in this permanent change of wardrobe and of jargon. The most important is the obsession with the "right interpretation". This delusion is adhered to with incomprehensible tenacity, although its logical inconsistency and its empirical lack of foundation are obvious. If ten people read a literary text, the result is ten different readings. Everyone knows that. Innumerable, completely uncontrollable factors enter into the act of reading: the social and psychological history of the reader, his expectations and interests, his state of mind at that moment, the situation in which he's reading – factors which are not only absolutely legitimate and therefore to be taken seriously, but are simply the conditions that allow something like reading to come about at all. The result is consequently not determined by the text and not determinable. In this sense the reader is always right and no one can take away the freedom to make whatever use of a text which suits him.

This freedom includes the right to leaf back and forward, to skip whole passages, to read sentences against the grain, to misunderstand them, to reshape them, to spin sentences out and embroider them with every possible association, to draw conclusions from the text, of which the text knows nothing, to be annoyed at it, to be happy because of it, to forget it, to plagiarize it and to throw the book in which it is printed into the corner at any time he likes. Reading is an anarchic act. Interpretation, especially the single correct one, exists to frustrate this act.

Its expression is consequently always authoritarian, it produces either subordination or resistance. Where resistance stirs, it is forced to assert its own theoretical or institutional authority. Insofar as this stands on feet of clay – which fortunately is ever more frequently the case – it attempts to borrow what it lacks elsewhere. Hence the recourse to the author, who is coolly assumed to be ready to make himself the accomplice of interpretation and betray his reader, by explaining in the final instance as it were how he meant it, consequently how it is to be understood, and that's it.

Things are not as bad as all that, one might say. No one pays any attention to these poetry interpretations unless forced to do so in order to earn a living. As far as the Germanists are concerned, after all no one pressganged them into the difficult duty which they perform year in year out on society's behalf; it's an activity which *consenting adults* agree to: given this condition Anglo-Saxon law declares most perversions to be permissible. But as for literature, it owes its charm not least to the fact that everyone is free to ignore it – a right of which the majority of our fellow citizens make full use, and the defence of which should be close to the heart of every writer. Certainly it would be theoretically conceivable to introduce a state compulsion to read the products of poetry, analogous to general compulsory education, and there may be colleagues who would hope for an improvement in their income as a result, yet such a measure is hardly to be feared. How little the poets would be helped by it is demonstrated by the example of the architects, who as a rule certainly earn more, but are pursued by the smouldering hatred of all those who are forced to inhabit their works. Everyone who lives in a city knows that architecture, in contrast to poetry, is a terrorist art.

Only for the minors among our fellow citizens is the right to free choice of reading matter invalid. Already held prisoner every day in concrete bunkers which the community has erected for this sole purpose, they are compelled to read poems endlessly and, what is even more shocking, to interpret poems in which, in most cases, they have displayed no interest whatsoever.

I know very well that the German teachers have not gratuitously brought about this repellent state of affairs under which they too presumably suffer. The true culprits are to be found in the undergrowth of institutions which are as far removed from an ordinary school as Kafka's Castle. Involved are a horde of bureaucrats and curriculum researchers who are extraordinarily difficult to pin down. Their true intentions are obscure. What impels them to the project of raising hundreds of thousands of sub-Germanists in our secondary schools and to inflict the interpretation of poems as forced labour we do not know. We shall never find out. It's small wonder that in such circumstances conspiracy theories run riot. I have already mentioned two of them. People who labour under the delusion that poetry is a revolutionary act of extraordinary explosive force have tried to draw the conclusion that discussing them during the German lesson is comparable to an innoculation; society protects itself from subversion through poems by carefully destroying them. The skills of the German teacher can be compared to those of a bomb disposal expert: with the aid of interpretation the fuse is unscrewed from the dangerous product.

The contrary dogma, according to which poetry appears suspect for the opposite reason, believes on the other hand, that poems are stuffed down the poor pupils' throats in order to reconcile them to existing conditions: the sweet poison is calculated to suffocate every hint of rebellion in them and to make them meek supporters of the status quo. Both these hypotheses seem as nonsensical to me as the phenomenon which they want to explain. It would certainly be nice if capitalism stood on such shaky foundations that it found it necessary to "stabilize" its rule through the interpretation of poems, yet I fear that its persistence relies on much more tangible facts. And why poems of all things? Why are whole school classes not dragged off by force to pop concerts in order then, as an exercise, to "extract" the "correct" interpretation of Pink Floyd?

No, there's not much to be gained in this case by explanatory ideological critique. That much is already clear in any case from the fact that the ritual of "running through," "classification," and interpreting of poetry in teaching is not tied to any particular conception of literature. From this perspective it makes no difference whatsoever whether it's traditional or progressive German teaching. The ideological prefixes are quite different in Munich and Bremen, Graz and Weimar, but in each place the texts have to be ground through the mill of correct interpretation until they have been transformed into a smooth powder. As long as the technocratic function of this work remains constant, the contents and methods can be exchanged without any difficulty. And it's nothing more than historical chance that poems are the preferred raw material for this purpose. They are first of all cheap and secondly always available in sufficient quantities. Behind the ritual of interpretation there always stands another, that of examination, and of an examination that determines the life of schoolgirls and schoolboys, since it regulates access to the universities, and so to many professions. But "the essential content of an examination is still always the examination itself... The contents of the teaching which precede it are immaterial, since they represent arbitrary exchange values with which one acquires marks, which is ultimately what counts." Of course the smarter students grasped that a long time ago. They know very well that the object of their class essay is not the poem at all, that it's much more important rigorously to avoid every reading of one's own and instead to guess the "correct interpretation" in the teacher's head, in order to reproduce it as accurately as possible.

A recent publication, the so called *Book of Standards, German*, demonstrates with all the plainness one could wish for, what needs to be done in order to transform a harmless poem into a technocratic cudgel and to use it to strike young heads with the greatest possible accuracy. The full title of this remarkable document reads: *Decisions of the Conference of Ministers of Education and Culture. Standard Examination Requirements in the School Leaving Certificate. German.* The jargon in which this *Book of Standards* is drawn up, already reveals that the ministers themselves cannot possibly be the authors; these gentlemen are politicians, and in this capacity they are careful not to leave the level of dull intelligibility. The work I'm talking about, on the other hand, is a result of interdisciplinary co-operation with the aim of the dullest unintelligibility. Hundreds of incumbents of tenured posts in educational and behavioural psychology, in curriculum research and from the bureaucracies of the ministries have made sure that this goal has been achieved.

Despite a natural feeling of nausea I cannot resist listing a few of the aims and intentions which the authors are pursuing, in their own words:

They want above all to regulate, supplement, effectively expedite, safeguard, standardize, integrate, revise, incorporate and allocate.

It further seems urgent to them, to develop discipline specific learning goal descriptions and learning goal systems, to classify the learning goals into learning goal areas, to describe the learning goal levels with sufficient accuracy, and to carefully differentiate the learning goal control levels from one another....

I would like to end my memorandum with a few conciliatory words. Stuff all the copies of the *Book of Standards, German* that you come across into the nearest waste-paper basket immediately! Sabotage the decisions of the Standing Conference of Ministers of Education and Culture wherever you can! Fight against the ugly vice of interpretation! Fight against the even uglier vice of correct interpretation! Never force a defenceless human being to open his mouth and swallow a poem he doesn't like! Practise the virtue of compassion towards the young people who are entrusted to you. Always remember: A child feels pain just as much as you do. Please also remember, by the way, my colleagues and myself. For besides the countless victims from the ranks of underage youth, at whom the *Book of Standards, German* is aimed, almost a dozen authors, who are evidently supposed to serve as suppliers of cudgels, are also listed by name: Brecht, Benn, Frisch, Dürrenmatt, Arp, Gomringer, Bender, Solzhenitsyn, Eich, Domin and Enzensberger. That is an impertinence. For each one of us, for you, for my butcher's daughter and for myself, these technocrats, who are not capable of composing even a single German sentence, have one of their ready-to-use martyrs' stakes ready. Are we going to bind one another to them? As far as I'm concerned, you have nothing to fear from me. On this conciliatory note, I beg you: lower your raised hand, before it is too late!

Chapter 60
Veronica Forrest-Thomson

Veronica Forrest-Thomson (1947–75) was a poet and theorist whose work established a powerful alignment of William Empson's thinking about poetry, Wittgenstein's philosophy of language, and aspects of structuralist and post-structuralist theory. During her lifetime she published four books and pamphlets of poetry: Identikit, Twelve Academic Questions *(1970),* Language-Games *(1971), and* Cordelia: *or,* "A Poem Should Not Mean But Be." *Another collection,* On the Periphery, *was published posthumously in 1976. Her work on poetics,* Poetic Artifice: A Theory of Twentieth-Century Poetry, *was published in 1978 and was followed in 1990 by her* Collected Poems and Translations. *Poetry and theory were continuous rather than opposed activities in Forrest-Thomson's work. Her poetry explores how it is that language becomes poetic by its attention both to examples of ordinary or technical language and to traditional poetic forms. But these explorations are not narrowly technical. They take up the challenge implied in Wittgenstein's statement from his* Tractatus *that "the limits of my language are the limits of my world." If this is so, do we have experiences in language of approaching this limit? And how might the form of poetry work on this threshold?*

Some of these questions are taken up in the following extract from Poetic Artifice. *Forrest-Thomson is critical of a tendency to pass from a poem's language to what the poem is about, thereby ignoring the semantically non-meaningful devices – including rhythm and sound but also punctuation and typographical design – that make the poem an artifice or an action on language. Forrest-Thomson does not want to ignore the referential aspects of poetry, but she does want to show how the devices that make up poetic form have a decisive role in composing our sense of what a poem is about.*

Continuity in Language

Even animals are not shut off from this wisdom, but show they are clearly initiated into it. For they do not stand stock still before things of sense as if they were things

> per se *with being in themselves: they despair of this reality altogether, and, in complete assurance of the nothingness of things, they fall-to without more ado and eat them up.*
>
> Hegel, *Phenomenology of Mind*

Language is common both to the realm of poetry and to the domain of ordinary experience, and this is one of the main factors with which a study of poetic language must deal. For our ordinary non-poetic language gives us the world which we generally regard as non-verbal: a world of emotions, objects, and states of affairs. This is the language we use every day (from now on I shall call it, for simplicity's sake, "ordinary language") and it is this language upon which Artifice must work to create its alternative imaginary orders. Of course, poetry deals also with the more specialised languages of, say, science, philosophy, religion, and cookery, but these do not present the same basic problem. For in them the non-verbal is already highly mediated, and Artifice has only to work on their alien structures of words, which must be absorbed and transformed into poetry.

When dealing with ordinary language, however, poetry has to confront the assumption that there is a non-verbal situation existing outside language which it is poetry's task to present. Ezra Pound claims that "in the art of Daniel and Cavalcanti, I have seen that precision which I miss in the Victorians, that explicit rendering, be it of external nature, or of emotion. Their testimony is of the eyewitness, their symptoms are first hand." This may stand as the type of such assumptions (though, to do Pound justice, he never believed that technique could be by-passed in such external rendering).

We have already come across these assumptions in our reading of Sonnet 94 and, while it is easy to refute the notion that Shakespeare is talking directly about his love life or any specific person or persons, it is not so easy to do away with the idea that there is emotion in that poem, that there are attitudes which emerge from that arrangement of words, and that these attitudes and emotions are not entirely explicable as the result of the words' meaning as part of technique. In point of fact it is not entirely clear why we should want to do away with the notion that there is feeling in poetry, for we should find ourselves very quickly arguing that poetry is of no interest at all. What is clear is that we cannot locate the emotion in either our minds or the poet's mind as situations outside the poem. If this were the case then T. E. Hulme would be right to claim that poetry was shorthand for a language of feeling that would hand over sensations bodily, and we should all be dying to get rid of the poetry to enter empathetic, kinaesthetic and inarticulate rapture.

But is this the case? No.... Where, then, can we safely situate these troublesome emotions? Where else but in the language of the poem itself, in those non-semantic features for which I have claimed the power to select and define the thematic synthesis that the reader should insert in the poem. For these features I now claim the further power to generate the required emotional reactions and, by their relationship to the

From *Poetic Artifice: A Theory of Twentieth-Century Poetry* (New York: St. Martin's Press, 1978), pp. 18–24, 27–8.

level of meaning, to delimit the non-verbal context which the poem uses as a fiction in its structure.

In a poem which begins

> From fairest creatures we desire increase

the language is working to achieve both continuity and discontinuity with a world of ordinary experience. The sentence implies the existence of 'fairest creatures' – animate beings ranked high on an evaluative scale – and suggests an attitude held by a significant portion of mankind ('we'). 'Increase' takes for granted, as elements which are fed into the poem, a whole background of natural processes. But the continuity which relates the poetic line to other situations in which its various words might be used is dominated by a discontinuity which distances and reorganises. The play of sound in "creatures . . . increase", intensified by the vowel of 'we', creates a structural solidarity unusual in ordinary language; the conventions of verse insist that we notice this, as a distinctive value with an important role. This assertion of the form of the linguistic material itself exerts pressure on external references, limiting them to what the poetic structure requires. The phonetic solidarity of 'creatures . . . increase' acts as a kind of proof of semantic appropriateness: we need not look outside the poem for any particular creatures (from a biographical situation) or any attested desire. The desire has been made an appropriate one by the artifice of the line, and 'creatures' are simply whatever should multiply. In short, the fact that we are reading a poem rather than a letter, speech, etc., calls us to relate the formal pattern to the meaning. This is achieved by lifting the meaning away from direct reference to an external state of affairs and preparing it for its part in a thematic synthesis, where the external contexts are evoked only to be made fictional.

Our reading must work through the level of meaning into the external world and then, via the non-semantic levels of Artifice, back into the poem, enriched by the external contexts of reference in which it found itself momentarily merged. This is what continuity in poetic language means. Without it the reader would have no way of making connections between poetic language and any other kind of language or between poetic language and the experience given him by the world of ordinary language which he inhabits most of the time. He would then retreat into either tendentious inarticulateness outside poetry – as did the Dadaists – or into tendentious Naturalisation which allows no play to the non-meaningful devices of Artifice – as so many critics and even poets have done in the last fifty years. Either manoeuvre deprives poetry of its essential strength of give and take with its environment, and both deprive it of its essential power over that environment. This power depends . . . on the non-meaningful levels of language. If poetry cannot control the meanings and feelings generated by the words it uses, its worth is reduced. If it cannot control experience by verbal relationships that channel it in a structural attitude, then its worth is less than that of the latest *News of the World* 'confession'.

Poetry's dealings with emotions, objects, and situations all fall under the general problem of continuity and discontinuity: the way in which poetry retains its contact with the world articulated by ordinary language while distancing itself from these customary modes of articulation. The power of poetry depends on its ability to maintain continuity while achieving discontinuity, but it is difficult to show precisely how this is done in particular cases. The best way to approach the problem is to study the various strategies and technical devices by which poetry distances itself from ordinary language and through which it limits the kind of external material which is assimilated and subjected to new organisation and articulation.

Several of Wittgenstein's remarks can give us a perspective on the problem and help to set the stage for discussion. First, 'the limits of my language mean the limits of my world.' The basis of continuity between poetry and the rest of one's experience is the essentially verbal nature of that experience: the fact that it takes shape through language. What we can know of experience always lies within language. And, correspondingly, 'to imagine a language means to imagine a form of life'. The world is not something static, irredeemably given by a natural language. When language is re-imagined the world expands with it. The continuity which makes it possible to read the world into words provides that the world may be enlarged or enriched by the enlargement of one's awareness of language and/or awareness of others' enlargement of their awareness of language. However, 'awareness' and 'knowledge' are perhaps the wrong words if they suggest that this expansion involves simply an accretion of information. As Wittgenstein says, 'the grammar of the word "knows" is evidently closely related to that of "can", "is able to". But also closely related to that of "understands" ("Mastery" of a technique).' The knowledge of both the poet and the reader of poetry is a kind of mastery, an ability to see how a use of language filters external contexts into the poem and subjects them to new distancing and articulation. The knowledge of readers and writers of poetry is an ability to exclude and to include and to grasp imaginative relations which are implicit in the words of the poem when they are read in terms of the conventions of poetry. It is mastery of these conventions that underlies the experience of 'seeing as' which the poem produces. To quote from Wittgenstein once more, '"Now he's seeing it like *this*", "now like *that*" would only be said of someone *capable* of making certain applications of the figure quite freely. The substratum of this experience is the mastery of a technique.'

A study of the way in which the conventions and formal devices of poetry direct the assimilation of external contexts and produce the discontinuity which gives poetry its power over those contexts will also be an account of the kind of mastery which is required of the reader of poetry. Learning to read poetry is a matter of acquiring the ability to hold together, simultaneously, continuity and discontinuity in the requisite proportions.

To see what is involved in the achievement of continuity and discontinuity, to see how poetry modifies and distances itself from the external contexts it assimilates, we might start with the most elementary case of poetic convention. If one takes a passage of prose and rearranges it on the page as verse, the language itself remains the same and hence any changes in its effects can be attributed to the new type of awareness with which we approach the verse passage. Any differences, in short, can be identified as effects which result from the conventional level: it is by convention that we read and organise the verse passage in ways that make it different from prose.

...If we rearrange prose as poetry in order to bring out rhythmic patterns we can only bring out elements or patterns which were dormant in the prose. Indeed, this is why the convention of free verse was developed in the first place: to make us aware of the poetry in our prose, of the imaginative alternatives that exist even in ordinary language. But the fact that resulting poetic rhythms were already there in the prose only makes more evident the fact that the differences between the prose and verse passage are the result of a change in conventional expectations, modes of attention, and interpretive strategies, rather than the result of any alteration of the linguistic material itself.

By way of example, I propose to rearrange as free verse what no-one, except perhaps certain members of the journalistic profession, would claim to be latent literature: a paragraph from a *Times* leader. The first paragraph of the first leader for Friday, December 15th, 1972, in its original form runs as follows:

> AT THE HEAD OF THE BBC
>
> The Government have taken their time in appointing the new chairman of the BBC, which is a measure both of the importance now attached to the office and of the difficulty in persuading somebody of the necessary quality to take it on a part-time basis at £6,000 a year. But in choosing Sir Michael Swann they have made a good selection, and a very much better one than might have been expected after such a delay. Both his record at Edinburgh, where he has been Principal and Vice-Chancellor of the university since 1965, and his comments on his appointment suggest that he will bring the right approach to his new responsibilities.

I have not kept the original line-endings but this is immaterial since the alignment is governed by the requirements of the printer which have no relation to the matter in hand. That is, no violation of material rules is involved since there is no continuum in newspapers between the meaning of the paragraph and the way it is arranged. Quite otherwise with the rules of rearranging the paragraph as verse, as a poem entitled 'At the head of the BBC':

> The Government have taken their time
> in appointing a new chairman of the
> BBC
> which is a measure both
> of the importance now attached to the office
> and of the difficulty in persuading somebody
> of the necessary quality
> to take it
> on a part-time basis
> at £6,000 a year

There is no need to look...for poetic figures or traditional stress rhythm...For twentieth-century poetry has evolved a whole new set of conventions for showing which words are dominant on any scale. Poems may or may not use traditional metre, rhythm, and rhyme, but they do generally stick to the convention that beginnings and ends of lines are marked as important in the thematic synthesis.

In the example above this is seen in lines 1, 3, 6, and in the body of the other lines where there is an ironic tone. 'Taken their time' stresses the Government's dilatoriness; 'BBC' casts a sardonic eye on that institution; 'somebody' suggests a frenetic haste to find 'anybody'. As for the other lines, 'necessary quality' suggests, given the previous ironic tinge, that the Government is being self-important; 'to take it' suggests that they have been begging anybody to accept it (which is at variance with the pomp); 'on a part-time basis' still contrasts the supposed importance with the casualness it has in fact. And 'at £6,000 a year' increases the irony (especially for those who are underpaid and overworked) by implying that £6,000 a year is a paltry sum for anyone to accept for a part-time job.

This ironic tone could be made blatant by increasing the use of poetic conventions:

At the 'head' of the BBC

The Government

                    Have taken their time

in appointing the

                    'new chairman' of the BBC

which is a measure both

                    of the 'importance'

now 'attached'

                    to the 'office' and of the difficulty

of persuading

                    somebody of the 'necessary quality'

to take it on a 'part-time basis' at

                    £6,000 a year

          BUT

In choosing Sir Michael Swann

                    they have made a

'good selection' and

                    a very much better one

than might have been expected

                    after such a delay.

BOTH his record at Edinburgh

                    where he has been

'Principal and Vice-Chancellor' of the university

                    since 1965

AND his 'comments on his appointment'

                    suggest

that he will bring 'the right approach' to his new 'responsibilities'.

The line-spacing across the page, which is the first thing to catch the eye, is a formal convention much used in all poetry but especially in poetry of this century, where neither stress or syllable metre is accepted as the norm and where other means must therefore be found to signal the importance of phrases and, if possible, to distinguish a dominant rhythm. The title already introduces another important convention, by no means confined to this century, but which has come to have a much greater importance that it had before: the use of quotation marks. Here they indicate the distance, the ironic distance, of the poet from the world of officialdom which he (for convenience's sake let us stick to one gender) regards with amused and slightly embittered annoyance.

How do we know that this is his attitude? From the way in which he uses the poetic convention of quotation marks to enclose official jargon. This is another mark of continuity between poetry and other languages: the conventions of poems see to it that the other languages are subordinated. And it is another instance of the way in which we can deduce from internal relations an attitude that might be supposed to exist outside the poem. The line-endings themselves would not do this, for they do not tell what kind of stress should be given to the words that end and begin, and I have chosen not to feed through these words into the formal pattern, for this is difficult without metre and would be obfuscatory for the present purpose.

The irony is increased by the use of capitalised 'BUT', 'BOTH', 'AND', which use necessary breaks in syntax to give the rudiments of a formal structure to the layout and thus link the levels of theme, meaning, and form to preserve continuity. The same is true of the italics; they focus attention and determine which contexts are appropriate. My suggestion that 'somebody', for instance, could imply a frantic search for 'anybody' is now converted into a definite thematic implication by the conjunction of three kinds of contentional features: line-breaks, which give importance, quotation marks, which by that stage in the poem have established ironic distance, and italics. The point is that these conventions do not conjoin in a void; they operate with meanings of the words to modify and filter the external contexts which the meanings involve; only thus is a thematic synthesis possible. Naturally it is not much of a synthesis since we have left out image-complexes and formal patterns, but bringing these in would have swamped and obscured the austere demonstration that even so slight a re-arrangement can open up imaginative possibilities in a dull piece of prose. And it would have obscured the more important point that it is through linking conventional expectations and the external contexts implied by syntax and lexis that these contexts may become indicators of the emotion or attitude the words are to carry. . . .

. . . In short, continuity in language – the relation between poetic discourse and other kinds of discourse which directly imply a world – requires discontinuity, a dislocation that occurs when one passes from the latter to the former. This is the central paradox of poetry. Mr Booth puts it thus:

> Art must distort; if it is to justify its existence, it must be other than the reality whose difficulty necessitates artistic mediation. It must seem as little a distortion as possible, because its audience wants comprehension of incomprehensible reality itself. We do not want so much to live in *a* world organised on human principles as to live in *the* world so organised. Art must seem to reveal a humanly ordered reality rather than replace a random one.

Such a general statement of the paradox helps us to see why our particular problem of poetry's situation between fact and fiction needs the special solution towards which I am working, for it highlights the questions of mediation. We have all been taught, by Marx, Freud, *The Golden Bough*, and contemporary developments in Anthropology and Linguistics, that the human consciousness cannot get at reality itself without mediation. This applies whether the agents of mediation be, as for [structuralism] a pattern inherent in the human mind which imposes binary form on the inchoate, or, as for Marx, the self-justifying ideological structures which produce a social class's 'objective reality', or again, as for Freud, the operations of condensation and displacement which order the world as figures of desire. Most relevant for us, perhaps, is the insistence of Benjamin Lee Whorf and of the linguists who attend to semantics that as a language changes from one society to another so does the world in which the members of the society live.

'All this the world knows well yet none knows well to shun the heaven that leads men to this hell', for literary theory has not kept up, has not kept that fact of mediation firmly in view. Critics have been slow to realize that literature, being based on language, cannot . . . get at the things behind language in some special way and that there may, in fact, be nothing (at least for the human mind) more real than forms of language. . . . Need one emphasize that it is scarcely praise to tell a poet that his greatest genius lies in not being a poet, in transcending those features of his art that make it an art, in lapsing into dependence on the level of meaning as 'BBC' does, and thus immersing and obscuring his art so that it becomes a 'comment on life'. This view makes his art subservient to life as we know it rather than a subversion and reinvention of that life through artifice; it makes us ignore mediation and take the 'reality' given us by ordinary language as the final court of appeal.

Luckily not all poetic theorists have succumbed to this view, and I shall hope to show that not all poets have put their theories into this realistic straitjacket. In some literary styles, notably, but not entirely, those developed in this century, the connection between verbal form and the extension of verbal meaning into the non-verbal world may be openly questioned. The implication that 'reality' is a product of linguistic rules may emerge. As Paul de Man claims, 'literature, unlike everyday language, begins on the far side of this knowledge; it is the only form of language free from the fallacy of unmediated expression'. De Man goes on to connect this fact with the priority of form over meaning and sees this latter as an analogue, essential to our understanding of literature, of the priority of fiction over reality. . . .

Chapter 61
Geoffrey Hill

Geoffrey Hill (1932–) is a poet, critic, and scholar whose work has been shaped by a passionate attention to the relation between poetry and Christianity. From the time of his first book of poetry, For the Unfallen, *published in 1959, Hill's writing has been both exacting and ambitious. Secular and religious history informs his work as a burden of guilt and obligation. Responsible poets inherit a past that is pervaded by the violence that runs through the history of European Christendom, and, in that inheritance, an anguished question about the relation between suffering and salvation. Yet that same history is also an inheritance of cultural achievement in the creation of institutions as well as works of art. Hence "burden" can take on a different and older meaning, as an aspect of the craft of making songs. Hill's work shows a dedication to the idea of poetry as a created artifact. His poems are learned, intricate, and carefully wrought, but also experimental in his refusal to fall into a single manner or idiom.* Mercian Hymns, *published in 1971, fuses together an ancient and legendary history of the English midlands with modern experience in a series of highly compressed poems. In this sequence Hill gave a new inflection to Eliot's concept of tradition. Critical opinion is divided by Hill's poetry. Some regard him as one of the great English poets working today. Others find his poetry obscure and intimidating. In addition to his work as a poet, Hill has published three collections of critical essays:* The Lords of Limit *in 1984,* The Enemy's Country *in 1991, and* Style and Faith *in 2003. He has worked at universities in Britain and the United States and is currently Professor of Literature and Religion at Boston University.*

"Poetry as 'Menace' and 'Atonement'" was first given as an inaugural lecture at the University of Leeds in 1977. It was subsequently published in The University of Leeds Review in 1978. A complete text of the essay can be found in The Lords of Limit. *In the following extract Hill explores certain dilemmas that he sees as characteristic of modern poetry. "Atonement" carries both an aesthetic and a penitential meaning. It describes the sense of reconciliation and harmony that can come with the "technical perfecting of a poem." But it also refers to the need for the modern artist to "atone for his own illiberal pride," and, in doing so, to take on a vicarious role in atoning for the refusal of modern culture to live within the bounds of a Christian understanding of natural order. Hill*

elaborates this argument in his discussion of the work of Eliot and Auden where he notes that the devotion in their later work to Christian ideals of penitence did not result in the renunciation of rhetorical mastery. Hill proposes an alternative idea of the poet, not a linguistic maestro but "homo faber," the devoted craftsman. The "menace" of his title is deliberately distanced from modern ideas of the subversive, destructive poet as social renegade and outcast. Poetry's menace arises from the high claims made for it, and from the intricate and demanding structures that Hill sees as characteristic of Romantic and modern poetry, a poetry that can torment its readers by its difficulty.

Poetry as "Menace" and "Atonement"

> *Thus my noblest capacity becomes my deepest perplexity; my noblest opportunity, my uttermost distress; my noblest gift, my darkest menace.*

My title may well strike you as exemplary in a fashion, being at once assertive and non-committal. The quotation-marks around 'menace' and 'atonement' look a bit like raised eyebrows. 'Menace' from what, and to whom? 'Atonement' by whom, and for what? Is one perhaps offering to atone for the menace of one's own jargon? In fact, though my title may appear 'challenging', it presents little more than a conflation of two modernist clichés. That it does so is an act of choice but the choice is exercised in order to demonstrate the closeness of a constraint. Behind the façade of challenge is the real challenge: that of resisting the attraction of terminology itself, a power at once supportive and coercive. There is for me also the challenge of the occasion, and a matter of decorum. I cannot disguise from myself the awareness that I have been drawn towards my present theme by way of the technical and metaphysical problems which I have encountered as a practitioner of verse. To what extent I should disguise this awareness from my audience is a question that causes me some perplexity. I am committed to speak, *ex cathedra*, as a professor of English Literature, not as a poet in residence. My distinguished predecessor, A. Norman Jeffares, is a scholar with an unrivalled knowledge of the life and work of one of the greatest of modern poets, W. B. Yeats. In taking poetry, and particularly modern poetry, as my own theme I shrink from any implication of special pleading, disdain the 'confessional mode' as currently practised, but distrust enigmas. That I have had some practice in the making of verse is evidence to be noted, I think; if only as a glint of improper goliardic song in the margin of a proper gospel.

Milton's dictum that poetry, though 'lesse suttle and fine', is 'more simple, sensuous and passionate' than rhetoric is a saying to which I am sympathetically inclined. Ideally my thesis would be equally deserving of sympathy. That it is here presented garnished and groaning with obliquities is due less to a simple sensuous and passionate wilfulness than to an obvious yet crucial fact. Language, the element in which a poet works, is also

From *The Lords of Limit* (London: André Deutsch, 1984), pp. 1–10.

the medium through which judgments upon his work are made. That commonplace image, founded upon the unfinished statues of Michelangelo, 'mighty figures straining to free themselves from the imprisoning marble', has never struck me as being an ideal image for sculpture itself; it seems more to embody the nature and condition of those arts which are composed of words. The arts which use language are the most impure of arts, though I do not deny that those who speak of 'pure poetry' are attempting, however inadequately, to record the impact of a real effect. The poet will occasionally, in the act of writing a poem, experience a sense of pure fulfilment which might too easily and too subjectively be misconstrued as the attainment of objective perfection. It seems less fanciful to maintain that, however much a poem is shaped and finished, it remains to some extent within the 'imprisoning marble' of a quotidian shapelessness and imperfection. At the same time I would claim the utmost significance for matters of technique and I take no cynical view of those rare moments in which the inertia of language, which is also the coercive force of language, seems to have been overcome.

Ideally, as I have already implied, my theme would be simple; simply this: that the technical perfecting of a poem is an act of atonement, in the radical etymological sense – an act of at-one-ment, a setting at one, a bringing into concord, a reconciling, a uniting in harmony; and that this act of atonement is described with beautiful finality by two modern poets: by W. B. Yeats when he writes in a letter of September 1936, to Dorothy Wellesley, that 'a poem comes right with a click like a closing box' and by T. S. Eliot in his essay of 1953, 'The Three Voices of Poetry':

> when the words are finally arranged in the right way – or in what he comes to accept as the best arrangement he can find – [the poet] may experience a moment of exhaustion, of appeasement, of absolution, and of something very near annihilation, which is in itself indescribable.

Anyone who has experienced that moment in which a poem 'comes right' must, I believe, give instinctive assent to such statements. And yet, in admitting this word 'instinctive', do I not put my argument in jeopardy and betray my deepest conviction? For it is not my intention to say anything which could either excite or placate those who associate creativity with random spontaneity and who regard form and structure as instruments of repression and constraint. It is as well to be reminded that my phrase was 'instinctive *assent*', and if 'instinct' is a 'natural or spontaneous tendency or inclination', 'assent' is 'agreement with a statement . . . or proposal that does not concern oneself'. From the depths of the self we rise to a concurrence with that which is not-self. For so I read those words of Pound: 'The poet's job is to *define* and yet again define till the detail of surface is in accord with the root in justice'.

I am attempting to convey, through these preliminary remarks, my belief that a debate of this nature is committed to a form of mimesis. The speaker must submit to an exemplary ordeal, analogous to that ordeal which Empson disarmingly calls 'the effort of writing a good bit of verse'. 'Mimesis', though, is an alluring term and exemplary ordeals are supposed to be ascetic. Define and yet again define. When Auerbach, in his book *Mimesis*, refers to a 'method of posing the problem so that the desired solution is contained in the very way in which the problem is posed' he acknowledges a pattern which is both austere and seductive. In posing the problem we 'show what it is like' to come up against rawness and contingency but not for a moment do we seriously put our mastery in hazard. When D. M. MacKinnon, on the other hand, remarks that Plato may have recognized, in the life and death of Socrates, 'a concretion, one might say a *mimesis*, of the way in which things ultimately are' we are possibly shaken out of our self-containment, our passionate attachment to those forms of hermetic mastery which must be so rebuked by life. But Romantic art is thoroughly familiar with the reproaches of life. Accusation, self-accusation, are the very life-blood of its most assured rhetoric: As Yeats puts it, in his poem 'The Circus Animals' Desertion':

> Those masterful images, because complete
> Grew in pure mind, but out of what began?
> A mound of refuse or the sweepings of a street,
> Old kettles, old bottles, and a broken can,
> Old iron, old bones, old rags, that raving slut
> Who keeps the till. Now that my ladder's gone,
> I must lie down where all the ladders start,
> In the foul rag-and-bone shop of the heart.

How is it possible, though, to revoke 'masterful images' in images that are themselves masterful? Can one renounce 'completion' with epithets and rhyme-patterns that in themselves retain a certain repleteness? T. S. Eliot's 'Marina' has been described as a 'poem that stammers into the hardly sayable' but I do not understand this remark. Though Eliot advocates humility and surrender, I do not think that he ever consciously surrenders rhetorical mastery. 'And why should he?' would be a fair question; but if I observe that 'Marina' seems to me to be an extremely eloquent poem and eminently 'sayable', I do so in the context of that obsessive self-critical Romantic monologue in which eloquence and guilt are intertwined, and for which the appropriate epigraph would be one abrupt entry in Coleridge's 1796 Notebook: 'Poetry – excites us to artificial feelings – makes us callous to real ones'.

There is a striking paragraph in Hannah Arendt's essay on Walter Benjamin in which she argues that to describe him and his work at all adequately 'one would have to make a great many negative statements'; as, for example, 'his erudition was great, but he was no scholar... he was greatly attracted... by theology... but he was no theologian and he was not particularly interested in the Bible... he thought poetically, but he was neither a poet nor a philosopher'. This quotation is central, indeed crucial, to the presentation of my argument. I have already conceded that, however challenging my title may appear, it nonetheless conforms. It is a not unfamiliar modernist theory which 'requires art to be destructive', which 'takes the violence of novelty as essential to success'. I may choose to ignore this theory, but I can't seem to be ignorant of it. I have to say, therefore, that the 'menace' to which I propose to refer is not that species of anti-bourgeois terrorism with which the names of Baudelaire, the Surrealists and Antonin Artaud have been indiscriminately linked. Nor is it the menace of the poetry of Négritude as polemically invoked by Sartre in writing of Césaire: 'Surrealism, a European poetic movement, is stolen from the Europeans by a Negro who turns it against them'. Nor is it that menace to which Hugh Kenner alludes in his epitaph for the American poet H. D.: 'Her grown life was a series of self-destructions, her poetic discipline one of these'.

As for 'atonement', the modern age is not unfamiliar with a literature of penitence; there is even, one may add, a literature of penitential literature. Thomas Mann is on record as saying that his novel *Doctor Faustus* is 'confession and sacrifice through and through'. The sin of Mann's protagonist, the composer Adrian Leverkühn, is in some respects similar to that which Maritain termed '"angelism," the refusal of the creature to submit to or be ruled by any of the exigencies of the created natural order'. And yet, of course, such a refusal to submit to these exigencies has itself been seen as the crime of capitalism, imperialism, modern technology and technological warfare. So there is a sense in which the modern artist is called upon to atone for his own illiberal pride and a sense in which he is engaged in vicarious expiation for the pride of the culture which itself rejects him. He can't win; but, you might say, he can't lose either; for in the words of Grotowski, in his book *Towards a Poor Theatre*, the actor 'does not sell his body but sacrifices it. He repeats the atonement; he is close to [secular] holiness'. It is, you may well feel, the sort of testimonial at which one looks twice.

Hannah Arendt, on the other hand, is reluctant to 'recommend' Walter Benjamin to our attention, to adjust his solitary witness to any of our recommended categories. One respects her scruple and her strategy. The 'negative statements' through which she vindicates, against the current of assumption, the man she believes Benjamin to be, themselves constitute a form of Romantic mimesis. Readers of the *Biographia Literaria* may note that Coleridge's concern is not so much with thought as with 'the mind's self-experience in the act of thinking' and that this 'self-experience' is most clearly realized by the process of win[ning one's] way up against the stream' or of observing how 'human nature itself [fights] up against [the] wilful resignation of intellect' to the dominion of common assumption and mechanical categorization. For Matthew Arnold, in his essay 'The Function of Criticism at the Present Time', the crucial vindication of Burke's integrity is his capacity to 'return . . . upon himself'; and a recent critic has described the Odes of Keats in precisely these terms: 'There was for Keats a certain justness, perhaps even a necessity, in beginning the first of the Odes [of 1819: the "Ode to Psyche"] by a return upon himself'. It is, of course, a frequently observed fact that the first word of the final stanza of Keats's 'Ode to a Nightingale' ('Forlorn! the very word is like a bell') echoes the last word of the preceding stanza ('Of perilous seas, in faery lands forlorn'). The echo is not so much a recollection as a revocation; and what is revoked is an attitude towards art and within art. The menace that is flinched from is certainly mortality ('Where youth grows pale, and spectre-thin, and dies') but it is also the menace of the high claims of poetry itself. 'Faery lands forlorn' reads like an exquisite pastiche of a Miltonic cadence: 'Stygian cave forlorn' ('L'Allegro', 1.3); 'these wilde Woods forlorn' (*Paradise Lost*, ix, 910). We perhaps too readily assume that the characteristic Romantic mode is an expansive gesture ('Hail to thee, blithe Spirit! Bird thou never wert'). That which MacKinnon has described, in speaking of Kant, as a 'tortuous and strenuous argument, whose structure torments the reader' is equally a paradigm of Romantic-Modernist method:

> Not, I'll not, carrion comfort, Despair, not feast on thee;
> Not untwist – slack they may be – these last strands of man
> In me or, most weary, cry *I can no more.* I can;
> Can something, hope, wish day come, not choose not to be.

These lines by Hopkins may also be said to embody the positive virtue of negative statements, which I have already remarked in Hannah Arendt's essay.

As I have also previously remarked, we are not unfamiliar with a modern literature of penitence, nor indeed with that required secondary reading which is at times, and not inappropriately, a penance in itself. One is, so to speak, 'winning one's way up against the stream'. In the past twenty years or so, in both Europe and North America, there has been a proliferation of studies devoted to aspects of the interrelationship of theology and literature, or 'the coinherence of religion and culture', to use the wider terms which some prefer. Professor Nathan A. Scott and his colleagues in the Divinity School of the University of Chicago have produced, and have inspired others to produce, a considerable body of criticism and exegesis which may fairly be described as being ecumenically nourished by the work of the Catholic Maritain and the Protestants Tillich and Bonhoeffer. It would seem unreasonable not to concur with Scott's précis of the situation; his suggestion that among 'the principal motives that underlie the general movement of [literary] criticism in our period' is the attempt 'to offer some resistance to the reductionist tendency of modern scientism', and that such 'resistance' is vulnerable to its own reductionist tendency whereby the precious autonomy of the poem may appear as no more than a structure of grammar and syntax. Scott is opposed to both 'reductionist scientism' and aesthetic hermeticism. He quotes with approval Vivas' view of the aesthetic experience as 'intransitive attention' and de Rougemont's definition of the work of art as 'a calculated trap for meditation'. The key terms for Scott's argument are 'attention' and 'meditation' because both words suggest not only an active contemplation of minute particulars and a resistance to sentimental substitution but also an 'ultimate concern' for 'the world of existence that transcends the work'. My reservations, I have already implied, relate not so much to principle as to practice. Although he recognizes that the artist only 'makes good his vocational claim . . . by the extent of the success with which he shapes the substance of experience', Scott's interpretation of what constitutes 'substance of experience' strikes me as being more simply discursive and more tenuous than his endorsement of such terms as 'intransitive attention' leads one to expect. Having been told, in the course of a single essay on Saul Bellow, that *Henderson the Rain King* is an 'adventure in atonement', that 'the comedy of *Herzog* is a comedy of redemption', that 'the drama [in the late books] becomes explicitly a drama of reconciliation', it is with a peculiar urgency of assent that one recalls MacKinnon's remark: 'the language of repentance is not a kind of bubble on the surface of things' or encounters Henry Rago's proper insistence that 'when the language is that of the imagination, we can be grateful enough to read that language as it asks to be read: in the very density of the medium, without the violence of interpolation or reduction'.

It is, I think, crucial at this point to draw a distinction between, on the one hand, a formal acknowledgement of the human condition of anxiety or guilt and, on the other, 'the empirical guilty conscience'. It is one thing to talk of literature as a medium through which we convey our awareness, or indeed our conviction, of an inveterate human condition of guilt or anxiety; it is another to be possessed by a sense of language itself as a manifestation of empirical guilt. In G. K. Chesterton's study, *Charles Dickens*, he remarks that 'a saint after repentance will forgive himself for a sin; a man about town will never forgive himself for a *faux pas*. There are ways of getting absolved for murder; there are no ways of getting absolved for upsetting the soup'. In Helen Waddell's novel *Peter Abelard*, we encounter the thought again, shorn of its risible bathos and delivered with a becoming genial ironic *gravitas* by Gilles de Vannes, Canon of Notre Dame:

> For one can repent and be absolved of a sin, but there is no canonical repentance for a mistake.

Out of context this has just the right weight and edge to enhance the thesis and the occasion. But it may be that Chesterton grasped the truth of the matter. Under scrutiny, this is the essence to which my term 'empirical guilt' is reduced: to an anxiety about *faux pas*, the perpetration of 'howlers', grammatical solecisms, misstatements of fact, misquotations, improper attributions. It is an anxiety only transiently appeased by the thought that misquotation may be a form of re-creation. This thought, originally proposed by Dr Matthew Hodgart in 1953, is subjected to intense and challenging scrutiny by Professor Christopher Ricks in an article in *The Times Literary Supplement*. Ricks's essay vindicates one's anxiety but nothing relieves it. Well, if one feels like this about it, why carry on? And why carry on so? And in public too!

'No man but a blockhead ever wrote, except for money.' Like Boswell, I feel a little distress at the good Doctor's blunt remark and like Boswell I hasten to add that 'numerous instances to refute this will occur to all who are versed in the history of literature'. If, however, we choose to take Johnson's words as a figure of speech implying that all men write from impure motives, whether from that 'necessity' which he himself cites, or from a desire for 'wreaths of fame and interest', or for 'erotic honey', or whatever, Johnson's cynicism may seem more sustainable. If that is so, let us postulate yet another impure motive, remorse, and let us suggest that a man may continue to write and to publish in a vain and self-defeating effort to appease his own sense of empirical guilt. It is ludicrous, of course. 'A knitting editor once said "if I make a mistake there are jerseys all over England with one arm longer than the other".' Set that beside Nadezhda Mandelstam's account of the life and death of her husband, the Russian poet Osip Mandelstam, and one can scarcely hope to be taken seriously. Men are imprisoned and tortured and executed for the strength of their beliefs and their ideas, not for upsetting the soup. And yet one must, however barely, hope to be taken seriously. It seems to me one of the indubitable signs of Simone Weil's greatness as an ethical writer that she associates the act of writing not with a generalized awareness of sin but with specific crime, and proposes a system whereby 'anybody, no matter who, discovering an avoidable error in a printed text or radio broadcast, would be entitled to bring an action before [special] courts empowered to condemn a convicted offender to prison or hard labour.' It may well strike others as unassailable evidence that the woman was merely an obsessional neurotic. Perhaps one could phrase the matter more moderately and say that one does not regard it as at all eccentric to endorse the view that grammar is a 'social and public institution', or to share W. K. Wimsatt's belief in 'the fullness of [the poet's] responsibility as public performer in a complex and treacherous medium'.

Stephen Spender, in his useful little book on Eliot, raises the question of the distinction between "legal crime' and "sin' in Eliot's thought. In *The Elder Statesman*, Lord Claverton declares:

> It's harder to confess the sin that no one believes in
> Than the crime that everyone can appreciate.
> For the crime is in relation to the law
> And the sin is in relation to the sinner.

Spender says that 'the point Eliot is trying to make is of course that "sin" is worse than "crime"'. The logic, if it is logic, underlying Claverton's words is that it is made more objectively difficult to confess if no one apart from oneself believes that there is anything which needs to be confessed. Spender is sceptical of the manner in which Eliot demonstrates his distinction and his priorities; and I would agree that some scepticism is justified. In *The Family Reunion* and *The Elder Statesman* 'sin' is more important than 'crime' partly because the criminal act is ultimately revealed to be either non-existent or very much less than one had been led to imagine. Reflecting upon his last play *The Elder Statesman*, one is inclined to wonder how far Eliot has succeeded in distinguishing 'sin' from those other mental or psychic states which solipsists might confuse with it. The late Harry Guntrip once suggested:

> It may be that the practical and relevant approach to the problem of sin for this age is by the study of the devastations, personal, social, and spiritual, which are the product of anxiety.

Doubtless he has a very strong case; but to Eliot, despite the portrayal of 'pathological despondency', 'psychic impotence', in *The Waste Land* and other poems, it would seem, possibly, a blurring of categories, an abdication of priorities. Yet that which Claverton retrospectively describes, and what he immediately undergoes when accosted by Gornez and Mrs Carghill, seems very like one aspect of that condition which Guntrip calls 'anxiety'. But that is precisely Eliot's point, you will fairly remonstrate. In a secular age we experience anxiety until we learn to read ourselves aright and know that we act and suffer as creatures of sin. Even so, I still maintain that something has eluded Eliot, eluded him in 'the very density of the medium'. Grover Smith, in his essay on *The Elder Statesman*, says that 'Claverton, troubled by his role in [the past lives of Gomez and Mrs Carghill], is indifferent to their future, though neither has wronged him so much as he has wronged them. He makes no atoning gesture'; but Smith seems to imply that this is an ironic profundity of Eliot's making. It seems to me, however, that in determining the order of priority between 'sin' and 'anxiety' 'the kind of pleasure that poetry gives' is to be experienced through contact with the force-fields of these conflicting yet colluding entities. To control such forces demands an *askesis* rather different from the 'ascetic rule' which Eliot laid down for himself in the writing of dramatic verse:

> the ascetic rule to avoid poetry which could not stand the test of strict dramatic utility.

That 'poetry' which is excluded on utilitarian grounds is, I would argue, that very element which could master the violence of the conflict and collusion between the sacramental and the secular, between the dogmatic exclusiveness of 'sin' and the rich solipsistic possibilities of 'anxiety'. I would further suggest that Eliot's asceticism in the three post-war verse-plays is too often a kind of resignation, or what W. W. Robson, in an acute criticism of the later essays, calls 'abstention'. He is left with a language that is at once aloof and ingratiating, unambiguous yet ambivalent. In the essay 'Poetry and Drama' Eliot speaks of 'a fringe of indefinite extent, of feeling which we can only detect, so to speak, out of the corner of the eye and can never completely focus . . . At such moments, we touch the border of those feelings which only music can express'. As Eliot well knew, however, a poet must also turn back, with whatever weariness, disgust, love barely distinguishable from hate, to confront 'the indefinite extent' of language itself and seek his 'focus' there. In certain contexts the expansive, outward gesture towards the condition of music is a helpless gesture of surrender, oddly analogous to that stylish aesthetic of despair, that desire for the ultimate integrity of silence, to which so much eloquence has been so frequently and indefatigably devoted.

Edward Mendelson, the editor of the posthumous *Collected Poems* of W. H. Auden, has said that 'as he grew older Auden became increasingly distrustful of vivid assertions, increasingly determined to write poems that were not breathtaking but truthtelling' and has endorsed the poet's motives and actions with his own suggestion that 'the local vividness of a line or passage can blind a reader into missing a poem's overall shape'. I would suggest, however, that the proof of a poet's craft is precisely the ability to affect an at-one-ment between the 'local vividness' and the 'overall shape', and that this is his truthtelling. When the poem 'comes right with a click like a closing box', what is there effected is the atonement of aesthetics with rectitude of judgment. The suggestion that the proof of a poet's integrity is a conviction that he must sacrifice 'vividness' to 'shape' seems to me to stem from a very dubious philosophy of authorial responsibility to the 'reader'. My argument is thus obliged to distinguish between this matter of 'empirical guilt' which is involved with 'the density of the medium' and the principles of Christian penitence and humility which were, it seems reasonable to suggest, the disciplines of conscience within which Eliot and Auden increasingly worked. One is left with the awkward observation that the acceptance of a principle of penitential humility in the conduct of life does not necessarily inhibit a readiness to accept the status of 'maestro' conferred by a supportive yet coercive public. It's worse than awkward, it's damned awkward; it cannot but be seen as a churlish refusal to concede honour where honour is due. I would reply that it is not a matter of *ad hominem* rebuke but a suggestion that fashionable adulation of the 'maestro' when there is so little recognition of the 'fabbro', 'homo faber', is one aspect of what C. K. Stead mordantly but not unfairly calls the 'struggle between poets and "poetry-lovers"', except that the very word 'struggle' suggests purpose and engagement. As Jon Silkin has remarked, 'it is not disagreement we have now but deafness'. Deafness, yes; and arbitrary assumption. To 'assume' is literally 'to take to oneself, adopt, usurp'; and the fashion in which society can 'take up' and 'drop' the poet (as John Clare was taken up, and dropped) is a form of usurpation which has little or no connection with intrinsic value. . . .

Part V
1980–2000

Chapter 62
Shoshana Felman

Shoshana Felman (1940–) is a literary theorist and cultural historian who has both absorbed and transformed the intellectual legacy of Lacanian psychoanalysis. In doing so she has questioned the authority of psychoanalysis as a method for discovering the unconscious contents of literary works or writers' minds. Unlike an earlier generation of literary critics who believed that psychoanalysis could become the basis for a new hermeneutic capable of disclosing the fundamental and hidden meanings of poems, novels, and plays, Felman has argued that psychoanalysis is implied in literature, not applied to it. The act of interpretation is no less subject to the activity of the unconscious than the art of literary invention. Neither poet nor text occupy the position of a patient waiting to be told by the critical analyst what their true meanings are. This revision of the place of psychoanalysis in literary interpretation has been accompanied by other changes in emphasis: an attention to the formal and structural elements in literary works rather than their hidden meanings, and a concern with the traditions of interpretation that build up around an author or a work. Felman's work has drawn on other sources than psychoanalysis, as in her study of Byron's Don Juan, The Scandal of the Speaking Body, *where she uses the speech act theory of the English philosopher, J. L. Austin, to deepen an understanding of the relation between language and the unconscious. More recently, Felman has written about the trauma of the Holocaust in her book,* Testimony: Crises of Witnessing *(1993) and the complex cultural meanings of show trials in her* The Juridicial Unconscious: Trials and Traumas in the Twentieth Century *(2003). She is the Thomas E. Donnelly Professor of French and Comparative Literature at Yale University.*

In the following excerpt from "On Reading Poetry: Reflections on the Limits and Possibilities of Psychoanalytical Approaches" Felman takes the work of Edgar Allan Poe as a significant example of the effects of poetry. Tracing the contradictions in Poe's reputation – at once a genius and a source of corruption that needs to be resisted – Felman tries to identify what it is that creates the disturbance associated with powerful poetry. Drawing on Lacan's response to Poe's short story, The Purloined Letter, *and treating it as an "allegory of poetic writing," Felman notes the poetic effects created in it by the repetition of a structure and a signifier. Poems contain within themselves the "signifier of poeticity," but this is not to be identified with a meaning in the usual sense.*

On Reading Poetry: Reflections on the Limits and Possibilities of Psychoanalytical Approaches

To account for poetry in psychoanalytical terms has traditionally meant to analyze poetry as a symptom of a particular poet. I would here like to reverse this approach, and to analyze a particular poet as a symptom of poetry.

No poet, perhaps, has been as highly acclaimed and, at the same time, as violently disclaimed as Edgar Allan Poe. The most controversial figure on the American literary scene, "perhaps the most thoroughly misunderstood of all American writers," "a stumbling block for the judicial critic," Edgar Allan Poe has had the peculiar fortune of being at once the most admired and the most decried of American poets. In the history of literary criticism, no other poet has engendered as much disagreement and as many critical contradictions. It is my contention that this critical disagreement is itself symptomatic of a *poetic effect*, and that the critical contradictions to which Poe's poetry has given rise are themselves indirectly significant of the nature of poetry.

The Poe-etic effect: a literary case history

No other poet has been so often referred to as a "genius," in a sort of common consensus shared even by his detractors. Joseph Wood Krutch, whose study of Poe tends to belittle Poe's stature and to disparage the value of his artistic achievement, nevertheless entitles his monograph *Edgar Allan Poe: A Study in Genius*. So do many other critics, who acknowledge and assert Poe's "genius" in the very titles of their essays, and thus propose to study "The Genius of Poe" (J. M. S. Robertson), *Le Génie d'Edgar Poe* (Camille Mauclair, Paris, 1925), *Edgar Allan Poe: His Genius and His Character* (John Dillon, New York, 1911), *The Genius and Character of Edgar Allan Poe* (John R. Thompson, privately printed, 1989), *Genius and Disaster: Studies in Drugs and Genius* (Jeannet A. Marks, New York, 1925), "Affidavits of Genius: French Essays on Poe" (Jean A. Alexander). "It happens to us but few times in our lives," writes Thomas W. Higginson, "to come consciously into the presence of that extraordinary miracle we call genius. Among the many literary persons whom I have happened to meet,... there are not half a dozen who have left an irresistible sense of this rare quality; and among these few, Poe." For Constance M. Rourke, "Poe has become a symbol for the type of genius which rises clear from its time"; the English poet A. Charles Swinburne speaks of "the special quality of [Poe's] strong and delicate genius"; the French poet Mallarmé describes his translations of Poe as "a monument to

From *The Literary Freud: Mechanics of Defense and the Poetic Will*, ed. Joseph H. Smith (New Haven, Conn.: Yale University Press, 1980), pp. 119–25, 132–48.

the genius who . . . exercised his influence in our country;" and the American poet James Russell Lowell, one of Poe's harshest critics, who, in his notorious versified verdict, judged Poe's poetry to include "two fifths sheer fudge," nonetheless asserts: "Mr. Poe has that indescribable something which men have agreed to call *genius*; . . . Let talent writhe and contort itself as it may, it has no such magnetism. Larger of bone and sinew it may be, but the wings are wanting."

However suspicious and unromantic the critical reader might wish to be with respect to "that indescribable something which men have agreed to call genius," it is clear that Poe's poetry produces, in a uniquely striking and undeniable manner, what might be called a *genius-effect*: the impression of some undefinable but compelling *force* to which the reader is subjected. To describe "this power, *which is felt*," as one reader puts it, Lowell speaks of "magnetism"; other critics speak of "magic." "Poe," writes Bernard Shaw, "constantly and inevitably *produced magic* where his greatest contemporaries produced only beauty." T. S. Eliot quite reluctantly agrees: "Poe had, to an exceptional degree, the feeling for the incantatory element in poetry, of that which may, in the most nearly literal sense, be called 'the magic of verse.' "

Poe's "magic" is thus ascribed to the ingenuity of his versification, to his exceptional technical virtuosity. And yet, the word *magic*, "in the most nearly literal sense," means much more than just the intellectual acknowledgment of an outstanding technical skill; it connotes the effective action of something which exceeds both the understanding and the control of the person who is subjected to it; it connotes a force to which the reader has no choice but to submit. "No one could tell us what it is," writes Lowell, still in reference to Poe's genius, "and yet there is none who is not *inevitably aware* of . . . its power." "Poe," said Bernard Shaw, "*inevitably* produced magic." There is something about Poe's poetry which, like fate, is experienced as *inevitable*, unavoidable (and not just as irresistible). What is more, once this poetry is read, its inevitability is there to stay; it becomes lastingly inevitable: "it will *stick to the memory* of every one who reads it," writes P. Pendleton Cooke. And T. S. Eliot: "Poe is the author of a few . . . short poems . . . which do somehow *stick in the memory*."

This is why Poe's poetry can be defined, and indeed has been, as a poetry of *influence* par excellence, in the sense emphasized by Harold Bloom: "to inflow" = to have power over another. The case of Poe in literary history could in fact be accounted for as one of the most extreme and most complex cases of "the anxiety of influence," of the anxiety unwittingly provoked by the "influence" irresistibly emanating from this poetry. What is unique, however, about Poe's influence, as about the "magic" of his verse, is the extent to which its action is unaccountably insidious, exceeding the control, the will, and the awareness of those who are subjected to it. "Poe's influence," writes T. S. Eliot, "is . . . puzzling":

> In France the influence of his poetry and of his poetic theories has been immense. In England and America it seems almost negligible. . . . And yet one cannot be sure that one's own writing has *not* been influenced by Poe. (*Recognition*, p. 205; Eliot's italics)

Studying Poe's influence on Baudelaire, Mallarmé, and Valéry, Eliot goes on to comment:

> Here are three literary generations, representing almost exactly a century of French poetry. Of course, these are poets very different from each other.... But I think we can trace the development and descent of one particular theory of the nature of poetry through these three poets and it is a theory which takes its origin in the theory... of Edgar Poe. And the impression we get of the influence of Poe is the more impressive, because of the fact that Mallarmé, and Valéry in turn, did not merely derive from Poe through Baudelaire: each of them subjected himself to that influence directly, and has left convincing evidence of the value which he attached to the theory and practice of Poe himself....
>
> I find that by trying to look at Poe through the eyes of Baudelaire, Mallarmé and Valéry, I become more thoroughly convinced of his importance, of the importance of his *work* as a whole. (*Recognition*, pp. 206, 219; Eliot's italics)

Curiously enough, while Poe's worldwide importance and effective influence is beyond question, critics nonetheless continue to protest and to proclaim, as loudly as they can, that Poe is *un*important, that Poe is *not* a major poet. In an essay entitled "Vulgarity in Literature" (1931) and taxing Poe with "vulgarity," Aldous Huxley argues:

> Was Edgar Allan Poe a major poet? It would surely never occur to any English-speaking critic to say so. And yet, in France, from 1850 till the present time, the best poets of each generation – yes, and the best critics, too; for, like most excellent poets, Baudelaire, Mallarmé, Paul Valéry are also admirable critics – have gone out of their way to praise him.... We who are speakers of English..., we can only say, with all due respect, that Baudelaire, Mallarmé, and Valéry were wrong and that *Poe is not one of our major poets.* (*Recognition*, p. 160)

Poe's detractors seem to be unaware, however, of the paradox that underlies their enterprise: it is by no means clear why anyone should take the trouble to write – at length – about a writer of no importance. Poe's most systematic denouncer, Ivor Winters, thus writes:

> *The menace* lies not, primarily, in his impressionistic admirers among literary people of whom he still has some, even in England and in America, where a familiarity with his language ought to render his crudity obvious, for these individuals in the main do not make themselves permanently very effective; *it lies rather in the impressive body of scholarship*.... When a writer is supported by a sufficient body of such scholarship, a very little philosophical elucidation will suffice to establish him in the scholarly world as a writer whose greatness is self-evident.

The irony which here escapes the author is that, in writing his attack on Poe, what the attacker is in fact doing is adding still another study to the bulk of "the impressive body of scholarship" in which, in his own terms, "the menace lies"; so that, paradoxically enough, through Ivor Winters' study, "the menace" – that is, the possibility of taking Poe's "greatness as a writer" as "self-evident" – will indeed increase. I shall here precisely argue that, regardless of the value-judgment it may pass on Poe, this impressive bulk of Poe scholarship, the very quantity of the critical literature to which Poe's poetry has given rise, is itself an indication of its effective poetic power, of the strength with which it drives the reader to an *action*, compels him to a *reading-act*. The elaborate written denials of Poe's value, the loud and lengthy negations of his importance, are therefore very like psychoanalytical negations. It is clear that if Poe's text in effect were unimportant, it would not seem so important to proclaim, argue, and prove that he is unimportant. The fact that it so much *matters* to proclaim that Poe *does not matter* is but evidence of the extent to which Poe's poetry is, in effect, a *poetry that matters.*

Poe might thus be said to have a *literary case history,* most revealing in that it incarnates, in its controversial forms, the paradoxical nature of a strong *poetic effect*: the very poetry which, more than any other, is experienced as *irresistible* has also proved to be, in literary history, the poetry most *resisted,* the one that, more than any other, has provoked resistances.

This apparent contradiction, which makes of Poe's poetry a unique case in literary history, clearly partakes of the paradoxical nature of an *analytical effect.* The enigma it presents us with is the enigma of "the analytical" par excellence, as stated by Poe himself, whose amazing intuitions of the nature of what he calls "analysis" are strikingly similar to the later findings of psychoanalysis:

> The mental features discoursed of as the analytical are, in themselves, but little susceptible of analysis. *We appreciate them only in their effects.*

Because of the very nature of its strong "effects," of the reading-*acts* that it provokes, Poe's text (and not just Poe's biography or his personal neurosis) is clearly an analytical case in the history of literary criticism, a case that suggests something crucial to understand in psychoanalytic terms. It is therefore not surprising that Poe, more than any other poet, has been repeatedly singled out for psychoanalytical research, has persistently attracted the attention of psychoanalytic critics....

If the thrust of the discourse of applied psychoanalysis is, indeed, in tracing poetry to a clinical reality, to *reduce* the poetic to a "cause" outside itself, the crucial limitation of this process of reduction is, however, that the cause, while it may be *necessary,* is by no means a *sufficient* one. "Modern psychiatry," judiciously writes David Galloway, "may greatly aid the critic of literature, but...it cannot thus far explain why other men, suffering from deprivations or fears or obsessions similar to Poe's, failed to demonstrate his particular creative talent. Though no doubt Marie Bonaparte was correct in seeing Poe's own art as a defense against madness, we must be wary of identifying the *necessity* for this defense, in terms of Poe's own life, with the *success* of this defense, which can only be measured in his art."

That the discourse of applied psychoanalysis is limited precisely in that it does not account for Poe's poetic *genius* is in fact the crucial point made by Freud himself in his prefatory note to Marie Bonaparte's study:

> FOREWORD
>
> In this book my friend and pupil, Marie Bonaparte, has shown the light of psychoanalysis on the life and work of a great writer with pathologic trends.

> Thanks to her interpretative effort, we now realize how many of the characteristics of Poe's works were conditioned by his personality, and can see how that personality derived from intense emotional fixations and painful infantile experiences. *Investigations such as this do not claim to explain creative genius*, but they do reveal the factors which awake it and the sort of subject matter it is destined to choose....
>
> Sigm. Freud

No doubt, Freud's remarkable superiority over some (most) of his disciples – including Marie Bonaparte – proceeds from his acute *awareness* of the very *limitations* of his method, an awareness that in his followers seems most often not to exist.

I would like here to raise a question which, springing out of this limitation of applied psychoanalysis, has, amazingly enough, never been asked as a serious question: is there a way *around* Freud's perspicacious reservation, warning us that studies like those of Bonaparte "do not claim to explain creative genius"? Is there, in other words, a way – a different way – in which psychoanalysis *can* help us to account for poetic genius? Is there an alternative to applied psychoanalysis? – an alternative that would be capable of touching, in a psychoanalytic manner, upon the very specificity of that which constitutes the poetic?

Before endeavoring to articulate the way in which this question might be answered, I would like to examine still another manner in which Poe's text has been psychoanalytically approached: Jacques Lacan's "Seminar" on Poe's short story, "The Purloined Letter."

Jacques Lacan: The approach of textual problematization

"The Purloined Letter," as is well known, is the story of the double theft of a compromising letter, originally sent to the queen. Surprised by the unexpected entrance of the king, the queen leaves the letter on the table in full view of any visitor, where it is least likely to appear suspicious and therefore to attract the king's attention. Enters the Minister D., who, observing the queen's anxiety and the play of glances between her and the unsuspicious king, analyzes the situation, figures out, recognizing the addresser's handwriting, what the letter is about, and steals it – by substituting for it another letter which he takes from his pocket – under the very eyes of the challenged queen, who can do nothing to prevent the theft without provoking the king's suspicions, and who is therefore reduced to silence. The queen then asks the prefect of police to search the minister's apartment and person, so as to find the letter and restore it to her. The prefect uses every conceivable secret-police technique to search every conceivable hiding place on the minister's premises, but to no avail: the letter remains undiscovered.

Having exhausted his resources, the prefect consults Auguste Dupin, the famous "analyst," as Poe calls him (i.e., an amateur detective who excels in solving problems by means of deductive logic), to whom he tells the whole story. (It is, in fact, from this narration of the prefect of police to Dupin and in turn reported by the first-person narrator, Dupin's friend, who is also present, that we, the readers, learn the story.)

On a second encounter between the prefect of police and Dupin, the latter, to the great surprise of the prefect and of the narrator, produces the purloined letter out of his drawer and hands it to the prefect in return for a large amount of money. The prefect leaves, and Dupin explains to the narrator how he came into possession of the letter: he had deduced that the minister, knowing that his premises would be thoroughly combed by the police, had concluded that the best principle of concealment would be to leave the letter in the open, in full view: in that way the police, searching for hidden secret drawers, would be outwitted, and the letter would not be discovered precisely because it would be too self-evident. On this assumption, Dupin called on the minister in his apartment and, glancing around, soon located the letter most carelessly hanging from the mantelpiece in a card-rack. A little later, a disturbance in the street provoked by a man in Dupin's employ drew the minister to the window, at which moment Dupin quickly replaced the letter with a facsimile, having slipped the real one into his pocket.

I will not enter here into the complexity of the psychoanalytic issues involved in Lacan's "The Seminar on *The Purloined Letter*," nor will I try to deal exhaustively with the nuanced sophistication of the seminar's rhetoric and theoretical propositions; I will confine myself to a few specific points that bear upon the methodological issue of Lacan's psychoanalytic treatment of the literary material.

What Lacan is concerned with at this point of his research is the psychoanalytic problematics of the "repetition-compulsion," as elaborated in Freud's speculative text, *Beyond the Pleasure Principle.* The thrust of Lacan's endeavor, with respect to Poe, is thus to point out – so as to elucidate the nature of Freudian repetition – the way in which the story's plot, its sequence of events (as, for Freud, the sequence of events in a life-story), is entirely contingent on, overdetermined by, a principle of repetition that governs it and inadvertently structures its dramatic and ironic impact. "There are two scenes," remarks Lacan, "the first of which we shall straightway designate the primal scene,... since the second may be considered its repetition in the very sense we are considering today." The "primal scene" takes place in the queen's boudoir: it is the theft of the letter from the queen by the minister; the second scene – its repetition – is the theft of the letter from the minister by Dupin, in the minister's hotel.

What constitutes repetition for Lacan, however, is not the mere thematic resemblance of the double *theft*, but the whole structural situation in which the repeated theft takes place: in each case, the theft is the outcome of an intersubjective relationship between three terms; in the first scene, the three participants are the king, the queen, and the minister; in the second, the three participants are the police, the minister, and Dupin. In much the same way as Dupin takes the place of the minister in the first scene (the place of the letter's robber), the minister in the second scene takes the place of the queen in the first (the dispossessed possessor of the letter); whereas the police, for whom the letter remains invisible, take the place formerly occupied by the king. The two scenes thus mirror each other, in that they dramatize the repeated exchange of "three glances, borne by three subjects, incarnated each time by different characters." What is repeated, in other words, is not a psychological act committed as a function of the individual psychology of a character, but three functional *positions in a structure* which, determining three different *viewpoints*, embody three different relations to the act of seeing – of seeing, specifically, the purloined letter.

> The first is a glance that sees nothing: the King and the Police.
> The second, a glance which sees that the first sees nothing and deludes itself as to the secrecy of what it hides: the Queen, then the Minister.
> The third sees that the first two glances leave what should be hidden exposed to whomever would seize it: the Minister, and finally Dupin.

...

"What interests us today," insists Lacan,

> is the manner in which the subjects relay each other in their displacement during the intersubjective repetition. We shall see that their displacement is determined by the place which a pure signifier – the purloined letter – comes to occupy in their trio. And that is what will confirm for us its status as repetition automatism.

The purloined letter, in other words, becomes itself – through its insistence in the structure – a symbol or a signifier of the *unconscious*, to the extent that it "is destined... to signify the annulment of what it signifies" – the necessity of its own *repression*, of the repression of its message: "It is not only the meaning but the text of the message which it would be dangerous to place in circulation." But in much the same way as the repressed *returns* in the *symptom*, which is its repetitive symbolic substitute, the purloined letter ceaselessly returns in the tale – as a signifier of the repressed – through its repetitive displacements and replacements. "This is indeed what happens in the repetition compulsion," says Lacan. Unconscious desire, once repressed, survives in displaced symbolic media which govern the subject's life and actions without his ever being aware of their meaning or of the repetitive pattern they structure:

> If what Freud discovered and rediscovers with a perpetually increasing sense of shock has a meaning, it is that the displacement of the signifier determines the subjects in their acts, in their destiny, in their refusals, in their blindnesses, in their end and in their fate, their innate gifts and social acquisitions notwithstanding, without regard for character or sex, and that, willingly or not, everything that might be considered the stuff of psychology, kit and caboodle, will follow the path of the signifier.

In what sense, then, does the second scene in Poe's tale, while repeating the first scene, nonetheless differ from it? In the sense, precisely, that the second scene, through the repetition, allows for an understanding, for an *analysis* of the first. This analysis through repetition is to become, in Lacan's ingenious reading, no less than an *allegory of psychoanalysis*. The intervention of Dupin, who restores the letter to the queen, is thus compared, in Lacan's interpretation, to the intervention of the analyst, who rids the patient of the symptom. The analyst's effectiveness, however, does not spring from his intellectual strength but – insists Lacan – from his position in the (repetitive) structure. By virtue of his occupying the third position – that is, the *locus* of the unconscious of the subject as a place of substitution of letter for letter (of signifier for signifier) – the analyst, through transference, allows at once for a repetition of the trauma, and for a symbolic substitution, and thus effects the drama's denouement.

It is instructive to compare Lacan's study of the psychoanalytical repetition compulsion in Poe's text to Marie Bonaparte's study of Poe's repetition compulsion through his text.[1] Although the two analysts study the same author and focus on the same psychoanalytic concept, their approaches are strikingly different. To the extent that Bonaparte's study of Poe has become a classic, a model of applied psychoanalysis which illustrates and embodies the most common understanding of what a psychoanalytic reading of a literary text might be, I would like, in pointing out the differences in Lacan's approach, to suggest the way in which those differences at once put in question the traditional approach and offer an alternative to it.

1. *What does a repetition compulsion repeat? Interpretation of difference as opposed to interpretation of identity*

For Marie Bonaparte, what is compulsively repeated through the variety of Poe's texts is the *same* unconscious fantasy: Poe's (sadonecrophiliac) desire for his dead mother. For Lacan, what is repeated in the text is not the content of a fantasy but the symbolic displacement of a signifier through the insistence of a signifying chain; repetition is not of *sameness* but of *difference*, not of independent terms or of analogous themes but of a structure of differential interrelationships, in which what *returns* is always *other*. Thus, the triangular structure repeats itself only through the *difference* of the characters who successively come to occupy the three positions; its structural significance is perceived only *through* this difference. Likewise, the significance of the letter is situated in its *displacement*, that is, in its repetitive movements toward a *different* place. And the second scene, being, for Lacan, an allegory of analysis, is important not just in that it *repeats* the first scene, but in the way this repetition (like the transferential repetition of a psychoanalytical experience) *makes a difference*: brings about a solution to the problem. Thus, whereas Marie Bonaparte analyzes repetition as the insistence of identity, for Lacan, any possible insight into the reality of the unconscious is contingent upon a perception of repetition, not as a confirmation of identity, but as the insistence of the indelibility of a difference.

2. *An analysis of the signifier as opposed to an analysis of the signified*

In the light of Lacan's reading of Poe's tale as itself an allegory of the psychoanalytic reading, it might be illuminating to define the difference in approach between Lacan and Bonaparte in terms of the story. If the purloined letter can be said to be a sign of the unconscious, for Marie Bonaparte the analyst's task is to uncover the letter's *content*, which she believes – as do the police – to be *hidden* somewhere in the real, in some secret biographical *depth*. For Lacan, on the other hand, the analyst's task is not to read the letter's hidden referential content, but to situate the superficial indication of its textual movement, to analyze the paradoxically invisible symbolic evidence of its displacement, its structural insistence, in a signifying chain. "There is such a thing," writes Poe, "as being too profound. Truth is not always in a well. In fact, as regards the most important knowledge, I do believe she is invariably superficial." Espousing Poe's insight, Lacan makes the principle of symbolic evidence the guideline for an analysis not of the signified but of the signifier – for an analysis of the unconscious (the repressed) not as hidden but on the contrary as *exposed* – in language – through a significant (rhetorical) displacement.

This analysis of the signifier, the model of which can be found in Freud's interpretation of dreams, is nonetheless a radical reversal of the traditional expectations and presuppositions involved in the common psychoanalytical approach to literature, and its invariable search for hidden meanings. Indeed, not only is Lacan's reading of "The Purloined Letter" subversive of the traditional model of psychoanalytical reading; it is, in general, a type of reading that is methodologically unprecedented in the whole history of literary criticism. The history of reading has accustomed us to the assumption – usually unquestioned – that reading is finding meaning, that interpretation – of whatever method – can dwell but on the meaningful. Lacan's analysis of the signifier opens up a radically new assumption, an assumption which is nonetheless nothing but an insightful logical and methodological consequence of Freud's discovery: that what *can* be read (and perhaps what *should* be read) is not just meaning, but the lack of meaning; that significance lies not just in consciousness, but, specifically, in its disruption; that the signifier can be analyzed in its effects without its signified being known; that the lack of meaning – the discontinuity in conscious understanding – can and should be interpreted as such, without necessarily being transformed into meaning. "Let's take a look," writes Lacan:

> We shall find illumination in what at first seems to obscure matters: the fact that the tale leaves us in virtually total ignorance of the sender, no less than of the contents, of the letter.
>
> The signifier is not functional.... We might even admit that the letter has an entirely different (if no more urgent) meaning for the Queen than the one understood by the Minister. The sequence of events would not be noticeably affected, not even if it were strictly incomprehensible to an uninformed reader.
>
> But that this is the very effect of the unconscious in the precise sense that we teach that the unconscious means that man is inhabited by the signifier.

Thus, for Lacan, what is analytical par excellence is not (as is the case for Bonaparte) the *readable*, but the *unreadable*, and the *effects* of the unreadable. What calls for analysis is the insistence of the unreadable in the text.

Poe, of course, had said it all in his insightful comment, previously quoted, on the nature of what he too – amazingly enough, before the fact – called "the analytical":

> The mental features discoursed of as the analytical are, in themselves, but little susceptible of analysis. We appreciate them only in their effects.

But, oddly enough, what Poe himself had said so strikingly and so explicitly about "the analytical" had itself remained totally unanalyzed, indeed unnoticed, by psychoanalytic scholars before Lacan, perhaps because it, too, according to its own (analytical) logic, had been "a little too self-evident" to be perceived.

3. *A textual as opposed to a biographical approach*

The analysis of the signifier implies a theory of textuality for which Poe's biography, or his so-called sickness, or his hypothetical personal psychoanalysis, become irrelevant. The presupposition – governing enterprises like that of Marie Bonaparte – that poetry can be interpreted only as autobiography is obviously limiting and limited. Lacan's textual analysis for the first time offers a psychoanalytical alternative to the previously unquestioned and thus seemingly exclusive biographical approach.

4. *The analyst/author relation: a subversion of the master/slave pattern and of the doctor/patient opposition*

Let us remember how many readers were unsettled by the humiliating and sometimes condescending psychoanalytic emphasis on Poe's "sickness," as well as by an explanation equating the poetic with the psychotic. There seemed to be no doubt in the minds of psychoanalytic readers that if the reading situation could be assimilated to the psychoanalytic situation, the poet was to be equated with the (sick) patient, with the analysand on the couch. Lacan's analysis, however, radically subverts not just this clinical status of the poet, but along with it the "bedside" security of the interpreter. If Lacan is not concerned with Poe's sickness, he is quite concerned, nonetheless, with the *figure of the poet* in the tale, and with the hypotheses made about his specific competence and incompetence. Let us not forget that both the minister and Dupin are said to be poets, and that it is their *poetic* reasoning that the prefect fails to understand and which thus enables both to outsmart the police. "D—, I presume, is not altogether a fool," comments Dupin early in the story, to which the prefect of police replies:

> "Not altogether a fool, . . . but then he's a poet, which I take to be only one remove from a fool."
>
> "True," said Dupin, after a long and thoughtful whiff from his meerchaum, "although I have been guilty of certain doggerel myself."

A question Lacan does not address could here be raised by emphasizing still another point that would normally tend to pass unnoticed, since, once again, it is at once so explicit and so ostentatiously insignificant: why does Dupin say that he too is *guilty* of poetry? In what way does the status of the poet involve guilt? In what sense can we understand the *guilt of poetry*?

Dupin, then, draws our attention to the fact that both he and the minister are poets, a qualification with respect to which the prefect feels that he can but be condescending. Later, when Dupin explains to the narrator the prefect's defeat as opposed to his own success in finding the letter, he again insists upon the prefect's blindness to a logic or to a "principle of concealment" which has to do with poets and thus (it might be assumed) is specifically *poetic*:

> This functionary [the prefect] has been thoroughly mystified; and the remote source of his defeat lies in the supposition that the Minister is a *fool*, because he has acquired renown as a *poet*. All fools are poets; this the Pretect *feels*; and he is merely guilty of a *non distributio medii* in thence inferring that all poets are fools.

In Baudelaire's translation of Poe's tale into French, the word fool is rendered, in its strong, archaic sense, as: *fou*, "mad." Here, then, is Lacan's paraphrase of this passage in the story:

> After which, a moment of derision [on Dupin's part] at the Prefect's error in deducing that because the Minister is a poet, he is not far from being mad, an error, it is argued, which would consist, . . . simply in a false distribution of the middle term, since it is far from following from the fact that all madmen are poets.
>
> Yes indeed. But we ourselves are left in the dark as to the poet's superiority in the art of concealment.

Both this passage in the story and this comment by Lacan seem to be marginal, incidental. Yet the hypothetical *relationship between poetry and madness* is significantly relevant to the case of Poe and to the other psychoanalytical approaches we have been considering. Could it not be said that the error of Marie Bonaparte (who, like the prefect, engages in a search for *hidden* meaning) lies precisely in the fact that, like the prefect once again, she simplistically *equates* the poetic with the psychotic, and so, blinded by what she takes to be the poetic *incompetence*, fails to see or understand the specificity of poetic *competence*? Many psychoanalytic investigations diagnosing the poet's sickness and looking for his poetic secret on (or in) his person (as do the prefect's men) are indeed very like police investigations; and like the police in Poe's story, they fail to find the letter, fail to see the textuality of the text.

Lacan, of course, does not say all this – this is not what is at stake in his analysis. All he does is open up still another question where we have believed we have come in possession of some sort of answer:

> Yes indeed. But we ourselves are left in the dark as to the poet's superiority in the art of concealment.

This seemingly lateral question, asked in passing and left unanswered, suggests, however, the possibility of a whole different focus or perspective of interpretation in the story. If "The Purloined Letter" is specifically the story of "the poet's superiority in the art of concealment," then it is not just an allegory of psychoanalysis but also, at the same time, an allegory of poetic writing. And Lacan is himself a poet to the extent that a thought about poetry is what is superiorly concealed in his "Seminar."

In Lacan's interpretation, however, "the poet's superiority" can only be understood as the structural superiority of the third position with respect to the letter: the minister in the first scene, Dupin in the second, both, indeed, poets. But the third position is also – this is the main point of Lacan's analysis – the position of the analyst. It follows that, in Lacan's approach, the status of the poet is no longer that of the (sick) patient but, if anything, that of the analyst. If the poet is still the object of the accusation of being a "fool," his folly – if in fact it does exist (which remains an open question) – would at the same time be the folly of the analyst. The clear-cut opposition between madness and health, or between doctor and patient, is unsettled by the odd functioning of the purloined letter of the unconscious, which no one can possess or master. "There is no metalanguage," says Lacan: there is no language in which interpretation can itself escape the effects of the unconscious; the interpreter is not more immune than the poet to unconscious delusions and errors.

5. *Implications, as opposed to application, of psychoanalytic theory*

Lacan's approach no longer falls into the category of what has been called "applied psychoanalysis," since the concept of "application" implies a relation of *exteriority* between the applied science and the field which it is supposed, unilaterally, to inform. Since, in Lacan's analysis, Poe's text serves to *re-interpret Freud* just as Freud's text serves to interpret Poe; since psychoanalytic theory and the literary text mutually inform – and displace – each other; since the very position of the interpreter – of the analyst – turns out to be not *outside*, but *inside* the text, there is no longer a clear-cut opposition or a well-defined border between literature and psychoanalysis: psychoanalysis could be intraliterary just as much as literature is intrapsychoanalytic. The methodological stake is no longer that of the *application* of psychoanalysis *to* literature, but rather, of their *interimplication* in each other.

If I have dealt at length with Lacan's innovative contribution and with the different methodological example of his approach, it is not so much to set this example up as a new model for imitation, but rather to indicate the way in which it suggestively invites us to go beyond itself (as it takes Freud beyond itself), the way in which it opens up a whole new range of as yet untried possibilities for the enterprise of reading. Lacan's importance in my eyes does not, in other words, lie specifically in the new dogma his "school" proposes, but in his outstanding demonstration that *there is more than one way* to implicate psychoanalysis in literature; that *how* to implicate psychoanalysis in literature is itself a question for interpretation, a challenge to the ingenuity and insight of the interpreter, and not a *given* that can be taken in any way for granted; that what is of analytical relevance in a text is not necessarily and not exclusively "the unconscious of the poet," let alone his sickness or his problems in life; that to situate in a text the analytical as such – to situate the object of analysis or the textual point of its implication – is not necessarily to recognize a *known*, to find an answer, but also, and perhaps more challengingly, to locate an *unknown*, to find a question.

The Poe-etic analytical

Let us now return to the crucial question we left in suspension earlier, after having raised it by reversing Freud's reservation concerning Marie Bonaparte's type of research: *can* psychoanalysis give us an insight into the specificity of the poetic? We can now supplement this question with a second one: where can we situate the analytical with respect to Poe's poetry?

The answers to these questions, I would suggest, might be sought in two directions. (1) In a direct reading of a poetic text by Poe, trying to locate in the poem itself a signifier of poeticity and to analyze its functioning and its effects; to analyze – in other words – how poetry as such works through signifiers (to the extent that signifiers, as opposed to meanings, are always signifiers of the unconscious). (2) In an analytically informed reading of literary history itself, inasmuch as its treatment of Poe obviously constitutes a (literary) *case history.* Such a reading has never, to my knowledge, been undertaken with respect to any writer: never has literary history itself been viewed as an analytical object, as a subject for a psychoanalytic interpretation. And yet it is overwhelmingly obvious, in a case like Poe's, that the discourse of literary history itself points to some unconscious determinations which structure it but of which it is not aware. What is the unconscious of literary history? Can the question of the *guilt of poetry* be relevant to that unconscious? Could literary history be in any way considered a repetitive unconscious *transference* of the guilt of poetry?

Literary history, or more precisely, the critical discourse surrounding Poe, is indeed one of the most visible ("self-evident") *effects* of Poe's poetic signifier, of his text. Now, how can the question of the peculiar effect of Poe be dealt with analytically? My suggestion is: by locating what seems to be unreadable or incomprehensible in this effect; by situating the most prominent discrepancies or discontinuities in the overall critical discourse concerning Poe, the most puzzling critical contradictions, and by trying to interpret those contradictions as symptomatic of the unsettling specificity of the Poe-etic effect, as well as of the necessary contingence of such an effect on the unconscious.

Before setting out to explore and to illustrate these two directions for research, I would like to recapitulate the primary historical contradictions analyzed at the opening of this study as a first indication of the nature of the poetic. According to its readers' contradictory testimonies, Poe's poetry, let it be recalled, seemed to be at once the most *irresistible* and the most *resisted* poetry in literary history. Poe is felt to be at once the most unequaled master of "conscious art" *and* the most tortuous unconscious case, as such doomed to remain "the perennial victim of the *idée fixe*, and of amateur psychoanalysis." Poetry, I would thus argue, is precisely the effect of a deadly struggle between consciousness and the unconscious; it has to do with resistance and with what can neither be resisted nor escaped. Poe is a symptom of poetry to the extent that poetry is both what most resists a psychoanalytical interpretation and what most depends on psychoanalytical effects.

Editor's Note

1 Felman refers here to her earlier discussion, not included in this extract, of Marie Bonaparte's *The Life and Works of Edgar Allan Poe, A Psychoanalytic Interpretation*, translated by John Rodber (London: Imago Press, 1949). The work was first published in French in 1933.

Chapter 63
Charles Bernstein

Charles Bernstein (1950–) is a poet, critic, and theorist who for a number of years was a leading figure in the Language school of poets. His work renews the experimental ambitions of earlier American modernists such as William Carlos Williams, Gertrude Stein, and Charles Olson. Like them he has a continuing preoccupation with inventing new poetic forms as "a process of pushing whatever way." But in his work this preoccupation takes on a new edge and urgency. The experimental impulse of American modernism joins forces with a radical social critique that draws on the work of Adorno, Benjamin, and Marx. Capitalism is an economic form that has colonized the languages of art and daily life alike, as well as producing a politics of unprecedented violence. Poetry's care for language becomes a mode of resisting the process whereby if an experience is to have value it must be translatable into a monetary equivalent. At the center of Bernstein's work is an effort to reinvent the connection between experimental poetic forms and opposition to the prevailing social order. This is not a matter of writing poems with an explicit political content but of creating experiences in and of language that suspend our customary and, for Bernstein, deeply suspect ways of making sense.

Bernstein has been a prolific poet and theorist since the publication of his first book, Asylums, *in 1975. For a brief period in the late 1970s and early 1980s, Bernstein and fellow poet, Bruce Andrews, edited a bimonthly journal of poetics and poetry,* L=A=N=G=U=A=G=E. *"The Dollar Value of Poetry" was first published in the journal, and republished in 1983 in an anthology drawn from the journal,* The L=A=N=G=U=A=G=E Book. *It draws on some familiar ideas about poetry – for example, that it resists translation and paraphrase – but gives them a new direction and force by placing them in the context of a culture where value is determined by a specific kind of translation known as the dollar. Poetry can recover experiences that do not fit the requirements of "uniform exposition." But to do this it must become a means of imagining states of language as well as "forms of life."*

The Dollar Value of Poetry

Social force is bound to be accompanied by lies. That is why all that is highest in human life, every effort of thought, every effort of love, has a corrosive action on the established order. Thought can just as readily, and on good grounds, be stigmatized as revolutionary on the one side, as counter-revolutionary on the other. In so far as it is ceaselessly creating a scale of values "that is not of this world", it is the enemy of forces which control society.

Simone Weil in *Oppression and Liberty*

So writing might be exemplary – an instance broken off from and hence not in the service of this economic and cultural – social – force called capitalism. A chip of uninfected substance; or else, a "glimpse", a crack into what otherwise might . . . ; of still, "the fact of its own activity", autonomy, self-sufficiency, "in itself and for itself" such that. . . . In any case, an appeal to an "other" world, as if access is not blocked to an experience (experiencing) whose horizon is not totally a product of the coercive delimiting of the full range of language (the limits of language the limits of experience) by the predominating social forces. An experience (released in the reading) which is non-commoditized, that is where the value is not dollar value (and hence transferable and instrumental) but rather, what is from the point of view of the market, no value (a negativity, inaudible, invisible) – that non-generalizable residue that is specific to each particular experience. It is in this sense that we speak of poetry as being untranslatable and un-paraphrasable, for what is untranslatable is the sum of all the specific conditions of the experience (place, time, order, light, mood, position, to infinity) made available by reading. That the political value of poems resides in the concreteness of the experiences they make available is the reason for the resistance to any form of normative standardization in the ordering of words in the unit or the sequencing of these units, since determining the exact nature of each of these is what makes for the singularity of the text. (It is, for example, a misunderstanding of the fact of untranslatability that would see certain "concretist" tendencies as its most radical manifestation since what is not translatable is the experience released in the reading while in so far as some "visual poems" move toward making the understanding independent of the language it is written in, i.e. no longer requiring translation, they are, indeed, no longer so much writing as works of visual art.)

Certainly, one method is the restoration of memory's remembering on its own terms, organizing along the lines of experience's trace, a reconstruction released from the pressures of uniform exposition – "the only true moments" the ones we have lost, which, in returning to them, come to life in a way that now reveals what they had previously concealed – the social forces that gave shape to them. So what were the

From *The L=A=N=G=U=A=G=E Book*, ed. Bruce Andrews and Charles Bernstein (Carbondale, Ill.: Southern Illinois University Press, 1984), pp. 138–40.

unseen operators now are manifest as traces of the psychic blows struck by the social forces (re)pressing us into shape (i.e.: "a sigh is the sword of an angel king"). "*What we do is to bring our words back*" – *to make our experiences visible*, or again: to see the conditions of experience. So that, in this way, a work may also be constructed – an "other" world *made* from whatever materials are ready to hand (not just those of memory) – structuring, in this way, possibilities otherwise not allowed for.

Meanwhile, the social forces hold sway in all the rules for the "clear" and "orderly" functioning of language and Caesar himself is the patron of our grammar books. Experience dutifully translated into these "most accessible" codes loses its aura and is reduced to the digestible contents which these rules alone can generate. There is nothing difficult in the products of such activity because there is no distance to be travelled, no gap to be aware of and to bridge from reader to text: what purports to be an experience is transformed into the blank stare of the commodity – there only to mirror our projections with an unseemly rapidity possible only because no experience of "other" is in it. – Any limits put on language proscribe the limits of what will be experienced, and, as Wittgenstein remarks, the world can easily be reduced to only the straight rows of the avenues of the industrial district, with no place for the crooked winding streets of the old city. "To imagine a language is to imagine a form of life" – think of that first "imagine" as the active word here.

"Is there anybody here who thinks that following the orders takes away the blame?" Regardless of "what" is being said, use of standard patterns of syntax and exposition effectively rebroadcast, often at a subliminal level, the basic constitutive elements of the social structure – they perpetuate them so that by constant reinforcement we are no longer aware that decisions are being made, our base level is then an already preconditioned world view which this de-formed language "repeats to us inexorably" but not *necessarily.* Or else these formations (underscored constantly by all "the media" in the form they "communicate" "information" "facts") take over our form of life (see *Invasion of the Body Snatchers* and *Dawn of the Dead* for two recent looks at this), as by posthypnotic suggestion we find ourselves in the grip of – living out – *feeling* – the attitudes programmed into us by the phrases, etc, and their sequencing, that are continually being repeated to us – language control = thought control = reality control: it must be "de-centered", "community controlled", taken out of the service of the capitalist project. For now, an image of the anti-virus: indigestible, intransigent.

Chapter 64
Czeslaw Milosz

Czeslaw Milosz (1911–) is a Polish poet, novelist, and critic who left his native country in 1951 initially for France and then for the United States. Much of his work both in poetry and prose has been preoccupied with making sense of the violent and complex history of twentieth-century Europe. Yet his sense of the poet's duty to address the fate and the future of civilizations works in a counterpoint with a lyrical and metaphysical sensibility that delights in contemplating the world rather than arguing about it. In 1953 he published a major work of political analysis, The Captive Mind, *which diagnosed the various ways that Polish intellectuals had adapted to communism. The poetry he published before the Second World War was marked by an apocalyptic pessimism. In later work he has combined great formal sophistication with a belief in the capacity of poetry to exorcise evil, or, at least to keep open the possibility of hope. In 1961 Milosz moved to the United States and some of his later work, including the prose work,* Visions of San Francisco Bay, *published in translation in 1982, has drawn on his experience of migration. He was awarded the Nobel Prize for Literature in 1971.*

"On Hope" was originally given as one of the Charles Eliot Norton lectures at Harvard University in 1982, and was published in the following year in The Witness of Poetry. *In the following excerpt, Milosz characteristically balances pessimistic evidence with the possibility of hope in his account of an emerging global culture. Anticipating "humanity's emergence as a new elemental force" and a possible overcoming of distinctions between elite and popular culture, Milosz detects a new kind of historical consciousness that finds its precedents in a number of twentieth-century poets such as Robert Graves and Constantine Cavafy.*

On Hope

. . . I am going to ask a simple question. What if the lament so widely spread in poetry today proves to be a prophetic response to the hopeless situation in which mankind has

From *The Witness of Poetry* (Cambridge, Mass.: Harvard University Press, 1983), pp. 101–3, 104–8, 109–16.

found itself? In that case, poetry would have proven once again that it is more conscious than the average citizen, or that it simply intensifies what is always present but veiled in people's minds.

In the nineteenth century the belief in the decline and imminent fall of Western civilization found expression first in Russian thought, and in that respect Dostoevsky is no exception. The same belief was soon to appear in Western Europe. The Parisian review *Le Décadent* said in 1886: "It would be nonsense to conceal the state of decadence that we have reached. Religion, mores, justice, everything is tending toward decline." What was called decadence soon became a movement and a fashion among bohemians, just as existentialism would a few decades later. Also, around 1900 the serene science fiction of Jules Verne was replaced by ominous predictions of general catastrophe or of the rule by machines which elude human control. The Slavic word *robota* entered common usage in various languages as "robot," an invention of the Czech writer, Karel Čapek.

Technology as a subject for science fiction also imperceptibly acquired a political shade, producing images of a future society which were not hopeful. Perhaps a farewell to nineteenth-century optimism had already been made in H. G. Wells's *The Time Machine* (1895), while our century created novels about the totalitarian systems of tomorrow, such as Yevgeny Zamyatin's *We* (1926), Aldous Huxley's *Brave New World* (1932), and George Orwell's *1984* (1948). On an equal footing I would put two novels by Stanisław Ignacy Witkiewicz, which are little known in the West: *Farewell to Autumn* (1927) and *Insatiability* (1930; published in English in 1977). This literature of anticipation corresponds to a universal and nearly obsessive preoccupation with the future, which is understandable, for great changes occur in an individual's immediate environment in the course of a single lifetime. We sense, again, "l'accéleration de l'histoire."

It is interesting to reflect on the extent to which certain writers' predictions have been fulfilled. In one sense, Dostoevsky was in appearance only writing about his contemporaries. He said once, "Everything depends upon the twentieth century," and he tried to guess what man would be like then.... Dostoevsky, we now see, fully deserves the title of prophet, if only as the author of *The Possessed.* Nevertheless, when reading him we seem to discover the limitations to any prophesying. Such prophecies probably always resemble a column of type that has been skewed, so that the particular lines are changed in order and the sequence of sentences is broken; or to use another comparison, they are like a series of mirrors where it is difficult to tell reality from illusion. That is, all the data are there, correctly foreseen, only their relations and proportions are disturbed. Thus the future is always seen as through a glass, darkly.

...We still have not fully grasped what the year 1914 meant for Europe and how violently the scales of its destiny were tipped then. The pessimistic poetry written by decadents may just be the future encoded and seen darkly. What actually does come to pass is always a little bit different from our conscious or unconscious expectations, but that "bit" denotes a radical divergence. Too many things have happened since that time not to make the mind-set from 1900 completely foreign to us, even though we recognize that the questions tormenting the decadents were well founded....

One could make a catalogue of the ominous forecasts appearing today in both science fiction and poetry. In view of an atmosphere conducive to borrowing themes and the uncertain nature of prophecy, we should treat those anxieties with a dose of suspicion. This does not mean that a sober appraisal of the human situation at the end of the twentieth century will be particularly reassuring. And since a poet, as I have said, should be faithful to reality, evaluating it with a sense of hierarchy, I shall not be digressing if I turn my attention for a moment to matters that preoccupy politicians and economists.

We are on the way toward the unification of our planet. For the time being, that unification proceeds in science and technology, which are the same everywhere. This is the result of the victory of a single civilization, the one that arose on the small Western European peninsula. Thanks to the quarrels of its theologians, that civilization developed the mechanism of abstract thought, which was subsequently applied to scientific discoveries. It has overcome and nearly destroyed the more static civilizations, closed in on themselves. A variety of technical inventions, from weapons to the automobile, transistor, and television, were its means of conquest and, by the same token, its philosophical representatives. At the same time, the European peninsula exported its internal crisis, primarily the crisis of its political form, to the whole planet. The scientific-technical revolution took place within the framework of monarchies ruled by kings whose authority had divine sanction, and this presupposed vertical structure: the divine above, the human below. A radical change occurred when the source of authority was shifted to the people, to a "general will" expressed by voting. The model taken by Rousseau from the assemblies of the entire population of a small Swiss canton proved to be more and more abstract when applied in countries with many millions of inhabitants, and as soon as the methods of influencing public opinion began to gain in complexity. If the nineteenth century seemed everywhere to move toward democracy, the twentieth century brought it a series of defeats. Democracy has shown little ability to expand beyond the area of its origin, the Western European peninsula and North America. What is more, the inhabitants of the countries with democratic systems have, in their majority, been affected by a lack of faith in the validity of democracy and in the possibility of defending it against the encroachments of an aggressive totalitarian system.

That system, too, derives the language it uses to sing its own praises from the notion of general will, modifying the notion accordingly. The rulers appear as an incarnation of a general will that, if left to itself, would not know its own true desires. One of the features of totalitarianism, which often cites Karl Marx, is to treat the population as children who shouldn't be allowed to play with matches, that is, to express their opinion in free elections. Yet fictitious elections are preserved, and this reminds us of the Western European origin of democracy's rival. Of course, the basic conflict is camouflaged by making the redistribution of wealth the primary social task. The real quarrel, however, is about the source of authority.

Our planet is small, and its unification into one global state is not unplausible. It could be accomplished, for instance, by conquest. Atomic war is a possibility, yet perhaps no more so than the use of a poison gas was in World War II, and today's pacifist movements are not free of hysteria. Infantry has been a decisive factor in all wars of this century, and this can incline us to suppose it will be decisive in the future as well.

Today the entire earth resembles the Greek peninsula at the time of the Peloponnesian war, at least in the sense that democracy has for its enemy countries that begin the military training of their youth in childhood. Yet both the modern Athens and the modern Sparta are afflicted by grave diseases, and their policies are to a considerable extent marked by their sickliness. A decline of civic virtues is occurring in the West, so that young generations cease to view the state as *their own* (worthy of being served and defended even at the sacrifice of one's life). In this respect, the year 1940 in France set the pattern of peace at any price, even by surrendering to the enemy. Still, that disease and others of a similar kind seem to be related functionally to the West's extraordinary creative capability, as if disintegration were a necessary condition to its progress. A decadent from 1900 would be struck today by the unprecedented development of science, technology, medicine, and the arts, precisely in the era which, according to his predictions, was to see nothing but ruin. And the apparent health of the totalitarian system, with its official cult of the state and the military virtues, conceals the disease of stagnation in every field of human endeavor except arms production. Now, as the century draws to its close, there is no doubt left as to the parasitic character of any state based upon a monopoly of ownership and power. It feeds on what remains from the organic past – not yet completely eradicated – or on technology, science, and art imported from outside. To imagine a worldwide totalitarian state is to imagine a dark age of sterility and inertia....

The fate of civilization – the only one, for the others have lost the game – is not comforting, and that is why some poets are now zealous readers of Nostradamus' apocalpytic prophecies. When looking for hope, we must turn to the internal dynamic responsible for having brought us to this precise point. Things begin to look strange once we reflect on the notions of "health" and of "decay," both of which seem to be highly misleading. Time was out of joint not only for Hamlet but for Shakespeare as well, and it would be difficult to maintain that he exaggerated the case. In fact, by the sixteenth century, the modern era was already at its beginnings, with all the good and evil it was to bring. Since that time, poets have tended to visualize an order located somewhere else, in a different place or time. Such longing, by its nature eschatological, is directed against every "here and now" and becomes one of the forces contributing to incessant change. Is this decay? It undoubtedly is, if it means an inability to relate to existing forms. One may advance the hypothesis that what happens in the West is similar to the processes initiated in an organism by bacteria which are indispensable to its proper functioning. It is possible that the Western branch of civilization disintegrates because it creates, and creates because it disintegrates. The fate of Kierkegaard's philosophy may serve as an example. It grew out of the disintegrations occurring within Christianity, in any case within Protestantism; in turn, his reading of Kierkegaard seems to have influenced Niels Bohr, creator of the quantum theory of the atom.

It is possible that we are witnessing a kind of race between the lifegiving and the destructive activity of civilization's bacteria, and that an unknown result awaits in the future. No computer will be able to calculate so many pros and cons – thus a poet with his intuition remains one strong, albeit uncertain, source of knowledge.

Putting economy and politics aside, I will now return to my own reasons for, if not optimism, then at least opposition to hopelessness.

We can do justice to our time only by comparing it to that of our grandfathers and great-grandfathers. Something happened, whose importance still eludes us, and it seems very ordinary, though its effects will both last and increase. The exceptional quality of the twentieth century is not determined by jets as a means of transportation or a decrease in infant mortality or the birth-control pill. It is determined by humanity's emergence as a new elemental force; until now humanity had been divided into castes distinguished by dress, mentality, and mores. The transformation can be clearly observed only in certain countries, but it is gradually occurring everywhere and causing the disappearance of certain mythical notions, widespread in the past century, about the specific and presumably eternal features of the peasant, worker, and intellectual. Humanity as an elemental force, the result of technology and mass education, means that man is opening up to science and art on unprecedented scale.

. . . Citizens in a modern state, no longer mere dwellers in their village and district, know how to read and write but are unprepared to receive nourishment of a higher intellectual order. They are sustained artificially on a lower level by television, films, and illustrated magazines – media that are for the mind what too small slippers were for women's feet in old China. At the same time, the elite is engaged in what is called "culture," consisting mostly of rituals attended out of snobbery and borne with boredom. Thus elemental humanity's openness to science and art is only potential, and much time will pass before it becomes a fact everywhere.

A poet, however, presupposes the existence of an ideal reader, and the poetic act both anticipates the future and speeds its coming. . . . It seems to me that this will be connected, in one or another way, with a new dimension entered on by elemental humanity – and here I expect some surprise from my audience – the dimension of the past of our human race. This would not seem too probable, since mass culture appears quickly inclined to forget important events and even recent ones, and less and less history is taught in the schools. Let us consider, though, what is happening at the same time.

Never before have the painting and music of the past been so universally accessible through reproductions and records. Never before has the life of past civilizations been so graphically recreated, and the crowds that now visit museums and galleries are without historical precedent. Thus technology, which forces history out of the classroom, compensates, perhaps even generously, for what it is destroying. Daring to make a prediction, I expect, perhaps quite soon, in the twenty-first century, a radical turning away from the Weltanschauung marked principally by biology, and this will result from a newly acquired historical consciousness. Instead of presenting man through those traits that link him to higher forms of the evolutionary chain, other of his aspects will be stressed: the exceptionality, strangeness, and loneliness of that creature mysterious to itself, a being incessantly transcending its own limits. Humanity will increasingly be turning back to itself, increasingly contemplating its entire past, searching for a key to its own enigma, and penetrating, through empathy, the soul of bygone generations and of whole civilizations.

Premonitions of this can be found in the poetry of the twentieth century. In 1900 education was of course the privilege of a small elite and included training in Latin and Greek, remnants of the humanist ideal. Some acquaintance with the poets of antiquity read in the original was also required. That period is closed, and Latin has even disappeared from the Catholic liturgy, with not much chance for revival. But, at the same time, judging by poetry, say Robert Graves's, the past of the Mediterranean – Jewish, Greek, Roman – has begun to have an even more intense existence in our consciousness than it had for our educated predecessors, though in a different way. One could multiply examples from poets. Also, the presence of mythical figures taken from European literature or from literary legend is more vivid than at any previous time, figures such as Hamlet, Lear, Prospero, François Villon, Faust.

From this perspective, it is worthwhile to mention the adventures of one poet, at least a few of whose poems belong to the canon of twentieth-century art and who deserves the name of forerunner, even though his work as a whole is uneven. A Greek from Alexandria, Constantine Cavafy was born in 1863. After many attempts at writing in the spirit of fin-de-siècle, he dared to embrace an idea alien to the highly subjectivist literary fashion of his contemporaries. He identified himself with the entire Hellenic world, from Homeric times up through the dynasty of the Seleucids and Byzantium, incarnating himself in them, so that his journey through time and space was also a journey into his own interior realm, his history as a Hellene. Maybe the impulse came from his familiarity with English poetry, primarily with Robert Browning and his personae taken from Renaissance Italy. Perhaps he had also read the poems of Pierre Louys, *Songs of Bilitis.* Be that as it may, Cavafy's best poems are meditations on the past, which is brought closer so that characters and situations from many centuries back are perceived by the reader as kindred. Cavafy seems to belong in the second half of this century, but this is an illusion resulting from his late arrival in world poetry, through translations. In fact, nearly unknown in his lifetime (though T. S. Eliot published him in his *Criterion*) and only gradually discovered after his death in 1933, he wrote his most famous poems before World War 1. "Waiting for the Barbarians" dates from 1898; "Ithaka" in the first version from 1894, in the second from 1910; "King Dimitrios" from 1900; "Dareios" and "In Alexandria, 31 B.C." came a little later, in 1917.

Since I have tried to present my Polish background and have used examples taken from Polish poetry in these lectures, it would perhaps be proper to note that the presence of the Hellenic past in Cavafy is particularly understandable for a Polish poet. The true home of the Polish poet is history, and though Polish history is much shorter than that of Greece, it is no less rich in defeats and lost illusions. In Cavafy's decision to exploit his own Hellenic history, his Polish reader recognizes the idea he had already discovered when reading poets of his own tongue: that we apprehend the human condition with pity and terror not in the abstract but always in relation to a given place and time, in one particular province, one particular country.

I have chosen to quote Cavafy's "Dareios" probably because the character appearing in it is treated with condescending humor and that character is in addition a poet worrying about fame. He seeks fame both as praise from the lips of a monarch and as recognition from malicious critics. This portrait of a poet from two thousand years ago fits into my slightly ironic approach to my own profession, which may be noticeable in what I have said here about its peculiarities.

Dareios

Phernazis the poet is at work
on the crucial part of his epic:
how Dareios, son of Hystaspis,
took over the Persian kingdom.
(It's from him, Dareios, that our glorious king,
Mithridatis, Dionysos and Evpator, descends.)
But this calls for serious thought: Phernazis has to analyze
the feelings Dareios must have had:
arrogance, maybe, and intoxication? No – more likely
a certain insight into the vanities of greatness.
The poet thinks deeply about the question.

But his servant, rushing in,
cuts him short to announce very important news:
the war with the Romans has begun:
most of our army has crossed the borders.
The poet is dumbfounded. What a disaster!
How can our glorious king,
Mithridatis, Dionysos and Evpator,
bother about Greek poems now?
In the middle of a war – just think, Greek poems!

Phernazis gets all worked up. What a bad break!
Just when he was sure to distinguish himself
with his *Dareios*, sure to make
his envious critics shut up once and for all.
What a setback, terrible setback to his plans.

And if it's only a setback, that wouldn't be too bad.
But can we really consider ourselves safe in Amisos?
The town isn't very well fortified,
and the Romans are the most awful enemies.

Are we, Cappadocians, really a match for them?
Is it conceivable?
Are we to compete with the legions?
Great gods, protectors of Asia, help us.

But through all his nervousness, all the turmoil,
the poetic idea comes and goes insistently:
arrogance and intoxication – that's the most likely, of course:
arrogance and intoxication are what Dareios must have felt.

As we learn from the commentary to Cavafy's poem, the poet Phernazis is a fictitious character. The city in which he lives, Amisos, was situated on the shore of Pontus, or the Black Sea. Mithridatis IV (Evpator) was a king of Pontus, who started a war with

Rome in 71 B.C. and thus it is then that the action of the poem takes place. Amisos was taken by the Romans three years later, and king Mithridatis lost the war to Pompeius in 66 B.C.

I have just alluded to identification with people of the past, to a feeling of fraternity that helps us penetrate the curtain of time. The poet Phernazis illustrates a secret of the poetic vocation. His worries, as war breaks out and the fate of his city and country is at stake, are comic. And yet, simultaneously with his professional malady – his oversensitivity to favorable opinions of his work – something else takes hold of him: "But through all his nervousness, all the turmoil / the poetic idea comes and goes insistently." A poet cannot break totally away from his little game of pride and humiliation, but at the same time he is liberated, again and again, from his ego by "the poetic idea." All of this acquires a peculiar expressiveness precisely because the city of Amisos, the poet Phernazis, and the king of the realm are for us mere shades asking us to give them life, as the shades of Hades do in Homer.

To make present what is gone by. We are even inclined to believe that a poet receives more than one life just because he is able to walk the streets of a city that existed two thousand years ago. But perhaps it is precisely this that people are seeking in their incessant search for the past in reproductions of old art, in architecture, in fashion, and in crowded museums. A one-dimensional man wants to acquire new dimensions by putting on the masks and dress, the manners of feeling and thinking, of other epochs.

More serious matters seem to be involved here as well. "From where will a renewal come to us, to us who have spoiled and devastated the whole earthly globe?" asks Simone Weil. And she answers, "Only from the past, if we love it." At first sight this is an enigmatic formulation, and it is difficult to guess what she has in mind. Her aphorism acquires meaning in the light of her other pronouncements. Thus she says elsewhere: "Two things cannot be reduced to any rationalism: Time and Beauty. We should start from them." Or: "Distance is the soul of beauty." The past is "woven with time the color of eternity." In her opinion, it is difficult for a man to reach through to reality, for he is hindered by his ego and by imagination in the service of his ego. Only a distance in time allows us to see reality without coloring it with our passions. And reality seen that way is beautiful. This is why the past has such importance: "The sense of reality is pure in it. Here is pure joy. Here is pure beauty. Proust." When quoting Simone Weil I think of what made me personally so receptive to her theory of purification. It probably was not the work of Marcel Proust, so dear to her, but a work I read much earlier, in childhood, and my constant companion ever since – *Pan Tadeusz*, by Adam Mickiewicz, a poem in which the most ordinary incidents of everyday life change into a web of fairytale, for they are described as occurring long ago, and suffering is absent because suffering only affects us, the living, not characters invoked by all-forgiving memory.

Humanity will also explore itself in the sense that it will search for reality purified, for the "color of eternity," in other words, simply for beauty. Probably this is what Dostoevsky, skeptical as he was about the fate of civilization, meant when he affirmed that the world will be saved by beauty. This means that our growing despair because of the discrepancy between reality and the desire of our hearts would be healed, and the world which exists objectively – perhaps as it appears in the eyes of God, not as it is perceived by us, desiring and suffering – will be accepted with all its good and evil.

I have offered various answers to the question why twentieth-century poetry has such a gloomy, apocalyptic tone. It is quite likely that the causes cannot be reduced to one. The separation of the poet from the great human family; the progressing subjectivization that becomes manifest when we are imprisoned in the melancholy of our individual transience; the automatisms of literary structures, or simply of fashion – all this undoubtedly has weight. Yet if I declare myself for realism as the poet's conscious or unconscious longing, I should pay what is due to a sober assessment of our predicament. The unification of the planet is not proceeding without high cost. Through the mass media poets of all languages receive information on what is occurring across the surface of the whole earth, on the tortures inflicted by man on man, on starvation, misery, humiliation. At a time when their knowledge of reality was limited to one village or district, poets had no such burden to bear. Is it surprising that they are always morally indignant, that they feel responsible, that no promise of the further triumphs of science and technology can veil these images of chaos and human folly? And when they try to visualize the near future, they find nothing there except the probability of economic crisis and war.

This is not the place to say what will happen tomorrow, as the fortune tellers and futurologists do. The hope of the poet, a hope that I defend, that I advance, is not enclosed by any date. If disintegration is a function of development, and development a function of disintegration, the race between them may very well end in the victory of disintegration. For a long time, but not forever – and here is where hope enters. It is neither chimerical or foolish. On the contrary, every day one can see signs indicating that now, at the present moment, something new, and on a scale never witnessed before, is being born: humanity as an elemental force conscious of transcending Nature, for it lives by memory of itself, that is, in History.

Chapter 65
Adrienne Rich

Adrienne Rich (1929–) published her first book of poetry, A Change of World, *in 1951. It won the Yale Series Younger Poets Award and W. H. Auden in his introduction to the book described Rich's poems as "neatly and modestly dressed."* A Change of World *was typical of Rich's early work in its formal accomplishment and emotional containment, although the poem "Aunt Jennifer's Tigers" indicated the future direction her work would take. By the time of her book* Necessities of Life *was published in 1966, a major change in her work was becoming evident. Rich's poetry increasingly engaged with the major political events of the 1960s: the civil rights movement, resistance to the Vietnam War, and the emergence of feminism. Her poetry marked the ways in which these engagements changed her identity. She became a leading figure in the feminist movement and since the early 1970s has written a series of highly influential essays, including "The Lesbian Continuum" and "Towards a Woman Centred University," as well as volumes of poetry that explore the complex connections between personal life and political commitment. In the preface to her 1973 collection,* Diving into the Wreck, *Rich described one purpose of her poetry as "breaking down the barriers between Vietnam and the lover's bed."*

"Blood, Bread, and Poetry: The Location of a Poet" was originally given as a talk at the Institute of Humanities at the University of Massachusetts, Amherst, in 1983 and was published the following year in the Massachusetts Review. *In the following excerpt, Rich takes her own development as a poet as an epitome of the problems and the opportunities for poetry in the United States. On the one hand, poetry is celebrated as a "decorative garnish on the buffet table of the university curriculum." On the other, it is ignored as an economically valueless activity. The cultural significance of poetry can only be renewed by breaking out of the charmed circle that prohibits a connection between poetry and the lived experience of particular political realities.*

Blood, Bread, and Poetry: The Location of the Poet

The Miami airport, summer 1983: a North American woman says to me, "You'll love Nicaragua: everyone there is a poet." I've thought many times of that remark, both while there and since returning home. Coming from a culture (North American, white- and male-dominated) which encourages poets to think of ourselves as alienated from the sensibility of the general population, which casually and devastatingly marginalizes us (so far, no slave labor or torture for a political poem – just dead air, the white noise of the media jamming the poet's words) – coming from this North American dominant culture which so confuses us, telling us poetry is neither economically profitable nor politically effective and that political dissidence is destructive to art, coming from this culture that tells me I am destined to be a luxury, a decorative garnish on the buffet table of the university curriculum, the ceremonial occasion, the national celebration – what am I to make, I thought, of that remark? *You'll love Nicaragua: everyone there is a poet.* (Do I love poets in general? I immediately asked myself, thinking of poets I neither love nor would wish to see in charge of my country.) Is being a poet a guarantee that I will love a Marxist-Leninist revolution? Can't I travel simply as an American radical, a lesbian feminist, a citizen who opposes her government's wars against its own people and its intervention in other people's lands? And what effectiveness has the testimony of a poet returning from a revolution where "everyone is a poet" to a country where the possible credibility of poetry is not even seriously discussed?

Clearly, this well-meant remark triggered strong and complex feelings in me. And it provided, in a sense, the text on which I began to build my talk here tonight.

I was born at the brink of the Great Depression; I reached sixteen the year of Nagasaki and Hiroshima. The daughter of a Jewish father and a Protestant mother, I learned about the Holocaust first from newsreels of the liberation of the death camps. I was a young white woman who had never known hunger or homelessness, growing up in the suburbs of a deeply segregated city in which neighborhoods were also dictated along religious lines: Christian and Jewish. I lived sixteen years of my life secure in the belief that though cities could be bombed and civilian populations killed, the earth stood in its old indestructible way. The process through which nuclear annihilation was to become a part of all human calculation had already begun, but we did not live with that knowledge during the first sixteen years of my life. And a recurrent theme in much poetry I read was the indestructibility of poetry, the poem as a vehicle for personal immortality.

I had grown up hearing and reading poems from a very young age, first as sounds, repeated, musical, rhythmically satisfying in themselves, and the power of concrete, sensuously compelling images:

From *Blood, Bread, and Poetry: Selected Prose 1979–1985* (New York: W. W. Norton, 1986), pp. 167–71, 172–5, 176–7, 178–85, 186–7.

All night long they hunted
   And nothing did they find
But a ship a-sailing,
   A-sailing with the wind.
One said it was a ship,
   The other he said, Nay,
The third said it was a house
   With the chimney blown away;
And all the night they hunted
   And nothing did they find
But the moon a-gliding
   A-gliding with the wind....

Tyger! Tyger! burning bright
   In the forest of the night,
What immortal hand or eye
   Dare frame thy fearful symmetry?

But poetry soon became more than music and images; it was also revelation, information, a kind of teaching. I believed I could learn from it – an unusual idea for a United States citizen, even a child. I thought it could offer clues, intimations, keys to questions that already stalked me, questions I could not even frame yet: *What is possible in this life? What does "love" mean, this thing that is so important? What is this other thing called "freedom" or "liberty" – is it like love, a feeling? What have human beings lived and suffered in the past? How am I going to live my life?* The fact that poets contradicted themselves and each other didn't baffle or alarm me. I was avid for everything I could get; my child's mind did not shut down for the sake of consistency.

I was angry with my friend,
I told my wrath, my wrath did end.
I was angry with my foe,
I told it not, my wrath did grow.

As an angry child, often urged to "curb my temper," I used to ponder those words of William Blake, but they slid first into my memory through their repetitions of sound, their ominous rhythms.

Another poem that I loved first as music, later pondered for what it could tell me about women and men and marriage, was Edwin Arlington Robinson's "Eros Turannos":

She fears him, and will always ask
   What fated her to choose him;
She meets in his engaging mask
   All reasons to refuse him;
But what she meets and what she fears
   Are less than are the downward years,
Drawn slowly to the foamless weirs
   Of age, were she to lose him....

And, of course, I thought that the poets in the anthologies were the only real poets, that their being in the anthologies was proof of this, though some were classified as "great" and others as "minor." I owed much to those anthologies: *Silver Pennies*; the constant outflow of volumes edited by Louis Untermeyer; *The Cambridge Book of Poetry for Children*; Palgrave's *Golden Treasury*; the *Oxford Book of English Verse*. But I had no idea that they reflected the taste of a particular time or of particular kinds of people. I still believed that poets were inspired by some transcendent authority and spoke from some extraordinary height. I thought that the capacity to hook syllables together in a way that heated the blood was the sign of a universal vision.

Because of the attitudes surrounding me, the aesthetic ideology with which I grew up, I came into my twenties believing in poetry, in all art, as the expression of a higher world view, what the critic Edward Said has termed "a quasi-religious wonder, instead of a human sign to be understood in secular and social terms." The poet achieved "universality" and authority through tapping his, or occasionally her, own dreams, longings, fears, desires, and, out of this, "speaking as a man to men," as Wordsworth had phrased it. But my personal world view at sixteen, as at twenty-six, was itself being created by political conditions. I was not a man; I was white in a white-supremacist society; I was being educated from the perspective of a particular class; my father was an "assimilated" Jew in an anti-Semitic world, my mother a white southern Protestant; there were particular historical currents on which my consciousness would come together, piece by piece. My personal world view was shaped in part by the poetry I had read, a poetry written almost entirely by white Anglo-Saxon men, a few women, Celts and Frenchmen notwithstanding. Thus, no poetry in the Spanish language or from Africa or China or the Middle East. My personal world view, which like so many young people I carried as a conviction of my own uniqueness, was not original with me, but was, rather, my untutored and half-conscious rendering of the facts of blood and bread, the social and political forces of my time and place.

I was in college during the late 1940s and early 1950s. The thirties, a decade of economic desperation, social unrest, war, and also of affirmed political art, was receding behind the fogs of the Cold War, the selling of the nuclear family with the mother at home as its core, heightened activity by the FBI and CIA, a retreat by many artists from so-called "protest" art, witch-hunting among artists and intellectuals as well as in the State Department, anti-Semitism, scapegoating of homosexual men and lesbians, and with a symbolic victory for the Cold War crusade in the 1953 electrocution of Ethel and Julius Rosenberg. . . .

Because of Yeats, who by then had become my idea of the Great Poet, the one who more than others could hook syllables together in a way that heated my blood, I took a course in Irish history. It was taught by a Boston Irish professor of Celtic, one of Harvard's tokens, whose father, it was said, had been a Boston policeman. He read poetry aloud in Gaelic and in English, sang us political ballads, gave us what amounted to a mini-education on British racism and imperialism, though the words were never mentioned. He also slashed at Irish self-romanticizing. People laughed about the Irish history course, said it must be full of football players. In and out of the Harvard Yard, the racism of Yankee Brahmin toward Boston Irish was never questioned, laced as it was with equally unquestioned class arrogance. Today, Irish Boston both acts out and takes the weight of New England racism against Black and Hispanic people. It was, strangely enough, through poetry that I first began to try to make sense of these things.

"Strangely enough," I say, because the reading of poetry in an elite academic institution is supposed to lead you – in the 1980s as back there in the early 1950s – not toward a criticism of society, but toward a professional career in which the anatomy of poems is studied dispassionately. Prestige, job security, money, and inclusion in an exclusive fraternity are where the academic study of literature is supposed to lead. Maybe I was lucky because I had started reading poetry so young, and not in school, and because I had been writing poems almost as long as I had been reading them. I should add that I was easily entranced by pure sound and still am, no matter what it is saying; and any poet who mixes the poetry of the actual world with the poetry of sound interests and excites me more than I am able to say. In my student years, it was Yeats who seemed to do this better than anyone else. There were lines of Yeats that were to ring in my head for years:

Many times man lives and dies
Between his two eternities,
That of race and that of soul,
And ancient Ireland knew it all....

Did she in touching that lone wing
Recall the years before her mind
Became a bitter, an abstract thing
Her thought some popular enmity:
Blind and leader of the blind
Drinking the foul ditch where they lie?

I could hazard the guess that all the most impassioned, seductive arguments against the artist's involvement in politics can be found in Yeats. It was this dialogue between art and politics that excited me in his work, along with the sound of his language – never his elaborate mythological systems. I know I learned two things from his poetry, and those two things were at war with each other. One was that poetry can be "about," can root itself in, politics. Even if it is a defense of privilege, even if it deplores political rebellion and revolution, it can, may have to, account for itself politically, consciously situate itself amid political conditions, without sacrificing intensity of language. The other, that politics leads to "bitterness" and "abstractness" of mind, makes women shrill and hysterical, and is finally a waste of beauty and talent: "Too long a sacrifice/ can make a stone of the heart." There was absolutely nothing in the literary canon I knew to counter the second idea. Elizabeth Barrett Browning's anti-slavery and feminist poetry, H.D.'s anti-war and woman-identified poetry, like the radical – yes, revolutionary – work of Langston Hughes and Muriel Rukeyser, were still buried by the academic literary canon. But the first idea was extremely important to me: a poet – one who was apparently certified – could actually write about political themes, could weave the names of political activists into a poem:

MacDonagh and MacBride
And Connally and Pearce
Now and in time to come

Wherever green is worn
Are changed, changed utterly:
A terrible beauty is born.

As we all do when young and searching for what we can't even name yet, I took what I could use where I could find it. When the ideas or forms we need are banished, we seek their residues wherever we can trace them. But there was one major problem with this. I had been born a woman, and I was trying to think and act as if poetry – and the possibility of making poems – were a universal – a gender-neutral – realm. In the universe of the masculine paradigm, I naturally absorbed ideas about women, sexuality, power from the subjectivity of male poets – Yeats not least among them. The dissonance between these images and the daily events of my own life demanded a constant footwork of imagination, a kind of perpetual translation, and an unconscious fragmentation of identity: woman from poet. Every group that lives under the naming and image-making power of a dominant culture is at risk from this mental fragmentation and needs an art which can resist it. . . .

It was in the pain and confusion of that inward wrenching of the self, which I experienced directly as a young woman in the fifties, that I started to feel my way backward to an earlier splitting, the covert and overt taboos against Black people, which had haunted my earliest childhood. And I began searching for some clue or key to life, not only in poetry but in political writers. The writers I found were Mary Wollstonecraft, Simone de Beauvoir, and James Baldwin. Each of them helped me to realize that what had seemed simply "the way things are" could actually be a social construct, advantageous to some people and detrimental to others, and that these constructs could be criticized and changed. The myths and obsessions of gender, the myths and obsessions of race, the violent exercise of power in these relationships could be identified, their territories could be mapped. They were not simply part of my private turmoil, a secret misery, an individual failure. I did not yet know what I, a white woman, might have to say about the racial obsessions of white consciousness. But I did begin to resist the apparent splitting of poet from woman, thinker from woman, and to write what I feared was political poetry. And in this I had very little encouragement from the literary people I knew, but I did find courage and vindication in words like Baldwin's: "Any real change implies the breakup of the world as one has always known it, the loss of all that gave one an identity, the end of safety." I don't know why I found these words encouraging – perhaps because they made me feel less alone.

Mary Wollstonecraft had seen eighteenth-century middle-class Englishwomen brain-starved and emotionally malnourished through denial of education; her plea was to treat women's minds as respectfully as men's – to admit women as equals into male culture. Simone de Beauvoir showed how the male perception of Woman as Other dominated European culture, keeping "woman" entrapped in myths which robbed her of her independent being and value. James Baldwin insisted that *all* culture was politically significant, and described the complexity of living with integrity as a Black person, an artist in a white-dominated culture, whether as an Afro-American growing up in Harlem, U.S.A., or as an African in a country emerging from a history of colonialism. He also alluded to "that as yet unwritten history of the Negro woman";

and he wrote in 1954 in an essay on Gide that "when men [heterosexual or homosexual] can no longer love women they also cease to love or respect or trust each other, which makes their isolation complete." And he was the first writer I read who suggested that racism was poisonous to white as well as destructive to Black people.

The idea of freedom – so much invoked during World War II – had become pretty abstract politically in the fifties. Freedom – then as now – was supposed to be what the Western democracies believed in and the "Iron Curtain" Soviet-bloc countries were deprived of. The existentialist philosophers who were beginning to be read and discussed among young American intellectuals spoke of freedom as something connected with revolt. But in reading de Beauvoir and Baldwin, I began to taste the concrete reality of being unfree, how continuous and permeating and corrosive a condition it is, and how it is maintained through culture as much as through the use of force....

But there were many voices then, as there are now, warning the North American artist against "mixing politics with art." I have been trying to retrace, to delineate, these arguments, which carry no weight for me now because I recognize them as the political declarations of privilege. There is the falsely mystical view of art that assumes a kind of supernatural inspiration, a possession by universal forces unrelated to questions of power and privilege or the artist's relation to bread and blood. In this view, the channel of art can only become clogged and misdirected by the artist's concern with merely temporary and local disturbances. The song is higher than the struggle, and the artist must choose between politics – here defined as earth-bound factionalism, corrupt power struggles – and art, which exists on some transcendent plane. This view of literature has dominated literary criticism in England and America for nearly a century. In the fifties and early sixties there was much shaking of heads if an artist was found "meddling in politics"; art was mystical and universal, but the artist was also, apparently, irresponsible and emotional and politically naïve.

In North America, moreover, "politics" is mostly a dirty word, associated with low-level wheeling and dealing, with manipulation. (There is nothing North Americans seem to fear so much as manipulation, probably because at some level we know that we belong to a deeply manipulative system.) "Politics" also suggested, certainly in the fifties, the Red Menace, Jewish plots, spies, malcontents conspiring to overthrow democracy, "outside agitators" stirring up perfectly contented Black and/or working people. Such activities were dangerous and punishable, and in the McCarthy era there was a great deal of fear abroad....

Perhaps many white North Americans fear an overtly political art because it might persuade us emotionally of what we think we are "rationally" against; it might get to us on a level we have lost touch with, undermine the safety we have built for ourselves, remind us of what is better left forgotten. This fear attributes real power to the voices of passion and of poetry which connect us with all that is not simply white chauvinist/male supremacist/straight/puritanical – with what is "dark," "effeminate," "inverted," "primitive," "volatile," "sinister." Yet we are told that political poetry, for example, is doomed to grind down into mere rhetoric and jargon, to become one-dimensional, simplistic, vituperative; that in writing "protest literature" – that is, writing from a perspective which may not be male, or white, or heterosexual, or middle-class – we sacrifice the "universal"; that in writing of injustice we are limiting our scope, "grinding a political axe." So political poetry is suspected of immense subversive power, yet accused of being, by definition, bad writing, impotent, lacking in breadth. No wonder if the North American poet finds herself or himself slightly crazed by the double messages.

By 1956, I had begun dating each of my poems by year. I did this because I was finished with the idea of a poem as a single, encapsulated event, a work of art complete in itself; I knew my life was changing, my work was changing, and I needed to indicate to readers my sense of being engaged in a long, continuing process. It seems to me now that this was an oblique political statement – a rejection of the dominant critical idea that the poem's text should be read as separate from the poet's everyday life in the world. It was a declaration that placed poetry in a historical continuity, not above or outside history.

In my own case, as soon as I published – in 1963 – a book of poems which was informed by any conscious sexual politics, I was told, in print, that this work was "bitter," "personal"; that I had sacrificed the sweetly flowing measures of my earlier books for a ragged line and a coarsened voice. It took me a long time not to hear those voices internally whenever I picked up my pen. But I was writing at the beginning of a decade of political revolt and hope and activism. The external conditions for becoming a consciously, self-affirmingly political poet were there, as they had not been when I had begun to publish a decade earlier. Out of the Black Civil Rights movement, amid the marches and sit-ins in the streets and on campuses, a new generation of Black writers began to speak – and older generations to be reprinted and reread; poetry readings were infused with the spirit of collective rage and hope. As part of the movement against United States militarism and imperialism, white poets also were writing and reading aloud poems addressing the war in Southeast Asia. In many of these poems you sensed the poet's desperation in trying to encompass in words the reality of napalm, the "pacification" of villages, trying to make vivid in poetry what seemed to have minimal effect when shown on television. But there was little location of the self, the poet's own identity as a man or woman. As I wrote in another connection, "The enemy is always outside the self, the struggle somewhere else." I had – perhaps through reading de Beauvoir and Baldwin – some nascent idea that "Vietnam and the lovers' bed," as I phrased it then, were connected; I found myself, in the late sixties, trying to describe those relations in poetry. Even before I called myself a feminist or a lesbian, I felt driven – for my own sanity – to bring together in my poems the political world "out there" – the world of children dynamited or napalmed, of the urban ghetto and militarist violence, and the supposedly private, lyrical world of sex and of male/female relationships. . . .

By the end of the 1960s an autonomous movement of women was declaring that "the personal is political." That statement was necessary because in other political movements of that decade the power relation of men to women, the question of women's roles and men's roles, had been dismissed – often contemptuosly – as the sphere of personal life. Sex itself was not seen as political, except for interracial sex. Women were now talking about domination, not just in terms of economic exploitation, militarism, colonialism, imperialism, but within the family, in marriage, in child rearing, in the heterosexual act itself. Breaking the mental barrier that separated private from public life felt in itself like an enormous surge toward liberation. For a woman thus engaged, every aspect of her life was on the line. We began naming and acting on issues we had been told were trivial, unworthy of mention: rape by husbands or lovers; the boss's hand groping the employee's breast; the woman beaten in her home with no place to go; the woman sterilized when she sought an abortion; the lesbian penalized for her private life by loss of her child, her lease, her job. We pointed out that women's unpaid work in the home is central to every economy, capitalist or socialist. And in the crossover between personal and political, we were also pushing at the limits of experience reflected in literature, certainly in poetry.

To write directly and overtly as a woman, out of a woman's body and experience, to take women's existence seriously as theme and source for art, was something I had been hungering to do, needing to do, all my writing life. It placed me nakedly face to face with both terror and anger; it did indeed *imply the breakdown of the world as I had always known it, the end of safety,* to paraphrase Baldwin again. But it released tremendous energy in me, as in many other women, to have that way of writing affirmed and validated in a growing political community. I felt for the first time the closing of the gap between poet and woman.

Women have understood that we needed an art of our own: to remind us of our history and what we might be; to show us our true faces – all of them, including the unacceptable; to speak of what has been muffled in code or silence; to make concrete the values our movement was bringing forth out of consciousness raising, speakouts, and activism. But we were – and are – living and writing not only within a women's community. We are trying to build a political and cultural movement in the heart of capitalism, in a country where racism assumes every form of physical, institutional, and psychic violence, and in which more than one person in seven lives below the poverty line. The United States feminist movement is rooted in the United States, a nation with a particular history of hostility both to art and to socialism, where art has been encapsulated as a commodity, a salable artifact, something to be taught in MFA programs, that requires a special staff of "arts administrators"; something you "gotta have" without exactly knowing why. As a lesbian-feminist poet and writer, I need to understand how this *location* affects me, along with the realities of blood and bread within this nation.

...As women, I think it essential that we admit and explore our cultural identities, our national identities, even as we reject the patriotism, jingoism, nationalism offered to us as "the American way of life." Perhaps the most arrogant and malevolent delusion of North American power – of white Western power – has been the delusion of destiny, that white is at the center, that white is endowed with some right or mission to judge and ransack and assimilate and destroy the values of other peoples. As a white feminist artist in the United States, I do not want to perpetuate that chauvinism, but I still have to struggle with its pervasiveness in culture, its residues in myself.

Working as I do in the context of a movement in which artists are encouraged to address political and ethical questions, I have felt released to a large degree from the old separation of art from politics. But the presence of that separation "out there" in North American life is one of many impoverishing forces of capitalist patriarchy. I began to sense what it might be to live, and to write poetry, as a woman, in a society which took seriously the necessity for poetry, when I read Margaret Randall's anthology of contemporary Cuban women poets *Breaking the Silences.* This book had a powerful effect on me – the consistently high level of poetry, the diversity of voices, the sense of the poets' connections with world and community, and, in their individual statements, the affirmation of an organic relation between poetry and social transformation:

> Things move so much around you.
> Even your country has changed. You yourself have
> changed it.
>
> And the soul, will it change? You must change it.
> Who will tell you otherwise?
> Will it be a desolate journey?
> Will it be tangible, languid
> without a hint of violence?
> As long as you are the person you are today
> being yesterday's person as well,
> you will be tomorrow's...
> the one who lives and dies
> to live like this.

It was partly because of that book that I went to Nicaragua. I seized the opportunity when it arose, not because I thought that everyone would be a poet, but because I had been feeling more and more ill informed, betrayed by the coverage of Central America in the United States media. I wanted to know what the Sandinistas believed they stood for, what directions they wanted to take in their very young, imperiled revolution. But I also wanted to get a sense of what art might mean in a society committed to values other than profit and consumerism. What was constantly and tellingly manifested was a *belief* in art, not as commodity, not as luxury, not as suspect activity, but as a precious resource to be made available to all, one necessity for the rebuilding of a scarred, impoverished, and still-bleeding country. And returning home I had to ask myself: What happens to the heart of the artist, here in North America? What toll is taken of art when it is separated from the social fabric? How is art curbed, how are we made to feel useless and helpless, in a system which so depends on our alienation?

Alienation – not just from the world of material conditions, of power to make things happen or stop happening. Alienation from our own roots, whatever they are, the memories, dreams, stories, the language, history, the sacred materials of art....

I write in full knowledge that the majority of the world's illiterates are women, that I live in a technologically advanced country where 40 percent of the people can barely read and 20 percent are functionally illiterate. I believe that these facts are directly connected to the fragmentations I suffer in myself, that we are all in this together. Because I can write at all – and I think of all the ways women especially have been prevented from writing – because my words are read and taken seriously, because I see my work as part of something larger than my own life or the history of literature, I feel a responsibility to keep searching for teachers who can help me widen and deepen the sources and examine the ego that speaks in my poems – not for political "correctness," but for ignorance, solipsism, laziness, dishonesty, automatic writing. I look everywhere for signs of that fusion I have glimpsed in the women's movement, and most recently in Nicaragua. I turn to Toni Cade Bambara's *The Salt Eaters* or Ama Ata Aidoo's *Our Sister Killjoy* or James Baldwin's *Just Above My Head*; to paintings by Frida Kahlo or Jacob Lawrence; to poems by Dionne Brand or Judy Grahn or Audre Lorde or Nancy Morejón; to the music of Nina Simone or Mary Watkins. This kind of art – like the art of so many others uncanonized in the dominant culture – is not produced as a commodity, but as part of a long conversation with the elders and with the future. (And, yes, I do live and work believing in a future.) Such artists draw on a tradition in which political struggle and spiritual continuity are meshed. Nothing need be lost, no beauty sacrificed. The heart does not turn to a stone.

Chapter 66
Richard Poirier

Richard Poirier (1925–) is a critic and editor who, over the last thirty years, has developed an account of poetic language based on his readings of nineteenth- and twentieth-century American poets and novelists. He has distanced himself from that mode of critical thinking that looks to literature as a form of cultural redemption or salvation. For Poirier, literature's value is to be found instead in its performative action in and on language. The literary text is not a formally balanced artifact but the scene of an engagement between the language that a writer inherits and the idiom that he or she seeks to create. This engagement is both never-ending and endlessly renewed. The energies of verbal performance it produces are manifested in the distinctive patterns of figurative language that become the hallmark of a writer's style. The drama of writing has both ethical and existential implications. The poet's discovery of a style is the creation of a context of freedom, something that Poirier has described as "an environment" in which the poet can "sound publicly what he privately is." Poirier's preoccupation with style as a manifestation of freedom is one indication of the American accent of his work. But he is equally alert to the ways in which stylistic freedom can rapidly congeal into constraining conventions. For Poirier language is always social, always in use, always imbued with a history of its earlier uses. These inherited facts about language can be experienced either as a comforting tradition or a deadly constraint. The work of the strong poet, exemplified for Poirier by Robert Frost and Wallace Stevens, "dramatizes the story of its own struggle with the terminologies to which it has married itself. Its struggle with language never ends, but like some marital arguments can produce always greater density and complexity."

The following excerpt comes from the introductory chapter of The Renewal of Literature: Emersonian Reflections, *first published in 1987. In it Poirier argues for an understanding of poetic language that draws on the insights of the nineteenth-century American philosopher, Emerson, and the pragmatism of William James. At the center of this poetics is a belief in language as a form of action in the world as well as a means of representing it. The art of poetry is not in pursuit of an equivalent to a divine or originating word but is animated by what Poirier describes as "nothing except the desire that there should be more than nothing."*

Prologue: The Deed of Writing

Writing may be either the record of a deed or a deed. It is nobler when it is a deed....

Thoreau, *Journal*, January 7, 1844

Of all the arts, literature has been put, I think, in the most unenviable position. It is the designated place where everyone in every sort of need or trouble is advised to go looking for something, told he can find something or recover it, that he ought "to reclaim a legacy," as is suggested by the title of a recent study from the National Endowment for the Humanities. Something literature promises to restore has been adulterated, it is said, by popular culture or diminished by history or neglected by society or besmirched by ideologues – our aspirations, our civility, our self-esteem, some knowledge that will redeem the horrors of recent history and remind us of how really good and creative we can be. Literature is supposed to hold all of this in trust, in a relatively uncontaminated form.

It will be clear as I go along that I find reclamation projects of this kind quite fruitless. They are the expression, usually, of some disguised cultural or social agenda which none of the great writers summoned from the past could possibly endorse. Still more perplexing is that the whole venture fails to take account of how literature is troubled within itself, how much, in fact, it shows the futility of this quest for truth, values, and exaltations.

From the beginning, literature has expressed this same need to find something that is missing, call it "nature" or "reality." So that the nostalgia of literary-cultural zealots is already going begging, so to speak, on the very spot where they look to have it satisfied. The illusion of literature's resourcefulness will not abate, however, despite what literature itself has to say about it, and any diminution of its popularity is the immediate occasion for pronouncements, by those who use it as a cultural and political resource, that a savage torpor is upon us. No one has ever, I think, made similar protestations about a decline of interest in musical recitals or dance recitals or gallery shows, since these involve forms of art neither commonly shared with the general populace nor obliged to use a material – language – which belongs more or less to everyone. Especially when alleged disaffections from literature can be blamed, quite egregiously, on enthusiasms for other entertainment media, the complaints are accompanied by a proportionate insistence that the schools ought to take a hand, that reading is a cure, that cultural salvation itself may be advanced by more assiduous attention to certain revered texts.

Reading for cultural renovation has a long and self-perpetuating history. F. R. Leavis, for example – in his vastly influential magazine *Scrutiny*, published from Downing

From *The Renewal of Literature: Emersonian Reflections* (New York: Random House, 1987), pp. 3–6, 7–12, 13–15.

College, Cambridge University, England, from 1932 to 1953, and in a series of books equally important to the pedagogy of English literary studies – makes no distinction between, on the one hand, his "great traditions" in fiction and poetry and, on the other, the vitalizing, restorative cultural values that, as he often emphatically puts it, are "there," specific to the words on the page. They were "there" all the more because, in the modern world as he posited it, they could be nowhere else. Leavis is an exceptionally brilliant expositor of a cultural-literary position that has been recurrently and widely held, not least by Matthew Arnold, as far back as Spenser's "A Letter of the Authors" to *The Faerie Queene.* He "followed all the antique Poets historicall," Spenser says, so as to choose as his hero King Arthur, a man protected from modern – that is, sixteenth-century – cultural degeneration, "furthest from the daunger of envy, and suspition of present time." No "present time" has ever, apparently, known itself to be as exemplary as later times assume and need it to be, which may be why, in its literature, life is so often reflected in an "antique mirror."

Whatever might turn out to be the relation of literature to life or to culture, it is impossible to measure just how important or effective the relation is. . . . Relatively few of the vast proliferations of people in the last five hundred years were readers of literature even when they could read at all. Furthermore, from George Chapman, the translator of Homer and author in 1594 of the aptly titled "The Shadow of Night," to Wordsworth in the nineteenth century on to Eliot in the twentieth, writers have warned that it was exactly the cultural necessity and virtue of their work that made it "difficult" to read. "Away, then," wrote Wordsworth in "Essay, Supplementary to the Preface" (1815), "with the senseless iteration of the word *popular*, applied to new works in poetry, as if there were no test of excellence in this first of the fine arts but that all men should run after its productions, as if urged by an appetite, or constrained by a spell!" Poetry can imagine itself like the goblet, hidden in Frost's poem "Directive," and "Under a spell so the wrong ones can't find it, / So can't get saved, as Saint Mark says they mustn't." Meanwhile, canon formation, in response to imagined cultural crises, has taken its cues from Matthew as much as from Mark: "Wide is the gate, and broad is the way, that leadeth to destruction, and many there be which go in thereat; Because strait is the gate, and narrow is the way, which leadeth unto life, and few there be that find it" (7: 13–14). Literature is a very restricted passage into life, if it is one at all. It is never even all at once everything that is sometimes literature. English literature, including the "best" of the most sacrosanct authors, changes shape every twenty years or so, and, as we shall see presently, American literature as it is now conceived was until quite recently kept in hiding or repressed.

Literature is so variable a factor in any situation that it is absurd to suppose that it is some sort of thing waiting neutrally to arbitrate real or imagined cultural crises. More likely it creates crises that do not exist for the people who are supposed to feel them most but who somehow refuse to do so. This was especially true, I think, of the Waste Land ethos during the second quarter of this century. Or it is used factionally to promote the social or political interests of a nation or a group, as was English literature by the British in occupied India. It is forever being exploited, most notably by poets and novelists talking about one another. A stunning case in point is in the criticism of T. S. Eliot, notably his defense of Joyce's *Ulysses.* The novel was received in England with facile incomprehension and hostility, and Eliot was courageous in his efforts to champion it in his *Dial* essay of 1923 and in publishing some of its early chapters in *The Egoist* in 1919, when he was assistant editor. If *The Waste Land*, published like *Ulysses* in 1922, is not significantly indebted to the novel, except for phrases here and there, mostly in the "Hades" and "Proteus" episodes, its status owes something to the promotional effort that goes on in Eliot's "Ulysses, Order and Myth." The essay more aptly describes Eliot's methods and ambitions in the poem than Joyce's book. It makes the book sound pretentiously full of cultural malaise, announces that "the novel is dead," and that Joyce has discovered what Eliot calls "the mythical method" by which it is possible to create "a continuous parallel between contemporaneity and antiquity." That Joyce now and again uses such a technique is obvious enough, though it is scarcely central to the work; that it constitutes a "scientific discovery" might surprise readers of Dante or Spenser or Milton. The claim for "method" is, however, merely preliminary to the larger extravagance by which Eliot goes on to make a cause and effect relationship between the writing method he describes – again, essentially his own – and what he considers contemporary conditions: "It is simply a way of controlling, of ordering, of giving a shape and a significance to the immense panorama of futility and anarchy which is contemporary history." Eliot had been much closer to the spirit of *Ulysses* in an earlier "London Letter" dated August 1922, in *The Dial*, where he said, "It is at once the exposure and the burlesque of that of which it is the perfection."...

My intention is not to attack Eliot, least of all as a poet. Rather, I propose him as a vivid example, and others will follow, of how writers like to endow their own practices with historical inevitability and large consequence. This in turn promotes the notion that in their work the rest of us can recover meanings that would otherwise yield to chaos or to the blandishments of meaningless pleasure. Wordsworth is a compelling illustration because he issues one of the most effective arguments ever made *against* treating literature as a source of adaptable knowledge even while he manages, in the 1800 Preface to *Lyrical Ballads*, to sound superficially as if he were writing in the pages of *The American Scholar* or for one of the innumerable panels that meet every so often to recommend a solution to the plight of the humanities in the age of video:

> For a multitude of causes, unknown to former times, are now acting with a combined force to blunt the discriminating powers of the mind, and, unfitting it for all voluntary exertion, to reduce it to a state of almost savage torpor. The most effective of these causes are the great national events which are daily taking place, and the increasing accumulation of men in cities, where the uniformity of their occupations produces a craving for extraordinary incident, which the rapid communication of intelligence hourly gratifies.... The invaluable works of our elder writers, I had almost said the works of Shakespeare and Milton, are driven into neglect by... this degrading thirst after outrageous stimulation.

Wordsworth is one of the heroes of this book because he does *not* mean what he appears to mean at the end of this passage. He could not show – no one has ever been able to show – any connection between the neglect of "the invaluable works of our elder writers" and the "savage torpor" of the population, or that the latter would be lessened by more attention to the former. The difference between Wordsworth and those who in our own time like to think that such connections do exist is that he suspects, and they are anxious not to, that the source of degeneration lies in economic, demographic, and cultural factors that have little to do with literature or the taste for it. The argument nowadays that "we" are in trouble because there is trouble in the centers of the culture, like the universities or literary criticism or the humanities, is merely one more journalistic-political maneuver designed to obscure the failures in our political-economic-social arrangements. Wordsworth might not have looked favorably over the past few decades on popular entertainment or urban life, but he would most likely have located the trauma of the sixties, for example, in the war in Vietnam and the fight for racial equality. He would not have confused the disasters of the period with what were in fact clumsy responses to them on college campuses or at rock concerts, whose violence was in any case negligible compared to what happens regularly at adult festivals of patriotic masculinity like hockey and soccer games. And in the seventies and eighties, he might object to feminist ideological protests without blaming them for a decline in those literary standards of civilization which, as it turns out, had never over the centuries managed to create a more civilized sense of the equality of women. Debates on all these issues are so flat minded by now that it is necessary to add that I am *not* in favor of making universities the center of political protest and that I am convinced that the practice, as against the theory, of feminist criticism of literature has in many cases weakened the critical enterprise. But the causes of what is importantly troubling the Western world lie elsewhere.

It would be nice indeed if cultural and social crises could be solved or ameliorated by more and closer readings of the "elder writers," or if the modern age really could, in Eliot's phrase, be "made possible for art" by Joyce's invention of "the mythic method," though it has been around for half a millennium. Besides, life in the twentieth century was made possible for art without the "method," as in Proust, Lawrence, Woolf, Forster, Frost, among many others, while Eliot's own poetry seems to me best read when you forget about the "method" and forget about the "panorama of futility and anarchy which is contemporary history." Most writers, most readers even more so, want to believe in such magnifications of literary method and literary meaning. The belief is essential to the notion that the writing and reading of literature have a culturally redemptive power. I am arguing that this belief cannot be sustained by the actual operations of language in literary texts. Writing that can be called literature tends, it seems to me, to be discernibly on edge about its own rhetorical status, especially when the rhetoric is conspicuously indebted to any of the great, historically rooted institutions, as in the theological-mythological-literary saturations of idiom in *Paradise Lost* or *Ulysses*. Part of the excitement derives from the way such works resist as well as absorb the meanings which their adopted language makes available to them, and to us.

These proposals will require a lot of demonstration and amplification. In the process I will have things to say about a number of writers, English, American, and European, but mainly about Emerson and some of those in his lineage, including Thoreau and Whitman, and, especially, William James, Frost, and Stevens. Why this grouping? First, because, as with a related figure like Wordsworth, they offer a way to think about literature and about life that seems to me a crucial alternative to the dominant modernist and so-called post-modernist ways of thinking. Second, because they still remain insufficiently understood and assimilated, especially within the academic-journalistic practices of Anglo-American criticism in the past several decades, including what has been going on recently under mostly French provenance. And third, because neither temperament nor circumstance induced them to claim that problems importantly affecting the production of literature have to do primarily with the burdens of inherited culture, aside from language itself, or with particular historical crises. They do not transform their difficulties with language into the cultural-historical heroics usually attributed to modernist writing.

Of course, like writers of any nation or any historical period, they are committed to the idea of a great national literature – wherein does any writer have a better chance for immortality? – and, like writers of any generation, each of these Americans knew, with Emerson in "The American Scholar," that "genius is always the enemy of genius by over influence," and that new writers are required to be "new." They necessarily concerned themselves with these matters, but not, I am suggesting, to any exceptional degree, and they mostly avoided the vulgar forms of literary nationalism. (When, for example, Whitman first addresses the issue in the opening lines of the 1855 preface to *Leaves of Grass* – he was only later to become jingoistic in his prose – he does so in a very relaxed manner: "America does not repel the past," he says, "is not so impatient as has been supposed.") As for the cultural blankness or bareness of America, they tend to see it as a cultural opportunity when it is not an image of more personal deprivations. When negatively conceived, the denuded landscapes in American writing are frequently an image not of cultural bareness at all, but of creative-sexual impotence. As a result, the Emersonian inclination is to locate the problem of literary production mostly in language rather than in historical circumstance, in the obscure origins of language, and in the mysteries of its transmissions and transformations.

The linguistic issue for them has something but not a lot to do with the fact that the language of American literature is not native to America; Whitman goes so far as to concede in the same preface that "the English language befriends the frank American expression." Far more important is the feeling that the bequest of language, to British no less than to American writers, carries with it certain inducements that are not distinguishable from obligations. As Emerson says of a Gothic cathedral in the essay "History," language "affirms that it was done by us, and not done by us." Each of us is enjoined to find himself or herself within the given discourse, but only by a process that resists and promises to transform it. There is nothing sacred on the far side of language except the desire that the words should exist. The desire itself will atrophy if its inheritors leave language in the forms in which they have received it or even if they rest content for long with any new forms they may have given it. We need to keep messing up the idiom, as Stevens suggests . . . : "speech," according to "The Creations of Sound," "is not dirty silence / Clarified. It is silence made still dirtier."

Let me expand further on these propositions. Literature generates its substance, its excitements, its rhetoric, and its plots often with the implicit intention, paradoxically, to get free of them and to restore itself to some preferred state of naturalness, authenticity, and simplicity. The implication is that if any of these actually did or could exist in an uncorrupted state, then literature itself would be unnecessary, a possibility to which I will return later on. Another way to put it, which will help explain why my emphasis on the Emersonians is not merely an American emphasis, is to say that literature implicitly idealizes that condition of bareness, that thinness of social and cultural circumstance, which, according to Henry James and other observers, was supposed to be the special plight of American writers. For Emerson, William James, and Stevens, however, leaving aside for a moment the differences in their lives and social opportunities, "bareness" is, as I have said, very often salutary, something to be sought after, no matter how much Emerson complained that Concord could be a dreary place for any man of talent.

What is the supposed virtue of bareness? That with nothing to depend on, nothing to lean or rely on, the naked and true self can and will emerge, compelled into expression, or that "something" will emerge. To quote one of the most beautiful passages from Stevens's "The Rock":

> As if nothingness contained a métier,
> A vital assumption, an impermanence
> In its permanent cold, an illusion so desired
>
> That the green leaves came and covered the high rock,
> That the lilacs came and bloomed, like a blindness cleaned,
> Exclaiming bright sight, as it was satisfied,
>
> In a birth of sight. . . .

Emerson can say in "Experience" that "the God [is] the native of these bleak rocks. That need makes in morals the capital virtue of self-trust. We must hold hard to this poverty, however scandalous, and by more vigorous self-recoveries, after the sallies of action, possess our axis more firmly." Poverty allows us, without having to burrow through layers of impediment, to "recover" a self that has been discernible (though he allows that it might also have been lost) in "the sallies of action." Melville, however, posits a very different condition. He envisioned masks, piles, heaps beyond or beneath which there was possibly nothing at all. Ahab imagines that Moby Dick "heaps me," and next to the passage from Emerson should be placed a passage from *Moby-Dick* inspired by Melville's visit in 1849 to the fourteenth- and fifteenth-century Gothic and Renaissance Hotel de Cluny in Paris. Obviously, he has in mind not merely European accumulations on top of some imaginary human essence, but an accumulation more ancient still which can never be gotten past:

> Winding far down from within the very heart of this spiked Hotel de Cluny where we here stand – however grand and wonderful, now quit it; – and take your way, ye nobler, sadder souls, to those vast Roman halls of Thermes; where far beneath the fantastic towers of man's upper earth, his root of grandeur, his whole awful essence sits in bearded state; an antique buried beneath antiquities, and throned on torsoes!

The renowned differences between Emerson and Melville are implicit in their contrasting measure of how much waste obscures the "real" self, if there is one, and the unlikelihood, in Melville's case, that the self can ever be liberated from it. And yet the difference between the two writers has been exaggerated, I think; even though the self in Emerson is not "an antique buried beneath antiquities," an endlessly layered invention, it is still no less in danger of being trapped in language, in the conformities which make language possible. This, as I have been implying, is the prior condition which any literature or work of literature discovers for itself.... Emerson has his own vision akin to Melville's Hotel de Cluny, though far less despairing. It is, as he says in the *Journals* for June–August 1845, that "literature has been before us wherever we go," an admission that initiates a long passage about literary prepossession of the continent that will be discussed later on. The "axis" which Emerson would "possess more firmly" is the capacity for actions belied in this passage from *Moby-Dick* (though not, of course, in Melville's own treatment of language), actions by which you might modify this inheritance of language and thus achieve a modification in human consciousness and history.

While it has been simplified, the difference between Emerson and Melville is, then, real and important. It is akin to the difference between the Emersonian heritage and the modernism of Eliot, and it can be located quite specifically: in the word "action" and in the sense of the efficacy of action. "Action" is a key term which American pragmatism, especially William James's version of it, took over from Emerson, along with the word "transition," which is equally central. Both words, as I hope gradually to make clear, point to an alliance of pragmatism with the workings of language in literature, with poetic making. American pragmatism never assumes that in the beginning was the Word or word. It does not deny that God is a necessary functional term; but it refuses to credit the *problem* of logocentrism. It cannot be a problem when, as James says in "Conclusions" to *A Pluralistic Universe*, "our thoughts determine our acts, and our acts redetermine the previous nature of the world."

To further explore some connections between pragmatism and the act of literary troping, the turning of a word, consider the first invention of that creature who eventually would conceive of the word "man." I ask you to suppose that its first invention was its own muteness. Muteness is not something attributable to a rock or a stone, a tree or a beast. For anything to imagine its own muteness it would have to desire not to be mute, to desire already to be other than what it is, to become different and to make a difference. Suppose that the next invention was the sound that erased the muteness, and that this was followed by the invention of other sounds intended to change those first ones and to change also the sounds of nature, as when Frost allows Adam in "Never Again Would Birds' Song Be the Same," to believe "that the birds there in all the garden round / From having heard the daylong voice of Eve / Had added to their own an oversound, / Her tone of meaning but without the words."

But here, in this possible scenario, we encounter a mystery or a missing element. And it is at this point that most people want to fill the gap with the word "soul" or the word "God." And why not? The human desire to make its presence known to itself and to the world, to make a difference to and in the world – must it not, even in its original muteness, have expected that there really *was* something waiting to be discovered, something "inside" that no other creature possessed? Exactly at this point pragmatism reveals its tough-mindedness as against the tender-minded who want to bring into the story a necessary God and a necessary soul. A pragmatist, by which I mean some version of Emerson, might have to use the words "God" or "soul," but would go on to suppose, as I do, that there was in fact really nothing outside to depend on and nothing inside either, nothing except the desire that there should be more than nothing.

That, if I may say so, is why works of art are not required to exist. There is nothing outside of them that requires their existence. If Shakespeare had never existed we would not miss his works, for there would be nothing missing. This is perhaps the most obvious, important, and repressed fact about artistic production. Critics and artists now and again do boast of being compelled by historical necessity or admit to working on assignment, and yet all that compels Shakespeare or Mozart or Rembrandt or Balanchine is that same desire which brought muteness into the act of sound or motion. The difference is that artistic acts have precedents, while that first act did not. An artistic act can take advantage of the vocabularies of prior works of art, but if the result is merely an imitation, then it might as well have remained mute; what it accomplishes will offer no testimony within itself of its need to exist. And that, I suspect, is why most inferior artists need and like to explain their works as having been historically necessitated....

Chapter 67
Jeremy Cronin

Jeremy Cronin (1949–) is a poet, politician, and critic who was imprisoned for seven years in 1976 for his opposition to the apartheid regime in South Africa. After his release Cronin went into exile in England and then Zambia, returning to South Africa in 1990. His first collection of poetry, Inside, *was published in 1983, and this was followed in 1997 by* Even the Dead *and in 1999 by* Inside and Out. *Cronin's poetry draws on both European and African traditions, combining forms that come from a poetry of the printed page with the techniques and idioms of oral poetry. Poetry, criticism, and politics are part of a single continuum in Cronin's work. He is currently Deputy General Secretary of the South African Communist Party and a member of the South African Parliament for the African National Congress Party.*

The following excerpts from "Even under the Rine of Terror" comes from an article first published in Research in African Literatures *in 1988. Within a very different cultural and historical context, it is concerned with an issue raised by Amy Lowell in 1917, the difference between a poetry of the printed page and a poetry composed or improvised for public performance. For Cronin this provokes a question about how poetry becomes valuable. The poetry he discusses displays the formal devices that Jakobson would have recognized as poetic. In the context of apartheid South Africa, these formal devices become charged with political and cultural significance that arise in the moment of performance.*

"Even under the Rine of Terror…": Insurgent South African Poetry

In the recent treason trial of sixteen United Democratic Front and trade union leaders, the apartheid prosecutor produced a weighty indictment running to over three hundred pages. The bulk of the indictment consisted in long quotations from

From *Research in African Literatures*, vol. 19, no. 1 (1988).

the proceedings of political rallies. The speeches were taped, one presumes, by police informers and then transcribed: there are extensive quotations from speeches made and quotations and translations of songs sung and slogans chanted. There is also evidence on the wording on banners, T-shirts, buttons, pamphlets, and flyers. Among this mass of forensic detail, as part of the allegedly treasonable material, there are a few poems, also taped and lovingly transcribed from the same events.

Besides the obvious question (Just who and what *is* treasonable in apartheid South Africa?), there is another irony in this indictment. The state prosecutor has understood more about current black poetry in South Africa than many an academic commentator. The prosecutor has, unwittingly, anthologized the poetry more accurately than is commonly the case in academic appraisal, for this is a poetry that can only be understood and analysed in its relationship to a range of traditional and contemporary oral and verbal practices: songs, chants, slogans, funeral orations, political speeches, sermons, and graffiti. It can be understood only in terms of the context of its major mode of presentation and reception. The book and the small magazine are perhaps not entirely insignificant modes of presentation and reception for this poetry, but they are mostly secondary and exceptional. When the book or magazine arrives within the university library, or in the academic's study, it tends willy-nilly to be collocated within a continuum that runs, if South African poetry is in question, from Thomas Pringle through Roy Campbell and William Plomer. Without wishing to disparage the academic reproduction and consumption of poetry, I find it necessary to understand that the conventional modes are more or less entirely inappropriate to deal with much contemporary black poetry in South Africa.

To talk about this poetry, written over the last two or three years, we must contextualize it within the rolling wave of semi-insurrectionary uprisings, mass stayaways, political strikes, consumer boycotts, huge political funerals (involving anything up to seventy thousand mourners at a time), factory occupations, rent boycotts, school and university boycotts, mass rallies, and physical confrontation over barricades with security forces. This wave of mobilization and struggle has spread into the smallest rural village. It has interwoven with a substantial organizational renaissance: youth, civic, religious, women's, trade union, and student organizations have sprung up and spread countrywide.

An emergent (and insurgent) national political culture is an integral part of this rolling wave of mass struggle. Journalists, photographers, and television crews are the only ones so far to have described some of the features of this emergent culture from the outside. Very little academic analysis has yet been done. The *South African Labour Bulletin* has had a brief and lively debate on working-class culture. There have been a few articles on trade union theatre. Some of the earlier academic writing on "Soweto poetry" is relevant, but somewhat left behind by the speed of unfolding events.

In the hope of assisting tentative beginnings, I shall present, descriptively, and to the best of my ability with all the limitations of the written word, a sampling of poetry performances that have occurred in the last two years. Through adopting this somewhat empirical approach, I hope to give at least an idea of the crucially important context of the poetry. . . .

A student conference

Glynn Thomas Hostel, Soweto, July 1984 – AZASO, the black university and college students' organization is holding its national conference. Five hundred delegates from all over South Africa, some from AZASO branches in the bantustans where they are compelled to operate clandestinely, are present. The atmosphere is vibrant; for three days the student delegates are locked in intense political discussions, papers, reports, workshops, and elections. The debates and discussions flow over into the hostel rooms and reach into the small hours of the morning. The national question, socialism, Afghanistan, the trade unions – the topics are diverse. For plenary sessions delegates pack into the hostel canteen. There is barely enough space and not enough chairs; one-third of the delegates are left standing, crammed up against walls and into corners. Sometimes emotions run away, and the chairperson or an older guest speaker is compelled to ask for discipline. 'Please, comrades, our task is not to make it easy for the enemy to arrest us. This place is certainly bugged. Comrades must please refrain from wild rhetoric; let us preserve a militant discipline.'

At the end of a paper, or discussion, to give minds awash with stimulation a moment of relaxation, the hall takes off on a series of liberation songs. The singing unfailingly brings the half-dozen stout mamas on the kitchen staff dancing and ululating out from behind the sinks and dishes. They do a little swaying, clapping lap of honour, down the aisles, up to the makeshift stage and round again. Cheers, *amandlas*, vivas, and then silence again as delegates return to the next discussion paper.

The interludes are not all song. Through the three days of conference, there are several poetry performances, notably by two young students from the University of the North, Turfloop. In fact, their performances are in popular demand. 'Poem! Poem!' is a request that gets called out fairly frequently between breaks in the days' sessions. The poetry of the two Turfloop students consists in a set of chanted refrains, one voice leading: 'Cuppa-ta-lismmmma! cuppa-ta-lismmmma! cummmma to me-e-e-e! with the other voice weighing in behind in response, 'I-I-I-I a-m-m-m-m-a cuppa-ta-lismmmma.' They have obviously worked out a broad structure and a basic set of refrains, but the performance is considerably extemporaneous. Sometimes the two voices are at separate ends of the canteen, more by chance than design, I guess. They then call to each other across the heads of the five hundred delegates:

> Cuppa-ta-lismmmma, cuppa-ta-lismma
> A spectre is a hauntinnnga you
> This accordinnnnga the gospel
> Of Marx and Engels
> Cuppa-ta-lissssmmma!

The interplay continues for some time with the second voice ('Capitalism') finally fading away with a long groan to enthusiastic foot stomping from those present.

The voices perform the poetry with a slow lilt, and from the reaction of the audience, much enjoyment is derived from the phonetic exaggeration. The principal features of this are an increased stress and duration of the repeated nasal sounds, particularly *m* sounds. Some of these are held for a full two or three seconds. There is also a tendency to lengthen penultimate syllables or to shift lengthened final syllables (particularly nasals) into penultimates with the addition of a little, lilting schwa as in 'l'mmmmmmma', or 'cuppa-ta-lismmmmmma'. This gives the English a pronounced, indeed, an exaggerated African texture.

The poetic thickening of language carries a playfulness as well as implications of appropriation and nationalization. 'Capitalism', the signifier, is taken over, smacked about on the lips, and transformed. Stylistically the poem bears all the marks of its context and function – a relaxing interlude that is, nevertheless, in key with the political ambience.

The political rally

Poetry performances somewhat like the above occur fairly often in a variety of contexts, such as mass funerals for political martyrs, rallies, and commemorative church hall meetings. Perhaps the finest current practitioner of this line of poetry is Mzwakhe Mbuli. It was he who brought the house down with his poem, 'I Am the Voice of International Anger', before an audience of fourteen thousand at the national launch of the United Democratic Front in August 1983. Mzwakhe is tall and angular with bulging pop eyes. His rhythms are somewhat influenced by the reggae, or dub talking poetry of Linton Kwesi Johnson. He performs at speed, with a heavily syncopated intonation, the mostly three- and four-beat rhythms poked out in the air with two long forefingers.

Ig-nor-rant
I am ignorant
I am ignorant
I have been fortunate
In the business of ignorancy
I am South African
Without residency
I can read,
I can write,
However ignorant I may be
I know Mandela is in Pollsmoor jail
Though I do not know why.
Oh people of Afrika
Help me before it is too late
Emancipate me
From my ignorancy.

Mzwakhe breaks the rhythm, stops, leans into the microphone, and whispers:

For freedom is getting rusty
On the pavements of oppression.

Sometimes Mzwakhe performs alone. At other times he performs with his group, Khuvangano. Some of the poems are then spoken by one voice, pitched over a freedom song that has dropped down to a hum in the remaining three or four voices of the group. The audience will also tend to take up the humming, particularly if it is a well-known freedom song. This style of declamation over a backdrop of humming might derive from African church rituals.

I say this because I have seen very similar oral performances (he does not call them 'poetry' but 'prayers of remembrance') by Aubrey Mokoena. Mokoena is a well-known political figure and was one of the sixteen charged in the treason trial mentioned above. He is also a part-time preacher. The two occasions on which I have seen him perform were at a mass rally of the Cape Youth Congress (CAYGO), and at the funeral of seven alleged ANC guerillas gunned down in Guguletu, Cape Town. On both occasions Mokoena led the hundreds-strong audience in singing the mourning song, 'Thina Sizwe'. After a minute or so of singing, Mokoena asked those present to drop down to a hum while, microphone in hand, he paced the dais, invoking a long litany of fallen martyrs, of leaders languishing in jail, and of those forced into exile. Mokoena's phrasing is more preacherly, more grand compared to the jerky syncopations of Mzwakhe. But there are also many common elements. . . .

A poetry of testament

There is another poetry which is fairly widespread, but which is first written down, or even scratched out, before it is performed. This is a poetry of testament, inscribed on cell walls, smuggled out of jails on rolls of toilet paper, or left behind under pillows in the townships. These are poems that involve a slight heightening of language to carry a special meaning, to give significance to the unspeakable. On what evidence I have, I would guess that all over South Africa there are black mothers with little pieces of paper, four- or five-line poems left behind by a son or daughter who has gone in the night to join up with the clandestine liberation movement. The poem, found a day later, is sometimes the last a parent will hear of a child. In the samples I have seen, the language is often clumsy, or formulaic ('for the motherland', "shed my blood'). But, however spurious this may seem to a literary criticism that measures the "authentic" in terms of 'individuality' and 'originality', the sincerity and meaningfulness of those little scraps is real enough. The existential acts with which they are integrated speak as loud as the words themselves.

A similar poetry is being smuggled out of jails. The following poem was written by a young member of the Bridgton Youth Organization, Bridgton being the 'coloured' ghetto in Oudtshoorn. The writer is probably a high school student. The poem, entitled 'Mothers of Bhongolethu' (which is the local African township), is dated '9.45 am, 30/6/85'; it is very much a poem of time and place. It was written in detention immediately after one of the countless massacres and widescale arrests:

Mothers of Bhongolethu,
You gave birth to the most

oppressed youth of our nation.
. . .
The enemy rejoiced in their death
But we don't mourn.
Mothers of Bhongolethu,
let us mobilize,
to continue their struggle.
Let us avenge their death.

Our sons and daughters were
not armed on that day.
But the soldiers of Africa
are marching into our
townships.
The day will come when we
will be ready,
ready to avenge the death
of our martyrs.

Mothers of Bhongolethu
do not despair.
Do not mourn . . .
But take courage in the
blood of our children.
In the blood that nurtures
the tree of Freedom.

The most moving of all are the short poems that come from the political prisoners on death row. On the eve of his hanging, young Benjamin Moloise sent out this poem:

I am proud to be what I am . . .
The storm of oppression will be followed
By the rain of my blood
I am proud to give my life
My one solitary life.

The last poem of Moloise, like that of Solomon Mahlangu, another young guerilla executed in Pretoria Maximum Security Prison, has since been repeated at many mass rallies, and so, like most of the other poems we have considered so far, it achieves its major form of reception in public gatherings. Indeed the words of both Mahlangu and Moloise have been incorporated within dozens of longer performed poems.

Some general poetic features

I have, in passing, already noted many of the poetic features of the poetry I have been describing. In the interests of moving in the direction of a little more analysis, it is useful to consider in more general terms some of the notable features.

The gestural. The poetry is, clearly, largely a poetry of performance. The bodily presence of the poet becomes an important feature of the poetics. Arm gestures, clapping, and head nodding are often used expressively and deictically. The poets also draw freely from the current political lexis of gesture: the clenched fist salute of people's power (*Amandla ngawethu*); the index finger pointing emphatically down to signal *Ngo*! ('Here and now!') after the chanted call *Inkululeko* ('Freedom'); or the slow, hitchhiker-like thumb sign to signal 'Let it come back' (*Afrika... Mayibuye*). These latter collective gestures are used freely within poems and, more often, as framing devices before and after the performance of a poem. The slogans and gestures will be taken up by the whole audience. They act phatically, as channel openers or closers and as a means of focussing attention on the performer.

The clothing of the performer should also be noted. As often as not it is unexceptional. However, quite a few poets, especially those who adopt a more bardic tone, don dashikis as an integral part of their performance. The several trade union praise poets also tend to wear special clothing, traditional skins and ornamentation, or a modern-day facsimile of the kind already noted.

Verbal stylistic features. The most notable verbal stylistic features are those commonly associated with principally oral literatures: the style tends to be additive, aggregative, formulaic, and 'copious'.

In Qwa Qwa
I found no one
In Lebowa
I was unfortunate
In Transkei
I talked about pass laws
Transkei citizenship card
Was the answer
In Bophuthatswana
I talked about democratic and social rights
Sun City was the answer
In Kwa Venda
I talked about people's security
The building of Thohoyandou police station
Was the answer
In Ciskei
I talked about trade unionism
The banning of SAAWU
Was the answer
(etc., etc.)
Ma-Afrika,
   I have travelled!

The repetitive and formulaic features assist the performing poet mnemonically. But these features also assist the audience to hear and understand the poem. Walter J. Ong notes the limitations of oral, as opposed to written, communication:

> Thought requires some sort of continuity. Writing establishes in the text a "line" of continuity outside the mind. If distraction confuses or obliterates from the mind the context out of which emerges the material I am now reading, the context can be retrieved by glancing back over the text selectively. Backlooping can be entirely occasional, purely *ad hoc*.... In oral discourse, the situation is different. There is nothing to backloop into outside the mind, for the oral utterance has vanished as soon as it is uttered.... Redundancy, repetition of the just-said, keeps both speaker and hearer surely on the track.[1]

Apart from these universal features and limitations of the oral, it should be remembered that the poetry we are considering is often performed in the worst imaginable acoustic situations. It is sometimes performed, for instance, in open township soccer fields or crowded halls with no public address systems. The poets are also pitching their poems to audiences that are generally very different from the quiet, reverential salon audience that will occasionally receive poetry of another kind. The poets have to take their chances in between militant mass singing, rousing political speeches, or routine organizational business. They perform to an audience that, generally, warmly acclaims their poetry. But it is an audience which, nevertheless, does not sit tightly in respectful silence. There are women with dying babies on their backs; there are youngsters crawling and toddling underfoot. People are getting up or sitting down. And all the while, hovering just outside the venue, radio transmitters bleeping, are the police with, as often as not, a helicopter rattling overhead.

Agonistically toned features. Another significant feature of much of this poetry is, again, noted by Ong as typical of all oral cultures.

> Many, if not all, oral or residually oral cultures strike literates as extraordinarily agonistic in their verbal performances and indeed in their lifestyle. Writing fosters abstractions that disengage knowledge from the arena where human beings struggle with one another.... By keeping knowledge embedded in the human lifeworld, orality situates knowledge within a context of struggle.... Bragging about one's own prowess and/or verbal tongue-lashings of an opponent figure regularly in encounters between characters in narrative: in the *Iliad*, in *Beowulf*, throughout medieval European romance, in *The Mwindo Epic* and countless other African stories... in the Bible, as between David and Goliath (1 Sam. 17: 43–47). Standard in oral societies across the world, reciprocal name-calling has been filled with a specific name in linguistics: flyting (or fliting).... The other side of agonistic name-calling or vituperation in oral or residually oral cultures is the fulsome expression of praise which is found everywhere in connection with orality.[2]

There are, in South Africa, strong indigenous traditions of praise poetry. We have already noted the existence, specifically within the trade union movement, of a proletarian reworking and updating of this tradition. But strong agonistic tones are a feature throughout:

> Even under the reign of terror [pronounced 'rine']
> The land is still mine
> My land is immovable

I am the beats
Admire me
I am the beats
From the drums of change
   In Afrika.

However, the most notable case of agonistically toned performance is the marching, defiant *toyi-toyi* chant. It is the national favourite with militant youth on the barricades, in their street battles with the army and police armoured cars. The *toyi-toyi* involves a lead voice incanting a long litany of names, some admired like u-Nelson Mandê-ê-ê-êla, Ol-eeee-va Tambo, or Joe Slovo, with appropriate epithets: *ubaba wethu* ('our father'), i-chief commander, and so forth. Other names are vilified: Le Grange, P. W. Botha, Gatsha Buthelezi. While the lead voice, mostly hidden anonymously deep within the folds of the crowd, incants, the rest of the squad, group, or crowd, as the case may be, replies to each name with approbation:

Hayyiii! . . .
Hayyiii! Hayyiii!

or with contempt:

Voetsek! . . .
Voetsek! Voetsek! ('Go to hell')

All the while, the entire group will be marching or marking time, knees high, at the double. The *toyi-toyi* litany is also freely sprinkled with onomatopoeic evocations of bazookas and 'ukka four seven' ('AK 47') assault rifles being fired off, of land mines exploding, and of 'freedom potatoes' ('grenati') going off:

Goosh! . . .
Goosh! Goosh!

Whether the *toyi-toyi* is a song, a chant, a march, a war cry, or a poem is a scholastic point. Functionally, like much of the emergent culture and all of the poetry I have described, it serves to mobilize and unite large groups of people. It transforms them into a collective that is capable of facing down a viciously oppressive and well-equipped police and army. In acting together, under the shadow of the apartheid guns, the mobilized people are forcing open space to hold proscribed meetings, to elect and mandate their own leadership, to discuss basic matters, to resolve crime in their streets, to bury their dead, to raise illegal banners, to unban their banned organizations, to discover their strength, and even to make their own poetry. In short, through it all, liberated zones are being opened up in industrial ghettos and rural locations, where the people are beginning – tenuously it is true – to govern themselves in this land of their birth.

Notes

1 Walter J. Ong, *Orality and Literacy: The Technologizing of the Word* (London: Methuen, 1982), pp. 39–40.
2 Ong, *Orality and Literacy*, pp. 43–5.

Chapter 68
Jacques Derrida

Jacques Derrida (1930–) is one of the most influential and controversial of late twentieth-century thinkers. In a series of remarkable essays, first published in the 1960s, Derrida invented the form of thought called "deconstruction." As its name implies, deconstruction concerns itself with the conditions and limits of philosophical and literary "constructions" or forms. For Derrida these conditions have often been set, and less often questioned, by an intellectual system, western metaphysics, that dates back to ancient Greek philosophy and continues to operate in more recent intellectual movements such as phenomenology and structuralism. A characteristic feature of this system is to think in terms of a binary structure of two concepts or ideas, such that one is privileged over the other. Thus Derrida argues speech is given priority over writing, the literal is given priority over the metaphoric, and so on. In a series of patient and detailed readings, Derrida demonstrates that these binary structures cannot sustain their own coherence. The first and dominant term turns out to depend for its validity on the second and lesser term. What seems to give structure can be shown to question that structure. The process of deconstruction discloses these complications in the language of thought, but does not stand outside them. Radically misunderstood as a form of nihilism, deconstruction instead opens up our taken-for-granted assumptions to new kinds of questions and to the possibility of creating new kinds of value. This is indicated in the course of Derrida's own thought. If his early work was dedicated to a critique of concepts in literary criticism and philosophy, his later work has extended that critique to basic questions in ethics and politics, as, for example, in his recent work on friendship and hospitality.

Derrida has written extensively about literature, including studies of poets such as Paul Valéry, Paul Celan, and François Ponge. The following text, "Che cos'è la poesia?," was originally published in an Italian journal, Poesia, *in November 1988. The editors of the journal had asked a succession of writers to respond to the question "What is poetry?." Derrida's reply tests the possibility of answering the question at all. He argues that to do so we must "renounce knowledge" and return to some of the simplest conceptions we have about poetry: that it is something learnt by heart, for example. But his answer also takes the form of an enigmatic fable about a hedgehog and its survival. As Derrida has made clear elsewhere, the hedgehog alludes to two writers: the German Romantic author Schlegel who compared the fragmentary work of art's detachment from its surroundings to a hedgehog's relation to its environment; and Heidegger who uses the Grimms' fable, "The Hedgehog and the Hare" as an allegory for a paradox about time, the thing that arrives but is always already there.*

Che cos'è la poesia?

In order to respond to such a question – *in two words, right?* – you are asked to know how to renounce knowledge. And to know it well, without ever forgetting it: demobilize culture, but never forget in your learned ignorance what you sacrifice on the road, in crossing the road.

Who dares to ask me that? Even though it remains inapparent, since disappearing is its law, the answer sees *itself (as) dictated (dictation).* I am *a* dictation, pronounces poetry, learn me by heart, copy me down, guard and keep me, look out for me, look at me, dictated dictation, right before your eyes: soundtrack, *wake*, trail of light, photograph of the feast in mourning.

It sees itself, the response, dictated to be poetic, by being poetic. And for that reason, it is obliged to address itself to someone, singularly to you but as if to the being lost in anonymity, between city and nature, an imparted secret, at once public and private, *absolutely* one and the other, absolved from within and from without, neither one nor the other, the animal thrown onto the road, absolute, solitary, rolled up in a ball, *next to (it)self.* And for that very reason, it may get itself run over, *just so*, the *hérisson, istrice* in Italian, in English, hedgehog.

And if you respond otherwise depending on each case, taking into account the space and time which you are *given* with this *demand* (already you are speaking Italian), by the demand itself, according to *this* economy but also in the imminence of some traversal *outside* yourself, away from *home*, venturing toward the language of the other in view of an impossible or denied translation, necessary but desired like a death – what would all of this, the very thing in which you have just begun to turn deliriously, have to do, at that point, with poetry? Or rather, with the *poetic*, since you intend to speak about an *experience*, another word for voyage, here the aleatory rambling of a trek, the strophe that turns but never leads back to discourse, or back home, at least is never reduced to poetry – written, spoken, even sung.

Here then, right away, *in two words*, so as not to forget:

1. *The economy of memory.* A poem must be brief, elliptical by vocation, whatever may be its objective or apparent expanse. Learned unconscious of *Verdichtung* and of the retreat.

2. *The heart.* Not the heart in the middle of sentences that circulate risk-free through the interchanges and let themselves be translated into any and all languages.

From *A Derrida Reader: Between the Blinds*, edited and trans. Peggy Kamuf (New York: Columbia University Press, 1991), pp. 223–37.

Not simply the heart archieved by cardiography, the object of sciences or technologies, of philosophies and bio-ethico-juridical discourses. Perhaps not the heart of the Scriptures or of Pascal, nor even, this is less certain, the one that Heidegger prefers to them. No, a story of "heart" poetically enveloped in the idiom "*apprendre par coeur*," whether in my language or another, the English language (to learn by heart), or still another, the Arab language (*hafiza a'n zahri kalb*) – a single trek with several tracks.

Two in one: the second axiom is rolled up in the first. The poetic, let us say it, would be that which you desire to learn, but from and of the other, thanks to the other and under dictation, by heart; *imparare a memoria.* Isn't that already it, the poem, once a token is given, the advent of an event, at the moment in which the traversing of the road named translation remains as improbable as an accident, one which is all the same intensely dreamed of, required there where what it promises always leaves something to be desired? A grateful recognition goes out toward that very thing and precedes cognition here: your benediction before knowledge.

A fable that you could recount as the gift of the poem, it is an emblematic story: someone writes *you,* to you, of you, on you. No, rather a mark addressed to you, left and confided with you, is accompanied by an injunction, in truth it is instituted in this very order which, in its turn, constitutes you, assigning your origin or giving rise to you: destroy me, or rather render my support invisible to the outside, in the world (this is already the trait of all dissociations, the history of transcendences), in any case do what must be done so that the provenance of the mark remains from now on unlocatable or unrecognizable. Promise it: let it be disfigured, transfigured or rendered indeterminate in its *port* – and in this word you will hear the shore of the departure as well as the referent toward which a translation is portered. Eat, drink, swallow my letter, carry it, transport it in you, like the law of a writing become your body: *writing in (it)self.* The ruse of the injunction may first of all let itself be inspired by the simple possibility of death, by the risk that a vehicle poses to every finite being. You hear the catastrophe coming. From that moment on imprinted directly on the trait, come from the heart, the mortal's desire awakens in you the movement (which is contradictory, you follow me, a double restraint, an aporetic constraint) to guard from oblivion this thing which in the same stroke exposes itself to death and protects itself – in a word, the address, the retreat of the *hérisson,* like an animal on the autoroute rolled up in a ball. One would like to take it in one's hands, undertake to learn it and understand it, to keep it for oneself, near oneself.

You love – keep that in its singular form, we could say in the irreplaceable *literality of the vocable* if we were talking about poetry and not only about the poetic in general. But our poem does not hold still within names, nor even within words. It is first of all thrown out on the roads and in the fields, thing beyond languages, even if it sometimes happens that it recalls itself in language, when it gathers itself up, rolled up in a ball on itself, it is more threatened than ever in its retreat: it thinks it is defending itself, and it loses itself.

Literally: you would like to retain by heart an absolutely unique form, an event whose intangible singularity no longer separates the ideality, the ideal meaning as one says, from the body of the letter. In the desire of this absolute inseparation, the absolute non-absolute, you breathe the origin of the poetic. Whence the infinite resistance to the transfer of the letter which the animal, in its name, nevertheless calls out for. That is the distress of the *hérisson.* What does the distress, *stress* itself, want? *Stricto sensu,* to put on guard. Whence the prophecy: translate me, watch, keep me yet awhile, get going, save yourself, let's get off the autoroute.

Thus the dream of *learning by heart* arises in you. Of letting your heart be traversed by the dictated dictation. In a single trait – and that's the impossible, that's the poematic experience. You did not yet know the heart, you learn it thus. From this experience and from this expression. I call a poem that very thing that teaches the heart, invents the heart, *that which,* finally, the word *heart* seems to mean and which, in my language, I cannot easily discern from the word itself. *Heart,* in the poem "learn by heart" (to be learned by heart), no longer names only pure interiority, independent spontaneity, the freedom to affect oneself actively by reproducing the beloved trace. The memory of the "by heart" is confided like a prayer – that's safer – to a certain exteriority of the automaton, to the laws of mnemotechnics, to that liturgy that mimes mechanics on the surface, to the automobile that surprises your passion and bears down on you as if from an outside: *auswendig,* "by heart" in German.

So: your heart beats, gives the downbeat, the birth of rhythm, beyond oppositions, beyond outside and inside, conscious representation and the abandoned archive. A heart down there, between paths and autostradas, outside of your presence, humble, close to the earth, low down. Reiterate(s) in a murmur: never repeat... In a single cipher, the poem (the learning by heart, learn it by heart) seals together the meaning and the letter, like a rhythm spacing out time.

In order to respond in two words: *ellipsis,* for example, or *election, heart, hérisson,* or *istrice,* you will have had to disable memory, disarm culture, know how to forget knowledge, set fire to the library of poetics. The unicity of the poem depends on this condition. You must celebrate, you have to commemorate amnesia, savagery, even the stupidity of the "by heart": the *hérisson.* It blinds itself. Rolled up in a ball, prickly with spines, vulnerable and dangerous, calculating and ill-adapted (because it makes itself into a ball, sensing the danger on the autoroute, it exposes itself to an accident). No poem without accident, no poem that does not open itself like a wound, but no poem that is not also just as wounding. You will call poem a silent incantation, the aphonic wound that, of you, from you, I want to learn by heart. It thus takes place, essentially, without one's having to do it or make it: it *lets itself* be done, without activity, without work, in the most sober *pathos,* a stranger to all production, especially to creation. The poem falls to me, benediction, coming of (or from) the other. Rhythm but dissymmetry. There is never anything but some poem, before any *poiesis.* When, instead of "poetry," we said "poetic," we ought to have specified: "poematic." Most of all do not let the *hérisson* be led back into the circus or the menagerie of *poiesis*: nothing to be done (*poiein*), neither "pure poetry," nor pure rhetoric, nor *reine Sprache,* nor "setting-forth-of-truth-in-the-work." Just this contamination, and this crossroads, this accident here. This turn, the turning around of *this* catastrophe. The gift of the poem cites nothing, it has no title, its histrionics are over, it comes along without your expecting it, cutting short the breath, cutting all ties with discursive and especially literary poetry. In the very ashes of this genealogy. Not the phoenix, not the eagle, but the *hérisson,* very lowly, low down, close to the earth. Neither sublime, nor incorporeal, angelic, perhaps, and for a time.

You will call poem from now on a certain passion of the singular mark, the signature that repeats its dispersion, each time beyond the *logos*, a-human, barely domestic, not reappropriable into the family of the subject: a converted animal, rolled up in a ball, turned toward the other and toward itself, in sum, a thing – modest, discreet, close to the earth, the humility that you surname, thus transporting yourself in the name beyond a name, a catachrestic *hérisson*, its arrows held at the ready, when this ageless blind thing hears but does not see death coming.

The poem can roll itself up in a ball, but it is still in order to turn its pointed signs toward the outside. To be sure, it can reflect language or speak poetry, but it never relates back to itself, it never moves by itself like those machines, bringers of death. Its event always interrupts or derails absolute knowledge, autotelic being in proximity to itself. This "demon of the heart" never gathers itself together, rather it loses itself and gets off the track (delirium or mania), it exposes itself to chance, it would rather let itself be torn to pieces by what bears down upon it.

Without a subject: poem, perhaps there is some, and perhaps it *leaves itself*, but I never write any. A poem, I never sign(s) it. The other sign(s). The *I* is only at the coming of this desire: to learn by heart. Stretched, tendered forth to the point of subsuming its own support, thus without external support, without substance, without subject, absolute of writing in (it)self, the "by heart" lets itself be elected beyond the body, sex, mouth, and eyes; it erases the borders, slips through the hands, you can barely hear it, but it teaches us the heart. Filiation, token of election confided as legacy, it can attach itself to any word at all, to the thing, living or not, to the name of *hérisson*, for example, between life and death, at nightfall or at daybreak, distracted apocalypse, proper and common, public and secret.

– But the poem you are talking about, you are getting off the track, it has never been named thus, or so arbitrarily.

– You just said it. Which had to be demonstrated. Recall the question: "What is . . . ?" (*ti esti, was ist . . . , istoria, episteme, philosophia*). "What is . . . ?" laments the disappearance of the poem – another catastrophe. By announcing that which is just as it is, a question salutes the birth of prose.

Chapter 69
Thomas Yingling

Thomas Yingling (1950–92) was, at the time of his death, emerging as a leading figure in a generation of intellectuals and activists concerned with the relation between sexuality, culture, and power. Michel Foucault's analysis of the role of discourse in creating sexual identities informed Yingling's work as did Eve Kosofsky Sedgwick's argument that the definitions of homosexual and heterosexual identity were central to an understanding of western cultural modernity. In Yingling's case, the work of critical analysis was animated by the political activism of the gay liberation movement and the crisis provoked by AIDS. His study of Hart Crane, Hart Crane and the Homosexual Text, *was published in 1990.* Aids and the National Body, *a posthumous collection of essays, poems, and other writing, was published in 1997.*

The following excerpt on the homosexual lyric comes from chapter 4 of Yingling's book on Hart Crane. In it Yingling develops an analysis of Crane's distinctive modernity and addresses a critical objection to the obscurity of some of Crane's poems. For Yingling, Crane's modernity and his obscurity are different aspects of Crane's distinctive lyricism. Both, that is, are the result of Crane's "refiguration of mimesis." In Crane, lyric language does not express the inner states of the writer. The lyric "I" is not a source and focus of experience, but an unstable moment in the dialectic between self and culture. The lyric poem is a construction in language, rather than the expression of a feeling: what Crane himself described as the invention in the poem of "a single, new word, *never before spoken and impossible to actually enunciate, but self-evident as an active principle in the reader's consciousness."*

The Homosexual Lyric

...Crane's indebtedness to the discourses of modernism has been documented elsewhere, and includes subjects as well as styles: his interest in machinery and technology,

From *Hart Crane and the Homosexual Text* (Chicago: University of Chicago Press, 1990), pp. 115–25.

for instance, an interest shared by a large number of artists, photographers, and writers; his linguistic density, which is his verbal equivalent of montage or cubist effect – the attempt to create simultaneity of reference and perspective in one synchronic structure. But perhaps the most "modern" development in Crane's work was his refiguration of mimesis. Crane does not represent external objects or even internalized processes and meditations in the manner Abrams suggests is conventional for Romantic poetry and that we find as the first assumption of Eliot's poetry. It is true that the city or the machine might enter Crane's work, but they enter it as objects enter the visual field in Steiglitz's photographs, for instance, as structure, idea, abstraction. Crane differs from Williams, Eliot, and Moore (and most of the writers who have taught us to read modernist texts) in that his work is not dependent upon representation in the same way as theirs. I will not take the time here to quibble about Williams's or Stevens's many variations on the abstract and the concrete (such as *Kora in Hell*, which seems experimental and antimimetic in ways analogous to Crane's antimimetic work). We should perhaps think of Crane's work as having most in common with Constructivist or conceptual art, for it is often more presentational than representational in its effect, breaking the planes and contours of illusion and making one aware of the fact that it is written work – not an imitation of a "real" interior monologue nor a description of a "real" world but a piece of language that foregrounds its textuality. As Suzanne Clarke Doeren has suggested, Crane's poetry is one where "a language system takes over the subject," where there is no illusion that language functions transparently to signify the internal state of mind of a speaker or writer. Crane's is perhaps the first lyric poetry in English (and perhaps the only poetry in English until Charles Olson's or John Ashbery's) that is designed to be read as a constructed verbal artifact rather than as mimetic of any natural discourse. The lyric focus in Crane seems, finally, to be neither the minimal unit of the image, as in Imagist work, nor the maximal unit of the poem conceived as organic whole, as in Romantic lyrics or dramatic monologues that trace psychologized themes. Lyricality in Crane is that point where language breaks its transparency and forces the reader to authorize his relation to it, and for Crane this characteristically occurs on intermediate levels of meaning: in syntax and semantics. Doeren writes that "Crane's poems seem to come into existence at the point where . . . a subject becomes some other form of language: a verb, an object, a preposition," and it is precisely in this use of language as a thick, palpable medium for construction that Crane's texts take their place beside other modernist experiments with aesthetic media.

The standard reading of Crane's deviation from poetic norms draws on prose statements such as the following. . . . "It is as though a poem gave the reader as he left it a single, new *word*, never before spoken and impossible to actually enunciate, but self-evident as an active principle in the reader's consciousness henceforward." Crane's poems are explicitly tied to this search for the "new word," for what he terms in "The Wine Menagerie" "new anatomies" of the "new thresholds" on which humanity stands. But it is important to see that if Crane's poems are initiatory and almost literally liminal, they are not unconstructed moments. Just as the silences of homosexuality are not unstructured but are a set of conditions that mark the relation of homosexuality to other cultural practices, the antistructural quality of Crane's difficult poems nevertheless maps a set of differential relations for the production of meaning. Crane's characteristic poems seem interested neither in a literally transcribed homosexual reality nor in an imaginary realm completely interiorized and private (the assumption behind dismissals by Moore and others that the poems were no doubt meaningful but too obscure to be read); rather, Crane's most characteristic texts are interested in linguistic meaning and subjectivity as they occur through the difficulty of textuality.

"Chaplinesque" (1921) is an interim text that provides useful contrast to the early homosexual poems discussed above and the difficult, prophetic poems of 1923–26 that come after it. It seems to have been particularly pleasing to Crane, and he was confounded by his friends' confused responses to it. Stylistically it is a step toward the dense semiosis that attends Crane's full development; thematically it is a rather sentimental and even maudlin poem that suggests the poignancy of innocence in a world that crushes it (the Chaplin thematic). On its surface, the poem would appear to have nothing to do with homosexuality, but it marks the beginning of Crane's disintegration of the speaking subject (although that subject appears here as "we"), and it is on this point of pronominal identification that we can begin to see the discursive outcomes of Crane's poetic response to homosexuality. The poem opens:

> We make our meek adjustments,
> Contented with such random consolations
> As the wind deposits
> In slithered and too ample pockets.

So much depends in this case not on chickens, rain, and wheelbarrows, but on who steps in to define and fill the vacuum of that "we." Who makes meek adjustment to the world? Who, later in the poem, will defy the law and "Dally the doom of that inevitable thumb / That slowly chafes its puckered index toward us"? Who "can still love the world, who find / A famished kitten on the step, and know / Recesses for it from the fury of the street"? For whom does Chaplin speak? For whom does the poem speak?

In discussing this poem, R. W. B. Lewis acknowledges that the text is (in its own words) "evasive," but Lewis does not imagine that one of the things evaded here is a more direct address to the social condition of the homosexual subject. This is not to suggest that "Chaplinesque" is intentionally "about" that subject but is, rather, to suggest that one of the strongest referents of subjectivity for Crane in 1921 was his experience as a homosexual – that the "we" of "Chaplinesque" is constructed in sight of the practice of homosexuality, its alienations and consequent, compensatory nostalgias. The poem is, that is, *and perhaps despite its intentions,* an allegory of homosexual desire and its articulation within the "American restrictions" of the Midwest ca. 1921. The next to last stanza tries to find virtue in the meek adjustment and "smirk" or "dull squint" of "innocence" and "surprise" with which this subject meets the "inevitable thumb" of the law (patriarchal repressions), and it suggests that a subjectivity grounded in desire always exceeds those social mechanisms and technologies that seek to control or euphemize it – the heart lives on:

And yet these fine collapses are not lies
More than the pirouettes of any pliant cane;
Our obsequies are, in a way, no enterprise.
We can evade you, and all else but the heart:
What blame to us if the heart live on.

The "fine collapses" of obsequy, euphemism, and poetry are not lies, Crane claims, and he locates the authority for their "truth" in the heart – signifying here both a center of consciousness and the center of desire. It is social pressure ("enterprise" picks up here on a whole discourse of antimaterialist writing in the period) which forces the lie: the "victim" of that pressure remains blameless in his own heart.

Crane has not by any means made a full transition into the advanced poetry of a decentered subjectivity in "Chaplinesque." The poem ends with a rather trite assertion of transformation that seems a restatement of Emerson's claim that he was everywhere defeated yet born to victory:

The game enforces smirks; but we have seen
The moon in lonely alleys make
A grail of laughter of an empty ash can,
And through all sound of gaiety and quest
Have heard a kitten in the wilderness.

In some sense the preposterousness of the final image marks a limit to Crane's naturalized Romanticism (how far from "The Tyger!"); two years later, when composing "Possessions," his rhetoric of transformation will be truly apocalyptic. But the closure marked here is also part of the poem's homosexual textuality, for the homosexual's heart needs to be defended as blameless, and the reality of its consolations asserted: loneliness in cruisey alleyways can become laughter; a genuine tenderness can be located amid the hubbub "of gaiety and quest." The tenor of this final stanza is clearly of a piece with the more optimistic moments in Crane's letters from Cleveland, and it provides in its reconstruction of a homosexual "we" something Crane felt sorely lacking at this time: a community in which he could discuss the contours of his existence, the "fine collapses" of his life, as if they were not inherently illegitimate as subjects for poetry.

Crane's investigation of homosexuality as cognate to the textual indeterminacy of subjectivity is nowhere as openly displayed as in the 1923 poem "Possessions." Of those poems written in this period, "Possessions" is the one that most makes a critical consideration of its homosexual referents unavoidable. Robert Martin has called it "the first poem of the modern urban homosexual in search of sex, his hesitations the result of fear and self-oppression." But it is important to our understanding of both Crane and his construction of homosexuality as a possibility and an impossibility of meaning to see that "Possessions" does not dramatize that search in a straightforward fashion. It does not present an individual confronting or ruminating on this as a psychic or social problem. "Possessions" employs the first-person pronoun, and there is some attempt to locate that person within a landscape that produces him as meaningful, but it is not by any means a dramatic monologue. Crane employs the

"I" here not so much to relate an individual's experience as to provide a field for those emotional and intellectual conflicts that do battle through him. Thus, Martin's claim that this is "the first poem of the modern urban homosexual in search of sex" is only partially correct. The problematic nature of the search for sex is only part of the poem's concern, and this is how Crane's text differs from Whitman's *Calamus*, for instance, or from a John Ashbery poem about cruising, "The Ongoing Story," both of which see homosexuality as transparent to the individual and not as a system in which the individual's meaning and desire are already written for him. In "City of Orgies," for instance, Whitman claims it is the "frequent and swift flash of eyes offering me love" that "repay me," and while there are poems in *Calamus* such as "Of the Terrible Doubt of Appearances" and "Earth, My Likeness" that suggest some difficulty in the expression of homosexual desire, Whitman's more typical texts on homosexuality locate it internal to the subject and transparent to his real self. Ashbery's "The Ongoing Story," which is not perhaps representative of his most skeptical interrogations of identity, locates the act of cruising as one stable field in a life otherwise uninterpretable and unstable: "It's as though I'd been left with the empty street / A few seconds after the bus pulled out." Personal and poetic closure are achieved in the following:

> you,
> In your deliberate distinctness, whom I love and gladly
> Agree to walk into the night with,
> Your realness is real to me though I would never take any of it
> Just to see how it grows. A knowledge that people live close by is,
> I think, enough. And even if only first names are ever exchanged
> The people who own them seem rock-true and marvelously self-sufficient.[1]

In the context of the poem – and in the context of Ashbery's entire oeuvre – there is perhaps some irony in this comfort which defines reality as the realness of others. Certainly the marvelous self-sufficiency of others offered at the close of the poem is proven to be an illusion by the knowledge elsewhere evident in it that one's own self-sufficiency is a fiction. But the poem does not destabilize the reading subject as does Crane's "Possessions." Crane's investigation of homosexuality, which occurs historically somewhere between the mystical naïveté of Whitman discovering the homoeroticism that is identical to his "self" and the inside joke of Ashbery's New York, where everything – including homosexuality – has always been known all along, is settled on a historical threshold where desire is no longer a secret excitement securely anchored within a Romantic self but is not yet a cultural cliché enabling only parody. "Possessions" presents homosexuality as a text but it understands the subject as lost within that text.

A closer inspection of the poem suggests that what is rejected from the outset in "Possessions" is less the practice of homosexuality than the constricting representations of it available to the homosexual and to the homosexual poet. In an almost polemical fashion, "Possessions" rejects the rhetorical construction of homosexuality as a "fixed stone of lust" and replaces it at the poem's close with a more idealized vision of "bright stones wherein our smiling plays." The poem is an attempt to depict homosexual existence as more than a "Record of rage and partial appetites," this last phrase nicely balanced to suggest that desire is both determined (one always favors or is partial to something) and fragmentary (desire is also partial and never whole; it never makes one whole, especially if it is taboo). But if homosexuality inscribes one as the field of rage and partial appetite, dividing the subject from proper knowledge of himself in his possession of sexual object after sexual object, the poem insists that this is preparatory to an "inclusive" moment when a "pure possession . . . /Whose heart is fire" will – as in the golden halo effect of Crane's letters – transform possessor and possessed into a single being.

A diachronic reading of the poem does not neatly display what I have here suggested is the poem's impact; the poem seems alternately to come into and go out of focus, to hesitate, as Martin suggests, and part of that hesitation or indeterminacy is due to its skewed syntax. If Crane claimed this text to be an example of how he "work[ed] hard for a more perfect lucidity," it is not immediately possible to grant that this poem exemplifies that work. Although the poem is brief and its major outlines are clear, there is considerable obscurity in specific passages and in the relation of details to the larger structure. Without intending it, Robert Combs suggests that the poem is an allegory of homosexual desire: "The difficulty of this poem lies chiefly in the way Crane delays interpretational clues which serve gradually to orient the reader. . . . 'Trust,' 'rain,' and 'key' in the first stanza are like elements in a mysterious allegory that seem to need interpretation by the last word 'lust'." It would seem to be Crane's strategy to keep syntactic relations, as homosexual desire itself remains, indeterminate in the opening of the poem. We can see only textual units, possible events, attitudes, and locations that exist in juxtaposition but without any continuity or englobing frame of reference. It is a world of contiguous and accidental relations:

> Witness now this trust! The rain
> That steals softly direction
> And the key, ready to hand – sifting
> One moment in sacrifice (the direst)
> Through a thousand nights the flesh
> Assaults outright for bolts that linger
> Hidden, – O undirected as the sky
> That through its black foam has no eyes
> For this fixed stone of lust. . . .

We see here only an act of implied entry; "the key, ready to hand," is a phallic object employed to cross some threshold, but that threshold remains undefined (although this act of unlocking certainly bristles with sexual innuendoes and is linked figuratively to the erotic "bolts that linger / Hidden"). The desire in this opening is overwhelming in its sequential duration ("a thousand nights") and in the intensity of its passion ("the flesh / Assaults outright"), and it occurs under a vacuous yet menacing sky that certainly draws its significance from religious injunctions that traditionally have "[had] no eyes" for homosexuality. If one accepts the pun on "eyes," this "black foam" of heaven at once names and negates homosexual identity, it robs one of one's "I," and its rain (reign) "steals softly direction" until one does not know which way one is going. This moment, "sift[ed]" from a thousand, occurs within the context of cosmic alienation, and one of its meanings as a "moment in sacrifice" would appear to be that the homosexual sacrifices himself on a "fixed stone", a pagan altar of lust.

If the first stanza articulates homosexuality as a broken syntax, the second stanza asks the reader to contemplate the magnitude of such displaced meaning when it is cast across the course of a lifetime (signified here as the accumulation of "an hour").

> Accumulate such moments to an hour:
> Account the total of this trembling tabulation.
> I know the screen, the distant flying taps
> And stabbing medley that sways –
> And the mercy, feminine, that stays
> As though prepared.

There is in this stanza little referential clarity; although it is possible to say that something in the last four lines seems to assuage the emptiness of the "trembling tabulation," it is not possible to say what exactly that is. It is a "screen," "distant flying taps," a "stabbing medley that sways," and "mercy, feminine, that stays / As though prepared." We see in the vocabulary of distance a vague outline perhaps of longing or romance, in the stabbing medley that sways a sense perhaps of poignancy and seduction. And if mercy is feminine, that suggestion is perhaps less surprising than its appearance here, an appearance that makes the alienation of the first stanza even more overtly masculine in retrospect. How that mercy stays and for what or how it is prepared seem indecipherable; "stays" can mean both "remains" and "supports," and "prepared" could mean, to follow out the religious imagery of the preceding stanza, "pre-ordained," prepared from before. In any case, this second stanza suggests alternatives to the opening of the poem: intersubjectivity and mercy are presented as being "real" qualities of homosexuality meant to counter its representation as nothing more than predatory lust.

The third stanza accepts the heavy burden of interpretation in the phrases "fixed stone of lust" and "take up the stone." But it does so without speech, "As quiet as you can make a man," and assigns that burden to an individual "Wounded by apprehensions out of speech."

> And I, entering, take up the stone
> As quiet as you can make a man...
> In Bleecker Street, still trenchant in a void,
> Wounded by apprehensions out of speech,
> I hold it up against a disk of light –
> I turning, turning on smoked forking spires,
> The city's stubborn lives, desires.

The difficult, unspeakable quality of homosexuality stands clearly behind this construction. Nevertheless, the poet "hold[s] ... up against a disk of light" this stone that represents the "city's stubborn lives, desires." If the "turning, turning on smoked forking spires" seems to suggest a demonic skewering appropriate to Bosch's *Garden of Earthly Delights* (and thus to be a continuation of the vocabulary of punishment and wounding that surrounds homosexuality), we need to see as well that this refers to the poet's textual production. The "forking spires" (both phallic and religious aspirations) are the double-pronged instrument of writing he uses to hold this topic up for inspection. Crane's "General Aims and Theories," which postdates this poem by two years but is nonetheless relevant to this text, may serve as a gloss on how Crane conceives the poet's civic function:

> It seems to me that a poet will accidentally define his time well enough simply by reacting honestly and to the full extent of his sensibilities to the states of passion, experience, and rumination that fate forces on him, first hand. He must, of course, have a sufficiently universal basis of experience to make his imagination selective and valuable. His picture of the "period," then, will simply be a by-product of his curiosity and the relation of his experience to a postulated "eternity."

What we see in this image of the stone of lust held up to the light makes a claim for the poet's relevance similar to that offered in "General Aims and Theories": "Possessions" examines homosexuality (the "stubborn lives, desires" of the city that are at stake here as the "passion" and "experience" fate forced on Crane) against the background of "a postulated 'eternity'" in order to define it for this time. No longer an unshakable paradigm or "fixed stone" of lust, homosexuality begins here to be figured contiguously – in the syntagmatic placing of one term against another. Thus, Crane reverses not only the meaning of homosexuality as a "fixed stone of lust" but (perhaps more significantly) the location of meaning in the fixity of metaphor and paradigm, that possibility of unshakable meaning out of which the poem's initial sense of alienation arose.

The opening lines of the last stanza quite clearly locate the dilemma of homosexuality (on the "horns" of which one is tossed) within a problematic of language and representation.

> Tossed on these horns, who bleeding dies,
> Lacks all but piteous admissions to be spilt
> Upon the page whose blind sum finally burns
> Record of rage and partial appetites.
> The pure possession, the inclusive cloud
> Whose heart is fire shall come, – the white wind rase
> All but bright stones wherein our smiling plays.

If homosexuality as a "fixed stone of lust" is traditionally figured as a wound or lack (both of which tropes appear in the poem), what it seems most crucially to lack are "piteous admissions . . . split/Upon the page." Although these admissions are "piteous," and the homosexual still cloaked in the rhetoric of guilt, more open textual representations would allow some challenge to negative paradigms of the private and public implications of the homosexual life. Such representations, when themselves tabulated, would (unlike the trembling moments at the beginning of the poem) "finally [burn]" the "Record of rage and partial appetites" that are the legacy of the paradigm of lust. This image of burning transforms the demonic language of the text; the "pure possession" or "inclusive cloud / Whose heart is fire shall come" and possess or repossess the now dispossessed homosexual man. The figure of the "bright stones wherein our smiling plays" also reverses the punishing god (and the altar of sacrifice) from the opening stanza and replaces it with a vision that can only be called, according to the poem's terms, "feminine." In the poem's final lines we see on a cosmic scale the "mercy, feminine, that stays / As though prepared" that has been the homosexual's internalized source of comfort and trust up to this point, that longed-for inclusive cloud that sanctions homosexual desire. What "Possessions" finds in "trust" is neither transcendence of the body nor foreclosure of homosexual desire but their positive integration into myth. What the poem seeks is a visionary love that can accommodate the homosexual and no longer isolate him as an example of lust.

Written two years after "Possessions," "Passage" presents a narrative of poetic coming to power. The poem does not explicitly examine the discursive problems of homosexuality, but in tracing a problematic development or rite of passage into self-awareness, "Passage" is an instance of homosexual autobiography. It is perhaps the most well made of Crane's shorter, visionary lyrics, and its success is due in part to the fact that it brackets homosexuality as a textual problem and therefore avoids the difficulties of articulation seen in "Possessions" or "Recitative." But in its revision of two Whitman texts, "Passage to India" and "Out of the Cradle Endlessly Rocking," it engages the question of homosexual autobiography, depicting the self as literally textual – a book – alienated from any transcendental, Emersonian illusion of transparency, self-reliance, or fructifying presence. The poem trades on metaphors familiar to readers of modern American poetry from Stevens's "The Idea of Order at Key West" (which also refigures "Out of the Cradle"), but here the speaker himself "hear[s] the sea" and attempts to present to the reader knowledge of an unmediated vision. "Passage" is "The Idea of Order" without the woman by the sea or the inescapable mediation that provides the logic of epistemology in Stevens.

But if the poem is built upon a desire for self-discovery and passage into mature and unmediated power, its promise of "an improved infancy" cannot be redeemed. In Emersonian terms, the self succumbs to Necessity – for Crane, this has to do with the inescapable otherness of the "I." "Passage" unwrites a naive Romantic subjectivity in its rejection of the trope of recovered memory and writes instead a subject divided from himself, forced to thieve his life in a writing where textuality and difference intervene. Unlike the cognitive ego privileged by memorial Romantic texts such as Wordsworth's, the subject in "Passage" does not recover an originary self-knowledge and -authorization but is actually annihilated by his "too well-known biography." The speechlessness etymologically implied in the "improved infancy" that inaugurates the poet's quest is exposed in the end as an impossibility; man is condemned to speech, to a written life where desire is not transparent to its object but is opaque and mediated even when the object of desire is self-knowledge....

Editor's Note

1 This quotation comes from John Ashbery's poem, *A Wave* (New York: Viking Press, 1984).

Chapter 70
Marjorie Perloff

Marjorie Perloff (1931–) has developed, through her detailed readings of a wide range of American and European experimental poets, an argument for the continuing vitality and possibility of poetry as an avant-garde art. From one perspective her criticism exemplifies a postmodern poetics. She has distanced herself from the early modernist poets, Yeats and Pound amongst them, who have found an authority for their poetry in an appeal to ideas of the natural (as in Pound's dictum, "the natural object is always the adequate symbol"), and has developed an alternative poetics based on a notion of "radical artifice." Poetic artifice works on the language forms that constantly emerge in a culture, displacing or estranging them from their customary uses. Poems of radical artifice create constructions in language that in turn invite constructive acts from their readers, but they do not imagine that the work of the poetry is to return language to its natural or original state. However, attaching the label "postmodern" to Perloff's writing can be misleading. She has a marked skepticism towards postmodernism as a global cultural theory of the kind developed by Fredric Jameson in the United States or Jean-François Lyotard in France. Hers is a version of postmodernism dedicated to ideals of artistic experiment. Her most recent work suggests she has grown tired of the label altogether, preferring to develop an argument for a poetics of the twenty-first century that will draw its inspiration from the early twentieth-century work of avant-garde poets such as Velimir Khlebnikov.

Some of these issues surface in the following extracts from the first chapter of her book, Radical Artifice, *first published in 1991. Perloff starts with a question about the impact of computer technology on the art of poetry. Noting that a standard response is to oppose poetry to technologies of this kind, she goes on to explore a different possibility, one that is exemplified in a poem/happening of John Cage's called* Lecture on the Weather. *Perloff's account of modern poetry assumes that certain poetic styles or schools become obsolete or exhausted. A changing culture requires new forms. If she rejects Pound's nostalgia for the "natural object" she would probably accept another of Pound's requirements, that poetry should "make it new."*

Avant-Garde or Endgame?

There is constant surprise at the new tricks language plays on us when we get into a new field.

Wittgenstein, *Lectures and Conversations* (1938)

I

. . . The impact of electronic technology on our lives is now the object of intense study, but what remains obscure is the role, if any, this technology has in shaping the ostensibly private language of poetry. Current thinking is sharply divided on this question but few of the answers are optimistic. Perhaps the most common response to what has been called the digital revolution has been simple rejection, the will, we might say, *not to change*, no matter how "different" the world out there seems to be. In recent years, for example, a movement has emerged that calls itself the New Formalism, or sometimes the New Narrative or Expansive poetry. The main thrust of New Formalist poetics, as Frederick Feirstein and Frederick Turner explain in their Introduction to a collection of New Formalist manifestos, is to move "beyond the short free verse autobiographical lyric" of the present, returning poetry to meter (which is almost invariably equated with iambic pentameter) and narrative. The "successful" narrative poem, writes Robert McDowell, should have "a beginning, a middle, and an end," its time frame should be "compressed," its characters should be "memorable" in being "consistent" ("an act must logically follow acts preceding it"), its locale specific and "identifiable," and its subject "compelling." E. A. Robinson, Robert Frost, Robinson Jeffers – these are New Formalist heroes, with the lofty Englit tradition (Milton to Wordsworth and Arnold) squarely behind these "robinets."

No doubt, the New Formalists do have a genuine grievance against the dominant lyric mode of the seventies and eighties, with its repetitive dwelling on delicate insight and "sensitive" response, its nostalgia for the "natural," and its excessive reliance on simulated speech and breath pause as determinants of line breaks and verse structure. But the real issue is not whether to write in free verse or iambic pentameter, any more than it is whether to foreground the lyric self or to have that self tell a "compelling" story. More properly put, the question would be: given the particular options (and nonoptions) of writing at the turn of the twenty-first century, what significant role can poetic language play? "The whole purpose of a lyric poem," writes Frederick Feirstein, "is to sing: to sing in a natural, not puffed up, way so that one can reach an audience." But what is a "natural" as opposed to a "puffed up" way of singing that will reach "an audience" accustomed to VCRs, FAX machines, Walkmans, laser printers, cellular phones, answering machines, computer games, and video terminals? And why should lyric be "natural" rather than artificial? Did Donne's

From *Radical Artifice* (Chicago: University of Chicago Press, 1991), pp. 1, 2–3, 4–5, 14–28.

lyric "sing" in a natural way? Or Pope's? What, for that matter, is natural about the heroic couplet or the Spenserian stanza? Or even Dickinson's four-line hymn stanza – is that natural?

...But this is not to say that the New Formalist critique of free verse is merely frivolous. What it tells us...is that the dominant modes of mid-century seem to be played out. Naked Poetry, Confessional Poetry, Open Form, Projective Verse – what could sound, in 1990, more tired? And the same holds true for comparable developments in the other arts: the happening, the body sculpture, the "live" performance piece in the white-walled art gallery, the *Learning from Las Vegas* slot-machine decor, and "ugly is beautiful" tract house which is really custom-built and costs millions – these paradoxically seem to belong to a time now more remote than the avant-garde of the 1910s and 1920s or, for that matter, more remote than the fin-de-siècle Vienna of Wittgenstein. What is it that has happened and where are we going? And what does our avant-garde – if that word still has meaning – look like?

I say "if" because the news that the avant-garde is dead is now widely circulated. In his influential *Theory of the Avant-Garde* (German edition, 1974; English translation, 1984), Peter Bürger defines the avant-garde as that specific movement in the early twentieth century which sought, not to develop, as had been the case in Impressionism or Cubism or Fauvism, a particular style, nor to attack prior schools of art, but to call into question the very role of "art" as an institution in a bourgeois society. Whereas medieval and Renaissance art, so the argument goes, was subject to "collective performance" and "collective reception," the bourgeois art of the post-Enlightenment was largely produced by isolated individuals for other isolated individuals. Divorced from the "praxis of life," it became increasingly autonomous and elitist, culminating in the Aestheticism of the late nineteenth century. It is this autonomy, this institutionalization of capitalist art as "unassociated with the life praxis of men [*sic*]" that Dada and Surrealism challenged....

But what about "the end of philosophy"? The "end of criticism"? Wouldn't these endgames have to follow "the end of art"? In conversation with John Cage in 1988, I posed the question: "What do you think of the current view that innovation is no longer possible, that indeed the avant-garde is dead?" Cage reflected a minute and said with a smile, "Even them?" A similar point was made by Marcel Broodthaers in a gallery publication:

> The aim of all art is commercial.
> My aim is equally commercial.
> The aim of criticism is just as commercial.
> Guardian of myself and of others,
> I do not know truly who to kick.

Touché. Criticism is not somewhere outside and beyond the "great arc of disintegration and decay" within which we live: if art undergoes the commodification of "late capitalism," so, inevitably, does critical theory. Or perhaps, as I prefer to think, the parameters can be redefined. In a recent essay on postmodernism for the *Socialist Review*, Charles Bernstein writes:

> *We can act*: we are not trapped in the postmodern condition if we are willing to differentiate between works of art that suggest new ways of conceiving of our present world and those that seek rather to debunk any possibilities for meaning. To do this, one has to be able to distinguish between, on the one hand, a fragmentation that attempts to valorize the concept of a free-floating signifier unbounded to social significance… and, on the other, a fragmentation that reflects a conception of meaning as prevented by conventional narration and so uses disjunction as a method of tapping into other possibilities available within language. Failure to make such distinctions is similar to failing to distinguish between youth gangs, pacifist anarchists, Weatherpeople, anti-Sandinista contras, Salvadoran guerrillas, Islamic terrorists, or US state terrorists. Perhaps all of these groups are responding to the "same" stage of multi-national capitalism. But the crucial point is that the responses cannot be understood as the same, unified as various interrelated "symptoms" of late capitalism. Nor are the "dominant" practices the exemplary ones that tell the "whole" story.

Like Cage's and Broodthaers's, Bernstein's is a refusal, so to speak, on the part of the *maker* of art to provide its receptor with so many exempla of a theory already in place. It is also a refusal to make easy generalizations: to take just one example, our penchant for the comparison of "profitable 'postmodern' artworld commodities to what were, in their own time, obscure and noncommercial 'modern' artworks," the comparison serving mainly to point up the telling symptoms of contemporary decline and fall. Indeed, perhaps it would be more useful to work the other way around and to consider, more closely than we usually do, what really happens on the video screen, at the computer terminal, or in the advertising media, and then to see how poetic or art discourse positions itself vis-à-vis these powerful new environments.…

II

Information theory provides us with a starting point. In a series of volumes beginning with *Hermes* (1968), for example, Michel Serres has studied the meaning and function of *noise*, the word being defined as "the set of those phenomena of interference that become obstacles to communication." "Obstacles" may be a misleading word here, Serres's point being that *noise* is not only incidental but *essential* to communication, whether at the level of writing (e.g., "waverings in the graphic forms, failures in the drawing, spelling errors, and so on"), of speech ("stammerings, mispronunciations, regional accents, dysphonias, and cacophonies"), or of the technical means of communciation ("background noise, jamming, static, cut-offs, hysteresis, various interruptions").

If, for example, a letter is written in careless or illegible script, there is interference in the reading process, which is to say that noise slows down communication. "The cacographer and the epigraphist" exchange roles, struggling as they do with noise as the common enemy: "*To hold a dialogue is to suppose a third man and to seek to exclude him.*" This third man, says Serres, is the *demon*, the "prosopopeia of noise." Demon, because, with the exception of mathematics, "the kingdom of quasi-perfect communication," the "third man" is never successfully excluded. Indeed, in order for the "pure" discourse of mathematics to be possible, one must shut out the entire empiricist domain; "one must close one's eyes and cover one's ears to the song and the beauty of the sirens."

Noise as unanticipated excess, as sirens' song – the phenomenon has always, of course, been with us. But given the complex electronic modes of communication that now exist, the possibility increases that what is received differs from what was sent. The garbled or gratuitous FAX message is an obvious example.... In this sense, what the Russian Futurists called *ostranenie* ("making strange") increasingly becomes a function of the actual dissemination of the message, its sender not necessarily being equivalent to its original producer and its receiver hence playing a greatly enlarged role in the processing of the text.

This brings us to a consideration of the computer terminal itself. In an important recent essay, Richard A. Lanham points out that the use of the personal computer and its electronic display "is forcing a radical realignment of the alphabetic and graphic components of ordinary textual communication." In the conventional printed book, after all, the written surface is, so Lanham reminds us, "not to be read aesthetically; that would only interfere with purely literate transparency." On the contrary, a page of print should stand to the thought conveyed "as a fine crystal goblet stands to the wine it contains." Such "unintermediated thought," such "unselfconscious transparency" has become, says Lanham, "a stylistic, one might almost say a cultural, ideal for Western civilization. The best style is the style not noticed; the best manners the most unobtrusive."

Enter pixeled ("pixels" are "picture elements," the dots which electronically paint the letters onto the computer screen) print, which calls the basic stylistic decorum of the "transparent" page into question. "Electronic typography is both creator-controlled and reader-controlled." I can, for example (especially with the MacIntosh) use a wide variety of Roman and Greek styles, redesign the shapes of the letters, make them brighter or dimmer, alter the alphabetic-graphic ratio of conventional literacy, alter the "normal" figure-ground relationships, and so on – all by touching a key. I can "transform" what is usually thought of as prose into what is usually thought of as poetry, simply by hitting the "indent" key and lineating the text. I can illuminate the text in various ways, use different colors, reformat it in italics or capitals, and so on. The textual surface has, in other words, become what Lanham calls "permanently bistable":

> We are always looking first AT [the text] and then THROUGH it, and this oscillation creates a different implied ideal of decorum, both stylistic and behavioral. Look THROUGH a text and you are in the familiar world of the Newtonian Interlude, where facts were facts, the world just "out there," folks sincere central selves, and the best writing style dropped from the writer as "simply and directly as a stone falls to the ground," just as Thoreau counseled. Look AT a text, however, and we have deconstructed the Newtonian world into Pirandello's and yearn to "act naturally." We have always had ways of triggering this oscillation, but the old ways – printing prose consecutively and verse not, layering figures of sound and arrangement on the stylistic surface until it squeaked – were clumsy, slow, unchangeable, and above all author-controlled.... The difference is profound.... You return, by electronic ambages, to that Renaissance *sprezzatura* of rehearsed spontaneity which Newtonian science so unceremoniously set aside.

Lanham's analysis seems to me an excellent antidote to the more abstract – and generally gloomy – explanations of the fate of "literature" under "late" or "multinational" capitalism, or within "consumer culture." For one thing, it refuses to grant large-scale explanatory force to designations that, as even Fredric Jameson has recently remarked with respect to his own use of the term "late capitalism," have become identified "as leftist logo[s] which [are] ideologically and politically booby-trapped." For another, if we take the longer historical view and consider such earlier nontransparent page design as that of the medieval scribe, who inevitably elaborated on his alphabet design in the interest of visual beauty, we can see that, for better or worse, we are now at a moment when transparency – the typography that is "as transparent as a crystal goblet" – can once again give way to what the Russian Futurists called "the word as such" (*slovo kak takovoe*).

Not only does the boundary between "verse" and "prose" break down but also the boundary between "creator" and "critic." For as I read X's text on the computer screen, I can, again with the flick of a finger, change it in any number of ways, reformat it to my liking, "improve it." Indeed, in the "interactive fiction" being written for the computer, the reader can choose the story's outcome, according to a series of possible moves. And in digitalized music programs, the distinction between time and space breaks down, the "composer" using the "Music Mouse" to make geometric motions that are then translated, by the computer, into sounds.

Such "digital equivalency," Lanham believes, "means that we can no longer pursue literary study by itself: the other arts will form part of literary study in an essential way." Indeed, "the personal computer itself constitutes the ultimate postmodern work of art. It introduces and focuses all the rhetorical themes advanced by the arts from Futurism onward.... The interactive audience which outrageous Futurist evenings forced upon Victorian conventions of passive silence finds its perfect fulfillment in the personal computer's radical enfranchisement of the perceiver. Cage's games of chance and Oldenburg's experiments in visual scaling become everyday routines in home computer graphics."

Such enthusiastic claims for the computer will strike many of us as excessively McLuhanesque, as too optimistic and uncritical of the culture within which and on which such technology operates. In what sense, after all, can such acquired behavior as computer formatting, largely conditioned as it is by the "hidden persuaders" of our culture, be considered "art"? What about the binary choices computer screen-prompts impose on the writer-reader, the necessity of always choosing between "yes" or "no," "up" or "down"? And, most disturbing, what about the gap between computer operation (a skill to be learned) and the internal computer system, which remains essentially inaccessible to the user?... For the moment, however, I want to take up Lanham's very interesting suggestion that computer textuality transforms the way we *receive* as well as the way we create written texts and hence has important implications for the larger study of rhetoric.

Consider, for example, Lanham's discussion of *prose*, that little word taken for granted ever since Monsieur Jourdain was told (incorrectly, as it happens, since the short utterance units of speech are not its equivalent) that what he was speaking was prose. Lanham writes:

> So used are we to thinking black-and-white, continuous printed prose the norm of conceptual utterance, that it has taken a series of theoretical attacks and technological metamorphoses to make us see it for what it is: an act of extraordinary stylization, of remarkable, expressive self-denial. The lesson has been taught by theorists, from Marinetti to Burke and Derrida, and by personal computers which restore to the reader whole ranges of expressivity – graphics, fonts, typography, layout, color – which the prose stylist has abjured. Obviously these pressures will not *destroy* prose, but they may change its underlying decorum. And perhaps engender, at long last, a theory of prose style as radical artifice rather than native transparency.

This distinction between the prose of "radical artifice" and that of "native transparency" has been made by many of the poets I shall be discussing in subsequent chapters. Indeed, Lanham's proposals for a "returning rhetorical paideia" that might govern our study of electronic text, whether verbal, visual, or musical, are extremely useful in shifting attention away from content – the New Formalist prescription, say, that a poem tell a "good story," or the Foucaultian prescription that every narrative is a coded account of power struggle – to the larger formal and theoretical issues relating to poetry today. But since Lanham's concerns are avowedly pedagogical rather than more specifically aesthetic, some qualification may be in order.

The most cursory survey of contemporary poetics would show that, at least as far as what Charles Bernstein calls "official verse culture" is concerned, technology, whether computer technology or the video, audio, and print media, remains, quite simply, the enemy, the locus of commodification and reification against which a "genuine" poetic discourse must react. In part . . . the most interesting poetic and artistic compositions of our time do position themselves, consciously or unconsciously, against the languages of TV and advertising, but the dialectic between the two is highly mediated. It is by no means a case, as poets sometimes complain, of "competing" with television, of pitting the "authentic" individual self against an impersonal, exploitative other that commodifies the consciousness of the duped masses. For authenticity, as Jed Rasula has recently suggested, is itself a commodity, a product based on a now-specious "ideology of privacy" that adheres to the following principles:

> (1) it must demonstrate a restraint of the stimulations or aggressions that inhere in charged or intense language; (2) it must display fidelity to the poet's personal life; (3) this fidelity, this "being true to life" must affirm a certain sufficiency inherent in all of us: (4) it must be an innocuous artifact and in no way seek to challenge its status as private concern of a handful of consumers.

The myth of "private concern" (e.g., "let me tell you what happened to me yesterday") runs headlong, so Rasula suggests, into the reality of non-privacy in our world. "It's no longer a matter of 'meeting the world halfway,'" he writes; "there's no such thing as privacy – privacy has been deleted. Leisure time is now archaic. What is now called leisure or free time is, instead, a differently calibrated sort of duty, the zone of bricolage in which we cut and snip and sort and paste our attentions, so we become prosthetic supplements to the total-body effect of the media, the coherent and pervasive final report that drifts along just out the door." Which is to say, that "instead of producing objects for the subject, ours is a system that produces subjects for the object."

Most contemporary writing that currently passes by the name of "poetry" belongs in this category which Rasula wittily calls PSI, for "Poetry Systems Incorporated, a subsidiary to data management systems." The business of this particular corporation is to produce the specialty item known as "the self," and it is readily available in popular magazines and at chain bookstores, its "corporate newsletter" being the *New York Times Book Review.* The "reader" for "PSI product" is, as is normal for TV, a digit, "a statistical guarantor of the precise scale of another kind of beast known as 'the audience.'" To this PSI-product audience, the "poem" is a form of instant uplift. Read one now and again and you'll participate in a ritual of "sensitivity" and "self-awareness." It is the mechanism of the poetry reading on campuses and in "poetry centers" across the United States.

At the same time, we are witnessing a poetic more consonant with the reading-writing mechanism of the new electronic "page." Like Serres and Lanham, Rasula places his emphasis on the writer *as reader.* "Normal channels," he suggests, "are the media of compliance. They are the means by which the unknown audience consents to captivity by testing positive to a numeracy syndrome, agreeing to a certain effacement in order to personally 'typify' some statistical groundswell." But when the audience – the reader – refuses "captivity" and demands a textuality that cannot be absorbed into or accommodated by the Mediaspeak or image field of "normal" telediscourse or digital display, a new interaction is produced, returning us, in Lanham's words "from a closed poetic to an open rhetoric."

III

Let us see how this might work in practice. The dominant poetic of the American sixties, a poetic . . . of strenuous authenticity, the desire to present a self as natural, as organic, and as unmediated as possible, was likely to produce such "deep image" poems as the following by James Wright:

From a Bus Window in Central Ohio,
Just before a Thunder Shower

Cribs loaded with roughage huddle together
Before the north clouds.
The wind tiptoes between poplars.
The silver maple leaves squint
Toward the ground.
An old farmer, his scarlet face
Apologetic with whiskey, swings back a barn door
And calls a hundred black-and-white Holsteins
From the clover field.

Here the poem is conceived as an act of witnessing. The speaker-observer must capture the exact nuance of the moment, beginning with the long documentary title that tells us just where and when the recorded experience took place. A "Bus Window in Central

Ohio, Just before a Thunder Shower" – a changeless place, as it were, in the heart of the nation (buses have been around for a long time), and a natural occurrence. The poem's images, presented directly in a series of simple declarative present-tense sentences, graphically convey that moment of strange quiet that precedes a storm, the moment when the corn cribs seem to "huddle together," the wind to "tiptoe between poplars," and, in an especially vivid metaphor, the "silver maple leaves [to] squint / Toward the ground." It is also the moment when the old farmer, perfectly attuned as he is to the elements despite his habitual but "apologetic" drinking, knows that it is time to call in the cows.

Such short imagistic poems depend for their effect on what Robert Lowell called "the grace of accuracy," a quality Wright had in abundance. No word is wasted: the perceiver's eye moves from the ground to the sky and back again, capturing for the reader the precise *frisson* that precedes the Ohio thunderstorm. The observer himself remains outside the picture frame ("bus window"), a seemingly impassive observer, even as everything that is seen and felt is filtered through his consciousness, defining a moment of ominous waiting, a foreboding of pain yet to come. Even the sound features – the slow trochaic rhythm, stressed diphthongs, and the alliteration and assonance (e.g., "The *silv*er map*le lea*ves squ*int*") emphasizing the integrity of the line, which is unpunctuated by caesurae – contribute to the sense that we are witnessing a "calm before the storm."

"Perfect" as such small "deep image" poems are, they are also oddly unambitious.... their minimalism may be said to mask a certain fear – the fear, perhaps, of confronting more of "Central Ohio" than the phenomenology of impending thunderstorms, the reluctance, moreover, to relate nature to culture, to consider the implications of using what has become a fairly standard free-verse form (a set of short, irregular lines surrounded by white space) and a fixed subject position in a world that increasingly questions the validity of such conventions. In this respect, we might compare "From a Bus Window" to a poetic construct like John Cage's *Lecture on the Weather*, written more than a decade later for the Bicentennial of the United States and performed at irregular intervals since then.

In his headnote to "Preface to *Lecture on the Weather*" (the only text available in print), Cage explains that when the work was first commissioned by the Canadian Broadcasting Corporation, Richard Coulter suggested that it might be based on texts of Benjamin Franklin, but *Poor Richard's Almanac* did not strike Cage's fancy and he turned instead to his beloved Henry David Thoreau, specifically the *Essay on Civil Disobedience*, the *Journal*, and *Walden*.

In the Preface to the resulting *Lecture on the Weather*, Cage sketches in the background of the project:

> The first thing I thought of doing in relation to this work was to find an anthology of American aspirational thought and subject it to chance operations. I thought the resultant complex would help to change our present intellectual climate. I called up Dover and asked whether they published such an anthology. They didn't. I called a part of Columbia University concerned with American History and asked about aspirational thought. They knew nothing about it. I called the Information Desk of the New York Public Library at

> 42nd Street. The man who answered said: You may think I'm not serious but I am; if you're interested in aspiration, go to the Children's Library on 52nd Street. I did. I found that anthologies for children are written by adults: they are what adults think are good for children. The thickest one was edited by [Henry Steele] Commager (*Documents of American History*). It is a collection of legal judgments, presidential reports, congressional speeches. I began to realize that what is called balance between the branches of our government is not balance at all: all the branches of our government are occupied by lawyers.
>
> Of all professions the law is the least concerned with aspiration. It is concerned with precedent, not with discovery.

How to subvert this state of affairs, how to subordinate precedent to discovery, all the while paying homage to the qualities of American ingenuity, pragmatism, and good sense epitomized for Cage in the person of Thoreau – this is the problematic addressed in *Lecture on the Weather*, a media work that deconstructs the media, a "lecture" whose words cannot be heard, a choral composition whose "voices" are disembodied presences, a performance piece that anyone can perform but in which no one is in the spotlight.

To begin with, *Lecture on the Weather* is not a lecture at all, but an elaborate rule-generated collage-work:

> Subjecting Thoreau's writings to *I Ching* chance operations to obtain collage texts, I prepared parts for twelve speaker-vocalists (or -instrumentalists), stating my preference that they be American men who had become Canadian citizens. Along with these parts go recordings by Maryanne Amacher of breeze, rain, and finally thunder and in the last (thunder) section a film by Luis Frangella representing lightning by means of briefly projected negatives of Thoreau's drawings.

Here, as so often in his "production notes," Cage assumes a casual air that his actual work belies. For one thing, the agreed-upon time-length for the spoken parts is rigidly fixed ("at least 22′45″[5′ × 4′33″] and not more than 36′24″[8′ × 4′33″]") the numerical reference being, of course, to Cage's famous early prepared piano piece 4′33″. Again, the "entrance" of the taped sound events – breeze, rain, and thunder – is precisely timed, the breeze "to be faded in at the beginning," the rain "to be faded in after 11 or 12% of the total agreed-upon performance time-length has elapsed," and the thunder "to enter abruptly after 63 to 70%...has elapsed." Further directions indicate when the lights are to be lowered, when the "lightning" slides are to be projected, and inform the performers that the recording of thunder should "stop abruptly" before those of breeze and rain fade out, but that "this stop [should not] interrupt a thunderclap."

Thus, although the Thoreau texts themselves are chosen by chance operations, their actual collocation, together with sounds and visual images, is a strictly planned mathematical system. Since no single passage from Thoreau is repeated twice, and since each of the twelve text-sets must have the same length, the performance of the simultaneous reading is anything but random. The chance operation, in this context, is more properly understood as a form of constraint, a rule-generated process within which "weather conditions" occur.

Weather: "The condition of the atmosphere at a given place and time with respect to heat or cold, quantity of sunshine, presence or absence of rain, hail, thunder, fog, etc., violence or gentleness of the winds. Also the condition of the atmosphere regarded as subject to vicissitudes" (*OED*). Here is the key to Cage's composition, in which a strict rule-bound process is subjected to the "vicissitudes" of the "atmosphere at a given place and time." Specific events (whether the speaker-vocalists stand or sit and where they are located in relation to the audience, how or whether the audience is seated, whether the performance space is large or small, open or closed, etc.) inevitably differ from performance to performance....

Here, then, is a text peculiarly for the times. *Lecture on the Weather* is a verbal-visual-musical composition that relies on current technology for its execution. There is no complete written text, since the printed page cannot reproduce the simultaneous visual and sound features of the "lecture." The coordination of vocal elements, sound, and film image is achieved by elaborate computer calculations. Yet, so the "lecture" implies, the availability of such technology by no means implies that we are now slaves to automation and commodification, that we have come to the endgame of art. On the contrary, Cage is suggesting that even as the early New England settlers achieved a sense of community out of mutual deprivation, hardship, and want, two hundred years later, our own "deprivation" (the glut, for example, of "aspirational" writing as well as of media discourse) can be overcome, not by finding books in the library that will talk *about* community, but by finding ways to actually have it happen.

"An adequate theory of prose," Richard Lanham suggests, would reconceive prose style "as radical artifice rather than native transparency." That, too, is the paradox of *Lecture on the Weather*. Cage is too often misunderstood as the champion of the natural, the advocate of art as a "purposeless play" that is "simply a way of waking up to the very life we're living, which is so excellent once one gets one's mind and one's desires out of its way and lets it act of its own accord." And in the "Preface to *Lecture on the Weather*," Cage cites Thoreau as saying, "Music is continuous; only listening is intermittent."

What Cage means by such statements is that the art construct must consistently tap into "life," must use what really happens in the external world as its materials, and that, vice versa, "life" is only "lived" when we perceive it as form and structure. But nothing is less *transparent* than a composition like *Lecture on the Weather*, in which the resources of such various media as film, soundtrack, pictogram, musical instrument, and of various genres like lecture, poem, journal, and drama are integrated by means of what Lanham calls "radical artifice." Indeed, the Duchamp readymade, which has had a profound influence on Cage's work and which Peter Bürger takes to be a kind of end point of avant-garde art (the "provocation" produced by the claim that an "ordinary" urinal could be construed as a work of art "cannot be repeated indefinitely"), here finds its antithetical match. Let me try to explain.

If the readymade is an "ordinary" industrial object, the "lecture on the weather" is a fabricated, simulated natural event. If the readymade turns a useful object (urinal, bicycle wheel, snow shovel, bottle rack) into an impersonal work of art, the "lecture" on weather turns the simulated event into one that behaves like a real one, causing the audience to take shelter from the cruel elements. Finally, if the readymade was appropriate to its modernist moment, a witty critique of "high art" pieties and prejudices in the early twentieth century, works like *Lecture on the Weather* are nothing if not appropriate to our moment, calling into question as they do our preoccupation with the lecture format – not only university lecture, of course, but any "address" A makes to B and C, whether on radio or TV, whether formal political address or the promotion of a new cosmetic product.

Whatever lectures we give or we attend, after all, none of us are likely to think of them as dangerous; on the contrary, the lecture is regarded as a little island of safety in a world of crowding, assault, and the unfriendly elements, like the tiptoeing hiss of the wind "between poplars" in Wright's weather poem. Accordingly, Cage created a lecture that would assault us with frightening noises and images, that would make us wish we were merely driving in freeway traffic. We might call it a case of defamiliarization, but defamiliarization of a sort the Russian Formalists, who disseminated the concept, would be hard put to recognize, the object of a work like *Lecture on the Weather* being, not to make the stone stony, but to stage an "event" that can change our environment and how we respond to it.

Such simulation is, of course, a case of marked artifice. Whereas Modernist poetics was overwhelmingly committed, at least in theory, to the "natural look," whether at the level of speech (Yeats's "natural words in the natural order"), the level of image (Pound's "the natural object is always the adequate symbol"), or the level of verse form ("free" verse being judged for the better part of the century as somehow more "natural" than meter and stanzaic structure), we are now witnessing a return to *artifice*, but a "radical artifice," to use Lanham's phrase, characterized by its opposition, not only to "the language really spoken by men" but also to what is loosely called Formalist (whether New or Old) verse, with its elaborate poetic diction and self-conscious return to "established" forms and genres. Artifice, in this sense, is less a matter of ingenuity and manner, of elaboration and elegant subterfuge, than of the recognition that a poem or painting or performance text is a *made thing* – contrived, constructed, chosen – and that its reading is also a construction on the part of its audience. At its best, such construction empowers the audience by altering its perceptions of how things happen. Thus, even though a work like *Lecture on the Weather* is a collage of found texts – extracts from Thoreau, replicas of bird calls, recordings of thunder – its "weather" is charged with possibilities.

Chapter 71
Eavan Boland

Eavan Boland (1944–) is a poet, critic, and teacher whose work has shown a commitment to the possibilities of lyric form and voice at the same time as she has raised serious questions about the constraints imposed on the woman poet by tradition and ideology. From the time of her first book of poems, New Territory, *published in 1967, Boland's work has moved between domestic and political subjects. Her poems trace a personal quest to find what she has described as the "relation of the voice to the line" and, by doing so, dissolve "all the borrowed voices of my apprenticeship." But this personal quest has to encounter the complicated legacies of Irish history and tradition. Boland writes out of an acute awareness that women may have been the objects of Irish writing, but they have rarely been its authors. Finding a voice has thus involved a recognition of an absence in tradition as well as of its power to determine what the subjects and forms of poetry should be. Boland's recent work has included* An Origin Like Water: Collected Poems 1967–87, In A Time of Violence *(1994), and a book of prose,* Object Lessons, *published in 1995. She is a Professor of English and Director of the Creative Writing program at Stanford University.*

"The Woman Poet: Her Dilemma" is taken from Object Lessons. *In the following extract Boland sets out the different forces that stand between being a woman who writes poems and becoming a woman poet. Some of these are readily identifiable: the "Romantic Heresy" that sets limits on what is to count as poetic experience, and, from a very different perspective, the effects of feminist ideology in decreeing what is to count as appropriate feeling. But beyond these is something less palpable: a sense of incompatibility between being a woman and being a poet. Boland's experience tells her that these difficulties persist, but they are not insurmountable. Women can have a "destiny in the form" of poetry.*

The Woman Poet: Her Dilemma

I

I believe that the woman poet today inherits a dilemma. That she does so inevitably, no matter what cause she espouses and whatever ideology she advocates or shuns. That when she sits down to work, when she moves away from her work, when she tries to be what she is struggling to express, at all these moments the dilemma is present, waiting and inescapable.

The dilemma I speak of is inherent in a shadowy but real convergence between new experience and an established aesthetic. What this means in practical terms is that the woman poet today is caught in a field of force. Powerful, persuasive voices are in her ear as she writes. Distorting and simplifying ideas of womanhood and poetry fall as shadows between her and the courage of own experience. If she listens to these voices, yields to these ideas, her work will be obstructed. If, however, she evades the issue, runs for cover and pretends there is no pressure, then she is likely to lose the resolution she needs to encompass the critical distance between writing poems and being a poet. A distance which for women is fraught in any case, as I hope to show, with psychosexual fear and doubt.

Dramatize, dramatize, said Henry James. And so I will. Imagine, then, that a woman is going into the garden. She is youngish; her apron is on, and there is flour on her hands. It is early afternoon. She is going there to lift a child who for the third time is about to put laburnum pods into its mouth. This is what she does. But what I have omitted to say in this small sketch is that the woman is a poet. And once she is in the garden, once the child, hot and small and needy, is in her arms, once the frills of shadow around the laburnum and the freakish gold light from it are in her eyes, then her poetic sense is awakened. She comes back through the garden door. She cleans her hands, takes off her apron, sets her child down for an afternoon sleep. Then she sits down to work.

Now it begins. The first of these powerful, distracting voices comes to her. For argument's sake, I will call it the Romantic Heresy. It comes to her as a whisper, an insinuation. What she wants to do is write about the laburnum, the heat of the child, common human love – the mesh of these things. But where, says the voice in her ear, is the interest in all this? How are you going to write a poem out of these plain Janes, these snips and threads of an ordinary day? Now, the voice continues, listen to me, and I will show you how to make all this poetic. A shade here, a nuance there, a degree of distance, a lilt of complaint, and all will be well. The woman hesitates. Suddenly the moment that seemed to her potent and emblematic and true appears commonplace, beyond the pale of art. She is shaken. And there I will leave her, with her doubts and fears, so as to look more closely at what it is that has come between her and the courage of that moment.

From *Object Lessons: The Life of the Woman and the Poet in Our Time* (Manchester: Carcanet Press, 1995), pp. 239–54.

The Romantic Heresy, as I have chosen to call it, is not romanticism proper, although it is related to it. "Before Wordsworth," writes Lionel Trilling, "poetry had a subject. After Wordsworth its prevalent subject was the poet's own subjectivity." This shift in perception was responsible for much that was fresh and revitalizing in nineteenth-century poetry. But it was also responsible for the declension of poetry into self-consciousness, self-invention.

This type of debased romanticism is rooted in a powerful, subliminal suggestion that poets are distinctive not so much because they write poetry as because in order to do so, they have poetic feelings about poetic experiences. That there is a category of experience and expression which is poetic and all the rest is ordinary and therefore inadmissible. In this way a damaging division is made between the perception of what is poetic on the one hand and, on the other, what is merely human. Out of this emerges the aesthetic which suggests that in order to convert the second into the first, you must romanticize it. This idea gradually became an article of faith in nineteenth-century postromantic English poetry. When Matthew Arnold said at Oxford, "the strongest part of our religion is its unconscious poetry," he was blurring a fine line. He was himself one of the initiators of a sequence of propositions by which the poetry of religion became the religion of poetry.

There are obvious pitfalls in all of this for any poet. But the dangers for a woman poet in particular must be immediately obvious. Women are a minority within the expressive poetic tradition. Much of their actual experience lacks even the most rudimentary poetic precedent. "No poet," says Eliot, "no artist of any kind has his complete meaning alone." The woman poet is more alone with her meaning than most. The ordinary routine day that many women live – must live – to take just one instance, does not figure largely in poetry. Nor the feelings that go with it. The temptations are considerable, therefore, for a woman poet to romanticize these routines and these feelings so as to align them with what is considered poetic.

Now let us go back to the woman at her desk. Let us suppose that she has recovered her nerve and her purpose. She remembers what is true: the heat, the fear that her child will eat the pods. She feels again the womanly power of the instant. She puts aside the distortions of romanticism. She starts to write again, and once again she is assailed. But this time by another and equally persuasive idea.

And this is feminist ideology or at least one part of it. In recent years feminism has begun to lay powerful prescriptions on writing by women. The most exacting of these comes from that part of feminist thinking which is separatist. Separatist prescriptions demand that women be true to the historical angers which underwrite the women's movement, that they cast aside preexisting literary traditions, that they evolve not only their own writing but the criteria by which to judge it. I think I understand some of these prescriptions. I recognize that they stem from the fact that many feminists – and I partly share the view – perceive a great deal in preexisting literary expression and tradition which is patriarchal, not to say oppressive. I certainly have no wish to be apologetic about the separatist tendency because it offends or threatens or bores – and it does all three – the prevailing male literary establishments. That does not concern me for a moment. There is still prejudice – the Irish poetic community is among the most chauvinist – but as it happens, that is not part of this equation.

What does concern me is that the gradual emphasis on the appropriate subject matter and the correct feelings has become as constricting and corrupt within feminism as within romanticism. In the grip of romanticism and its distortions, women can be argued out of the truth of their feelings, can be marginalized, simplified and devalued by what is, after all, a patriarchal tendency. But does the separatist prescription offer more? I have to say – painful as it may be to dissent from one section of a movement I cherish – that I see no redemption whatsoever in moving from one simplification to the other.

So here again is the woman at her desk. Let us say she is feminist. What is she to make of the suggestion by a poet like Adrienne Rich that "to be a female human being, trying to fulfill female functions in a traditional way, is in direct conflict with the subversive function of the imagination?"

Yet the woman knows that whether or not going into the garden and lifting her child are part of the "traditional way," they have also been an agent and instrument of subversive poetic perception. What is she to do? Should she contrive an anger, invent a disaffection? How is she to separate one obligation from the other, one truth from the other? And what is she to make of the same writer's statement that "to the eye of the feminist, the work of Western male poets now writing reveals a deep, fatalistic pessimism as to the possibilities of change . . . and a new tide of phallocentric sadism." It is no good to say she need not read these remarks. Adrienne Rich is a wonderful poet and her essay – "When We Dead Awaken" – from which these statements are quoted is a central statement in contemporary poetry. It should be read by every poet. So there is no escape. The force or power of this stance, which I would call separatist, but may more accurately be called antitraditional, must be confronted.

Separatist thinking is a persuasive and dangerous influence on any woman poet writing today. It tempts her to disregard the whole poetic past as patriarchal betrayal. It pleads with her to discard the complexities of true feeling for the relative simplicity of anger. It promises to ease her technical problems with the solvent of polemic. It whispers to her that to be feminine in poetry is easier, quicker and more eloquent than the infinitely more difficult task of being human. Above all, it encourages her to feminize her perceptions rather than humanize her femininity.

But women have a birthright in poetry. I believe, though an antitraditional poet might not agree, that when a woman poet begins to write, she very quickly becomes conscious of the silences which have preceded her, which still surround her. These silences will become an indefinable part of her purpose as a poet. Yet as a working poet she will also – if she is honest – recognize that these silences have been at least partly redeemed within the past expressions of other poets, most of them male. And these expressions also will become part of her purpose. But for that to happen, she must have the fullest possible dialogue with them. She needs it; she is entitled to it. And in order to have that dialogue, she must have the fullest dialogue also with her own experience, her own present as a poet. I do not believe that separatism allows for this.

Very well. Let us say that after all this inner turmoil the woman is still writing. That she has taken her courage with both hands and has resisted the prescriptions both of romanticism and separatism. Yet for all that, something is still not right. Once again she hesitates. But why? "Outwardly," says Virginia Woolf, "what is simpler than to write books? Outwardly what obstacles are there for a woman rather than for a man? Inwardly I think the case is very different. She still has many ghosts to fight, many prejudices to overcome." Ghosts and prejudices. Maybe it is time we took a look at these.

II

I am going to move away from the exploratory and theoretical into something more practical. Let us say, for argument's sake, that it is a wet Novemberish day in a country town in Ireland. Now, for the sake of going a bit further, let us say that a workshop or the makings of one have gathered in an upstairs room in a school perhaps or an adult education center. The surroundings will – they always are on these occasions – be just a bit surreal. There will be old metal furniture, solid oak tables, the surprising gleam of a new video in the corner. And finally, let us say that among these women gathered here is a woman called Judith. I will call her that [as] a nod in the direction of Virginia Woolf's great essay *A Room of One's Own*. And when I – for it is I who am leading the workshop – get off the train or out of the car and climb the stairs and enter that room, it is Judith – her poems already in her hand – who catches my eye and holds my attention.

"History," says Butterfield, "is not the study of origins; rather it is the analysis of all the mediations by which the past has turned into our present." As I walk into that room, as Judith hands me her poems, our past becomes for a moment a single present. I may know, she may acknowledge, that she will never publish, never evolve. But equally I know we have been in the same place and have inherited the same dilemma.

She will show me her work diffidently. It will lack almost any technical finish – lineation is almost always the chief problem – but that will not concern me in the least. What will concern me, will continue to haunt me, is that it will be saying to me – not verbally but articulately nonetheless – I write poetry, but I am not a poet. And I will realize, without too much being said, that the distance between writing poetry and being a poet is one that she has found in her life and her time just too difficult, too far and too dangerous to travel. I will also feel – whether or not I am being just in the matter – that the distance will have been more impassable for her than for any male poet of her generation. Because it is a preordained distance, composed of what Butterfield might call the unmediated past. On the surface that distance seems to be made up of details: lack of money, lack of like minds and so on. But this is deceptive. In essence the distance is psychosexual, made so by a profound fracture between her sense of the obligations of her womanhood and the shadowy demands of her gift.

In his essay on Juana de Asbaje, Robert Graves sets out to define that fracture. "Though the burden of poetry," he writes, "is difficult enough for a man to bear, he can always humble himself before an incarnate Muse and seek instruction from her.... The case of a woman poet is a thousand times worse: since she is herself the Muse, a Goddess without an external power to guide or comfort her, and if she strays even a finger's breadth from the path of divine instinct, must take a violent self-vengeance."

I may think there is a certain melodrama in Graves's commentary. Yet in a subterranean way this is exactly what women fear. That the role of poet, added to that of woman, may well involve them in unacceptable conflict. The outcome of that fear is constant psychosexual pressure. And the result of that pressure is a final reluctance to have the courage of her own experience. All of which adds up to that distance between writing poems and being a poet, a distance which Judith – even as she hands me her work – is telling me she cannot and must not travel.

I will leave that room angered and convinced. Every poet carries within them a silent constituency, made of suffering and failed expression. Judith and the "compound ghost" that she is – for she is, of course, an amalgam of many women – is mine. It is difficult, if not impossible, to explain to men who are poets – writing as they are with centuries of expression behind them – how emblematic are the unexpressed lives of other women to the woman poet, how intimately they are her own. And how, in many ways, that silence is as much part other tradition as the troubadours are of theirs. "You who maintain that some animals sob sorrowfully, that the dead have dreams," writes Rimbaud, "try to tell the story of my downfall and my slumber. I no longer know how to speak."

How to speak. I believe that if a woman poet survives, if she sets out on that distance and arrives at the other end, then she has an obligation to tell as much as she knows of the ghosts within her, for they make up, in essence, her story as well. And that is what I intend to do now.

III

I began writing poetry in the Dublin of the early sixties. Perhaps began is not the right word. I had been there or thereabouts for years: scribbling poems in boarding school, reading Yeats after lights out, reveling in the poetry on the course.

Then I left school and went to Trinity. Dublin was a coherent space then, a small circumference in which to be and become a poet. A single bus journey took you into college for the day. Twilights over Stephen's Green were breathable and lilac-colored. Coffee beans turned and gritted off the blades in the windows of Roberts' and Bewleys. A single cup of it, moreover, cost ninepence in old money and could be spun out for hours of conversation. The last European city. The last literary smallholding.

Or maybe not. "Until we can understand the assumptions in which we are drenched," writes Adrienne Rich, "we cannot know ourselves." I entered that city and that climate knowing neither myself nor the assumptions around me. And into the bargain, I was priggish, callow, enchanted by the powers of the intellect.

If I had been less of any of these things, I might have looked about me more. I might have taken note of my surroundings. If history is the fable agreed upon, then literary traditions are surely the agreed fiction. Things are put in and left out, are preselected and can be manipulated. If I had looked closely, I might have seen some of the omissions. Among other things, I might have noticed that there were no women poets, old or young, past or present in my immediate environment. Sylvia Plath, it is true, detonated in my consciousness, but not until years later. Adrienne Rich was to follow, and Bishop later still. As it was, I accepted what I found almost without question. And soon enough, without realizing it, without inquiring into it, I had inherited more than a set of assumptions. I had inherited a poem.

This poem was a mixture really, a hybrid of the Irish lyric and the British movement piece. It had identifiable moving parts. It usually rhymed, was almost always stanzaic, had a beginning, middle and end. The relation of music to image, of metaphor to idea was safe, repetitive and derivative. "Ladies, I am tame, you may stroke me," said Samuel Johnson to assorted fashionable women. If this poem could have spoken, it might have said something of the sort. I suppose it was no worse, if certainly no better, than the model most young poets have thrust upon them. The American workshop poem at the moment is just as pervasive and probably no more encouraging of scrutiny. Perhaps this was a bit more anodyne; the "bien-fait poem," as it has since been called; the well-made compromise.

This, then, was the poem I learned to write, labored to write. I will not say it was a damaging model because it was a patriarchal poem. As it happens, it was, but that matters less than that I had derived it from my surroundings, not from my life. It was not my own. That was the main thing. . . .

When a woman writer leaves the center of a society, becomes a wife, mother and housewife, she ceases automatically to be a member of that dominant class which she belonged to when she was visible chiefly as a writer. As a student, perhaps, or otherwise as an apprentice. Whatever her writing abilities, henceforth she ceases to be defined by them and becomes defined instead by subsidiary female roles. Jean Baker Miller, an American psychoanalyst, has written about the relegation to women of certain attitudes which a society is uneasy with. "Women," she says, "become the carriers for society of certain aspects of the total human experience, those aspects which remain unsolved." Suddenly, in my early thirties, I found myself a "carrier" of these unsolved areas of experience. Yet I was still a writer, still a poet. Obviously something had to give.

What gave, of course, was the aesthetic. The poem I had been writing no longer seemed necessary or true. On rainy winter afternoons, with the dusk drawn in, the fire lighted and a child asleep upstairs, I felt assailed and renewed by contradictions. I could have said, with Éluard, "there is another world, but it is in this one." To a degree I felt that, yet I hesitated. "That story I cannot write," says Conrad, "weaves itself into all I see, into all I speak, into all I think." So it was with me. And yet I remained uncertain of my ground.

On the one hand, poetic convention – conventions, moreover, which I had breathed in as a young poet – whispered to me that the daily things I did, things which seemed to me important and human, were not fit material for poetry. That is, they were not sanctioned by poetic tradition. But, the whisper went on, they could become so. If I wished to integrate these devalued areas into my poetry, I had only to change them slightly. And so on. And in my other ear, feminist ideology – to which I have never been immune – argued that the life I lived was fit subject for anger and the anger itself the proper subject for poetry.

Yet in my mind and in the work I was starting to do a completely different and opposed conviction was growing: that I stood at the center of the lyric moment itself, in a mesh of colors, sensualities and emotions that were equidistant from poetic convention and political feeling alike. Technically and aesthetically I became convinced that if I could only detach the lyric mode from traditional romantic elitism and the new feminist angers, then I would be able at last to express that moment.

The precedents for this were in painting rather than poetry. Poetry offered spiritual consolation but not technical example. In the genre painters of the French eighteenth century – in Jean Baptiste Chardin in particular – I saw what I was looking for. Chardin's paintings were ordinary in the accepted sense of the word. They were unglamorous, workaday, authentic. Yet in his work these objects were not merely described; they were revealed. The hare in its muslin bag, the crusty loaf, the woman fixed between menial tasks and human dreams – these stood out, a commanding text. And I was drawn to that text. Romanticism in the nineteenth century, it seemed to me, had prescribed that beauty be commended as truth. Chardin had done something different. He had taken truth and revealed its beauty.

From painting I learned something else of infinite value to me. Most young poets have bad working habits. They write their poems in fits and starts, by feast or famine. But painters follow the light. They wait for it and do their work by it. They combine artisan practicality with vision. In a house with small children, with no time to waste, I gradually reformed my working habits. I learned that if I could not write a poem, I could make an image, and if I could not make an image, I could take out a word, savor it and store it.

I have gone into all this because to a certain extent, the personal witness of a woman poet is still a necessary part of the evolving criteria by which women and their poetry must be evaluated. Nor do I wish to imply that I solved my dilemma. The dilemma persists; the crosscurrents continue. What I wished most ardently for myself at a certain stage of my work was that I might find my voice where I had found my vision. I still think this is what matters most and is threatened most for the woman poet.

I am neither a separatist nor a postfeminist. I believe that the past matters, yet I do not believe we will reach the future without living through the womanly angers which shadow this present. What worries me most is that women poets may lose their touch, may shake off their opportunities because of the pressures and temptations of their present position.

It seems to me, at this particular time, that women have a destiny in the form. Not because they are women; it is not as simple as that. Our suffering, our involvement in the collective silence do not – and will never – of themselves guarantee our achievement as poets. But if we set out in the light of that knowledge and that history, determined to tell the human and poetic truth, and if we avoid simplification and self-deception, then I believe we are better equipped than most to discover the deepest possibilities and subversions within poetry itself. Artistic forms are not static. Nor are they radicalized by aesthetes and intellectuals. They are changed, shifted, detonated into deeper patterns only by the sufferings and self-deceptions of those who use them. By this equation, women should break down barriers in poetry in the same way that poetry will break the silence of women. In the process it is important not to mistake the easy answer for the long haul.

Chapter 72
Seamus Heaney

Seamus Heaney (1939–) is an Irish poet who since the early 1970s has published a body of work whose insight and authority matches that of Yeats. Heaney's poetry avoids the mythological systems and stately eloquence of some of Yeats's work, but he is like his predecessor in his sustained engagement with the history and politics of Ireland. These are not abstract categories of judgment in Heaney's poetry. History and politics are discovered in the intimacies of family history, the inflections of daily speech, and in the continuing dialogue in Heaney's work between his delight in the art of poetry and his obligation to the demands of his culture. If these are constants in his poetry there have also been significant changes. His work from the time of his first book, Death of a Naturalist *(1966) to* Field Work *(1979) is shaped by a metaphor of poetry as a digging down into a familial and historical past. His later work, including* The Haw Lantern *(1987),* Seeing Things *(1991), and* Electric Light *(2001), while remaining dedicated to poetry as an art of memory and commemoration, has been drawn to metaphors of ascent and transcendence. He was awarded the Nobel Prize for Literature in 1995.*

In addition to his work as a poet, Heaney has published six collections of essays, some of them based on lectures given at universities in Britain and the United States. The following excerpt comes from the first lecture Heaney gave as Oxford Professor of Poetry, a post he held from 1989 to 1994. These lectures were subsequently published in 1995 in the volume, The Redress of Poetry. *In it Heaney considers the ethical and political obligations of poetry and how these can be phrased in a language of commitment to an oppressed minority or gender. The argument that identifies poetry's value with its political stance is in danger of missing the point about how poetry works in the world. It identifies the nature of poetry's redress too narrowly as the correction of a specific injustice. What poetry offers instead is a capacity to disclose "a glimpsed alternative, a revelation of potential that is denied or constantly threatened by circumstances." And if this is to happen, poetry must sustain itself as an art that delights in language.*

The Redress of Poetry

Professors of poetry, apologists for it, practitioners of it, from Sir Philip Sidney to Wallace Stevens, all sooner or later are tempted to show how poetry's existence as a form of art relates to our existence as citizens of society – how it is 'of present use'. Behind such defences and justifications, at any number of removes, stands Plato, calling into question whatever special prerogatives or useful influences poetry would claim for itself within the *polis*. Yet Plato's world of ideal forms also provides the court of appeal through which poetic imagination seeks to redress whatever is wrong or exacerbating in the prevailing conditions. Moreover, 'useful' or 'practical' responses to those same conditions are derived from imagined standards too: poetic fictions, the dream of alternative worlds, enable governments and revolutionaries as well. It's just that governments and revolutionaries would compel society to take on the shape of their imagining, whereas poets are typically more concerned to conjure with their own and their readers' sense of what is possible or desirable or, indeed, imaginable. The nobility of poetry, says Wallace Stevens, 'is a violence from within that protects us from a violence without'. It is the imagination pressing back against the pressure of reality.

Stevens, as he reaches this conclusion in his essay 'The Noble Rider and the Sounds of Words', is anxious to insist that his own words are intended to be more than merely sonorous, and his anxiety is understandable. It is as if he were imagining and responding to the outcry of some disaffected heckler in the crowd of those whom Tony Harrison calls 'the rhubarbarians', one crying out against the mystification of art and its appropriation by the grandees of aesthetics. 'In our time', the heckler protests, echoing something he has read somewhere, 'the destiny of man presents itself in political terms'. And in his understanding, and in the understanding of most people who protest against the ascription to poetry of any metaphysical force, those terms are going to derive from the politics of subversion, of redressal, of affirming that which is denied voice. Our heckler, in other words, will want poetry to be more than an imagined response to conditions in the world; he or she will urgently want to know why it should not be an applied art, harnessed to movements which attempt to alleviate those conditions by direct action.

The heckler, therefore, is going to have little sympathy with Wallace Stevens when he declares the poet to be a potent figure because the poet 'creates the world to which we turn incessantly and without knowing it, and…gives life to the supreme fictions without which we are unable to conceive of [that world]' – meaning that if our given experience is a labyrinth, its impassability can still be countered by the poet's imagining some equivalent of the labyrinth and presenting himself and us with a vivid experience of it. Such an operation does not intervene in the actual but by offering consciousness a chance to recognize its predicaments, foreknow its capacities and rehearse its comebacks in all kinds of venturesome ways, it does constitute a beneficent event, for poet and audience alike. It offers a response to reality which has a liberating

From *The Redress of Poetry* (New York: Farrar, Straus and Giroux, 1995), pp. 1–9.

and verifying effect upon the individual spirit, and yet I can see how such a function would be deemed insufficient by a political activist. For the activist, there is going to be no point in envisaging an order which is comprehensive of events but not in itself productive of new events. Engaged parties are not going to be grateful for a mere image – no matter how inventive or original – of the field of force of which they are a part. They will always want the redress of poetry to be an exercise of leverage on behalf of *their* point of view; they will require the entire weight of the thing to come down on their side of the scales.

So, if you are an English poet at the Front during World War I, the pressure will be on you to contribute to the war effort, preferably by dehumanizing the face of the enemy. If you are an Irish poet in the wake of the 1916 executions, the pressure will be to revile the tyranny of the executing power. If you are an American poet at the height of the Vietnam War, the official expectation will be for you to wave the flag rhetorically. In these cases, to see the German soldier as a friend and secret sharer, to see the British government as a body who might keep faith, to see the South-East Asian expedition as an imperial betrayal, to do any of these things is to add a complication where the general desire is for a simplification.

Such countervailing gestures frustrate the common expectation of solidarity, but they do have political force. Their very power to exacerbate is one guarantee of their effectiveness. They are particular instances of a law which Simone Weil announced with typical extremity and succinctness in her book *Gravity and Grace*. She writes there:

> If we know in what way society is unbalanced, we must do what we can to add weight to the lighter scale ... we must have formed a conception of equilibrium and be ever ready to change sides like justice, 'that fugitive from the camp of conquerors'.

Clearly, this corresponds to deep structures of thought and feeling derived from centuries of Christian teaching and from Christ's paradoxical identification with the plight of the wretched. And in so far as poetry is an extension and refinement of the mind's extreme recognitions, and of language's most unexpected apprehensions, it too manifests the workings of Weil's law.

'Obedience to the force of gravity. The greatest sin.' So Simone Weil also writes in *Gravity and Grace*. Indeed her whole book is informed by the idea of counterweighting, of balancing out the forces, of redress – tilting the scales of reality towards some transcendent equilibrium. And in the activity of poetry too, there is a tendency to place a counter-reality in the scales – a reality which may be only imagined but which nevertheless has weight because it is imagined within the gravitational pull of the actual and can therefore hold its own and balance out against the historical situation. This redressing effect of poetry comes from its being a glimpsed alternative, a revelation of potential that is denied or constantly threatened by circumstances. And sometimes, of course, it happens that such a revelation, once enshrined in the poem, remains as a standard for the poet, so that he or she must then submit to the strain of bearing witness in his or her own life to the plane of consciousness established in the poem.

In this century, especially, from Wilfred Owen to Irina Ratushinskaya, there have been many poets who from principle, in solitude, and without any guarantee of success, were drawn by the logic of their work to disobey the force of gravity. These figures have become the types of an action that gains value in proportion to its immediate practical ineffectiveness. In their case, the espousal of that which critics used to call 'vision' or 'moral commitment' grew exorbitant and carried them beyond the charmed circle of artistic space and further, beyond domestic privacy, social conformity, and minimal ethical expectation, into the solitary role of the witness. Characteristically, figures of such spiritual stamina incline to understate the heroic aspect of their achievement and insist upon the strictly artistic discipline at the heart of their vocation. Yet the fact remains that for the writers I have mentioned, and others like them – Osip Mandelstam and Czeslaw Milosz, for instance – the redress of poetry comes to represent something like an exercise of the virtue of hope as it is understood by Vaclav Havel. Indeed, what Havel has to say about hope can also be said about poetry: it is

> a state of mind, not a state of the world. Either we have hope within us or we don't; it is a dimension of the soul, and it's not essentially dependent on some particular observation of the world or estimate of the situation... It is an orientation of the spirit, an orientation of the heart; it transcends the world that is immediately experienced, and is anchored somewhere beyond its horizons. I don't think you can explain it as a mere derivative of something here, of some movement, or of some favourable signs in the world. I feel that its deepest roots are in the transcendental, just as the roots of human responsibility are... It is not the conviction that something will turn out well, but the certainty that something makes sense, regardless of how it turns out.

Of course, when a contemporary lifts a pen or gazes into the dead-pan cloudiness of a word processor, considerations like these are well in the background. When Douglas Dunn sits down at his desk with its view above the Tay Estuary or Anne Stevenson sees one of her chosen landscapes flash upon her inward eye, neither is immediately haunted by the big questions of poetics. All these accumulated pressures and issues are felt as an abiding anxiety but they do not enter as guiding factors within the writing process itself. The movement is from delight to wisdom and not vice versa. The felicity of a cadence, the chain reaction of a rhyme, the pleasuring of an etymology, such things can proceed happily and as it were autistically, in an area of mental operations cordoned off by and from the critical sense. Indeed, if one recalls W. H. Auden's famous trinity of poetic faculties – making, judging, and knowing – the making faculty seems in this light to have a kind of free pass that enables it to range beyond the jurisdiction of the other two.

It is only right that this should be the case. Poetry cannot afford to lose its fundamentally self-delighting inventiveness, its joy in being a process of language as well as a representation of things in the world. To put it in W. B. Yeats's terms, the will must not usurp the work of the imagination. And while this may seem something of a truism, it is nevertheless worth repeating in a late twentieth-century context of politically approved themes, post-colonial backlash and 'silence-breaking' writing of all kinds. In these circumstances, poetry is understandably pressed to give voice to much that has hitherto been denied expression in the ethnic, social, sexual and political life. Which is to say that its power as a mode of redress in the first sense – as agent for proclaiming and correcting injustices – is being appealed to constantly. But in discharging this function, poets are in danger of slighting another imperative, namely, to redress poetry *as* poetry, to set it up as its own category, an eminence established and a pressure exercised by distinctly linguistic means.

Not that it is not possible to have a poetry which consciously seeks to promote cultural and political change and yet can still manage to operate with the fullest artistic integrity. The history of Irish poetry over the last 150 years is in itself sufficient demonstration that a motive for poetry can be grounded to a greater or lesser degree in programmes with a national purpose. Obviously, patriotic or propagandist intent is far from being a guarantee of poetic success, but in emergent cultures the struggle of an individual consciousness towards affirmation and distinctness may be analogous, if not coterminous, with a collective straining towards self-definition; there is a mutual susceptibility between the formation of a new tradition and the self-fashioning of individual talent. Yeats, for example, began with a desire 'to write short lyrics or poetic drama where every speech would be short and concentrated', but, typically, he endowed this personal stylistic ambition with national significance by relating it to 'an Irish preference for a swift current' and contrasting it with 'the English mind... meditative, rich, deliberate', which 'may remember the Thames valley'.

At such moments of redefinition, however, there are complicating factors at work. What is involved, after all, is the replacement of ideas of literary excellence derived from modes of expression originally taken to be canonical and unquestionable. Writers have to start out as readers, and before they put pen to paper, even the most disaffected of them will have internalized the norms and forms of the tradition from which they wish to secede. Whether they are feminists rebelling against the patriarchy of language or nativists in full cry with the local accents of their vernacular, whether they write Anglo-Irish or Afro-English or Lallans, writers of what has been called 'nation language' will have been wrong-footed by the fact that their own literary formation was based upon models of excellence taken from the English language and its literature. They will have been predisposed to accommodate themselves to the consciousness which subjugated them. Naturally, black poets from Trinidad or Lagos and working-class writers from Newcastle or Glasgow will be found arguing that their education in Shakespeare or Keats was little more than an exercise in alienating them from their authentic experience, devalorizing their vernacular and destabilizing their instinctual at-homeness in their own non-textual worlds: but the truth of that argument should not obliterate other truths about language and self-valorization which I shall come to presently.

In any movement towards liberation, it will be necessary to deny the normative authority of the dominant language or literary tradition. At a special moment in the Irish Literary Revival, this was precisely the course adopted by Thomas MacDonagh, Professor of English at the Royal University in Dublin, whose book on *Literature in Ireland* was published in 1916, the very year he was executed as one of the leaders of the Easter Rising. With more seismic consequences, it was also the course adopted by

James Joyce. But MacDonagh knew the intricacies and delicacies of the English lyric inheritance which he was calling into question, to the extent of having written a book on the metrics of Thomas Campion. And Joyce, for all his hauteur about the British Empire and the English novel, was helpless to resist the appeal of, for example, the songs and airs of the Elizabethans. Neither MacDonagh nor Joyce considered it necessary to proscribe within his reader's memory the riches of the Anglophone culture whose authority each was, in his own way, compelled to challenge. Neither denied his susceptibility to the totally persuasive word in order to prove the purity of his resistance to an imperial hegemony. Which is why both these figures are instructive when we come to consider the scope and function of poetry in the world. They remind us that its integrity is not to be impugned just because at any given moment it happens to be a refraction of some discredited cultural or political system.

Poetry, let us say, whether it belongs to an old political dispensation or aspires to express a new one, has to be a working model of inclusive consciousness. It should not simplify. Its projections and inventions should be a match for the complex reality which surrounds it and out of which it is generated. *The Divine Comedy* is a great example of this kind of total adequacy, but a haiku may also constitute a satisfactory comeback by the mind to the facts of the matter. As long as the coordinates of the imagined thing correspond to those of the world that we live in and endure, poetry is fulfilling its counterweighting function. It becomes another truth to which we can have recourse, before which we can know ourselves in a more fully empowered way. In fact, to read poetry of this totally adequate kind is to experience something bracing and memorable, something capable of increasing in value over the whole course of a lifetime.

There is nothing exaggerated about such a claim. Jorge Luis Borges, for example, makes a similar point about what happens between the poem and the reader:

> The taste of the apple (states Berkeley) lies in the contact of the fruit with the palate, not in the fruit itself; in a similar way (I would say) poetry lies in the meeting of poem and reader, not in the lines of symbols printed on pages of a book. What is essential is . . . the thrill, the almost physical emotion that comes with each reading.

Borges goes on to be more precise about the nature of that thrill or 'physical emotion' and suggests that it fulfils the continual need we experience to 'recover a past or prefigure a future' – a formulation, incidentally, which has a suggestive truth at the communal as well as at the personal level.

The issue is clarified further if we go back to Borges's first book of poems, and his note of introduction:

> If in the following pages there is some successful verse or other, may the reader forgive me the audacity of having written it before him. We are all one; our inconsequential minds are much alike, and circumstances so influence us that it is something of an accident that you are the reader and I the writer – the unsure, ardent writer – of my verses.

Disingenuous as this may be, it nevertheless touches on something so common that it is in danger of being ignored. Borges is talking about the fluid, exhilarating moment which lies at the heart of any memorable reading, the undisappointed joy of finding that everything holds up and answers the desire that it awakens. At such moments, the delight of having all one's faculties simultaneously provoked and gratified is like gaining an upper hand over all that is contingent and (as Borges says) 'inconsequential'. There is a sensation both of arrival and of prospect, so that one does indeed seem to 'recover a past' and 'prefigure a future', and thereby to complete the circle of one's being. When this happens, we have a distinct sensation that (to borrow a phrase from George Seferis's notebooks) poetry is 'strong enough to help'; it is then that its redress grows palpable. . . .

Chapter 73
Helen Vendler

Helen Vendler (1933–) has written prolifically on the work of twentieth-century poets as well as publishing important studies on Keats's odes, Shakespeare's sonnets, and the poetry of George Herbert. Vendler has proved single-minded in her dedication to poetry as a genre, but her work on twentieth-century poetry is marked by its diversity: book-length studies of Wallace Stevens and Seamus Heaney, but also sympathetic readings of the poetry of Allan Ginsberg and Jorie Graham amongst many others. Vendler has acknowledged the stimulus given to her thinking by the work of the critic, Paul de Man, but she has deliberately refused affiliation with any school of modern criticism, whether "de Manian" deconstruction, new historicism, or theories of identity or the "subject." For Vendler criticism begins with the encounter of the reader with the poem, and develops into a recognition of the individual signature of the poet's work. This requires what she has described as an understanding of a poem's "functional, stylistic elements" and it is her contention that such an understanding is constrained by the ideological imperatives of theory. Vendler discovers the relevant contexts for understanding these elements in the individual oeuvre of a poet and in the literary tradition that informs the poem. What good criticism discovers is how strong poets transform the stylistic field of poetry. Vendler is a critic who believes in originality. The practice of close reading is the means to disclose this originality in a poet's work. She is currently the A. Kingsley Porter University Professor at Harvard.

Vendler is no stranger to polemic as the following excerpt shows. It comes from her 1995 book, Soul Says, *and presents a sustained defence of lyric form as the central genre of poetry against what she describes as the "jealous appropriation of literature into . . . socially marked categories" of "locale, religion, language, ethnicity, race and sexuality." The abstractions of lyric permit an identification not of the social self but of "soul," "where the human being becomes a set of warring passions independent of time and space."*

Introduction: *Soul Says*

The senses and the imagination together furnish rhythms for the poet. The rhythms of the poet translate themselves back, in the mind of the reader, into the senses and the imagination. What is it about the critic that cannot rest content with this silent transaction? Most of the time the critic is just another reader, and can put a book down, whether with appreciation or with irritation, without any wish to write something about that book. Yet certain books will not let the critic look away; they demand a fuller response, and they will not let go until another set of words, this time in the critic's own prose, renders again the given of the book. Something in the book – or in a single poem – is "a hatching that stared and demanded an answering look." That phrase is Wallace Stevens'; and though he used it about the poet's response to life (newborn every day), it is equally true of the critic's response to a significant piece of writing. Emily Dickinson called her response to life "my letter to the world / That never wrote to me." Criticism is also a letter to the world, more meditated than conversation, more widely aimed than scholarship.

The significant poem, for me, can be about anything, or almost anything. I have never been drawn in a positive way to subject matter: that is, I do not respond more enthusiastically to a poem about women than to a poem about men, a poem about nature than a poem about the city, a political poem than a metaphysical poem. Though I grew up in a city, my favorite poems, from Keats's "To Autumn" to Stevens' "The Auroras of Autumn," have often been ones using metaphors from nature; I have liked Protestant poets (from Milton to Clampitt) and Jewish poets (from Ginsberg to Goldbarth) as well as Catholic poets (from Hopkins to Péguy); though I can read only Romance languages, my two indispensable contemporary foreign poets are Paul Celan and Czeslaw Milosz, whom I cannot read in the original. Though I am white, I could not do without the poetry of Langston Hughes and Rita Dove. I have written on both gay and "straight" writers. I bring up these questions of locale, religion, language, ethnicity, race, and sexuality because these days they appear so much in writing about literature, and because there is a jealous appropriation of literature into such socially marked categories.

At first I found it hard to understand, when such categories were ritually invoked, why people felt they could respond only to literature that replicated their own experience of race, class, or gender. I heard many tales beginning, "I never found literature meaningful to me till I read . . ." and there would follow, from a woman, a title like *Jane Eyre*, or, from a black, a title like *Invisible Man*. After a while, it dawned on me that these accounts mostly issued from readers of novels. The first time I heard Toni Morrison speak, she told of going from novel to novel "looking for me," and, for a long time, not finding herself, or her story, anywhere. Then, when she found representations of black women in fiction, they were being victimized, or killed, or exploited, a fact that filled her with anger. Since I was not a novel reader, I had never

From *Soul Says: On Recent Poetry* (Cambridge, Mass.: Belknap Press of Harvard University Press, 1995), pp. 1–8.

gone on that quest for a socially specified self resembling me. The last thing I wanted from literature was a mirror of my external circumstances. What I wanted was a mirror of my feelings, and that I found in poetry.

An adolescent reader of poetry finds herself in a world of the first-person pronoun: "My heart aches, and a drowsy numbness pains my sense"; "I awoke in the midsummer not-to-call night"; "How do I love thee? Let me count the ways." The all-purpose pronouns "I" and "you" are tracks along which any pair of eyes can go, male or female, black or white, Jewish or Catholic, urban or rural. Poetry answered so completely to my wish for a mirror of feelings that novels seemed by comparison overburdened, "loose and baggy monsters," and I cheerfully left them aside.

It now is clear to me how completely the traditional lyric desires a stripping-away of the details associated with a socially specified self in order to reach its desired all-purpose abstraction. "Oh, wert thou in the cauld blast, / I'd shelter thee, I'd shelter thee": yes, it was in Scots, but the feeling was easily transferable to me in America. "Thine eyen two will sley me sodenly": yes, it was said by a man to a woman, but it was equally sayable by a woman to a man. "Never seek to tell thy love / Love that never told can be": advice as sinister to a young woman as to a young man. I plunged on, untroubled by any sense of difference or apartness; and if a poet was a castaway, I too was a castaway; if a poet regretted Fern Hill, I too had a house I regretted and had lost; if Auden wrote about the shield of Achilles, Homer was mine as much as his. Perhaps my high school training in the antiphonal singing of Psalms lay behind my willing self-investiture in any poetic "I": "Out of the depths I have cried to thee, O Lord, Lord, hear my voice." We in the choir were to take such words as our own, as generations of Jews and Christians and atheists have done. And if it was not literally true when I said, "They have pierced my hands and my feet; they have numbered all my bones," I knew it was metaphorically true of all suffering, my own included. Metaphor, not mimesis, was my native realm. Everything said in a poem was a metaphor for something in my inner life, and I learned about future possibilities within my inner life from the poetry I read with such eagerness.

Lyric, from the Psalms to "The Waste Land," seemed, when I was seventeen, to be the voice of the soul itself. This, I take it, is what Jorie Graham means in calling one of her poems "Soul Says," which I have borrowed as the title for this collection of essays about lyric poetry. In lyric poetry, voice is made abstract. It may tell you one specific thing about itself – that it is black, or that it is old, or that it is female, or that it is celibate. But it will not usually tell you, if it is black, that it grew up in Atlanta rather than Boston; or, if it is old, how old it is; or, if it is female, whether it is married; or, if it is celibate, when it took its vows. That is, the range of things one would normally know about a voice in a novel one does not know about a voice in a lyric. What one does know, if it is socially specified at all, is severely circumscribed. (There are exceptions that prove the rule, but I am here concerned with the rule.)

What is the use of abstraction in lyric? And why are most lyrics abstract? And what of the somewhat socially specific lyric – one that ends, for instance, with the words "Black like me," as one of Hughes's poems does? Does it offer a track for my feet, or can only a black reader walk its path? And when the exception comes along, a poem full of novelistic detail like Ginsberg's "Kaddish," how is it that it keeps to its lyric intent?

What is the human interest in shedding most, or all, of the detail in which one necessarily lives? What is gained, and what is lost, when a poet – one now nameless and sourceless and vanished – writes,

> Western wind, when wilt thou blow,
> The small rain down can rain?
> Christ, that my love were in my arms,
> And I in my bed again!

When we look for analogies to such work in the other arts, we might speak of the sketch, the *Lied*, the solo dance. What are they to the oil painting, the opera, the corps de ballet? Their first appeal is the appearance of spontaneity; no one can pretend that the *Mona Lisa* has been dashed off, or that *Aida* has been artlessly uttered. The lyric, though, has the look of casual utterance, of immediate outspokenness: "When I see birches bend to left and right, / I like to think some boy's been swinging them." And it has the look of encounter, of naked circumstance: "Since there's no help, come, let us kiss and part." And it can happen, or seem to happen, even prematurely, as the poet, stunned by a death, must, as he says to the laurels, "shatter your leaves before the mellowing year." While the rhythm of fiction is long-breathed and deliberate in pursuit, the rhythm of lyric is wayward, even hesitant, but always intense, and surprising:

> Let us go, then, you and I,
> While the evening is spread out upon the sky,
> Like a patient etherised upon a table.

Spontaneity, intensity, circumstantiality; a sudden freeze-frame of disturbance, awakening, pang; an urgent and inviting rhythm; these are among the characteristics of lyric, but there is one other that is even more characteristic, and that is compression. In view of the length of certain lyrics (from "The Epithalamion" on), this claim can seem dubious; but as soon as one recognizes that the single day Spenser covers in his wedding poem is the equivalent of the one day Joyce covers in *Ulysses*, the compression of the lyric (especially from a poet so given to digressive expansion as Spenser) is positively striking.

What does compression have to do with the abstraction to which Jorie Graham gives the name "soul," by contrast to the more socially specified human unit we normally call, these days, the "self?" If the normal home of selfhood is the novel, which ideally allows many aspects of the self, under several forms, to expatiate and take on substance, then the normal home of "soul" is the lyric, where the human being becomes a set of warring passions independent of time and space. It is generally thought that the lyric is the genre of "here" and "now," and it is true that these index words govern the lyric moment. But insofar as the typical lyric exists only in the here and now, it exists nowhere, since life as it is lived is always bracketed with a there and a then. Selves come with a history: souls are independent of time and space. "I tried each thing," says Ashbery; "only some were immortal and free." The lyric is the gesture of immortality and freedom; the novel is the gesture of the historical and of the spatial.

Readers read with design. The historically minded read socially mimetic literature as a source for information retrieval: What can we learn from the novels of Dickens about notions of criminality in nineteenth-century England? How did working women describe themselves in their journals? For such readers, no lyric source can seem as rich as a novel. The psychologically minded read literature as a source of culturally coded discourse on the passions; for such readers, the novel offers a multitude of characters interacting in highly motivated ways, impelled by a variety of interests and feelings. The lyric might seem, by contrast, impoverished, existing as it does without much of a plot, and without any significant number of dramatis personae.

In fact, the lyric has come in for a good deal of criticism on this account. The sonneteers are reproved for not allowing a voice to the female object of their desire; and if Elizabeth Barrett Browning is no more disposed than Petrarch to allow her beloved to get a word in edgewise, her "suppression of the other" is to be blamed, it is suggested, on the bad male example of her predecessors. Even Bakhtin, with his subtle and comprehensive mind, thought the lyric to be monologic and therefore (given his taste for the dialogic and the heteroglossic) a disappointing genre. Such judgments stem from a fundamental misunderstanding of the lyric. When soul speaks, it speaks with a number of voices (as the writers of psychomachia knew). But the voices in lyric are represented not by characters, as in a novel or drama, but by changing registers of diction, contrastive rhythms, and varieties of tone. There is no complex lyric that does not contain within itself a congeries of forces, just as there is no sonata of Mozart's that – voiced though it is by a single instrument – does not contain forms of call and response in many emotional tonalities. The "plot" of a lyric resembles that of a sonata: "As if a magic lantern threw the nerves in patterns on a screen" (Prufrock). And since almost every word in lyric language has a long history, each word appears as a "character" heavy with motivation, desire, and import. When these "characters" undergo the binding force of syntax, sound, and rhythm, they are being subjected to what, in a novel or play, we would call "fate." The "destiny" of the words in a lyric must be as complex as the destinies of human beings in life, or the lyric would not be, in its way, adequate to the portion of life it undertakes to represent, the life that the soul lives when it is present to itself and alone with its own passions.

Rhythms have historical meaning, and so do stanza forms; genres have historical meaning, and so do personae. The satisfactions of lyric, for those attached to this form revealing the inner life, are as rich as the satisfactions of novels and plays for those attached to the forms revealing life in society. The interaction of the "soul" and the "self" within a single person is one of the great themes of lyric when it decides to face outward rather than inward: this is the undertaking of poets like Yeats and Ginsberg. They solve the problem differently: Yeats coerces his occult historical systems into a concern with the fate of a single soul; Ginsberg alternates painful social detail and exalted meditation. Yet even such "social" poets remain within the rule of abstraction, so that Ginsberg can ask himself, knowing that he is not writing a novel about his mother's life, "O mother what have I left out / O mother what have I forgotten." Lyric is indexical, not exhaustive; it mentions, and the reader is to expand the mention to the whole arc of experience of which the mention is the sign.

The virtues of lyric – extreme compression, the appearance of spontaneity, an intense and expressive rhythm, a binding of sense by sound, a structure which enacts the experience represented, an abstraction from the heterogeneity of life, a dynamic play of semiotic and rhythmic "destiny" – are all summoned to give a voice to the "soul" – the self when it is alone with itself, when its socially constructed characteristics (race, class, color, gender, sexuality) are felt to be in abeyance. The biological characteristics ("black like me") are of course present, but in the lyric they can be reconstructed in opposition to their socially constructed form, occasioning one of lyric's most joyous self-proclaimings: "I am I, am I; / All creation shivers / With that sweet cry" (Yeats).

The poets about whom I have written in the essays in this book are poets whom I admire. There is really nothing to say about an inept poem except to enumerate its absences – "This poem has no energy; this poem relies on clichés and has no original diction; this poem has no compelling occasion; this poem has no tensile strength or compression; this poem has no enabling structure." It is not interesting for a critic to compile a list of lacks. In all the poets here, there is presence rather than absence, force rather than feebleness, originality rather than derivativeness, strenuousness rather than slackness, daring rather than timidity, idiosyncrasy rather than typicality. In almost all of these cases, one can say, "That's Bidart," or "Gary Snyder, of course," or "Graham, unmistakably," or "Heaney, yes." That is, one could not mistake Snyder for Dove, or Clampitt for Heaney, or Glück for Graham, or Goldbarth for Ginsberg. Each has left a mark on language, has found a style. And it is that style – the compelling aesthetic signature of each – that I respond to as I read, and want to understand and describe.

When I was asked to write, for *Antaeus*, a self-portrait under the rubric "The I of Writing," I had to think about myself in the act of undertaking the sort of writing I do – a writing that takes its origin from an earlier piece of writing, one which I feel at first blindly and dumbly, and then gradually come to know with some degree of accurate understanding. This is what I said in my self-portrait as a writer:

> "Not I, not I, but the wind that blows through me." Writing, I am deaf and blind; then suddenly I wake to the radio, and to ground covered with snow. Not asleep in body, not asleep in mind, but asleep in the senses and awake in an away, an otherness. The otherness is felt by my hand as it rewrites words – *the bronze decor, a shadow of a magnitude, so strength first found a way.* The hand is not female, the hand is not male; its *celestial stir* moves in a hyperspace neither here nor there, neither once nor now. The timeless hand moves in a place where memory cannot be remembered because it is part of a manifold undivided in time. The hand has no biography and no ideas; it traces a contour pliable under its touch. The braille of the poet's words brushes my fingers and moves through them into my different calligraphy. The calligraphy tells less than the fingers feel; *sumptuous despair* loses its dark glamour as the hand falters after it. But the hand loves the contour, tracing obscure lineaments, translating them into language. Is the language signed? Only namelessly by its century and its country of origin, influencing invisibly the contour it has felt. The hand is anonymous, mine and not mine, even if my name signs what it has written.

This passage is, I now see, written within the sphere of lyric, where I am as anonymous as the poet of "Western wind," though as much within my century as he within his. To me, what soul says seems convincing, and self seems a contingent adventitiousness always in tension with it. Yeats reversed the terms, and made "self" mean the abstraction of carnal voice, while "soul" was the abstraction of discarnate voice. These are terms that can be defined at will; the Yeatsian "self" is what Jorie Graham calls "soul." Each is the abstracted voice of the whole person, body and mind, riven by the feelings always coursing from the senses to the passions, struggling to say what words, when formally arranged, can say as the experience of the inner life makes itself articulate and available to others. It is through poets such as those I reflect on here that the coming centuries will be able to know, as Stevens put it, "what we felt at what we saw."

Chronology

Literature, the arts, philosophy, science and technology		Political events
Texts included in the anthology are in bold type.		
	1900	
Yeats, **The Symbolism of Poetry** Freud, *The Interpretation of Dreams* First exhibition of Picasso's work Planck's Quantum Theory		Labour Representation Committee, Britain First Pan-African Conference
	1901	
Henry James, *The Sacred Fount* Kipling, *Kim* Mann, *Buddenbrooks* Norris, *Octopus* Invention of instant coffee		Death of Queen Victoria
	1902	
Hardy, *Poems of the Past and Present* Masefield, *Salt-Water Ballads* Robinson, *Captain Craig* Conrad, *Heart of Darkness* Gide, *L'Immoraliste*		End of Boer War

William James, *Varieties of Religious Experience*
Lenin, *What is to be Done?*

Discovery of hormones

1903

Rilke, **Letter to Lou Andreas-Salomé**
Bridges, *Now in Wintry Delights*
Kipling, *The Five Nations*
Masefield, *Ballads*

Henry James, *The Ambassadors*

Wright brothers' flight

Women's Social and Political Union (WSPU) founded in Britain.

Mass European emigration to USA

1904

Swinburne, *Collected Poems*
Sandburg, *In Reckless Ecstasy*

Conrad, *Nostromo*
Henry James, *The Golden Bowl*

Chekov, *The Cherry Orchard*

Cézanne, *Mont Sainte-Victoire* paintings (–1906)

Russo-Japanese War (–1905)

Anglo-French Entente

1905

Wilde, *De Profundis* (posthumous)

Einstein's Special Theory of Relativity

Debussy, *La Mer*

Freud, *Three Essays on the Theory of Sexuality*

Mutiny on battleship *Potemkin*, Russia

First Russian Revolution

Sinn Fein movement, Ireland

Independence of Norway

1906

Yeats, *Poems (1899–1905)*

Galsworthy, *The Man of Property*
Sinclair, *The Jungle*

Picasso, *Les Demoiselles d'Avignon* (–1907)

Muslim League founded, India

Russian Duma elected

1907

Rilke, **Letter to Clara Rilke**
Kipling, *Collected Verse*

Anglo-Russian Entente

British Labour Party founded

Rilke, *New Poems*, vol. 1

Conrad, *The Secret Agent*

Adams, *The Education of Henry Adams*
William James, *Pragmatism*

Cubist exhibition, Paris

First electric washing machine

1908

Freud, **Creative Writers and Day-Dreaming**

Pound, *A Lume Spento*
Rilke, *New Poems*, vol. 2

Stein, *Three Lives*
Wells, *Tono-Bungay*

Labour government in Australia

Young Turk majority in Ottoman Parliament

1909

Pound, *Personae*
Yeats, *Poems: Second Series*
Hardy, *Time's Laughingstock and Other Verses*
Williams, *Poems*

Schoenberg, *Five Orchestral Pieces*

T. H. Morgan begins genetic research in USA

Bleriot flies across English Channel
Production line for cars, Ford USA

Old age pensions begin, Britain

1910

Yeats, *The Green Helmet*
Pound, *Provenca*
Péguy, *Le Mystère de la charité de Jeanne d'Arc*
Tsvetaeva, *Evening Album*

Rilke, *Notebook of Malte Laurid Briggs*
Forster, *Howard's End*
Wells, *The History of Mr Polly*

First Post-Impressionist exhibition, London

British constitutional crisis over power of the House of Lords

Union of South Africa

Japan annexes Korea

Russell and Whitehead, *Principia Mathematica* (–1913)

1911

Hulme, **Romanticism and Classicism**

Brooke, *Poems*
Pound, *Canzoni*

Conrad, *Under Western Eyes*

Braque, *The Portuguese*

Rutherford's nuclear model of the atom
Amundsen reaches South Pole

National Insurance Act, Britain

1912

Marinetti, **Technical Manifesto of Futurist Literature**
Tagore, **Poet Yeats**

Kipling, *Collected Verse*
Amy Lowell, *A Dome of Many Colored Glass*
Pound, *Ripostes*
Tagore, *Gitanjali*
Mayakovsky, *A Slap in the Face for Public Taste*
Monro (ed.) *Georgian Poetry 1911–12*
Tsvetaeva, *The Magic Lantern*

Mann, *Death in Venice*

Formation of the African National Congress, (ANC)

Sinking of the *Titanic*

Sun Yatsen establishes republic in China

1913

Frost, *A Boy's Will*
Williams, *The Tempers*
Apollinaire, *Alcools*
Lawrence, *Love Poems and Others*
Mandelstam, *Stones*

Lawrence, *Sons and Lovers*
Proust, *A la recherche du temps perdu* (–1927)

Matisse, *Portrait of Madame Matisse*

Stravinsky, *The Rite of Spring*

Suffragette demonstrations, London

Ulster Volunteers formed, Ireland

Bohr's theory of the electronic structure of atoms

Husserl, *Phenomenology*

Armory Show, New York

1914

Thomas, **Robert Frost**

Dickinson, *The Single Hound* (posthumous)
Frost, *North of Boston*
Amy Lowell, *Sword Blades and Poppy Seeds*
Yeats, *Responsibilities*
Hardy, *Satires of Circumstance*
Pound (ed.) *Des Imagistes*
Stein, *Tender Buttons*

Joyce, *Dubliners*

Irish Home Rule Bill passed, Britain

Panama Canal opens

Assassination of Archduke Franz Ferdinand in Sarajevo leads to the start of First World War

1915

Brooke, *1914 and Other Poems*
Masters, *Spoon River Anthology*
Mayakovsky, *A Cloud in Trousers*
The Backbone Flute
Pound, *Cathay*
Amy Lowell (ed.), *Some Imagist Poets* (–1917)

Conrad, *Victory*
Ford, *The Good Soldier*
Lawrence, *The Rainbow*
Woolf, *The Voyage Out*

Duchamp, *The Large Glass* (–1923)

Einstein's General Theory of Relativity

Zeppelin raids on London

Sinking of *SS Lusitania*

1916

Pound, *Lustra*
Mayakovsky, *War and the World*
Amy Lowell, *Men, Women, and Ghosts*
Edward Thomas, *Six Poems*
Lawrence, *Amores*
Graves, *Over the Brazier*

Battles of Verdun, Somme, and Jutland

Easter Rising, Ireland

Arab revolt against Ottoman Turks (–1918)

Frost, *Mountain Interval*

Joyce, *Portrait of the Artist as a Young Man*
Kafka, *Metamorphosis*

D. W. Griffith, *Birth of a Nation*

1917

Amy Lowell, **Poetry as Spoken Art**
Apollinaire, **The New Spirit and the Poets**

Eliot, *Prufrock and Other Observations*
Edward Thomas, *Poems*
Mayakovsky, *Man*
Lawrence, *Look! We have Come Through*
Pasternak, *My Sister Life*
Williams, *Al Que Quiere!*
Valéry, *La Jeune Parque*
Hardy, *Moments of Vision*
Graves, *Fairies and Fusiliers*

Diaghilev Ballet's production of *Parade* in Paris

First recording of New Orleans jazz

Margaret Sanger jailed in the USA for setting up a birth control clinic

Pulitzer prizes first awarded

Battle of Passchendaele
Russian Revolution: Tzar Nicolas abdicates. Lenin becomes leader of revolutionary government

USA enters First World War

Balfour Declaration on Palestine

1918

Pound, **A Retrospect**

Apollinaire, *Calligrammes*
Edward Thomas, *Last Poems* (posthumous)
Block, *The Twelve*
G. M. Hopkins, *Poems* (posthumous)
Kipling, *Twenty Poems*
Amy Lowell, *Can Grande's Castle*
Lawrence, *New Poems*

Strachey, *Eminent Victorians*
Spengler, *Decline of the West*
Stopes, *Married Love*

End of First World War (November 11)

Votes for women aged 30 and over in Britain

Influenza pandemic (–1919)

German Communist Party founded

1919

Tzara, **Note on Poetry**
Khlebnikov, **On Poetry, On Contemporary Poetry**
Eliot, **Tradition and the Individual Talent, Reflections on Contemporary Poetry**

Eliot, *Poems*
Hardy, *Collected Poems*
Amy Lowell, *Pictures of the Floating World*
Pound, *The Fourth Canto*
Yeats, *The Wild Swans at Coole*
Graves, *Treasure Box*
Vallejo, *The Black Heralds*
Waley, *170 Chinese Poems*

Anderson, *Winesburg, Ohio*

Keynes, *The Economic Consequences of the Peace*

Relativity scientifically proven

Treaty of Versailles

Amristsar massacre, India

Arab rebellion against British in Egypt

Alcock and Brown fly Atlantic

First woman MP elected to British Parliament

1920

Lawrence, **Preface to *New Poems* (American Edition)**
Williams, **Prologue to *Kora in Hell***

Owen, *Poems* (posthumous)
Pound, *Hugh Selwyn Mauberley*
Williams, *Kora in Hell: Improvisations*
Graves, *Country Sentiment*

Lawrence, *Women in Love*
Mansfield, *Bliss and Other Stories*
Wharton, *The Age of Innocence*

League of Nations founded

Irish Republican Army (IRA) formed

Marcus Garvey in New York

Women's vote in USA

Formation of Nazi Party, Munich

French and British Communist parties founded

1921

Amy Lowell, *Legends*
Williams, *Sour Grapes*
Yeats, *Michael Robartes and the Dancer*
Tsvetaeva, *Mileposts*
Moore, *Poems*
Graves, *The Pier Glass*

Irish Free State established

Irish Civil War (–1924)

Chinese Communist Party founded

Italian Communist Party founded

Pirandello, *Six Characters in Search of an Author*

Chaplin, *The Kid*

Birth control clinic established in London

Washington Conference on Disarmament

1922

Eliot, *The Waste Land*
Valéry, *Charmes*
Amy Lowell, *A Critical Fable*
Tsvetaeva, *Mileposts Book 1*
The Maiden-Tsar
Hardy, *Late Lyrics and Earlier*
Vallejo, *Trilce*

Joyce, *Ulysses*
Woolf, *Jacob's Room*
Lewis, *Babbit*

Wittgenstein, *Tractatus Logico-Philosophicus*
Weber, *Society and Economy*

Lang, *Dr Mabuse*
Murnau, *Nosferatu*

USSR formed

British Broadcasting Company (BBC) established
Mussolini's fascists take power, Italy

1923

Lawrence, *Birds, Beasts and Flowers*
Masefield, *Collected Poems*
Rilke, *Duino Elegies*
Sonnets to Orpheus
Williams, *Spring and All*
Stevens, *Harmonium*
Tsvetaeva, *Psyche Craft*
Graves, *Whipperginny*
Frost, *Selected Poems New Hampshire*

Lawrence, *Kangaroo*

Le Corbusier: *Vers une architecture*

IBM founded
First talking picture
BBC begins radio transmission

Hyper-inflation in Germany

Ottoman empire ends

French occupy Ruhr

Stalin gains control of Soviet Communist Party

1924

Tzara, *Sept Manifestes Dada*

Tsvetaeva, *The Swain: A Fairy Tale*
Moore, *Observations*
Neruda, *Twenty Love Poems*

Forster, *A Passage to India*
Mann, *The Magic Mountain*

O'Casey, *Juno and the Paycock*

De Mille, *The Ten Commandments*

Boom in US economy

Death of Lenin

First Labour government, Britain

1925

Crane, **General Aims and Theories**

Eliot, *Poems 1909–25*
H.D., *Collected Poems*
Pound, *A Draft of XVI Cantos*
Montale, *Cuttlefish Bones*
Amy Lowell, *What's O'Clock*
Hardy, *Human Shows, Far Phantasies*

Compton Burnet, *Pastors and Masters*
Woolf, *Mrs Dalloway*
Stein, *The Making of Americans*
Fitzgerald, *The Great Gatsby*
Kafka, *The Trial* (posthumous)

Surrealist Exhibition, Paris

Eisenstein, *Battleship Potemkin*
Chaplin, *The Gold Rush*

Hitler, *Mein Kampf* (–1926)

Chiang Kai-shek's campaign to unify China

Locarno Pact to ease international tension

1926

Langston Hughes, **The Negro Artist and the Racial Mountain**
Mayakovsky, ***How Are Verses Made?***
Richards, **Science and Poetry**

Brecht, *Taschenpostille*
Éluard, *Capitale de la douleur*
Pound, *Personae: The Collected Poems*
Tsvetaeva, *After Russia*

General Strike, Britain (May 3–12)

Germany joins League of Nations

Gramsci imprisoned in Italy

Macdiarmid, *The Drunk Man Looks at the Thistle*
Langston Hughes, *The Weary Blues*
Crane, *White Buildings: Poems*
Riding, *The Close Chaplet*

Gide, *Les Faux-Monnayeurs*
Hemingway, *The Sun Also Rises*

T. E. Lawrence, *The Seven Pillars of Wisdom*
Tawney, *Religion and the Rise of Capitalism*

Lang, *Metropolis*
Jean Renoir, *Nana*

1927

Graves and Riding, ***A Survey of Modernist Poetry***

Riding, *Voltaire: A Biographical Fantasy*
Graves, *Poems (1914–1927)*
Langston Hughes, *Fine Clothes to the Jew*

Woolf, *To the Lighthouse*
Hemingway, *Men Without Women*

Heidegger, *Being and Time*
Lindbergh's solo flight of the Atlantic

Trotsky expelled from Soviet Communist Party

Guomindang advances in China

Sacco and Vanzetti executed, USA

1928

Auden, *Poems*
Frost, *West-Running Brook*
Lorca, *Gypsy Ballads*
Pound, *Selected Poems* (ed. Eliot)
Riding, *Love as Love, Death as Death*
Hardy, *Winter Words*
Yeats, *The Tower*

Lawrence, *Lady Chatterley's Lover*
Waugh, *Decline and Fall*
Woolf, *Orlando*

Brecht, *The Threepenny Opera*

Collectivization in USSR

Kellog Pact, renouncing war as an instrument of policy, signed by 65 states

Women aged 21 and over given vote in Britain

Buñuel, *Un Chien Andalou*
Eisenstein, *October*
Disney, *Mickey Mouse*

Small TV service operating in New York

Penicillin discovered

1929

Éluard, *L'Amour la poesie*
Cullen, *The Black Christ and Other Poems*
Frost, *The Lovely Shall Be Choosers*
Lawrence, *Pansies*

Faulkner, *The Sound and the Fury*
Graves, *Goodbye to All That*
Woolf, *A Room of One's Own*

Hitchcock, *Blackmail*

Wall Street Crash; World Economic Depression begins

1930

Empson, ***Seven Types of Ambiguity***

Auden, *Poems*
Breton and Éluard, *L'Immaculée conception*
Crane, *The Bridge*
Eliot, *Ash Wednesday*
Frost, *Collected Poems*
Lawrence, *Nettles*
Riding, *Though Gently*
Dos Passos, *The 42nd Parallel*
Faulkner, *As I Lay Dying*
Musil, *The Man Without Qualities*, vol. 1
Waugh, *Vile Bodies*

Buñuel, *L'Age d'or*

Freud, *Civilization and Its Discontents*

Planet Pluto discovered

Gandhi leads Salt March in India

London Round-Table Conferences on the future of India

1931

Burke, **The Poetic Process**
Seferis, *Turning Point*
Lorca, *Poems of the Deep Song*
Riding, *Laura and Francisca*
Stevens, *Harmonium* (revised edition)

Spanish Republic formed

Japan occupies Manchuria
British National Government (–1935)

Ungaretti, *The Joy*

Woolf, *The Waves*

Dali, *The Persistence of Memory*

Lang, *M*
Chaplin, *City Lights*

1932

Éluard, **Poetry's Evidence**
Leavis, ***New Bearings in English Poetry***

Auden, *The Orators: An English Study*
Eliot, *Sweeney Agonistes*
Lawrence, *Last Poems* (posthumous)
Williams, *The Cod Head*
Yeats, *Words for Music Perhaps*

Dos Passos, *Nineteen Nineteen*
Huxley, *Brave New World*

Cockcroft and Walton split atom
Cologne–Bonn autobahn opened in Germany

F. D. Roosevelt elected President of the USA

14 million unemployed in USA

Saudi Arabia and Iraq become independent kingdoms

Gandhi campaigns for Indian untouchables

1933

Breton, **Automatic Writing**
Lorca, **Play and Theory of the Duende**

Frost, *The Lone Striker*
Graves, *Poems 1930–33*
Milosz, *A Poem of Congealed Time*
Neruda, *Residence on the Earth 1*
Riding, *The Life of the Dead Poet: A Lying Word*
Yeats, *The Winding Stair Collected Poems*

Stein, *The Autobiography of Alice B. Toklas*
Malraux, *La Condition Humaine*

Lorca, *Blood Wedding*
Orwell, *Down and Out in Paris and London*

Hitler appointed Chancellor of Germany

First New Deal, USA

Anti-Semitic laws passed in Germany

1934

Auden, *Poems*
Lorca, *Lament for Ignacio Sanchez Mejias*
Pound, *Homage to Sextus Propertius*
Riding, *Americans*
Williams, *Collected Poems 1921–31*
Dylan Thomas, *Eighteen Poems*

Beckett, *More Pricks Than Kicks*
Fitzgerald, *Tender is the Night*
Waugh, *A Handful of Dust*
Miller, *Tropic of Cancer*

Radioactivity discovered

Night of the Long Knives: Hitler purges his rivals

Stalin's purges begin

Purified National Party established in South Africa with apartheid ideology

Long March begins in China (–1935)

1935

Stein, **Poetry and Grammar**
Tsvetaeva, **Poets with History**

Frost, *Three Poems*
Moore, *Selected Poems*
Riding, *The Second Leaf*
Stevens, *Ideas of Order*
Seferis, *Mythistoreme*
Ungaretti, *Sentiment of Time*
Williams, *An Early Martyr*

Isherwood, *Mr Norris Changes Trains*

Gershwin, *Porgy and Bess*

Nuremberg Laws: German Jews lose citizenship

Italy invades Abyssinia

1936

Auden, *Look Stranger*
Eliot, *Collected Poems 1909–35*
Frost, *A Further Range*
Milosz, *Three Winters*
Moore, *The Pangolin and Other Verse*
Stevens, *Owl's Clover*
Dylan Thomas, *Twenty-Five Poems*
Williams, *Adam & Eve & the City*

Faulkner, *Absalom, Absalom*
Dos Passos, *The Big Money*

Ayer, *Language, Truth and Logic*
Keynes, *General Theory*

Spanish Civil War (–1939)

Popular Front Government, France

Abdication of Edward VIII, Britain

Moscow show trials begin

Japan invades China

Mao Zedong, *Strategic Problems of Revolutionary War*

Chaplin, *Modern Times*

BBC: first public TV service

1937

Auden, *Spain*
Auden, MacNeice, *Letters from Iceland*
Jones, *In Parenthesis*
Stevens, *The Man with the Blue Guitar and Other Poems*

Woolf, *The Years*

Picasso, *Guernica*

Turing, "On Computable Numbers"

Photocopier patented in the USA

Arab/Jewish conflict, Palestine

Truce in Chinese Civil War

Bombing of Guernica, Spain

1938

Benjamin, **Modernism**

Cummings, *Collected Poems*
Graves, *Collected Poems*
Riding, *Collected Poems*
Williams, *Complete Collected Poems 1906–38*
Yeats, *New Poems*

Beckett, *Murphy*
Bowen, *Death of the Heart*
Green, *Brighton Rock*

Orwell, *Homage to Catalonia*

Nuclear fission

Nylon patented in the USA

Austrian Anschluss with Germany

Kristallnacht

Czechoslovakia cedes Sudentland

Munich crisis

IRA bombings in England

1939

Frost, **The Figure a Poem Makes**
Valéry, **Poetry and Abstract Thought**
Auden and Isherwood, *Journey to a War*
Eliot, *Old Possum's Book of Practical Cats*

Nazi/Soviet Pact

Franco becomes leader of Spain

Germany invades Poland

Britain and France declare war on Germany. Second World War begins

Frost, *Collected Poems* (revised edition)
A Considerable Speck
MacNeice, *Autumn Journal*
Montale, *Occasions*
Dylan Thomas, *The Map of Love*
Yeats, *Last Poems*

Joyce, *Finnegans Wake*
Isherwood, *Goodbye to Berlin*
West, *The Day of the Locust*

Brecht, *The Life of Galileo*
Mother Courage

Jean Renoir, *Les Règles du jeu*
Ford, *Stagecoach*
Cukor and Fleming, *Gone with the Wind*

Pauling's discovery of the nature of the chemical bond

1940

Auden, *Another Time*
Lorca, *Poet in New York* (posthumous)
Pound, *Cantos LII–LXXI*
Zukofsky, *First Half of "A"–9*

Stead, *The Man Who Loved Children*
Wright, *Native Son*

Germany occupies France, Belgium, Norway, Netherlands, Denmark

Churchill appointed Prime Minister of Britain

British evacuation from Dunkirk

Vichy Government in France

German bombing of Britain

Battle of Britain

Assassination of Trotsky, Mexico City

1941

Heidegger, **Hölderlin**

Auden, *The Double Man*
Moore, *What Are You?*
Williams, *The Broken Span*
Zukofsky: *55 Poems*

Welles, *Citizen Kane*

German invasion of Soviet Union

Japan bombs Pearl Harbor; United States at war with Japan, Germany, and Italy

Stalin becomes Prime Minister of USSR

1942

Stevens, **The Noble Rider and the Sound of Words**
Langston Hughes, *Shakespeare in Harlem*
Stevens, *Parts of a World*
Notes Towards a Supreme Fiction
Frost, *A Witness Tree*

Camus, *L'Étranger*
Welty, *The Robber Bridegroom*

Construction of nuclear reactor

German defeats at battles of Stalingrad and El Alamein

Japanese defeat at battle of Midway

Wansee meeting in Berlin leads to Nazi policy of systematic extermination of European Jews

1943

Eliot, *Four Quartets*
Langston Hughes, *Jim Crow's Last Stand*

Sartre, *L'Être et le Neant*

German defeat at the battle of the Kursk salient

Allied bombing of Germany

Allied invasion of Italy; Mussolini deposed

1944

Heidegger, **Hölderlin**

Auden, *For the Time Being*
Robert Lowell, *Land of Unlikeness*
Moore, *Nevertheless*
Williams, *The Wedge*

Powell and Pressburger, *The Canterbury Tale*

D Day: Allied invasion of France

Liberation of Paris

Japanese defeat at battle of Leyte Gulf

Civil War begins in Greece (–1949)

Bretton Woods conference

World Bank created after Bretton Woods

1945

Césaire, **Poetry and Knowledge**

Auden, *Collected Poems*
Frost, *A Masque of Reason*
Larkin, *The North Ship*
Milosz, *Rescue*
Stevens, *Esthetique du Mal*
Descriptions Without Place

Stead, *For Love Alone*

War ends in Europe with German surrender (May)

Atomic bombs dropped on Hiroshima and Nagasaki

Japan surrenders (September)

United Nations formed

Death of Roosevelt

Brecht, *Caucasian Chalk Circle*

Rossellini, *Rome, Open City*

Britten, *Peter Grimes*

Bebop jazz, New York

Labour Party wins British Election

Civil War in China (–1949)

1946

Heidegger, **Hölderlin**

Bishop, *North and South*
Graves, *Poems 1938–45*
Frost, *The Courage to be New*
Robert Lowell, *Lord Weary's Castle*
Zukofsky, *Anew*
Williams, *Paterson Book 1*

Cold War begins

Italian Republic formed

National Health Service, Britain

Peron president in Argentina

Jordan independence from British empire

1947

Auden, *The Age of Anxiety*
Brecht, *Selected Poems*
Frost, *Steeple Bush*
Stevens, *Transport to Summer*

Bellow, *The Victim*
Lowry, *Under the Volcano*

Genet, *The Maids*
Tennessee Williams, *A Streetcar Named Desire*

Transistor invented, US

India independence

Nationalization of fuel, power, and transport in Britain

CIA founded

Puppet Communist states in Eastern Europe

1948

Breton, *Poèmes*
Graves, *Collected Poems (1914–47)*
Olson, *Y & X*
Pound, *The Pisan Cantos*
The Cantos
Stevens, *A Primitive Like an Orb*
Walcott, *Twenty-Five Poems*
Williams, *The Clouds*
Paterson Book 2

Mailer, *The Naked and the Dead*

Vinyl LP successfully marketed in USA

Berlin airlift

Gandhi assassinated

State of Israel founded

Apartheid legislation in South Africa

Malayan emergency (–1960)

1949

Frost, *Complete Poems*
W. S. Graham, *The White Threshold*
Walcott, *Epitaph for the Young*
Williams, *The Pink Church*
Paterson Book 3

Orwell, *1984*
Wilson, *The Wrong Set*

Miller, *Death of a Salesman*

De Beauvoir, *Le Deuxième Sexe*

De Sica, *The Bicycle Thieves*

Berliner Ensemble founded

Manchester Mark I Computer

COMECON and NATO formed

Republic of Ireland established

Communist regime in Hungary

People's Republic of China under Chairman Mao

Federal Republic of Germany founded

1950

Olson, **Projective Verse**
Zukofsky, **A Statement for Poetry**

Auden, *Collected Shorter Poems 1930–44*
Robert Lowell, *Poems 1938–49*
Neruda, *General Song*
Stevens, *The Auroras of Autumn*
Williams, *Collected Later Poems*

Green, *Nothing*
Lessing, *The Grass is Singing*

Ionesco, *The Bald Prima Donna*

Pollock, *Autumn Rhythm*

Turing, *Computing Machinery and Intelligence*

First successful kidney transplant

Stereophonic sound on two-track tape

Schuman Plan: European Coal and Steel Community formed

Korean War (–1953)

China conquers Tibet

1951

Auden, *Nones*
Graves, *Poems and Satires 1951*

Churchill elected Prime Minister of Britain (–1955)

Langston Hughes, *Montage of a Dream Deferred*
Larkin, *XX Poems*
Robert Lowell, *The Mills of the Kavanaughs*
Moore, *Collected Poems*
Rich, *A Change of World*
Olson, *Letter for Melville 1951*
Williams, *Paterson Book 4*
Collected Early Poems

Powell, *A Question of Upbringing*
Salinger, *The Catcher in the Rye*

Huston, *The African Queen*

Anzas Pact in the Pacific

Cyprus bids for independence from British empire

1952

Creeley, *Le Fou*
Jones, *The Anethemata*
O'Hara, *A City Winter*
Olson, *This*
Dylan Thomas, *Collected Poems*

Hemingway, *The Old Man and the Sea*
Ellison, *Invisible Man*
Green, *Doting*
Stead, *The People with Dogs*

Bacon, *Study for the Head of a Screaming Pope*

Britain tests atomic bomb

European Coal and Steel Community formed

Elizabeth II becomes Queen of England

1953

Barthes, **Is There Any Poetic Writing?**

Ashbery, *Turandot and Other Poems*
Berryman, *Homage to Mistress Bradstreet*
O'Hara, *Oranges*
Olson, *In Cold Hell, in Thicket*
The Maximus Poems 1–10
Milosz, *Daylight*
Stevens, *Selected Poems*
Walcott, *Poems*

Miller, *The Crucible*
Dylan Thomas, *Under Milk Wood*

Death of Stalin

Egyptian Republic established

McCarthy hearings in the USA

Mau Mau emergency in Kenya (–1957)

End of Korean War

Wittgenstein, *Philosophical Investigations*

Ozu, *Tokyo Story*
Crick and Watson discover structure of DNA

Color TV service in USA

1954

Lacan, **The Subject from Homeostasis and Insistence**

Gunn, *Fighting Terms*
Neruda, *Elemental Odes*
Stevens, *Collected Poems*
Williams, *The Desert Music*

Kingsley Amis, *Lucky Jim*
Baldwin, *Go Tell It on the Mountain*
Lamming, *The Emigrants*
Murdoch, *Under the Net*
Welty, *The Ponder Heart*

Fortran developed in USA

French defeat by Viet Minh at Dien Bien Phu

Geneva Conference on Vietnam

British troops withdraw from Egypt

Algerian revolt against French rule begins

1955

Davie, **What is Modern Poetry?**
Blanchot, **Mallarmé's Experience**
Lacan, **Metaphor and Metonymy**
Auden, *The Shield of Achilles*
Bishop, *Poems: North and South-A Cold Spring*
Creeley, *All That is Lovely in Men*
Davie, *Brides of Reason*
W. S. Graham, *The Nightfishing*
Graves, *Collected Poems 1955*
Larkin, *The Less Deceived*
Rich, *The Diamond Cutters*
Williams, *The Journey to Love*

Beckett, *Molloy*
Gaddis, *The Recognitions*
Nabokov, *Lolita*

Marcuse, *Eros and Civilization*

West Germany joins NATO

Warsaw Pact formed

Bandung Conference of Third World nations

1956

Ashbery, *Some Trees*
Auden, *The Old Man's Road*
Ginsberg, *Howl and Other Poems*
Bishop, *Poems*
Creeley, *If You*
Herbert, *The Cord of Light*
Moore, *Like a Bulwark*
O'Hara, *Meditations in an Emergency*
Olson, *The Maximus Poems 11–22*
Zukofsky, *Some Time, Short Poems*

Beckett, *Malone Dies*

Osborne, *Look Back in Anger*

Elvis Presley, "Heartbreak Hotel"

First commercial nuclear power station in Britain

20th Congress of Soviet Communist Party; Kruschev denounces Stalin

Suez Crisis; petrol rationing in Britain

Hungarian Uprising

Civil war begins in Vietnam

1957

Larkin, **The Pleasure Principle**
Adorno, **On Lyric Poetry and Society**
Lacan, **The Agency of the Letter**
Auden, *Reflections on a Forest*
Davie, *A Winter Talent*
Gunn, *The Sense of Movement*
Ted Hughes, *The Hawk in the Rain*
Levertov, *Here and Now*

Robbe-Grillet, *La Jalousie*
Kerouac, *On The Road*
Pasternak, *Dr Zhivago*

Barthes, *Mythologies*
Hoggart, *The Uses of Literacy*

Bergman, *The Seventh Seal*

Treaty of Rome: European Economic Community formed

Ghana's independence from British empire

1958

Betjeman, *Collected Poems*
Williams, *Paterson Book 5*
Zukofsky, *Barely and Widely*

Achebe, *Things Fall Apart*
Levi, *If This Is a Man*

Fifth French Republic founded with De Gaulle as President

Great Leap Forward in China

British West Indies Federation (–1962)

Murdoch, *The Bell*
Sillitoe, *Saturday Night and Sunday Morning*

Lévi-Strauss, *Structural Anthropology*
Raymond Williams, *Culture and Society*

Rothko, *The Seagram Murals*

Silicon chip invented by Texas Instruments

Campaign for Nuclear Disarmament (CND) founded in Britain

1959

Auden, *Selected Poetry*
Davie, *The Forests of Lithuania*
Graves, *Collected Poems 1959*
Hill, *For the Unfallen: Poems 1952–8*
Langston Hughes, *Selected Poems*
Robert Lowell, *Life Studies*
Moore, *O to be a Dragon*
Zukofsky, *"A" 1–12*

Burroughs, *The Naked Lunch*
Grass, *The Tin Drum*

Godard, *A Bout de souffle*

Miles Davis, "Kind of Blue"

North Sea gas discovered

Cuban Revolution: Castro comes to power

Independence of Cyprus from Britain

Tibetan uprising against Chinese rule

Alaska and Hawaii become part of USA

Jamaica granted self-government within the West Indies Federation

European Free Trade Association (EFTA) founded

1960

Jakobson, **Closing Statement**
Auden, *Homage to Clio*
Ashbery, *The Poems*
Ted Hughes, *Lupercal*
O'Hara, *Second Avenue, Odes*
Olson, *The Maximus Poems*
Plath, *The Colossus*

Lasers built in USA
Oral contraceptives marketed

Sharpeville massacre, South Africa

Congolese independence

Vietnam War (–1975)

OPEC formed

OECD formed

American U2 spy plane shot down by USSR

1961

Dorn, **What I See in the *Maximus* Poems**
Ginsberg, **When the Mode of the Music Changes**
O'Hara, **Personism: A Manifesto**

Davie, *New and Selected Poems*
Dorn, *The Newly Fallen*
Frost, *Dedication: The Gift Outright*
Ginsberg, *Kaddish and Other Poems 1958–60*
Gunn, *My Sad Captains*
Baraka/Jones, *Preface to a 20 Volume Suicide Note*
Robert Lowell, *Imitations*
Olson, *Maximus, From Dogtown 1*

Heller, *Catch-22*
Spark, *The Prime of Miss Jean Brodie*
Naipaul, *A House for Mr Biswas*
Updike, *Rabbit Run*

First manned space flight

Berlin Wall built

South Africa becomes a republic

Kennedy President of USA

Bay of Pigs

1962

Auden, **The Poet and the City**
Ginsberg, **Abstraction in Poetry**

Ashbery, *The Tennis Court Oath*
Creeley, *For Love: Poems 1950–1960*
Frost, *In the Clearing*
Moore, *Eight Poems*
Stevie Smith, *Selected Poems*
Walcott, *In a Green Night: Poems 1948–60*
Williams, *Pictures from Breughel*

Kesey, *One Flew Over the Cuckoo's Nest*
Lessing, *The Golden Notebook*

Austin, *How To Do Things With Words*
Beatles, "Love Me Do"
Boulez, *Pli selon Pli*

Warhol, "Marilyn" series

First satellite television broadcast

Cuban missile crisis

Commonwealth Immigrants Act, Britain

Vatican II (–1965)

Jamaica, Trinidad and Tobago, and Uganda became independent of British rule

1963

Eliot, *Collected Poems: 1909–62*
Ginsberg, *Reality Sandwiches 1953–60*
Rich, *Snapshots of a Daughter-in-Law: Poems 1954–62*
Williams, *Paterson Books 1–5*

The Beatles, "Please Please Me"

President Kennedy assassinated

French veto British bid to join European Economic Community

Nuclear Test-ban Treaty

Organization for African Unity (OAU) formed

1964

Baraka Jones, **Hunting Is Not Those Heads on the Wall**
Creeley, **A Sense of Measure**

Baraka/Jones, *The Dead Lecturer*
Davie, *Events and Wisdoms: Poems 1957–1963*
Dorn, *From Gloucester Out*
Graves, *Man Does, Woman Is*
Hill, *Preghiere*
Larkin, *The Whitsun Weddings*
Robert Lowell, *For the Union Dead*
Milosz, *Bobo's Metamorphosis*
Moore, *The Arctic Ox*
O'Hara, *Lunch Poems*
Roethke, *The Far Field*
Zukofsky, *Found Objects 1962–26*

Selby, *Last Exit to Brooklyn*

Holye and Narlikar propound new theory of gravity
First word processor

Civil Rights Act, USA

Race Relations Act, Britain

Civil war in the Sudan

Palestine Liberation Organization (PLO) formed

Mandela sentenced to life imprisonment, South Africa

1965

Baraka/Jones, **State/Meant**

Auden, *About the House*
Bishop, *Questions of Travel*
Dorn, *Geography*
Heaney, *Eleven Poems*
O'Hara, *Love Poems: Tentative Title*
Plath, *Ariel* (posthumous)
Walcott, *The Castaway and Other Poems*
Zukofsky, *All: The Collected Shorter Poems 1923–58*

UDI in Rhodesia

War between India and Pakistan

Military coup in Indonesia

Bellow, *Herzog*
Drabble, *The Millstone*
Mailer, *An American Dream*
Ngugi, *The River Between*
Soyinka, *The Interpreters*

Dylan, "Highway 61 Revisited"

Pinter, *The Homecoming*

1966

Auden, *Collected Shorter Poems 1927–1957*
Ashbery, *Rivers and Mountains*
Bunting, *Briggflatts*
Creeley, *About Women Poems 1950–1965*
Heaney, *Death of a Naturalist*
Moore, *Tell Me, Tell Me: Granite, Steel and Other Topics*
Rich, *Necessities of Life: Poems 1962–65*

Pynchon, *The Crying of Lot 49*

Dylan, "Blonde on Blonde"

Sontag, "Against Interpretation"

Bergman, *Persona*

Cultural Revolution in China (–1968)

Major US offensive against Viet Cong

Civil Rights rally, Jackson, Mississippi

France withdraws from NATO

Assassination of Verwoerd, Prime Minister of South Africa

1967

Ashbery, *Selected Poems*
Bishop, *Selected Poems*
Dorn, *The North Atlantic Turbine*
Robert Lowell, *Near the Ocean*
Moore, *The Complete Poems*
Snyder, *The Back Country*
Ponge, *Le Savon*
Pound, *Selected Cantos*
Rich, *Selected Poems*

Carter, *The Magic Toyshop*
Márquez, *A Hundred Years of Solitude*
Ngugi, *A Grain of Wheat*

Derrida, *L'Ecriture et la difference*

Six day Arab/Israeli War

Biafra War (–1970)

European Economic Community (EEC) becomes European Community (EC)

France vetoes Britain's second bid to enter EC

1968

Ashbery, **The Invisible Avant-Garde**
Herrnstein Smith, **Closure and Anti-Closure in Modern Poetry**

Auden, *Collected Longer Poems*
Dorn, *Gunslinger Book 1*
Graves, *Poems 1965–1968*
Ginsberg, *Planet News 1961–1967*
Gunn, *Touch*
Hill, *King Log*
Mahon, *Night-Crossing*
Olson, *Maximus Poems IV, V, VI*
Prynne, *Kitchen Poems*

Updike, *Couples*
Vidal, *Myra Breckinridge*

Bell and Hewish discover the pulsar

Tet Offensive in Vietnam

Assassination of Martin Luther King

Assassination of Robert Kennedy

Warsaw Pact armies invade, Czechoslovakia

Student protests in Europe

1969

Genette, **Poetic Language, Poetics of Language**

Auden, *City Without Walls and Other Poems*
Bishop, *The Complete Poems*
Davie, *Essex Poems 1963–67*
Dorn, *Gunslinger Book 2*
Heaney, *Door into the Dark*
Robert Lowell, *Notebook 1967–1968*
Milosz, *City Without a Name*
Rich, *Leaflets: Poems 1965–1968*
Walcott, *The Gulf and Other Poems*

Fowles, *The French Lieutenant's Woman*
Roth, *Portnoy's Complaint*
Vonnegut, *Slaughterhouse 5*

Greer, *The Female Eunuch*

Woodstock rock music festival

First man on the moon

Open University established in Britain

First Concorde flight

Chinese/Soviet frontier war

Renewal of Protestant/Catholic hostility in Northern Ireland; British troops deployed in Northern Ireland

Brandt becomes West German Chancellor

Gadaffi comes to power in Libya

Strategic Arms Limitation talks (SALT) begin between USA and USSR

1970

de Man, **Intentional Structure of the Romantic Image**

Baraka/Jones, *It's Nation Time*
Ashbery, *The Double Dream of Spring*
Creeley, *The Finger: Poems 1966–1969*
Davie, *Six Epistles to Eva Hesse*
Ted Hughes, *Crow*
Olson, *Archaeologist of Morning*

Bellow, *Mr Sammler's Planet*

Allende becomes President of Chile

West German policy of Ostpolitik

Continuing disturbance in Northern Ireland. Recruitment by Provisional IRA

Kent State University shooting, USA

1971

Auden, *Academic Graffiti*
Forrest-Thomson, *Language-Games*
Gunn, *Moly*
Hill, *Mercian Hymns*
Rich, *The Will to Change: Poems 1968–1970*
Zukofsky, *All: The Collected Shorter Poems 1923–1964*

Fellini, *Roma*

Rawls, *A Theory of Justice*

Decimal currency introduced in Britain

Interment policy introduced in Northern Ireland

1972

Ashbery, *Three Poems*
Auden, *Epistle to a Godson and Other Poems*
Baraka/Jones, *Spirit Reach*
Creeley, *A Day Book*
Davie, *Collected Poems, 1950–1970*
Ginsberg, *The Fall of America: Poems of These States 1965–71, New Year Blues*
Heaney, *Wintering Out*
Murray, *Poems Against Economics*
O'Hara, *Collected Poems* (posthumous)
Zukofsky, "A"–24

Atwood, *Surfacing*
Berger, *G*
Calvino, *Invisible Cities*

Bangladesh formed after India/Pakistan War

US/USSR détente. SALT 1 signed

US recognizes Communist China

British government imposes direct rule in Northern Ireland

Miners' strike in Britain

Overthrow of Allende government in Chile; Military dictatorship begins

Coppola, *The Godfather*
Fassbinder, *The Bitter Tears of Petra von Kant*

1973

Robert Lowell, *For Lizzie and Harriet*
The Dolphin
Rich, *Diving into the Wreck: Poems 1971–1972*
Walcott, *Another Life*

Ballard, *Crash*
Pynchon, *Gravity's Rainbow*
Jong, *Fear of Flying*

CT body scanner first used

Yom Kippur War: Israel against Arab states

USA withdraws from Vietnam War

OPEC raises price of oil

Britain, Denmark, and Ireland join the European Community

Industrial unrest in Britain

1974

Kristeva, **The Ethics of Linguistics**
Walcott, **The Muse of History**

Auden, *Thank You Fog* (posthumous)
Baraka/Jones, *Hard Facts*
Davie, *The Shires: Poems*
Dorn, *Recollections of Gran, Apacheria*
Forrest-Thomson, *Cordelia*
Gunn, *Mandrakes*
Larkin, *High Windows*
Milosz, *Where the Sun Rises and Where It Sets*
Murray, *Lunch and Counter Lunch*

Le Carré, *Tinker, Tailor, Soldier, Spy*
Morrison, *Sula*
Solzhenitsyn, *The Gulag Archipelago* (–1978, 3 vols.)

Watergate scandal leads to resignation of Nixon as President of USA

Turkish invasion of Cyprus

Democracy restored in Portugal

IRA bombing in mainland Britain

1975

Ashbery, *Self Portrait in a Convex Mirror*
Bernstein, *Asylums*
Dorn, *Gunslinger, Book 1–4*
Enzensberger, *Mausoleum*
Graves, *Collected Poems 1975*
Heaney, *North*

End of Vietnam War

Civil war in Lebanon

Angola and Mozambique independent from Portugal

Sex Discrimination Act, Britain

Ted Hughes, *Cave Birds*
Mahon, *The Snow Party*
Rich, *Poems Selected and New 1950–1974*
Zukofsky, *"A" 22 and 23*

Bellow, *Humboldt's Gift*
Bradbury, *The History Man*
Doctorow, *Ragtime*
McEwan, *First Love, Last Rites*
Weldon, *Female Friends*

Dylan, "Blood on the Tracks"

Spielberg, *Jaws*

Emergence of hip hop and rap music in New York

Apollo and Soyuz dock in space

Death of Franco, Spain

1976

Enzensberger, **A Modest Proposal**

Bernstein, *Parsing*
Creeley, *Selected Poems*
Forrest-Thomson, *On the Periphery* (posthumous)
Gunn, *Jack Straw's Castle*
Walcott, *Sea Grapes*

Storey, *Saville*

Bicentenary celebrations of US independence

Death of Mao

Soweto massacre, South Africa

IMF supports British economy

1977

Ashbery, *Houseboat Days*
Bishop, *Geography III*
Davie, *In the Stopping Train*
Ginsberg, *Mind Breaths: Poems 1972–1977*
Ted Hughes, *Gaudete*
Lowell, *Day by Day*
Murray, *Ethnic Radio*

Carter, *The Passion of New Eve*

Lucas, *Star Wars*
Wenders, *The American Friend*

Democratic elections in Spain

Deng Xiaoping gains power in China

1978

Forrest-Thomson, **Continuity in Language**

Dorn, *Hello, La Jolla*
Enzensberger, *The Sinking of the Titanic*
Hill, *Tenebrae*
Raine, *The Onion, Memory*
Rich, *The Dream of a Common Language: Poems 1974–1977*
Edward Thomas, *Collected Poems* (posthumous)

Coover, *The Public Burning*
Murdoch, *The Sea, the Sea*

Said, *Orientalism*

First test-tube baby born

Camp David Accord between Israel, Egypt, and USA

Civil war in Chad and Nicaragua

Boat people leave Vietnam

1979

Ashbery, *As We Know*
Baraka/Jones, *Am/Track*
Bernstein, *Senses of Responsibility*
Creeley, *Later*
Heaney, *Field Work*
Ted Hughes, *Remains of Elmet*
Read, *Arcadia*
Zukofsky, *A* (posthumous)

Gordimer, *Burger's Daughter*
Naipaul, *A Bend in the River*
Styron, *Sophie's Choice*

Coppola, *Apocalypse Now*

Rise of Islamic fundamentalism

Shah of Iran deposed

USSR invades Afghanistan

Pol Pot deposed in Cambodia

Thatcher elected British Prime Minister

Iran/US hostage crisis

1980

Felman, **The Poe-etic Effect**

Bernstein et al., *Legend*
Boland, *In Her Own Image*
Jorie Graham, *Hybrids of Plants and of Ghosts*
Paulin, *The Strange Museum*

Zimbabwe becomes an independent state

Iran/Iraq War (–1988)

Solidarity movement in Poland

US government funds Contras in Nicaragua

Eco, *The Name of the Rose*
Golding, *Rites of Passage*

John Lennon murdered

1981

Bernstein, *The Occurrence of Tune*
Davie, *Three for Water Music, and the Shires*
Enzensberger, *Thirty-Three Poems*
Rich, *A Wild Patience Has Taken Me This Far: Poems 1978–1981*
Wright, *The Southern Cross*
Walcott, *The Fortunate Traveller*

Rushdie, *Midnight's Children*

Lucian Freud, *Large Interior W11* (–1983)

Identification of AIDS in USA

Space shuttle Columbia

Reagan inaugurated as US President

President Sadat of Egypt assassinated

Split in British Labour Party; Social Democratic Party formed

Privatization of public corporations and increasing unemployment in Britain

1982

Boland, *Night Feed*
Creeley, *The Collected Poems, 1945–1975*
Fenton, *The Memory of War*
Ginsberg, *Plutonian Ode*
Gunn, *The Passages of Joy*
Mahon, *The Hunt by Night*

Brink, *A Chain of Voices*
Coetzee, *Waiting for the Barbarians*
Keneally, *Schindler's Ark*
Walker, *The Color Purple*
White, *A Boy's Own Story*

Michael Jackson, *Thriller*

Cordless telephones
CDs first marketed in Japan

Falklands War between Britain and Argentina

Israel invades Lebanon

PLO takes refuge in Tunis

Famine in Ethiopia

1983

Bernstein, **The Dollar Value of Poetry**
Milosz, **On Hope**

US troops invade Grenada

Bishop, *Complete Poems* (posthumous)
Cronin, *Inside*
Davie, *Collected Poems 1970–1983*
Enzensberger, *Poems*
Heaney, *Sweeney Astray*
Jorie Graham, *Erosion*
Muldoon, *Quoof*
C. K. Williams, *Tar*

Swift, *Waterland*

Civilian government in Argentina

Cruise missiles installed in Britain and Germany; active protest from peace movements

1984

Rich, **Blood, Bread, and Poetry**

Ashbery, *A Wave*
Ginsberg, *Many Loves*
Motion, *Dangerous Play: Poems 1974–1984*
Raworth, *Tottering State: Selected and New Poems 1963–1983*
Rich, *The Fact of a Doorframe: Poems Selected and New 1950–1984*
Heaney, *Station Island*
Walcott, *Midsummer*

Acker, *Blood and Guts in High School*
Carter, *Nights at the Circus*
Coetzee, *Life and Times of Michael K*
Gibson, *Neuromancer*

Springsteen, "Born in the USA"
Increasing use of fax, word processors, and PCs

Indira Gandhi assassinated

Hong Kong agreement between Britain and China

Miners' strike in Britain

IRA bomb attack on British cabinet in Brighton

1985

Ginsberg, *Collected Poems 1947–1980*
Mahon, *Antarctica*
Hugo Williams, *Writing Home*

Ackroyd, *Hawksmoor*
Atwood, *The Handmaid's Tale*
Barnes, *Flaubert's Parrot*
Harris, *The Guyana Quartet*

The Smiths, "Meat is Murder"

Gorbachev becomes General Secretary of the Soviet Communist Party

Anti-apartheid movement grows in South Africa

Eritrean Liberation Front continues war against Ethiopia

Anglo-Irish Agreement

1986

Creeley, *Memory Gardens*
Enzesnberger, *Poems 1950–1985*
Ted Hughes, *Flowers and Insects*
Rich, *Your Native Land, Your Life*

DeLillo, *White Noise*

Chernobyl disaster

US bombs Libya

Spain and Portugal join EC

Single European Act

1987

Ashbery, *April Galleons*
Boland, *The Journey and Other Poems*
Bernstein, *The Sophist*
Dove, *Thomas and Beulah*
Jorie Graham, *The End of Beauty*
Heaney, *The Haw Lantern*
Muldoon, *Meeting the British*
Walcott, *The Arkansas Testament*
C. K. Williams, *Flesh and Blood*

Auster, *The New York Trilogy*
Farah, *Maps*
Morrison, *Beloved*
Roth, *The Counterlife*

Palestinian Intifada begins

US/USSR treaty for intermediate missiles

Stock market crisis

China suppresses Tibet protest

1988

Cronin, "**Even Under the Rine of Terror**"
Derrida, **Che cos'è la poesia?**

Creeley, *The Company*
Davie, *To Scorch or Freeze: Poems about the Sacred*
Rich, *Time's Power: Poems 1985–1988*

Achebe, *The African Trilogy*
Lodge, *Nice Work*
Moorcock, *Mother London*
Rushdie, *The Satanic Verses*
Hollinghurst, *The Swimming Pool Season*

Hawking, *A Brief History of Time*

War between Iran and Iraq ends

PLO recognizes Israel

Lockerbie disaster

1989

Ted Hughes, *Moortown Diary*
Sebald, *After Nature*
Martin Amis, *London Fields*
Ishiguro, *The Remains of the Day*
Kelman, *A Disaffection*

Bicentennial celebrations of the French Revolution in France
AIDS reported in over 150 countries

Exon Valdez oil spill

Collapse of Communist governments in Eastern Europe; Berlin Wall comes down

Tiananmen Square massacre

Iranian fatwah against Salman Rushdie

Death of Ayatollah Khomeini in Iran

Namibian independence

1990

Yingling, **The Homosexual Lyric**

Boland, *Outside History*
Davie, *Collected Poems*
Dorn, *Abhorrences*
Walcott, *Omeros*

Byatt, *Possession: A Romance*

Butler, *Gender Trouble*

Wong Kar Wei, *Days of Being Wild*

Mandela freed from jail, South Africa

Iraq invades Kuwait

East and West Germany united

ANC talks with South African government

End of Cold War

1991

Perloff, **Avant-Garde or Endgame?**

Ashbery, *Flow Chart*
Heaney, *Seeing Things*
Rich, *An Atlas of a Difficult World: Poems 1988–1991*

Martin Amis, *Time's Arrow*
Carter, *Wise Children*
Okri, *Famished Road*
Ellis, *American Psycho*

Nirvana, *Nevermind*

Civil war begins in Yugoslavia

2nd Gulf War: UN Coalition against Iraq; Iraq driven out of Kuwait

Attempted coup in Soviet Union; Yeltsin comes to power

1992

Ashbery, *Hotel Lautremont*
Bernstein, *Rough Trades*
Gunn, *The Man with Night Sweats*

Intensifying conflict in Yugoslavia; siege of Sarajevo by Serbian forces.

Clinton elected US President

C. K. Williams, *A Dream of Mind*

Crace, *Arcadia*
Ondaatje, *The English Patient*
Roberts, *Daughters of the House*

1993

Jorie Graham, *Materialism*
Rich, *Collected Early Poems* 1950–1970
Riley, *Mop Mop Georgette*
Mahon, *Selected Poems*
Walcott, *Poems 1965–1980*

Philips, *Crossing the River*
Proulx, *The Shipping News*
Sebald, *The Emigrants*
Tremain, *Sacred Country*

Czechoslovakia divided into two republics

Bombing of World Trade Center

Israel/PLO peace accord

1994

Bernstein, *Dark City*
Boland, *In a Time of Violence*
Hill, *New and Collected Poems*
Motion, *The Price of Everything*

Brodkey, *Profane Friendship*
Heller, *Closing Time*

Bhabha, *The Location of Culture*

Oasis, *Definitely, Maybe*

Inauguration of Channel Tunnel

Mandela becomes President of South Africa

Continuing war and cease-fires in Bosnia-Herzegovina

North American Free Trade Agreement between Mexico, USA, and Canada

Israel withdraws from Jericho and Gaza Strip. Creation of Palestinian National Authority

British coal industry privatized

1995

Boland, **The Woman Poet: Her Dilemma**
Heaney, **The Redress of Poetry**
Vendler, ***Soul Says***

Ashbery, *Can You Hear, Bird*
Baraka/Jones, *Transbluencey: Selected Poems 1961–1995*
Doty, *My Alexandria*
Enzensberger, *Kiosk: New Poems*
Rich, *Dark Fields of the Republic, 1991–1995*

Fourth UN World Conference on Women, Beijing

Oklahoma bombing

NATO air attacks on Serb forces in Bosnia

Cease-fire in Bosnia, Dayton peace agreement

Assassination of Rabin, Prime Minister of Israel

Ted Hughes, *New Selected Poems, 1957–94*

Ford, *Independence Day*

Rushdie, *The Moor's Last Sigh*
Sebald, *The Rings of Saturn*
Shields, *The Stone Doors*

1996

Baraka/Jones, *Funk Lore: New Poems 1984–1995*
Boland, *An Origin Like Water*
Enzensberger, *Poems 1950–1995*
Graham, *The Dream of a Unified Field: Selected Poems 1974–1994*
Heaney, *The Spirit Level*
Mahon, *The Hudson Letter*
Murray, *Subhuman Redneck Poems*

Swift, *Last Orders*

Comprehensive Test-Ban Treaty

Mitchell Commission Report on Northern Ireland

IRA ends cease-fire: bombings in Britain

BSE crisis in Britain

Israeli offensive in Lebanon

1997

Cronin, *Even the Dead*
Graham, *The Errancy*
Hill, *Canaan*
Ted Hughes, *Tales from Ovid*
Motion, *Salt Water*
Walcott, *The Bounty*

DeLillo, *Underworld*
McEwan, *Enduring Love*
Roy, *The God of Small Things*

Bob Dylan, *Time Out of Mind*

Labour government elected in Britain; Tony Blair becomes Prime Minister

Return of Hong Kong by Britain to China

IRA cease-fire

Tourist massacre in Luxor, Egypt

Death of Diana, Princess of Wales

1998

Ashbery, *Wakefulness*
Hill, *Triumph of Love*
Ted Hughes, *Birthday Letters*
Muldoon, *Hay*

Roth, *American Pastoral*
Makhmalbaf, *The Silence*

Lewinsky scandal leads to inquiry into impeachment of President Clinton

Escalating violence in Algeria

Northern Ireland Peace Agreement

Economic crisis in Japan

Nuclear tests in India and Pakistan

Publication of Truth and Reconciliation Report, South Africa

1999

Ashbery, *Girls on the Run: A Poem*
Cronin, *Inside and Out*
Mahon, *Collected Poems*

Coetzee, *Disgrace*
Morrison, *Paradise*
Tremain, *Music and Silence*

Kiorastami, *The Wind Will Carry Us*

Introduction of the Euro

Trial and acquittal of President Clinton

Kosovo crisis, NATO air strikes in Serbia

Columbine High School massacre, USA

US fails to ratify Comprehensive Test-Ban Treaty

India/Pakistan conflict in Kashmir

Resignation of President Yeltsin, Russia

Riots at WTO meeting, Seattle

2000

Ashbery, *Your Name Here*
Bernstein, *Republics of Reality: 1975–1995*
Graham, *Swarm*
Hill, *Speech! Speech!*
Walcott, *Tiepolo's Hound*

Bellow, *Ravelstein*
Kundera, *Identity*
Rushdie, *The Ground Beneath Her Feet*
Zadie Smith, *White Teeth*

Judicial ruling against the Microsoft monopoly

Putin elected President of Russia

Overthrow of Milosevic in Serbia

Fuel protests in Britain

Israeli withdrawal from Lebanon

Failure of climate change talks in The Hague

Bush declared President of USA after contested election result

Select Bibliography

Adorno, Theodor. *Prisms*, trans. by Samuel and Shierry Weber. Cambridge, Mass: MIT Press, 1981.

Agamben, Georgio. *The End of the Poem: Studies in Poetics*, trans. D. Heller-Roazen. Stanford: Stanford University Press, 1999.

Altieri, Charles. *Painterly Abstraction in Modernist American Poetry*. Pennsylvania: Pennsylvania State University Press, 1995.

Bernstein, Charles. *Contents Dream: Essays 1975–84*. Los Angeles: Sun and Moon Press, 1986.

Bloom, Harold. *The Anxiety of Influence: A Theory of Poetry*, 2nd edn. Oxford and New York: Oxford University Press, 1997.

Bradbury, Malcolm and McFarlane, James (eds.) *Modernism: 1890–1930*. Harmondsworth: Penguin, 1976.

Brown, Dennis. *The Poetry of Postmodernity: Anglo-American Encodings*. Basingstoke: Macmillan, 1994.

Bruns, Gerald. *Modern Poetry and the Idea of Language*. New Haven and London: Yale University Press, 1974.

Caygill, Howard. *Walter Benjamin: The Colour of Experience*. London: Routledge, 1998.

Clark, Suzanne. *Sentimental Modernism: Women Writers and the Revolution of the Word*. Bloomington: University of Indiana Press, 1991.

Conte, Joseph. *Unending Design: The Forms of Postmodern Poetry*. Ithaca: Cornell University Press, 1991.

Crawford, Robert, *The Modern Poet: Poetry, Academia and Knowledge since the 1750s*. Oxford and New York: Oxford University Press, 2001.

Davidson, Michael. *Ghostlier Demarcations: Modern Poetry and the Material World*. Berkeley: University of California Press, 1997.

Davie, Donald. *Thomas Hardy and British Poetry*. London: Routledge and Kegan Paul, 1973.

de Man, Paul. *Blindness and Insight: Essays in the Rhetoric of Contemporary Criticism*, 2nd edn., revised. London: Methuen, 1983.

Dickie, Margaret and Travisano, Thomas (eds.) *Gendered Modernisms*. Philadelphia: University of Pennsylvania Press, 1996.

Donoghue, Dennis. *Connoisseurs of Chaos: Ideas of Order in Modern American Poetry*. New York: Columbia University Press, 1984.

Easthope, Anthony. *Poetry as Discourse.* London: Methuen, 1983.

Easthope, Anthony and Thompson, John (eds.) *Contemporary Poetry Meets Modern Theory.* Toronto: University of Toronto Press, 1991.

Ellman, Maud. *Poetic Impersonality.* Brighton: Harvester Press, 1987.

Emig, Rainer. *Modernism in Poetry.* London: Longman, 1995.

Erikson, Jon. *The Fate of the Object: From Modern Object to Postmodern Sign in Performance, Art, and Poetry.* Ann Arbor: University of Michigan Press, 1995.

Fenton, James. *The Strength of Poetry.* Oxford: Oxford University Press, 2001.

Friedrich, Hugo, *The Structure of Modern Poetry from the mid-19th Century to the mid-20th Century.* Evanston: Northwestern University Press, 1974.

Gilbert, Sandra and Gubar, Susan. *No Man's Land* (3 vols). New Haven and London: Yale University Press, 1988, 1989, 1994.

Gioia, Dana. *Can Poetry Matter? Essays in Poetry and American Culture.* St. Paul: Graywolf Press, 1992.

Guetti, James. *Wittgenstein and the Grammar of Literary Experience.* Athens and London: University of Georgia Press, 1993.

Hamburger, Michael. *The Truth of Poetry: Tensions in Modern Poetry from Baudelaire to the 1960s.* London: Weidenfeld and Nicolson, 1969.

Heaney, Seamus. *Finders Keepers.* London: Faber, 2002.

Hoge, Cynthia. *Scheming Women: Poetry, Privilege and the Politics of Subjectivity.* Albany: State University of New York Press, 1995.

Hollander, John. *Modern Poetry: Essays in Criticism.* New York and Oxford: Oxford University Press, 1968.

Homberger, Eric. *The Art of the Real: Poetry in England and America since 1939.* London: Dent, 1977.

Hosak, Chorwa and Parker, Patricia (eds.) *Lyric Poetry: Beyond New Criticism.* Ithaca: Cornell University Press, 1985.

Johnson, Barbara. *The Critical Difference: Essays in the Contemporary Rhetoric of Reading.* Baltimore and London: Johns Hopkins University Press, 1980.

Kenner, Hugh. *The Pound Era.* Berkeley: University of California Press, 1988.

Kermode, Frank. *Romantic Image.* London: Routledge and Kegan Paul, 1957.

—— *An Appetite for Poetry.* London: Fontana, 1990.

Kristeva, Julia. *Revolution in Poetic Language,* trans. Margaret Weller. New York: Columbia University Press, 1984.

Lacoue-Labarthe, Philippe and Nancy, Jean-Luc. *The Literary Absolute,* trans. Philip Barnard and Cheryl Lester. Albany: State University of New York Press, 1988.

Langbaum, Robert. *The Poetry of Experience.* Harmondsworth: Penguin, 1974 (first published 1957).

Langenbach, James. *Modern Poetry after Modernism.* New York and Oxford: Oxford University Press, 1997.

Lentricchia, Frank. *The Gaiety of Language: An Essay on the Radical Poetics of W. B. Yeats and Wallace Stevens.* Berkeley: University of California Press, 1968.

Longley, Edna. *Poetry in the Wars.* Newcastle upon Tyne: Bloodaxe Books, 1986.

Lucas, John. *Modern English Poetry from Hardy to Hughes.* London: Batsford, 1986.

Mazarro, Jerome. *Postmodern American Poetry.* Urbana: University of Illinois Press, 1980.

McGann, Jerome. *Black Riders: The Visible Language of Modernism.* Princeton: Princeton University Press, 1993.

Miller, Nancy K. (ed.) *The Poetics of Gender.* New York and Guilford: Columbia University Press, 1986.

Montefiore, Jan. *Feminism and Poetry: Language, Experience and Identity in Women's Writing.* London: Pandora Press, 1987.

O'Brien, Sean. *The Deregulated Muse.* Newcastle upon Tyne: Bloodaxe Books, 1998.

Perelman, Bob. *The Marginalization of Poetry: Language Writing and Literary History.* Princeton and Chichester: Princeton University Press, 1996.

Perkins, David. *A History of Modern Poetry: Modernism and After.* Cambridge, Mass. and London: Belknap Press of the University of Harvard Press, 1987.

Perloff, Marjorie. *The Poetics of Indeterminacy: Rimbaud to Cage.* Princeton: Princeton University Press, 1981.

Raban, Jonathan. *The Society of the Poem.* London: Harrap, 1971.

Ramazani, Jahan. *The Poetry of Mourning: The Modern Elegy from Hardy to Heaney.* Chicago: University of Chicago Press, 1994.

Rifaterre, Michel. *The Semiotics of Poetry.* London: Methuen, 1980.

Riley, Denise. *The Words of Selves: Identification, Solidarity, Irony.* Stanford: Stanford University Press, 2000.

Scott, Clive. *The Poetics of French Verse: Studies in Reading.* Oxford: Clarendon Press, 1998.

Smith, Stan. *The Origins of Modernism: Eliot, Pound, Yeats and the Rhetoric of Renewal.* Hemel Hempstead: Harvester Wheatsheaf, 1994.

Trotter, David. *The Making of the Reader: Language and Subjectivity in Modern American, English and Irish Poetry.* London: Macmillan, 1984.

Welsh, Andrew. *Roots of Lyric: Primitive Poetry and Modern Poetics.* Prinecton: Princeton University Press, 1978.

Woods, Gregory. *Articulate Flesh, Male Homo-Eroticism and Modern Poetry.* New Haven: Yale University Press, 1987.

Thematic Index

Index